# Java™ I/O

# Other Java™ resources from O'Reilly

**Related titles**

Java™ in a Nutshell
Head First Java™
Head First EJB™
Programming Jakarta Struts
Tomcat: The Definitive Guide
Learning Java™

Java™ Extreme Programming
Cookbook
Java™ Servlet and JSP™
Cookbook™
Hardcore Java™
JavaServer™ Pages

**Java Books Resource Center**

*java.oreilly.com* is a complete catalog of O'Reilly's books on Java and related technologies, including sample chapters and code examples.

*OnJava.com* is a one-stop resource for enterprise Java developers, featuring news, code recipes, interviews, weblogs, and more.

**Conferences**

O'Reilly brings diverse innovators together to nurture the ideas that spark revolutionary industries. We specialize in documenting the latest tools and systems, translating the innovator's knowledge into useful skills for those in the trenches. Visit *conferences.oreilly.com* for our upcoming events.

Safari Bookshelf (*safari.oreilly.com*) is the premier online reference library for programmers and IT professionals. Conduct searches across more than 1,000 books. Subscribers can zero in on answers to time-critical questions in a matter of seconds. Read the books on your Bookshelf from cover to cover or simply flip to the page you need. Try it today for free.

SECOND EDITION

# Java™ I/O

*Elliotte Rusty Harold*

Beijing · Cambridge · Farnham · Köln · Paris · Sebastopol · Taipei · Tokyo

**Java™ I/O, Second Edition**
by Elliotte Rusty Harold

Published by O'Reilly Media, Inc., 1005 Gravenstein Highway North, Sebastopol, CA 95472.

O'Reilly books may be purchased for educational, business, or sales promotional use. Online editions are also available for most titles (*safari.oreilly.com*). For more information, contact our corporate/institutional sales department: (800) 998-9938 or *corporate@oreilly.com*.

| | |
|---|---|
| **Editor:** Deb Cameron | **Indexer:** Johnna VanHoose Dinse |
| **Developmental Editor:** Mike Loukides | **Cover Designer:** Karen Montgomery |
| **Production Editor:** Philip Dangler | **Interior Designer:** David Futato |
| **Copyeditor:** Rachel Wheeler | **Illustrators:** Robert Romano and Jessamyn Read |
| **Proofreader:** Lydia Onofrei | |

**Printing History:**

| | |
|---|---|
| March 1999: | First Edition. |
| May 2006: | Second Edition. |

 This book uses RepKover™, a durable and flexible lay-flat binding.

ISBN: 0-596-52750-0
[M]

# Table of Contents

## Part I.    Basic I/O

## Part II.   Data Sources

## Part III.   Filter Streams

# Preface

In many ways, this book is a prequel to my previous book, *Java Network Programming* (O'Reilly). When writing that book, I more or less assumed that readers were familiar with basic input and output in Java™—that they knew how to use input streams and output streams, convert bytes to characters, connect filter streams to each other, and so forth.

However, after that book was published, I began to notice that a lot of the questions I got from readers weren't as much about network programming itself as they were about input and output (I/O in programmer vernacular). When Java 1.1 was released with a vastly expanded java.io package and many new I/O classes spread out across the rest of the class library, it became obvious that a book that specifically addressed I/O was required. This is that book. More specifically, it is that book updated and expanded to cover the even more impressive I/O capabilities introduced in Java 1.4, 5, and 6. The I/O class libraries in Java are more powerful and interesting than ever, and this book shows you how to take full advantage of them. Techniques you'll learn here include:

- Reading and writing files
- Communicating over network sockets
- Filtering data
- Interpreting a wide variety of formats for integer and floating-point numbers
- Passing data between threads
- Encrypting and decrypting content
- Calculating digital signatures for streams
- Compressing and decompressing data
- Writing objects to streams
- Copying, moving, and renaming files and directories
- Choosing files from a GUI interface
- Reading and writing non-English text in a variety of character sets

- Talking directly to modems and other serial port devices
- Controlling printers and other parallel port devices
- Managing and communicating with USB devices
- Transmitting data wirelessly with Bluetooth
- Communicating with the outside world from small devices such as cell phones and PDAs

Java is the first language to provide a cross-platform I/O library that is powerful enough to handle all these diverse tasks. Java is the first programming language with a modern, object-oriented approach to input and output. Java's I/O model is more powerful and more suited to real-world tasks than any other major language used today. *Java I/O* is the first and still the only book to fully expose the power and sophistication of this library.

## What's New in This Edition

The first edition of this book was inspired by the wealth of I/O functionality added in Java 1.1, and this edition was motivated in large part by the new I/O package introduced in Java 1.4. Therefore, this edition assumes you're working with at least Java 1.4, though most of the basic material will work as far back as Java 1.1.

Java 1.4 introduced a huge amount of new material relevant to I/O. The most obvious additions are the java.nio packages that provide nonblocking and memory-mapped I/O. Chapters 14–16 cover these powerful new abilities in depth. java.nio also exposes character set conversion code that's been present in the JDK since 1.1 but hasn't had a public API before now. This is the primary subject of Chapter 19.

Many still-relevant pre-1.4 topics have been added and expanded as well. The ProgressMonitorInputStream is covered here for the first time. Many more details are offered about object serialization including serialPersistentFields, writeReplace( ), readResolve( ), and javadoc tags for serialization. JAR files and the java.util.jar package now get their own chapter (Chapter 11). Among other topics, I explain the Pack200 compression format and evangelize the increasingly popular technique of hiding noncode resources like images and data files inside JAR files.

Java 5 continues to build on the basic I/O functionality of Java 1.4 and earlier. Many new classes and methods from those versions are covered here including the Flushable and Closable interfaces. Most shockingly, Java 5 finally brings variable-length argument lists and the printf family of functions, the lack of which helped inspire the first edition. You'll find that these functions are even more powerful in Java than they are in C and can handle not only numbers but also dates and several other object types.

I/O in Java isn't finished evolving yet. Java 6 introduces some interesting new classes including Console and IOError. You'll learn about these right up front in Chapter 1.

---

Java 6 also introduces several useful new methods including a much-improved file-system API that enables you to inspect file attributes and determine the free space on a disk. Finally, I added Swing's FileSystemView, an oft-overlooked class that provides much information about the user's view of the filesystem.

However, since most programmers (yours truly included) are not yet developing in Java 5 on a daily basis, I'll be careful to note which methods, classes, and packages are only available in Java 5 or 6. In any case, when I discuss a method, class, or interface that's only available in Java 5 or 6, its signature will be suffixed with a comment indicating that. For example, this FileDialog constructor was introduced for the first time in Java 5:

```
public FileDialog(Dialog parent, String title) // Java 5
```

There've been many interesting developments outside the core JDK, too. Some of the most exciting developments have occurred in the world of small devices, both peripherals such as GPS receivers that connect to a host computer and devices such as Palm Pilots that are themselves increasingly powerful computers. Treatment of both of these has been dramatically expanded in this edition.

For those readers working with serial and parallel port devices, I've upgraded the Java Communications API chapter to version 3.0. However, in 2006 more and more devices use faster USB ports instead. Consequently, Chapter 23 covers the new Java USB API in depth. For smaller devices that can't quite run full Java but need to perform I/O nonetheless, J2ME offers the Generic Connection Framework (GCF). Chapter 24 covers this alternative to the traditional I/O framework. Finally, Chapter 25 uses the GCF to communicate over one of the newest I/O buses, the Bluetooth API used for wireless communications with a variety of peripherals.

Finally, the existing content has been rewritten from page 1 to bring it up to date with the latest thinking in Java code and style as well as to make it clearer, more compact, and more accurate. For example, exception handling and multithreading is much improved in this edition's examples. Streams are closed more reliably. Exceptions are thrown rather than caught where appropriate, and synchronization is avoided throughout. I expect you'll find this edition even better than the first.

# Organization of the Book

This book has 25 chapters that are divided into seven parts:

## Part I: Basic I/O

Traditional I/O in Java is based on a single metaphor, the stream. Programs read data out of input streams and write data onto output streams. For the most part, you don't need to know whether the stream is a file, network socket, or something else, as long as you have a stream that points to it. Our exploration of I/O in Java naturally begins with this most fundamental abstraction.

Chapter 1, *Introducing I/O*

Chapter 1 describes the architecture and design of the java.io package, including the reader/stream dichotomy. It discusses some basic preliminaries about the int, byte, and char data types and introduces the IOException thrown by many I/O methods. It introduces the console and offers some stern warnings about its proper use. Finally, it offers a cautionary message about how the security manager can interfere with most kinds of I/O, sometimes in unexpected ways.

Chapter 2, *Output Streams*

Chapter 2 explores the OutputStream class you need in order to write data onto any output stream. You'll learn about the three overloaded versions of write( ) as well as flush( ) and close( ). You'll see several examples, including a simple subclass of OutputStream that acts like */dev/null* and a text area component that gets its data from an output stream.

Chapter 3, *Input Streams*

The third chapter introduces the InputStream class. You'll learn about the three overloaded variants of the read( ) method and when to use each. You'll see how to skip over data and check how much data is available as well as how to place a bookmark in an input stream and reset back to that point. You'll also learn how and why to close input streams. This is all drawn together with a StreamCopier program that copies data read from an input stream onto an output stream. This program is used repeatedly over the next several chapters.

# Part II: Data Sources

Part II talks about the two most common targets of I/O, the filesystem and the network. While both are accessed using input and output streams, some critical differences in setup and performance characteristics make them worth exploring separately.

Chapter 4, *File Streams*

The majority of I/O involves reading or writing files. Chapter 4 introduces the FileInputStream and FileOutputStream classes, concrete subclasses of InputStream and OutputStream that let you read and write files. Also in this chapter, I begin developing a File Viewer program, an example that will grow as the book progresses. This initial version prints the raw bytes in a file in both decimal and hexadecimal format.

Chapter 5, *Network Streams*

From its first days, Java, more than any other common programming language, has always had the network in mind. Java is the first programming language to provide as much support for network I/O as it does for file I/O, perhaps even more. Chapter 5 introduces the URL, URLConnection, Socket, and ServerSocket classes, all fertile sources of streams. Examples in this chapter include several simple web and email clients.

# Part III: Filter Streams

Some of the most interesting possibilities arise when you use streams not just for input and output but also for processing. Streaming processing simplifies code, vastly reduces memory usage, and dramatically increases perceived performance. A lot can happen when you don't try to read everything into a memory structure at once. Filter streams are Java's mechanism for processing data as you read or write rather than doing it after the fact.

Chapter 6, *Filter Streams*

Chapter 6 introduces filter streams. Filter input streams read data from a preexisting input stream such as a FileInputStream and work with or change the data before it is delivered to the client program. Filter output streams write data to a preexisting output stream such as a FileOutputStream and process the data before it is written onto the underlying stream. Multiple filters can be chained onto a single underlying stream to combine the functionality offered by several filters. Filter streams are used for encryption, compression, translation, buffering, and much more. At the end of this chapter, I redesign the File Viewer program around filter streams to make it more extensible.

Chapter 7, *Print Streams*

Chapter 7 introduces PrintStream. The most familiar example of a PrintStream is System.out, which is used for the very first Hello World example. However, starting in Java 5, the familiar PrintStream class has become a lot more powerful and interesting. Besides basic console output, it now provides extensive capabilities for formatting numbers and dates in a straightforward and easy fashion.

Chapter 8, *Data Streams*

Chapter 8 introduces data streams for writing strings, integers, floating-point numbers, and other data that's commonly presented at a level higher than mere bytes. The DataInputStream and DataOutputStream classes read and write the primitive Java data types (boolean, int, double, etc.) and strings in a particular, well-defined, platform-independent format. Along the way, you'll develop classes to read and write little-endian numbers, and you'll extend the File Viewer program to handle big- and little-endian integers and floating-point numbers of varying widths.

Chapter 9, *Streams in Memory*

Chapter 9 shows you how streams can move data from one part of a running Java program to another. There are three main ways to do this. Sequence input streams chain several input streams together so that they appear as a single stream. Byte array streams allow output to be stored in byte arrays and input to be read from byte arrays. Finally, piped input and output streams turn output from one thread into input for another thread.

Chapter 10, *Compressing Streams*

Chapter 10 explores the java.util.zip package that reads and writes data in zip and gzip formats. Java uses these classes to read and write JAR archives and to display PNG images. However, the java.util.zip classes can also be used for general-purpose compression and decompression. In the final example, I add support for compressed files is added to the File Viewer program.

Chapter 11, *JAR Archives*

Many Java programs store content in JAR archives. Among other advantages, this makes it easy to bundle many different files and resources into a single distributable. Chapter 11 explores the java.util.jar package used to read these archives. In this chapter, you'll learn when to replace filesystems with unitary JAR archives, how to put content into those archives, and how to get that content back out again.

Chapter 12, *Cryptographic Streams*

The core Java API contains two cryptography-related filter streams in the java. security package, DigestInputStream and DigestOutputStream. There are two more in the javax.crypto package, CipherInputStream and CipherOutputStream, available in the Java Cryptography Extension™ (JCE for short). Chapter 12 shows you how to use these classes to encrypt and decrypt data using a variety of algorithms, including DES and Blowfish. You'll also learn how to calculate message digests for streams that can be used for digital signatures. In the final example, I add support for encrypted files to the File Viewer program.

Chapter 13, *Object Serialization*

Most I/O is performed with bytes. Occasionally, larger types like ints, floats, and doubles are converted to bytes and written as well. However, most actual programming is done with classes and objects. Object serialization lets you read and write almost arbitrary objects onto a stream. This chapter shows you how to read and write objects as well as how to customize the format used for serialization.

## Part IV: New I/O

Java 1.4 introduced a completely new I/O model based on channels and buffers instead of streams. This model doesn't replace traditional stream-based I/O for many uses. However, it is significantly faster in one important use case: servers that process many simultaneous clients.

Chapter 14, *Buffers*

Chapter 14 introduces the buffer classes that underlie all of the new I/O models. It demonstrates the use of the new I/O classes to read and write files and shows how memory-mapped I/O enables you to read and write truly huge files efficiently with limited memory.

Chapter 15, *Channels*

Chapter 15 moves the new I/O model onto the network with channels. You'll learn how to combine channels through scattering and gathering, how to communicate over sockets with channels, and how to transmit UDP packets in the new I/O model.

Chapter 16, *Nonblocking I/O*

The real performance gain of new I/O is in highly multiprocessing servers. This chapter demonstrates the use of nonblocking I/O to dramatically increase the number of simultaneous clients one program can serve. You'll learn about selectors, selection keys, attachments, and pipe channels.

## Part V: The File System

When we think of I/O, the first thing that comes to mind is files. Part V discusses operations on files themselves as distinct from the contents of those files. This includes moving, deleting, renaming, and choosing them.

Chapter 17, *Working with Files*

Files can be moved, deleted, renamed, and copied. Files usually have metadata such as the time the file was created, the icon for the file, and the permissions that determine which users can read or write the file. Chapter 17 shows you how to do all this and elaborates the precautions you need to take to make your file code portable across all major platforms that support Java.

Chapter 18, *File Dialogs and Choosers*

Filenames are problematic, even if you don't have to worry about cross-platform idiosyncrasies. Users forget names, mistype them, can't remember the exact path to files they need, and more. The proper way to ask a user to choose a file is to show him a list of the files and ask him to pick one. Most graphical user interfaces provide standard graphical widgets for selecting a file. In Java, the platform's native file selector widget is exposed through the java.awt.FileDialog class. Like many native peer-based classes, however, FileDialog doesn't behave the same way or provide the same services on all platforms. Therefore, Swing provides a pure Java implementation of a file dialog, the javax.swing.JFileChooser class. Chapter 18 shows you how to use both of these classes. The final example adds a Swing-based GUI to the File Viewer program.

## Part VI: Text

I/O is based on bytes, but much of that I/O has a larger structure as text. Part VI explores how text is represented in Java and how it can be manipulated through special text streams called readers and writers.

Chapter 19, *Character Sets and Unicode*

All Java chars and strings are given in Unicode. However, since there's also a lot of non-Unicode legacy text in the world, in a dizzying array of encodings, Java provides the classes you need in order to read and write text in these encodings as well. Chapter 19 introduces you to the multitude of character sets used around the world and the java.nio.charsets package used to make sense out of this panoply.

Chapter 20, *Readers and Writers*

A language that supports international text must separate the reading and writing of raw bytes from the reading and writing of characters, since in an international system, they are no longer the same thing. Classes that read and write characters must be able to parse a variety of character encodings, not just ASCII, and translate them to and from the language's native String and char types. The Reader and Writer classes perform this task. Chapter 20 shows you how to use these classes to add support for multilingual text to the File Viewer program.

Chapter 21, *Formatted I/O with java.text*

Computers process numbers, not words. When outputting binary numbers as decimal strings for humans to read, the java.text.NumberFormat class controls the width, precision, and alignment of the resulting numeric strings. NumberFormat can also localize numbers with different character sets, thousands separators, decimal points, and digit characters. Chapter 21 shows you how to use this class and its subclasses for traditional tasks such as lining up the decimal points in a table of prices, and nontraditional tasks such as formatting numbers in Egyptian Arabic.

# Part VII: Devices

Not everything is a filesystem or a network. I/O also includes talking to other kinds of devices: laboratory sensors, PDAs, and human input devices such as mice and keyboards. While common devices such as mice and keyboards are addressed through higher-level APIs, less common devices such as laboratory equipment are not. This section shows you how to communicate with different kinds of peripherals and small devices that don't have traditional filesystems or network connections.

Chapter 22, *The Java Communications API*

Chapter 22 introduces the Java Communications API, a standard extension that allows Java applications to send and receive data to and from the serial and parallel ports of the host computer. The Java Communications API allows your programs to communicate with essentially any device connected to a serial or parallel port, such as a printer, scanner, or modem.

Chapter 23, *USB*

Serial and parallel ports are still found on a lot of legacy equipment, but most new devices have moved on. USB is the next generation serial connector, and Java supports it. Chapter 23 shows you how to talk to a variety of USB devices using the Java USB API. In particular, it demonstrates collecting data from a USB-enabled laboratory temperature probe.

Chapter 24, *The J2ME Generic Connection Framework*

Some small devices are computers in their own rights: Palm Pilots, cell phones, programmable calculators, and others. However, these devices don't always have the CPU speed, memory, or battery life necessary to run a full-scale Java VM. Many of them run one of a variety of slimmed-down virtual machines that collectively go by the name J2ME. The standard java.io and java.net packages are too heavyweight to fit in many such small devices. This chapter introduces the smaller, simpler Generic Connection Framework (GCF) and javax.microedition. io package that replace the standard I/O library on small devices.

Chapter 25, *Bluetooth*

Increasingly, small devices don't even need cables in order to connect to a host system. Instead, they transmit data over the air using Bluetooth. Chapter 25 explores the Java API for Bluetooth and shows you how Java programs can talk to Bluetooth devices wirelessly using the GCF. One example shows how to read location data from a Bluetooth GPS receiver.

Chapters 1 through 6 provide the basic background you'll need to do any sort of work with I/O in Java. After that, you should feel free to jump around wherever your interests take you. There are, however, some interdependencies between specific chapters. Figure P-1 should help you map out possible paths through the book.

A few examples in later chapters depend on material from earlier chapters—for instance, many examples use the FileInputStream class discussed in Chapter 4—but they should not be difficult to understand on the whole.

# Who You Are

This book assumes you have a basic familiarity with Java. You should be thoroughly familiar with the syntax of the language. You should be comfortable with object-oriented programming, including terminology like instances, objects, and classes. You should know what a reference is and what that means for passing arguments to and returning values from methods. You should already have written simple applications and applets.

For the most part, I try to keep the examples relatively straightforward so that they require only minimal understanding of other parts of the class library outside the I/O classes. This may lead some to deride these as "toy examples." However, I find that such examples are far more conducive to understanding and learning than are full-blown, sophisticated programs that fill page after page with graphical user interface (GUI) code just to demonstrate a two-line point about I/O. Occasionally, however, a graphical example is simply too tempting to ignore, as in the JStreamedTextArea class in Chapter 2 or the File Viewer application developed throughout most of the book. I

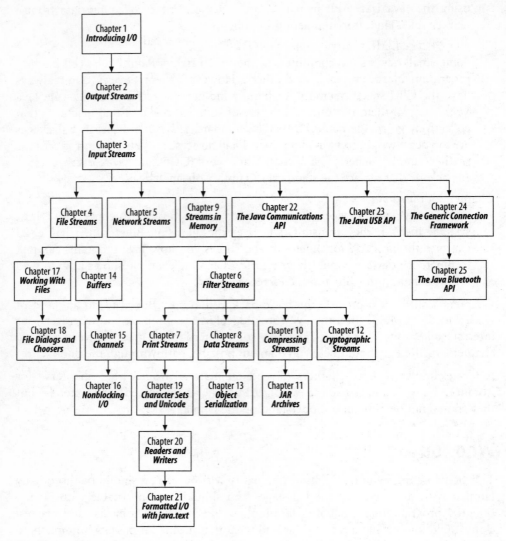

*Figure P-1. Chapter prerequisites*

will try to keep the GUI material to a minimum, but a familiarity with the basics of the AWT and Swing will be assumed.

When you encounter a topic that requires a deeper understanding of I/O than is customary—for instance, the exact nature of strings—I'll cover that topic as well, at least briefly. However, this is not a language tutorial, and the emphasis will always be on the I/O-specific features.

# About the Examples

Although many of the examples are toys unlikely to be reused, a few of the classes I develop have real value. Please feel free to reuse them or any parts of them in your own code; no special permission is required. Such classes are placed somewhere in the com.elharo package, generally mirroring the java package hierarchy. For instance, Chapter 2's NullOutputStream class is in the com.elharo.io package. When working with these classes, don't forget that the compiled *.class* files must reside in directories matching their package structure inside your classpath and that you'll have to import them in your own classes before you can use them. The web page for this book, at *http://www.oreilly.com/catalog/javaio2/*, includes a JAR file that can be installed in your classpath.

# Conventions Used in This Book

The following formatting conventions are used in this book:

*Italic*
> Used for emphasis and to signify the first use of a term. Italic is also used for commands, filenames, and URLs.

Constant width
> Used in all Java code and generally for anything that you would type literally when programming, including keywords, data types, constants, method names, variables, class names, and interface names.

*Constant width italic*
> Used as a placeholder to indicate an item that should be replaced with an actual value in your program.

**Constant width bold**
> Used for user input on the command line.

# Request for Comments

I enjoy hearing from readers, whether with general comments about how this could be a better book, specific corrections, or other topics you would like to see covered. You can reach me by sending email to *elharo@metalab.unc.edu*. Please realize, however, that I receive several hundred pieces of email a day and cannot personally respond to each one.

I'm especially interested in hearing about mistakes. If you find one, I'll post it on my web page for this book at *http://www.cafeaulait.org/books/javaio2/* and on the O'Reilly web site at *http://www.oreilly.com/catalog/javaio2/*. Before reporting errors, please check one of those pages to see if I already know about it and have posted a fix.

# Safari Enabled

 When you see the Safari® Enabled icon on the back cover of your favorite technology book, that means the book is available online through the O'Reilly Network Safari Bookshelf.

Safari offers a solution that's better than e-books. It's a virtual library that lets you easily search thousands of top technology books, cut and paste code samples, download chapters, and find quick answers when you need the most accurate, current information.

Try it for free at *http://safari.oreilly.com*.

# Acknowledgments

Many people were involved in the production of this book. All these people deserve much thanks and credit. My editor, Mike Loukides, got this book rolling and provided many helpful comments that substantially improved it. Deb Cameron stepped up to the plate to edit this second edition. Clairemarie Fisher O'Leary, Chris Maden, and Robert Romano deserve a special commendation for putting in all the extra effort needed for a book that makes free use of Arabic, Cyrillic, Chinese, and other non-Roman scripts. Tim O'Reilly and the whole crew at O'Reilly deserve special thanks for building a publisher that's willing to give a book the time and support it needs to be a good book rather than rushing it out the door to meet an artificial deadline.

Many people looked over portions of the manuscript and provided helpful comments. These included Scott Bortman, Bob Eckstein, and Avner Gelb. Bruce Schneier and Jan Luehe both lent their expertise to the cryptography chapter. Ron Hitchens shone light into many of the darker areas of the new I/O APIs. Ian Darwin was invaluable in handling the details of the Java Communications API. Jonathan Knudsen helped out with Bluetooth and The GCF. IBM's Dan Streetman assisted with understanding the Java USB API (as well as writing the open source reference implementation I used), and Avetana's Moritz Gmelin was equally helpful with some tricky points of working with the Java Bluetooth API.

Finally, I'd like to save my largest thanks for my wife, Beth, without whose support and assistance this book would never have happened.

—Elliotte Rusty Harold
Brooklyn, NY
May 2, 2006

# PART I

# Basic I/O

# CHAPTER 1

# Introducing I/O

Input and output, I/O for short, are fundamental to any computer operating system or programming language. Only theorists find it interesting to write programs that don't require input or produce output. At the same time, I/O hardly qualifies as one of the more "thrilling" topics in computer science. It's something in the background, something you use every day—but for most developers, it's not a topic with much sex appeal.

But in fact, there are plenty of reasons Java programmers should find I/O interesting. Java includes a particularly rich set of I/O classes in the core API, mostly in the java.io and java.nio packages. These packages support several different styles of I/O. One distinction is between byte-oriented I/O, which is handled by input and output streams, and character-I/O, which is handled by readers and writers. Another distinction is between the old-style stream-based I/O and the new-style channel- and buffer-based I/O. These all have their place and are appropriate for different needs and use cases. None of them should be ignored.

Java's I/O libraries are designed in an abstract way that enables you to read from external data sources and write to external targets, regardless of the kind of thing you're writing to or reading from. You use the same methods to read from a file that you do to read from the console or from a network connection. You use the same methods to write to a file that you do to write to a byte array or a serial port device.

Reading and writing without caring where your data is coming from or where it's going is a very powerful abstraction. Among other things, this enables you to define I/O streams that automatically compress, encrypt, and filter from one data format to another. Once you have these tools, programs can send encrypted data or write zip files with almost no knowledge of what they're doing. Cryptography or compression can be isolated in a few lines of code that say, "Oh yes, make this a compressed, encrypted output stream."

In this book, I'll take a thorough look at all parts of Java's I/O facilities. This includes all the different kinds of streams you can use and the channels and buffers that offer high-performance, high-throughput, nonblocking operations on servers. We're also going to investigate Java's support for Unicode. We'll look at Java's powerful facilities for formatting I/O. Finally, we'll look at the various APIs Java provides for low-level I/O through various devices including serial ports, parallel ports, USB, Bluetooth, and other hardware you'll find in devices that don't necessarily look like a traditional desktop computer or server.

I won't go so far as to say, "If you've always found I/O boring, this is the book for you!" I will say that if you do find I/O uninteresting, you probably don't know as much about it as you should. I/O is the means for communication between software and the outside world. Java provides a powerful and flexible set of tools for doing this crucial part of the job. Having said that, let's start with the basics.

# What Is a Stream?

A stream is an ordered sequence of bytes of indeterminate length. Input streams move bytes of data into a Java program from some generally external source. Output streams move bytes of data from Java to some generally external target. (In special cases, streams can also move bytes from one part of a Java program to another.)

The word *stream* is derived from an analogy between a sequence and a stream of water. An input stream is like a siphon that sucks up water; an output stream is like a hose that sprays out water. Siphons can be connected to hoses to move water from one place to another. Sometimes a siphon may run out of water if it's drawing from a finite source like a bucket. On the other hand, if the siphon is drawing water from a river, it may well operate indefinitely. So, too, an input stream may read from a finite source of bytes such as a file or an unlimited source of bytes such as System.in. Similarly, an output stream may have a definite number of bytes to output or an indefinite number of bytes.

Input to a Java program can come from many sources. Output can go to many different kinds of destinations. The power of the stream metaphor is that the differences between these sources and destinations are abstracted away. All input and output operations are simply treated as streams using the same classes and the same methods. You don't need to learn a new API for every different kind of device. The same API that reads files can read network sockets, serial ports, Bluetooth transmissions, and more.

## Where Do Streams Come From?

The first source of input most programmers encounter is System.in. This is the same thing as stdin in C—generally some sort of console window, probably the one in which the Java program was launched. If input is redirected so the program reads from a file, then System.in is changed as well. For instance, on Unix, the following command redirects stdin so that when the MessageServer program reads from System. in, the actual data comes from the file *data.txt* instead of from the console:

```
% java MessageServer < data.txt
```

The console is also available for output through the static field out in the java.lang. System class, that is, System.out. This is equivalent to stdout in C parlance and may be redirected in a similar fashion. Finally, stderr is available as System.err. This is most commonly used for debugging and printing error messages from inside catch clauses. For example:

```
try {
  //... do something that might throw an exception
}
catch (Exception ex) {
  System.err.println(ex);
  }
```

Both System.out and System.err are print streams—that is, instances of java.io. PrintStream. These will be discussed in detail in Chapter 7.

Files are another common source of input and destination for output. File input streams provide a stream of data that starts with the first byte in a file and finishes with the last byte in that file. File output streams write data into a file, either by erasing the file's contents and starting from the beginning or by appending data to the file. These will be introduced in Chapter 4.

Network connections provide streams too. When you connect to a web server, FTP server, or some other kind of server, you read the data it sends from an input stream connected from that server and write data onto an output stream connected to that server. These streams will be introduced in Chapter 5.

Java programs themselves produce streams. Byte array input streams, byte array output streams, piped input streams, and piped output streams all move data from one part of a Java program to another. Most of these are introduced in Chapter 9.

Perhaps a little surprisingly, GUI components like TextArea and JTextArea do not produce streams. The issue here is ordering. A group of bytes provided as data for a stream must have a fixed order. However, users can change the contents of a text area or a text field at any point, not just at the end. Furthermore, they can delete text from the middle of a stream while a different thread is reading that data. Hence, streams aren't a good metaphor for reading data from GUI components. You can, however, use the strings they do produce to create a byte array input stream or a string reader.

# The Stream Classes

Most of the classes that work directly with streams are part of the java.io package. The two main classes are java.io.InputStream and java.io.OutputStream. These are abstract base classes for many different subclasses with more specialized abilities.

The subclasses include:

| | |
|---|---|
| BufferedInputStream | BufferedOutputStream |
| ByteArrayInputStream | ByteArrayOutputStream |
| DataInputStream | DataOutputStream |
| FileInputStream | FileOutputStream |
| FilterInputStream | FilterOutputStream |
| ObjectInputStream | ObjectOutputStream |
| PipedInputStream | PipedOutputStream |
| PrintStream | PushbackInputStream |
| SequenceInputStream | |

The java.util.zip package contains four input stream classes that read data in compressed format and return it in uncompressed format and four output stream classes that read data in uncompressed format and write in compressed format. These will be discussed in Chapter 10.

| | |
|---|---|
| CheckedInputStream | CheckedOutputStream |
| DeflaterOutputStream | GZIPInputStream |
| GZIPOutputStream | InflaterInputStream |
| ZipInputStream | ZipOutputStream |

The java.util.jar package includes two stream classes for reading files from JAR archives. These will be discussed in Chapter 11.

| | |
|---|---|
| JarInputStream | JarOutputStream |

The java.security package includes a couple of stream classes used for calculating message digests:

| | |
|---|---|
| DigestInputStream | DigestOutputStream |

The Java Cryptography Extension (JCE) adds two classes for encryption and decryption:

| | |
|---|---|
| CipherInputStream | CipherOutputStream |

These four streams will be discussed in Chapter 12.

Finally, a few random stream classes are hiding inside the sun packages—for example, sun.net.TelnetInputStream and sun.net.TelnetOutputStream. However, these are deliberately hidden from you and are generally presented as instances of java.io.InputStream or java.io.OutputStream only.

# Numeric Data

Input streams read bytes and output streams write bytes. Readers read characters and writers write characters. Therefore, to understand input and output, you first need a solid understanding of how Java deals with bytes, integers, characters, and other primitive data types, and when and why one is converted into another. In many cases Java's behavior is not obvious.

## Integer Data

The fundamental integer data type in Java is the int, a 4-byte, big-endian, two's complement integer. An int can take on all values between –2,147,483,648 and 2,147,483,647. When you type a literal integer such as 7, –8345, or 3000000000 in Java source code, the compiler treats that literal as an int. In the case of 3000000000 or similar numbers too large to fit in an int, the compiler emits an error message citing "Numeric overflow."

longs are 8-byte, big-endian, two's complement integers that range all the way from –9,223,372,036,854,775,808 to 9,223,372,036,854,775,807. long literals are indicated by suffixing the number with a lower- or uppercase L. An uppercase L is preferred because the lowercase l is too easily confused with the numeral 1 in most fonts. For example, 7L, –8345L, and 3000000000L are all 64-bit long literals.

Two more integer data types are available in Java, the short and the byte. shorts are 2-byte, big-endian, two's complement integers with ranges from –32,768 to 32,767. They're rarely used in Java and are included mainly for compatibility with C.

bytes, however, are very much used in Java. In particular, they're used in I/O. A byte is an 8-bit, two's complement integer that ranges from –128 to 127. Note that like all numeric data types in Java, a byte is signed. The maximum byte value is 127. 128, 129, and so on through 255 are not legal values for bytes.

Java has no short or byte literals. When you write the literal 42 or 24000, the compiler always reads it as an int, never as a byte or a short, even when used in the right-hand side of an assignment statement to a byte or short, like this:

```
byte b = 42;
short s = 24000;
```

However, in these lines, a special *assignment conversion* is performed by the compiler, effectively casting the int literals to the narrower types. Because the int literals are constants known at compile time, this is permitted. However, assignments from int variables to shorts and bytes are not—at least not without an explicit cast. For example, consider these lines:

```
int i = 42;
byte b = i;
```

Compiling these lines produces the following errors:

```
Error:   Incompatible type for declaration.
Explicit cast needed to convert int to short.
ByteTest.java  line 6
```

This occurs even though the compiler is theoretically capable of determining that the assignment does not lose information. To correct this, you must use explicit casts, like this:

```
int i = 42;
byte b = (byte) i;
```

Even the addition of two byte variables produces an integer result and thus cannot be assigned to a byte variable without a cast. The following code produces the same error:

```
byte b1 = 22;
byte b2 = 23;
byte b3 = b1 + b2;
```

For these reasons, working directly with byte variables is inconvenient at best. Many of the methods in the stream classes are documented as reading or writing bytes. However, what they really return or accept as arguments are ints in the range of an unsigned byte (0–255). This does not match any Java primitive data type. These ints are then converted into bytes internally.

For instance, according to the Java class library documentation, the read( ) method of java.io.InputStream returns "the next byte of data, or –1 if the end of the stream is reached." Upon reflection, this sounds suspicious. How is a –1 that appears as part of the stream data to be distinguished from a –1 indicating end of stream? In point of fact, the read( ) method does not return a byte; its signature shows that it returns an int:

```
public abstract int read( ) throws IOException
```

This int is not a Java byte with a value between –128 and 127 but a more general unsigned byte with a value between 0 and 255. Hence, –1 can easily be distinguished from valid data values read from the stream.

The write( ) method in the java.io.OutputStream class is similarly problematic. It returns void but takes an int as an argument:

```
public abstract void write(int b) throws IOException
```

This int is intended to be an unsigned byte value between 0 and 255. However, there's nothing to stop a careless programmer from passing in an int value outside that range. In this case, the 8 low-order bits are written and the top 24 high-order bits are ignored:

```
b = b & 0x000000FF;
```

 Although this is the behavior described in the *Java Language Specifica-tion*, since the `write( )` method is abstract, actual implementation of this scheme is left to the subclasses, and a careless programmer could do something different.

On the other hand, real Java bytes are used in methods that read or write arrays of bytes. For example, consider these two `read( )` methods from `java.io.InputStream`:

```
public int read(byte[] data) throws IOException
public int read(byte[] data, int offset, int length) throws IOException
```

While the difference between an 8-bit byte and a 32-bit int is insignificant for a single number, it can be very significant when several thousand to several million numbers are read. In fact, a single byte still takes up four bytes of space inside the Java virtual machine, but a byte array occupies only the amount of space it actually needs. The virtual machine includes special instructions for operating on byte arrays but does not include any instructions for operating on single bytes. They're just promoted to ints.

Although data is stored in the array as signed Java bytes with values between −128 and 127, there's a simple one-to-one correspondence between these signed values and the unsigned bytes normally used in I/O. This correspondence is given by the following formula:

```
int unsignedByte = signedByte >= 0 ? signedByte : 256 + signedByte;
```

## Conversions and Casts

Since bytes have such a small range, they're often converted to ints in calculations and method invocations. Often, they need to be converted back, generally through a cast. Therefore, it's useful to have a good grasp of exactly how the conversion occurs.

Casting from an int to a byte—for that matter, casting from any wider integer type to a narrower type—takes place through truncation of the high-order bytes. This means that as long as the value of the wider type can be expressed in the narrower type, the value is not changed. The int 127 cast to a byte still retains the value 127.

On the other hand, if the int value is too large for a byte, strange things happen. The int 128 cast to a byte is not 127, the nearest byte value. Instead, it is −128. This occurs through the wonders of two's complement arithmetic. Written in hexadecimal, 128 is 0x00000080. When that int is cast to a byte, the leading zeros are truncated, leaving 0x80. In binary, this can be written as 10000000. If this were an unsigned number, 10000000 would be 128 and all would be fine, but this isn't an unsigned number. Instead, the leading bit is a sign bit, and that 1 does not indicate $2^7$ but a minus sign. The absolute value of a negative number is found by taking the complement (changing all the 1 bits to 0 bits and vice versa) and adding 1. The complement of 10000000 is 01111111. Adding 1, you have 01111111 + 1 = 10000000 = 128 (decimal). Therefore, the byte 0x80 actually represents −128. Similar calculations show that the int 129 is cast to the byte −127, the int 130 is cast to the byte −126, the int 131 is cast to the byte −125, and so on. This continues through the int 255, which is cast to the byte −1.

 In this book, as in Java source code, all numbers preceded by 0x are read as hexadecimal.

When 256 is reached, the low-order bytes of the int are filled with zeros. In other words, 256 is 0x00000100. Thus, casting it to a byte produces 0, and the cycle starts over. This behavior can be reproduced algorithmically with this formula, though a cast is obviously simpler:

```
int byteValue;
int temp = intValue % 256;
if ( intValue < 0) {
  byteValue =  temp < -128 ? 256 + temp : temp;
}
else {
  byteValue =  temp > 127 ? temp - 256 : temp;
}
```

# Character Data

Numbers are only part of the data a typical Java program needs in order to read and write. Many programs also handle text, which is composed of characters. Since computers only really understand numbers, characters are encoded by assigning each character in a given script a number. For example, in the common ASCII encoding, the character *A* is mapped to the number 65; the character *B* is mapped to the number 66; the character *C* is mapped to the number 67; and so on. Different encodings may encode different scripts or may encode the same or similar scripts in different ways.

Java understands several dozen different character sets for a variety of languages, ranging from ASCII to the Shift Japanese Input System (SJIS) to Unicode. Internally, Java uses the Unicode character set. Unicode is a superset of the 1-byte Latin-1 character set, which in turn is an 8-bit superset of the 7-bit ASCII character set.

## ASCII

ASCII, the American Standard Code for Information Interchange, is a 7-bit character set. Thus it defines $2^7$, or 128, different characters whose numeric values range from 0 to 127. These characters are sufficient for handling most of American English. It's an often-used lowest common denominator format for different computers. If you were to read a byte value between 0 and 127 from a stream, then cast it to a char, the result would be the corresponding ASCII character.

ASCII characters 0–31 and character 127 are nonprinting control characters. Characters 32–47 are various punctuation and space characters. Characters 48–57 are the digits 0–9. Characters 58–64 are another group of punctuation characters. Characters 65–90 are the capital letters A–Z. Characters 91–96 are a few more punctuation marks. Characters 97–122 are the lowercase letters a–z. Finally, characters 123–126 are a few remaining punctuation symbols. The complete ASCII character set is shown in Table A-1 in the Appendix.

## Latin-1

ISO 8859-1, Latin-1, is an 8-bit character set that's a strict superset of ASCII. It defines $2^8$, or 256, different characters whose numeric values range from 0 to 255. The first 128 characters—that is, those numbers with the high-order bit equal to 0—correspond exactly to the ASCII character set. Thus 65 is ASCII A and Latin-1 A; 66 is ASCII B and Latin-1 B; and so on. Where Latin-1 and ASCII diverge is in the characters between 128 and 255 (characters with the high-order bit equal to 1). ASCII does not define these characters. Latin-1 uses them for various accented letters such as *ü* needed for non-English languages written in a Roman script, additional punctuation marks and symbols such as ©, and additional control characters. The upper, non-ASCII half of the Latin-1 character set is shown in Table A-2 in the Appendix. If you were to read an unsigned byte value from a stream, then cast it to a char, the result would be the corresponding Latin-1 character.

## Unicode

Latin-1 suffices for most Western European languages (with the notable exception of Greek), but it doesn't have anywhere near the number of characters required to represent Cyrillic, Greek, Arabic, Hebrew, or Devanagari, not to mention pictographic languages like Chinese and Japanese. Chinese alone has over 80,000 different characters. To handle these scripts and many others, the Unicode character set was invented. Unicode has space for over one million different possible characters. Only about 100,000 are used in practice, the rest being reserved for future expansion. Unicode can handle most of the world's living languages and a number of dead ones as well.

The first 256 characters of Unicode are identical to the characters of the Latin-1 character set. Thus 65 is ASCII A and Unicode A; 66 is ASCII B and Unicode B, and so on.

Unicode is only a character set. It is not a character encoding. That is, although Unicode specifies that the letter A has character code 65, it doesn't say whether the number 65 is written using one byte, two bytes, or four bytes, or whether the bytes used are written in big- or little-endian order. However, there are certain standard encodings of Unicode into bytes, the most common of which are UTF-8, UTF-16, and UTF-32.

UTF-32 is the most naïve encoding. It simply represents each character as a single 4-byte (32-bit) int.

UTF-16 represents most characters as a 2-byte, unsigned short. However, certain less common Chinese characters, musical and mathematical symbols, and characters from dead languages such as Linear B are represented in four bytes each. The Java virtual machine uses UTF-16 internally. In fact, a Java char is not really a Unicode character. Rather it is a UTF-16 code point, and sometimes two Java chars are required to make up one Unicode character.

Finally, UTF-8 is a relatively efficient encoding (especially when most of your text is ASCII) that uses one byte for each of the ASCII characters, two bytes for each character in many other alphabets, and three-to-four bytes for characters from Asian languages. Java's *.class* files use UTF-8 internally to store string literals.

## Other Encodings

ASCII, Latin-1, and Unicode are hardly the only character sets in common use, though they are the ones handled most directly by Java. There are many other character sets, both that encode different scripts and that encode the same scripts in different ways. For example, IBM mainframes have long used a non-ASCII character set called EBCDIC. EBCDIC has most of the same characters as ASCII but assigns them to different numbers. Macintoshes commonly use an 8-bit encoding called MacRoman that matches ASCII in the lower 128 places and has most of the same characters as Latin-1 in the upper 128 characters, though in different positions. DOS (including the DOS shell in Windows) uses character sets such as Cp850 that include box drawing characters such as ⌊ and ✦. Big-5 and SJIS are encodings of Chinese and Japanese, respectively, that include most of the numerous characters used in those scripts.

The exact details of each encoding are fairly involved and should really be handled by experts. Fortunately, the Java class library includes a set of reader and writer classes written by such experts. Readers and writers convert to and from bytes in particular encodings to Java chars without any extra effort. For similar reasons, you should use a writer rather than an output stream to write text, as discussed in Chapter 20.

## The char Data Type

Text in Java is primarily composed of the char primitive data type, char arrays, and Strings, which are stored as arrays of chars internally. Just as you need to understand bytes to really grasp how input and output streams work, so too do you need to understand chars to understand how readers and writers work.

In Java, a char is a 2-byte, unsigned integer—the only unsigned type in Java. Thus, possible char values range from 0 to 65,535. Each char represents a particular character in the Unicode character set. chars may be assigned to by using int literals in this range; for example:

```
char copyright = 169;
```

chars may also be assigned to by using char literals—that is, the character itself enclosed in single quotes:

```
char copyright = '©';
```

Sun's *javac* compiler can translate many different encodings to Unicode by using the -encoding command-line flag to specify the encoding in which the file is written. For example, if you know a file is written in ISO 8859-1, you might compile it as follows:

```
% javac -encoding 8859_1 CharTest.java
```

The list of available encodings is given in Table A-4.

With the exception of Unicode itself, most character sets understood by Java do not have equivalents for all the Unicode characters. To encode characters that do not exist in the character set you're programming with, you can use *Unicode escapes*. A Unicode escape sequence is an unescaped backslash, followed by any number of *u* characters, followed by four hexadecimal digits specifying the character to be used. For example:

```
char copyright = '\u00A9';
```

Unicode escapes may be used not just in char literals, but also in strings, identifiers, comments, and even in keywords, separators, operators, and numeric literals. The compiler translates Unicode escapes to actual Unicode characters before it does anything else with a source code file.

> Unicode escapes are a relic of times when most text editors could not handle Unicode. Fortunately, this hasn't been the case for years. Today, Java source code should be written in Unicode (preferably UTF-8) and any non-ASCII characters typed directly. In 2006, Unicode escapes serve only to obfuscate code.

# Readers and Writers

Streams are primarily intended for data that can be read as pure bytes—basically, byte data and numeric data encoded as binary numbers of one sort or another. Streams are specifically not intended for reading and writing text, including both ASCII text, such as "Hello World," and numbers formatted as text, such as "3.1415929". For these purposes, you should use readers and writers.

Input and output streams are fundamentally byte-based. Readers and writers are based on characters, which can have varying widths depending on the character set.

For example, ASCII and Latin-1 use 1-byte characters. UTF-32 uses 4-byte characters. UTF-8 uses characters of varying width (between one and four bytes). Since characters are ultimately composed of bytes, readers take their input from streams. However, they convert those bytes into chars according to a specified encoding format before passing them along. Similarly, writers convert chars to bytes according to a specified encoding before writing them onto some underlying stream.

The java.io.Reader and java.io.Writer classes are abstract superclasses for classes that read and write character-based data. The subclasses are notable for handling the conversion between different character sets. The core Java API includes nine reader and eight writer classes, all in the java.io package:

| | |
|---|---|
| BufferedReader | BufferedWriter |
| CharArrayReader | CharArrayWriter |
| FileReader | FileWriter |
| FilterReader | FilterWriter |
| InputStreamReader | LineNumberReader |
| OutputStreamWriter | PipedReader |
| PipedWriter | PrintWriter |
| PushbackReader | StringReader |
| StringWriter | |

For the most part, these classes have methods that are extremely similar to the equivalent stream classes. Often the only difference is that a byte in the signature of a stream method becomes a char in the signature of the matching reader or writer method. For example, the java.io.OutputStream class declares these three write() methods:

```
public abstract void write(int i) throws IOException
public void write(byte[] data) throws IOException
public void write(byte[] data, int offset, int length) throws IOException
```

The java.io.Writer class, therefore, declares these three write() methods:

```
public void write(int i) throws IOException
public void write(char[] data) throws IOException
public abstract void write(char[] data, int offset, int length) throws IOException
```

As you can see, the signatures match except that in the latter two methods the byte array data has changed to a char array. There's also a less obvious difference not reflected in the signature. While the int passed to the OutputStream write() method is reduced modulo 256 before being output, the int passed to the Writer write() method is reduced modulo 65,536. This reflects the different ranges of chars and bytes.

java.io.Writer also has two more write() methods that take their data from a string:

```
public void write(String s) throws IOException
public void write(String s, int offset, int length) throws IOException
```

Because streams don't know how to deal with character-based data, there are no corresponding methods in the java.io.OutputStream class.

# Buffers and Channels

Streams are reasonably fast as long as an application has to read from or write to only one at a time. In fact, the bottleneck is more likely to be the disk or network you're reading from or writing to than the Java program itself. The situation is a little dicier when a program needs to read from or write to many different streams simultaneously. This is a common situation in web servers, for example, where a single process may be communicating with hundreds or even thousands of different clients simultaneously.

At any given time, a stream may *block*. That is, it may simply stop accepting further requests temporarily while it waits for the actual hardware it's writing to or reading from to catch up. This can happen on disks, and it's a major issue on network connections. Clearly, you don't want to stop sending data to 999 clients just because one of them is experiencing network congestion. The traditional solution to this problem prior to Java 1.4 was to put each connection in a separate thread. Five hundred clients requires 500 threads. Each thread can run independently of the others so that one slow connection doesn't slow down everyone.

However, threads are not without overhead of their own. Creating and managing threads takes a lot of work, and few virtual machines can handle more than a thousand or so threads without serious performance degradation. Spawning several thousand threads can crash even the toughest virtual machine. Nonetheless, big servers need to be able to communicate with thousands of clients simultaneously.

The solution invented in Java 1.4 was nonblocking I/O. In nonblocking I/O, streams are relegated mostly to a supporting role while the real work is done by channels and buffers. Input buffers are filled with data from the channel and then drained of data by the application. Output buffers work in reverse: the application fills them with data that is subsequently drained out by the target. The design is such that the writer and reader don't always have to operate in lockstep with each other. Most importantly, the client application can queue reads and writes to each channel. It does not have to stop processing simply because the other end of the channel isn't quite ready. This enables one thread to service many different channels simultaneously, dramatically reducing the load on the virtual machine.

Channels and buffers are also used to enable memory-mapped I/O. In memory-mapped I/O, files are treated as large blocks of memory, essentially as big byte arrays. Particular parts of a mapped file can be read with statements such as int x = file.getInt(1067) and written with statements such as file.putInt(x, 1067). The data is stored directly to disk at the right location without having to read or write all the data that precedes or follows the section of interest.

Channels and buffers are a little more complex than streams and bytes. However, for certain kinds of I/O-bound applications, the performance gains are dramatic and worth the added complexity.

## The Ubiquitous IOException

As far as computer operations go, input and output are unreliable. They are subject to problems completely outside the programmer's control. Disks can develop bad sectors while a file is being read. Construction workers drop their backhoes through the cables that connect your WAN. Users unexpectedly cancel their input. Telephone repair crews shut off your modem line while trying to repair someone else's. (This last one actually happened to me while writing this chapter. My modem kept dropping the connection and then not getting a dial tone; I had to hunt down the Verizon "repairman" in my building's basement and explain to him that he was working on the wrong line.)

Because of these potential problems and many more, almost every method that performs input or output is declared to throw an IOException. IOException is a checked exception, so you must either declare that your methods throw it or enclose the call that can throw it in a try/catch block. The only real exceptions to this rule are the PrintStream and PrintWriter classes. Because it would be inconvenient to wrap a try/catch block around each call to System.out.println( ), Sun decided to have PrintStream (and later PrintWriter) catch and eat any exceptions thrown inside a print( ) or println( ) method. If you do want to check for exceptions inside a print( ) or println( ) method, you can call checkError( ):

```
public boolean checkError( )
```

The checkError( ) method returns true if an exception has occurred on this print stream, false if one hasn't. It tells you only that an error occurred. It does not tell you what sort of error occurred. If you need to know more about the error, you'll have to use a different output stream or writer class.

IOException has many subclasses—15 in java.io alone—and methods often throw a more specific exception that subclasses IOException; for instance, EOFException on an unexpected end of file or UnsupportedEncodingException when you try read text in an unknown character set. However, methods usually declare only that they throw an IOException.

The java.io.IOException class declares no public methods or fields of significance—just the usual two constructors you find in most exception classes:

```
public IOException( )
public IOException(String message)
```

The first constructor creates an IOException with an empty message. The second provides more details about what went wrong. Of course, IOException has the usual methods inherited by all exception classes such as toString( ) and printStackTrace( ).

 Java 6 also adds an IOError class that is "Thrown when a serious I/O error has occurred." Xueming Shen snuck this class in the backdoor solely to avoid declaring that methods in the new Console class throw IOException like they should. I am not sure if this wart will remain in the final version of Java 6 or not. At the time of this writing, I am lobbying strenuously to get this removed, or at least replaced by a runtime exception instead of an error.

## The Console: System.out, System.in, and System.err

The console is the default destination for output written to System.out or System.err and the default source of input for System.in. On most platforms the console is the command-line environment from which the Java program was initially launched, perhaps an *xterm* or a DOS prompt as shown in Figure 1-1. The word *console* is something of a misnomer, since on Unix systems the console refers to a very specific command-line shell rather than to command-line shells overall.

```
D:\JAVA\Java IO Author Review\tests>type WriteHello.java
import java.io.*;

public class WriteHello {

  public static void main(String[] args) throws IOException {

    byte[] hello = {72, 101, 108, 108, 111, 32, 87, 111, 114, 108, 100, 33, 10, 13};
    System.out.write(hello);

  }
}
D:\JAVA\Java IO Author Review\tests>java WriteHello
Hello World!
```

*Figure 1-1. A DOS console on Windows*

Many common misconceptions about I/O occur because most programmers' first exposure to I/O is through the console. The console is convenient for quick hacks and toy examples commonly found in textbooks, and I will use it for that in this book, but it's really a very unusual source of input and destination for output, and good Java programs avoid it. It behaves almost, but not completely, unlike anything else you'd want to read from or write to. While consoles make convenient examples in programming texts like this one, they're a horrible user interface and really have little place in modern programs. Users are more comfortable with a well-designed

GUI. Furthermore, the console is unreliable across platforms. Many smaller devices such as Palm Pilots and cell phones have no console. Web browsers running applets sometimes provide a console that can be used for output. However, this is hidden by default, normally cannot be used for input, and is not available in all browsers on all platforms.

## System.out

System.out is the first instance of the OutputStream class most programmers encounter. In fact, it's often encountered before students know what a class or an output stream is. Specifically, System.out is the static out field of the java.lang.System class. It's an instance of java.io.PrintStream, a subclass of java.io.OutputStream.

System.out corresponds to stdout in Unix or C. Normally, output sent to System.out appears on the console. As a general rule, the console converts the numeric byte data System.out sends to it into ASCII or Latin-1 text. Thus, the following lines write the string "Hello World!" on the console:

```
byte[] hello = {72, 101, 108, 108, 111, 32, 87, 111, 114, 108, 100, 33, 10,
                13};
System.out.write(hello);
```

## System.err

Unix and C programmers are familiar with stderr, which is commonly used for error messages. stderr is a separate file pointer from stdout, but often means the same thing. Generally, stderr and stdout both send data to the console, whatever that is. However, stdout and stderr can be redirected to different places. For instance, output can be redirected to a file while error messages still appear on the console.

System.err is Java's version of stderr. Like System.out, System.err is an instance of java.io.PrintStream, a subclass of java.io.OutputStream. System.err is most commonly used inside the catch clause of a try/catch block, as shown here:

```
try {
  // Do something that may throw an exception.
}
catch (Exception ex) {
  System.err.println(ex);
}
```

Finished programs shouldn't have much need for System.err, but it is useful while you're debugging.

Libraries should never print anything on System.err. In general, libraries should not talk to the user at all, unless that is their specific purpose. Instead, libraries should inform the client application of any problems they encounter by throwing an exception or invoking a callback method in some sort of error-handler object. Yes, Xerces, I'm talking to you. (The Xerces XML parser, now built into Java 5 has a really annoying habit of reporting even nonfatal errors by printing them on System.err.)

## System.in

System.in is the input stream connected to the console, much as System.out is the output stream connected to the console. In Unix or C terms, System.in is stdin and can be redirected from a shell in the same fashion. System.in is the static in field of the java.lang.System class. It's an instance of java.io.InputStream, at least as far as is documented.

Past what's documented, System.in is really a java.io.BufferedInputStream. BufferedInputStream doesn't declare any new methods; it just overrides the ones already declared in java.io.InputStream. Buffered input streams read data in large chunks into a buffer, then parcel it out in requested sizes. This can be more efficient than reading one character at a time. Otherwise, the data is completely transparent to the programmer.

The main significance of this is that bytes are not available to the program at the moment the user types them on System.in. Instead, input enters the program one line at a time. This allows a user typing into the console to backspace over and correct mistakes. Java does not allow you to put the console into "raw mode," wherein each character becomes available as soon as it's typed, including characters such as backspace and delete.

The user types into the console using the platform's default character set, typically ASCII or some superset thereof. The data is converted into numeric bytes when read. For example, if the user types "Hello World!" and hits the Enter key, the following bytes are read from System.in in this order:

    72, 101, 108, 108, 111, 32, 87, 111, 114, 108, 100, 33, 10, 13

Many programs that run from the command line and read input from System.in require you to enter the "end of stream" character, also known as the "end of file" or EOF character, to terminate a program normally. How this is entered is platform-dependent. On Unix and the Mac, Ctrl-D generally indicates end of stream. On Windows, Ctrl-Z does. In some cases it may be necessary to type this character alone on a line. That is, you may need to hit Enter/Ctrl-Z or Enter/Ctrl-D before Java will recognize the end of stream.

## Redirecting System.out, System.in, and System.err

In a shell, you often redirect stdout, stdin, or stderr. For example, to specify that output from the Java program OptimumBattingOrder goes into the file *yankees06.out* and that input for that program is read from the file *yankees06.tab*, you might type:

```
% java OptimumBattingOrder < yankees06.tab > yankees06.out
```

Redirection in a DOS shell is the same.

It's sometimes convenient to be able to redirect System.out, System.in, and System.err from inside the running program. The following three static methods in the java.lang.System class do exactly that:

```
public static void setIn(InputStream in)
public static void setOut(PrintStream out)
public static void setErr(PrintStream err)
```

For example, to specify that data written on System.out is sent to the file *yankees99.out* and that data read from System.in comes from *yankees99.tab*, you could write:

```
System.setIn(new FileInputStream("yankees99.tab"));
System.setOut(new PrintStream(new FileOutputStream("yankees99.out")));
```

## The Console Class // Java 6

While working on Java 6, Sun finally got tired of all the sniping from the Python and Ruby communities about how hard it was to just read a line of input from the console. This is a one liner in most scripting languages, but traditionally it's been a little involved in Java.

 The reason reading a line of input from the console is relatively involved in Java compared to some other languages is because in 2006 no one needs to do this outside of a CS 101 course. Real programs use GUIs or the network for user interfaces, not the console, and Java has always been focused on getting real work done rather than enabling toy examples.

Java 6 adds a new java.lang.Console class that provides a few convenience methods for input and output. This class is a singleton. There's never more than one instance of it, and it always applies to the same shell that System.in, System.out, and System.err point to. You retrieve the single instance of this class using the static System.console() method like so:

```
Console theConsole = System.console();
```

This method returns null if you're running in an environment such as a cell phone or a web browser that does not have a console.

There are several ways you might use this class. Most importantly, it has a simple readLine( ) method that returns a single string of text from the console, not including the line-break characters:

```
public String readLine() throws IOError
```

This method returns null on end of stream. It throws an IOError if any I/O problem is encountered. (Again, this is a design bug, and I am trying to convince Sun to fix this before final release. This method should throw an IOException like any normal method if there's a problem.)

You can optionally provide a formatted prompt before reading the line:

```
public String readLine(String prompt, Object... formatting)
```

The prompt string is interpreted like any printf( ) string and filled with arguments to its right. *All* this does is format the prompt. This is not a scanf( ) equivalent. The return value is the same as for the no-args readLine( ) method.

Console also has two readPassword( ) methods:

```
public char[] readPassword()
public char[] readPassword(String prompt, Object... formatting)
```

Unlike readLine( ), these do not echo the characters typed back to the screen. Also note that they return an array of chars rather than a String. When you're finished with the password, you can overwrite the characters in the array with zeros so that the password is not held in memory for longer than it needs to be. This limits the possibility of the password being exposed to memory scanners or stored on the disk due to virtual memory.

For output, Console has two methods, printf( ) and format( ):

```
public Console format(String format, Object... arguments)
public Console printf(String format, Object... arguments)
```

There is no difference between these two methods. They are synonyms. For example, this code fragment prints a three-column table of the angles between 0 and 360 degrees in degrees, radians, and grads on the console using only printf( ). Each number is exactly five characters wide with one digit after the decimal point.

```
Console console = System.console();
for (double degrees = 0.0; degrees < 360.0; degrees++) {
  double radians = Math.PI * degrees / 180.0;
  double grads = 400 * degrees / 360;
  console.printf("%5.1f %5.1f %5.1f\n", degrees, radians, grads);
}
```

Here's the start of the output:

```
0.0   0.0   0.0
1.0   0.0   1.1
2.0   0.0   2.2
3.0   0.1   3.3
...
```

Chapter 7 explores printf( ) and its formatting arguments in greater detail.

The console normally buffers all output until a line break is seen. You can force data to be written to the screen even before a line break by invoking the flush( ) method:

```
formatter.flush();
formatter.close();
```

Finally, if these methods aren't enough for you, you can work directly with the console's associated PrintWriter and Reader:

```
public PrintWriter writer()
public Reader      reader()
```

Chapter 20 explores these two classes.

Example 1-1 is a simple program that uses the Console class to answer a typical homework assignment: ask the user to enter an integer and print the squares of the numbers from 1 to that integer. In keeping with the nature of such programs, I've deliberately left at least three typical student bugs in the code. Identifying and correcting them is left as homework for the reader.

*Example 1-1. CS 101 Homework*

```
import java.io.*;

class Homework {

  public static void main(String[] args) {
    Console console = System.console();
    String input = console.readLine(
      "Please enter a number between 1 and 10: ");
    int max = Integer.parseInt(input);
    for (int i = 1; i < max; i++) {
      console.printf("%d\n", i*i);
    }
  }
}
```

Here's what the program looks like when it runs:

```
C:\>java Homework
Please enter a number between 1 and 10: 4
1
4
9
```

# Security Checks on I/O

One of the original fears about downloading executable content like applets from the Internet was that a hostile applet could erase your hard disk or read your Quicken files. Nothing has happened to change that since Java was introduced. This is why

Java applets run under the control of a security manager that checks each operation an applet performs to prevent potentially hostile acts.

The security manager is particularly careful about I/O operations. For the most part, the checks are related to these questions:

- Can the program read a particular file?
- Can the program write a particular file?
- Can the program delete a particular file?
- Can the program determine whether a particular file exists?
- Can the program make a network connection to a particular host?
- Can the program accept an incoming connection from a particular host?

The short answer to all these questions when the program is an applet is "No, it cannot." A slightly more elaborate answer would specify a few exceptions. Applets can make network connections to the host they came from; applets can read a few very specific files that contain information about the Java environment; and trusted applets may sometimes run without these restrictions. But for almost all practical purposes, the answer is almost always no.

Because of these security issues, you need to be careful when using code fragments and examples from this book in an applet. Everything shown here works when run in an application, but when run in an applet, it may fail with a SecurityException. It's not always obvious whether a particular method or class will cause problems. The write( ) method of BufferedOutputStream, for instance, is completely safe when the ultimate destination is a byte array. However, that same write( ) method will throw an exception when the destination is a file. An attempt to open a connection to a web server may succeed or fail depending on whether or not the web server you're connecting to is the same one the applet came from.

Consequently, this book focuses very much on applications. There is very little I/O that can be done from an applet without running afoul of the security manager. The problem may not always be obvious—not all web browsers properly report security exceptions—but it is there. If you can make an applet work when it's run as a standalone application and you cannot get it to work inside a web browser, the problem is likely a conflict with the browser's security manager.

# CHAPTER 2
# Output Streams

The java.io.OutputStream class declares the three basic methods you need to write bytes of data onto a stream. It also has methods for closing and flushing streams:

```
public abstract void write(int b) throws IOException
public void write(byte[] data) throws IOException
public void write(byte[] data, int offset, int length) throws IOException
public void flush() throws IOException
public void close() throws IOException
```

OutputStream is an abstract class. Subclasses provide implementations of the abstract write(int b) method. They may also override the four nonabstract methods. For example, the FileOutputStream class overrides all five methods with methods that call native code to write files. Although OutputStream is abstract, often you only need to know that the object you have is an OutputStream; the more specific subclass of OutputStream is hidden from you. For example, the getOutputStream() method of java.net.URLConnection has this signature:

```
public OutputStream getOutputStream() throws IOException
```

Depending on the type of URL associated with this URLConnection object, the actual class of the output stream that's returned may be a sun.net.TelnetOutputStream, a sun.net.smtp.SmtpPrintStream, a sun.net.www.http.KeepAliveStream, or something else completely. All you know as a programmer, and all you need to know, is that the object returned is some kind of OutputStream.

Furthermore, even when working with subclasses whose types you know, you still need to be able to use the methods inherited from OutputStream. And since methods that are inherited are not included in the API documentation, it's important to remember that they're there. For example, the java.io.DataOutputStream class does not declare a close() method, but you can still call the method it inherits from its superclass.

# Writing Bytes to Output Streams

The fundamental method of the `OutputStream` class is `write( )`:

```
public abstract void write(int b) throws IOException
```

This method writes a single unsigned byte of data whose value should be between 0 and 255. If you pass a number larger than 255 or smaller than 0, it's reduced modulo 256 before being written.

Example 2-1, AsciiChart, is a simple program that writes the printable ASCII characters (32 to 126) on the console. The console interprets the numeric values as ASCII characters, not as numbers. This is a feature of the console, not of the `OutputStream` class or the specific subclass of which `System.out` is an instance. The `write( )` method merely sends a particular bit pattern to a particular output stream. How that bit pattern is interpreted depends on what's connected to the other end of the stream.

*Example 2-1. The AsciiChart program*

```java
import java.io.*;

public class AsciiChart {

  public static void main(String[] args) {

    for (int i = 32; i < 127; i++) {
      System.out.write(i);
      // break line after every eight characters.
      if (i % 8 == 7) System.out.write('\n');
      else System.out.write('\t');
    }
    System.out.write('\n');
  }
}
```

Notice the use of the char literals `'\t'` and `'\n'`. The compiler converts these to the numbers 9 and 10, respectively. When these numbers are written on the console, the console interprets them as a tab and a linefeed, respectively. The same effect could have been achieved by writing the if clause like this:

```java
if (i % 8 == 7) System.out.write(10);
else System.out.write(9);
```

Here's the output:

```
% java AsciiChart
 !      "       #       $       %       &       '
 (      )       *       +       ,       -       .       /
 0      1       2       3       4       5       6       7
 8      9       :       ;       <       =       >       ?
 @      A       B       C       D       E       F       G
 H      I       J       K       L       M       N       O
 P      Q       R       S       T       U       V       W
```

| X | Y | Z | [ | \ | ] | ^ | _ |
|---|---|---|---|---|---|---|---|
| ` | a | b | c | d | e | f | g |
| h | i | j | k | l | m | n | o |
| p | q | r | s | t | u | v | w |
| x | y | z | { | \| | } | ~ | |

The write( ) method can throw an IOException, so you'll need to wrap most calls to this method in a try/catch block, or declare that your own method throws IOException. For example:

```
try {
  for (int i = 32; i <= 127; i++) out.write(i);
}
catch (IOException ex) {
  System.err.println(ex);
}
```

Observant readers will have noticed that Example 2-1 did not actually catch any IOExceptions. The PrintStream class, of which System.out is an instance, overrides write( ) with a variant that does not throw IOException. This is very unusual, and PrintStream is almost the only class that does this. I'll have more to say about PrintStream, including this very unsafe behavior, in Chapter 7.

## Writing Arrays of Bytes

It's often faster to write data in large chunks than it is to write it byte by byte. Two overloaded variants of the write( ) method do this:

```
public void write(byte[] data) throws IOException
public void write(byte[] data, int offset, int length) throws IOException
```

The first variant writes the entire byte array data. The second writes only the subarray of data starting at offset and continuing for length bytes. For example, the following code fragment blasts the bytes in a string onto System.out:

```
String s = "How are streams treating you?";
byte[] data = s.getBytes( );
System.out.write(data);
```

Conversely, you may run into performance problems if you attempt to write too much data at a time. The exact turnaround point depends on the eventual destination of the data. Files are often best written in small multiples of the block size of the disk, typically 1024, 2048, or 4096 bytes. Network connections often require smaller buffer sizes—128 or 256 bytes. The optimal buffer size depends on too many system-specific details for anything to be guaranteed, but I often use 128 bytes for network connections and 1024 bytes for files.

Example 2-2 is a simple program that constructs a byte array filled with an ASCII chart, then blasts it onto the console in one call to write( ).

*Example 2-2. The AsciiArray program*

```java
import java.io.*;

public class AsciiArray {

  public static void main(String[] args) {

    byte[] b = new byte[(127-31)*2];
    int index = 0;
    for (int i = 32; i < 127; i++) {
      b[index++] = (byte) i;
      // Break line after every eight characters.
      if (i % 8 == 7) b[index++] = (byte) '\n';
      else b[index++] = (byte) '\t';
    }
    b[index++] = (byte) '\n';
    try {
      System.out.write(b);
    }
    catch (IOException ex) {
      System.err.println(ex);
    }
  }
}
```

The output is the same as in Example 2-1. Because of the nature of the console, this particular program probably isn't a lot faster than Example 2-1, but it certainly could be if you were writing data into a file rather than onto the console. The difference in performance between writing a byte array in a single call to write( ) and writing the same array by invoking write( ) once for each component of the array can easily be a factor of a hundred or more. *really?*

# Closing Output Streams

When you're through with a stream, you should close it. This allows the operating system to free any resources associated with the stream. Exactly what these resources are depends on your platform and varies with the type of stream. However, many systems have finite resources. For example, on some personal computer operating systems, no more than several hundred files can be open at once. Multiuser operating systems have larger limits, but limits nonetheless.

To close a stream, invoke its close( ) method:

```java
public void close() throws IOException
```

For example, again assuming out is an OutputStream, calling out.close( ) closes the stream and frees any underlying resources such as file handles or network ports associated with the stream.

Once you have closed an output stream, you probably can't write anything else onto that stream. Attempting to do so normally throws an IOException, though there are a few classes where this doesn't happen.

 Again, System.out is a partial exception because, as a PrintStream, all exceptions it throws are eaten. Once you close System.out, you can't write to it. Trying to do so won't throw any exceptions; however, your output will not appear on the console.

Not all streams need to be closed—byte array output streams do not need to be closed, for example. However, streams associated with files and network connections should always be closed when you're done with them. For example, if you open a file for writing and neglect to close it when you're through, then other processes may be blocked from reading or writing to that file. Often, files are closed like this:

```
try {
  OutputStream out = new FileOutputStream("numbers.dat");
  // Write to the stream...
  out.close( );
}
catch (IOException ex) {
  System.err.println(ex);
}
```

However, this code fragment has a potential leak. If an IOException is thrown while writing, the stream won't be closed. It's more reliable to close the stream in a finally block so that it's closed whether or not an exception is thrown. To do this you need to declare the OutputStream variable outside the try block. For example:

```
// Initialize this to null to keep the compiler from complaining
// about uninitialized variables
OutputStream out = null;
try {
  out = new FileOutputStream("numbers.dat");
  // Write to the stream...
}
catch (IOException ex) {
  System.err.println(ex);
}
finally {
  if (out != null) {
    try {
      out.close( );
    }
    catch (IOException ex) {
      System.err.println(ex);
    }
  }
}
```

Variable scope and nested try-catch-finally blocks make this a little uglier, yet it's quite a bit safer. The code can be a little cleaner if you have the option of propagating any IOExceptions thrown rather than catching them; that is, if the method that contains this code is declared to throw IOException. In that case, a typical call to close( ) works like this:

```
// Initialize this to null to keep the compiler from complaining
// about uninitialized variables
OutputStream out == null;
try {
  out = new FileOutputStream("numbers.dat");
  // Write to the stream...
}
finally {
  if (out != null) out.close();
}
```

## The Closeable Interface

Java 5 added a Closeable interface that the OutputStream class implements:

```
package java.io;

public interface Closeable {
  void close( ) throws IOException;
}
```

InputStream, Channel, Formatter, and various other things that can be closed also implement this interface. Personally I've never figured out the use case that justifies this extra interface, but it's there if for some reason you want to write a method that accepts only arguments that can be closed, or some such.

# Flushing Output Streams

Many output streams buffer writes to improve performance. Rather than sending each byte to its destination as it's written, the bytes are accumulated in a memory buffer ranging in size from several bytes to several thousand bytes. When the buffer fills up, all the data is sent at once. The flush( ) method forces the data to be written whether or not the buffer is full:

```
public void flush( ) throws IOException
```

This is not the same as any buffering performed by the operating system or the hardware. These buffers will not be emptied by a call to flush( ). (Then sync( ) method in the FileDescriptor class, discussed in Chapter 17, can sometimes empty these buffers.)

If you use a stream for only a short time, you don't need to flush it explicitly. It should flush automatically when the stream is closed. This should happen when the program exits or when the close( ) method is invoked. You flush an output stream explicitly only if you want to make sure data is sent before you're through with the stream. For example, a program that sends bursts of data across the network periodically should flush after each burst of data is written to the stream.

Flushing is often important when you're trying to debug a crashing program. All streams flush automatically when their buffers fill up, and all streams should be flushed when a program terminates normally. If a program terminates abnormally, however, buffers may not get flushed. In this case, unless there is an explicit call to flush( ) after each write, you can't be sure the data that appears in the output indicates the point at which the program crashed. In fact, the program may have continued to run for some time past that point before it crashed.

System.out, System.err, and some (but not all) other print streams automatically flush after each call to println( ) and after each time a new line character ('\n') appears in the string being written. You can enable or disable auto-flushing in the PrintStream constructor.

## The Flushable Interface

Java 5 added a Flushable interface that the OutputStream class implements:

```
package java.io;

public interface Flushable {
  void flush( ) throws IOException;
}
```

Formatter and various other things that can be flushed also implement this interface. I've never figured out the use case that justifies *this* extra interface either, but it's there if for some reason you want to write a method that accepts only objects that can be flushed as arguments, or some such.

# Subclassing OutputStream

OutputStream is an abstract class that mainly describes the operations available with any OutputStream object. Specific subclasses know how to write bytes to particular destinations. For instance, a FileOutputStream uses native code to write data in files. A ByteArrayOutputStream uses pure Java to write its output in an expanding byte array.

Recall that there are three overloaded variants of the write( ) method in OutputStream, one abstract, two concrete:

```
public abstract void write(int b) throws IOException
public void write(byte[] data) throws IOException
public void write(byte[] data, int offset, int length) throws IOException
```

Subclasses must implement the abstract write(int b) method. They often also override the third variant, write(byte[], data int offset, int length), to improve performance. The implementation of the three-argument version of the write( ) method in OutputStream simply invokes write(int b) repeatedly—that is:

```
public void write(byte[] data, int offset, int length) throws IOException {
  for (int i = offset; i < offset+length; i++) write(data[i]);
}
```

Most subclasses can provide a more efficient implementation of this method. The one-argument variant of write( ) merely invokes write(data, 0, data.length); if the three-argument variant has been overridden, this method will perform reasonably well. However, a few subclasses may override it anyway.

Example 2-3 is a simple program called NullOutputStream that mimics the behavior of */dev/null* on Unix operating systems. Data written into a null output stream is lost.

*Example 2-3. The NullOutputStream class*

```
package com.elharo.io;

import java.io.*;

public class NullOutputStream extends OutputStream {

  private boolean closed = false;

  public void write(int b) throws IOException {
    if (closed) throw new IOException("Write to closed stream");
  }

  public void write(byte[] data, int offset, int length)
   throws IOException {
    if (data == null) throw new NullPointerException("data is null");
    if (closed) throw new IOException("Write to closed stream");
  }

  public void close() {
    closed = true;
  }
}
```

The no-op flush( ) method inherited from the superclass is good enough here since this stream really doesn't need flushing. However, note that this class does need to check whether the stream is closed before writing anything, and check whether the array passed in to write( ) is null. Most subclasses will need to make similar checks.

By redirecting System.out and System.err to a null output stream in the shipping version of your program, you can disable any debugging messages that might have slipped through quality assurance. For example:

```
OutputStream out = new NullOutputStream( );
PrintStream ps = new PrintStream(out);
System.setOut(ps);
System.setErr(ps);
```

# A Graphical User Interface for Output Streams

As an example, I'm going to show a subclass of javax.swing.JTextArea that can be connected to an output stream. As data is written onto the stream, it is appended to the text area in the default character set. (This isn't ideal. Since text areas contain text, a writer would be a better source for this data. In later chapters, I'll expand on this class to use a writer instead. For now, this makes a neat example.) This subclass is shown in Example 2-4.

The actual output stream is contained in an inner class inside the JStreamedTextArea class. Each JStreamedTextArea component contains a TextAreaOutputStream object in its theOutput field. Client programmers access this object via the getOutputStream( ) method. The JStreamedTextArea class has four overloaded constructors that imitate the four constructors in the javax.swing.JTextArea class, each taking a different combination of text, rows, and columns. The first three constructors merely pass their arguments and suitable defaults to the most general fourth constructor using this( ). The fourth constructor calls the most general superclass constructor, then calls setEditable(false) to ensure that the user doesn't change the text while output is streaming into it.

*Example 2-4. The JStreamedTextArea component*

```
package com.elharo.io.ui;

import javax.swing.*;
import java.io.*;

public class JStreamedTextArea extends JTextArea {

  private OutputStream theOutput = new TextAreaOutputStream( );

  public JStreamedTextArea( ) {
    this("", 0, 0);
  }

  public JStreamedTextArea(String text) {
    this(text, 0, 0);
  }

  public JStreamedTextArea(int rows, int columns) {
    this("", rows, columns);
  }

  public JStreamedTextArea(String text, int rows, int columns) {
    super(text, rows, columns);
    setEditable(false);
  }

  public OutputStream getOutputStream( ) {
    return theOutput;
```

*Example 2-4. The JStreamedTextArea component (continued)*

```
}

private class TextAreaOutputStream extends OutputStream {

  private boolean closed = false;

  public void write(int b) throws IOException {
    checkOpen( );
    // recall that the int should really just be a byte
    b &= 0x000000FF;
    // must convert byte to a char in order to append it
    char c = (char) b;
    append(String.valueOf(c));
  }

  private void checkOpen( ) throws IOException {
      if (closed) throw new IOException("Write to closed stream");
  }

  public void write(byte[] data, int offset, int length)
   throws IOException {
    checkOpen( );
    append(new String(data, offset, length));
  }

  public void close( ) {
      this.closed = true;
  }

 }
}
```

The TextAreaOutputStream inner class is quite simple. It extends OutputStream and thus must implement the abstract method write( ). It also overrides the primary array write( ) method to provide a more efficient implementation. Finally, it overrides close( ) to make sure that no writes take place after the stream is closed.

To use this class, simply add an instance of it to a container such as an applet or a window, much as you'd add a regular text area. Next, invoke its getOutputStream( ) method to get a reference to the output stream for the area, then use the usual write( ) methods to write into the text area. Often, these steps will take place at different times in different methods.

Figure 2-1 shows a program using a JStreamedTextArea to display data downloaded from *http://www.oreilly.com/*. The application in this picture will be developed in Chapter 5.

*Figure 2-1. The JStreamedTextArea component*

I'll revisit and improve this class in future chapters using techniques I haven't discussed yet. In particular, I'll pay much more attention to the issue of character sets and encodings.

# CHAPTER 3

# Input Streams

java.io.InputStream is the abstract superclass for all input streams. It declares the three basic methods needed to read bytes of data from a stream. It also has methods for closing streams, checking how many bytes of data are available to be read, skipping over input, marking a position in a stream and resetting back to that position, and determining whether marking and resetting are supported.

## The read( ) Method

The fundamental method of the InputStream class is read( ). This method reads a single unsigned byte of data and returns the integer value of the unsigned byte. This is a number between 0 and 255:

```
public abstract int read( ) throws IOException
```

read( ) is declared abstract; therefore, InputStream is abstract. Hence, you can never instantiate an InputStream directly; you always work with one of its concrete subclasses.

The following code reads 10 bytes from the System.in input stream and stores them in the int array data:

```
int[] data = new int[10];
for (int i = 0; i < data.length; i++) {
  data[i] = System.in.read( );
}
```

Notice that although read( ) is reading a byte, it returns an int. If you want to store the raw bytes instead, you can cast the int to a byte. For example:

```
byte[] b = new byte[10];
for (int i = 0; i < b.length; i++) {
  b[i] = (byte) System.in.read( );
}
```

Of course, this produces a signed byte instead of the unsigned byte returned by the read( ) method (that is, a byte in the range −128 to 127 instead of 0 to 255). As long as you're clear in your mind and in your code about whether you're working with signed or unsigned data, you won't have any trouble. Signed bytes can be converted back to ints in the range of 0 to 255 like this:

```
int i = (b >= 0) ? b : 256 + b;
```

When you call read( ), you also have to catch the IOException that it might throw, or declare that your methods throw it. However, there's no IOException if read( ) encounters the end of the input stream; in this case, it returns −1. You use this as a flag to watch for the end of stream. The following code fragment shows how to catch the IOException and test for the end of the stream:

```
try {
  InputStream in = new FileInputStream("file.txt");
  int[] data = new int[10];
  for (int i = 0; i < data.length; i++) {
    int datum = in.read( );
    if (datum == -1) break;
    data[i] = datum;
  }
}
catch (IOException ex) {
  System.err.println(ex.getMessage( ));
}
```

The read( ) method normally waits as long as it needs to in order to get a byte of data. Most input streams do not time out. (A few network streams are exceptions.) Input can be slow, so if your program is doing anything else of importance, try to put I/O in its own thread.

Example 3-1 is a program that reads data from System.in and prints the numeric value of each byte read on the console using System.out.println( ).

*Example 3-1. The StreamPrinter class*

```
import java.io.*;

public class StreamPrinter {

  public static void main(String[] args) {
    try {
      while (true) {
        int datum = System.in.read( );
        if (datum == -1) break;
        System.out.println(datum);
      }
    }
    catch (IOException ex) {
      System.err.println("Couldn't read from System.in!");
    }
  }
}
```

# Reading Chunks of Data from a Stream

Input and output are often the performance bottlenecks in a program. Reading from or writing to disk can be hundreds of times slower than reading from or writing to memory; network connections and user input are even slower. While disk capacities and speeds have increased over time, they have never kept pace with CPU speeds. Therefore, it's important to minimize the number of reads and writes a program actually performs.

All input streams have overloaded read( ) methods that read chunks of contiguous data into a byte array. The first variant tries to read enough data to fill the array. The second variant tries to read length bytes of data starting at position offset into the array. Neither of these methods is guaranteed to read as many bytes as you want. Both methods return the number of bytes actually read, or −1 on end of stream.

```
public int read(byte[] data) throws IOException
public int read(byte[] data, int offset, int length) throws IOException
```

The default implementation of these methods in the java.io.InputStream class merely calls the basic read( ) method enough times to fill the requested array or sub-array. Thus, reading 10 bytes of data takes 10 times as long as reading 1 byte of data. However, most subclasses of InputStream override these methods with more efficient methods, perhaps native, that read the data from the underlying source as a block.

For example, to attempt to read 10 bytes from System.in, you could write the following code:

```
try {
  byte[] b = new byte[10];
  System.in.read(b);
}
catch (IOException ex) {
  System.err.println("Couldn't read from System.in!");
}
```

Reads don't always succeed in getting as many bytes as you want. Conversely, there's nothing to stop you from trying to read more data into the array than will fit. If you do this, read( ) throws an ArrayIndexOutOfBoundsException. For example, the following code loops repeatedly until it either fills the array or sees the end of stream:

```
try {
  byte[] b = new byte[100];
  int offset = 0;
  while (offset < b.length) {
    int bytesRead = System.in.read(b, offset, b.length - offset);
    if (bytesRead == -1) break; // end of stream
    offset += bytesRead;
  }
}
catch (IOException ex) {
  System.err.println("Couldn't read from System.in!");
}
```

# Counting the Available Bytes

It's sometimes convenient to know how many bytes can be read before you attempt to read them. The InputStream class's available( ) method tells you how many bytes you can read without blocking. It returns 0 if there's no data available to be read.

```
public int available( ) throws IOException
```

For example:

```
try {
  byte[] b = new byte[100];
  int offset = 0;
  while (offset < b.length) {
    int a = System.in.available( );
    int bytesRead = System.in.read(b, offset, a);
    if (bytesRead == -1) break; // end of stream
    offset += bytesRead;
  }
}
catch (IOException ex) {
  System.err.println("Couldn't read from System.in!");
}
```

There's a potential bug in this code. There may be more bytes available than there's space in the array to hold them. One common idiom is to size the array according to the number available( ) returns, like this:

```
try {
  byte[] b = new byte[System.in.available( )];
  System.in.read(b);
}
catch (IOException ex) {
  System.err.println("Couldn't read from System.in!");
}
```

This works well if you're going to perform a single read. For multiple reads, however, the overhead of creating multiple arrays is excessive. You should probably reuse the array and create a new array only if more bytes are available than will fit in the array.

The available( ) method in java.io.InputStream always returns 0. Subclasses are supposed to override it, but I've seen a few that don't. You may be able to read more bytes from the underlying stream without blocking than available( ) suggests; you just can't guarantee that you can. If this is a concern, place input in a separate thread so that blocked input doesn't block the rest of the program.

# Skipping Bytes

The skip( ) method jumps over a certain number of bytes in the input:

```
public long skip(long bytesToSkip) throws IOException
```

The argument to skip( ) is the number of bytes to skip. The return value is the number of bytes actually skipped, which may be less than bytesToSkip. −1 is returned if the end of stream is encountered. Both the argument and return value are longs, allowing skip( ) to handle extremely long input streams. Skipping is often faster than reading and discarding the data you don't want. For example, when an input stream is attached to a file, skipping bytes just requires that the position in the file be changed, whereas reading involves copying bytes from the disk into memory. For example, to skip the next 80 bytes of the input stream in:

```
try {
  long bytesSkipped = 0;
  long bytesToSkip = 80;
  while (bytesSkipped < bytesToSkip) {
    long n = in.skip(bytesToSkip - bytesSkipped);
    if (n == -1) break;
    bytesSkipped += n;
  }
}
catch (IOException ex) {
  System.err.println(ex);
}
```

## Closing Input Streams

As with output streams, input streams should be closed when you're through with them to release any native resources such as file handles or network ports that the stream is holding onto. To close a stream, invoke its close( ) method:

```
public void close( ) throws IOException
```

Once you have closed an input stream, you should no longer read from it. Most attempts to do so will throw an IOException (though there are a few exceptions).

Not all streams need to be closed—System.in generally does not need to be closed, for example. However, streams associated with files and network connections should always be closed when you're done with them. As with output streams, it's best to do this in a finally block to guarantee that the stream is closed, even if an exception is thrown while the stream is open. For example:

```
// Initialize this to null to keep the compiler from complaining
// about uninitialized variables
InputStream in = null;
try {
  URL u = new URL("http://www.msf.org/");
  in = u.openStream( );
  // Read from the stream...

}
catch (IOException ex) {
  System.err.println(ex);
}
```

```
        finally {
          if (in != null) {
            try {
              in.close();
            }
            catch (IOException ex) {
              System.err.println(ex);
            }
          }
        }
```

If you can propagate any exceptions that are thrown, this strategy can be a little shorter and simpler. For example:

```
// Initialize this to null to keep the compiler from complaining
// about uninitialized variables
InputStream in = null;
try {
  URL u = new URL("http://www.msf.org/");
  in = u.openStream();
  // Read from the stream...
}
finally {
  if (in != null) in.close();
}
```

## Marking and Resetting

It's often useful to be able to read a few bytes and then back up and reread them. For example, in a Java compiler, you don't know for sure whether you're reading the token <, <<, or <<= until you've read one too many characters. It would be useful to be able to back up and reread the token once you know which token you've read.

Some (but not all) input streams allow you to mark a particular position in the stream and then return to it. Three methods in the java.io.InputStream class handle marking and resetting:

```
public void    mark(int readLimit)
public void    reset() throws IOException
public boolean markSupported()
```

The markSupported( ) method returns true if this stream supports marking and false if it doesn't. If marking is not supported, reset( ) throws an IOException and mark( ) does nothing. Assuming the stream does support marking, the mark( ) method places a bookmark at the current position in the stream. You can rewind the stream to this position later with reset( ) as long as you haven't read more than readLimit bytes. There can be only one mark in the stream at any given time. Marking a second location erases the first mark.

The only two input stream classes in java.io that always support marking are BufferedInputStream (of which System.in is an instance) and ByteArrayInputStream.

---

However, other input streams such as DataInputStream may support marking if they're chained to a buffered input stream first.

 This is a truly bizarre design. It's almost always a bad idea to put methods in a superclass that aren't applicable to all subclasses. The proper solution to this problem would be to define a Resettable interface that declares these three methods and then have subclasses implement that interface or not as they choose. You could then tell whether marking and resetting were supported with a simple instanceof Resettable test. All I can offer by way of explanation here is that this design was invented ten years ago in Java 1.0, when not all the people working on Java were fully adept at object-oriented design.

# Subclassing InputStream

Immediate subclasses of InputStream must provide an implementation of the abstract read( ) method. They may also override some of the nonabstract methods. For example, the default markSupported( ) method returns false, mark( ) does nothing, and reset( ) throws an IOException. Any class that allows marking and resetting must override these three methods. Subclasses should also override available( ) to return something other than 0. Furthermore, they may override skip( ) and the other two read( ) methods to provide more efficient implementations.

Example 3-2 is a simple class called RandomInputStream that "reads" random bytes of data. This provides a useful source of unlimited data you can use in testing. A java.util.Random object provides the data.

*Example 3-2. The RandomInputStream class*

```
package com.elharo.io;

import java.util.*;
import java.io.*;

public class RandomInputStream extends InputStream {

  private Random generator = new Random( );
  private boolean closed = false;

  public int read( ) throws IOException {
    checkOpen( );
    int result = generator.nextInt( ) % 256;
    if (result < 0) result = -result;
    return result;
  }

  public int read(byte[] data, int offset, int length) throws IOException {
    checkOpen( );
    byte[] temp = new byte[length];
```

*Example 3-2. The RandomInputStream class (continued)*

```java
    generator.nextBytes(temp);
    System.arraycopy(temp, 0, data, offset, length);
    return length;

  }

  public int read(byte[] data) throws IOException {
    checkOpen();
    generator.nextBytes(data);
    return data.length;

  }

  public long skip(long bytesToSkip) throws IOException {
    checkOpen();
    // It's all random so skipping has no effect.
    return bytesToSkip;
  }

  public void close() {
      this.closed = true;
  }

  private void checkOpen() throws IOException {
      if (closed) throw new IOException("Input stream closed");
  }

  public int available() {
    // Limited only by available memory and the size of an array.
    return Integer.MAX_VALUE;
  }
}
```

The no-argument read( ) method returns a random int in the range of an unsigned byte (0 to 255). The other two read( ) methods fill a specified part of an array with random bytes. They return the number of bytes read (in this case the number of bytes created).

## An Efficient Stream Copier

As a useful example of both input and output streams, in Example 3-3, I'll present a StreamCopier class that copies data between two streams as quickly as possible. (I'll reuse this class in later chapters.) This method reads from the input stream and writes onto the output stream until the input stream is exhausted. A 1K buffer is used to try to make the reads efficient. A main( ) method provides a simple test for this class by reading from System.in and copying to System.out.

*Example 3-3. The StreamCopier class*

```java
package com.elharo.io;

import java.io.*;

public class StreamCopier {

  public static void main(String[] args) {

    try {
      copy(System.in, System.out);
    }
    catch (IOException ex) {
      System.err.println(ex);
    }

  }

  public static void copy(InputStream in, OutputStream out)
   throws IOException {

    byte[] buffer = new byte[1024];
    while (true) {
      int bytesRead = in.read(buffer);
      if (bytesRead == -1) break;
      out.write(buffer, 0, bytesRead);
    }

  }

}
```

Here's a simple test run:

```
D:\JAVA\ioexamples\03> java com.elharo.io.StreamCopier
this is a test
this is a test
0987654321
0987654321
^Z
```

Input was not fed from the console (DOS prompt) to the StreamCopier program until the end of each line. Since I ran this on Windows, the end-of-stream character is Ctrl-Z. On Unix, it would have been Ctrl-D.

# PART II

# Data Sources

# CHAPTER 4

# File Streams

Until now, most of the examples in this book have used the streams System.in and System.out. These are convenient for examples, but in real life, you'll more commonly attach streams to data sources like files and network connections. The java.io.FileInputStream and java.io.FileOutputStream classes, which are concrete subclasses of java.io.InputStream and java.io.OutputStream, provide methods for reading and writing data in files. What they don't provide is file management, like finding out whether a file is readable or writable or moving a file from one directory to another. For that, you may want to flip forward to Chapter 17, which talks about the File class itself and the way Java works with files.

## Reading Files

java.io.FileInputStream is a concrete subclass of java.io.InputStream. It provides an input stream connected to a particular file. FileInputStream has all the usual methods of input streams, such as read( ), available( ), skip( ), and close( ), which are used exactly as they are for any other input stream. FileInputStream( ) has three constructors, which differ only in how the file to be read is specified:

```
public FileInputStream(String fileName) throws IOException
public FileInputStream(File file) throws FileNotFoundException
public FileInputStream(FileDescriptor fdObj)
```

The first constructor uses a string containing the name of the file. The second constructor uses a java.io.File object. The third constructor uses a java.io.FileDescriptor object.

To read a file, just pass the name of the file into the FileInputStream( ) constructor. Then use the read( ) method as normal. For example, the following code fragment reads the file *README.TXT*, then prints it on System.out:

```
try {
  FileInputStream fis = new FileInputStream("README.TXT");
  for (int n = fis.read(); n != -1; n = fis.read()) {
    System.out.write(n);
```

```
    }
  }
  catch (IOException ex) {
    System.err.println(ex);
  }
  System.out.println( );
```

Java looks for files in the *current working directory*. Generally, this is the directory you were in when you typed **java *program_name*** to start running the program. You can open a file in a different directory by passing a full or relative path to the file from the current working directory. For example, to read the file */etc/hosts* no matter which directory is current, you can do this:

```
FileInputStream fis = new FileInputStream("/etc/hosts");
```

Filenames are platform-dependent, so hardcoded filenames should be avoided wherever possible. This example depends on a Unix-style pathname. It is not guaranteed to work on other platforms such as Windows or Mac OS 9, though it might. Using a filename to create a FileInputStream violates Sun's rules for "100% Pure Java." Some runtime environments such as Apple's Macintosh Runtime for Java include extra code to translate from Unix-style filenames to the native style. However, for maximum cross-platform awareness, you should use File objects instead. These can be created directly from filenames as described in Chapter 17, supplied by the user through a GUI such as a Swing JFileChooser, or returned by various methods scattered throughout the API and class libraries. Much of the time, code that uses a File object adapts more easily to unexpected filesystem conventions. One particularly important trick is to create multisegment paths by successively appending new File objects for each directory like so:

```
File root = new File("/");
File dir = new File(root, "etc");
File child = new File(dir, "hosts");
FileInputStream fis = new FileInputStream(child);
```

However, this still assumes that the root of the filesystem is named "/", which isn't likely to be a true on a non-Unix system. It's better to use the File.listRoots( ) method:

```
File[] roots = File.listRoots( )
File dir = new File(roots[0], "etc");
File child = new File(dir, "hosts");
FileInputStream fis = new FileInputStream(child);
```

However, although this code is more platform independent, it still assumes a particular file layout structure. This can vary not just from platform to platform, but from one PC to the next, even those running the same operating system. For more robustness, you'll want to get at least a directory, if not a complete file, by invoking a method that adapts to the local system. Possibilities include:

- Ask the user to choose a file with a Swing JFileChooser.
- Ask the user to choose a file with an AWT FileDialog.

- Ask a third-party library such as MRJ Adapter's `SpecialFolder` for a known location such as the preferences folder or the desktop folder.
- Create a temporary file with the `File.createTempFile( )` method.
- Find the user's home directory with `System.getProperty("user.home")`.
- Find the current working directory with `System.getProperty("user.dir")`.

This list is not exhaustive; there are other approaches. Which one is appropriate depends on the use case. Details of these approaches are addressed in future chapters.

If the file you're trying to read does not exist when the `FileInputStream` object is constructed, the constructor throws a `FileNotFoundException` (a subclass of `java.io.IOException`). If for some other reason a file cannot be read—for example, the current process does not have read permission for the file—some other kind of `IOException` is thrown.

Example 4-1 reads a filename from the command line, then copies the named file to `System.out`. The `StreamCopier.copy( )` method from Example 3-3 in the previous chapter does the actual reading and writing. Notice that that method does not care whether the input is coming from a file or going to the console. It works regardless of the type of the input and output streams it's copying. It will work equally well for other streams still to be introduced, including ones that did not even exist when `StreamCopier` was created.

*Example 4-1. The FileTyper program*

```java
import java.io.*;
import com.elharo.io.*;

public class FileTyper {

  public static void main(String[] args) throws IOException {
    if (args.length != 1) {
      System.err.println("Usage: java FileTyper filename");
      return;
    }
    typeFile(args[0]);
  }

  public static void typeFile(String filename) throws IOException {
    FileInputStream fin = new FileInputStream(filename);
    try {
      StreamCopier.copy(fin, System.out);
    }
    finally {
      fin.close( );
    }
  }
}
```

Untrusted code is not usually allowed to read or write files. If an applet tries to create a FileInputStream, the constructor will throw a SecurityException.

The FileInputStream class has one method that's not declared in the InputStream superclass: getFD( ).

```
public final FileDescriptor getFD() throws IOException
```

This method returns the java.io.FileDescriptor object associated with this stream. FileDescriptor objects are discussed in Chapter 17. For now, all you can do with this object is use it to create another file stream.

It is possible to open multiple input streams to the same file at the same time, though it's rarely necessary to do so. Each stream maintains a separate pointer that points to the current position in the file. Reading from the file does not change the file in any way. Writing to the file is a different story, as you'll see in the next section.

# Writing Files

The java.io.FileOutputStream class is a concrete subclass of java.io.OutputStream that provides output streams connected to files. This class has all the usual methods of output streams, such as write( ), flush( ), and close( ), which are used exactly as they are for any other output stream.

FileOutputStream( ) has three main constructors, differing primarily in how the file is specified:

```
public FileOutputStream(String filename) throws IOException
public FileOutputStream(File file) throws IOException
public FileOutputStream(FileDescriptor fd)
```

The first constructor uses a string containing the name of the file; the second constructor uses a java.io.File object; the third constructor uses a java.io.FileDescriptor object. To write data to a file, just pass the name of the file to the FileOutputStream( ) constructor, then use the write( ) methods as usual. If the file does not exist, all three constructors will create it. If the file does exist, any data inside it will be overwritten.

A fourth constructor also lets you specify whether the file's contents should be erased before data is written into it (append == false) or whether data is to be tacked onto the end of the file (append == true):

```
public FileOutputStream(String name, boolean append) throws IOException
```

Output streams created by the other three constructors simply overwrite the file; they do not provide an option to append data to the file.

Java looks for files in the current working directory. You can write to a file in a different directory by passing a full or relative path to the file from the current working directory. For example, to append data to the *\Windows\java\javalog.txt* file no matter which directory is current, you would do this:

```
FileOutputStream fout =
 new FileOutputStream("/Windows/java/javalog.txt", true);
```

Although Windows uses a backslash as the directory separator, Java still expects you to use a forward slash as in Unix. Hardcoded pathnames are dangerously platform-dependent. Using this constructor automatically classifies your program as impure Java. As with input streams, a slightly less dangerous alternative builds a File object a piece at a time like so:

```
File[] roots = File.listRoots()
File windows = new File(roots[0], "Windows");
File java = new File(windows, "java");
File javalog = new File(java, "javalog.txt");
FileInputStream fis = new FileInputStream(javalog);
```

Untrusted code is normally not allowed to write files either. If an applet tries to create a FileOutputStream, the constructor throws a SecurityException.

The FileOutputStream class has one method that's not declared in java.io. OutputStream: getFD( ).

```
public final FileDescriptor getFD( ) throws IOException
```

This method returns the java.io.FileDescriptor object associated with this stream.

Example 4-2 reads two filenames from the command line, then copies the first file into the second file. The StreamCopier class from Example 3-3 in the previous chapter does the actual reading and writing.

*Example 4-2. The FileCopier program*

```
import java.io.*;
import com.elharo.io.*;

public class FileCopier {

  public static void main(String[] args) {

    if (args.length != 2) {
      System.err.println("Usage: java FileCopier infile outfile");
    }
    try {
      copy(args[0], args[1]);
    }
    catch (IOException ex) {
      System.err.println(ex);
    }
  }

  public static void copy(String inFile, String outFile)
    throws IOException {
```

*Example 4-2. The FileCopier program (continued)*

```
  FileInputStream  fin = null;
  FileOutputStream fout = null;

  try {
    fin  = new FileInputStream(inFile);
    fout = new FileOutputStream(outFile);
    StreamCopier.copy(fin, fout);
  }
  finally {
    try {
      if (fin != null) fin.close();
    }
    catch (IOException ex) {
    }
    try {
      if (fout != null) fout.close();
    }
    catch (IOException ex) { }
  }
 }
}
```

Since we're no longer writing to System.out and reading from System.in, it's important to make sure the streams are closed when we're done. This is a good use for a finally clause, as we need to make sure the files are closed whether the reads and writes succeed or not.

Java is better about closing files than most languages. As long as the VM doesn't terminate abnormally, the files will be closed when the program exits. Still, if this class is used inside a long-running program like a web server, waiting until the program exits isn't a good idea; other threads and processes may need access to the files.

Example 4-2 has one bug: the program does not behave well if the input and output files are the same. While it would be straightforward to compare the two filenames before copying, this is not safe enough. Once aliases, shortcuts, symbolic links, and other factors are taken into account, a single file may have multiple names. The full solution to this problem will have to wait until Chapter 17, where I discuss canonical paths and temporary files.

# File Viewer, Part 1

I often find it useful to be able to open an arbitrary file and interpret it in an arbitrary fashion. Most commonly, I want to view a file as text, but occasionally it's useful to interpret it as hexadecimal integers, IEEE 754 floating-point data, or something else. In this book, I'm going to develop a program that lets you open any file and view its contents in a variety of different ways. In each chapter, I'll add a piece to the program until it's fully functional. Since this is only the beginning of the program, it's important to keep the code as general and adaptable as possible.

Example 4-3 reads a series of filenames from the command line in the main( ) method. Each filename is passed to a method that opens the file. The file's data is read and printed on System.out. Exactly how the data is printed on System.out is determined by a command-line switch. If the user selects text format (-a), the data will be assumed to be Latin-1 text and will be printed as chars. If the user selects decimal dump (-d), then each byte should be printed as unsigned decimal numbers between 0 and 255, 16 to a line. For example:

```
000 234 127 034 234 234 000 000 000 002 004 070 000 234 127 098
```

Leading zeros maintain a constant width for the printed byte values and for each line. For hex dump format (-h), each byte should be printed as two hexadecimal digits. For example:

```
CA FE BA BE 07 89 9A 65 45 65 43 6F F6 7F 8F EE E5 67 63 26 98 9E 9C
```

Hexadecimal encoding is easier, because each byte is always exactly two hex digits. The static Integer.toHexString( ) method converts each byte read into two hexadecimal digits.

Text format is the default and is the simplest to implement. This conversion can be accomplished merely by copying the input data to the console.

*Example 4-3. The FileDumper program*

```java
import java.io.*;
import com.elharo.io.*;

public class FileDumper {

  public static final int ASC = 0;
  public static final int DEC = 1;
  public static final int HEX = 2;

  public static void main(String[] args) {

    if (args.length < 1) {
      System.err.println("Usage: java FileDumper [-ahd] file1 file2...");
      return;
    }

    int firstArg = 0;
    int mode = ASC;

    if (args[0].startsWith("-")) {
      firstArg = 1;
      if (args[0].equals("-h")) mode = HEX;
      else if (args[0].equals("-d")) mode = DEC;
    }

    for (int i = firstArg; i < args.length; i++) {
      try {
        if (mode == ASC) dumpAscii(args[i]);
```

*Example 4-3. The FileDumper program (continued)*

```
        else if (mode == HEX) dumpHex(args[i]);
        else if (mode == DEC) dumpDecimal(args[i]);
      }
      catch (IOException ex) {
        System.err.println("Error reading from " + args[i] + ": "
          + ex.getMessage( ));
      }
      if (i < args.length-1) {  // more files to dump
        System.out.println("\r\n--------------------------------------\r\n");
      }
    }
  }
}

public static void dumpAscii(String filename) throws IOException {

  FileInputStream fin = null;
  try {
    fin = new FileInputStream(filename);
    StreamCopier.copy(fin, System.out);
  }
  finally {
    if (fin != null) fin.close( );
  }
}

public static void dumpDecimal(String filename) throws IOException {

  FileInputStream fin = null;
  byte[] buffer = new byte[16];
  boolean end = false;

  try {
    fin = new FileInputStream(filename);
    while (!end) {
      int bytesRead = 0;
      while (bytesRead < buffer.length) {
        int r = fin.read(buffer, bytesRead, buffer.length - bytesRead);
        if (r == -1) {
          end = true;
          break;
        }
        bytesRead += r;
      }
      for (int i = 0; i < bytesRead; i++) {
        int dec = buffer[i];
        if (dec < 0) dec = 256 + dec;
        if (dec < 10) System.out.print("00" + dec + " ");
        else if (dec < 100) System.out.print("0" + dec + " ");
        else System.out.print(dec + " ");
      }
      System.out.println( );
    }
```

*Example 4-3. The FileDumper program (continued)*

```java
      }
      finally {
        if (fin != null) fin.close( );
      }
  }

  public static void dumpHex(String filename) throws IOException {

      FileInputStream fin = null;
      byte[] buffer = new byte[24];
      boolean end = false;

      try {
        fin = new FileInputStream(filename);
        while (!end) {
          int bytesRead = 0;
          while (bytesRead < buffer.length) {
            int r = fin.read(buffer, bytesRead, buffer.length - bytesRead);
            if (r == -1) {
              end = true;
              break;
            }
            bytesRead += r;
          }
          for (int i = 0; i < bytesRead; i++) {
            int hex = buffer[i];
            if (hex < 0) hex = 256 + hex;
            if (hex >= 16) System.out.print(Integer.toHexString(hex) + " ");
            else System.out.print("0" + Integer.toHexString(hex) + " ");
          }
          System.out.println( );
        }
      }
      finally {
        if (fin != null) fin.close( );
      }
  }
}
```

When `FileDumper` is used to dump its own *.class* file in hexadecimal format, it produces the following output:

```
D:\JAVA\ioexamples\04> java FileDumper -h FileDumper.class
ca fe ba be 00 00 00 2e 00 78 0a 00 22 00 37 09 00 38 00 39 08 00 3a 0a
00 3b 00 3c 08 00 3d 0a 00 3e 00 3f 08 00 40 0a 00 3e 00 41 08 00 42 0a
00 21 00 43 0a 00 21 00 44 0a 00 21 00 45 09 00 38 00 46 08 00 47 07 00
48 0a 00 0f 00 49 0a 00 4a 00 4b 07 00 4c 0a 00 3b 00 4d 0a 00 0f 00 4e
...
```

In later chapters, I'll add a graphical user interface and many more possible interpretations of the data in the file, including floating-point, big- and little-endian integer, and various text encodings.

# CHAPTER 5

# Network Streams

From its first days, Java, more than any other common programming language, has had the network in mind. Java is the first programming language to provide as much support for network I/O as it does for file I/O, perhaps even more (Java's URL, URLConnection, Socket, and ServerSocket classes are all fertile sources of streams). The exact type of the stream used by a network connection is typically hidden inside the undocumented sun classes. Thus, network I/O relies primarily on the basic InputStream and OutputStream methods, which you can wrap with any higher-level stream that suits your needs: buffering, cryptography, compression, or whatever your application requires.

## URLs

The java.net.URL class represents a Uniform Resource Locator such as *http://www.cafeaulait.org/books/javaio2/*. Each URL unambiguously identifies the location of a resource on the Internet. The URL class has six constructors. All are declared to throw MalformedURLException, a subclass of IOException.

```
public URL(String url) throws MalformedURLException
public URL(String protocol, String host, String file)
 throws MalformedURLException
public URL(String protocol, String host, int port, String file)
 throws MalformedURLException
public URL(String protocol, String host, int port, String file,
  URLStreamHandler handler)  throws MalformedURLException
public URL(URL context, String url) throws MalformedURLException
public URL(URL context, String url, URLStreamHandler handler)
   throws MalformedURLException
```

Each constructor throws a MalformedURLException if its arguments do not specify a valid URL. Often, this means a particular Java implementation does not have the right protocol handler installed. Thus, given a complete absolute URL such as *http://www.poly.edu/schedule/fall2006/bgrad.html#cs*, you construct a URL object like so:

```
URL u = null;
try {
```

```
      u = new URL("http://www.poly.edu/schedule/fall2006/bgrad.html#cs");
    }
    catch (MalformedURLException ex) {
      // this shouldn't happen for a syntactically correct http URL
    }
```

You can also construct the URL object by passing its pieces to the constructor:

```
URL u = new URL("http", "www.poly.edu", "/schedule/ fall2006/bgrad.html#cs");
```

You don't normally need to specify a port for a URL. Most protocols have default ports. For instance, the HTTP port is 80. Sometimes the port used does change, and in that case you can use this constructor:

```
URL u = new URL("http", "www.poly.edu", 80, "/schedule/ fall2006/bgrad.html#cs ");
```

Finally, many HTML files contain relative URLs. The last two constructors create URLs relative to a given URL and are particularly useful when parsing HTML. For example, the following code creates a URL pointing to the file *08.html*, taking the rest of the URL from u1:

```
URL u1 = new URL("http://www.cafeaualit.org/course/week12/07.html");
URL u2 = new URL(u1, "08.html");
```

Once a URL object has been constructed, you can retrieve its data in two ways. The openStream( ) method returns a raw stream of bytes from the source. The getContent( ) method returns a Java object that represents the data. When you call getContent( ), Java looks for a content handler that matches the MIME type of the data. It is the openStream( ) method that is of concern in this book.

The openStream( ) method makes a socket connection to the server and port specified in the URL. It returns an input stream from which you can read the data at that URL. Any headers that come before the actual data or file requested are stripped off before the stream is opened. You only get the raw data.

```
public InputStream openStream( ) throws IOException
```

Example 5-1 shows you how to connect to a URL entered on the command line, download its data, and copy that to System.out.

*Example 5-1. The URLTyper program*

```
import java.net.*;
import java.io.*;

public class URLTyper {

  public static void main(String[] args) throws IOException {

    if (args.length != 1) {
      System.err.println("Usage: java URLTyper url");
      return;
    }
```

*Example 5-1. The URLTyper program (continued)*

```
    InputStream in = null;
    try {
      URL u = new URL(args[0]);
      in = u.openStream( );
      for (int c = in.read(); c != -1; c = in.read( )) {
        System.out.write(c);
      }
    }
    catch (MalformedURLException ex) {
      System.err.println(args[0] + " is not a URL Java understands.");
    }
    finally {
      if (in != null) in.close( );
    }
  }
}
```

For example, here are the first few lines you see when you connect to *http://www. oreilly.com/*:

```
$ java URLTyper http://www.oreilly.com/
<!DOCTYPE HTML PUBLIC "-//W3C//DTD HTML 4.01 Transitional//EN">
<html xmlns="http://www.w3.org/1999/xhtml" lang="en-US" xml:lang="en-US">
<head>
<title>oreilly.com -- Welcome to O'Reilly Media, Inc. -- computer books, softwar
e conferences, online publishing</title>
<meta name="keywords" content="O'Reilly, oreilly, computer books,
technical books, UNIX, unix, Perl, Java, Linux, Internet, Web, C, C++, Windows,
Windows NT, Security, Sys Admin, System Administration, Oracle, PL/SQL, online b
ooks, books online, computer book online, e-books, ebooks, Perl Conference, Open
 Source Conference, Java Conference, open source, free software, XML, Mac OS X,
.Net, dot net, C#, PHP, CGI, VB, VB Script, Java Script, javascript, Windows 200
0, XP, bioinformatics, web services, p2p" />
...
```

Most network connections, even on LANs, are slower and less reliable sources of data than files. Connections across the Internet are even slower and less reliable, and connections through a modem are slower and less reliable still. One way to enhance performance under these conditions is to buffer the data: to read as much data as you can into a temporary storage array inside the class, then parcel it out as needed. In the next chapter, you'll learn about the BufferedInputStream class that does exactly this.

Untrusted code running under the control of a security manager—e.g., applets that run inside a web browser—are normally allowed to connect only to the host they were downloaded from. This host can be determined from the URL returned by the getCodeBase( ) method of the Applet class. Attempts to connect to other hosts throw security exceptions. You can create URLs that point to other hosts, but you may not download data from them using openStream( ) or any other method. (This security restriction for applets applies to any network connection, regardless of how you get it.)

# URL Connections

URL connections are closely related to URLs, as their name implies. Indeed, you get a reference to a URLConnection by using the openConnection( ) method of a URL object; in many ways, the URL class is only a wrapper around the URLConnection class. URL connections provide more control over the communication between the client and the server. In particular, URL connections provide not just input streams by which the client can read data from the server, but also output streams to send data from the client to the server.

The java.net.URLConnection class is an abstract class that handles communication with different kinds of servers, such as FTP servers and web servers. Protocol-specific subclasses of URLConnection, which are hidden inside the sun packages, handle different kinds of servers.

## Reading Data from URL Connections

URL connections take place in five steps:

1. The URL object is constructed.
2. The openConnection( ) method of the URL object creates the URLConnection object.
3. The parameters for the connection and the request properties that the client sends to the server are set up.
4. The connect( ) method makes the connection to the server, perhaps using a socket for a network connection or a file input stream for a local connection. The response header information is read from the server.
5. Data is read from the connection using the input stream returned by getInputStream( ) or a content handler returned by getContent( ). Data can be sent to the server using the output stream provided by getOutputStream( ).

This scheme is very much based on the HTTP protocol. It does not fit other schemes that have a more interactive "request, response, request, response, request, response" pattern instead of HTTP/1.0's "single request, single response, close connection" pattern. In particular, FTP doesn't really fit this pattern.

URLConnection objects are not constructed directly in your own programs. Instead, you create a URL for the particular resource and call that URL's openConnection( ) method. This gives you a URLConnection. Then the getInputStream( ) method returns an input stream that reads data from the URL. (The openStream( ) method of the URL class is just a thin veneer over the getInputStream( ) method of the URLConnection class.) If the connection cannot be opened, for example because the remote host is unreachable, connect( ) throws an IOException. For example, this code repeats the main body of Example 5-1 using a URLConnection to open the stream:

```
URL u = new URL(args[0]);
URLConnection connection = u.openConnection( );
```

```
      in = connection.getInputStream( );
      for (int c = in.read(); c != -1; c = in.read( )) {
        System.out.write(c);
      }
```

# Writing Data on URL Connections

Writing data to a URLConnection is similar to reading data. However, you must first inform the URLConnection that you plan to use it for output. Then, instead of getting the connection's input stream and reading from it, you get the connection's output stream and write to it. This is commonly used for HTTP POST and PUT. Here are the steps for writing data on a URLConnection:

1. Construct the URL object.
2. Call the openConnection( ) method of the URL object to create the URLConnection object.
3. Pass true to setDoOutput( ) to indicate that this URLConnection will be used for output.
4. If you also want to read input from the stream, invoke setDoInput(true) to indicate that this URLConnection will be used for input.
5. Create the data you want to send, preferably as a byte array.
6. Call getOutputStream( ) to get an output stream object. Write the byte array calculated in step 5 onto the stream.
7. Close the output stream.
8. Call getInputStream( ) to get an input stream object. Read and write it as usual.

Example 5-2 uses these steps to implement a simple mail client. It forms a *mailto* URL from an email address entered on the command line. Input for the message is copied from System.in onto the output stream of the URLConnection using a StreamCopier. The end-of-stream character signals the end of the message.

*Example 5-2. The MailClient class*

```
import java.net.*;
import java.io.*;

public class MailClient {

  public static void main(String[] args) {

    if (args.length == 0) {
      System.err.println("Usage: java MailClient username@host.com");
      return;
    }

    try {
      URL u = new URL("mailto:" + args[0]);
```

*Example 5-2. The MailClient class (continued)*

```
    URLConnection uc = u.openConnection( );
    uc.setDoOutput(true);
    uc.connect( );
    OutputStream out = uc.getOutputStream( );
    for (int c = System.in.read(); c != -1; c = System.in.read( )) {
      out.write(c);
    }
    out.close( );
  }
  catch (IOException ex) {
    System.err.println(ex);
  }
 }
}
```

For example, to send email to the author of this book:

```
$ java MailClient elharo@metalab.unc.edu
hi there!
^D
```

MailClient suffers from a few restrictions. The proper way to detect the end of the message is to look for a period on a line by itself. Proper or not, that style of user interface is really antiquated, so I didn't bother to implement it. To do so properly, you'll need to use a Reader or a Writer; they're discussed in Chapter 20. Furthermore, it works only in Java environments that support the *mailto* protocol; thus, it works under Sun's JDK but may not work in other VMs. It also requires that the local host be running an SMTP server, or that the system property mail.host must contain the name of an accessible SMTP server, or that a machine in the local domain named *mailhost* be running an SMTP server. Finally, the security manager must permit network connections to that server, although this is not normally a problem in an application.

# Sockets

Before data is sent across the Internet from one host to another, it is split into packets of varying but finite size called *datagrams*. Datagrams range in size from a few dozen bytes to about 60,000 bytes. Anything larger, and often things smaller, must be split into smaller packets before it's transmitted. The advantage of this scheme is that if one packet is lost, it can be retransmitted without requiring redelivery of all other packets. Furthermore, if packets arrive out of order, they can be reordered at the receiving end of the connection.

Fortunately, packets are invisible to the Java programmer. The host's native networking software splits data into packets on the sending end and reassembles packets on the receiving end. Instead, the Java programmer is presented with a higher-level abstraction called a *socket*. The socket provides a reliable connection for the transmission of data between two hosts. It isolates you from the details of packet encodings, lost and retransmitted packets, and packets that arrive out of order. A socket performs four fundamental operations:

- Connects to a remote machine
- Sends data
- Receives data
- Closes the connection

A socket may not connect to more than one remote host. However, a socket may both send data to and receive data from the remote host it's connected to.

The java.net.Socket class is Java's interface to a network socket and allows you to perform all four fundamental socket operations. It provides raw, uninterpreted communication between two hosts. You can connect to remote machines; you can send data; you can receive data; you can close the connection. No part of the protocol is abstracted out, as is the case with URL and URLConnection. The programmer is completely responsible for the interaction between the client and the server.

To open a connection, call one of the Socket constructors, specifying the host to which you want to connect. Each Socket object is associated with exactly one remote host. To connect to a different host, you must create a new Socket object:

```
public Socket(String host, int port)
  throws UnknownHostException, IOException
public Socket(InetAddress address, int port) throws IOException
public Socket(String host, int port, InetAddress localAddress, int localPort)
  throws IOException
public Socket(InetAddress address, int port, InetAddress localAddress,
  int localPort) throws IOException
```

The host argument is a string like "www.oreilly.com" or "duke.poly.edu" that specifies the particular host to connect to. It may even be a numeric, dotted quad string such as "199.1.32.90". This argument may also be passed as a java.net.InetAddress object.

The port argument is the port on the remote host to connect to. A computer's network interface is logically subdivided into 65,536 different ports. As data traverses the Internet in packets, each packet carries both the address of the host it's going to and a port number on that host. A host reads the port number from each packet it receives to decide which program should receive that chunk of data. Many services run on well-known ports. For example, HTTP servers generally listen on port 80.

The optional localAddress and localPort arguments specify which address and port on the local host the socket connects from, assuming more than one is available. Most hosts have many available ports but only one address. These two arguments are optional. If they're left out, the constructor will choose reasonable values.

Data is sent across the socket via streams. These are the methods to get both streams for the socket:

```
public InputStream  getInputStream( ) throws IOException
public OutputStream getOutputStream( ) throws IOException
```

There's also a method to close the socket:

```
public void close( ) throws IOException
```

This closes the socket's input and output streams as well. Any attempt to read from or write to them after the socket is closed throws an IOException.

Example 5-3 is yet another program that connects to a web server and downloads a specified URL. However, since this one uses raw sockets, it needs to both send the HTTP request and read the headers in the response. These are not parsed away as they are by the URL and URLConnection classes; you use an output stream to send the request explicitly and an input stream to read the data—including HTTP headers— back. Only HTTP URLs are supported.

*Example 5-3. The SocketTyper program*

```java
import java.net.*;
import java.io.*;

public class SocketTyper {

  public static void main(String[] args) throws IOException {

    if (args.length != 1) {
      System.err.println("Usage: java SocketTyper url1");
      return;
    }

    URL u = new URL(args[0]);
    if (!u.getProtocol( ).equalsIgnoreCase("http")) {
      System.err.println("Sorry, " + u.getProtocol( )
        + " is not supported");
      return;
    }

    String host = u.getHost( );
    int port    = u.getPort( );
    String file = u.getFile( );
    if (file == null) file = "/";
    // default port
    if (port <= 0) port = 80;

    Socket s = null;
    try {
      s = new Socket(host, port);
      String request = "GET " + file + " HTTP/1.1\r\n"
        + "User-Agent: SocketTyper\r\n"
        + "Accept: text/*\r\n"
```

*Example 5-3. The SocketTyper program (continued)*

```
        + "Host: " + host + "\r\n"
        + "\r\n";
      byte[] b = request.getBytes("US-ASCII");

      OutputStream out = s.getOutputStream( );
      InputStream in = s.getInputStream( );
      out.write(b);
      out.flush( );

      for (int c = in.read(); c != -1; c = in.read( )) {
        System.out.write(c);
      }
    }
    finally {
      if (s != null && s.isConnected()) s.close( );
    }
  }
}
```

For example, when SocketTyper connects to *http://www.oreilly.com/*, here is what you see:

```
$ java SocketTyper http://www.oreilly.com/
HTTP/1.1 200 OK
Date: Mon, 23 May 2005 14:03:17 GMT
Server: Apache/1.3.33 (Unix) PHP/4.3.10 mod_perl/1.29
P3P: policyref="http://www.oreillynet.com/w3c/p3p.xml",CP="CAO DSP COR CURa ADMa
 DEVa TAIa PSAa PSDa IVAa IVDa CONo OUR DELa PUBi OTRa IND PHY ONL UNI PUR COM N
AV INT DEM CNT STA PRE"
Last-Modified: Mon, 23 May 2005 08:20:30 GMT
ETag: "20653-db8c-4291924e"
Accept-Ranges: bytes
Content-Length: 56204
Content-Type: text/html
X-Cache: MISS from www.oreilly.com

<!DOCTYPE HTML PUBLIC "-//W3C//DTD HTML 4.01 Transitional//EN">
<html xmlns="http://www.w3.org/1999/xhtml" lang="en-US" xml:lang="en-US">
<head>
...
```

Notice the header lines here, which you didn't see in Example 5-1. When you use the URL class to download a web page, the associated protocol handler consumes the HTTP header before you get a stream.

# Server Sockets

Each connection has two ends: the client, which initiates the connection, and the server, which responds to the connection. So far, I've only discussed the client side and assumed that a server existed out there for the client to talk to. To implement a server, you need to write a program that waits for other hosts to connect to it. A server socket binds to a particular port on the local machine (the server). Then it listens for incoming connection attempts from remote machines (the clients). When the server detects a connection attempt, it accepts the connection. This creates a socket between the two machines over which the client and the server communicate.

Multiple clients can connect to a server simultaneously. Incoming data is distinguished by the port to which it is addressed and the client host and port from which it came. The server can tell which service (such as HTTP or FTP) the data is intended for by checking the port at which it arrives. It knows where to send any response by looking at the client address and port stored with the data.

No more than one server socket can listen to a particular port at one time. Therefore, since a server may need to handle many connections at once, server programs tend to be multithreaded. (Alternately, they can use nonblocking I/O. We'll explore this starting in Chapter 16.) Generally, the server socket listening on the port only accepts the connections. It passes off the actual processing of each connection to a separate thread. Incoming connections are stored in a queue until the server can accept them. On most systems, the default queue length is between 5 and 50. Once the queue fills up, further incoming connections are refused until space in the queue opens up.

The `java.net.ServerSocket` class represents a server socket. The constructors receive the port to bind to, the queue length for incoming connections, and the IP address:

```
public ServerSocket(int port) throws IOException
public ServerSocket(int port, int backlog) throws IOException
public ServerSocket(int port, int backlog, InetAddress bindAddr)
 throws IOException
```

Normally, you only specify the port you want to listen on:

```
ServerSocket ss = new ServerSocket(80);
```

When you create a `ServerSocket` object, it attempts to bind to the port given by the port argument. If another server socket is already listening to the port, the constructor throws an `IOException`—more specifically, a `java.net.BindException`. Only one server socket can listen to a particular port at a time. This includes server sockets opened by non-Java programs. For example, if there's already an HTTP server running on port 80, you won't be able to bind to port 80.

 On Unix systems, including Mac OS X but not Windows, the program must be running as root to bind to a port between 1 and 1023. Otherwise, `accept()` throws a `BindException`.

0 is a special port number. It tells Java to pick an available port. You can then find out which port it has picked with the `getLocalPort()` method:

```
public int getLocalPort()
```

This is useful if the client and the server have already established a separate channel of communication over which the chosen port number can be communicated. For example, the FTP protocol uses two sockets. The client makes the initial connection to the server on a socket it will use to send commands. The client also opens a server socket on a random port on the local host. One of the commands it sends tells the server the port number on which the client is listening. The server then opens a socket to the client's server port, which it uses to send files. Because commands and data are sent over two different sockets, a long file doesn't tie up the command channel.

Once you have a ServerSocket, you wait for incoming connections by calling the accept( ) method. This method blocks until a connection attempt occurs and then returns a Socket that you can use to communicate with the client.

```
public Socket accept( ) throws IOException
```

The close( ) method terminates the ServerSocket:

```
public void close( ) throws IOException
```

That's pretty much all there is to the ServerSocket, except for a few methods dealing with socket options and some other details. In particular, there aren't methods for getting input and output streams. Instead, accept( ) returns a client Socket object: this Socket's getInputStream( ) or getOutputStream( ) methods return the streams used to communicate. For example:

```
ServerSocket ss = new ServerSocket(2345);
Socket s = ss.accept( );
OutputStream out = s.getOutputStream( );
// send data to the client...
s.close( );
```

Notice in this example, I closed the Socket s, not the ServerSocket ss. ss is still bound to port 2345. You get a new socket for each connection and reuse the server socket. For example, the next code fragment repeatedly accepts connections:

```
ServerSocket ss = new ServerSocket(2345);
while (true) {
  Socket s = ss.accept( );
  OutputStream out = s.getOutputStream( );
  // send data to the client...
  s.close( );
}
```

The program in Example 5-4 listens for incoming connections on port 2345. When it detects one, it answers with the client's address and port and its own. Then it closes the connection.

*Example 5-4. The HelloServer program*

```
import java.net.*;
import java.io.*;

public class HelloServer {
```

*Example 5-4. The HelloServer program (continued)*

```
public static void main(String[] args) throws IOException {

    int port = 2345;
    ServerSocket ss = new ServerSocket(port);
    while (true) {
      try {
        Socket s = ss.accept( );

        String response = "Hello " + s.getInetAddress( ) + " on port "
         + s.getPort( ) + "\r\n";
        response += "This is " + s.getLocalAddress( ) + " on port "
         + s.getLocalPort( ) + "\r\n";
        OutputStream out = s.getOutputStream( );
        out.write(response.getBytes("US-ASCII"));
        out.flush( );
        s.close( );
      }
      catch (IOException ex) {
        // This is an error on one connection. Maybe the client crashed.
        // Maybe it broke the connection prematurely. Whatever happened,
        // it's not worth shutting down the server for.
      }
    }  // end while
  } // end main
} // end HelloServer
```

Here's some output from this server. The server is running on *utopia.poly.edu*. The client is connecting from *titan.oit.unc.edu*. Note how the port from which the connection comes changes each time; like most client programs, the telnet program picks an arbitrary local port for outgoing connections:

```
$ telnet utopia.poly.edu
Trying 128.238.3.21...
Connected to utopia.poly.edu.
Escape character is '^]'.
Hello titan.oit.unc.edu/152.2.22.14 on port 50361
This is utopia.poly.edu/128.238.3.21 on port 2345
Connection closed by foreign host.
% telnet utopia.poly.edu
Trying 128.238.3.21...
Connected to utopia.poly.edu.
Escape character is '^]'.
Hello titan.oit.unc.edu/152.2.22.14 on port 50362
This is utopia.poly.edu/128.238.3.21 on port 2345
Connection closed by foreign host.
```

 If you aren't able to make a connection to this server, check your firewall rules. For security, most modern networks install firewalls in either the router, the local host, or both that prevent all connections to unrecognized services and ports. You may need to configure your firewall(s) to allow connections to port 2345 to run this program.

# URLViewer

Example 5-5 is the URLViewer program foreshadowed in Chapter 2. URLViewer is a simple application that provides a window in which you can view the contents of a URL. It assumes that those contents are more or less ASCII text. (In future chapters, I'll remove that restriction.) The application has a text field in which the user can type a URL, a Load button that the user presses to load the specified URL, and a JStreamedTextArea component from Chapter 2 that displays the text from the URL. Each of these corresponds to a field in the URLViewer class.

*Example 5-5. The URLViewer program*

```java
import java.awt.*;
import java.awt.event.*;
import java.io.*;
import javax.swing.*;
import java.net.*;
import com.elharo.io.ui.*;

public class URLViewer extends JFrame
 implements ActionListener {

  private JTextField theURL = new JTextField();
  private JButton loadButton = new JButton("Load");
  private JStreamedTextArea theDisplay = new JStreamedTextArea(60, 72);

  public URLViewer() {
    super("URL Viewer");
    this.getContentPane().add(BorderLayout.NORTH, theURL);
    JScrollPane pane = new JScrollPane(theDisplay);
    this.getContentPane().add(BorderLayout.CENTER, pane);
    Panel south = new Panel();
    south.add(loadButton);
    this.getContentPane().add(BorderLayout.SOUTH, south);
    theURL.addActionListener(this);
    loadButton.addActionListener(this);
    this.setLocation(50, 50);
    this.setDefaultCloseOperation(JFrame.EXIT_ON_CLOSE);
    this.pack();
  }

  public void actionPerformed(ActionEvent event) {
    try {
      URL u = new URL(theURL.getText());
      InputStream in = u.openStream();
      OutputStream out = theDisplay.getOutputStream();
      theDisplay.setText("");
      for (int c = in.read(); c != -1; c = in.read()) {
        out.write(c);
      }
      in.close();
    }
```

*Example 5-5. The URLViewer program (continued)*

```
    catch (IOException ex) {
      theDisplay.setText("Invalid URL: " + ex.getMessage( ));
    }
  }

  public static void main(String args[]) {
    final URLViewer me = new URLViewer( );
    // To avoid deadlock don't show frames on the main thread
    SwingUtilities.invokeLater(
      new Runnable( ) {
        public void run( ) {
          me.show( );
        }
      }
    );
  }
}
```

The URLViewer class itself extends JFrame. The constructor builds the interface, which consists of a JTextField to type the URL into, a JStreamedTextArea component from Chapter 2 that is placed inside a JScrollPane, and a Load button that can be pressed to download the content of the URL.

The streamed text area is filled when the user clicks the Load button or presses Enter inside the URL text field. The URLViewer object listens to both of these components. The URLViewer's actionPerformed( ) method constructs a URL from the text in the text field, then opens an input stream from the URL in the text field. Data from the URL's input stream pours into the text area's output stream. When that's finished, the input stream is closed. The output stream, however, is left open so the user can view new URLs.

# PART III

# Filter Streams

# CHAPTER 6

# Filter Streams

Filter input streams read data from a preexisting input stream such as a `FileInputStream` and have an opportunity to work with or change the data before it is delivered to the client program. Filter output streams write data to a preexisting output stream such as a `FileOutputStream` and have an opportunity to work with or change the data before it is written onto the underlying stream. Multiple filters can be chained onto a single underlying stream. Filter streams are used for encryption, compression, translation, buffering, and much more.

The word *filter* is derived by analogy with a water filter. A water filter sits between the pipe and faucet, filtering out impurities. A stream filter sits between the source of the data and its eventual destination and applies a specific algorithm to the data. As drops of water are passed through the water filter and modified, so too are bytes of data passed through the stream filter. Of course, there are some big differences—most notably, a stream filter, in addition to removing things you don't want, can add data or some other kind of annotation to the stream; it may even produce a stream that is completely different than its original input (for example, by compressing the original data).

## The Filter Stream Classes

`java.io.FilterInputStream` and `java.io.FilterOutputStream` are concrete superclasses for input and output stream subclasses that somehow modify or manipulate data of an underlying stream:

```
public class FilterInputStream extends InputStream
public class FilterOutputStream extends OutputStream
```

Each of these classes has a single protected constructor that specifies the underlying stream from which the filter stream reads or writes data:

```
protected FilterInputStream(InputStream in)
protected FilterOutputStream(OutputStream out)
```

These constructors set protected InputStream and OutputStream fields, called in and out, inside the FilterInputStream and FilterOutputStream classes, respectively:

```
protected InputStream in
protected OutputStream out
```

Since the constructors are protected, only subclasses can create filter streams. Each subclass implements a particular filtering operation. Most of the time, references to a filter stream are either references to a more specific subclass such as BufferedInputStream or they're polymorphic references to InputStream or OutputStream with no hint of the filter remaining. In other words, it's rare to declare a variable with the explicit type FilterInputStream or FilterOutputStream.

Beyond the constructors, both FilterInputStream and FilterOutputStream declare exactly the methods of their respective superclasses. For FilterInputStream, these are:

```
public int  read() throws IOException
public int  read(byte[] data) throws IOException
public int  read(byte[] data, int offset, int length) throws IOException
public long skip(long n) throws IOException
public int  available() throws IOException
public void close() throws IOException
public void mark(int readlimit)
public void reset() throws IOException
public boolean markSupported()
```

For FilterOutputStream, these are:

```
public void write(int b) throws IOException
public void write(byte[] data) throws IOException
public void write(byte[] data, int offset, int length) throws IOException
public void flush() throws IOException
public void close() throws IOException
```

Each of these methods merely passes its arguments to the corresponding method in the underlying stream. For example, the skip() method in FilterInputStream behaves like this:

```
public long skip(long n) throws IOException {
  in.skip(n);
}
```

The close() method in FilterOutputStream behaves like this:

```
public void close() throws IOException {
  out.close();
}
```

Thus, closing a filter stream closes the underlying stream. You cannot close one filter stream and then open up another on the same underlying stream, nor can you close one filter stream in a chain but still read from the underlying stream or other streams in the chain. Attempting to do so throws an IOException. Once a stream is closed—no matter which filter stream it's chained to—it's closed for good.

Since the constructors are protected, you don't use these classes directly. Instead, you create subclasses and use those. Since FilterOutputStream does not have a no-argument constructor, it's essential to give all subclasses explicit constructors and use super( ) to invoke the FilterOutputStream constructor. Your subclass will probably also want to override the write(int b) and write(byte[] data, int offset, int length) methods to perform its filtering. The write(byte[] data) method merely invokes write(data, 0, data.length), so if you've overridden the three-argument write( ) method, you probably don't need to override write(byte[] data) as well. Depending on circumstances, you may or may not need to override some of the other methods.

The PrintableOutputStream class shown in Example 6-1 is a subclass of FilterOutputStream that truncates all data to the range of printable ASCII characters: byte values 32–126, plus 9, 10, and 13 (tab, linefeed, and carriage return). Every time a byte in that range is passed to write( ), it is written onto the underlying output stream, out. Every time a byte outside that range is passed to write( ), a question mark is written onto the underlying output stream, out. Among other things, this class provides a quick and dirty way to read ASCII string literals embedded in a *.class* or *.exe* file.

*Example 6-1. The PrintableOutputStream class*

```
package com.elharo.io;

import java.io.*;

public class PrintableOutputStream extends FilterOutputStream {

  public PrintableOutputStream(OutputStream out) {
    super(out);
  }

  public void write(int b) throws IOException {

    // carriage return, linefeed, and tab
    if (b == '\n' || b == '\r' || b == '\t') out.write(b);
    // non-printing characters
    else if (b < 32 || b > 126) out.write('?');
    // printing, ASCII characters
    else out.write(b);
  }

  public void write(byte[] data, int offset, int length) throws IOException {
    for (int i = offset; i < offset+length; i++) {
      this.write(data[i]);
    }
  }
}
```

To use this class, or any other filter output stream, you must chain it to another stream that actually writes the bytes to their eventual target. For example, to chain a PrintableOutputStream to System.out, you would write:

```
PrintableOutputStream pos = new PrintableOutputStream(System.out);
```

If the filter stream subclass only overrides methods from the superclass and does not add any, it's common to just declare the variable as type OutputStream or InputStream. For example, the previous statement can be rewritten like this:

```
OutputStream out = new PrintableOutputStream(System.out);
```

Sometimes the underlying stream is created directly inside the constructor:

```
OutputStream out =
    new PrintableOutputStream(new FileOutputStream("data.txt"));
```

However, the sheer length of the stream class names tends to make this style of coding inconvenient.

Multiple streams can be chained together in sequence to get the benefits of each. For example, to create a buffered, printable file output stream, you would chain a file output stream to a buffered output stream, which you'd then chain to a printable output stream. For example:

```
FileOutputStream fout = new FileOutputStream("data.txt");
BufferedOutputStream bout = new BufferedOutputStream(fout);
PrintableOutputStream pout = new PrintableOutputStream(bout);
```

Sometimes this is done using only a single OutputStream variable:

```
OutputStream out = new FileOutputStream("data.txt");
out = new BufferedOutputStream(out);
out = new PrintableOutputStream(out);
```

This keeps you from accidentally writing onto or reading from anything but the last stream in the chain. There are reasons you might sometimes need to read from or write to a stream deeper in the chain, but such reasons are unusual, and you shouldn't do it by accident.

Example 6-2 uses the PrintableOutputStream class to extract ASCII strings from a file. First it chains either System.out or a file output stream to a printable output stream, then it opens a file input stream from a file named on the command line and copies it into the printable output stream, thereby converting it to printable ASCII characters.

*Example 6-2. The StringExtractor class*

```
import com.elharo.io.*;
import java.io.*;

public class StringExtractor {

  public static void main(String[] args) {

    if (args.length < 1) {
      System.out.println("Usage: java StringExtractor inFile");
```

*Example 6-2. The StringExtractor class (continued)*

```
      return;
    }
    try {
      InputStream in = new FileInputStream(args[0]);
      OutputStream out;
      if (args.length >= 2) {
        out = new FileOutputStream(args[1]);
      }
      else out = System.out;

      // Here's where the output stream is chained
      // to the ASCII output stream.
      PrintableOutputStream pout = new PrintableOutputStream(out);
      for (int c = in.read(); c != -1; c = in.read()) {
          pout.write(c);
      }
      out.close();
    }
    catch (FileNotFoundException e) {
      System.out.println("Usage: java StringExtractor inFile outFile");
    }
    catch (IOException ex) {
      System.err.println(ex);
    }
  }
}
```

Here's the output produced by running StringExtractor on its own *.class* file:

```
$ java StringExtractor  StringExtractor.class
???????.?D
????    ??????
?!?"??#
???$??%
???$??&
?       ?'
?(?)
?       ?*
?+?,??-??.??/   ???0
?!?1??2??3???<init>???( )V???Code???LineNumberTable???main???
([Ljava/lang/String;)V??SourceFile???StringExtractor.java
???????4??5?6??"Usage: java StringExtractor
inFile??7??8?9???java/io/FileInputStream????9???
java/io/FileOutputStream??#com/elharo/io/PrintableOutputStream????:??;??
<?=??>????@??A?????java/io/FileNotFoundException??
*Usage: java StringExtractor inFile
outFile???java/io/IOException??B?6??8?C???StringExtractor???java/lang/Object???
java/lang/System???out???Ljava/io/PrintStream;???java/io/PrintStream???println???
(Ljava/lang/String;)V???(Ljava/io/OutputStream;)V???java/io/InputStream???read???
( )I???write???(I)V???java/io/OutputStream???close???err???(Ljava/lang/Object;)V
?!????????????????????????????????*???????????????????????
?????????????????????r*??????????????????Y*?2???L*????????Y*?2???M??????M??        Y,??
???L??????????L???+?????????Z?]?????Z?i?????????N?????????        ???
```

Although a lot of information is clearly lost in this translation, a surprising amount is retained—you have every string literal in the file and the names of all the classes and methods referenced by this class.

Filter input streams are created similarly. Since FilterInputStream does not have a no-argument constructor, all subclasses require explicit constructors and must use super( ) to invoke the FilterInputStream constructor. The subclass overrides the read( ) and read(byte[] data, int offset, int length) methods in order to do the actual filtering. The read(byte[] data) method merely invokes read(data, 0, data. length), so if you've overridden the three-argument read( ) method, you probably don't need to override read(byte[] data) as well. Depending on circumstances, you may or may not need to override some of the other methods. For example, the PrintableInputStream class shown in Example 6-3 truncates all data read to the range of printable ASCII characters. As with PrintableOutputStream, any character not in that range is replaced by a question mark.

*Example 6-3. The PrintableInputStream class*

```
package com.elharo.io;

import java.io.*;

public class PrintableInputStream extends FilterInputStream {

  public PrintableInputStream(InputStream in) {
    super(in);
  }

  public int read( ) throws IOException {

    int b = in.read( );
    // printing, ASCII characters
    if (b >= 32 && b <= 126) return b;
    else if (b == '\n' || b == '\r' || b == '\t') return b;
    // nonprinting characters
    else return '?';

  }

  public int read(byte[] data, int offset, int length) throws IOException {

    int result = in.read(data, offset, length);
    for (int i = offset; i < offset+result; i++) {
      // Do nothing with the printing characters.
      if (data[i] == '\n'|| data[i] == '\r' || data[i] == '\t' || data[i] == -1) ;
      // nonprinting characters
      else if (data[i] < 32 || data[i] > 126) data[i] = (byte) '?';
    }
    return result;
  }
}
```

# The Filter Stream Subclasses

The java.io package contains many useful filter stream classes. The BufferedInputStream and BufferedOutputStream classes buffer reads and writes by first putting data into a buffer (an internal array of bytes). Thus, an application can read or write bytes to the stream without necessarily calling the underlying native methods. The data is read from or written into the buffer in blocks; subsequent accesses go straight to the buffer. This improves performance in many situations. Buffered input streams also allow the reader to back up and reread data.

The java.io.PrintStream class allows very simple printing of primitive values, objects, and string literals. It uses the platform's default character encoding to convert characters into bytes. This class traps all IOExceptions and is primarily intended for debugging. System.out and System.err are the most popular examples of the PrintStream class, but you can connect a PrintStream filter to other output streams as well. For example, you can chain a PrintStream to a FileOutputStream to write formatted strings into a file. These classes will be discussed in the next chapter.

The PushbackInputStream class has a 1-byte pushback buffer so a program can "unread" the last character read. The next time data is read from the stream, the unread character is reread.

The ProgressMonitorInputStream class shows the user a running tally of how much data has been read and how much remains to be read.

The DataInputStream and DataOutputStream classes read and write primitive Java data types and strings in a machine-independent way. (Big-endian for integer types, IEEE-754 for floats and doubles, a variant of UTF-8 for strings.) These classes will be discussed in Chapter 8. The ObjectInputStream and ObjectOutputStream classes extend DataInputStream and DataOutputStream with methods to read and write arbitrary Java objects as well as primitive data types. These will be taken up in Chapter 13.

The java.util.zip package also includes several filter stream classes. The filter input streams in this package decompress compressed data; the filter output streams compress raw data. Because compressed files are particularly vulnerable to corruption, this package also provides filters that maintain a running checksum of the data in a file. These will be discussed in Chapter 10.

The java.util.security package contains the DigestInputStream and DigestOutputStream filter streams; these calculate message digests of the data that passes through them. The Java Cryptography Extension (JCE) adds two more filter streams to this package, CipherInputStream and CipherOutputStream, which can encrypt or decrypt data using a variety of algorithms. These filter streams will be discussed in Chapter 12.

# Buffered Streams

Buffered input streams read more data than they initially need into a buffer (an internal array of bytes). When one of the stream's read( ) methods is invoked, data is removed from the buffer rather than from the underlying stream. When the buffer runs out of data, the buffered stream refills its buffer from the underlying stream. Likewise, buffered output streams store data in an internal byte array until the buffer is full or the stream is flushed; then the data is written out to the underlying output stream in one swoop. In situations where it's almost as fast to read or write several hundred bytes from the underlying stream as it is to read or write a single byte, a buffered stream can provide a significant performance boost.

There are two BufferedInputStream constructors and two BufferedOutputStream constructors:

```
public BufferedInputStream(InputStream in)
public BufferedInputStream(InputStream in, int size)
public BufferedOutputStream(OutputStream out)
public BufferedOutputStream(OutputStream out, int size)
```

The first argument is the underlying stream from which data will be read or to which data will be written. The size argument is the number of bytes in the buffer. If a size isn't specified, a 2048-byte buffer is used. The best size for the buffer depends on the platform and is generally related to the block size of the disk (at least for file streams). Less than 512 bytes is probably too small and more than 8,192 bytes is probably too large. Ideally, you want an integral multiple of the block size of the disk. However, you might want to use smaller buffer sizes for unreliable network connections. For example:

```
URL u = new URL("http://java.sun.com");
BufferedInputStream bis = new BufferedInputStream(u.openStream( ), 256);
```

Example 6-4 copies files named on the command line to System.out with buffered reads and writes.

*Example 6-4. A BufferedStreamCopier*

```
package com.elharo.io;
import java.io.*;

public class BufferedStreamCopier {

  public static void main(String[] args) {

    try {
      copy(System.in, System.out);
    }
    catch (IOException ex) {
      System.err.println(ex);
    }
  }
}
```

*Example 6-4. A BufferedStreamCopier (continued)*

```
  public static void copy(InputStream in, OutputStream out)
   throws IOException {

    BufferedInputStream bin = new BufferedInputStream(in);
    BufferedOutputStream bout = new BufferedOutputStream(out);

    while (true) {
      int datum = bin.read();
      if (datum == -1) break;
      bout.write(datum);
    }
    bout.flush();
  }
}
```

This copy( ) method copies byte by byte, which is normally not very efficient. However, almost all the copies take place in memory, because the input stream and the output stream are buffered. Therefore, this is reasonably quick.

The output stream is deliberately flushed. The data reaches its eventual destination in the underlying stream out only when the stream is flushed or the buffer fills up. Therefore, it's important to call flush( ) explicitly before the method returns.

## BufferedInputStream Details

BufferedInputStream only overrides and inherits methods from InputStream. It does not declare any new methods of its own. Marking and resetting are supported.

In Java 1.2 and later, the two multibyte read( ) methods try to fill the specified array or subarray completely by reading repeatedly from the underlying input stream. They return only when the requested number of bytes have been read, the end of stream is reached, or the underlying stream would block. Most other input streams attempt only one read from the underlying stream or data source before returning.

The buffer and the current state of the buffer are stored in protected fields. The buffer itself is a byte array called buf; the number of bytes in the buffer is an int named count; the index of the next byte that will be returned by read( ) is an int called pos; the mark, if any, is an int called markpos; the read-ahead limit before the mark is invalidated is an int called marklimit. Subclasses of BufferedInputStream can directly access all these fields, which can be important for performance.

```
    protected byte[] buf
    protected int    count
    protected int    pos
    protected int    markpos
    protected int    marklimit
```

## BufferedOutputStream Details

BufferedOutputStream stores the buffered data in a protected byte array named buf and the index of the next place in the array where a byte will be stored in an int field named pos. BufferedOutputStream does not expose the number of bytes in the buffer.

```
protected byte buf[]
protected int  pos
```

Otherwise, BufferedOutputStream has the same write( ), flush( ), and close( ) methods every OutputStream has. These methods are invoked exactly as they would be for any output stream. The only difference is that writes place data in the buffer rather than directly on the underlying output stream. BufferedOutputStream does not declare any new methods.

# PushbackInputStream

The java.io.PushbackInputStream class provides a pushback buffer so a program can "unread" bytes. In other words, it can add bytes to the stream and then read them. These may be bytes the program has read from the underlying InputStream or they may be completely different bytes. In effect, PushbackInputStream allows programs to add data to a stream while they're reading it. The next time data is read from the stream, the unread bytes are reread.

```
public void unread(int b) throws IOException
public void unread(byte[] data, int offset, int length) throws IOException
public void unread(byte[] data) throws IOException
```

By default, the buffer is only 1 byte long, and trying to unread more than 1 byte throws an IOException. However, you can change the default buffer size with the second constructor:

```
public PushbackInputStream(InputStream in)
public PushbackInputStream(InputStream in, int size)
```

Unread data is pushed onto a stack. In other words, the last byte you unread is the first byte you read. This code fragment prints 2, 1, 0; not 0, 1, 2:

```
PushbackInputStream in = new PushbackInputStream(System.in, 5);
in.unread(0);
in.unread(1);
in.unread(2);
System.out.println(in.read( ));
System.out.println(in.read( ));
System.out.println(in.read( ));
```

One common use for PushbackInputStream is tokenizing source code. For example, suppose a compiler is reading the Java statement int count=7;. Because Java variable names can have any length, the compiler doesn't know that the last character is t until it has read the equals sign (=). However, by the time it knows this, it has already read the equals sign. A PushbackInputStream allows the compiler to unread the equals sign and continue, this time treating the sign as an operator rather than as a piece of an identifier. Other times, the program may want to add something to the stream that wasn't there before and then read it in the usual way. For instance, to convert a Mac text file to a Windows text file, a program could unread a linefeed after it reads a carriage return.

Although both PushbackInputStream and BufferedInputStream use buffers, only a PushbackInputStream allows unreading, and only a BufferedInputStream allows marking and resetting. In a PushbackInputStream, markSupported( ) returns false.

The read( ) and available( ) methods are invoked exactly as they are with normal input streams. However, they first attempt to read from the pushback buffer.

# ProgressMonitorInputStream

I/O operations can be slow, especially when reading data from the network. User-centric programs should always give the user feedback, even if the feedback is no more significant than "No, I haven't frozen; I'm still running." For simple operations, an animated cursor like the Macintosh's spinning beach ball may be sufficient. For longer operations, you should display a progress bar that indicates how much of the operation has been accomplished and how much remains to be done, such as the one shown in Figure 6-1. ProgressMonitorInputStream is a unique filter stream hiding in the javax.swing package that displays progress bars that indicate how much of a stream has been read and how much remains to be read.

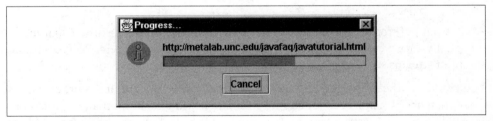

*Figure 6-1. A Swing progress bar*

ProgressMonitorInputStream is a FilterInputStream that you can chain to any other input stream in the usual way. If the data is read in less time than it normally takes for the user to notice a delay (as for a small file read from a disk), no dialog is shown. However, if the input begins to take a noticeable amount of time, Java pops up a progress bar that includes a cancel button. If the user presses that button, the current read( ) method throws an InterruptedIOException. Otherwise, input continues, and the progress bar is updated until the end of the stream is reached.

The primary method you need to be aware of in ProgressMonitorInputStream is the constructor:

```
public ProgressMonitorInputStream(Component parent,
  Object message, InputStream in)
```

The parent argument specifies the parent component of the progress monitor, though it may be null if no such component is available. The message argument is normally a String containing the message shown in the dialog. If some other type is used, its toString( ) method is invoked to provide the message. Finally, in is the underlying InputStream this stream is chained to. For example, this code fragment will use a progress monitor to keep the user updated about how far along it is while it's reading the file *lotsofdata.txt*:

```
File f = new File("lotsofdata.txt");
InputStream in = new FileInputStream(fin);
ProgressMonitorInputStream pin = new ProgressMonitorInputStream(
 null, f.getName( ), in);
```

The only other new method you need to know about in this class is getProgressMonitor( ):

```
public ProgressMonitor getProgressMonitor( )
```

This returns a reference to the actual progress monitor so that you can adjust its behavior with the methods of the javax.swing.ProgressMonitor class. For instance, you can change the default time before the progress monitor is shown or the maximum and minimum values used for the monitor. You also use this object to tell the ProgressMonitor how much data is expected through the setMaximum( ) method. For instance, when reading a file, the length( ) method in the File class reveals how many bytes you expect to read. That would be the maximum for the progress bar. For example:

```
ProgressMonitor pm = pin.getProgressMonitor( );
pm.setMaximum(f.length( ));
```

Aside from getProgressMonitor( ), ProgressMonitorInputStream has the usual methods of any InputStream class: read( ), close( ), markSupported( ), etc. Progress monitor input streams support marking and resetting only if the underlying stream does.

You read from the stream just as you read from any other stream. If the process takes more than about half a second, and it looks like it will take more than two seconds, Java will pop up a ProgressMonitor showing the user just how much is done and how much remains to be done. You can adjust these times using the methods of the ProgressMonitor class, but the defaults for everything except the maximum value are generally reasonable.

Programs that read data from the network take even longer than programs that read from files. Example 6-5 is a complete program that reads data from a URL given on the command line and copies it to System.out. It uses a ProgressMonitor to keep the user alerted as to its progress. It uses the content-length HTTP header to determine how much data will be sent in order to set the maximum value for the progress bar.

*Example 6-5. MonitoredSourceViewer*

```
import java.net.*;
import java.io.*;
import javax.swing.*;

public class MonitoredSourceViewer {

  public static void main (String[] args) {

    if  (args.length > 0) {
      try {
        // Open the URLConnection for reading
        URL u = new URL(args[0]);
        URLConnection uc = u.openConnection( );
        InputStream in = uc.getInputStream( );

        // Chain a ProgressMonitorInputStream to the
        // URLConnection's InputStream
        ProgressMonitorInputStream pin
         = new ProgressMonitorInputStream(null, u.toString( ), in);

        // Set the maximum value of the ProgressMonitor
        ProgressMonitor pm = pin.getProgressMonitor( );
        pm.setMaximum(uc.getContentLength( ));

        // Read the data
        for (int c = pin.read(); c != -1; c = pin.read( )) {
          System.out.print((char) c);
        }
        pin.close( );
      }
      catch (MalformedURLException ex) {
        System.err.println(args[0] + " is not a parseable URL");
      }
      catch (InterruptedIOException ex) {
        // User cancelled. Do nothing.
      }
      catch (IOException ex) {
        System.err.println(ex);
      }
    } //  end if

    // Since we brought up a GUI, we have to explicitly exit here
    // rather than simply returning from the main( ) method.
    System.exit(0);
  } // end main
} // end MonitoredSourceViewer
```

Figure 6-1 is the screenshot of a progress monitor taken from this program.
ProgressMonitorInputStream is a simple class that's very easy to program with and
that will make users' experiences much more pleasant.

# Multitarget Output Streams

As a final example, I present two slightly unusual filter output streams that direct their data to multiple underlying streams. The TeeOutputStream class in Example 6-6 has not one but two underlying streams. It does not modify the data that's written in any way; it merely writes that data on both of its underlying streams.

*Example 6-6. The TeeOutputStream class*

```java
package com.elharo.io;

import java.io.*;

public class TeeOutputStream extends FilterOutputStream {

  private OutputStream out1;
  private OutputStream out2;

  public TeeOutputStream(OutputStream stream1, OutputStream stream2) {
    super(stream1);
    out1 = stream1;
    out2 = stream2;
  }

  public void write(int b) throws IOException {
    out1.write(b);
    out2.write(b);
  }

  public void write(byte[] data, int offset, int length)
   throws IOException {
    out1.write(data, offset, length);
    out2.write(data, offset, length);
  }

  public void flush() throws IOException {
    out1.flush();
    out2.flush();
  }

  public void close() throws IOException {
    out1.close();
    out2.close();
  }
}
```

It would be possible to store one of the output streams in FilterOutputStream's protected out field and the other in a field in this class. However, it's simpler and cleaner to maintain the parallelism between the two streams by storing them both in the TeeOutputStream class.

Example 6-7 demonstrates how one might use this class to write a TeeCopier program that copies a file into two separate, new files.

*Example 6-7. The TeeCopier program*

```
import java.io.*;
import com.elharo.io.*;

public class TeeCopier {

  public static void main(String[] args) throws IOException {

    if (args.length != 3) {
      System.out.println("Usage: java TeeCopier infile outfile1 outfile2");
      return;
    }

    FileInputStream fin = new FileInputStream(args[0]);
    FileOutputStream fout1 = new FileOutputStream(args[1]);
    FileOutputStream fout2 = new FileOutputStream(args[2]);
    TeeOutputStream tout = new TeeOutputStream(fout1, fout2);
    BufferedStreamCopier.copy(fin, tout);
    fin.close();
    tout.close();
  }
}
```

# File Viewer, Part 2

One of many things Fred Brooks is famous for saying is, "plan to throw one away; you will anyhow."[*] Now that we've got filter streams in hand, I'm ready to throw out the monolithic design for the FileDumper program used in Chapter 4. I'm going to rewrite it using a more flexible, object-oriented approach that relies on multiple chained filters. This allows us to extend the system to handle new formats without rewriting all the old classes. (It also makes some of the examples in subsequent chapters smaller, since I won't have to repeat all of the code each time.) The basic idea is to make each interpretation of the data a filter input stream. Bytes from the underlying stream move into the filter; the filter converts the bytes into strings. Since more bytes generally come out of the filter than go into it (for instance, the single byte 32 is replaced by the four bytes "0", "3", "2", and " " in decimal dump format), the filter streams buffer the data as necessary.

The architecture revolves around the abstract DumpFilter class shown in Example 6-8. The public interface of this class is identical to that of FilterInputStream. Internally, a buffer holds the string interpretation of each byte as an array of bytes. The read( ) method returns bytes from this array as long as possible. An index field tracks the next available byte. When index reaches the length of the array, the abstract fill( ) method is invoked to read from the underlying stream and place data in the buffer.

---

[*] Frederick P. Brooks, *The Mythical Man-Month*, 20th Anniversary Edition (Reading: Addison-Wesley), 115.

By changing how the fill( ) method translates the bytes it reads into the bytes in the buffer, you can change how the data is interpreted.

*Example 6-8. DumpFilter*

```java
package com.elharo.io;
import java.io.*;

public abstract class DumpFilter extends FilterInputStream {

  // This is really an array of unsigned bytes.
  private int[] buf = new int[0];
  private int index = 0;

  public DumpFilter(InputStream in) {
    super(in);
  }

  public int read( ) throws IOException {

    int result;
    if (index < buf.length) {
      result = buf[index];
      index++;
    } // end if
    else {
      try {
        this.fill( );
        // fill is required to put at least one byte
        // in the buffer or throw an EOF or IOException.
        result = buf[0];
        index = 1;
      }
      catch (EOFException ex) {
        result = -1;
      }
    } // end else

    return result;
  }

  protected abstract void fill( ) throws IOException;

  public int read(byte[] data, int offset, int length) throws IOException {

    if (data == null) {
      throw new NullPointerException( );
    }
    else if ((offset < 0) || (offset > data.length) || (length < 0)
     || ((offset + length) > data.length) || ((offset + length) < 0)) {
      throw new ArrayIndexOutOfBoundsException( );
    }
    else if (length == 0) {
      return 0;
    }
```

*Example 6-8. DumpFilter (continued)*

```
    // Check for end of stream.
    int datum = this.read( );
    if (datum == -1) {
      return -1;
    }

    data[offset] = (byte) datum;

    int bytesRead = 1;
    try {
      for (; bytesRead < length ; bytesRead++) {

        datum = this.read( );

        // In case of end of stream, return as much as we've got,
        // then wait for the next call to read to return -1.
        if (datum == -1) break;
        data[offset + bytesRead] = (byte) datum;
      }
    }
    catch (IOException ex) {
      // Return what's already in the data array.
    }
    return bytesRead;
  }

  public int available( ) throws IOException {
    return buf.length - index;
  }

  public long skip(long bytesToSkip) throws IOException {

    long bytesSkipped = 0;
    for (; bytesSkipped < bytesToSkip; bytesSkipped++) {
      int c = this.read( );
      if (c == -1) break;
    }
    return bytesSkipped;
  }

  public void mark(int readlimit) {}

  public void reset( ) throws IOException {
    throw new IOException("marking not supported");
  }

  public boolean markSupported( ) {
    return false;
  }
}
```

The FilterInputStream class tacitly assumes that the number of bytes of input read from the underlying stream is the same as the number of bytes read from the filter stream. Somtimes this isn't true, as is the case here. For instance, the HexFilter will provide three bytes of data for every byte read from the underlying stream. The DecimalFilter will provide four. Therefore, we also have to override skip( ) and available( ). The skip( ) method reads as many bytes as possible, then returns. The available( ) method returns the number of bytes remaining in the buffer. For the uses we're putting these classes to, these methods aren't all that important, so I haven't bothered to provide optimal implementations. You can do better in subclasses, if you like.

The same problem applies to the mark( ) and reset( ) methods. These will mark and reset the underlying stream, but what we really desire is to mark and reset this stream. The easiest solution here is to deliberately not support marking and resetting. If marking and resetting is necessary, it's easy to chain this stream to a buffered stream as long as the buffered stream follows the dump filter in the chain rather than preceding it.

Concrete subclasses need to implement only a constructor or two and the fill( ) method. Example 6-9 shows the DecimalFilter class. Example 6-10 shows the HexFilter class. These two classes are very similar; each implements fill( ) and overrides available( ) (the latter mainly because it's straightforward to do). The algorithms used by the fill( ) methods for converting bytes to decimal and hexadecimal strings are essentially the same as those used by the dumpDecimal( ) and dumpHex( ) methods back in Chapter 4's FileDumper program.

*Example 6-9. DecimalFilter*

```
package com.elharo.io;
import java.io.*;

public class DecimalFilter extends DumpFilter {

  private int numRead = 0;
  private int breakAfter = 15;
  private int ratio = 4; // number of bytes of output per byte of input

  public DecimalFilter(InputStream in) {
    super(in);
  }

  protected void fill( ) throws IOException {

    buf = new int[ratio];
    int datum = in.read( );
    this.numRead++;
    if (datum == -1) {
      // Let read( ) handle end of stream.
      throw new EOFException( );
    }
```

*Example 6-9. DecimalFilter (continued)*

```
    String dec = Integer.toString(datum);
    if (datum < 10) { // Add two leading zeros.
      dec = "00" + dec;
    }
    else if (datum < 100) { // Add leading zero.
      dec = '0' + dec;
    }
    for (int i = 0; i < dec.length(); i++) {
      buf[i] = dec.charAt(i);
    }
    if (numRead < breakAfter) {
      buf[buf.length - 1] = ' ';
    }
    else {
      buf[buf.length - 1] = '\n';
      numRead = 0;
    }
  }

  public int available() throws IOException {
    return (buf.length - index) + ratio * in.available();
  }
}
```

*Example 6-10. HexFilter*

```
package com.elharo.io;
import java.io.*;

public class HexFilter extends DumpFilter {

  private int numRead = 0;
  private int breakAfter = 24;
  private int ratio = 3; // Number of bytes of output per byte of input.

  public HexFilter(InputStream in) {
    super(in);
  }

  protected void fill() throws IOException {

    buf = new int[ratio];
    int datum = in.read();
    this.numRead++;
    if (datum == -1) {
      // Let read() handle end of stream.
      throw new EOFException();
    }

    String hex = Integer.toHexString(datum);
    if (datum < 16) { // Add a leading zero.
      hex = '0' + hex;
    }
```

*Example 6-10. HexFilter (continued)*

```
    for (int i = 0; i < hex.length(); i++) {
      buf[i] = hex.charAt(i);
    }
    if (numRead < breakAfter) {
      buf[buf.length - 1] = ' ';
    }
    else {
      buf[buf.length - 1] = '\n';
      numRead = 0;
    }
  }

  public int available() throws IOException {
    return (buf.length - index) + ratio * in.available();
  }
}
```

The main( ) method and class in Example 6-11 are similar to what we've seen before. However, rather than selecting a method to dump the file, we select a dump filter to use. This allows multiple filters to be used in sequence—a feature that will be important when we want to decompress, decrypt, or perform other transformations on the data, in addition to interpreting it. The program is also easier to read and understand when split across the three classes.

*Example 6-11. FileDumper2*

```
import java.io.*;
import com.elharo.io.*;

public class FileDumper2 {

  public static final int ASC = 0;
  public static final int DEC = 1;
  public static final int HEX = 2;

  public static void main(String[] args) {

    if (args.length < 1) {
      System.err.println("Usage: java FileDumper2 [-ahd] file1 file2...");
      return;
    }

    int firstArg = 0;
    int mode = ASC;

    if (args[0].startsWith("-")) {
      firstArg = 1;
      if (args[0].equals("-h")) mode = HEX;
      else if (args[0].equals("-d")) mode = DEC;
    }

    for (int i = firstArg; i < args.length; i++) {
```

*Example 6-11. FileDumper2 (continued)*

```
    try {
      InputStream in = new FileInputStream(args[i]);
      dump(in, System.out, mode);

      if (i < args.length-1) {  // more files to dump
        System.out.println();
        System.out.println("------------------------------------");
        System.out.println();
      }
    }
    catch (IOException ex) {
      System.err.println(ex);
    }
  }
}

public static void dump(InputStream in, OutputStream out, int mode)
  throws IOException {

  // The reference variable in may point to several different objects
  // within the space of the next few lines. We can attach
  // more filters here to do decompression, decryption, and more.

  if (mode == ASC) ; // no filter needed, just copy raw bytes
  else if (mode == HEX) in = new HexFilter(in);
  else if (mode == DEC) in = new DecimalFilter(in);

  BufferedStreamCopier.copy(in, out);
  in.close();
  }
}
```

The main( ) method is responsible for choosing the file and format to be dumped. The dump( ) method translates an input stream onto an output stream using a particular filter. This allows the dump( ) method to be used by other classes as a more general translation service for streams. An alternative pattern would pass the filter as an argument to dump( ) rather than as an integer mode. This might make the program more flexible but would not allow us to easily chain several filters together, as we'll do in upcoming chapters.

# CHAPTER 7

# Print Streams

System.out is the first output stream most Java programmers encounter. System.err is probably the second. Both are instances of the java.io.PrintStream class. PrintStream is a subclass of FilterOutputStream that converts numbers and objects to text. System.out is primarily used for simple, character-mode applications and for debugging. Its *raison d'étre* is convenience, not robustness; print streams ignore many issues involved in internationalization and error checking. This makes System.out easy to use in quick-and-dirty hacks and simple examples, while simultaneously making it unsuitable for production code, which should use the java.io.PrintWriter class (discussed in Chapter 20) instead.

PrintStream is not limited to the console. PrintStream is a filter stream and thus can be connected to any other output stream: a FileOutputStream, a ByteArrayOutputStream, a TelnetOutputStream, or anything else you write to. Three constructors can be used to chain a PrintStream to an underlying stream:

```
public PrintStream(OutputStream out)
public PrintStream(OutputStream out, boolean autoFlush)
public PrintStream(OutputStream out, boolean autoFlush, String encoding)
 throws UnsupportedEncodingException
```

The out argument is just the underlying output stream. The autoFlush argument is a boolean. If it's true, the stream is flushed every time a linefeed character (\n) or byte is written, a println( ) method is invoked, or a byte array is written. The encoding argument names the character encoding used to convert strings to bytes. The last option is available only in Java 1.4 and later. Print streams in Java 1.3 and earlier (and all print streams created with the first two constructors) use the local system's default encoding, whatever that may be. Often this is not the encoding you need, so you should specify the encoding explicitly if possible.

Java 5 added four more constructors, though these are mostly just conveniences. They allow you to create a PrintStream that will write data in a file. The file to be written is specified with either a java.io.File object (which will be discussed in

Chapter 17) or a `String` containing the filename. You can also specify the character encoding used to write the file:

```
public PrintStream(String fileName) throws FileNotFoundException
public PrintStream(String fileName, String encoding)
 throws FileNotFoundException, UnsupportedEncodingException
public PrintStream(File file) throws FileNotFoundException
public PrintStream(File file, String encoding)
 throws FileNotFoundException, UnsupportedEncodingException
```

These constructors don't accomplish anything that chaining a `PrintStream` to a `FileOutputStream` won't do.

## Print Versus Write

The reason you might choose a `PrintStream` instead of a raw `OutputStream` is for its `print()` and `println()` methods. These methods each convert their argument to a `String` and then convert the `String` to bytes in a specific encoding before writing it to the underlying output stream. For example, consider this `PrintStream` connected to a file named *numbers.dat*:

```
PrintStream out = new PrintStream(new FileOutputStream("numbers.dat"));
```

Suppose we use a simple for loop to *write* the numbers from 0 to 127 in that file:

```
for (int i = 0; i <= 127; i++) out.write(i);
```

When we're done, the file contains 128 bytes: the first byte is 0, the second is 1, the third is 2, and so on. It's pure binary data. If you try to open it up in a text editor you'll see goop, as shown in Figure 7-1. Some of those binary numbers happen to be interpretable as ASCII text, but that's an accident. They're really just bytes. Many of them aren't printable.

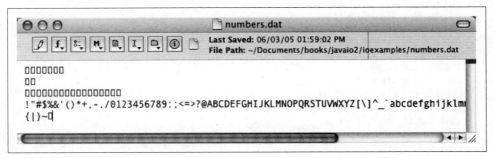

*Figure 7-1. A binary file in a text editor*

Now suppose instead of using the `write()` method we use the `print()` method:

```
for (int i = 0; i <= 127; i++) out.print(i);
```

This time the `PrintStream` does not write raw binary data in the file. Instead, it converts each number into its ASCII string equivalent and writes that string. For instance, instead of writing the byte 20, it writes the character 2 followed by the character 0. If you open the file in a text editor now, you'll see something like the screenshot shown in Figure 7-2.

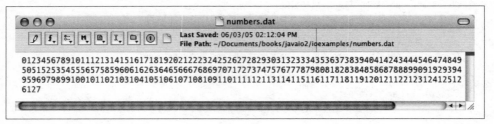

*Figure 7-2. A text file in a text editor*

 It's not absolutely guaranteed that the string will be written in ASCII. On a few IBM mainframes, EBCDIC might be used instead. However, given the range of characters used here, it's pretty likely that the resulting file will make sense when interpreted as ASCII. More on this point shortly.

The print1n( ) method prints a platform-specific line terminator after printing its argument. Suppose instead of using the print( ) method we use the print1n( ) method:

```
for (int i = 0; i <= 127; i++) out.println(i);
```

Then the output is even neater, as shown in Figure 7-3.

These examples used ints, but the PrintStream class has print( ) and print1n( ) methods for every Java data type. The method signatures are:

```
public void print(boolean b)
public void print(char c)
public void print(int i)
public void print(long l)
public void print(float f)
public void print(double d)
public void print(char[] s)
public void print(String s)
public void print(Object o)
public void println(boolean b)
public void println(char c)
public void println(int i)
public void println(long l)
public void println(float f)
public void println(double d)
public void println(char[] s)
public void println(String s)
public void println(Object o)
```

You can pass anything at all to a print( ) method. Whatever argument you supply is guaranteed to match at least one of these methods. Object types are converted to

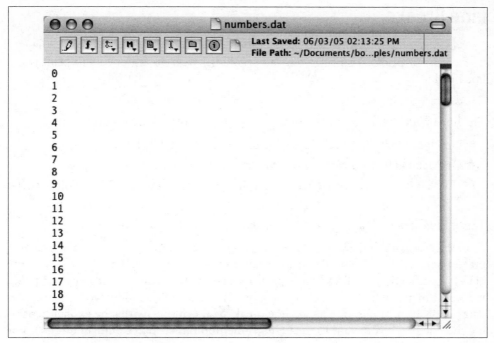

*Figure 7-3. A text file with line breaks*

strings by invoking their toString( ) methods. Primitive types are converted with the appropriate String.valueOf( ) methods.

One aspect of making System.out simple for quick jobs is not in the PrintStream class at all, but in the compiler. Because Java overloads the + operator to signify concatenation of strings, primitive data types, and objects, you can pass multiple variables to the print( ) and println( ) methods, which are then converted to strings and concatenated. For example, consider the line:

```
System.out.println("As of " + (new Date()) + " there have been over "
 + hits + " hits on the web site." );
```

The compiler rewrites this complicated expression as:

```
StringBuffer sb = new StringBuffer( );
sb.append("As of ");
Date d = new Date( );
sb.append(d);
sb.append(" there have been over ");
sb.append(hits);
sb.append(" hits on the web site.")
String s = sb.toString( );
System.out.println(s);
```

The StringBuffer append( ) method is overloaded in much the same way that the print( ) and println( ) methods are; as a result, it can handle any Java data type.

# Line Breaks

As previously mentioned, the println( ) method always adds a line break at the end of each line it prints. You can even call println( ) with no arguments to print just a line break:

```
public void println( )
```

The line break character varies from platform to platform. In particular:

- On Unix (including Mac OS X), it's a linefeed, \n, ASCII 10.
- On Mac OS 9, it's a carriage return, \r, ASCII 13.
- On Windows, it's a carriage return linefeed pair, \r\n, ASCII 13 followed by ASCII 10.

*This is almost never what you actually want!*

Most file formats and most network protocols care a great deal about which line break character is written.* For instance, if you're writing a web client or server, the HTTP specification requires that header lines end with carriage return linefeed pairs. It doesn't matter whether the client or server is a Mac, a PC, a Unix workstation, or a Palm Pilot. It must use \r\n as the line break. You can specify this by explicitly passing the line break you want to the print( ) method rather than calling println( ). For example:

```
for (int i = 0; i <= 127; i++) {
  out.print(i);
  out.print("\r\n");
}
```

 In practice, most HTTP servers and clients accept requests that use the wrong line breaks. However, some aren't so forgiving, and you really shouldn't count on this behavior.

If for some reason you want to know which line break character will be used, the line.separator system property will tell you:

```
String lineBreak = System.getProperty("line.separator");
```

Not all line breaks are created equal. If the PrintStream is set to autoFlush—that is, if the second argument to the constructor is true—after every call to println( ) and after every linefeed that's printed, the underlying stream will be flushed. Thus, out. println( ) and out.print("\n") both flush the stream. So does out.print("\r\n"), because it contains a linefeed. However, out.print("\r") does not cause an automatic flush.

---

* XML is a notable exception here. It treats linefeeds, carriage returns, and carriage return linefeed pairs equally.

# Error Handling

You may have noticed something a little funny with the code fragments in this chapter: I haven't put any try-catch blocks around them. That's not an oversight. `PrintStream` methods never throw `IOExceptions`. Each method in the class catches `IOException`. When an exception occurs, an internal flag is set to `true`. You can test this flag using the `checkError( )` method:

```
public boolean checkError( )
```

This method returns `true` if this print stream has ever encountered an error during its lifetime. Most of the time, you just ignore this, since print streams are only used in situations where exhaustive error checking is unnecessary.

There's also a protected `setError( )` method you can use to signal an error from a subclass:

```
protected void setError( )
```

Once an error has been set, there's no way to unset it. Generally, once a `PrintStream` has encountered an error, all further writes to it silently fail. It's not the failure but the silence that makes `PrintStream` unsuitable for most applications.

# printf( )

I was inspired to write the first edition of this book by the numerous questions I received about why there was no `printf( )` function in Java. Part of the goal of that edition was to explain to readers why they didn't actually need it. Thus, I was a little perturbed when Java 5 added `printf( )`. Personally, I still don't think Java needs `printf( )`, but it's here now, so let's talk about it.

The `printf( )` method makes heavy use of Java 5's new varargs feature. That is, a single method definition can support any number of arguments. In this case, the signature is:

```
public PrintStream printf(String format, Object... args)
```

A typical invocation looks like this:

```
System.out.printf("There are %f centimeters in %f inches.", 2.54*inches, inches);
```

If you're an old C hack, this is like coming home. The first argument is a format string containing both literal text and tags beginning with percent signs (%). To form the output, each tag is replaced by the corresponding argument that follows the format string. If the format string is the zeroth argument, the first tag is replaced by the first argument, the second tag by the second argument, and so forth. If there are more tags than arguments, `printf( )` throws a `java.util.MissingFormatArgumentException`. This is a subclass of `IllegalFormatException`, which is a runtime exception, so you don't have to catch it. If there are more arguments than tags, the extra arguments are silently ignored.

The letter(s) after the percent sign in the format tag specify how the number is interpreted. For instance, %f means that the number is formatted as a floating-point number with a decimal sign. %d formats the argument as a decimal integer. %x formats the number as a hexadecimal integer. %X also formats the number as a hexadecimal integer but uses the uppercase letters A–F instead of the lowercase letters a–f to represent 10–15.

 Most of the time, changing a lowercase conversion specifier to uppercase changes the formatted string from lowercase to uppercase. However, there are a few exceptions to this rule.

There are a couple of dozen tags for different kinds of data. Not all data is compatible. For instance, if you use %x to format a double as a hexadecimal integer, printf( ) throws a java.util.IllegalFormatConversionException. Again, this is a runtime exception and a subclass of IllegalFormatException.

So far, this isn't anything that can't be done easily with println( ) and string concatenation. What makes printf( ) more convenient for some uses is that the tags can also contain width and precision specifiers. For example, suppose we wrote the previous statement like this instead:

```
System.out.printf("There are %.3f centimeters in %.2f feet.", 2.54*feet, feet);
```

%.3f means that the centimeters will be formatted as a decimal number with exactly three digits after the decimal point. %.2f means that the number will be rounded to only two decimal places. This gives more legible output, like "There are 21.691 centimeters in 8.54 feet" instead of "There are 21.690925 centimeters in 8.539734 feet."

A number before the decimal point in the format tag specifies the minimum width of the formatted string. For instance, %7.3f formats a decimal number exactly seven characters wide with exactly three digits after the decimal point. Those seven characters include the decimal point, so there will be exactly three digits to the left of the decimal point. If the number is smaller than 100, it will be padded on the left with spaces to make seven characters. Zeros will be added to the right of the decimal point if necessary to pad it to three decimal places.

Consider this Java 1.4 code fragment that prints a three-column table of the angles between 0 and 360 degrees in degrees, radians, and grads, using only println( ):

```
for (double degrees = 0.0; degrees < 360.0; degrees++) {
  double radians = Math.PI * degrees / 180.0;
  double grads = 400 * degrees / 360;
  System.out.println(degrees + " " + radians + " " + grads);
}
```

Its output looks like this (not very pretty):

```
0.0 0.0 0.0
1.0 0.017453292519943295 1.1111111111111112
```

```
2.0 0.03490658503988659 2.2222222222222223
3.0 0.05235987755982988 3.3333333333333335
...
```

In Java 5, printf( ) can easily format each number exactly five characters wide with one digit after the decimal point:

```
for (double degrees = 0.0; degrees < 360.0; degrees++) {
  double radians = Math.PI * degrees / 180.0;
  double grads = 400 * degrees / 360;
  System.out.printf("%5.1f %5.1f %5.1f\n", degrees , radians, grads);
}
```

Here's the start of the output:

```
0.0   0.0   0.0
1.0   0.0   1.1
2.0   0.0   2.2
3.0   0.1   3.3
...
```

Notice how nicely everything lines up in a monospaced font? This is incredibly useful for the two dozen programmers using Java to generate reports for VT-100 terminals and letter-quality printouts on green-and-white barred computer paper. (Those readers who haven't written any software like that since 1984, and certainly those readers who weren't even born in 1984, should now see why I'm less than thrilled with the addition of this 1970s technology to a 21st-century language.)

Of course, programmers printing text in proportional-width fonts, GUI table components, HTML reports, XML documents styled with XSL stylesheets, and any other output format produced since 1992 may be less enamored of this style of programming. Anyway, Java has it now. You don't have to use it (or read the rest of this chapter) if you don't need it.

# Formatter

In fact, printf( ) is a little more general than System.out (though that's its primary justification). Besides printf( ), the PrintStream class also has a format( ) method:

```
public PrintStream format(String format, Object... args)
```

This does *exactly* the same thing as printf( ). That is, the previous example could be rewritten like this and produce identical output:

```
for (double degrees = 0.0; degrees < 360.0; degrees++) {
  double radians = Math.PI * degrees / 180.0;
  double grads = 400 * degrees / 360;
  System.out.format("%5.1f %5.1f %5.1f\n", degrees , radians, grads);
}
```

Why two methods, then? The format( ) method is used not just by PrintStream but also by the java.util.Formatter class:

```
public class Formatter implements Flushable, Closeable
```

printf( ) is there solely to make C programmers feel nostalgic.

Formatter is the object-oriented equivalent of sprintf( ) and fprintf( ) in C. Rather than writing its output onto the console, it writes it into a string, a file, or an output stream. Pass the object you want to write into to the Formatter constructor. For example, this code fragment creates a Formatter that writes data into a file named *angles.txt*:

```
Formatter formatter = new Formatter("angles.txt");
```

Once you've created a Formatter object, you can write to it using the format( ) method just as you would with System.out.format( ), except that the output goes into the file rather than onto the console:

```
for (double degrees = 0.0; degrees < 360.0; degrees++) {
  double radians = Math.PI * degrees / 180.0;
  double grads = 400 * degrees / 360;
  formatter.format("%5.1f %5.1f %5.1f\n", degrees , radians, grads);
}
```

Formatters are not output streams, but they can and should be flushed and closed just the same:

```
formatter.flush( );
formatter.close( );
```

## Constructors

Exactly where the output from a Formatter ends up depends on what argument you pass to the constructor. You've already seen the constructor that takes a filename:

```
public Formatter(String fileName) throws FileNotFoundException
```

If the named file does not exist in the current working directory, this constructor attempts to create it. If that fails for any reason other than a security violation, the constructor throws a FileNotFoundException. Security problems are reported with a SecurityException instead. If the file does exist, its contents are overwritten.

Instead of a filename, you can pass in a File object:

```
public Formatter(File file) throws FileNotFoundException
```

You can also use a Formatter to write onto a PrintStream or another kind of OutputStream:

```
public Formatter(PrintStream out)
public Formatter(OutputStream out)
```

or onto any Appendable object:

```
public Formatter(Appendable out)
```

The `Appendable` interface is a new Java 5 interface for anything onto which chars can be appended. This includes `StringBuffers` and `StringBuilders`. It also includes a number of classes we'll talk about later, such as `CharBuffer` and `Writer`.

Finally, the no-args constructor creates a `Formatter` with no specified destination for output:

```
public Formatter()
```

In this case, the `Formatter` writes everything onto a new `StringBuilder` object. You can retrieve this object using the `out()` method at any time before the `Formatter` is closed:

```
public Appendable out() throws FormatterClosedException
```

You might need to use this method if you want to write unformatted output onto the same `StringBuilder`, but more commonly you'll just use the `toString()` method to get the final result. For example:

```
Formatter formatter = new Formatter();
for (double degrees = 0.0; degrees < 360.0; degrees++) {
  double radians = Math.PI * degrees / 180.0;
  double grads = 400 * degrees / 360;
  formatter.format("%5.1f %5.1f %5.1f\n", degrees , radians, grads);
}
String table = formatter.toString();
```

## Character Sets

So far, I haven't paid a lot of attention to character set issues. As long as you stick to the ASCII character set, a single computer, and `System.out`, character sets aren't likely to be a problem. However, as data begins to move between different systems, it becomes important to consider what happens when the other systems use different character sets. For example, suppose I use a `Formatter` or a `PrintStream` on a typical U.S. or Western European PC to write the sentence "Au cours des dernières années, XML a été adapte dans des domaines aussi diverse que l'aéronautique, le multimédia, la gestion de hôpitaux, les télécommunications, la théologie, la vente au détail, et la littérature médiévale" in a file. Say I then send this file to a Macintosh user, who opens it up and sees "Au cours des derniËres annÈes, XML a ÈtÈ adapte dans des domaines aussi diverse que l'aÈronautique, le multimÈdia, la gestion de hÙpitaux, les tÈlÈcommunications, la thÈologie, la vente au dÈtail, et la littÈrature mÈdiÈvale." This is not the same thing at all! The confusion is even worse if you go in the other direction.

If you're writing to the console (i.e., `System.out`), you don't really need to worry about character set issues. The default character set Java writes in is usually the same one the console uses.

Actually, you may need to worry a little. On Windows, the console encoding is usually not the same as the system encoding found in the file.encoding system property. In particular, the console uses a DOS character set such as Cp850 that includes box drawing characters such as ╚ and ╬, while the rest of the system uses an encoding such as Cp1252 that maps these same code points to alphabetic characters like È and Î. To be honest, the console is reliable enough for ASCII, but anything beyond that requires a GUI.

However, there's more than one character set, and when transmitting files between systems and programs, it pays to be specific. In the previous example, if we knew the file was going to be read on a Macintosh, we might have specified that it be written with the MacRoman encoding:

```
Formatter formatter = new Formatter("data.txt", "MacRoman");
```

More likely, we'd just agree on both the sending and receiving ends to use some neutral format such as ISO-8859-1 or UTF-8. In some cases, encoding details can be embedded in the file you write (HTML, XML) or sent as out-of-band metadata (HTTP, SMTP). However, you do need some way of specifying and communicating the character set in which any given document is written. When you're writing to anything other than the console or a string, you should almost always specify an encoding explicitly. Three of the Formatter constructors take character set names as their second argument:

```
public Formatter(String fileName, String characterSet)
  throws FileNotFoundException
public Formatter(File file , String characterSet)
   throws FileNotFoundException
public Formatter(OutputStream out, String characterSet)
```

I'll have more to say about character sets in Chapter 19.

## Locales

Character sets are not the only localization issue in the Formatter class. For instance, in France, a decimal comma is used instead of a decimal point. Thus, a French user running the earlier degree table example would want to see this:

```
0,0   0,0   0,0
1,0   0,0   1,1
2,0   0,0   2,2
3,0   0,1   3,3
4,0   0,1   4,4
...
```

Sometimes Java adapts the format to the local conventions automatically, and sometimes it doesn't. For instance, if you want decimal commas, you have to write %,5.1f instead of %5.1f. The comma after the percent sign is a flag that tells the formatter to use the local conventions. (It does not actually say to use commas.) Java will now use commas only if the local conventions say to use commas. On a typical U.S. English system, the local convention is a decimal point, and that's what you'll get even if you format numbers as %,5.1f.

Of course, sometimes you don't want a program to adapt to the local conventions. For instance, many companies use PCs adapted to local languages and customs but still need to produce English documents that use American formats. Thus, as an optional third argument to the constructor, you can pass a java.util.Locale object:

```
public Formatter(String fileName, String characterSet, Locale locale)
  throws FileNotFoundException
public Formatter(File file, String characterSet, Locale locale)
  throws FileNotFoundException
public Formatter(OutputStream out, String characterSet, Locale locale)
```

For example, to force the use of American conventions regardless of where a program is run, you'd construct a Formatter like this:

```
Formatter formatter = new Formatter("data.txt", "ISO-8859-1", Locale.US);
```

You can also specify a locale when writing to an Appendable object or a StringBuilder:

```
public Formatter(Appendable out, Locale locale)
public Formatter(Locale locale)
```

Character encodings don't matter for these two cases because both Appendable and StringBuilder are defined in terms of characters rather than bytes—there's no conversion to be done. However, locales can change formatting even when the character set stays the same.

On occasion, you might wish to change the locale for one string you write but not for other strings (in a mixed English/French document, perhaps). In that case, you can pass a locale as the first argument to the format( ) method before the format string:

```
public Formatter format(Locale locale, String format, Object... args)
```

You can do the same thing with the printf( ) and format( ) methods in the PrintStream class:

```
public PrintStream printf(Locale locale, String format, Object... args)
```

Finally, I'll note that there's a getter method that returns the Formatter's current locale:

```
public Locale locale( )
```

## Error Handling

The Formatter class handles errors in much the same way PrintStream does. That is, it sweeps them under the rug and pretends they didn't happen. Notice how none of the methods mentioned so far threw IOException?

To find out if the Formatter has encountered an error, invoke its ioException( ) method:

```
public IOException ioException( )
```

This returns the last IOException thrown by the underlying output stream. If there was more than one, only the last one is available.

This is marginally better than PrintStream's boolean checkError( ) method. At least Formatter will tell you what the problem was. However, it still won't tell you unless you ask. For simple cases in which you don't have to write a lot of data before closing the Formatter and checking for any errors, this may be adequate. However, programs that need to write for an extended period of time should probably create strings using a Formatter but write them using a regular OutputStream. That way, if an I/O error does happen, you'll find out soon enough to do something about it.

## Format Specifiers

The Formatter class and the printf( ) method in PrintStream that depends on it support several dozen format specifiers. In addition to integer and floating-point numbers, Formatter offers a wide range of date and time formats. It also has a few general formatters that can display absolutely any object or primitive data type.

All format specifiers begin with percent signs. The minimum format specifier is a percent sign followed by an alphabetic conversion code. This code identifies what the corresponding argument is to be formatted as. For instance, %f formats a number with a decimal point, %d formats it as a decimal (base-10) integer, %o formats it as an octal integer, and %x formats it as a hexadecimal integer. None of these specifiers changes what the number actually is; they're just different ways of creating a string that represents the number.

To use a literal percent character in a format string, just double escape it. That is, %% is formatted as % in the output.

 To get the platform default line separator, use %n. (\n is always a linefeed regardless of platform. %n may be a carriage return, a linefeed, or a carriage return linefeed pair, depending on the platform.)

### Integer conversions

Integer conversions can be applied to all integral types (specifically, byte, short, int, and long, as well as the type-wrapper classes Byte, Short, Integer, Long, and also the java.math.BigInteger class). These conversions are:

%d

    A regular base-10 integer, such as 987

%o

    A base-8 octal integer, such as 1733

%x

A base-16 lowercase hexadecimal integer, such as 3db

%X

A base-16 uppercase hexadecimal integer, such as 3DB

Example 7-1 prints the number 1023 in all four formats.

*Example 7-1. Integer format specifiers*

```java
public class IntegerFormatExample {

  public static void main(String[] args) {
    int n = 1023;
    System.out.printf("Decimal:              %d\n", n);
    System.out.printf("Octal:                %o\n", n);
    System.out.printf("Lowercase hexadecimal: %x\n", n);
    System.out.printf("Uppercase hexadecimal: %X\n", n);
  }
}
```

Here's the output:

```
Decimal:               1023
Octal:                 1777
Lowercase hexadecimal: 3ff
Uppercase hexadecimal: 3FF
```

### Floating-point conversions

Floating-point conversions can be applied to all floating-point types: `float` and `double`, the type-wrapper classes `Float` and `Double`, and `java.math.BigDecimal`. These conversions are:

%f

A regular base-10 decimal number, such as 3.141593

%e

A decimal number in scientific notation with a lowercase e, such as 3.141593e+00

%E

A decimal number in scientific notation with an uppercase E, such as 3.141593E+00

%g

A decimal number formatted in either regular or scientific notation, depending on its size and precision, with a lowercase e if scientific notation is used

%G

A decimal number formatted in either regular or scientific notation, depending on its size and precision, with an uppercase E if scientific notation is used

%a

A lowercase hexadecimal floating-point number, such as 0x1.921fb54442d18p1

%A

An uppercase hexadecimal floating-point number, such as 0X1.921FB54442D18P1

Surprisingly, you cannot use these conversions on integer types such as int or BigDecimal. Java will not automatically promote the integer type to a floating-point type when formatting. If you try to use them, it throws an IllegalFormatConversionException.

Example 7-2 prints π in all of these formats.

*Example 7-2. Floating-point format specifiers*

```
public class FloatingPointFormatExample {

  public static void main(String[] args) {
    System.out.printf("Decimal:                %f\n", Math.PI);
    System.out.printf("Scientific notation:    %e\n", Math.PI);
    System.out.printf("Scientific notation:    %E\n", Math.PI);
    System.out.printf("Decimal/Scientific:     %g\n", Math.PI);
    System.out.printf("Decimal/Scientific:     %G\n", Math.PI);
    System.out.printf("Lowercase Hexadecimal: %a\n", Math.PI);
    System.out.printf("Uppercase Hexadecimal: %A\n", Math.PI);
  }
}
```

Here's the output:

```
Decimal:                3.141593
Scientific notation:    3.141593e+00
Scientific notation:    3.141593E+00
Decimal/Scientific:     3.14159
Decimal/Scientific:     3.14159
Lowercase Hexadecimal: 0x1.921fb54442d18p1
Uppercase Hexadecimal: 0X1.921FB54442D18P1
```

## Date and time conversions

Date and time conversions can be applied to java.util.Calendar and java.util.Date objects. They can also be applied to long and Long values, in which case the value is assumed to be the number of milliseconds since midnight, January 1, 1970. All date and time conversions begin with a t for lowercase or a T for uppercase. These conversions are:

%tH/%TH
> Two-digit hour using a 24-hour clock, ranging from 00 to 23

%tI/%TI
> Two-digit hour using a 12-hour clock, ranging from 01 to 12

%tk/%Tk
> One- or two-digit hour using a 24-hour clock, ranging from 0 to 23

%tl/%Tl
> One- or two-digit hour using a 12-hour clock, ranging from 1 to 12

**%tM/%TM**

Two-digit minutes, ranging from 00 to 59

**%tS/%TS**

Two-digit seconds, ranging from 00 to 60 (60 is used for leap seconds)

**%tL/%TL**

Three-digit milliseconds, ranging from 000 to 999

**%tN/%TN**

Nine-digit nanoseconds, ranging from 000000000 to 999999999

**%tp/%Tp**

Locale-specific morning/afternoon indicator, such as am or PM

**%tz/%Tz**

RFC 822 numeric time zone indicator as an offset from UMT (for instance, Eastern Standard Time is −0500)

**%tZ/%TZ**

An abbreviation for the time zone, such as edt or EST

**%ts/%Ts**

Seconds elapsed since midnight, January 1, 1970, Greenwich Mean Time

**%TQ**

Milliseconds elapsed since midnight, January 1, 1970, Greenwich Mean Time

**%tB/%TB**

Localized month, such as "January" or "JANVIER"

**%tb/%Tb**

Localized, abbreviated month, such as "Jan" or "JAN"

**%th/%Th**

Localized, abbreviated month, such as "Jan" or "JAN" (yes, %tb and %th are synonyms; I have no idea why)

**%tA/%TA**

Localized day name, such as "Tuesday" or "MARDI"

**%ta/%Ta**

Localized, abbreviated day, such as "Tue" or "TUE"

**%tC/%TC**

Two-digit century, ranging from 00 to 99

**%tY/%TY**

Year with at least four digits, ranging from 0001 to the indefinite future

**%ty/%Ty**

Two-digit year, ranging from 00 to 99

**%tj/%Tj**

Three-digit day of the year, ranging from 001 to 366

**%tm/%Tm**

Two-digit month, ranging from 01 to 13 (13 is used in some non-Gregorian lunar calendars)

**%td/%Td**

Two-digit day of the month, ranging from 01 to 31

**%te/%Te**

One- or two-digit day of the month, ranging from 1 to 31

**%tR/%TR**

Hours and minutes on a 24-hour clock, such as 03:23 or 14:07

**%tT/%TT**

Hours, minutes, and seconds on a 24-hour clock, such as 03:23:17 or 14:07:00

**%tr/%Tr**

Hours, minutes, and seconds on a 12-hour clock, such as 03:23:17 am or 02:07:00 PM

**%tD/%TD**

Date in the form month/day/year, such as 05/12/06

**%tF/%TF**

ISO 8601 standard date in the form year-month-day, such as 2006-05-12

**%tc/%Tc**

Date and time formatted like so: "Fri May 12 12:27:30 EDT 2006"

Example 7-3 prints the current date and time in all of these formats.

*Example 7-3. Date format specifiers*

```java
import java.util.Date;

public class DateFormatExample {

  public static void main(String[] args) {
    Date now = new Date( );
    System.out.printf("two-digit hour on a 24-hour clock: %tH/%TH\n", now, now);
    System.out.printf("two-digit hour on a 12-hour clock: %tI/%TI\n", now, now);
    System.out.printf("one- or two-digit hour on a 24-hour clock: %tk/%Tk\n",
      now, now);
    System.out.printf("one- or two-digit hour on a 12-hour clock: %tl/%Tl\n", now,
      now);
    System.out.printf("two-digit minutes ranging from 00 to 59: %tH/%TH\n",
      now, now);
    System.out.printf("two-digit seconds ranging from 00 to 60 : %tS/%TS\n",
      now, now);
    System.out.printf("milliseconds: %tL/%TL\n", now, now);
    System.out.printf("nanoseconds: %tN/%TN\n", now, now);
    System.out.printf("locale-specific morning/afternoon indicator: %tp/%Tp\n",
      now, now);
    System.out.printf("RFC 822 numeric time zone indicator: %tz/%Tz\n", now, now);
    System.out.printf("time zone abbreviation: %tZ/%TZ\n", now, now);
```

*Example 7-3. Date format specifiers (continued)*

```
    System.out.printf("seconds since the epoch: %ts/%Ts\n", now, now);
    System.out.printf("milliseconds since the epoch: %TQ\n", now);
    System.out.printf("localized month name: %tB/%TB\n", now, now);
    System.out.printf("localized, abbreviated month: %tb/%Tb\n", now, now);
    System.out.printf("localized, abbreviated month: %th/%Th\n", now, now);
    System.out.printf("localized day name: %tA/%TA\n", now, now);
    System.out.printf("localized, abbreviated day: %ta/%Ta\n", now, now);
    System.out.printf("two-digit century: %tC/%TC\n", now, now);
    System.out.printf("four-digit year: %tY/%TY\n", now, now);
    System.out.printf("two-digit year: %ty/%Ty\n", now, now);
    System.out.printf("three-digit day of the year: %tj/%Tj\n", now, now);
    System.out.printf("two-digit month: %tm/%Tm\n", now, now);
    System.out.printf("two-digit day of the month: %td/%Td\n", now, now);
    System.out.printf("one- or two-digit day of the month: %te/%Te\n", now, now);
    System.out.printf("hours and minutes on a 24-hour clock: %tR/%TR\n", now, now);
    System.out.printf("hours, minutes, and seconds on a 24-hour clock: %tT/%TT\n",
     now, now);
    System.out.printf("hours, minutes, and seconds on a 12-hour clock: %tr/%Tr\n",
     now, now);
    System.out.printf("month/day/year: %tD/%TD\n", now, now);
    System.out.printf("ISO 8601 standard date: %tF/%TF\n", now, now);
    System.out.printf("Unix date format: %tc/%Tc\n", now, now);
  }
}
```

Here's the output when this was run on Friday, June 24, 2005 at 6:43 PM EDT:

```
    two-digit hour on a 24-hour clock: 18/18
    two-digit hour on a 12-hour clock: 06/06
    one- or two-digit hour on a 24-hour clock: 18/18
    one- or two-digit hour on a 12-hour clock: 6/6
    two-digit minutes ranging from 00 to 59: 18/18
    two-digit seconds ranging from 00 to 60 : 50/50
    milliseconds: 859/859
    nanoseconds: 859000000/859000000
    locale-specific morning/afternoon indicator: pm/PM
    RFC 822 numeric time zone indicator: -0500/-0500
    time zone abbreviation: EDT/EDT
    seconds since the epoch: 1119653030/1119653030
    milliseconds since the epoch: 1119653030859
    localized month name: June/JUNE
    localized, abbreviated month: Jun/JUN
    localized, abbreviated month: Jun/JUN
    localized day name: Friday/FRIDAY
    localized, abbreviated day: Fri/FRI
    two-digit century: 20/20
    four-digit year: 2005/2005
    two-digit year: 05/05
    three-digit day of the year: 175/175
    two-digit month: 06/06
    two-digit day of the month: 24/24
    one- or two-digit day of the month: 24/24
    hours and minutes on a 24-hour clock: 18:43/18:43
```

```
hours, minutes, and seconds on a 24-hour clock: 18:43:50/18:43:50
hours, minutes, and seconds on a 12-hour clock: 06:43:50 PM/06:43:50 PM
month/day/year: 06/24/05/06/24/05
ISO 8601 standard date: 2005-06-24/2005-06-24
Unix date format: Fri Jun 24 18:43:50 EDT 2005/FRI JUN 24 18:43:50 EDT 2005
```

## Character conversions

Character conversions can be applied to char and java.lang.Character objects. They
can also be applied to byte, short, int, and the equivalent type-wrapper objects if the
integer falls into the range of Unicode code points (0 to 0x10FFFF). These conversions are:

%c

> A lowercase Unicode character

%C

> An uppercase Unicode character

## Boolean conversions

Boolean conversions can be applied to boolean primitive values and java.lang.Boolean
objects. They can also be applied to all object types, in which case they're considered to
be true if the object is nonnull and false if it is null. All other primitive types are considered to be true, regardless of value. These conversions are:

%b

> "true" or "false"

%B

> "TRUE" or "FALSE"

These conversions are not localized. Even in France, you'll see "true" and "false"
instead of "vrai" and "faux."

## General conversions

There are two more conversions that can be applied to any object and also to primitive types after autoboxing. These are:

%h/%H

> The lowercase/uppercase hexadecimal form of the object's hashCode, or "null" or
> "NULL" if the object is null.

%s/%S

> The result of invoking the object's formatTo( ) method if it implements
> Formattable; otherwise, the result of invoking its toString( ) method, or "null" if
> the object is null. With %S, this value is then converted to uppercase.

Example 7-4 prints a URL (which does not implement Formattable) in all of these
formats.

*Example 7-4. General format specifiers*

```java
import java.net.*;

public class GeneralFormatExample {

  public static void main(String[] args) throws MalformedURLException {
    URL u = new URL("http://www.example.com/Article.html");
    System.out.printf("boolean:   %b\n", u);
    System.out.printf("BOOLEAN:   %B\n", u);
    System.out.printf("hashcode:  %h\n", u);
    System.out.printf("HASHCODE:  %H\n", u);
    System.out.printf("string:    %s\n", u);
    System.out.printf("STRING:    %S\n", u);
  }
}
```

Here's the output from running this on a U.S.-localized system:

```
boolean:   true
BOOLEAN:   TRUE
hashcode:  79d2cef0
HASHCODE:  79D2CEF0
string:    http://www.example.com/Article.html
STRING:    HTTP://WWW.EXAMPLE.COM/ARTICLE.HTML
```

Be cautious about uppercasing. URL path components and many other things are case sensitive. *HTTP://WWW.EXAMPLE.ORG/ARTICLE.HTML* is not the same URL as *http://www.example.org/Article.html*.

## Format Modifiers

In addition to a conversion code, the format string can also specify a width, a precision, the argument it's replaced with, and any of several special-purpose flags. The most general format follows this pattern:

%[*argument_index*$][*flags*][*width*][.*precision*]conversion

Here is a quick definition of those parameters. More detail on each will follow:

*argument_index*
> The number of the argument with which to replace this tag

*flags*
> Indicators of various formatting options

*width*
> The minimum number of characters with which to format the replacement value

*precision*
> The number of characters after the decimal point; alternately, the maximum number of characters in the formatted string

These four options control exactly how a string is formatted as tags are replaced by values.

## Argument index

The argument index is specified when the order of the arguments does not match the order of the tags. For example:

```
out.printf("There are %2$f centimeters in %1$f feet.", feet, 2.54 * feet * 12);
```

In this case, indexes start with 1 rather than 0, which is unusual for Java. (The format string counts as argument 0.) If you reference a nonexistent argument, printf( ) throws a MissingFormatArgumentException.

The argument index is particularly useful when you want to repeat the same value more than once in a string, perhaps formatted differently each time. For example:

```
System.out.printf("Hexadecimal: %1$H Decimal: %1$f", Math.PI);
```

You can also repeat the previous argument by specifying a less than sigh (<) rather than an integer and a dollar sign ($). For instance, this statement is equivalent to the previous statement:

```
System.out.printf("Hexadecimal: %1$H Decimal: %<f", Math.PI);
```

## Flags

Flags indicate a variety of formatting options. Not all flags apply to all types. Using a flag to format a type that does not apply throws a FormatFlagsConversionMismatchException, a subclass of IllegalFormatException. However, you can combine multiple flags that do apply. Table 7-1 summarizes these flags.

*Table 7-1. Format flags*

| Flag | Signifies | Applies to |
| --- | --- | --- |
| - | Left-justify. | All |
| # | Alternate form. | General, integer, floating point |
| + | Include a sign even if positive. (Normally, only negative numbers have signs.) | Integer, floating point |
| space | Add a leading space to positive numbers. (This is where the sign would be and helps line up positive and negative numbers.) | Integer, floating point |
| 0 | Pad with zeros instead of spaces. | Integer, floating point |
| , | Use the locale-specific grouping separator instead of a period. | Integer, floating point |
| ( | Use instead of a minus sign to indicate negative numbers. | Integer, floating point |

For example, this statement prints a double formatted as a 20-character decimal padded with zeros, using a locale-specific grouping separator and parentheses for negative numbers:

```
System.out.printf("%(+0,20f", -Math.PI);
```

The result is (00000000003.141593).

The relative order of the flags does not matter. This statement prints the same thing:

```
System.out.printf("%,0+(20f", -Math.PI);
```

## Width

Each of the various conversions may be preceded by an optional width. This sets the *minimum* number of characters to print. For example, if you format an integer using the code %5d, it will always be printed at least five characters wide. If the integer has fewer than five digits, extra spaces are added on the left-hand side to make up five characters. If it has five or more digits, no extra spaces are added.

 The entire number is always printed. If the argument is larger than can fit in five places, all of it will be printed anyway, and subsequent columns may no longer line up properly.

For example, this statement prints five mathematical constants, each 12 places wide:

```
System.out.printf("%12f %12f %12f %12f %12f",
          Math.PI, Math.E, 1.0, 0.0, Math.sqrt(2));
```

By default, extra places are filled with space characters to right-justify the numbers. However, flags can be used to fill extra places with zeros or to left-justify the numbers instead.

This is the output:

```
    3.141593     2.718282     1.000000     0.000000     1.414214
```

Width is not limited to numeric types. You can specify a width for any format tag: date, time, boolean, and so on.

## Precision

Floating-point types (%e, %E, %f, %g, and %G) may also specify a precision in the form .3 or .5. The precision comes after the width but before the conversion code. This indicates how many places are used after the decimal point. For example, this statement formats the same five constants 15 places wide, with 3 places after the decimal point:

```
System.out.printf("%15.3f %15.3f %15.3f %15.3f %15.3f",
          Math.PI, Math.E, 1.0, 0.0, Math.sqrt(2));
```

This is the output:

```
    3.142          2.718          1.000          0.000          1.414
```

A precision can also be applied to strings and other nonnumeric, nondate types. In these cases, it specifies the maximum number of characters to write to the output.

Precision cannot be set for integral types, however. Attempting to do so throws an IllegalFormatPrecisionException. As usual, this is a subclass of IllegalFormatException and a runtime exception.

# Formattable

You can format your own custom classes by implementing the Formattable inter-face. In format strings, you use %s and %S to indicate where you want your custom class instances placed. The default formatting for objects matched to %s and %S is simply whatever is returned by toString( ). However, more often than not, this is just a debugging string not really meant for display to end users. If your class implements the java.util.Formattable interface, Java will use the return value of the object's formatTo( ) method instead. That method has this signature:

```
public void formatTo(Formatter formatter, int flags, int width, int precision)
```

The four arguments are:

formatter
> The Formatter that called formatTo. More importantly, this is the object onto which the output will be written. Your method will invoke this object's format( ) methods to write to the underlying stream.

flags
> A bitmasked constant providing the values of various flags set for this operation: ^, -, #, etc. You interpret these with the FormattableFlags class.

width
> The minimum number of characters your method must return. If the returned value has fewer characters than the specified minimum, it will be padded with spaces.

precision
> The maximum number of characters your method should return.

Earlier, I complained that the uppercasing in the URL class was too naïve because, when formatted, it changed the case of case-sensitive parts such as the path and the query string as well as case-insensitive parts such as the scheme and the hostname. There's another problem with the naïve uppercasing: the scheme and hostnames are defined in ASCII, but uppercasing isn't always. In particular, uppercasing the letter i in Turkey produces the capital dotted İ rather than the usual undotted capital I. For instance, www.microsoft.com uppercases as WWW.MİCROSOFT.COM, which will not resolve.

Example 7-5 demonstrates a FormattableURL class that uppercases only those parts of a URL that can be uppercased without changing its meaning. Ideally this would be a subclass of java.net.URL, but since URL is final, delegation is used instead. In essence, FormattableURL is a wrapper around a URL object that just provides the formatTo( ) method.

*Example 7-5. Implementing Formattable*

```
import java.util.*;
import java.net.*;
```

*Example 7-5. Implementing Formattable (continued)*

```java
public class FormattableURL implements Formattable {

  private URL delegate;

  public FormattableURL(URL url) {
    this.delegate = url;
  }

  public void formatTo(Formatter formatter, int flags, int width,
      int precision) {

    if (precision < -1) {
      throw new IllegalFormatPrecisionException(precision);
    }
    if (width < -1) {
      throw new IllegalFormatWidthException(width);
    }
    if (precision > width) {
      throw new IllegalFormatPrecisionException(precision);
    }

    // Check to see if we've been asked to use any flags we don't interpret
    int recognizedFlags
     = FormattableFlags.UPPERCASE | FormattableFlags.LEFT_JUSTIFY;
    boolean unsupportedFlags = ((~recognizedFlags) & flags) != 0;
    if (unsupportedFlags) {
      // We should really pass the flags to this constructor.
      // However, Java doesn't offer any reasonable way to get these.
      throw new IllegalFormatFlagsException("#");
    }

    boolean upperCase = (flags & FormattableFlags.UPPERCASE) != 0;

    StringBuffer sb = new StringBuffer();

    String scheme = delegate.getProtocol();
    if (upperCase && scheme != null) {
      scheme = scheme.toUpperCase(Locale.ENGLISH);
    }

    String hostname = delegate.getHost();
    if (upperCase && hostname != null) {
      hostname = hostname.toUpperCase(Locale.ENGLISH);
    }

    String userInfo = delegate.getUserInfo();

    int port = delegate.getPort();
    String path = delegate.getPath();
    String query = delegate.getQuery();
    String fragment = delegate.getRef();
```

*Example 7-5. Implementing Formattable (continued)*

```
    if (scheme != null) {
      sb.append(scheme);
      sb.append("://");
    }

    if (userInfo != null) {
      sb.append(userInfo);
      sb.append("@");
    }

    if (hostname != null) {
      sb.append(hostname);
    }

    if (port != -1) {
      sb.append(':');
      sb.append(port);
    }

    if (path != null) {
      sb.append(path);
    }

    if (query != null) {
      sb.append('?');
      sb.append(query);
    }

    if (fragment != null) {
      sb.append('#');
      sb.append(fragment);
    }

    boolean leftJustify = (flags & FormattableFlags.LEFT_JUSTIFY) != 0;

    // Truncate on the right if necessary
    if (precision < sb.length()) {
      sb.setLength(precision);
    }
    else {// Pad with spaces if necessary
      while (sb.length() < width) {
        if (leftJustify) sb.append(' ');
        else sb.insert(0, ' ');
      }
    }

    formatter.format(sb.toString());
  }
}
```

The formatTo( ) method first checks to see if the values passed make sense—that is, that the width is greater than or equal to the precision, and both are greater than or equal to −1. (−1 simply indicates that these values weren't set.) Assuming these checks pass, it splits the delegate URL into its component parts and uppercases the two case-insensitive parts (the scheme and the hostname) if the uppercase flag is set. It then appends all the other parts without changing their cases at all. Finally, if the precision is less than the string's length, the formatted string is truncated on the right. If the string's length is less than the specified width, the string is padded with spaces: on the right by default but on the left if the left-justified flag is set. If any other flags are present, an IllegalFormatFlagsException is thrown. Thus, it becomes possible to format a URL like this:

```
URL url = new URL("http://www.example.org/index.html?name=value#Fred");
System.out.printf("%60.40S\n", new FormattableURL(url));
```

# CHAPTER 8

# Data Streams

Data streams read and write strings, integers, floating-point numbers, and other data that's commonly presented at a higher level than mere bytes. The java.io. DataInputStream and java.io.DataOutputStream classes read and write the primitive Java data types (boolean, int, double, etc.) and strings in a particular, well-defined, platform-independent format. Since DataInputStream and DataOutputStream use the same formats, they're complementary. What a data output stream writes, a data input stream can read and vice versa. These classes are especially useful when you need to move data between platforms that may use different native formats for integers or floating-point numbers.

## The Data Stream Classes

The java.io.DataInputStream and java.io.DataOutputStream classes are subclasses of FilterInputStream and FilterOutputStream, respectively.

```
public class DataInputStream extends FilterInputStream implements DataInput
public class DataOutputStream extends FilterOutputStream
                        implements DataOutput
```

They have all the usual methods you expect in input and output stream classes, such as read( ), write( ), flush( ), available( ), skip( ), close( ), markSupported( ), and reset( ). (Data input streams support marking if, and only if, their underlying input stream supports marking.) However, the real purpose of DataInputStream and DataOutputStream is not to read and write raw bytes using the standard input and output stream methods. It's to read and interpret multibyte data like ints, floats, doubles, and chars.

# The DataInput and DataOutput Interfaces

The java.io.DataInput interface declares 15 methods that read various kinds of data:

```
public boolean readBoolean( ) throws IOException
public byte    readByte( ) throws IOException
public int     readUnsignedByte( ) throws IOException
public short   readShort( ) throws IOException
public int     readUnsignedShort( ) throws IOException
public char    readChar( ) throws IOException
public int     readInt( ) throws IOException
public long    readLong( ) throws IOException
public float   readFloat( ) throws IOException
public double  readDouble( ) throws IOException
public String  readLine( ) throws IOException
public String  readUTF( ) throws IOException
public void    readFully(byte[] data) throws IOException
public void    readFully(byte[] data, int offset, int length) throws IOException
public int     skipBytes(int n) throws IOException
```

These methods are all available from the DataInputStream class and any other class that implements DataInput. (In the core Java API, this includes DataInputStream, ObjectInputStream, RandomAccessFile, and several stream classes in the Java Image I/O API.)

Likewise, the java.io.DataOutput interface declares 14 methods, mostly complementary to those in DataInput:

```
public void write(int b) throws IOException
public void write(byte[] data) throws IOException
public void write(byte[] data, int offset, int length)
                   throws IOException
public void writeBoolean(boolean v) throws IOException
public void writeByte(int b) throws IOException
public void writeShort(int s) throws IOException
public void writeChar(int c) throws IOException
public void writeInt(int i) throws IOException
public void writeLong(long l) throws IOException
public void writeFloat(float f) throws IOException
public void writeDouble(double d) throws IOException
public void writeBytes(String s) throws IOException
public void writeChars(String s) throws IOException
public void writeUTF(String s) throws IOException
```

The writeBytes( ) and writeChars( ) methods are not matched by readBytes( ) and readChars( ) methods in DataInput. writeBytes( ) and writeChars( ) only write the actual bytes and chars. They do not write the length of the string passed as an argument to writeBytes( ) and writeChars( ), so the bytes and chars cannot easily be reassembled into a string.

Any class that implements these interfaces must use the binary data format summarized in Table 8-1.

*Table 8-1. Formats used by DataInput and DataOutput*

| Type | Written by | Read by | Format |
|------|-----------|---------|--------|
| boolean | writeBoolean(boolean b) | readBoolean( ) | One byte, 0 if false, 1 if true |
| byte | writeByte(int b) | readByte( ) | One byte, two's complement |
| byte array | write(byte[] data)<br>write(byte[]<br>data, int offset, int<br>length) | readFully(byte[]<br>data)<br>readFully(byte[]<br>data, int offset,<br>int length) | The bytes in the order they appear in the array or subarray |
| short | writeShort(int s) | readShort( ) | Two bytes, two's complement, big-endian |
| char | writeChar(int c) | readChar( ) | Two bytes, unsigned, big-endian |
| int | writeInt(int i) | readInt( ) | Four bytes, two's complement, big-endian |
| long | writeLong(long l) | readLong( ) | Eight bytes, two's complement, big-endian |
| float | writeFloat(float f) | readFloat( ) | Four bytes, IEEE 754, big-endian |
| double | writeDouble(double d) | readDouble( ) | Eight bytes, IEEE 754, big-endian |
| unsigned byte | N/A | readUnsignedByte( ) | One unsigned byte |
| unsigned short | N/A | readUnsignedShort( ) | Two bytes, big-endian, unsigned |
| String | writeBytes(String s) | N/A | The low-order byte of each char in the string from first to last |
| String | writeChars(String s) | N/A | Both bytes of each char in the string from first to last |
| String | writeUTF(String s) | readUTF( ) | A signed short giving the number of bytes in the encoded string, followed by a modified UTF-8 encoding of the string |

## Constructors

The DataInputStream and DataOutputStream classes have exactly the constructors you would expect:

```
public DataInputStream(InputStream in)
public DataOutputStream(OutputStream out)
```

These constructors chain the data streams to the underlying streams passed as arguments. For example, to read formatted data from a file called *data.txt* and write formatted data to *output.dat*, you would create the two streams dis and dos:

```
DataInputStream dis = new DataInputStream(new FileInputStream("data.txt"));
DataOutputStream dos = new DataOutputStream(
  new FileOutputStream("output.dat")
);
```

# Integers

The `DataOutputStream` class has methods for writing all of Java's primitive integer data types: byte, short, int, and long. The `DataInputStream` class has methods to read these types. It also has methods for reading two integer data types not directly supported by Java or the `DataOutputStream` class: the unsigned byte and the unsigned int.

## Integer Formats

While Java's platform independence guarantees that you don't have to worry about the precise data formats when working exclusively in Java, you frequently need to read data created by a program written in another language. Similarly, it's not unusual to have to write data that will be read by a program written in a different language. For example, most Java network clients talk to servers written in other languages, and most Java network servers talk to clients written in other languages. You cannot naïvely assume that the data format Java uses is a data format other programs will understand; you must take care to understand and recognize the data formats being used.

Although other schemes are possible, almost all modern computers have standardized on binary arithmetic performed on integers composed of an integral number of 8-bit bytes. Furthermore, they've standardized on two's complement arithmetic for signed numbers. In two's complement arithmetic, the most significant bit is 1 for a negative number and 0 for a positive number. The absolute value of a negative number is calculated by taking the complement of the number and adding 1. In Java terms, this means (-n == ~n + 1) is true where n is a negative int.

Regrettably, this is about all that's been standardized. One big difference between computer architectures is the size of an int. Probably the majority of modern computers still use 4-byte integers that can hold a value between –2,147,483,648 and 2,147,483,647. However, some systems are moving to 64-bit architectures where the native integer ranges from –9,223,372,036,854,775,808 to 9,223,372,036,854,775,807 and takes 8 bytes; and many older and smaller systems use 16-bit integers with a far narrower range (from –32,768 to 32,767). Exactly how many bytes a C compiler uses for each int is platform-dependent, which is one of many reasons C code isn't as portable as one might wish. The sizes of C's short and long are even less predictable and may or may not be the same as the size of a C int. Java always uses a 2-byte short, a 4-byte int, and an 8-byte long, and this is one of the reasons Java code is more portable than C code. However, you must be aware of varying integer widths when your Java code needs to communicate binary numbers with programs written in other languages.

C compilers also allow various unsigned types. For example, an unsigned byte is a binary number between 0 and 255; an unsigned 2-byte integer is a number between 0 and 65,535; an unsigned 4-byte integer is a number between 0 and 4,294,967,295. Java doesn't have any unsigned numeric data types (unless you count char), but the DataInputStream class does provide two methods to read unsigned bytes and unsigned shorts.

Perhaps worst of all, modern computers are split almost down the middle between those that use a big-endian and those that use a little-endian ordering of the bytes in an integer. In a little-endian design, used on X86 architectures, the most significant byte is at the highest address in memory. On the other hand, on a big-endian system, the most significant byte is at the lowest address in memory.

For example, consider the number 1,108,836,360. In hexadecimal, this number is written as 0x42178008. On a big-endian system, the bytes are ordered much as they are in a hex literal—that is, 42, 17, 80, 08. On the other hand, on a little-endian system, this order is reversed: 08, 80, 17, 42. If 1,108,836,360 is written into a file on a little-endian system and then read on a big-endian system without any special treatment, it comes out as 0x08801742, or 142,612,29—not the same thing at all.

Java uses big-endian integers exclusively. Data input streams read and data output streams write big-endian integers. Most Internet protocols that rely on binary numbers, such as the time protocol, implicitly assume "network byte order," which is a fancy way of saying "big-endian." And finally, almost all computers manufactured today, except those based on the X86 architecture, use big-endian byte orders, so X86 is really the odd one out. However, X86 is the 1000-pound gorilla of computer architectures, so it's impossible to ignore it or the data formats it supports. Later in this chapter, I'll develop a class for reading little-endian data.

## The Char Format

Unicode characters (more specifically, the UTF-16 code points used for Java chars) are two bytes long and are interpreted as an unsigned number between 0 and 65,535. This means they have an "endianness" problem too. The Unicode standard specifically does not require a particular endianness of text written in Unicode; both big- and little-endian encodings are allowed. The Unicode standard does suggest that character 65,279 (0xFEFF in hex) be placed at the beginning of each file of Unicode text. Thus, by reading the first character, you can determine the endianness of the file and take appropriate action. For example, if you're reading a Unicode file containing little-endian data using big-endian methods, the first character will appear as 0xFFFE (65,534), signaling that something is wrong. Java's data stream classes always read and write chars and strings in big-endian order.

# Writing Integers

The `DataOutputStream` class has the usual three `write()` methods you'll find in any output stream class:

```
public void write(int b) throws IOException
public void write(byte[] data) throws IOException
public void write(byte[] data, int offset, int length)
   throws IOException
```

These methods behave exactly as they do in the superclass, so I won't discuss them further here.

The `DataOutputStream` class also declares the following void methods that write signed integer types onto its underlying output stream:

```
public final void writeByte(int b)   throws IOException
public final void writeShort(int s) throws IOException
public final void writeInt(int i)    throws IOException
public final void writeLong(long l) throws IOException
```

Because Java doesn't fully support the byte or short types, the `writeByte()` and `writeShort()` methods each take an int as an argument. The excess bytes in the int are ignored before the byte or short is written. Thus `writeByte()` writes only the low-order byte of its argument. `writeShort()` writes only the low-order two bytes of its argument, higher-order byte first—that is, big-endian order. The `writeInt()` and `writeLong()` methods write all of the bytes of their arguments in big-endian order. These methods can throw IOExceptions if the underlying stream throws an IOException.

Example 8-1 fills a file called *1000.dat* with the integers between 1 and 1000. This filename is used to construct a `FileOutputStream`. This stream is then chained to a `DataOutputStream` whose `writeInt()` method writes the data into the file.

*Example 8-1. One thousand ints*

```java
import java.io.*;

public class File1000 {

  public static void main(String args[]) {

    DataOutputStream dos = null;

    try {
      dos = new DataOutputStream(new FileOutputStream("1000.dat"));
      for (int i = 1; i <= 1000; i++) {
        dos.writeInt(i);
      }
    }
    catch (IOException ex) {System.err.println(ex);}
    finally {
```

*Example 8-1. One thousand ints (continued)*

```
      try { if (dos != null) dos.close( ); }
      catch (IOException ex) { /* Not much else we can do */ }
    }
  }
}
```

Let me emphasize that the numbers written by this program or by any other data output stream are *binary numbers*. They are not text strings such as 1, 2, 3, 4, 5, ...999, 1000. If you try to open *1000.dat* with a text editor, you'll see a lot of gibberish or an error message. The data this program writes is meant to be read by other programs, not by people.

## Reading Integers

DataInputStream has the usual three read( ) methods it inherits from its superclass; these methods read a byte and return an int. They behave exactly as they do in the superclass, so I won't discuss them further:

```
    public int read( ) throws IOException
    public int read(byte[] data) throws IOException
    public int read(byte[] data, int offset, int length) throws IOException
```

The DataInputStream class declares the following methods that return signed integer types:

```
    public final byte  readByte( )  throws IOException
    public final short readShort( ) throws IOException
    public final char  readChar( )  throws IOException
    public final int   readInt( )   throws IOException
    public final long  readLong( )  throws IOException
```

Each of the integer read( ) methods read the necessary number of bytes and convert them into the appropriate integer type. readByte( ) reads a single byte and returns a signed byte between –128 and 127. readShort( ) reads two bytes and returns a short between –32,768 and 32,767. readInt( ) reads 4 bytes and returns an int between –2,147,483,648 and 2,147,483,647. readLong( ) reads 8 bytes and returns a long between –9,223,372,036,854,775,808 and 9,223,372,036,854,775,807. All numbers are read as big-endian.

–1 is a valid return value for these methods. Therefore, if the end of stream is encountered while reading, a java.io.EOFException, which is a subclass of java.io. IOException, is thrown. An EOFException can be thrown while more bytes of data remain in the stream. For example, readInt( ) reads 4 bytes. If only two bytes are left in the stream, those two bytes are read and the EOFException is thrown. However, at this point, those two bytes are lost. You can't go back and reread those two bytes as a short. (If the underlying stream supports marking and resetting, you could mark before each read and reset on an EOFException.)

The DataInputStream class also has two methods that read unsigned bytes and shorts:

```
public final int readUnsignedByte( ) throws IOException
public final int readUnsignedShort( ) throws IOException
```

Since Java has no unsigned byte or unsigned short data type, both of these methods return an int. readUnsignedByte( ) returns an int between 0 and 255, and readUnsignedShort( ) returns an int between 0 and 65,535. However, both methods still indicate end of stream with an EOFException rather than by returning −1.

Example 8-2 interprets a file as 4-byte signed integers, reads them, and prints them out. You might use this to read the output of Example 8-1. However, it is not necessarily the case that the program or person who created the file actually intended it to contain 32-bit, two's complement integers. The file contains bytes, and these bytes may be interpreted as ints, with the possible exception of one to three bytes at the end of the file (if the file's length is not an even multiple of 4 bytes). Therefore, it's important to be very careful about what you read.

*Example 8-2. The IntReader program*

```
import java.io.*;

public class IntReader {

  public static void main(String[] args) throws IOException {

    DataInputStream din = null;
    try {
      FileInputStream fin = new FileInputStream(args[0]);
      System.out.println("-----------" + args[0] + "-----------");
      din = new DataInputStream(fin);
      while (true) {
        int theNumber = din.readInt( );
        System.out.println(theNumber);
      } // end while
    } // end try
    catch (EOFException ex) {
      // normal termination
      din.close( );
    }
    catch (IOException ex) {
      // abnormal termination
      System.err.println(ex);
    }
  } // end main
} // end IntReader
```

This program opens the files named on the command line with a file input stream. The file input stream is chained to a data input stream, which reads successive integers until an IOException occurs. IntReader does not print an error message in the event of an EOFException since that now indicates normal termination.

# Floating-Point Numbers

Java understands two floating-point number formats, both specified by the IEEE 754 standard. Floats are stored in 4 bytes with a 1-bit sign, a 24-bit mantissa, and an 8-bit exponent. Float values range from $1.40129846432481707 \times 10^{-45}$ to $3.40282346638528860 \times 10^{38}$, either positive or negative. Doubles take up 8 bytes with a 1-bit sign, 53-bit mantissa, and 11-bit exponent. This gives them a range of $4.94065645841246544 \times 10^{-324}$ to $1.79769313486231570 \times 10^{308}$, either positive or negative. Both floats and doubles also have representations of positive and negative zero, positive and negative infinity, and not a number (NaN).

 Astute readers will notice that the number of bits given for floats and doubles adds up to 33 and 65 bits, respectively—one too many for the width of the number. The first bit of the mantissa of a nonzero number is assumed to be 1. With this trick, it is unnecessary to include the first bit of the mantissa. Thus, an extra bit of precision is gained for free.

These formats are supported by most modern RISC architectures and by all current X86 processors. Nowadays the only chips that don't natively support this format are a few embedded processors.

The DataInputStream class reads and the DataOutputStream class writes floating-point numbers of either 4 or 8 bytes in length, as specified in the IEEE 754 standard. They do not support the 10-byte and longer long double, extended double, and double double formats supported by some architectures and compilers. If you have to read floating-point data written in some format other than basic IEEE 754 float and double, you'll need to write your own class to convert the format to 4- or 8-byte IEEE 754.

## Writing Floating-Point Numbers

Two methods in the DataOutputStream class write floating-point numbers, writeFloat( ) and writeDouble( ):

```
public final void writeFloat(float f) throws IOException
public final void writeDouble(double d) throws IOException
```

Both of these methods throw an IOException if something goes wrong with the underlying stream. Otherwise, they're fairly innocuous and can convert any float or double to bytes and write it on the underlying stream.

Example 8-3 fills a file called *roots.dat* with the square roots of the numbers 0 to 1000. First, a FileOutputStream is opened to *roots.dat*. This stream is chained to a DataOutputStream, whose writeDouble( ) method writes the data into the file.

*Example 8-3. Writing doubles with a DataOutputStream*

```java
import java.io.*;

public class RootsFile {

  public static void main(String[] args) throws IOException {

    DataOutputStream dout = null;
    try {
      FileOutputStream fout = new FileOutputStream("roots.dat");
      dout = new DataOutputStream(fout);
      for (int i = 0; i <= 1000; i++) {
        dout.writeDouble(Math.sqrt(i));
      }
      dout.flush();
      dout.close();
    }
    finally {
      if (dout != null) dout.close();
    }
  }
}
```

## Reading Floating-Point Numbers

The DataInputStream class has two methods that read floating-point numbers, readFloat( ) and readDouble( ):

```java
public final float  readFloat() throws IOException
public final double readDouble() throws IOException
```

The readFloat( ) method reads 4 bytes, converts the data into a float, and returns it. The readDouble( ) method reads 8 bytes, converts the data into a double, and returns that. Both methods throw an EOFException if they can't read enough bytes. In this case, data may be lost without careful (and usually unnecessary) marking and resetting.

Example 8-4 reads a file specified on the command line and prints its contents interpreted as doubles.

*Example 8-4. The DoubleReader program*

```java
import java.io.*;

public class DoubleReader {

public static void main(String[] args) throws IOException {

    DataInputStream din = null;
    try {
      FileInputStream fin = new FileInputStream(args[0]);
      System.out.println("-----------" + args[0] + "-----------");
      din = new DataInputStream(fin);
```

*Example 8-4. The DoubleReader program (continued)*

```
    while (true) {
      int theNumber = din.readDouble( );
      System.out.println(theNumber);
    }  // end while
  } // end try
  catch (EOFException ex) {
    // normal termination
    din.close( );
  }
  catch (IOException ex) {
    // abnormal termination
    System.err.println(ex);
  }
} // end main
} // end DoubleReader
```

Here are the first few lines produced when this program is used to read the output of Example 8-4, RootsFile. You may recognize this output as the square roots of the integers between 0 and 9.

```
$ java DoubleReader roots.dat
-----------roots.dat-----------
0.0
1.0
1.4142135623730951
1.7320508075688772
2.0
2.23606797749979
2.449489742783178
2.6457513110645907
2.8284271247461903
3.0
...
```

# Booleans

The DataOutputStream class has a writeBoolean( ) method, and the DataInputStream class has a corresponding readBoolean( ) method:

```
public final void    writeBoolean(boolean b) throws IOException
public final boolean readBoolean( ) throws IOException
```

Although theoretically a single bit could be used to indicate the value of a boolean, in practice a whole byte is used. This makes alignment much simpler and the extra space it uses isn't large enough to create an issue on modern machines. The writeBoolean( ) method writes a 0 byte (0x00) to indicate false or a 1 byte (0x01) to indicate true. The readBoolean( ) method interprets 0 as false and any positive number as true. Negative numbers indicate end of stream and lead to an EOFException being thrown.

# Byte Arrays

As already mentioned, the `DataInputStream` class has the usual two methods for reading bytes into a byte array:

```
public int read(byte[] data) throws IOException
public int read(byte[] data, int offset, int length) throws IOException
```

Neither of these methods guarantees that all of the bytes requested will be read. Instead, you're expected to check the number of bytes actually read and then call `read()` again as necessary for different parts of the array. For example, to read 1024 bytes from the `InputStream` in into the byte array data:

```
int offset = 0;
while (true){
  int bytesRead = in.read(data, offset, data.length - offset);
  offset += bytesRead;
  if (bytesRead == -1 || offset >= data.length) break;
}
```

The `DataInputStream` class has two `readFully()` methods that provide this logic. Each reads repeatedly from the underlying input stream until the array data or a specified portion thereof is filled.

```
public final void readFully(byte[] data) throws IOException
public final void readFully(byte[] data, int offset, int length)
                throws IOException
```

If the data runs out before the array is filled and no more data is forthcoming, an `IOException` is thrown.

## Determining the Number of Bytes Written

The `DataOutputStream` class has a protected field called `written` that stores the number of bytes written to the output stream using any of its methods since the point it was constructed. The value of this field is returned by the public `size()` method:

```
protected int written
public final int size()
```

Every time you invoke `writeInt()`, `writeBytes()`, `writeUTF()`, or some other write method, the `written` field is incremented by the number of bytes written. This might be useful if for some reason you're trying to limit the number of bytes you write. For instance, you may prefer to open a new file when you reach some preset size rather than continuing to write into a very large file.

## Skipping Bytes

The `DataInputStream` class's `skipBytes()` method skips over a specified number of bytes without reading them. Unlike the `skip()` method of `java.io.InputStream` that

`DataInputStream` inherits, `skipBytes()` either skips over all of the bytes it's asked to skip or it throws an exception:

```
public final int  skipBytes(int n) throws IOException
```

`skipBytes()` blocks and waits for more data until n bytes have been skipped (successful execution) or until an exception is thrown. The method returns the number of bytes skipped, which is always n (because if it's not n, an exception is thrown and nothing is returned). On end of stream, it throws an `EOFException`. It throws an `IOException` if the underlying stream throws an `IOException`.

# Strings and chars

Because of the difficulties caused by different character sets, reading and writing text is one of the trickiest things you can do with streams. Most of the time, text should be handled with readers and writers, a subject we'll take up in Chapter 20. However, the `DataInputStream` and `DataOutputStream` classes do provide methods a Java program can use to read and write text that another Java program will understand. The text format used is a modified form of Unicode's UTF-8 encoding. It's unlikely that other, non-Java programs will understand this format.

This variant form of UTF-8 is intended for string literals embedded in compiled byte code and serialized Java objects and for communication between two Java programs. It is not intended for reading and writing arbitrary UTF-8 text. To read standard UTF-8, you should use an `InputStreamReader`; to write it, you should use an `OutputStreamWriter`.

## Writing Text

The `DataOutputStream` class has four methods that convert text into bytes and write them onto the underlying stream:

```
public final void writeChar(int c) throwsIOException
public final void writeChars(String s) throws IOException
public final void writeBytes(String s) throws IOException
public final void writeUTF(String s) throws IOException
```

The `writeChar()` method writes a single Java char. This method does not use UTF-8. It simply writes the two bytes of the char (i.e., a UTF-16 code point) in big-endian order. `writeChars()` writes each character in the `String` argument to the underlying output stream as a 2-byte char. And the `writeBytes()` method writes the low-order byte of each character in the `String` argument to the underlying output stream. Any information in the high-order byte is lost. In other words, it assumes the string contains only characters whose value is between 0 and 255.

The `writeUTF()` method, however, retains the information in the high-order byte as well as the length of the string. First it writes the number of characters in the string onto the underlying output stream as a 2-byte unsigned int between 0 and 65,535. Next it encodes the string in UTF-8 and writes the bytes of the encoded string to the underlying output stream. This allows a data input stream reading those bytes to completely reconstruct the string. However, if you pass a string longer than 65,535 characters to writeUTF( ), writeUTF( ) throws a java.io.UTFDataFormatException, which is a subclass of IOException, and doesn't write any of the data. For large blocks of text, you should use a Writer rather than a DataOutputStream. DataOutputStream is intended for files containing mixed binary and text data, not for those comprised purely of text content, such as XML documents.

## Reading Text

The DataInputStream class has three methods to read text data:

```
public final char   readChar( ) throws IOException
public final String readUTF( ) throws IOException
public static final String readUTF(DataInput in) throws IOException
```

The readChar( ) method reads two bytes from the underlying input stream and interprets them as a big-endian Java char. It throws an IOException if the underlying input stream's read( ) method throws an IOException. It throws an EOFException if there's only one byte left in the stream and therefore a complete char can't be read.

The no-args readUTF( ) method reads the length of the string and then reads and returns a string that was written in Java's pseudo-UTF-8 encoding with a 2-byte, unsigned length prefix (in other words, a string written by writeUTF( ) in DataOutputStream). This method throws an EOFException if the stream runs out of data before providing the promised number of characters. It throws a UTFDataFormatException if the bytes read are not valid UTF-8—for example, if 4 bytes in a row begin with the bit sequence 10. And, of course, it will propagate any IOException thrown by the underlying stream.

Finally, the static readUTF( ) method reads a UTF string from any DataInput object. It also expects Java's pseudo-UTF-8 format and is not suitable for general purpose text reading.

## The Deprecated readLine( ) Method

The DataInputStream class also has a commonly used but deprecated readLine( ) method:

```
public final String readLine( ) throws IOException
```

This method reads a single line of text from the underlying input stream and returns it as a string. A line of text is considered to be any number of characters, followed by a carriage return, a linefeed, or a carriage return/linefeed pair. The line terminator (possibly including both a carriage return and a linefeed) is read; however, it is not included in the string returned by readLine( ). The problem with readLine( ) is that it does not properly handle non-Latin-1 character sets. BufferedReader's readLine( )

method is supposed to be used instead. readLine( ) also has a nasty bug involving streams that end with carriage returns that can cause a program to hang indefinitely when reading data from a network connection.

# Little-Endian Numbers

It's likely that at some point in time you'll need to read a file full of little-endian data, especially if you're working on Intel hardware or with data written by native code on such a platform. Java has essentially no support for little-endian numbers. The LittleEndianOutputStream class in Example 8-5 and the LittleEndianInputStream class in Example 8-6 provide the support you need to do this. These classes are closely modeled on the java.io.DataInputStream and java.io.DataOutputStream classes. Some of the methods in these classes do exactly the same thing as the same methods in the DataInputStream and DataOutputStream classes. After all, a big-endian byte is no different from a little-endian byte. In fact, these two classes come very close to implementing the java.io.DataInput and java.io.DataOutput interfaces. Actually doing so would have been a bad idea, however, because client programmers expect objects implementing DataInput and DataOutput to use big-endian numbers, and it's best not to go against such common assumptions.

*Example 8-5. The LittleEndianOutputStream class*

```java
package com.elharo.io;

import java.io.*;

public class LittleEndianOutputStream extends FilterOutputStream {

  protected int written;

  public LittleEndianOutputStream(OutputStream out) {
    super(out);
  }

  public void write(int b) throws IOException {
    out.write(b);
    written++;
  }

  public void write(byte[] data, int offset, int length)
   throws IOException {
    out.write(data, offset, length);
    written += length;
  }

  public void writeBoolean(boolean b) throws IOException {
    if (b) this.write(1);
    else this.write(0);
  }
```

*Example 8-5. The LittleEndianOutputStream class (continued)*

```java
public void writeByte(int b) throws IOException {
  out.write(b);
  written++;
}

public void writeShort(int s) throws IOException {
  out.write(s & 0xFF);
  out.write((s >>> 8) & 0xFF);
  written += 2;
}

public void writeChar(int c) throws IOException {
  out.write(c & 0xFF);
  out.write((c >>> 8) & 0xFF);
  written += 2;
}

public void writeInt(int i) throws IOException {

  out.write(i & 0xFF);
  out.write((i >>> 8) & 0xFF);
  out.write((i >>> 16) & 0xFF);
  out.write((i >>> 24) & 0xFF);
  written += 4;

}

public void writeLong(long l) throws IOException {

  out.write((int) l & 0xFF);
  out.write((int) (l >>> 8) & 0xFF);
  out.write((int) (l >>> 16) & 0xFF);
  out.write((int) (l >>> 24) & 0xFF);
  out.write((int) (l >>> 32) & 0xFF);
  out.write((int) (l >>> 40) & 0xFF);
  out.write((int) (l >>> 48) & 0xFF);
  out.write((int) (l >>> 56) & 0xFF);
  written += 8;

}

public final void writeFloat(float f) throws IOException {
  this.writeInt(Float.floatToIntBits(f));
}

public final void writeDouble(double d) throws IOException {
  this.writeLong(Double.doubleToLongBits(d));
}

public void writeBytes(String s) throws IOException {
  int length = s.length();
  for (int i = 0; i < length; i++) {
```

*Example 8-5. The LittleEndianOutputStream class (continued)*

```java
      out.write((byte) s.charAt(i));
    }
    written += length;
  }

  public void writeChars(String s) throws IOException {
    int length = s.length( );
    for (int i = 0; i < length; i++) {
      int c = s.charAt(i);
      out.write(c & 0xFF);
      out.write((c >>> 8) & 0xFF);
    }
    written += length * 2;
  }

  public void writeUTF(String s) throws IOException {

    int numchars = s.length( );
    int numbytes = 0;

    for (int i = 0 ; i < numchars ; i++) {
      int c = s.charAt(i);
      if ((c >= 0x0001) && (c <= 0x007F)) numbytes++;
      else if (c > 0x07FF) numbytes += 3;
      else numbytes += 2;
    }

    if (numbytes > 65535) throw new UTFDataFormatException( );

    out.write((numbytes >>> 8) & 0xFF);
    out.write(numbytes & 0xFF);
    for (int i = 0 ; i < numchars ; i++) {
      int c = s.charAt(i);
      if ((c >= 0x0001) && (c <= 0x007F)) {
        out.write(c);
      }
      else if (c > 0x07FF) {
        out.write(0xE0 | ((c >> 12) & 0x0F));
        out.write(0x80 | ((c >>  6) & 0x3F));
        out.write(0x80 | (c & 0x3F));
        written += 2;
      }
      else {
        out.write(0xC0 | ((c >>  6) & 0x1F));
        out.write(0x80 | (c & 0x3F));
        written += 1;
      }
    }

    written += numchars + 2;

  }
```

*Example 8-5. The LittleEndianOutputStream class (continued)*

```
  public int size( ) {
    return this.written;
  }
}
```

Notice how all writing is done by passing byte values to the underlying output stream out (set in the constructor and inherited from the superclass, FilterOutputStream). The primary purpose of these methods is to convert the Java data type to bytes and then write them in a little-endian order. In general, the conversions are accomplished by shifting the bits of interest into the low-order eight bits and then masking it off. For example, consider the writeInt( ) method:

```
    public void writeInt(int i) throws IOException {
      out.write(i & 0xFF);
      out.write((i >>> 8) & 0xFF);
      out.write((i >>> 16) & 0xFF);
      out.write((i >>> 24) & 0xFF);
      written += 4;
    }
```

A Java int is composed of four bytes in big-endian order. Thus, the low-order byte is in the last eight bits. This byte needs to be written first in a little-endian scheme. The mask 0xFF has one bit in the low-order eight bits and zero bits everywhere else. By bitwise ANDing 0xFF with i, we select the low-order eight bits of i. The second-lowest order byte—that is, bits 16 to 23—is selected by first shifting the bits right without sign extension into the low-order bits. That's the purpose of (i >>> 8). Then this byte can be retrieved with the same 0xFF mask used before. The same is done for the second-to-lowest-order byte and the highest-order byte. Here, however, it's necessary to shift by 16 and 24 bits, respectively.

floats and doubles are written by first converting them to ints and longs using Float.floatToIntBits( ) and Double.doubleToLongBits( ) and then invoking writeInt( ) or writeLong( ) to write those bits in little-endian order.

Each method increments the protected field written by the number of bytes actually written. This tracks the total number of bytes written onto the output stream at any one time.

Example 8-6 shows the corresponding LittleEndianInputStream class, based on the DataInputStream class.

*Example 8-6. The LittleEndianInputStream class*

```
package com.elharo.io;

import java.io.*;

public class LittleEndianInputStream extends FilterInputStream {
```

*Example 8-6. The LittleEndianInputStream class (continued)*

```java
public LittleEndianInputStream(InputStream in) {
  super(in);
}

public boolean readBoolean() throws IOException {
  int bool = in.read();
  if (bool == -1) throw new EOFException();
  return (bool != 0);
}

public byte readByte(int b) throws IOException {
  int temp = in.read();
  if (temp == -1) throw new EOFException();
  return (byte) temp;
}

public int readUnsignedByte() throws IOException {
  int temp = in.read();
  if (temp == -1) throw new EOFException();
  return temp;
}

public short readShort() throws IOException {
  int byte1 = in.read();
  int byte2 = in.read();
  // only need to test last byte read
  // if byte1 is -1 so is byte2
  if (byte2 == -1) throw new EOFException();
  return (short) (((byte2 << 24) >>> 16) + (byte1 << 24) >>> 24);
}

public int readUnsignedShort() throws IOException {
  int byte1 = in.read();
  int byte2 = in.read();
  if (byte2 == -1) throw new EOFException();
  return ((byte2 << 24) >> 16) + ((byte1 << 24) >> 24);
}

public char readChar() throws IOException {
  int byte1 = in.read();
  int byte2 = in.read();
  if (byte2 == -1) throw new EOFException();
  return (char) (((byte2 << 24) >>> 16) + ((byte1 << 24) >>> 24));
}

public int readInt() throws IOException {

  int byte1 = in.read();
  int byte2 = in.read();
  int byte3 = in.read();
  int byte4 = in.read();
  if (byte4 == -1) {
```

*Example 8-6. The LittleEndianInputStream class (continued)*

```
      throw new EOFException( );
    }
  return (byte4 << 24)
    + ((byte3 << 24) >>> 8)
    + ((byte2 << 24) >>> 16)
    + ((byte1 << 24) >>> 24);

}

public long readLong( ) throws IOException {

  long byte1 = in.read( );
  long byte2 = in.read( );
  long byte3 = in.read( );
  long byte4 = in.read( );
  long byte5 = in.read( );
  long byte6 = in.read( );
  long byte7 = in.read( );
  long byte8 = in.read( );
  if (byte8 == -1) {
    throw new EOFException( );
  }
  return (byte8 << 56)
    + ((byte7 << 56) >>> 8)
    + ((byte6 << 56) >>> 16)
    + ((byte5 << 56) >>> 24)
    + ((byte4 << 56) >>> 32)
    + ((byte3 << 56) >>> 40)
    + ((byte2 << 56) >>> 48)
    + ((byte1 << 56) >>> 56);

}

public String readUTF( ) throws IOException {

  int byte1 = in.read( );
  int byte2 = in.read( );
  if (byte2 == -1) throw new EOFException( );
  int numbytes = (byte1 << 8) + byte2;
  char result[] = new char[numbytes];
  int numread = 0;
  int numchars = 0;

  while (numread < numbytes) {

    int c1 = readUnsignedByte( );

    // The first 4 bits of c1 determine how many bytes are in this char
    int test = c1 >> 4;
    if (test < 8) {  // one byte
      numread++;
      result[numchars++] = (char) c1;
    }
```

*Example 8-6. The LittleEndianInputStream class (continued)*

```
        else if (test == 12 || test == 13) { // 2 bytes
          numread += 2;
          if (numread > numbytes) throw new UTFDataFormatException();
          int c2 = readUnsignedByte();
          if ((c2 & 0xC0) != 0x80) throw new UTFDataFormatException();
          result[numchars++] = (char) (((c1 & 0x1F) << 6) | (c2 & 0x3F));
        }
        else if (test == 14) { // three bytes
          numread += 3;
          if (numread > numbytes) throw new UTFDataFormatException();
          int c2 = readUnsignedByte();
          int c3 = readUnsignedByte();
          if (((c2 & 0xC0) != 0x80) || ((c3 & 0xC0) != 0x80)) {
            throw new UTFDataFormatException();
          }
          result[numchars++] = (char)
            (((c1 & 0x0F) << 12) | ((c2 & 0x3F) << 6) | (c3 & 0x3F));
        }
        else { // malformed
          throw new UTFDataFormatException();
        }

    }  // end while

    return new String(result, 0, numchars);

  }

  public final double readDouble() throws IOException {
    return Double.longBitsToDouble(this.readLong());
  }

  public final float readFloat() throws IOException {
    return Float.intBitsToFloat(this.readInt());
  }

  public final int skipBytes(int n) throws IOException {
    for (int i = 0; i < n; i += (int) skip(n - i));
    return n;
  }
}
```

This class is used later in this chapter to view files containing little-endian numbers.

## Thread Safety

The LittleEndianInputStream class is not threadsafe. Consider the readInt() method:

```
    public int readInt() throws IOException {

        int byte1 = in.read();
        int byte2 = in.read();
```

```
    int byte3 = in.read( );
    int byte4 = in.read( );
    if (byte4 == -1  || byte3 == -1 || byte2 == -1 || byte1 == -1) {
      throw new EOFException( );
    }
    return (byte4 << 24) + (byte3 << 16) + (byte2 << 8) + byte1;
  }
```

If two threads are trying to read from this input stream at the same time, there is no guarantee that bytes 1 through 4 will be read in order. The first thread might read bytes 1 and 2, and then the second thread could preempt it and read any number of bytes. When the first thread regained control, it would no longer be able to read bytes 3 and 4 but would read whichever bytes happened to be next in line. It would then return an erroneous result.

A synchronized block would solve this problem neatly:

```
    public int readInt( ) throws IOException {

      int byte1, byte2, byte3, byte4;

      synchronized (this) {
        byte1 = in.read( );
        byte2 = in.read( );
        byte3 = in.read( );
        byte4 = in.read( );
      }
      if (byte4 == -1  || byte3 == -1 || byte2 == -1 || byte1 == -1) {
        throw new EOFException( );
      }
      return (byte4 << 24) + (byte3 << 16) + (byte2 << 8) + byte1;
    }
```

It isn't necessary to synchronize the entire method—only the four lines that read from the underlying stream. However, this solution is still imperfect. It is remotely possible that another thread has a reference to the underlying stream rather than to the little-endian input stream and could try to read directly from that. Therefore, you might be better off synchronizing on the underlying input stream in.

However, this would prevent another thread from reading from the underlying input stream only if the second thread also synchronized on the underlying input stream. In general, you can't count on this, so it's not really a solution. In fact, Java really doesn't provide a good means to guarantee thread safety when you have to modify objects you don't control that are passed as arguments to your methods.

LittleEndianOutputStream has equally severe problems. Consider the writeInt( ) method:

```
    public void writeInt(int i) throws IOException {

      out.write(i & 0xFF);
      out.write((i >>> 8) & 0xFF);
```

```
    out.write((i >>> 16) & 0xFF);
    // What happens if another thread preempts here?
    out.write((i >>> 24) & 0xFF);
    written += 4;
  }
```

Suppose a second thread preempts the running thread where indicated and writes unrelated data onto the output stream. The entire stream can be corrupted because the bytes of the int are separated. All the problems I've noted here are shared by DataInputStream and DataOutputStream, and similar problems crop up in other filter stream classes. This leads to the following general principle for threadsafe programming:

> *Never allow two threads to share a stream.*

The principle is most obvious for filter streams, but it applies to regular streams as well. Although writing or reading a single byte can be treated as an atomic operation, many programs will not be happy to read and write individual bytes. They'll want to read or write a particular group of bytes and will not react well to being interrupted.

# File Viewer, Part 3

In Chapter 4, I introduced a FileDumper program that could print the raw bytes of a file in ASCII, hexadecimal, or decimal. In this chapter, I'm going to expand that program so that it can interpret the file as containing binary numbers of varying widths. In particular, I'm going to make it possible to dump a file as shorts, unsigned shorts, ints, longs, floats, and doubles. Integer types may be either big-endian or little-endian. The main class, FileDumper3, is shown in Example 8-7. As in Chapter 4, this program reads a series of filenames and arguments from the command line in the main( ) method. Each filename is passed to a method that opens a file input stream from the file. Depending on the command-line arguments, a particular subclass of DumpFilter from Chapter 6 is selected and chained to the input stream. Finally, the StreamCopier.copy( ) method pours data from the input stream onto System.out.

*Example 8-7. The FileDumper3 class*

```
import java.io.*;
import com.elharo.io.*;

public class FileDumper3 {

  public static final int ASC = 0;
  public static final int DEC = 1;
  public static final int HEX = 2;
  public static final int SHORT = 3;
  public static final int INT = 4;
  public static final int LONG = 5;
```

*Example 8-7. The FileDumper3 class (continued)*

```java
public static final int FLOAT = 6;
public static final int DOUBLE = 7;

public static void main(String[] args) {

  if (args.length < 1) {
    System.err.println(
      "Usage: java FileDumper3 [-ahdsilfx] [-little] file1 file2...");
  }

  boolean bigEndian = true;
  int firstFile = 0;
  int mode = ASC;

  // Process command-line switches.
  for (firstFile = 0; firstFile < args.length; firstFile++) {
    if (!args[firstFile].startsWith("-")) break;
    if (args[firstFile].equals("-h")) mode = HEX;
    else if (args[firstFile].equals("-d")) mode = DEC;
    else if (args[firstFile].equals("-s")) mode = SHORT;
    else if (args[firstFile].equals("-i")) mode = INT;
    else if (args[firstFile].equals("-l")) mode = LONG;
    else if (args[firstFile].equals("-f")) mode = FLOAT;
    else if (args[firstFile].equals("-x")) mode = DOUBLE;
    else if (args[firstFile].equals("-little")) bigEndian = false;
  }

  for (int i = firstFile; i < args.length; i++) {
    try {
      InputStream in = new FileInputStream(args[i]);
      dump(in, System.out, mode, bigEndian);

      if (i < args.length-1) {  // more files to dump
        System.out.println();
        System.out.println("------------------------------------");
        System.out.println();
      }
    }
    catch (Exception ex) {
      System.err.println(ex);
    }
  }
}

public static void dump(InputStream in, OutputStream out, int mode,
 throws IOException {

  // The reference variable in may point to several different objects
  // within the space of the next few lines. We can attach
  // more filters here to do decompression, decryption, and more.

  if (bigEndian) {
```

*Example 8-7. The FileDumper3 class (continued)*

```
    DataInputStream din = new DataInputStream(in);
    switch (mode) {
      case HEX:
        in = new HexFilter(in);
        break;
      case DEC:
        in = new DecimalFilter(in);
        break;
      case INT:
        in = new IntFilter(din);
        break;
      case SHORT:
        in = new ShortFilter(din);
        break;
      case LONG:
        in = new LongFilter(din);
        break;
      case DOUBLE:
        in = new DoubleFilter(din);
        break;
      case FLOAT:
        in = new FloatFilter(din);
        break;
      default:
    }
  }
  else {
    LittleEndianInputStream lin = new LittleEndianInputStream(in);
    switch (mode) {
      case HEX:
        in = new HexFilter(in);
        break;
      case DEC:
        in = new DecimalFilter(in);
        break;
      case INT:
        in = new LEIntFilter(lin);
        break;
      case SHORT:
        in = new LEShortFilter(lin);
        break;
      case LONG:
        in = new LELongFilter(lin);
        break;
      case DOUBLE:
        in = new LEDoubleFilter(lin);
        break;
```

*Example 8-7. The FileDumper3 class (continued)*

```
    case FLOAT:
      in = new LEFloatFilter(lin);
      break;
    default:
    }
  }

  StreamCopier.copy(in, out);
  in.close();
  }
}
```

The main( ) method of this class reads the command-line arguments and uses the switches to determine the format of the input data. The dump( ) method reads the mode and the endianness, selects the appropriate filter, and copies the input onto the output. Table 8-2 shows the command-line switches. Eight of these switches select a particular format. One of them, -little, specifies the endianness of the data. Since there's no difference between big-endian and little-endian ASCII, decimal, and hexadecimal dumps, a total of 12 different filters are used here. Two of the switches, the HexFilter and the DecimalFilter, were introduced in Chapter 6. They haven't changed.

*Table 8-2. Command-line switches for FileDumper3*

| Switch | Format |
| --- | --- |
| -a | ASCII |
| -d | decimal dump |
| -h | hexadecimal |
| -s | short |
| -i | int |
| -l | long |
| -f | float |
| -x | double |
| -little | little-endian |

I've introduced ten new filters for big- and little-endian shorts, ints, longs, floats, and doubles. The big-endian filters read data from a data input stream. The little-endian filters read data from a little-endian input stream. To take advantage of code reuse, the big-endian filters are all subclasses of a new abstract subclass of DumpFilter called DataFilter, shown in Example 8-8. The little-endian filters are all subclasses of a new abstract subclass of DumpFilter called LEFilter, shown in Example 8-10. The hierarchy of these filters is shown in Figure 8-1.

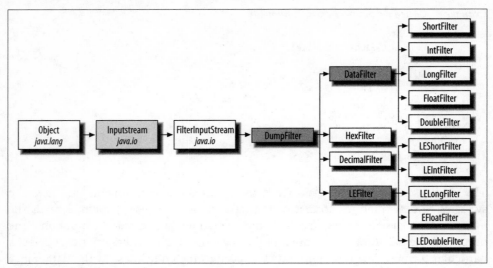

*Figure 8-1. Class hierarchy for filters*

*Example 8-8. DataFilter*

```java
package com.elharo.io;

import java.io.*;

public abstract class DataFilter extends DumpFilter {

  // The use of DataInputStream here is a little forced.
  // It would be more natural (though more complicated)
  // to read the bytes and manually convert them to an int.
  private DataInputStream din;

  public DataFilter(DataInputStream din) {
    super(din);
    this.din = din;
  }

  public int available() throws IOException {
    return (buf.length - index) + in.available();
  }
}
```

DataFilter makes sure that a data input stream is available to subclasses to read from. It also has enough information to provide a reasonable available( ) method. The actual implementation of the fill( ) method is left to specific subclasses like IntFilter. LEFilter, shwon in Example 8-9, is identical except for its use of a LittleEndianInputStream in place of a DataInputStream.

*Example 8-9. LEFilter*

```
package com.elharo.io;

import java.io.*;

public abstract class LEFilter extends DumpFilter {

  private LittleEndianInputStream lin;

  public LEFilter(LittleEndianInputStream lin) {
    super(lin);
    this.lin = lin;
  }

  public int available() throws IOException {
    return (buf.length - index) + lin.available();
  }
}
```

The concrete subclasses of these two classes are all very similar. Example 8-10 shows the simplest, IntFilter.

*Example 8-10. IntFilter*

```
package com.elharo.io;

import java.io.*;

public class IntFilter extends DataFilter {

  public IntFilter(DataInputStream din) {
    super(din);
  }

  protected void fill() throws IOException {
    int number = din.readInt();
    String s = Integer.toString(number)
     + System.getProperty("line.separator", "\r\n");
    byte[] b = s.getBytes("8859_1");
    buf = new int[b.length];
    for (int i = 0; i < b.length; i++) {
      buf[i] = b[i];
    }
  }
}
```

The fill() method reads an integer from the underlying DataInputStream din. That integer is converted to a string using the static Integer.toString() method. The string is then converted to bytes using the ISO 8859-1 (Latin-1) encoding.

The remaining DataFilter subclasses are very similar. For example, Example 8-11 shows the ShortFilter. Aside from the trivial difference in the class and constructor name, the only real difference is the use of readShort( ) instead of readInt() in the first line of the fill( ) method.

*Example 8-11. ShortFilter*

```java
package com.elharo.io;

import java.io.*;

public class ShortFilter extends DataFilter {

  public ShortFilter(DataInputStream din) {
    super(din);
  }

  protected void fill( ) throws IOException {
    int number = din.readShort( );
    String s = Integer.toString(number)
     + System.getProperty("line.separator", "\r\n");
    byte[] b = s.getBytes("8859_1");
    buf = new int[b.length];
    for (int i = 0; i < b.length; i++) {
      buf[i] = b[i];
    }
  }
}
```

The LongFilter, FloatFilter, and DoubleFilter are only slightly different, so I haven't put the source code in the book; it's available, with the rest of the examples, online. Likewise, I've omitted the similar set of filters for little-endian data. The little-endian filters all extend LEFilter; they are LEIntFilter, LEShortFilter, LELongFilter, LEFloatFilter, and LEDoubleFilter.

In later chapters, I'll add support for compressed and encrypted files, a graphical user interface, and various text interpretations of the data in a file. However, none of that will require changes to any of the filters we've developed here.

# CHAPTER 9

# Streams in Memory

In the last several chapters, you've learned how to use streams to move data between a running Java program and external sources and data stores. Streams can also be used to move data from one part of a Java program to another. This chapter explores three such classes. Sequence input streams chain several input streams together so that they appear as a single stream. Byte array streams allow output to be stored in byte arrays and input to be read from byte arrays. Finally, piped input and output streams allow output from one thread to become input for another thread.

## Sequence Input Streams

The `java.io.SequenceInputStream` class connects multiple input streams together in a particular order. A `SequenceInputStream` first reads all the bytes from the first stream in the sequence, then all the bytes from the second stream in the sequence, then all the bytes from the third stream, and so on. When the end of one stream is reached, that stream is closed; the next data comes from the next stream. This class has two constructors:

```
public SequenceInputStream(Enumeration e)
public SequenceInputStream(InputStream in1, InputStream in2)
```

The first constructor creates a sequence out of all the elements of the `Enumeration` e. This assumes all objects in the enumeration are input streams. If this isn't the case, a `ClassCastException` will be thrown the first time a read is attempted from an object that is not an `InputStream`. The use of an `Enumeration` instead of an `Iterator` is a little old-fashioned. However, this class goes all the way back to Java 1.0, and Sun has never felt compelled to enhance it. In Java 5, this constructor has been retrofitted with generics, making it a tad more typesafe:

```
public SequenceInputStream(Enumeration<? extends InputStream> e)
```

However, it does exactly the same thing.

The second constructor creates a sequence input stream that reads first from in1, then from in2. Note that in1 or in2 may themselves be sequence input streams, so repeated applications of this constructor allows a sequence input stream with an indefinite number of underlying streams to be created. For example, to read the home pages of both Yahoo and Google, you might do this:

```
URL u1 = new URL("http://www.yahoo.com/");
URL u2 = new URL("http://www.google.com");
SequenceInputStream sin = new SequenceInputStream(
  u1.openStream(), u2.openStream());
```

Example 9-1 reads a series of filenames from the command line, creates a sequence input stream from file input streams for each file named, and then copies the contents of all the files onto System.out.

*Example 9-1. The SequencePrinter program*

```
import java.io.*;
import java.util.*;

public class SequencePrinter {

  public static void main(String[] args) throws IOException {

    Vector theStreams = new Vector();

    for (int i = 0; i < args.length; i++) {
      FileInputStream fin = new FileInputStream(args[i]);
      theStreams.addElement(fin);
    }

    InputStream in = new SequenceInputStream(theStreams.elements());
    for (int i = in.read(); i != -1; i = in.read()) {
      System.out.write(i);
    }
  }
}
```

# Byte Array Streams

It's sometimes convenient to use stream methods to manipulate data in byte arrays. For example, you might receive an array of raw bytes that you want to interpret as double-precision, floating-point numbers. (This is common when using UDP to transfer data across the Internet, for example.) The quickest way to do this is to use a DataInputStream. However, before you can create a data input stream, you first need to create a raw, byte-oriented stream. This is what the java.io.ByteArrayInputStream class gives you. Similarly, you might want to send a group of double-precision, floating-point numbers across the network with UDP. Before you can do this, you have to convert the numbers into bytes. The simplest solution is to use a data output stream chained to a `java.io.ByteArrayOutputStream`. By chaining the data output stream to a byte array output stream, you can write the binary form of the floating-point numbers into a byte array, then send the entire array in a single packet.

## Byte Array Input Streams

The `ByteArrayInputStream` class reads data from a byte array using the methods of `java.io.InputStream`:

```
public class ByteArrayInputStream extends InputStream
```

`ByteArrayInputStream( )` has two constructors. Both take a byte array as an argument. This byte array is the buffer from which data will be read. The first constructor uses the entire buffer array as an input stream. The second constructor uses only the subarray of `length` bytes of `buffer` starting with the byte at `offset`.

```
public ByteArrayInputStream(byte[] buffer)
public ByteArrayInputStream(byte[] buffer, int offset, int length)
```

Other than these two constructors, the `ByteArrayInputStream` class just has the usual `read( )`, `available( )`, `close( )`, `mark( )`, and `reset( )` methods. Byte array input streams do support marking and resetting up to the full length of the stream. This is relatively straightforward to implement because, at any time, a byte array contains in memory all of the data in the stream. Unlike other kinds of streams, you don't have to worry that you'll try to reset further back than the buffer allows.

## Byte Array Output Streams

The `ByteArrayOutputStream` class writes data into the successive components of a byte array using the methods of `java.io.OutputStream`:

```
public class ByteArrayOutputStream extends OutputStream
```

This class has the following two constructors, plus the usual `write( )`, `close( )`, and `flush( )` methods:

```
public ByteArrayOutputStream( )
public ByteArrayOutputStream(int size)
```

The no-argument constructor uses a buffer of 32 bytes. The second constructor uses a user-specified buffer size. However, regardless of the initial size, the byte array output stream will expand its buffer as necessary to accommodate additional data.

To return the byte array that contains the written data, use the `toByteArray( )` method:

```
public byte[] toByteArray( )
```

There are also `toString( )` methods that convert the bytes into a string. The no-argument version uses the platform's default encoding. The second method allows you to specify the encoding to be used:

```
public String toString()
public String toString(String encoding) throws UnsupportedEncodingException
```

Another common use of ByteArrayOutputStream is to accumulate data into an internal buffer and then quickly write the entire buffer onto another stream.

The writeTo() performs this task:

```
public void writeTo(OutputStream out) throws IOException
```

Example 9-2 uses a byte array output stream to implement a simple form of buffering. An array is created to hold the first *n* Fibonacci numbers in binary form, where *n* is specified on the command line. (The Fibonacci numbers are the sequence 1, 1, 2, 3, 5, 8, 13, and so on, where each number is calculated by adding the previous two numbers in the sequence.) The array is filled using the methods of java.io. DataOutputStream. Once the array is created, a file is opened and the data in the array is written into the file. Then the file is closed. This way, the data can be written quickly without requiring the file to be open while the program is calculating.

*Example 9-2. The FibonacciFile program*

```java
import java.io.*;

public class FibonacciFile {

  public static void main(String args[]) throws IOException {

    int howMany = 20;

    // To avoid resizing the buffer, calculate the size of the
    // byte array in advance.
    ByteArrayOutputStream bout = new ByteArrayOutputStream(howMany*4);
    DataOutputStream dout = new DataOutputStream(bout);

    // First two Fibonacci numbers must be given
    // to start the process.
    int f1 = 1;
    int f2 = 1;
    dout.writeInt(f1);
    dout.writeInt(f2);

    // Now calculate the rest.
    for (int i = 3; i <= 20; i++) {
      int temp = f2;
      f2 = f2 + f1;
      f1 = temp;
      dout.writeInt(f2);
    }

    FileOutputStream fout = new FileOutputStream("fibonacci.dat");
    try {
      bout.writeTo(fout);
      fout.flush();
```

*Example 9-2. The FibonacciFile program (continued)*

```
    }
    finally {
      fout.close( );
    }
  }
}
```

You can use the FileDumper3 program from the previous chapter with the -i option to view the output. For example:

```
$ java FibonacciFile fibonacci.dat
$ java FileDumper3 -i fibonacci.dat
1
1
2
3
5
8
13
21
34
55
...
```

# Communicating Between Threads Using Piped Streams

The java.io.PipedInputStream class and java.io.PipedOutputStream classes provide a convenient means to move data from one thread to another. Output from one thread becomes input for the other thread, as shown in Figure 9-1.

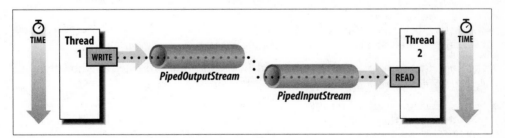

*Figure 9-1. Data moving between threads using piped streams*

```
    public class PipedInputStream  extends InputStream
    public class PipedOutputStream extends OutputStream
```

The PipedInputStream class has two constructors:

```
    public PipedInputStream( )
    public PipedInputStream(PipedOutputStream source) throws IOException
```

The no-argument constructor creates a piped input stream that is not yet connected to a piped output stream. The second constructor creates a piped input stream that's connected to the piped output stream source.

The PipedOutputStream class also has two constructors:

```
public PipedOutputStream(PipedInputStream sink) throws IOException
public PipedOutputStream( )
```

The no-argument constructor creates a piped output stream that is not yet connected to a piped input stream. The second constructor creates a piped output stream that's connected to the piped input stream sink.

Piped streams are normally created in pairs. The piped output stream becomes the underlying source for the piped input stream. For example:

```
PipedOutputStream pout = new PipedOutputStream( );
PipedInputStream  pin  = new PipedInputStream(pout);
```

This simple example is a little deceptive because these lines of code will normally be in different methods and perhaps even different classes. Some mechanism must be established to pass a reference to the PipedOutputStream into the thread that handles the PipedInputStream. Or you can create them in the same thread, then pass a reference to the connected stream into a separate thread. Alternately, you can reverse the order:

```
PipedInputStream  pin  = new PipedInputStream( );
PipedOutputStream pout = new PipedOutputStream(pin);
```

Or you can create them both unconnected, then use one or the other's connect( ) method to link them:

```
PipedInputStream  pin  = new PipedInputStream( );
PipedOutputStream pout = new PipedOutputStream( );
pin.connect(pout);
```

Otherwise, these classes just have the usual read( ), write( ), flush( ), close( ), and available( ) public methods like all stream classes.

PipedInputStream also has four protected fields and one protected method that are used to implement the piping:

```
protected static final int PIPE_SIZE
protected byte[] buffer
protected int in
protected int out
protected void receive(int b) throws IOException
```

PIPE_SIZE is a named constant for the size of the buffer. The buffer is the byte array where the data is stored, and it's initialized to be an array of length PIPE_SIZE. When a client class invokes a write( ) method in the piped output stream class, the write( ) method invokes the receive( ) method in the connected piped input stream to place the data in the byte array buffer. Data is always written at the position in the buffer given by the field in and read from the position in the buffer given by the field out.

There are two possible blocks here. The first occurs if the writing thread tries to write data while the reading thread's input buffer is full. When this occurs, the output stream enters an infinite loop in which it repeatedly waits for one second until some thread reads some data out of the buffer and frees up space. If this is likely to be a problem for your application, subclass PipedInputStream and make the buffer larger. The second possible block is when the reading thread tries to read and no data is present in the buffer. In this case, the input stream enters an infinite loop in which it repeatedly waits for one second until some thread writes some data into the buffer.

Although piped input streams contain an internal buffer, they do not support marking and resetting. The circular nature of the buffer would make this excessively complicated. You can always chain the piped input stream to a buffered input stream and read from that if you need marking and resetting.

The following program is a simple and somewhat artificial example that generates Fibonacci numbers in one thread and writes them onto a piped output stream while another thread reads the numbers from a corresponding piped input stream and prints them on System.out. This program uses three classes: FibonacciProducer and FibonacciConsumer, which are subclasses of Thread, and FibonacciDriver, which manages the other two classes. Example 9-3 shows the FibonacciProducer class, a subclass of Thread. This class does not directly use a piped output stream. It just writes data onto the output stream that it's given in the constructor.

*Example 9-3. The FibonacciProducer class*

```java
import java.io.*;

public class FibonacciProducer extends Thread {

  private DataOutputStream theOutput;
  private int howMany;

  public FibonacciProducer(OutputStream out, int howMany) {
    theOutput = new DataOutputStream(out);
    this.howMany = howMany;
  }

  public void run( ) {

    try {
      int f1 = 1;
      int f2 = 1;
      theOutput.writeInt(f1);
      theOutput.writeInt(f2);

      // Now calculate the rest.
      for (int i = 2; i < howMany; i++) {
        int temp = f2;
        f2 = f2 + f1;
        f1 = temp;
```

*Example 9-3. The FibonacciProducer class (continued)*

```
      if (f2 < 0) { // overflow
       break;
      }
      theOutput.writeInt(f2);
    }
   }
   catch (IOException ex) { System.err.println(ex); }
  }
}
```

Example 9-4 is the FibonacciConsumer class. It could just as well have been called the IntegerConsumer class since it doesn't know anything about Fibonacci numbers. Its run( ) method merely reads integers from its input stream until the stream is exhausted. At this point, the other end of the pipe closes and an IOException is thrown. The only way to tell the difference between this normal termination and a real exception is to check the exception message.

*Example 9-4. The FibonacciConsumer class*

```
import java.io.*;

public class FibonacciConsumer extends Thread {

  private DataInputStream theInput;

  public FibonacciConsumer(InputStream in) {
    theInput = new DataInputStream(in);
  }

  public void run( ) {

    try {
      while (true) {
        System.out.println(theInput.readInt( ));
      }
    }
    catch (IOException ex) {
      if (ex.getMessage( ).equals("Pipe broken")) {
        // normal termination
        return;
      }
      System.err.println(ex);
    }
  }
}
```

Example 9-5 is the FibonacciDriver class. It creates a piped output stream and a piped input stream and uses those to construct FibonacciProducer and FibonacciConsumer objects. These streams are a channel of communication between the two threads. As data is written by the FibonacciProducer thread, it becomes available for the FibonacciConsumer thread to read. Both the FibonacciProducer and the

FibonacciConsumer are run with normal priority so that when the FibonacciProducer blocks or is preempted, the FibonacciConsumer runs and vice versa.

*Example 9-5. The FibonacciDriver class*

```java
import java.io.*;

public class FibonacciConsumer extends Thread {

  private DataInputStream theInput;

  public FibonacciConsumer(InputStream in) {
    theInput = new DataInputStream(in);
  }

  public void run( ) {

    try {
      while (true) {
        System.out.println(theInput.readInt( ));
      }
    }
    catch (IOException ex) {
      if (ex.getMessage( ).equals("Pipe broken")
        || ex.getMessage( ).equals("Write end dead")) {
        // normal termination
        return;
      }
      ex.printStackTrace( );
    }
  }
}
```

You may be wondering how the piped streams differ from the stream copiers presented earlier in the book. The first difference is that the piped stream moves data from an output stream to an input stream. The stream copier always moves data in the opposite direction, from an input stream to an output stream. The second difference is that the stream copier actively moves the data by calling the read( ) and write( ) methods of the underlying streams. A piped output stream merely makes the data available to the input stream. It is still necessary for some other object to invoke the piped input stream's read( ) method to read the data. If no other object reads from the piped input stream, after about one kilobyte of data has been written onto the piped output stream, the writing thread blocks while it waits for the piped input stream's buffer to empty.

# CHAPTER 10
# Compressing Streams

The `java.util.zip` package, shown in Figure 10-1, contains six stream classes and another half dozen assorted classes that read and write data in zip, gzip, and inflate/deflate formats. Java uses these classes to read and write JAR archives and to display PNG images. The `java.util.zip` classes are well-suited for general-purpose compression and decompression.

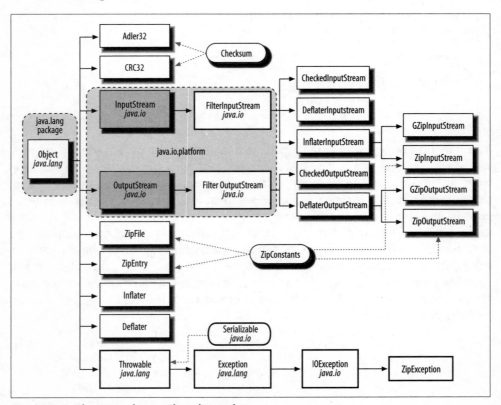

*Figure 10-1. The java.util.zip package hierarchy*

# Inflaters and Deflaters

The `java.util.zip.Deflater` and `java.util.zip.Inflater` classes provide compression and decompression services for all other classes. These two classes support several related compression formats, including zlib, deflate, and gzip. Each of these formats is based on the LZ77 compression algorithm (named after the inventors, Jakob Ziv and Abraham Lempel), though each has a different way of storing metadata that describes an archive's contents. Since compression and decompression are extremely CPU-intensive operations, these classes are usually implemented as Java wrappers around native methods written in C.

zip, gzip, and zlib all compress data in more or less the same way. Repeated bit sequences in the input data are replaced with pointers back to the first occurrence of that bit sequence. Other tricks are used, but this is basically how these compression schemes work, and it has certain implications for compression and decompression code. First, you can't randomly access data in a compressed file. To decompress the *n*th byte of data, you must first decompress bytes 1 through *n*–1 of the data. Second, a single twiddled bit doesn't just change the meaning of the byte it's part of. It also changes the meaning of bytes that come after it in the data, since subsequent bytes may be stored as copies of the previous bytes. Therefore, compressed files are much more susceptible to corruption than uncompressed files.

## Deflating Data

The `Deflater` class contains methods to compress blocks of data. You can choose the compression format, the level of compression, and the compression strategy. Deflating data with the `Deflater` class requires nine steps:

1. Construct a `Deflater` object.
2. Choose the strategy (optional).
3. Set the compression level (optional).
4. Preset the dictionary (optional).
5. Set the input.
6. Deflate the data repeatedly until `needsInput( )` returns true.
7. If more input is available, go back to step 5 to provide additional input data. Otherwise, go to step 8.
8. Finish the data.
9. If there are more streams to be deflated, reset the deflater.

More often than not, you don't use this class directly. Instead, you use a `Deflater` object indirectly through one of the compressing stream classes like `DeflaterInputStream` or `DeflaterOutputStream`. These classes provide more convenient programmer interfaces for stream-oriented compression than the raw `Deflater` methods.

## Constructing deflaters

`Deflater( )` has three constructors:

```
public Deflater(int level, boolean useGzip)
public Deflater(int level)
public Deflater( )
```

The most general constructor allows you to set the level of compression and the format used. Compression level is specified as an `int` between 0 and 9. 0 is no compression; 9 is maximum compression. Generally, the higher the compression level, the smaller the output will be and the longer the compression will take. Four mnemonic constants are available to select particular levels of compression. These are:

```
public static final int NO_COMPRESSION = 0;
public static final int BEST_SPEED = 1;
public static final int BEST_COMPRESSION = 9;
public static final int DEFAULT_COMPRESSION = -1;
```

If useGzip is true, gzip compression format is used. Otherwise, the zlib compression format is used. (zlib format is the default.) These formats are essentially the same except that zlib includes some extra header and checksum fields.

The `Deflater` class supports only a single compression method, deflation. This one method, used by zip, gzip, and zlib, is represented by the mnemonic constant `Deflater.DEFLATED`:

```
public static final int DEFLATED = 8;
```

## Choose a strategy

Java supports three compression strategies: filtered, Huffman, and default, represented by the mnemonic constants `Deflater.FILTERED`, `Deflater.HUFFMAN_ONLY`, and `Deflater.DEFAULT_STRATEGY`, respectively. The setStrategy( ) method chooses one of these strategies.

```
public void setStrategy(int strategy)
```

This method throws an `IllegalArgumentException` if an unrecognized strategy is passed as an argument. If no strategy is chosen explicitly, the default strategy is used. The default strategy concentrates primarily on emitting pointers to previously seen data, so it works well in data where runs of bytes tend to repeat themselves. In files where long runs of bytes are uncommon, but where the distribution of bytes is uneven, you may be better off with pure Huffman coding. Huffman coding simply uses fewer bits for more common characters like "e" and more bits for less common characters like "q." A third situation, common in some binary files, is where all bytes are more or less equally likely. When dealing with these sorts of files, the filtered strategy provides a good compromise, with some Huffman coding and some matching of data to previously seen values. Most of the time, the default strategy will do the best job, and, even if it doesn't, it will compress within a few percent of the optimal strategy, so it's rarely worth agonizing over which is the best solution.

---

## Set the compression level

The deflater compresses by trying to match the data it's looking at now to data it has already seen earlier in the stream. The compression level determines how far back in the stream the deflater looks for a match. The farther back it looks, the more likely it is to find a match and the longer the run of bytes it can replace with a simple pointer. However, looking farther back takes longer. Thus, compression level is a tradeoff between speed and file size. The tighter you compress, the more time it takes. Generally, the compression level is set in the constructor, but you can change it after the deflater is constructed by using the setLevel( ) method:

```
public void setLevel(int Level)
```

As with the Deflater( ) constructors, the compression level should be an int between 0 and 9 (no compression to maximum compression) or perhaps –1, signifying the default compression level. Any other value causes an IllegalArgumentException. It's good coding style to use one of the mnemonic constants Deflater.NO_COMPRESSION (0), Deflater.BEST_SPEED (1), Deflater.BEST_COMPRESSION (9), or Deflater.DEFAULT_COMPRESSION (–1) instead of an explicit value.

In limited testing with small files, I haven't found the difference between best speed and best compression to be noticeable, either in file size or the time it takes to compress or decompress. You may occasionally want to set the level to no compression (0) if you're deflating already compressed files such as GIF, JPEG, or PNG images before storing them in an archive. These file formats have built-in compression algorithms specifically designed for the type of data they contain, and Deflator's general-purpose deflation algorithm is unlikely to compress them further. It may even increase their size.

## Set the dictionary

The deflater builds a dictionary of phrases as it reads the text. The first time it sees a phrase, it puts the phrase in the dictionary. The second time it sees the phrase, it replaces the phrase with its position in the dictionary. However, it can't do this until it has seen the phrase at least once, so data early in the stream isn't compressed very well compared with data that occurs later in the stream. When you have a good idea that certain byte sequences appear in the data very frequently, you can preset the dictionary used for compression. You would fill the dictionary with the frequently repeated data in the text. For instance, if your text is composed completely of ASCII digits and assorted whitespace (tabs, carriage returns, and so forth), you could put those characters in your dictionary. This allows the early part of the stream to compress as effectively as later parts.

There are two setDictionary( ) methods. The first uses as the dictionary the entire byte array passed as an argument. The second uses the subarray of data starting at offset and continuing for length bytes.

```
public void setDictionary(byte[] data)
public void setDictionary(byte[] data, int offset, int length)
```

Presetting a dictionary is never necessary and requires detailed understanding of both the compression format used and the data to be compressed. Putting the wrong data in your dictionary can actually increase the file size. Unless you're a compression expert and you really need every last byte of space you can save, I recommend letting the deflater build the dictionary adaptively as the data is compressed.

I started with a highly compressible 44,392-byte text file (the output of running *FileDumper2.java* on itself in decimal mode). Without presetting the dictionary, it deflated to 3,859 bytes. My first attempt to preset the dictionary to the ASCII digits, space, and \r\n actually increased that size to 3,863 bytes. After carefully examining the data and custom-designing a dictionary to fit it, I was able to deflate the data to 3,852 bytes, saving a whopping 7 extra bytes, or 0.18 percent. Of course, the dictionary itself occupied 112 bytes, so it's debatable whether I really saved anything.

Exact details are likely to vary from file to file. The only real possible gain is for very short, very predictable files in which Java may not have enough data to build a good dictionary before the end of stream is reached. However, Java uses a pretty good algorithm for building an adaptive dictionary, and you're unlikely to do significantly better by hand. I recommend that you not worry about setting a dictionary and simply let the deflater build one for you.

If `Inflater.inflate()` decompresses the data later, the `Inflater.getAdler()` method will return the Adler-32 checksum of the dictionary needed for decompression. However, you'll need some other means to pass the dictionary itself between the deflater and the inflater. It is not stored with the deflated file.

### Set the input

Next, you must set the input data to be deflated with one of the `setInput()` methods:

```
public void setInput(byte[] input)
public void setInput(byte[] input, int offset, int length)
```

The first method prepares to deflate the entire array. The second method prepares to deflate the specified subarray starting at `offset` and continuing for `length` bytes.

### Deflate the data repeatedly until needsInput( ) returns true

Finally, you're ready to deflate the data. Once `setInput()` has filled the input buffer with data, it is deflated through one of two `deflate()` methods:

```
public int deflate(byte[] output)
public int deflate(byte[] output, int offset, int length)
```

The first method fills the `output` array with the bytes of compressed data. The second fills the subarray of `output` beginning at `offset` and continuing for `length` bytes. Both methods return the actual number of compressed bytes written into the array.

You do not know in advance how many compressed bytes will be written into output because you do not know how well the data will compress. You always have to check the return value. If deflate( ) returns 0, call needsInput( ) to see if more uncompressed input data is needed:

```
public boolean needsInput( )
```

When more data is needed, the needsInput( ) method returns true. At this point, you should invoke setInput( ) again to feed in more uncompressed input data, call deflate( ), and repeat the process until deflate( ) returns *and* there is no more input data to be compressed.

## Finish the deflation

Finally, when the input data is exhausted, invoke finish( ) to indicate that no more data is forthcoming and the deflater should finish with the data it already has in its buffer:

```
public void finish( )
```

The finished( ) method returns true when the end of the compressed output has been reached—that is, when all data stored in the input buffer has been deflated:

```
public boolean finished( )
```

After calling finish( ), invoke deflate( ) repeatedly until finished( ) returns true. This flushes out any data that remains in the input buffer.

## Reset the deflater and start over

This completes the sequence of method invocations required to compress data. If you'd like to use the same strategy, compression level, and other settings to compress more data with the same Deflater, call its reset( ) method:

```
public void reset( )
```

Otherwise, call end( ) to throw away any unprocessed input and free the resources used by the native code:

```
public void end( )
```

The finalize( ) method calls end( ) before the deflater is garbage-collected, even if you forget to invoke it explicitly:

```
protected void finalize( )
```

## An example

Let's look at a simple program that deflates files named on the command line. First, a Deflater object, def, is created with the default strategy, method, and compression level. A file input stream named fin is opened to each file. At the same time, a file output stream named fout is opened to an output file with the same name plus the three-letter extension *.dfl*. The program then enters a loop in which it tries to read

1024-byte chunks of data from fin, though care is taken not to assume that 1024 bytes are actually read. Any data that is successfully read is passed to the deflater's setInput() method. The data is repeatedly deflated and written onto the output stream until the deflater indicates that it needs more input. The process then repeats itself until the end of the input stream is reached. When no more input is available, the deflater's finish() method is called. Then the deflater's deflate() method is repeatedly invoked until its finished() method returns true. At this point, the program breaks out of the infinite read() loop and moves on to the next file.

Figure 10-2 is a flowchart demonstrating this sequence for a single file. One thing may seem a little fishy about this chart. After the deflater is finished, a repeated check is made to see if the deflater is, in fact, finished. The finish() method tells the deflater that no more data is forthcoming and it should work with whatever data remains in its input buffer. However, the finished() method does not actually return true until the input buffer has been emptied by calls to deflate(). Example 10-1 shows a sample program.

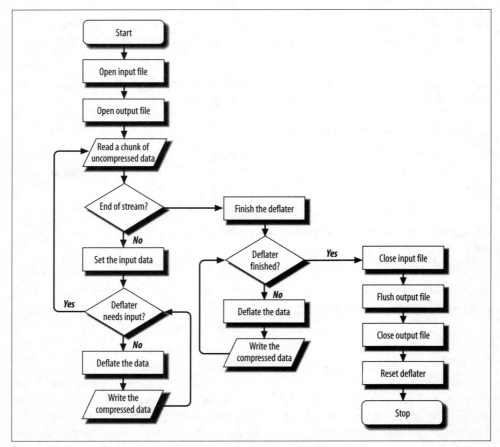

Figure 10-2. The deflation sequence

*Example 10-1. The DirectDeflater*

```java
import java.io.*;
import java.util.zip.*;

public class DirectDeflater {

  public final static String DEFLATE_SUFFIX = ".dfl";

  public static void main(String[] args) throws IOException  {

    Deflater def = new Deflater();
    byte[] input = new byte[1024];
    byte[] output = new byte[1024];

    for (int i = 0; i < args.length; i++) {
        FileInputStream fin = new FileInputStream(args[i]);
        FileOutputStream fout = new FileOutputStream(args[i] + DEFLATE_SUFFIX);

        while (true) { // read and deflate the data

          // Fill the input array.
          int numRead = fin.read(input);
          if (numRead == -1) { // end of stream
            // Deflate any data that remains in the input buffer.
            def.finish();
            while (!def.finished()) {
              int numCompressedBytes = def.deflate(output, 0, output.length);
              if (numCompressedBytes > 0) {
                fout.write(output, 0, numCompressedBytes);
              } // end if
            }  // end while
            break; // Exit while loop.
          } // end if
          else {  // Deflate the input.
            def.setInput(input, 0, numRead);
            while (!def.needsInput()) {
              int numCompressedBytes = def.deflate(output, 0, output.length);
              if (numCompressedBytes > 0) {
                fout.write(output, 0, numCompressedBytes);
              } // end if
            }  // end while
          }  // end else
        } // end while
        fin.close();
        fout.flush();
        fout.close();
        def.reset();
    }
  }
}
```

This program is more complicated than it needs to be because it has to read the file in small chunks. In Example 10-3 later in this chapter, you'll see a simpler program that achieves the same result using the `DeflaterOutputStream` class.

### Checking the state of a deflater

The `Deflater` class also provides several methods that return information about the deflater's state. The `getAdler()` method returns the Adler-32 checksum of the uncompressed data. This is *not* a `java.util.zip.Checksum` object but the actual `int` value of the checksum:

```
public int getAdler()
```

The `getTotalIn()` method returns the number of uncompressed bytes passed to the `setInput()` method:

```
public int getTotalIn()
```

The `getTotalOut()` method returns the total number of compressed bytes output so far via `deflate()`:

```
public int getTotalOut()
```

For example, to print a running total of the compression achieved by the `Deflater` object `def`, you might do something like this:

```
System.out.println((1.0 - def.getTotalOut()/def.getTotalIn())*100.0 +
"% saved");
```

## Inflating Data

The `Inflater` class contains methods to decompress blocks of data compressed in the zip, gzip, or zlib formats. This data may have been produced by Java's `Deflater` class or by some other program written in another language entirely, such as WinZip or gzip. Using an inflater is a little simpler than using a deflater since there aren't a lot of settings to pick. (Those were established when the data was compressed.) There are seven steps to inflating data:

1. Construct an `Inflater` object.
2. Set the input with the compressed data to be inflated.
3. Call `needsDictionary()` to determine if a preset dictionary is required.
4. If `needsDictionary()` returns true, call `getAdler()` to get the Adler-32 checksum of the dictionary. Then invoke `setDictionary()` to set the dictionary data.
5. Inflate the data repeatedly until `inflate()` returns 0.
6. If `needsInput()` returns true, go back to step 2 to provide additional input data.
7. The `finished()` method returns true.

If you want to decompress more data with this `Inflater` object, reset it.

You rarely use this class directly. Instead, you use an inflater indirectly through one of the decompressing stream classes like `InflaterInputStream` or `InflaterOutputStream`. These classes provide much more convenient programmer interfaces for stream-oriented decompression.

## Constructing inflaters

`Inflater( )` has two constructors:

```
public Inflater(boolean zipped)
public Inflater( )
```

By passing true to the first constructor, you indicate that data to be inflated has been compressed using the zip or gzip format. Otherwise, the constructor assumes the data is in the zlib format.

## Set the input

Once you have an `Inflater` to work with, you can start feeding it compressed data with `setInput( )`:

```
public void setInput(byte[] input)
public void setInput(byte[] input, int offset, int length)
```

As usual, the first variant treats the entire input array as data to be inflated. The second uses the subarray of input, starting at offset and continuing for length bytes.

## Check whether a preset dictionary was used

Next, determine whether this block of data was compressed with a preset dictionary. If it was, `needsDictionary( )` returns true:

```
public boolean needsDictionary( )
```

If `needsDictionary( )` does return true, you can get the Adler-32 checksum of the requisite dictionary with the `getAdler( )` method:

```
public int getAdler( )
```

This doesn't actually tell you what the dictionary is (which would be a lot more useful), but if you have a list of commonly used dictionaries, you can probably use the Adler-32 checksum to determine which of those were used to compress the data.

## Set the dictionary

If `needsDictionary( )` returns true, you'll have to use one of the `setDictionary( )` methods to provide the data for the dictionary. The first uses the entire `dictionary` byte array as the dictionary. The second uses the subarray of `dictionary`, starting at offset and continuing for length bytes.

```
public void setDictionary(byte[] dictionary)
public void setDictionary(byte[] dictionary, int offset, int length)
```

The dictionary is not generally available with the compressed data. Whoever writes files using a preset dictionary is responsible for determining some higher-level protocol for passing the dictionary used by the compression program to the decompression program. One possibility is to store the dictionary file, along with the compressed data, in an archive. Another possibility is that programs that read and write many very similar files may always use the same dictionary—one that is built into both the compression and decompression programs.

### Inflate the data

Once setInput( ) has filled the input buffer with data, it is inflated through one of two inflate( ) methods:

```
public int inflate(byte[] output) throws DataFormatException
public int inflate(byte[] output, int offset, int length)
    throws DataFormatException
```

The first method fills the output array with the uncompressed data. The second fills the specified subarray—beginning at offset and continuing for length bytes—with the uncompressed data. inflate( ) returns the number of uncompressed bytes written into the array. If this is 0, call needsInput( ) to see if you need to call setInput( ) again to insert more compressed input data:

```
public boolean needsInput( )
```

When more data is needed, needsInput( ) returns true. At this point, call setInput( ) again to feed in more compressed input data, call inflate( ), and repeat the process until there is no more input data to be decompressed. If no more data is needed after inflate( ) returns zero, it should mean decompression is finished, and the finished( ) method should return true:

```
public boolean finished( )
```

The inflate( ) methods throw a java.util.zip.DataFormatException if they encounter invalid data, which generally indicates a corrupted input stream. This is a direct subclass of java.lang.Exception, not an IOException.

### Reset the inflater

If you'd like to use the same settings to decompress more data with the same Inflater object, you can invoke its reset( ) method:

```
public void reset( )
```

Otherwise, call end( ) to throw away any unprocessed input and free the resources used by the native code:

```
public void end( )
```

The finalize( ) method calls end( ) before the inflater is garbage-collected, even if you forget to invoke it explicitly:

```
protected void finalize( )
```

## An example

Example 10-2 presents a simple program that inflates files named on the command line. First, an Inflater object, inf, is created. A file input stream named fin is opened to each file. At the same time, a file output stream named fout is opened to an output file with the same name minus the three-letter extension *.dfl*. The program then enters a loop in which it tries to read 1024-byte chunks of data from fin, though care is taken not to assume that 1024 bytes are actually read. Any data that is successfully read is passed to the inflater's setInput( ) method. This data is repeatedly inflated and written onto the output stream until the inflater indicates that it needs more input. The process then repeats itself until the end of the input stream is reached and the inflater's finished( ) method returns true. At this point, the program breaks out of the read( ) loop and moves on to the next file.

*Example 10-2. The DirectInflater*

```
import java.io.*;
import java.util.zip.*;

public class DirectInflater {

  public static void main(String[] args) {

    Inflater inf = new Inflater();
    byte[] input = new byte[1024];
    byte[] output = new byte[1024];

    for (int i = 0; i < args.length; i++) {

      try {
        if (!args[i].endsWith(DirectDeflater.DEFLATE_SUFFIX)) {
          System.err.println(args[i] + " does not look like a deflated file");
          continue;
        }
        FileInputStream fin = new FileInputStream(args[i]);
        FileOutputStream fout = new FileOutputStream(args[i].substring(0,
         args[i].length() - DirectDeflater.DEFLATE_SUFFIX.length()));

        while (true) { // Read and inflate the data.

          // Fill the input array.
          int numRead = fin.read(input);
          if (numRead != -1) { // End of stream, finish inflating.
            inf.setInput(input, 0, numRead);
          } // end if
          // Inflate the input.

          int numDecompressed = 0;
          while ((numDecompressed = inf.inflate(output, 0, output.length))
           != 0) {
            fout.write(output, 0, numDecompressed);
          }
          // At this point inflate() has returned 0.
```

*Example 10-2. The DirectInflater (continued)*

```
      // Let's find out why.
      if (inf.finished()) { // all done
        break;
      }
      else if (inf.needsDictionary()) { // We don't handle dictionaries.
        System.err.println("Dictionary required! bailing...");
        break;
      }
      else if (inf.needsInput()) {
        continue;
      }
    } // end while

    // Close up and get ready for the next file.
    fin.close();
    fout.flush();
    fout.close();
    inf.reset();
  } // end try
  catch (IOException ex) {System.err.println(ex);}
  catch (DataFormatException ex) {
    System.err.println(args[i] + " appears to be corrupt");
    System.err.println(ex);
  } // end catch
 }
 }
}
```

Once again, this program is more complicated than it needs to be because of the necessity of reading the input in small chunks. In Example 10-4, you'll see a much simpler program that achieves the same result via an InflaterOutputStream.

## Checking the state of an inflater

The Inflater class also provides several methods that return information about the Inflater object's state. The getAdler() method returns the Adler-32 checksum of the uncompressed data:

```
public int getAdler()
```

The getTotalIn() method returns the number of compressed bytes passed to the setInput() method:

```
public int getTotalIn()
```

The getTotalOut() method returns the total number of decompressed bytes output via inflate():

```
public int getTotalOut()
```

The getRemaining() method returns the number of compressed bytes left in the input buffer:

```
public int getRemaining()
```

# Compressing and Decompressing Streams

The `Inflater` and `Deflater` classes are a little raw. It would be more convenient to write uncompressed data onto an output stream and have the stream compress, without worrying about the mechanics of deflation. Similarly, it would be useful to have an input stream class that could read from a compressed file but return the uncompressed data. Java, in fact, has several classes that do exactly this. The `java.util.zip.DeflaterOutputStream` class is a filter stream that compresses the data it receives in deflated format before writing it out to the underlying stream. The `java.util.zip.InflaterInputStream` class inflates deflated data before passing it to the reading program. `java.util.zip.GZIPInputStream` and `java.util.zip.GZIPOutputStream` do the same thing except using the gzip format.

## The DeflaterOutputStream Class

`DeflaterOutputStream` is a filter stream that deflates data before writing it onto the underlying stream:

```
public class DeflaterOutputStream extends FilterOutputStream
```

Each stream uses a protected `Deflater` object called `def` to compress data stored in a protected internal buffer called `buf`:

```
protected Deflater def;
protected byte[] buf;
```

The same deflater must not be used in multiple streams at the same time, though Java takes no steps to guarantee that this won't happen.

The underlying output stream that receives the deflated data, the deflater object `def`, and the length of the byte array `buf` are all set by one of the three `DeflaterOutputStream` constructors:

```
public DeflaterOutputStream(OutputStream out, Deflater def, int bufferLength)
public DeflaterOutputStream(OutputStream out, Deflater def)
public DeflaterOutputStream(OutputStream out)
```

The underlying output stream must be specified. The buffer length defaults to 512 bytes, and the `Deflater` defaults to the default compression level, strategy, and method. Of course, the `DeflaterOutputStream` has all the usual output stream methods such as `write()`, `flush()`, and `close()`. It overrides three of these methods, but as a client programmer, you don't use them any differently than you would in any other output stream.

There's also one new method, `finish()`, which finishes writing the compressed data onto the underlying output stream but does not close the underlying stream:

```
public void finish() throws IOException
```

The close( ) method finishes writing the compressed data onto the underlying stream and then closes it:

```
public void close( ) throws IOException
```

Example 10-3 is a simple character-mode program that deflates files. Filenames are read from the command line. A file input stream is opened to each file; a file output stream is opened to that same filename with the extension *.dfl* (for deflated). Finally, the file output stream is chained to a deflater output stream, and a stream copier pours the data from the input file into the output file.

*Example 10-3. The FileDeflater program*

```java
import java.io.*;
import java.util.zip.*;

public class FileDeflater {

  public final static String DEFLATE_SUFFIX = ".dfl";

  public static void main(String[] args) {

    for (int i = 0; i < args.length; i++) {
      try {
        FileInputStream fin = new FileInputStream(args[i]);
        FileOutputStream fout = new FileOutputStream(args[i] + DEFLATE_SUFFIX);
        DeflaterOutputStream dos = new DeflaterOutputStream(fout);
        for (int c = fin.read(); c != -1; c = fin.read()) {
            dos.write(c);
        }
        dos.close( );
        fin.close( );
      }
      catch (IOException ex) {
        System.err.println(ex);
      }
    }
  }
}
```

This program is a lot simpler than Example 10-1, even though the two programs do the same thing. In general, a DeflaterOutputStream is preferable to a raw Deflater object for reasons of simplicity and legibility, especially if you want the default strategy, algorithm, and compression level. However, using the Deflater class directly does give you more control over the strategy, algorithm, and compression level. You can get the best of both worlds by passing a custom-configured Deflater object as the second argument to the DeflaterOutputStream( ) constructor.

# The InflaterInputStream Class

The `InflaterInputStream` class is a filter stream that inflates data while reading it from the underlying stream.

```
public class InflaterInputStream extends FilterInputStream
```

Each inflater input stream uses a protected `Inflater` object called `inf` to decompress data that is stored in a protected internal byte array called `buf`. There's also a protected `int` field called `len` that (unreliably) stores the number of bytes currently in the buffer, as opposed to storing the length of the buffer itself.

```
protected Inflater inf;
protected byte[] buf;
protected int len;
```

The same `Inflater` object must not be used in multiple streams at the same time.

The underlying input stream from which deflated data is read, the `Inflater` object `inf`, and the length of the byte array `buf` are all set by one of the three `InflaterInputStream( )` constructors:

```
public InflaterInputStream(InputStream in, Inflater inf, int bufferLength)
public InflaterInputStream(InputStream in, Inflater inf)
public InflaterInputStream(InputStream in)
```

The underlying input stream must be specified, but the buffer length defaults to 512 bytes and the `Inflater` defaults to an inflater for deflated streams (as opposed to zipped or gzipped streams). Of course, the `InflaterInputStream` has all the usual input stream methods such as `read( )`, `available( )`, and `close( )`. It overrides the following three methods:

```
public int  read( ) throws IOException
public int  read(byte[] data, int offset, int length) throws IOException
public long skip(long n) throws IOException
```

For the most part, you use these the same way you'd use any `read( )` or `skip( )` method. However, it's occasionally useful to know that the read method throws a new subclass of `IOException`—`java.util.zip.ZipException`—if the data doesn't adhere to the expected format. You should also know that `read( )`, `skip( )`, and all other input stream methods count the uncompressed bytes, not the compressed raw bytes that were actually read.

Example 10-4 is a simple character-mode program that inflates files. Filenames are read from the command line. A file input stream is opened from each file that ends in *.dfl*, and this stream is chained to an inflater input stream. A file output stream is opened to that same file minus the *.dfl* extension. Finally, a stream copier pours the data from the input file through the inflating stream into the output file.

*Example 10-4. The FileInflater program*

```
import java.io.*;
import java.util.zip.*;

public class FileInflater {

  public static void main(String[] args) {

    for (int i = 0; i < args.length; i++) {
      if (args[i].toLowerCase().endsWith(FileDeflater.DEFLATE_SUFFIX)) {
        try {
          FileInputStream fin = new FileInputStream(args[i]);
          InflaterInputStream iis = new InflaterInputStream(fin);
          FileOutputStream fout = new FileOutputStream(
           args[i].substring(0, args[i].length()-4));
          for (int c = iis.read(); c != -1; c = iis.read()) {
            fout.write(c);
          }
          fout.close();
        }
        catch (IOException ex) {
          System.err.println(ex);
        }
      }
      else {
        System.err.println(args[i] + " does not appear to be a deflated file.");
      }
    }
  }
}
```

## The GZIPOutputStream Class

Although zip files deflate their entries, raw deflated files are uncommon. More common are gzipped files. These are deflated files with some additional header information attached. The header specifies a checksum for the contents, the name of the compressed file, the time the file was last modified, and other information. The `java.util.zip.GZIPOutputStream` class is a subclass of `DeflaterOutputStream` that understands when and how to write this extra information to the output stream.

```
public class GZIPOutputStream extends DeflaterOutputStream
```

`GZIPOutputStream` has two constructors. Since `GZIPOutputStream` is a filter stream, both constructors take an underlying output stream as an argument. The second constructor also allows you to specify a buffer size. (The first uses a default buffer size of 512 bytes.)

```
public GZIPOutputStream(OutputStream out) throws IOException
public GZIPOutputStream(OutputStream out, int size) throws IOException
```

Data is written onto a gzip output stream as onto any other stream, typically with the `write()` methods. However, some of the data may be temporarily stored in the input buffer until more data is available. At that point, the data is compressed and written onto the underlying output stream. Therefore, when you are finished writing the data that you want to be compressed onto the stream, you should call finish( ):

```
public void finish( ) throws IOException
```

This writes all remaining data in the buffer onto the underlying output stream. It then writes a trailer containing a CRC value and the number of uncompressed bytes stored in the file onto the stream. This trailer is part of the gzip format specification that's not part of a raw deflated file. If you're through with the underlying stream as well as the gzip output stream, call close( ) instead of finish( ). If the stream hasn't yet been finished, close( ) finishes it, then closes the underlying output stream. From this point on, data may not be written to that stream.

```
public void close( ) throws IOException
```

Example 10-5 is a simple command-line program that reads a list of files from the command line and gzips each one. A file input stream reads each file. A file output stream chained to a gzip output stream writes each output file. The gzipped files have the same name as the input files plus the suffix *.gz*.

*Example 10-5. The GZipper*

```java
import java.io.*;
import java.util.zip.*;

public class GZipper {

  public final static String GZIP_SUFFIX = ".gz";

  public static void main(String[] args) {

    for (int i = 0; i < args.length; i++) {
      try {
        InputStream fin = new FileInputStream(args[i]);
        OutputStream fout = new FileOutputStream(args[i] + GZIP_SUFFIX);
        GZIPOutputStream gzout = new GZIPOutputStream(fout);
        for (int c = fin.read(); c != -1; c = fin.read()) {
          gzout.write(c);
        }
        gzout.close( );
      }
      catch (IOException ex) {
        System.err.println(ex);
      }
    }
  }
}
```

If this looks similar to Example 10-3, that's because it is. All that has changed is the compression format (gzip instead of deflate) and the compressed file suffix. However, since *gzip* and *gunzip* are available on virtually all operating systems—unlike raw deflate—you can test this code by unzipping the files it produces with the Free Software Foundation's (FSF) *gunzip* or some other program that handles gzipped files.

## The GZIPInputStream Class

The `java.util.zip.GZIPInputStream` class is a subclass of `InflaterInputStream` that provides a very simple interface for decompressing gzipped data:

```
public class GZIPInputStream extends InflaterInputStream
```

This class has two constructors:

```
public GZIPInputStream(InputStream in) throws IOException
public GZIPInputStream(InputStream in, int bufferLength) throws IOException
```

Since this is a filter stream, both constructors take an underlying input stream as an argument. The second constructor also accepts a length for the buffer into which the compressed data will be read. Otherwise, `GZIPInputStream` has the usual methods of an input stream: `read( )`, `skip( )`, `close( )`, `mark( )`, `reset( )`, and others. Marking and resetting are not supported. `read( )` and `close( )` are overridden:

```
public int read(byte[] data, int offset, int length) throws IOException
public void close( ) throws IOException
```

These methods work exactly like the superclass methods they override. The only thing you need to be aware of is that the `read( )` method blocks until sufficient data is available in the buffer to allow decompression.

Example 10-6 shows how easy it is to decompress gzipped data with `GZIPInputStream`. The `main( )` method reads a series of filenames from the command line. A `FileInputStream` object is created for each file and a `GZIPInputStream` is chained to that. The data is read from the file, and the decompressed data is written into a new file with the same name minus the *.gz* suffix. (A more robust implementation would handle the case where the suffix is not *.gz*.) You can test this program with files gzipped by Example 10-5 and with files gzipped by the FSF's *gzip* program.

*Example 10-6. The GUnzipper*

```
import java.io.*;
import java.util.zip.*;

public class GUnzipper {

  public static void main(String[] args) {

    for (int i = 0; i < args.length; i++) {
      if (args[i].toLowerCase( ).endsWith(GZipper.GZIP_SUFFIX)) {
        try {
          FileInputStream fin = new FileInputStream(args[i]);
          GZIPInputStream gzin = new GZIPInputStream(fin);
          FileOutputStream fout = new FileOutputStream(
```

*Example 10-6. The GUnzipper (continued)*

```
            args[i].substring(0, args[i].length( )-3));
          for (int c = gzin.read(); c != -1; c = gzin.read( )) {
            fout.write(c);
          }
          fout.close( );
        }
        catch (IOException ex) {System.err.println(ex);}
      }
      else {
        System.err.println(args[i] + " does not appear to be a gzipped file.");
      }
    }
  }
}
```

## Expanding Output Streams and Compressing Input Streams

You may have noticed that the compression stream classes are not fully symmetrical. You can expand the data being read from an input stream, and you can compress data being written to an output stream, but no classes compress data being read from an input stream or expand data being written to an output stream. Such classes aren't commonly needed. It's possible that you might want to read compressed data from a file and write uncompressed data onto the network, but as long as there are an input stream and an output stream, you can always put the compressor on the output stream or the decompressor on the input stream. In either case, the compressor and decompressor fall between the two underlying streams, so how they're chained doesn't really matter. Alternatively, you may have some reason to work with compressed data in memory; for example, your application might find it more efficient to store large chunks of text in compressed form. In this case, a byte array output stream chained to a deflater output stream will do the trick.

# Zip Files

Gzip and deflate are compression formats. Zip is both a compression and an archive format. This means that a single zip file may contain more than one uncompressed file, along with information about the names, permissions, creation and modification dates, and other information about each file in the archive. This makes reading and writing zip archives somewhat more complex and somewhat less amenable to a stream metaphor than reading and writing deflated or gzipped files.

The java.util.zip.ZipFile class represents a file in the zip format. Such a file might be created by zip, PKZip, WinZip, or any of the many other zip programs. The java.util.zip.ZipEntry class represents a single file stored in such an archive.

```
public class ZipFile  extends Object implements ZipConstants
public class ZipEntry extends Object implements ZipConstants
```

The java.util.zip.ZipConstants interface that both these classes implement is a rare, nonpublic interface that contains constants useful for reading and writing zip files. Most of these constants define the positions in a zip file where particular information, like the compression method used, is found. You don't need to concern yourself with it.

The ZipFile class contains two constructors. The first takes a filename as an argument. The second takes a java.io.File object as an argument. The third takes a File object and a mode indicating whether or not the file is to be deleted. This mode should be one of the two named constants ZipFile.READ or ZipFile.DELETE. If you specify ZipFile.DELETE, the file will be deleted automatically sometime after you open it and before you close it. However, you'll still be able to read its contents until the application exits. File objects will be discussed in Chapter 17. For now, I'll just use the constructor that accepts a filename. Functionally, these constructors are similar.

```
public ZipFile(String filename) throws ZipException, IOException
public ZipFile(File file) throws ZipException, IOException
public ZipFile(File file, int mode) throws IOException
```

ZipException is a subclass of IOException that indicates the data in the zip file doesn't fit the zip format. In this case, the zip exception's message will contain more details, like "invalid END header signature" or "cannot have more than one drive." While these may be useful to a zip expert, in general they indicate that the file is corrupted, and there's not much that can be done about it.

```
public class ZipException extends IOException
```

Both constructors attempt to open the specified file for random access. If the file is opened successfully with no exceptions, the entries( ) method will return a list of all the files in the archive:

```
public Enumeration entries( )
```

The return value is a java.util.Enumeration object containing one java.util.zip.ZipEntry object for each file in the archive. In Java 5, this method's signature has been genericized to make that a tad more obvious:

```
public Enumeration<? extends ZipEntry> entries( )
```

Example 10-7 lists the entries in a zip file specified on the command line. The toString( ) method is used implicitly to provide the name for each zip entry in the list.

*Example 10-7. ZipLister*

```
import java.util.*;
import java.util.zip.*;
import java.io.*;
```

*Example 10-7. ZipLister (continued)*

```
public class ZipLister {

  public static void main(String[] args) throws IOException {
    ZipFile zf = new ZipFile(args[0]);
    Enumeration e = zf.entries();
    while (e.hasMoreElements()) {
      System.out.println(e.nextElement());
    }
  }
}
```

Here are the first few lines that result from running this program on the *classes.jar* file (JAR files are just zip files that contain manifests) from the JDK:

```
$ java ZipLister /usr/local/java/lib/classes.jar
META-INF/
META-INF/MANIFEST.MF
com/
com/sun/
com/sun/tools/
com/sun/tools/javac/
com/sun/tools/javac/Main.class
com/sun/tools/javac/v8/
com/sun/tools/javac/v8/CommandLine.class
com/sun/tools/javac/v8/util/
com/sun/tools/javac/v8/util/ListBuffer$Enumerator.class
com/sun/tools/javac/v8/util/ListBuffer.class
...
```

To get a single entry in the zip file rather than a list of the entire contents, pass the name of the entry to the getEntry( ) method:

```
public ZipEntry getEntry(String name)
```

Of course, this requires you to know the name of the entry in advance. The name is simply the path and filename, such as *java/io/ObjectInputValidation.class*. For example, to retrieve the zip entry for *java/io/ObjectInputValidation.class* from the ZipFile zf, you might write:

```
ZipEntry ze = zf.getEntry("java/io/ObjectInputValidation.class");
```

You can also get the name with the getName( ) method of the ZipEntry class, discussed later in this chapter. This method, however, requires you to have a ZipEntry object already, so there's a little chicken-and-egg problem here.

Most of the time, you'll want more than the names of the files in the archive. You can get the actual contents of the zip entry using getInputStream( ):

```
public InputStream getInputStream(ZipEntry ze) throws IOException
```

This returns an input stream from which you can read the uncompressed contents of the zip entry (file). Example 10-8 is a simple unzip program that uses this input stream to unpack a zip archive named on the command line.

*Example 10-8. Unzipper*

```java
import java.util.*;
import java.util.zip.*;
import java.io.*;

public class Unzipper {

  public static void main(String[] args) throws IOException {
    ZipFile zf = new ZipFile(args[0]);
    Enumeration e = zf.entries();
    while (e.hasMoreElements()) {
      ZipEntry ze = (ZipEntry) e.nextElement();
      System.out.println("Unzipping " + ze.getName());
      FileOutputStream fout = new FileOutputStream(ze.getName());
      InputStream in = zf.getInputStream(ze);
      for (int c = in.read(); c != -1; c = in.read()) {
        fout.write(c);
      }
      in.close();
      fout.close();
    }
  }
}
```

This is not an ideal unzip program. For one thing, it blindly overwrites any files that already exist with the same name in the current directory. Before creating a new file, it should check to see if one exists and, if it does, ask whether the user wants to overwrite it. Furthermore, it can unzip files only into existing directories. If the archive contains a file in a directory that does not exist, a FileNotFoundException is thrown. Both problems are completely fixable, but fixing them requires the java.io.File class. You'll learn about this in Chapter 17.

Finally, two utility methods in java.util.zip.ZipFile relate to the "File" part of ZipFile rather than the "Zip" part:

```java
public String getName()
public void    close() throws IOException
```

The getName() method returns the full path to the file—for example, */usr/local/java/lib/classes.jar*. The close() method closes the zip file. Even after a file is closed, you can still get an entry or an input stream because the entries are read and stored in memory when the ZipFile object is first constructed. However, you cannot get the actual data associated with the entry. Attempts to do so will throw a NullPointerException.

## Zip Entries

The java.util.zip.ZipEntry class represents a file stored in a zip archive. A ZipEntry object contains information about the file but not the contents of the file. Most ZipEntry objects are created by non-Java tools and retrieved from zip files using the getEntry() or entries() methods of the ZipFile class. However, if you're writing your own program to write zip files using the `ZipOutputStream` class, you'll need to create new `ZipEntry` objects with this constructor:

```
public ZipEntry(String name)
```

Normally, the `name` argument is the name of the file that's being placed in the archive. It should not be null, or a `NullPointerException` will be thrown. It is also required to be less than 65,536 bytes long (which is plenty long for a filename).

There's also a copy constructor that copies the name, comment, modification time, CRC checksum, size, compressed size, method, comment, and, indeed, everything except the actual data of the file from an existing `ZipEntry` object:

```
public ZipEntry(ZipEntry e)
```

Nine methods return information about a specific entry in a zip file:

```
public String  getName( )
public long    getTime( )
public long    getSize( )
public long    getCompressedSize( )
public long    getCrc( )
public int     getMethod( )
public byte[]  getExtra( )
public String  getComment( )
public boolean isDirectory( )
```

The name is simply the relative path and filename stored in the archive, such as *com/sun/tools/javac/v8/CommandLine.class* or *java/awt/Dialog.class*. The time is the last time this entry was modified. It is given as a `long`, counting the number of milliseconds since midnight, January 1, 1970, Greenwich Mean Time. (This is not how the time is stored in the zip file, but Java converts the time before returning it.) −1 indicates that the modification time is not specified. The CRC is a 32-bit cyclic redundancy code for the data that's used to determine whether or not the file is corrupt. If no CRC is included, getCRC( ) returns −1.

The size is the original, uncompressed length of the data in bytes. The compressed size is the length of the compressed data in bytes. The getSize( ) and getCompressedSize( ) methods both return −1 if the size isn't known.

getMethod( ) tells you whether or not the data is compressed; it returns 0 if the data is uncompressed, 8 if it's compressed using the deflation format, and −1 if the compression format is unknown. 0 and 8 are the mnemonic constants `ZipEntry.STORED` and `ZipEntry.DEFLATED`.

Each entry may contain an arbitrary amount of extra data. If so, this data is returned in a byte array by the getExtra( ) method. Similarly, each entry may contain an optional string comment. If it does, the getComment( ) method returns it; if it doesn't, getComment( ) returns null. Finally, the isDirectory( ) method returns true if the entry is a directory and false if it isn't.

Example 10-9 is an improved ZipLister that prints information about the files in a zip archive.

*Example 10-9. FancyZipLister*

```java
import java.util.*;
import java.util.zip.*;
import java.io.*;

public class FancyZipLister {

  public static void main(String[] args) {

    for (int i = 0; i < args.length; i++) {
      try {
        ZipFile zf = new ZipFile(args[i]);
        Enumeration e = zf.entries();
        while (e.hasMoreElements()) {
          ZipEntry ze = (ZipEntry) e.nextElement();
          String name = ze.getName();
          Date lastModified = new Date(ze.getTime());
          long uncompressedSize = ze.getSize();
          long compressedSize = ze.getCompressedSize();
          long crc = ze.getCrc();
          int method = ze.getMethod();
          String comment = ze.getComment();

          if (method == ZipEntry.STORED) {
            System.out.println(name + " was stored at " + lastModified);
            System.out.println("with a size of  " + uncompressedSize
              + " bytes");
          }
          else if (method == ZipEntry.DEFLATED) {
            System.out.println(name + " was deflated at " + lastModified);
            System.out.println("from  " + uncompressedSize + " bytes to "
             + compressedSize + " bytes, a savings of "
             + (100.0 - 100.0*compressedSize/uncompressedSize) + "%");
          }
          else {
            System.out.println(name
              + " was compressed using an unrecognized method at "
              + lastModified);
            System.out.println("from  " + uncompressedSize + " bytes to "
             + compressedSize + " bytes, a savings of "
             + (100.0 - 100.0*compressedSize/uncompressedSize) + "%");
          }
          System.out.println("Its CRC is " + crc);
          if (comment != null && !comment.equals("")) {
            System.out.println(comment);
          }
          if (ze.isDirectory()) {
            System.out.println(name + " is a directory");
          }
```

*Example 10-9. FancyZipLister (continued)*

```
        System.out.println( );
      }
    }
    catch (IOException ex) {System.err.println(ex);}
  }
 }
}
```

Typical output looks like this:

```
$ java FancyZipLister temp.zip

test.txt was deflated at Wed Jun 11 15:57:32 EDT 1997
from  187 bytes to 98 bytes, a savings of 52.406417112299465%
Its CRC is 1981281836

ticktock.txt was deflated at Wed Jun 11 10:42:02 EDT 1997
from  1480 bytes to 405 bytes, a savings of 27.364864864864863%
Its CRC is 4103395328
```

There are also six corresponding set methods, which are used to attach information to each entry you store in a zip archive. However, most of the time it's enough to let the ZipEntry class calculate these for you:

```
public void setTime(long time)
public void setSize(long size)
public void setCrc(long crc)
public void setMethod(int method)
public void setExtra(byte[] extra)
public void setComment(String comment)
```

## The ZipOutputStream Class

The java.util.zip.ZipOutputStream class subclasses DeflaterOutputStream and writes compressed data in the zip format. ZipOutputStream implements the nonpublic java.util.zip.ZipConstants interface.

```
public class ZipOutputStream  extends DeflaterOutputStream
                       implements ZipConstants
```

Java supports two zip formats, uncompressed and compressed. These are slightly less well known as *stored* and *deflated*. They correspond to the mnemonic constants ZipOutputStream.STORED and ZipOutputStream.DEFLATED:

```
public static final int STORED = ZipEntry.STORED;
public static final int DEFLATED = ZipEntry.DEFLATED;
```

Deflated files are compressed by a Deflater object using the deflation method. Stored files are copied byte for byte into the archive without any compression. This is the right format for files that are already compressed but still need to go into the archive, such as a GIF image or an MPEG movie.

Because zip is not just a compression format like deflation or gzip but an archival format, a single zip file often contains multiple zip entries, each of which contains a deflated or stored file. Furthermore, the zip file contains a header with metainformation about the archive itself, such as the location of the entries in the archive. Therefore, it's not possible to write raw, compressed data onto the output stream. Instead, zip entries must be created for each successive file (or other sequence of data), and data must be written into the entries. The sequence of steps you must follow to write data onto a zip output stream is:

1. Construct a ZipOutputStream object from an underlying stream, most often a file output stream.
2. Set the comment for the zip file (optional).
3. Set the default compression level and method (optional).
4. Construct a ZipEntry object.
5. Set the metainformation for the zip entry.
6. Put the zip entry in the archive.
7. Write the entry's data onto the output stream.
8. Close the zip entry (optional).
9. Repeat steps 4 through 8 for each entry you want to store in the archive.
10. Finish the zip output stream.
11. Close the zip output stream.

Steps 4 and 8, the creation and closing of zip entries in the archive, are new. You won't find anything like them in other stream classes, but they are necessary. Attempts to write data onto a zip output stream using only the regular write( ), flush( ), and close( ) methods are doomed to failure.

### Constructing and initializing the ZipOutputStream

There is a single ZipOutputStream( ) constructor that takes as an argument the underlying stream to which data will be written:

```
public ZipOutputStream(OutputStream out)
```

For example:

```
FileOutputStream fout = new FileOutputStream("data.zip");
ZipOutputStream  zout = new ZipOutputStream(fout);
```

### Set the comment for the zip file

After the zip output stream has been constructed (in fact, at any point before the zip output stream is finished), you can add a single comment to the zip file with the setComment( ) method:

```
public void setComment(String comment)
```

The comment is an arbitrary ASCII string comment of up to 65,535 bytes. For example:

```
zout.setComment("Archive created by Zipper 1.0");
```

All high-order Unicode bytes are discarded before the comment is written onto the zip output stream. Attempts to attach a comment longer than 65,535 characters throw IllegalArgumentExceptions. Each zip output stream can have only one comment (though individual entries may have their own comments too). Resetting the comment erases the previous comment.

### Set the default compression level and method

Next, you may wish to set the default compression method with setMethod( ):

```
public void setMethod(int method)
```

You can change the default compression method from stored to deflated or deflated to stored. This default method is used only when the zip entry itself does not specify a compression method. The initial value is ZipOutputStream.DEFLATED (compressed); the alternative is ZipOutputStream.STORED (uncompressed). An IllegalArgumentException is thrown if an unrecognized compression method is specified. You can call this method again at any time before the zip output stream is finished. This sets the default compression method for all subsequent entries in the zip output stream. For example:

```
zout.setMethod(ZipOutputStream.STORED);
```

You can change the default compression level with setLevel( ) at any time before the zip output stream is finished:

```
public void setLevel(int level)
```

For example:

```
zout.setLevel(9);
```

As with the default method, the zip output stream's default level is only used when the zip entry itself does not specify a compression level. The initial value is Deflater. DEFAULT_COMPRESSION. Valid levels range from 0 (no compression) to 9 (high compression); an IllegalArgumentException is thrown if a compression level outside that range is requested. You can call setLevel( ) again at any time before the zip output stream is finished to set the default compression level for all subsequent entries in the zip output stream.

### Construct a ZipEntry object and put it in the archive

Data is written into the zip output stream in separate zip entries represented by ZipEntry objects. A zip entry must be opened before data is written, and each zip entry must be closed before the next one is opened. The putNextEntry( ) method opens a new zip entry on the zip output stream:

```
public void putNextEntry(ZipEntry ze) throws IOException
```

If a previous zip entry is still open, it's closed automatically. The properties of the ZipEntry argument ze specify the compression level and method. If ze leaves those unspecified, the defaults set by the last calls to setLevel( ) and setMethod( ) are used. The ZipEntry object may also contain a CRC checksum, the time the file was last modified, the size of the file, a comment, and perhaps some optional data with an application-specific meaning (for instance, the resource fork of a Macintosh file). These properties are set by the setTime( ), setSize( ), setCrc( ), setComment( ), and setExtra( ) methods of the ZipEntry class. (These properties are not set by the ZipOutputStream class since they will be different for each file stored in the archive.)

### Write the entry's data onto the output stream

Data is written into the zip entry using the usual write( ) methods of any output stream. Only one write( ) method is overridden in ZipOutputStream:

```
public void write(byte[] data, int offset, int length) throws IOException
```

### Close the zip entry

Finally, you may want to close the zip entry to prevent any further data from being written to it. For this, call the closeEntry( ) method:

```
public void closeEntry( ) throws IOException
```

If an entry is still open when putNextEntry( ) is called or when you finish the zip output stream, this method will be called automatically. Thus, an explicit invocation is usually unnecessary.

### Finish the zip output stream

A zip file stores metainformation in both the header and the tail of the file. The finish( ) method writes out this tail information:

```
public void finish( ) throws IOException
```

Once a zip output stream is finished, you cannot write any more data to it. However, data may be written to the underlying stream using a separate reference to the underlying stream. In other words, finishing a stream does not close it.

### Close the zip output stream

Most of the time, you will want to close a zip output stream at the same time you finish it. ZipOutputStream overrides the close() method inherited from java.util.zip. DeflaterOutputStream.

```
public void close( ) throws IOException
```

This method finishes the zip output stream and then closes the underlying stream.

## An example

Example 10-10 uses a zip output stream chained to a file output stream to create a single zip archive from a list of files named on the command line. The name of the output zip file and the files to be stored in the archive are read from the command line. An optional -d command-line flag can set the level of compression anywhere from 0 to 9.

*Example 10-10. The Zipper program*

```java
import java.util.zip.*;
import java.io.*;

public class Zipper {

  public static void main(String[] args) throws IOException {

    if (args.length < 2) {
      System.out.println("Usage: java Zipper [-d level] name.zip"+
                          " file1 file2...");
      return;
    }

    String outputFile = args[0];
    // Default to maximum compression
    int level = 9;
    int start = 1;
    if (args[0].equals("-d")) {
      try {
        level = Integer.parseInt(args[1]);
        outputFile = args[2];
        start = 3;
      }
      catch (Exception ex) {
        System.out.println("Usage: java Zipper [-d level] name.zip"
                          + " file1 file2...");
        return;
      }
    }

    FileOutputStream fout = new FileOutputStream(outputFile);
    ZipOutputStream zout = new ZipOutputStream(fout);
    zout.setLevel(level);
    for (int i = start; i < args.length; i++) {
      ZipEntry ze = new ZipEntry(args[i]);
      FileInputStream fin = new FileInputStream(args[i]);
      try {
        System.out.println("Compressing " + args[i]);
        zout.putNextEntry(ze);
        for (int c = fin.read(); c != -1; c = fin.read()) {
          zout.write(c);
        }
      }
```

*Example 10-10. The Zipper program (continued)*

```
    finally {
      fin.close( );
    }
  }
  zout.close( );
  }
}
```

## The ZipInputStream Class

Zip input streams read data from zip archives. As with output streams, it's generally best not to read the raw data. (If you must read the raw data, you can always use a bare file input stream.) Instead, the input is first parsed into zip entries. Once you've positioned the stream on a particular zip entry, you read decompressed data from it using the normal read( ) methods. Then the entry is closed, and you open the next zip entry in the archive. This sequence of steps reads data from a zip input stream:

1. Construct a ZipInputStream object from an underlying stream.
2. Open the next zip entry in the archive.
3. Read data from the zip entry using InputStream methods such as read( ).
4. Close the zip entry (optional).
5. Repeat steps 2 through 4 as long as there are more entries (files) remaining in the archive.
6. Close the zip input stream.

Steps 2 and 4, the opening and closing of zip entries in the archive, are specific to zip streams; you won't find anything like them in other input stream classes.

You probably noticed that the ZipInputStream class provides a second way to decompress zip files. The ZipFile class approach shown in the Unzipper program of Example 10-8 is the first. ZipInputStream uses one input stream to read from successive entries. The ZipFile class uses different input stream objects for different entries. Which to use is mainly a matter of aesthetics. There's not a strong reason to prefer one approach over the other, though the ZipInputStream is somewhat more convenient in the middle of a sequence of filters.

### Construct a ZipInputStream

There is a single ZipInputStream( ) constructor that takes as an argument the underlying input stream:

```
public ZipInputStream(InputStream in)
```

For example:

```
FileInputStream fin = new FileInputStream("data.zip");
ZipInputStream zin = new ZipInputStream(fin);
```

No further initialization or parameter setting are needed. A zip input stream can read from a file regardless of the compression method or level used.

### Open the next zip entry

A zip input stream reads zip entries in the order in which they appear in the file. You do not need to read each entry in its entirety, however. Instead, you can open an entry, close it without reading it, read the next entry, and repeat until you come to the entry you want. The getNextEntry( ) method opens the next entry in the zip input stream:

```
public ZipEntry getNextEntry( ) throws IOException
```

If the underlying stream throws an IOException, it's passed along by this method. If the stream data doesn't represent a valid zip file, a ZipException is thrown.

### Reading from a ZipInputStream

Once the entry is open, you can read from it using the regular read( ), skip( ), and available( ) methods of any input stream. (Zip input streams do not support marking and resetting.) Only two of these are overridden:

```
public int read(byte[] data, int offset, int length) throws IOException
public long skip(long n) throws IOException
```

The read( ) method reads and the skip( ) method skips the decompressed bytes of data.

### Close the zip entry

When you reach the end of a zip entry, or when you've read as much data as you're interested in, you may call closeEntry( ) to close the zip entry and prepare to read the next one:

```
public void closeEntry( ) throws IOException
```

Explicitly closing the entry is optional. If you don't close an entry, it will be closed automatically when you open the next entry or close the stream.

These three steps—open the entry, read from the entry, close the entry—may be repeated as many times as there are entries in the zip input stream.

### Close the ZipInputStream

When you are finished with the stream, you can close it using the close( ) method:

```
public void close( ) throws IOException
```

As usual for filter streams, this method also closes the underlying stream. Unlike zip output streams, zip input streams do not absolutely have to be finished or closed when you're through with them, but it's polite to do so.

## An example

Example 10-11 is an alternative unzipper that uses a `ZipInputStream` instead of a `ZipFile`. There's not really a huge advantage to using one or the other. Use whichever you find more convenient or aesthetically pleasing.

*Example 10-11. Another Unzipper*

```
import java.util.zip.*;
import java.io.*;

public class Unzipper2 {

  public static void main(String[] args) throws IOException {

    for (int i = 0; i < args.length; i++) {
      FileInputStream fin = new FileInputStream(args[i]);
      ZipInputStream zin = new ZipInputStream(fin);
      ZipEntry ze = null;
      while ((ze = zin.getNextEntry()) != null) {
        System.out.println("Unzipping " + ze.getName());
        FileOutputStream fout = new FileOutputStream(ze.getName());
        for (int c = zin.read(); c != -1; c = zin.read()) {
          fout.write(c);
        }
        zin.closeEntry();
        fout.close();
      }
      zin.close();
    }
  }
}
```

# Checksums

Compressed files are especially susceptible to corruption. While changing a bit from 0 to 1 or vice versa in a text file generally affects only a single character, changing a single bit in a compressed file often makes the entire file unreadable. Therefore, it's customary to store a checksum with the compressed file so that the recipient can verify that the file is intact. The zip format does this automatically, but you may wish to use manual checksums in other circumstances as well.

There are many different checksum schemes. A particularly simple example adds a parity bit to the data, typically 1 if the number of 1 bits is odd, 0 if the number of 1 bits is even. This checksum can be calculated by summing up the number of 1 bits and taking the remainder when that sum is divided by two. However, this scheme isn't very robust. It can detect single-bit errors, but in the face of bursts of errors, as often occur in transmissions over modems and other noisy connections, there's a 50-50 chance that corrupt data will be reported as correct.

Better checksum schemes use more bits. For example, a 16-bit checksum could sum up the number of 1 bits and take the remainder modulo 65,536. This means that in the face of completely random data, there's only 1 in 65,536 chances of corrupt data being reported as correct. This chance drops exponentially as the number of bits in the checksum increases. More mathematically sophisticated schemes can reduce the likelihood of a false positive even further.

The java.util.zip.Checksum interface defines four methods for calculating a checksum for a sequence of bytes. Implementations of this interface provide specific checksum algorithms.

```
public abstract void update(int b)
public abstract void update(byte[] data, int offset, int length)
public abstract long getValue( )
public abstract void reset( )
```

The update( ) methods calculate the initial checksum and update the checksum as more bytes are added to the sequence. As bytes increase, the checksum changes. For example, using the parity checksum algorithm described earlier, if the byte 255 (binary 11111111) were added to the sequence, the checksum would not change because an even number of 1 bits had been added. If the byte 7 (binary 00000111) were added to the sequence, the checksum's value would flip (from 1 to 0 or 0 to 1) because an odd number of ones had been added to the sequence.

The getValue( ) method returns the current value of the checksum. The reset( ) method returns the checksum to its initial value. Example 10-12 shows about the simplest checksum class imaginable—one that implements the parity algorithm described here.

*Example 10-12. The parity checksum*

```java
import java.util.zip.*;

public class ParityChecksum implements Checksum {

  private long checksum = 0;

  public void update(int b) {
    int numOneBits = 0;
    for (int i = 1; i < 256; i *= 2) {
      if ((b & i) != 0) numOneBits++;
    }
    checksum = (checksum + numOneBits) % 2;
  }

  public void update(byte data[], int offset, int length) {
    for (int i = offset; i < offset+length; i++) {
      this.update(data[i]);
    }
  }
}
```

*Example 10-12. The parity checksum (continued)*

```
  public long getValue( ) {
    return checksum;
  }

  public void reset( ) {
    checksum = 0;
  }
}
```

The java.util.zip package provides two concrete implementations of the Checksum interface, CRC32 and Adler32. Both produce 32-bit checksums. The Adler-32 algorithm is not quite as reliable as CRC-32 but can be computed much faster. Both of these classes have a single no-argument constructor:

```
    public CRC32( )
    public Adler32( )
```

They share the same five methods, four implementing the methods of the Checksum interface and one additional update( ) method that reads an entire byte array:

```
    public void update(int b)
    public void update(byte[] data, int offset, int length)
    public void update(byte[] data)
    public void reset( )
    public long getValue( )
```

Example 10-13, FileSummer, is a simple program that calculates and prints a CRC-32 checksum for any file. However, it's structured such that the static getCRC32( ) method can calculate a CRC-32 checksum for any stream.

*Example 10-13. FileSummer*

```
import java.io.*;
import java.util.zip.*;

public class FileSummer {

  public static void main(String[] args) throws IOException {
    FileInputStream fin = new FileInputStream(args[0]);
    System.out.println(args[0] + ":\t" + getCRC32(fin));
    fin.close( );
  }

  public static long getCRC32(InputStream in) throws IOException {

    Checksum cs = new CRC32( );

    // It would be more efficient to read chunks of data
    // at a time, but this is simpler and easier to understand.
```

*Example 10-13. FileSummer (continued)*

```
    for (int b = in.read(); b != -1; b = in.read()) {
      cs.update(b);
    }
    return cs.getValue();
  }
}
```

This isn't as useful as it might appear at first. Most of the time, you don't want to read the entire stream just to calculate a checksum. Instead, you want to look at the bytes of the stream as they go past on their way to some other, ultimate destination. You neither want to alter the bytes nor consume them. The CheckedInputStream and CheckedOutputStream filters allow you to do this.

## Checked Streams

The java.util.zip.CheckedInputStream and java.util.zip.CheckedOutputStream classes keep a checksum of the data they've read or written.

```
    public class CheckedInputStream extends FilterInputStream
    public class CheckedOutputStream extends FilterOutputStream
```

These are filter streams, so they're constructed from an underlying stream and an object that implements the Checksum interface.

```
    public CheckedInputStream(InputStream in, Checksum cksum)
    public CheckedOutputStream(OutputStream out, Checksum cksum)
```

For example:

```
    FileInputStream fin = new FileInputStream("/etc/passwd");
    Checksum cksum = new CRC32();
    CheckedInputStream cin = new CheckedInputStream(fin, cksum);
```

The CheckedInputStream and CheckedOutputStream classes have all the usual read( ), write( ), and other methods you expect in a stream class. Externally, these methods behave exactly like those in the superclass and do not require any special treatment.

Both CheckedOutputStream and CheckedInputStream have a getChecksum( ) method that returns the Checksum object for the stream. You can use this Checksum object to get the current value of the checksum for the stream.

```
    public Checksum getChecksum()
```

These methods return a reference to the actual Checksum object that's being used to calculate the checksum. It is not copied first. Thus, if a separate thread is accessing this stream, the value in the checksum may change while you're working with the Checksum object. Conversely, if you invoke one of this Checksum object's update( ) methods, it affects the value of the checksum for the stream as well.

# File Viewer, Part 4

Because of the nature of filter streams, it is relatively straightforward to add decompression services to the FileDumper program last seen in Chapter 8. Generally, you'll want to decompress a file before dumping it. Adding decompression does not require a new dump filter. Instead, it simply requires passing the file through an inflater input stream before passing it to one of the dump filters. We'll let the user choose from either gzipped or deflated files with the command-line switches –gz and –deflate. When one of these switches is seen, the appropriate inflater input stream is selected; it is an error to select both. Example 10-14, FileDumper4, demonstrates.

*Example 10-14. FileDumper4*

```java
import java.io.*;
import java.util.zip.*;
import com.elharo.io.*;

public class FileDumper4 {

  public static final int ASC = 0;
  public static final int DEC = 1;
  public static final int HEX = 2;
  public static final int SHORT = 3;
  public static final int INT = 4;
  public static final int LONG = 5;
  public static final int FLOAT = 6;
  public static final int DOUBLE = 7;

  public static void main(String[] args) {

    if (args.length < 1) {
      System.err.println("Usage: java FileDumper4 [-ahdsilfx] [-little]"+
                                  "[-gzip|-deflated] file1...");
    }

    boolean bigEndian = true;
    int firstFile = 0;
    int mode = ASC;
    boolean deflated = false;
    boolean gzipped = false;

    // Process command-line switches.
    for (firstFile = 0; firstFile < args.length; firstFile++) {
      if (!args[firstFile].startsWith("-")) break;
      if (args[firstFile].equals("-h")) mode = HEX;
      else if (args[firstFile].equals("-d")) mode = DEC;
      else if (args[firstFile].equals("-s")) mode = SHORT;
      else if (args[firstFile].equals("-i")) mode = INT;
      else if (args[firstFile].equals("-l")) mode = LONG;
      else if (args[firstFile].equals("-f")) mode = FLOAT;
      else if (args[firstFile].equals("-x")) mode = DOUBLE;
```

*Example 10-14. FileDumper4 (continued)*

```
      else if (args[firstFile].equals("-little")) bigEndian = false;
      else if (args[firstFile].equals("-deflated") && !gzipped) deflated = true;
      else if (args[firstFile].equals("-gzip") && !deflated) gzipped = true;
    }

  for (int i = firstFile; i < args.length; i++) {
    try {
      InputStream in = new FileInputStream(args[i]);
      dump(in, System.out, mode, bigEndian, deflated, gzipped);

      if (i < args.length-1) {  // more files to dump
        System.out.println( );
        System.out.println("-------------------------------------");
        System.out.println( );
      }
    }
    catch (Exception e) {
      System.err.println(e);
      e.printStackTrace( );
    }
  }
}

public static void dump(InputStream in, OutputStream out, int mode,
 boolean bigEndian, boolean deflated, boolean gzipped) throws IOException {

  // The reference variable in may point to several different objects
  // within the space of the next few lines. We can attach
  //  more filters here to do decompression, decryption, and more.
  if (deflated) {
    in = new InflaterInputStream(in);
  }
  else if (gzipped) {
    in = new GZIPInputStream(in);
  }

  if (bigEndian) {
    DataInputStream din = new DataInputStream(in);
    switch (mode) {
      case HEX:
        in = new HexFilter(in);
        break;
      case DEC:
        in = new DecimalFilter(in);
        break;
      case INT:
        in = new IntFilter(din);
        break;
      case SHORT:
        in = new ShortFilter(din);
        break;
      case LONG:
```

*Example 10-14. FileDumper4 (continued)*

```
          in = new LongFilter(din);
          break;
        case DOUBLE:
          in = new DoubleFilter(din);
          break;
        case FLOAT:
          in = new FloatFilter(din);
          break;
        default:
      }
    }
    else {
      LittleEndianInputStream lin = new LittleEndianInputStream(in);
      switch (mode) {
        case HEX:
          in = new HexFilter(in);
          break;
        case DEC:
          in = new DecimalFilter(in);
          break;
        case INT:
          in = new LEIntFilter(lin);
          break;
        case SHORT:
          in = new LEShortFilter(lin);
          break;
        case LONG:
          in = new LELongFilter(lin);
          break;
        case DOUBLE:
          in = new LEDoubleFilter(lin);
          break;
        case FLOAT:
          in = new LEFloatFilter(lin);
          break;
        default:
      }
    }
    StreamCopier.copy(in, out);
    in.close();
  }
}
```

Note how little I had to change to add support for compressed files. I simply
imported one package and added a couple of command-line switches and six lines of
code (which could easily have been two) to test for the command-line arguments and
add one more filter stream to the chain. Zip and JAR files would not be hard to support either. You'd just have to iterate through the entries in the archive and dump
each entry onto System.out. That's left as an exercise for the reader.

# CHAPTER 11

# JAR Archives

JAR archives are the standard means of packaging and distributing Java software. They are used by applets, servlets, standalone GUI applications, class libraries, Java-Beans, and more. The content in a JAR archive can be found by the class loader, regardless of the file's exact location in the filesystem, as long as it is somewhere in the classpath. This makes JARs a very convenient place to put configuration data, preferences, lookup tables, localization strings, and other noncode resources that need to be distributed with an application. In particular, storing such resources in JAR archives enables you to read them using standard streams without:

- Worrying that the user will have moved them. When the application is distributed as a single file rather than a collection of nested folders, it's harder for one file to be accidentally moved, deleted, or edited.

- Concerning yourself with the detailed filesystem conventions on the local platform. Even if the local system uses backslashes or colons as path separators or doesn't even have a filesystem (as is often the case in J2ME environments), the JAR file always uses standard Unix file and path conventions.

JAR files also improve performance, especially in applications such as applets and Java Web Start–launched applications that download their code from a server. First of all, the content in the JAR archive is compressed. More importantly, it is faster for a web browser to download one JAR file than to download all the individual files the archive contains, since only one HTTP connection is required. Storing resources in a JAR file makes your applications faster, more robust, harder to accidentally break, and easier to install.

Sun wisely decided not to define a new archive format for JAR files. Instead, they stuck with the tried-and-true zip format. However, a JAR file also contains some extra metadata you won't find in a typical zip file. To a pure zip tool, this metadata just looks like some files and directories in the archive. However, to a JAR tool, that extra metadata provides key information your programs can use.

To make the files contained in the archive available to Java, the complete path to the archive itself is added to the classpath. The JAR file is treated like a directory in the context of the classpath. This is sensible, because although the archive is a file to the filesystem, it behaves like a directory to Java. Alternately, you can just put the JAR file in the *jre/lib/ext* directory or the *jre/lib/endorsed* directory, where all class loaders will find it automatically.

## Meta-Information: Manifest Files and Signatures

Aside from the three-letter extension, the only distinction between a zip file and a JAR file is that a JAR file contains a manifest file that lists the contents of the archive as well as information about those contents. The manifest file, which provides meta-information about the contents of the archive in a particular format, is named *MANIFEST.MF* and is stored in the *META-INF* directory at the top of the archive. This directory and file are normally not present in the unarchived collection. Generally, a manifest is added as part of the archiving process.

At a minimum, a manifest file must contain this opening line:

```
Manifest-Version: 1.0
```

A manifest usually contains additional entries for some of the files in the archive. However, the manifest does not usually contain an entry for every file in the archive.

Blank lines separate entries from each other. Each entry is composed of a list of name/value pairs, one to a line. Names are separated from values by colons and whitespace, as in email headers. For example:

```
Name: com/elharo/awt/Filmstrip.class
Java-Bean: true
Last-modified: 09-07-2005
Depends-On: com/elharo/io/StreamCopier.class
Brad: Majors
Digest-Algorithms: MD5
MD5-Digest: XD4578YEEIK9MGX54RFGT7UJUI9810
```

This manifest defines an entry with the name *com/elharo/awt/Filmstrip.class*. This entry has six attributes: Java-Bean with the value true, Last-modified with the value 09-07-2005, Depends-On with the value com/elharo/io/StreamCopier.class, Brad with the value Majors, and so on. Each of these has a specific meaning in a particular context. For instance, the Java-Bean attribute with the value true means that this class is a JavaBean that can be loaded into a visual builder tool. Digest-Algorithms lists the types of message digests computed from the file, and MD5-Digest gives the value of one particular digest. Most of the attributes have application-specific meanings. Applications reading a JAR archive that don't understand a particular attribute should simply ignore it.

The files in the JAR archive may be signed using a digital signature algorithm. Different individuals may sign different files, and more than one person may sign each file. For each file that's signed, the *META-INF* directory will also contain a signature file. The signatures can be checked when a file is read from a JAR archive. If the signatures no longer match the files, an `IOException` can be thrown (though this behavior is configurable at the programmer level). If you're interested, the details are available in *Java Security* by Scott Oaks (O'Reilly).

## The jar Tool

Sun's JDK contains a simple command-line program called *jar* that packages a set of files or a directory structure into a JAR file. Its syntax is modeled after the Unix *tar* command. For instance, to verbosely compress the directory *com* into the file *javaio.jar* with the manifest file *javaio.mf*, you would type the following command line:

```
% jar cvmf javaio.mf javaio.jar com
added manifest
adding: com/ (in=0) (out=0) (stored 0%)
adding: com/elharo/ (in=0) (out=0) (stored 0%)
adding: com/elharo/io/ (in=0) (out=0) (stored 0%)
adding: com/elharo/io/StreamCopier.class (in=887) (out=552) (deflated 37%)
adding: com/elharo/io/NullOutputStream.class (in=374) (out=225) (deflated 39%)
adding: com/elharo/io/RandomInputStream.class (in=792) (out=487) (deflated 38%)
adding: com/elharo/io/NullOutputStream.java (in=263) (out=149) (deflated 43%)
adding: com/elharo/io/StreamCopier.java (in=764) (out=377) (deflated 50%)
```

This creates a file named *javaio.jar*. To extract files, change `cvmf` (*c* reate *v* erbose with *m* anifest *f* ile) to `xvf` (e*x* tract *v* erbose *f* ile). If you don't care to see each file as it's added or extracted, you can omit the `v` argument:

```
% jar xf javaio.jar
```

You can also use any other zip tool to create or unpack JAR archives. However, you'll have to include the *META-INF/MANIFEST.MF* file manually.

The JDK also includes a *jarsigner* tool that digitally signs JAR archives and verifies JAR archives signed by others using a public key system.

## The java.util.jar Package

The `java.util.jar` package, shown in Figure 11-1, contains two stream classes and another half dozen assorted classes and interfaces that assist in reading from and writing to JAR archives. As you can see, almost everything in this package is a subclass of a related class in the `java.util.zip` package. JAR files are zip files, and they are read and written just like zip files. This package mostly adds support for reading and writing manifests. You don't have to use the `java.util.jar` package at all—`java.util.zip` and the standard I/O and string classes are enough to do anything you need to do—but java.util.jar certainly does make your job easier when you need to read manifest entries.

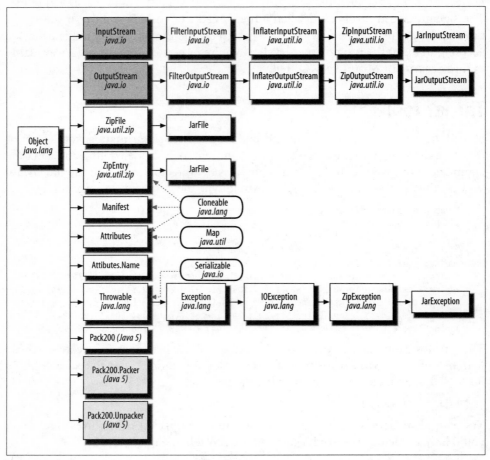

*Figure 11-1. The java.util.jar package hierarchy*

All of the classes in java.util.jar are used much like their superclasses are. For instance, to read a JAR file, follow these steps:

1. Construct a JarInputStream object from an underlying stream, most commonly a file input stream.

2. Open the next JAR entry in the archive.

3. Read data from the JAR entry using InputStream methods such as read( ).

4. Close the JAR entry (optional).

5. Repeat steps 2 through 4 as long as there are more entries (files) remaining in the archive.

6. Close the JAR input stream.

These are the same six steps you use to read a zip file, only with the java.util.zip classes replaced by their counterparts in java.util.jar.

# JarFile

The java.util.jar.JarFile class represents a file in the JAR format. It is a subclass of java.util.zip.ZipFile, and JarFile objects are almost exactly like ZipFile objects.

```
public class JarFile extends ZipFile
```

The JarFile class has five constructors:

```
public JarFile(String filename) throws IOException
public JarFile(String filename, boolean verify) throws IOException
public JarFile(String filename, boolean verify, int mode) throws IOException
public JarFile(File file) throws IOException
public JarFile(File file, boolean verify) throws IOException
```

The first argument specifies the file to read, either by name or with a java.io.File object. The optional second argument, verify, is important only for signed JAR files. If verify is true, signatures will be checked against the file's contents; if verify is false, signatures will not be checked against the file's contents. The default is to check signatures. An IOException is thrown if an entry does not match its signature. The optional third argument, mode, should be one of the named constants ZipFile. OPEN_READ or ZipFile.OPEN_DELETE, to indicate whether the file is opened in read-only or read-and-delete mode. JAR files cannot be opened for writing.

The JarFile class is so similar in interface and behavior to java.util.zip.ZipFile that I can spare you a lot of details about most of its methods. It declares only the following five methods (though of course you shouldn't forget about the others it inherits from its superclass):

```
public ZipEntry getEntry(String name)
public Enumeration entries()
public InputStream getInputStream(ZipEntry ze) throws IOException
public JarEntry getJarEntry(String name)
public Manifest getManifest() throws IOException
```

getEntry(), entries(), and getInputStream() are used exactly as they are for zip files. getJarEntry() is used almost exactly like getEntry(), except that it's declared to return an instance of JarEntry, a subclass of ZipEntry. Some extra work takes place in these methods to read the manifest file and verify signatures, but unless the signatures don't verify (in which case an IOException is thrown), none of this is relevant to the client programmer. The one really interesting new method in this list is getManifest(), which returns an instance of the java.util.jar.Manifest class. You can use this to read the entries in the manifest file, as described in the section on the Manifest class later in this chapter.

# JarEntry

JarEntry objects represent files stored inside a JAR archive. JarEntry is a subclass of java.util.zip.ZipEntry, and JarEntry objects are almost exactly like ZipEntry objects.

```
public class JarEntry extends ZipEntry
```

JarEntry has three constructors:

```
public JarEntry(String filename)
public JarEntry(ZipEntry entry)
public JarEntry(JarEntry entry)
```

You might use the first one if you were creating a JAR file from scratch, though that's rare. The other two are mainly for Java's internal use to allow the internal state of one JarEntry object to be quickly copied to a new JarEntry object.

JarEntry does not override any methods from ZipEntry. It inherits all of ZipEntry's assorted getter and setter and utility methods. It also provides two new methods:

```
public Attributes getAttributes() throws IOException
public Certificate[] getCertificates()
```

The getAttributes() method returns the attributes for this entry as documented in the manifest file of the archive. In brief, an Attributes object is a map of the name/value pairs for the entry. This will be discussed further in the next section. The getCertificates() method returns an array of java.security.cert.Certificate objects formed from any signature files for this entry stored in the archive. These can be used to allow some classes more access to the system than they would normally get.

# Attributes

The java.util.jar.Attributes class is mostly just a concrete implementation of the java.util.Map interface from the Collections API.

```
public class Attributes implements Map, Cloneable
```

An Attributes object is a container for an entry in a manifest file. Recall that the entry is composed of name/value pairs; the keys of the map are the names and the values of the entries are the values of the map. The Attributes class is accessed almost entirely through the methods of the Map interface and has three public constructors:

```
public Attributes()
public Attributes(int size)
public Attributes(Attributes a)
```

However, these constructors are primarily for Java's internal use. Most of the time, you'll simply retrieve `Attributes` objects from the `getAttributes()` method of `JarEntry` or the `getAttributes()` and `getMainAttributes()` methods of `Manifest`.

The `Attributes` class implements all the usual `Map` methods:

```
public Object      get(Object name)
public Object      put(Object name, Object value)
public Object      remove(Object name)
public boolean     containsValue(Object value)
public boolean     containsKey(Object name)
public void        putAll(Map attr)
public void        clear()
public int         size()
public boolean     isEmpty()
public Set         keySet()
public Collection  values()
public Set         entrySet()
public boolean     equals(Object o)
public int         hashCode()
```

The keys for this map should all be `Attributes.Name` objects. `Attributes.Name` is a public inner class called `Name` inside the `Attributes` class. However, it's simplest to just think of it as another class in `java.util.jar` with a somewhat funny name. This class has a single constructor:

```
public Attributes.Name(String name)
```

The `Attributes.Name` class represents the name half of the name/value pairs in a manifest file. Attribute names are restricted to the upper- and lowercase letters A–Z, the digits 0–9, the underscore, and the hyphen. The `Attributes.Name()` constructor checks to make sure that the name is legal and throws an `IllegalArgumentException` if it isn't.

`Attributes.Name` overrides the `equals()`, `hashCode()`, and `toString()` methods but has no other methods. It exists only to be a key in the `Attributes` map.

The `Attributes.Name` class defines some mnemonic constants that identify particular attribute names found in some kinds of JAR files. These are all `Attributes.Name` objects:

```
Attributes.Name.MANIFEST_VERSION          // "Manifest-Version"
Attributes.Name.SIGNATURE_VERSION         // "Signature-Version"
Attributes.Name.CONTENT_TYPE              // "Content-Type"
Attributes.Name.CLASS_PATH                // "Class-Path"
Attributes.Name.MAIN_CLASS                // "Main-Class"
Attributes.Name.SEALED                    // "Sealed"
Attributes.Name.IMPLEMENTATION_TITLE      // "Implementation-Title"
Attributes.Name.IMPLEMENTATION_VERSION    // "Implementation-Version"
Attributes.Name.IMPLEMENTATION_VENDOR     // "Implementation-Vendor"
Attributes.Name.IMPLEMENTATION_VENDOR_ID  // "Implementation-Vendor-Id"
Attributes.Name.IMPLEMENTATION_URL        // "Implementation-Vendor-URL"
Attributes.Name.SPECIFICATION_TITLE       // "Specification-Title"
```

```
Attributes.Name.SPECIFICATION_VERSION      // "Specification-Version"
Attributes.Name.SPECIFICATION_VENDOR       // "Specification-Vendor"
Attributes.Name.SIGNATURE_VERSION          // "Signature-Version"
Attributes.Name.EXTENSION_LIST             // "Extension-List"
Attributes.Name.EXTENSION_NAME             // "Extension-Name"
Attributes.Name.EXTENSION_INSTALLATION     // "Extension-Installation"
```

Since Attributes implements Cloneable as well as Map, it also provides a clone( ) method:

```
public Object clone( )
```

Unlike maps in general, Attributes maps contain only strings, raw strings as values, and strings embedded in Attributes.Name objects. Therefore, the Attributes class contains three extra map-like methods for getting and putting strings into the map:

```
public String putValue(String name, String value)
public String getValue(String name)
public String getValue(Attributes.Name name)
```

The last one takes an Attributes.Name object as an argument. Example 11-1 is a revised version of the FancyZipLister from Example 10-9. This program works with JAR files and prints the attributes of each entry as well as the information seen previously.

*Example 11-1. JarLister*

```java
import java.util.*;
import java.util.zip.*;
import java.util.jar.*;
import java.io.*;

public class JarLister {

  public static void main(String[] args) throws IOException {

    JarFile jf = new JarFile(args[0]);
    Enumeration e = jf.entries( );
    while (e.hasMoreElements( )) {
      JarEntry je = (JarEntry) e.nextElement( );
      String name = je.getName( );
      Date lastModified = new Date(je.getTime( ));
      long uncompressedSize = je.getSize( );
      long compressedSize = je.getCompressedSize( );
      long crc = je.getCrc( );
      int method = je.getMethod( );
      String comment = je.getComment( );

      if (method == ZipEntry.STORED) {
        System.out.println(name + " was stored at " + lastModified);
        System.out.println("with a size of  " + uncompressedSize
          + " bytes");
      }
      else if (method == ZipEntry.DEFLATED) {
```

*Example 11-1. JarLister (continued)*

```
        System.out.println(name + " was deflated at " + lastModified);
        System.out.println("from  " + uncompressedSize + " bytes to "
          + compressedSize + " bytes, a savings of "
          + (100.0 - 100.0*compressedSize/uncompressedSize) + "%");
      }
      else {
        System.out.println(name
          + " was compressed using an unrecognized method at "
          + lastModified);
        System.out.println("from  " + uncompressedSize + " bytes to "
          + compressedSize + " bytes, a savings of "
          + (100.0 - 100.0*compressedSize/uncompressedSize) + "%");
      }
      System.out.println("Its CRC is " + crc);
      if (comment != null && !comment.equals("")) {
        System.out.println(comment);
      }
      if (je.isDirectory()) {
        System.out.println(name + " is a directory");
      }
      Attributes a = je.getAttributes();
      if (a != null) {
        Object[] nameValuePairs = a.entrySet().toArray();
        for (int j = 0; j < nameValuePairs.length; j++) {
          System.out.println(nameValuePairs[j]);
        }
      }
      System.out.println();
    }
  }
}
```

# Manifest

What the java.util.jar classes add to the superclasses in java.util.zip is the ability to read the attributes of each JAR entry as well as the manifest for the entire JAR archive. Recall that a JAR archive should have exactly one manifest file. That manifest file has entries that apply to the entire file as well as entries for some (though perhaps not all) of the files stored in the archive. Although physically the manifest file belongs to the entire archive, logically parts of it belong to different entries in the archive. The java.util.jar.Manifest class represents this manifest file.

```
public class Manifest extends Object implements Cloneable
```

It has methods to get the entries and attributes of a manifest, to write the manifest onto an output stream, or to read entries from an input stream, as well as an assortment of utility methods. The Manifest class has three constructors:

```
public Manifest()
public Manifest(InputStream in) throws IOException
public Manifest(Manifest manifest)
```

The first constructor creates an empty manifest (one with no entries), the second reads the manifest from the given stream, and the third copies the manifest from the Manifest object passed as an argument. However, all three are mostly for the internal use of Java. Instead, client programmers use the getManifest( ) method of JarFile to retrieve the Manifest object for the manifest file in a particular archive. For example:

```
JarFile jf = new JarFile("classes.jar");
Manifest m = jf.getManifest( );
```

The Manifest class has three methods that return a map of the entries in the manifest. getEntries( ) returns a Map in which the keys are the entry names and the values are the Attributes objects for the entry:

```
public Map getEntries( )
```

Java 5 genericizes this method to specify that the keys are strings and the values are attributes:

```
public Map<String,Attributes> getEntries( )
```

The getMainAttributes( ) method returns an Attributes object representing the attributes in the manifest file that apply to the file as a whole rather than to any individual entry in the file, such as Manifest-Version:

```
public Attributes getMainAttributes( )
```

The getAttributes( ) method returns an Attributes object containing the name/value pairs of the named entry. The Name attribute is not included in this list:

```
public Attributes getAttributes(String entryName)
```

The clear( ) method (which client programmers have little reason to call) removes all entries and attributes from the manifest so that it can be reused:

```
public void clear( )
```

The Manifest class also contains methods to read a Manifest object from an input stream and write one onto an output stream. These methods are mostly for Java's private use:

```
public void write(OutputStream out) throws IOException
public void read(InputStream in) throws IOException
```

The write( ) method is particularly useless, since there's no good way to create a Manifest object and add attributes to it from within Java. I suppose you could write a manifest file on a byte array output stream, create a byte array input stream from the output stream's byte array, and read it back in, but that's really a kludge. Much more commonly, you'll simply work with Manifest objects returned by getManifest( ).

# JarInputStream

JarInputStream is a subclass of ZipInputStream that reads data from JAR archives.

```
public class JarInputStream extends ZipInputStream
```

Two constructors chain the JAR input stream to an underlying input stream:

```
public JarInputStream(InputStream in) throws IOException
public JarInputStream(InputStream in, boolean verify) throws IOException
```

By default, any signatures present in the JAR archive will be verified, and an IOException will be thrown if verification fails. However, you can turn off this behavior by passing false as the second argument to the constructor. For example:

```
FileInputStream fin = new FileInputStream("javaio.jar");
JarInputStream jin = new JarInputStream(fin, false);
```

When the JarInputStream object is constructed, the manifest, if present, is read from the stream and stored inside the class as a Manifest object. You do not get an opportunity to read the manifest from the stream yourself. However, you can retrieve the Manifest object with the getManifest( ) method:

```
public Manifest getManifest( )
```

Otherwise, a JAR input stream is used almost exactly like a zip input stream. You position the stream on a particular entry in the file and read data from it using the normal read( ) methods. Any necessary decompression is performed transparently. When you've finished reading an entry, you close it and position the stream on the next entry. Two methods, getNextEntry( ) and read( ), are overridden so that verification of signatures can be performed. A getNextJarEntry( ) method that returns a JarEntry instead of a ZipEntry is also available. This method can be used in place of getNextEntry( ), if you like:

```
public ZipEntry getNextEntry( ) throws IOException
public int read(byte[] data, int offset, int length) throws IOException
public JarEntry getNextJarEntry( ) throws IOException
```

# JarOutputStream

JarOutputStream is a subclass of ZipOutputStream.

```
public class JarOutputStream extends ZipOutputStream
```

You can specify a manifest for the archive in the constructor, but this is optional. If you don't provide a manifest, none is written onto the stream:

```
public JarOutputStream(OutputStream out, Manifest man) throws IOException
public JarOutputStream(OutputStream out) throws IOException
```

This class is even closer to ZipOutputStream than JarInputStream is to ZipInputStream. It overrides exactly one method, putNextEntry( ):

```
public void putNextEntry(ZipEntry ze) throws IOException
```

This is done in order to store the JAR magic number with each entry, but you don't need to know this. Other than the constructor invocation, you use this class exactly like you use `ZipOutputStream`.

# JarURLConnection

One of the simplest ways to get information from a JAR file is through the `java.net.JarURLConnection` class. This class represents an active connection to a JAR file, generally via either the HTTP or file protocols.

```
public abstract class JarURLConnection extends URLConnection
```

It provides methods to get the URL, name, manifest, JAR entries, attributes, and certificates associated with the JAR file and its entries. The only constructor in this class is protected. As with most `URLConnection` subclasses, you don't instantiate `JarURLConnection` directly. Instead, you create a URL object using the string form of a JAR URL and invoke its `openConnection( )` method. For example:

```
URL u = new URL(
  "jar:http://www.oreilly.com/javaio.jar!/com/elharo/io/StreamCopier.class");
URLConnection juc = u.openConnection( );
// ...
```

Notice the strange URL. A JAR URL is like a normal HTTP or file URL pointing to a JAR file, with the prefix "jar:" added to the URL's scheme (i.e., *jar:http:* or *jar:file:*). After the hostname, you place the path to the JAR file on the server. After the JAR filename, you add an exclamation point and a path to the particular entry you want within the JAR archive. For example, to refer to the file *StreamCopier.class* in the *com/elharo/io* directory of the JAR file *javaio.jar* located at *http://www.oreilly.com/*, you would use the JAR URL *jar:http://www.oreilly.com/javaio.jar!/com/elharo/io/StreamCopier.class*. If the entry is omitted, the URL refers to the JAR archive as a whole (for example, *jar:http://www.oreilly.com/javaio.jar!/*).

If you only want to read data from the connection using `getInputStream( )` from the `URLConnection` superclass, the previous code will suffice. If you want to use the methods of the `JarURLConnection` class directly, you should cast the object returned from `openConnection( )` to `JarURLConnection`. For example:

```
URL u = new URL(
  "jar:http://www.oreilly.com/javaio.jar!/com/elharo/io/StreamCopier.class");
JarURLConnection juc = (JarURLConnection) u.openConnection( );
// ...
```

Once you've done this, you can use eight methods that provide easy access to various meta-information about the JAR file and its contents. This meta-information comes from the archive's manifest or certificate files. The `getJarFileURL( )` method returns the URL of the JAR file for this connection:

```
public URL getJarFileURL( )
```

This is most useful if the URL refers to a particular entry in the file. In that instance, the URL returned by getJarFileURL( ) refers to the URL of the archive. For example:

```
URL u = new URL(
  "jar:http://www.oreilly.com/javaio.jar!/com/elharo/io/StreamCopier.class");
JarURLConnection juc = (JarURLConnection) u.openConnection();
URL base = juc.getURL();
```

The URL object base now refers to *http://www.oreilly.com/javaio.jar*.

The getEntryName( ) method returns the name of the JAR entry referred to by this JAR URL:

```
public String getEntryName()
```

It returns null if the JAR URL points to a JAR file as a whole rather than to one of the entries in the file.

The getJarFile( ) method returns an immutable JarFile object for the JAR archive referred to by this URL:

```
public abstract JarFile getJarFile() throws IOException
```

You can read the state of this object, but you cannot change it. Attempts to do so throw a java.lang.UnsupportedOperationException. This is a runtime exception, so you do not have to catch it.

The getJarEntry( ) method returns an immutable JarEntry object for the JAR entry referred to by this URL:

```
public JarEntry getJarEntry() throws IOException
```

You can read the state of this object, but you cannot change it. Attempts to do so throw a java.lang.UnsupportedOperationException .

The getManifest( ) method returns an immutable Manifest object constructed from the manifest file in the JAR archive:

```
public Manifest getManifest() throws IOException
```

It returns null if the archive doesn't have a manifest. Again, you cannot modify this Manifest object, and any attempt to do so will throw an UnsupportedOperationException.

The getAttributes( ) method returns an Attributes object representing the attributes of the JAR entry referred to by this URL:

```
public Attributes getAttributes() throws IOException
public Attributes getMainAttributes() throws IOException
```

It returns null if the URL refers to a JAR file rather than a particular entry. To get the attributes of the entire archive, use the getMainAttributes( ) method instead.

Finally, the getCertificates() method returns an array of java.security.cert. Certificate objects containing the certificates for the JAR entry referred to by this URL (if any):

```
public Certificate[] getCertificates() throws IOException
```

This method returns null if the URL refers to a JAR file rather than a JAR entry.

# Pack200

Java 5 introduced a new compression format called Pack200, designed specifically to compress JAR archives. Pack200 takes advantage of detailed knowledge of the format of JAR files to achieve much better compression at a lower cost than the general-purpose deflate algorithms used by zip, gzip, and the like. For example, every Java *.class* file begins with the 4-byte sequence 0xCAFEBABE (in hexadecimal). If you know that every *.class* file begins with these four bytes, you don't actually need to include them. You can strip them out when compressing and add them back in when decompressing, automatically saving four bytes per file in the archive. The algorithm has a lot of little Java-specific tricks like this. Pack200 won't compress *War and Peace* as well as zip, but it will compress *.class* files three to four times smaller than zip will.

The Pack200 format first reorganizes the archive to make it more suitable for compression, for instance by merging and sorting the constant pools in the different classes in the archive. It then throws away some details that zip would normally preserve but that aren't important to a JAR (Unix file permissions, for instance). Next, it compresses this carefully prepared archive with the deflate algorithm so that it can still be uncompressed with existing tools. Compared to a regular zip compression, a Pack200 compression is lossy; you don't get the same bytes out of it that went in. However, all the changes are changes that don't matter in the context of a JAR archive.

 There is one problem. Converting an archive into Pack200 format tends to break digital signatures, because it reorganizes the files stored in the archive (and the contents of those files) to enable greater compression. To digitally sign a Pack200 archive, you should first *normalize* it:

1. Compress it with Pack200.
2. Decompress it with Pack200.
3. Sign the decompressed archive.
4. Compress it again with Pack200.

Of course, use the same options for each compression and decompression. You may sometimes also need to set the SEGMENT_LIMIT property to -1.

The JDK includes two tools that compress and decompress JARs in the Pack200 format, called, simply enough, *pack200* and *unpack200*. These tools are customarily used to statically compress documents on a web server. If a browser indicates willingness to accept this format by including an Accept-encoding: pack200-gzip field in the HTTP header, the server will send it the *.pack.gz* form of the file rather than the original. While it would be possible for the server to compress these files on the fly, Pack200 compression normally takes more time than it would take to send the uncompressed file. Precompression with the *pack200* tool is preferable.

The Pack200 format is also available to your programs through the Pack200 class in the java.util.jar package:

```
public abstract class Pack200 extends Object
```

The Pack200 class itself doesn't do anything except provide instances of its inner Packer and Unpacker interfaces that actually compress and decompress files. These are returned by the static newPacker( ) and newUnpacker( ) methods:

```
public static Pack200.Packer newPacker( )
public static Pack200.Unpacker newUnpacker( )
```

To convert an existing archive to Pack200 format, you pass it to the pack( ) method:

```
public void pack(JarFile in, OutputStream out) throws IOException
public void pack(JarInputStream in, OutputStream out) throws IOException
```

This packs the existing JAR file or input stream and writes it onto an OutputStream you provide. (Files are not converted in place.) Close the OutputStream when you're done, as the pack( ) method does not close it for you. You can, in fact, pack several JAR files onto the same OutputStream by repeatedly invoking pack( ) and not closing the OutputStream until you're done.

Example 11-2 is a simple program that packs an existing JAR file using Pack200. The convention is that the file is suffixed with *.pack* (or *.pack.gz* if the *.pack* file is subsequently compressed further with gzip).

*Example 11-2. Packing a JAR archive*

```
import java.io.*;
import java.util.jar.*;

public class Packer200 {

  public static void main(String[] args) {

    OutputStream out = null;
    try {
      JarFile f = new JarFile(args[0]);
      Pack200.Packer packer = Pack200.newPacker( );
      out = new FileOutputStream(args[0] + ".pack");
      packer.pack(f, out);
    }
```

*Example 11-2. Packing a JAR archive (continued)*

```
    catch (IOException ex) {
      ex.printStackTrace( );
    }
    finally {
      if (out != null) {
        try {
          out.close( );
        }
        catch (IOException ex) {
          System.err.println("Error closing file: " + ex.getMessage( ));
        }
      }
    }
  }
}
```

Provided you're using Java 5, decompression of Pack200 archives is mostly automatic. The usual JARFile and JarInputStream classes can detect that an archive was compressed with Pack200 and decompress it accordingly. However, you might need to manually convert a Pack200 archive to a regular JAR archive for use with earlier versions of Java. For this purpose, the Pack200.Unpacker interface has an unpack( ) method:

```
    public void unpack(File in, OutputStream out) throws IOException
    public void unpack(InputStream in, OutputStream out) throws IOException
```

The unpack( ) method does not close its OutputStream either, and you can also unpack several Pack200 files onto the same OutputStream by repeatedly invoking unpack( ). Close the OutputStream when you're done.

Example 11-3 is a simple program that unpacks a Pack200 file. Unlike Example 11-2, the command-line *pack200* tool bundled with the JDK tends to run a final gzip over the entire packed archive when it's done to get even more compression. Thus, if the input filename ends in *.pack.gz*, a chained GZIPInputStream decompresses the file before passing it to the unpacker.

*Example 11-3. Unpacking a JAR archive*

```
import java.io.*;
import java.util.jar.*;
import java.util.zip.GZIPInputStream;

public class Unpacker200 {

  public static void main(String[] args) {

    String inName = args[0];
    String outName;
    if (inName.endsWith(".pack.gz")) {
      outName = inName.substring(0, inName.length( )-8);
    }
```

*Example 11-3. Unpacking a JAR archive (continued)*

```
    else if (inName.endsWith(".pack")) {
      outName = inName.substring(0, inName.length( )-5);
    }
    else {
      outName = inName + ".unpacked";
    }

    JarOutputStream out = null;
    InputStream in = null;
    try {
      Pack200.Unpacker unpacker = Pack200.newUnpacker( );
      out = new JarOutputStream(new FileOutputStream(outName));
      in = new FileInputStream(inName);
      if (inName.endsWith(".gz")) in = new GZIPInputStream(in);
      unpacker.unpack(in, out);
    }
    catch (IOException ex) {
      ex.printStackTrace( );
    }
    finally {
      if (out != null) {
        try {
          out.close( );
        }
        catch (IOException ex) {
          System.err.println("Error closing file: " + ex.getMessage( ));
        }
      }
      if (in != null) {
        try {
          in.close( );
        }
        catch (IOException ex) {
          System.err.println("Error closing file: " + ex.getMessage( ));
        }
      }
    }
  }
}
```

The default options are reasonable, but for extreme tuning you may want to set additional properties. For both the packer and unpacker, this is controlled by a map of properties. This map is returned by the properties( ) method:

```
public SortedMap<String,String> properties( )
```

The map is *live*. Modifying a property or adding a property to the map returned by this method immediately affects the behavior of the corresponding Packer or Unpacker object. For example, this code fragment tells the packer not to respect the original order of the archive entries:

```
Map properties = packer.properties( );
properties.put(Packer.KEEP_FILE_ORDER, Packer.FALSE);
```

Both the names and values in this map are strings, even when the strings hold values that are semantically numbers or Booleans. For instance, `Packer.FALSE` is the string `"false"`, not `Boolean.FALSE`. The names of all the standard properties and some of the possible values are available as named constants in the `Packer` class, as follows:

`Pack200.Packer.SEGMENT_LIMIT ("pack.segment.limit")`

Memory-limited J2ME environments may not be able to load the entire archive at once. The Pack200 algorithm can split archives into multiple *segments*, each of which can be decompressed separately from the other segments, at the cost of a somewhat larger total file size. The default value is `"1000000"` (one million bytes). If the archive grows larger than this, it will be split into multiple segments. You can adjust the segment size to fit the needs of your device, generally making it smaller for devices with less memory.

Two values are special: `"0"` stores each file and class in its own segment; `"-1"` stores the complete contents in a single segment regardless of size.

`Pack200.Packer.KEEP_FILE_ORDER ("pack.keep.file.order")`

Set `Pack200.Packer.TRUE` (`"true"`) if the JAR entries cannot be reordered during packing and `Pack200.Packer.FALSE` (`"false"`) if the JAR entries can be reordered during packing. The default is `"true"`, but `"false"` should improve the compression.

`Pack200.Packer.EFFORT ("pack.effort")`

A single digit (`"0"` to `"9"`) indicating the trade-off between time and compression. `"0"` is no compression at all; `"9"` is maximum compression.

`Pack200.Packer.DEFLATE_HINT ("pack.deflate.hint")`

By default each archive entry contains a hint for the decoder indicating how it was stored. If you set this property to either `Pack200.Packer.TRUE` or `Pack200.Packer.FALSE`, individual hints will not be used for each file in the archive. Instead, the entire archive will be hinted as either using compression (true) or not (false).

`Pack200.Packer.MODIFICATION_TIME ("pack.modification.time")`

The default value, `Pack200.Packer.KEEP`, maintains the last modification time of each entry in the archive. Setting this to `Pack200.Packer.LATEST` signals the compressor to set all entries within each archive segment to the same last modification time, thereby saving a little space.

`Pack200.Packer.UNKNOWN_ATTRIBUTE ("pack.unknown.attribute")`

This property defines what to do when a *.class* file being compressed contains an unrecognized attribute. The default value, `Pack200.Packer.PASS`, logs a warning and does not attempt to compress the file. Setting this to `Pack200.Packer.STRIP` indicates that any such attributes should be removed and the remaining file should be compressed. Setting this to `Pack200.Packer.ERROR` indicates that the entire operation should fail and an exception should be thrown.

`Pack200.Packer.PASS_FILE_PFX` ("pack.pass.file.")

> All files in the archive whose paths begin with this string are not compressed. For example, setting this to "com/elharo/io/ui" would exclude all files in the com.elharo.io.ui package and its subpackages from compression. This can be a complete filename to uniquely identify a file, as in "com/elharo/io/ui/StreamedTextArea.class".
>
> To exclude multiple prefixes, just set new properties that all begin with `Pack200.Packer.PASS_FILE_PFX` ("pack.pass.file."); for example, `Pack200.Packer.PASS_FILE_PFX+1` ("pack.pass.file.1"), `Pack200.Packer.PASS_FILE_PFX+2` ("pack.pass.file.2"), and so on.

`Pack200.Packer.CLASS_ATTRIBUTE_PFX` ("pack.class.attribute.")
`Pack200.Packer.FIELD_ATTRIBUTE_PFX` ("pack.field.attribute.")
`Pack200.Packer.METHOD_ATTRIBUTE_PFX` ("pack.method.attribute.")
`Pack200.Packer.CODE_ATTRIBUTE_PFX` ("pack.code.attribute.")

> These four values are used to specify what the Pack200 algorithm does with particular attributes in Java *.class* files. Each of these can be set to `Pack200.Packer.PASS`, `Pack200.Packer.STRIP`, or `Pack200.Packer.ERROR` to indicate what should happen to a particular attribute. For example, to remove the coverage table generated for the JCOV profiler, set the `Pack200.Packer.CODE_ATTRIBUTE_PFX+"CoverageTable"` ("pack.code.attribute.CoverageTable") property to `Pack200.Packer.STRIP`.
>
> Besides the three mnemonic constants, you can also set one of these values to a string in a special language defined in the Pack200 specification that specifies precisely how each attribute is laid out in the file. This is really quite advanced and only worth it if you're trying to squeeze every last byte out of a JAR to fit it into an extremely memory-constrained environment.

`Pack200.Packer.PROGRESS` ("pack.progress")

> This read-only property indicates the approximate percentage of the data that has been compressed; i.e., it is a number between 0 and 100. If this is "-1", the operation has stalled. This property applies to unpackers as well as packers.

Nonstandard properties not in this list are mostly ignored. You can set any property you like, but if it's not in this list, it won't change anything. There are a few undocumented properties that do not have mnemonic constants. The only one I've encountered is "strip.debug"; when it's set to "true", all debugging symbols are removed from the packed JAR.

For example, this code fragment sets up a packer for maximum compression, at the possible cost of taking more time and memory to compress and decompress:

```
Pack200.Packer packer = Pack200.newPacker();
Map<String, String> p = packer.properties();
p.put(Pack200.Packer.SEGMENT_LIMIT, "-1");
p.put(Pack200.Packer.KEEP_FILE_ORDER, Pack200.Packer.FALSE);
p.put(Pack200.Packer.DEFLATE_HINT, Pack200.Packer.TRUE);
```

```
        p.put(Pack200.Packer.MODIFICATION_TIME, Pack200.Packer.LATEST);
        p.put(Pack200.Packer.UNKNOWN_ATTRIBUTE, Pack200.Packer.STRIP);
        p.put(Pack200.Packer.EFFORT, "9");
```

I'm not sure the extra effort is really worth it, though. When testing this, the default options compressed the Saxon 8 JAR archive from 2,457,114 bytes to 628,945 bytes, an impressive 74.4% reduction. Adding these options reduced the final file size to 585,837 bytes, a savings of an additional 1.7%. However, the time to compress jumped dramatically from almost instantaneous to "go get a soda" territory (if not quite all the way to "brew a pot of coffee"), and this was on quite fast hardware. It might be worth doing this if you're only compressing once and then distributing the compressed archive many thousands of times, but I wouldn't try it when compressing archives dynamically.

Both Packer and Unpacker support PropertyChangeListener if you need to monitor the state of various properties:

```
        public void addPropertyChangeListener(PropertyChangeListener listener)
        public void removePropertyChangeListener(PropertyChangeListener listener)
```

Mostly, you'll set the properties yourself, so there's little need to listen for changes. However, monitoring the PROGRESS property does allow you to keep a progress bar or other indicator up to date, so users can tell whether they've got time to make some coffee or just to grab a soda out of the fridge. For instance, Example 11-4 is a simple program that shows a progress bar while the packer is compressing a JAR.

*Example 11-4. A ProgressMonitor for packing or unpacking*

```
import java.awt.Component;
import javax.swing.ProgressMonitor;
import java.beans.*;
import java.util.jar.Pack200;

public class PackProgressMonitor extends ProgressMonitor
 implements PropertyChangeListener {

  public PackProgressMonitor(Component parent) {
    super(parent, null, "Packing", -1, 100);
  }

  public void propertyChange(PropertyChangeEvent event) {
    if (event.getPropertyName().equals(Pack200.Packer.PROGRESS)) {
      String newValue = (String) event.getNewValue();
      int value = Integer.parseInt(newValue);
      this.setProgress(value);
    }
  }
}
```

I'm not sure how useful this is. While the compression can easily take long enough for the progress bar to pop up, the packing code doesn't seem to call propertyChange( ) very frequently. In my tests it was called only three times, once at 0, once at 50, and once at 100. Still, if an operation is going to take a while, it's better to show the user some sign of progress, even if it's a less than perfectly accurate one.

# Reading Resources from JAR Files

JAR files aren't just for classes. Any other resource a program needs can be stored there as well: sounds, pictures, text files, property lists, and more. They can be read using the same input streams and output streams we've been talking about since Chapter 1. The difference is that instead of getting those streams using constructors connected to the filesystem, you ask a ClassLoader to find them for you.

For example, my XOM class library (*http://www.xom.nu*) needs a file called *characters.dat* to operate. This file is a 64K lookup table of bit flags XOM consults to test whether various characters are XML name characters, XML name start characters, and so forth. The file contains just raw binary data, not a Java class, a serialized object file, or anything else fancy like that.

This lookup table could be distributed as a separate file along with XOM's JAR archive, but then I'd have to worry about it getting moved from where XOM expected to find it. More likely, the *xom.jar* archive would get copied somewhere else but someone would forget to copy *characters.dat* at the same time. Instead, I bundle it along with the rest of XOM's classes in the *nu/xom* directory, along with all the classes in the nu.xom package. This way, when I load the lookup table, I'm reasonably certain it'll still be there.

Loading *characters.dat* requires first finding a ClassLoader. The simplest way is to ask the class that needs the data for the loader that loaded it. For example, in XOM's case, this is the Verifier class:

```
ClassLoader loader = Verifier.class.getClassLoader( );
```

Most of the time that's all you need. However, if that ClassLoader doesn't find the resource, you can ask the current thread for its loader instead:

```
loader = Thread.currentThread().getContextClassLoader( );
```

Once you have a ClassLoader in hand, the getResourceAsStream( ) method will give you an input stream that reads from that JAR entry:

```
public InputStream getResourceAsStream(String path)
```

Pass this method the path to the resource inside the JAR archive starting from the root of the JAR. For example, XOM looks for *nu/xom/characters.dat*. This requests the resource named *characters.dat* located in the *xom* subdirectory of the *nu* directory at the top level of the JAR archive.

More accurately, it looks for one such resource found in some JAR file or top-level directory somewhere in the classpath. Theoretically, there could be more than one. The loader looks through all the classpath entries until it finds one that matches the path it's looking for. It then returns an InputStream from which you can read the resource's data. Like other input streams, you don't need to worry excessively about where the stream comes from. You read this stream just like you'd read a stream from a file or a network connection. In XOM's case, the InputStream is first chained to a DataInputStream that stores the entire file in a byte array for later random access:

```
InputStream raw = loader.getResourceAsStream("nu/xom/characters.dat");
DataInputStream  in = new DataInputStream(raw);
byte[] flags = new byte[65536];
in.readFully(flags);
```

You could do other things with this stream, of course; that's just what XOM happens to need to do.

For robustness, a little error checking never hurts. After all, someone could have unzipped the JAR file and moved the pieces around, or built her own copy of XOM without using my Ant *build.xml* file and left out *characters.dat*. It's unlikely, but it has been known to happen, so XOM tests for it. If there is a problem, there's not a lot XOM can do to fix it, so it throws a RuntimeException and gives up:

```
DataInputStream in = null;
try {
  InputStream raw = loader.getResourceAsStream("nu/xom/characters.dat");
  if (raw == null) {
    throw new RuntimeException("Broken XOM installation: "
      + "could not load nu/xom/characters.dat");
  }
  in = new DataInputStream(raw);
  flags = new byte[65536];
  in.readFully(flags);
}
catch (IOException ex) {
  throw new RuntimeException("Broken XOM installation: "
   + "could not load nu/xom/characters.dat");
}
finally {
  try {
    if (in != null) in.close();
  }
  catch (IOException ex) {
    // no big deal
  }
}
```

Several other methods in ClassLoader also find data (as opposed to code) resources stored in the classpath. The getResource( ) method returns a URL for the resource (or null if the loader can't find the resource) instead of an InputStream:

```
public URL getResource(String name)
```

You can then open a stream from that URL using the usual methods of the URL class:

```
URL resource = loader.getResource("nu/xom/characters.dat");
InputStream in = resource.openStream( );
```

Normally, I prefer to use getResourceAsStream( ) and skip the intermediate URL. However, this can be useful if you need to repeatedly access the same resource, since you can create many different streams from the same URL.

If you want all copies of a resource in the classpath, rather than just the first one, getResources( ) returns an Enumeration containing URL objects for each matching resource:

```
public Enumeration getResources(String name)
```

Three static methods, getSystemResource( ), getSystemResources( ), and getSystemResourceAsStream( ), behave the same, except that they always search using the system ClassLoader:

```
public static InputStream getSystemResourceAsStream(String path)
public static URL         getSystemResource(String name)
public static Enumeration getSystemResources(String name)
```

These methods are occasionally useful in a multiclassloader environment such as a servlet container.

# CHAPTER 12

# Cryptographic Streams

This chapter discusses filter streams for cryptography. The Java core API contains two of these in the `java.security` package, `DigestInputStream` and `DigestOutputStream`. The `javax.crypto` package contains two more, `CipherInputStream` and `CipherOutputStream`. All four of these streams use an engine object to handle the filtering. `DigestInputStream` and `DigestOutputStream` use a `MessageDigest` object while `CipherInputStream` and `CipherOutputStream` use a `Cipher` object. The streams rely on the programmer to properly initialize and—in the case of the digest streams—clean up after the engines. Therefore, we'll first look at the engine classes and then at the streams built around these engines.

## Hash Functions

Sometimes it's essential to know whether data has changed. For instance, crackers invading Unix systems often replace crucial files like */etc/passwd* or */usr/ucb/cc* with their own hacked versions that enable them to regain access to the system if the original hole they entered through is plugged. Therefore, if you discover your system has been penetrated, one of the first things you need to do is reinstall any changed files. Of course, this raises the question of how you identify the changed files, especially since anybody who's capable of replacing system executables is more than capable of resetting the last-modified date of the files. You can keep an offline copy of the system files; but this is costly and difficult, especially since multiple copies need to be stored for long periods of time. If you don't discover a penetration until several months after it occurred, you may need to roll back the system files to that point in time. Recent backups are likely to have been made after the penetration occurred and thus also likely to be compromised.

As a less threatening example, suppose you want to be notified whenever a particular web page changes. It's not hard to write a robot that connects to the site at periodic intervals, downloads the page, and compares it to a previously retrieved copy for changes. However, if you need to do this for hundreds or thousands of web pages, the space to store the pages becomes prohibitive. Peer-to-peer file sharing applications such as BitTorrent have similar needs. They need to know who's sharing which files without transferring the complete files. After a file is transferred, it must be checked to make sure it wasn't corrupted in transit.

All these tasks need a way to compare files at different times without storing the files themselves. A *hash function* reads an indefinite number of sequential bytes and assigns a number to that sequence of bytes. This number is called a *hash code* or *digest*. The size of the number depends on the hash function. It is not necessarily the same size as any Java primitive data type like int or long. For instance, digests calculated with the SHA algorithm are 20-byte numbers. You can store the digests of the files, then compare the digests. The digests are generally much smaller than the files themselves.

Hash functions are also used in digital signatures. To prove that you authored a document, you first calculate the hash function for the message, then encrypt the hash code with your private key. To check your signature, the recipient of the message decrypts the hash code with your public key and compares it to a new hash code they calculate for the document with the same hash function. If the two codes match, then only someone who knew your private key could have signed the message. Although you could simply encrypt the entire message with your private key rather than a hash code, public key algorithms are rather slow, and encrypting a 20-byte hash code is much faster than encrypting even a short email message. In Java, digital signatures are implemented through the java.security.Signature class. I won't talk much about that class in this book, but it is dependent on the MessageDigest classes I will discuss.

## Requirements for Hash Functions

There are better and worse hash functions. Strong hash functions make it extremely unlikely that two different documents share a hash value. Furthermore, hash functions used for cryptography must be one-way—that is, given a hash code, you should not be able to create a document with that hash code. A strong one-way hash function must meet several related criteria. These criteria include:

*Determinism*
> The same document always has the same hash code. The hash code does not depend on the time it's calculated, a random number, or anything other than the sequence of bytes in the document. Without this requirement, the same document could have different hash codes at different times, indicating that documents had changed when in fact they hadn't.

*Uniform distribution*
> Given any sample of the documents you wish to track, all hash codes are equally likely. For instance, if the hash code is a 64-bit long, even and odd numbers should be equally likely.

*Impossible to reverse engineer*

There should be no means easier than brute force to produce a document that matches a certain hash code. For instance, if I know the hash code is 9,423,456,789, I shouldn't be able to then create a file that happens to have that exact hash code.

*No collisions*

It should be difficult to find two documents that share a hash code. You cannot easily find two documents with the same hash code, regardless of what that hash code is. The previous criterion means that you can't change the document to match a hash code. This criterion says you can't change two documents to match each other.

*Sensitive dependence on initial conditions*

Small changes in a document produce large changes in its hash code. Without this requirement, somebody attempting to create a document with a given hash code could modify the document a little at a time until the hash code matched, much as you might adjust the hot and cold water faucets gradually until the water reaches a desired temperature. A hash function should act more like a faucet that can scald or freeze you after the tiniest nudge.

*Randomness*

The hash code does not say anything about the document it represents. The one-way hash function is not even partially invertible. For instance, knowing that the hash code is even should not suggest that the document being hashed contains an even number of bytes. Nor should it suggest that the document being hashed is 60% more likely to contain an even number of bytes than an odd number. While one-way hash functions need to be reproducible—that is, the same document always has the same hash code—they should otherwise be completely random. It is extremely hard, perhaps impossible, to prove that any function meets this criterion. Nonetheless, stronger functions come closer than weaker functions; and years of experience among cryptographers allow them to make reasonable guesses about what are and are not strong hash functions, even if their hunches can't be proved to a mathematical certainty.

The proper design of one-way hash functions is a well-studied field. It's easy to create weak one-way hash functions. However, it is much harder to create truly strong, reliable, one-way hash functions. Nonexperts tend to make nonobvious but serious mistakes when implementing hash functions. Therefore, this is a task that's best left to the experts. Fortunately, the Java core API contains some hash functions designed by experts that the rest of us can use without earning a PhD in applied mathematics first.

The hash codes used by the java.util.Hashtable class and returned by the hashCode( ) method of any Java object are only intended to be used as IDs for elements of a hash table, not as cryptographically strong digests. These sorts of hash codes have different requirements for utility. Most of the time, they only need to meet the first two of the six criteria, and in practice they often don't meet even those. The hashCode( ) method is a hash function but not necessarily a *one-way* hash function.

# The MessageDigest Class

The java.security.MessageDigest class is an abstract class that represents a hash code and its associated algorithm. Concrete subclasses (actually concrete subclasses of java.security.MessageDigestSPI, though the difference isn't relevant from a client's point of view) implement particular, professionally designed, well-known hash code algorithms. Thus, rather than constructing instances of this class directly, you ask the static MessageDigest.getInstance( ) factory method to provide an implementation of an algorithm with a particular name. Table 12-1 lists the standard names for several message digest algorithms. A stock installation of the JDK won't have all of these, but you can install more providers that support additional algorithms.

*Table 12-1. Message digest algorithms*

| Name | Algorithm |
| --- | --- |
| SHA-1 | Produces 20-byte digests; suitable for documents of less than 264 bits; recently compromised. |
| SHA | In Java, this is an alias for SHA-1. In other contexts, it refers to SHA-0, a compromised and withdrawn standard Java has never supported. It sometimes also refers to the whole family of Secure Hash Algorithms as defined in Secure Hash Standard, NIST FIPS 180-2 Secure Hash Standard (SHS); *http://csrc.nist.gov/publications/fips/fips180-2/fips180-2.pdf*. |
| SHA-256 | Produces 32-byte digests; suitable for documents of less than 264 bits. |
| SHA-384 | Produces 48-byte digests; suitable for documents of less than $2^{128}$ bits. |
| SHA-512 | Produces 64-byte digests; suitable for documents of less than $2^{128}$ bits. |
| MD2 | RSA Message Digest 2 as defined in RFC 1319 and RFC 1423 (RFC 1423 corrects a mistake in RFC 1319); produces 16-byte digests; suitable for use with digital signatures. |
| MD5 | RSA Message Digest 5 as defined in RFC 1321; produces 16-byte digests; quite fast on 32-bit machines. |
| RipeMD160 | RACE Integrity Primitives Evaluation Message Digest; produces 20-byte digests; designed in the open unlike the NSA-designed SHA formats. |
| Tiger | An algorithm invented by Ross Anderson and Eli Biham for efficiency on 64-bit platforms; produces 24-byte digests; used on the Gnutella file sharing network. |
| Whirlpool | An unpatented algorithm designed by Vincent Rijmen and Paulo S. L. M. Barreto; produces 64-byte digests; suitable for documents of less than $2^{256}$ bits. |

SHA-1 is a least common denominator available pretty much anywhere the MessageDigest class is. It's also available in many other non-Java software packages and used by numerous protocols including PGP, SSL, SSH, IPSec, and BitTorrent. It's also used in various proprietary systems such as the Microsoft XBox.

 The last couple of years have seen a flurry of attacks on hash functions. New, more practical attacks seem to be published every few months; and as an old NSA saying goes, "Attacks always get better; they never get worse." SHA-1, MD2, MD4, MD5, RIPEMD-160, and related algorithms are weakening by the month. New protocols and applications should use one of the more recent, more secure algorithms such as SHA-256, SHA-512, or Whirlpool. If the attacks improve, some of the older protocols that depend on SHA-1 may need to be revised or replaced as well.

## Calculating Message Digests

There are four steps to calculating a hash code for a file or other sequential set of bytes with a MessageDigest object; Figure 12-1 shows a flowchart for this process.

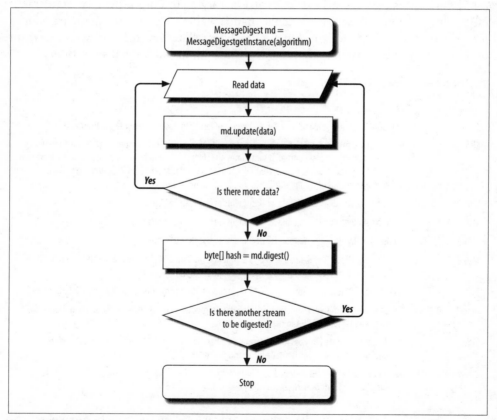

*Figure 12-1. The four steps to calculating a message digest*

1. Pass the name of the algorithm to the static `MessageDigest.getInstance()` factory method to get a new `MessageDigest` object.

2. Feed bytes into the `update()` method.

3. If more data remains, repeat step 2.

4. Invoke a `digest()` method to complete computation of the digest and return it as an array of bytes.

Once the `digest()` method has been invoked, the digest is reset. You can begin again at step 1 to calculate a new digest, but you cannot update the digest you've already created.

Example 12-1, `URLDigest`, is a simple program that uses the `MessageDigest` class to calculate the SHA-1 hash for a web page named on the command line. The `main()` method gets the input stream from a URL as discussed in Chapter 5 and passes it to `printDigest()`. The `printDigest()` method gets an SHA `MessageDigest` object named `sha` with the `getInstance()` factory method. It then repeatedly reads data from the input stream. All bytes read are passed to `sha.update()`. When the stream is exhausted, the `sha.digest()` method is called; it returns the SHA hash of the URL as an array of bytes, which is then printed.

*Example 12-1. URLDigest*

```java
import java.net.*;
import java.io.*;
import java.security.*;
import java.math.*;

public class URLDigest {

  public static void main(String[] args)
   throws IOException, NoSuchAlgorithmException {

    URL u = new URL(args[0]);
    InputStream in = u.openStream();
    MessageDigest sha = MessageDigest.getInstance("SHA");
    byte[] data = new byte[128];
    while (true) {
      int bytesRead = in.read(data);
      if (bytesRead < 0) break;
      sha.update(data, 0, bytesRead);
    }
    byte[] result = sha.digest();
    for (int i = 0; i < result.length; i++) {
      System.out.print(result[i] + " ");
    }
    System.out.println();
    System.out.println(new BigInteger(result));
  }
}
```

Here's a sample run. The digest is shown both as a list of bytes and as one very long integer. The java.math.BigInteger class converts the bytes to a decimal integer. This class was added to the core API precisely to support cryptography, where arithmetic with very large numbers is common.

```
$ java URLDigest http://www.oreilly.com/
54 9 -70 68 64 109 58 -80 -52 36 -69 51 -13 -90 40 -75 -114 78 59 76
30850243444129611042146325217902057252033804572
```

This output doesn't really mean anything to a human reader. However, if you were to run the program again, you'd get a different result if the web page had changed in some way. Even a small change that would be unlikely to be noticed by a human or an HTML parser—for instance, adding an extra space to the end of one line—would be picked up by the digest. If you only want to detect significant changes, you have to first filter the insignificant data from the stream in a predictable fashion before calculating the message digest.

## Creating Message Digests

There are no public constructors in java.security.MessageDigest. Instead, you use one of two MessageDigest.getInstance( ) factory methods to retrieve an object configured with a particular algorithm.

```
public static MessageDigest getInstance(String algorithm)
  throws NoSuchAlgorithmException
public static MessageDigest getInstance(String algorithm, String provider)
  throws NoSuchAlgorithmException, NoSuchProviderException
```

For example:

```
MessageDigest sha256 = MessageDigest.getInstance("SHA-256");
MessageDigest md2 = MessageDigest.getInstance("MD2", "Cryptix");
```

Each of these methods returns an instance of a MessageDigest subclass that's configured with the requested algorithm. These subclasses and the associated MessageDigestSPI classes that actually implement the algorithms are installed when you install a cryptographic provider.

Each provider offers a possibly redundant collection of message digest algorithms. The factory method design pattern used here allows for the possibility that a particular algorithm may be provided by different classes in different environments. For instance, the SHA-256 algorithm may be supplied by the sun.security.provider. SHA256 class on one system and by the cryptix.jce.provider.md.SHA256 class in another. Some standard algorithm names are listed in Table 12-1. If you request an algorithm that none of the installed providers can supply, getInstance( ) throws a NoSuchAlgorithmException. Most of the time, you're content to simply request an algorithm and let any provider that can fulfill your request provide it. However, if you want to specify a particular provider by name (for instance, because it has an especially fast native-code implementation of the algorithm), you can pass the provider name as the second argument to `MessageDigest.getInstance( )`. If the provider you request isn't found, `getInstance( )` throws a `NoSuchProviderException`.

## Feeding Data to the Digest

Once you have a `MessageDigest` object, you digest the data by passing bytes into one of three `update( )` methods. If you're digesting some other form of data, such as Unicode text, you must first convert that data to bytes.

```
public void update(byte input)
public void update(byte[] input)
public void update(byte[] input, int offset, int length)
public final void update(ByteBuffer input) // Java 5
```

For example:

```
byte[] data = new byte[128];
int bytesRead = in.read(data);
sha.update(data, 0, bytesRead);
```

The first `update( )` method takes a single byte as an argument. The second method takes an entire array of bytes. The third method takes the subarray of `input` beginning at `offset` and continuing for `length` bytes. All the bytes remaining in the buffer are digested.

In Java 5 and later, you can pass a `ByteBuffer` instead of an array of bytes. For the moment, you can think of a `ByteBuffer` as an object-oriented wrapper around an array that also keeps track of the current position within the array. We'll explore byte buffers in a couple of chapters. For now, the methods that operate directly on byte arrays will suffice.

You can call `update( )` repeatedly as long as you have more data to feed it. Example 12-1 passed in bytes as they were read from the input stream. The only restriction is that the bytes should not be reordered between calls to `update( )`.

## Finishing the Digest

Digest algorithms cannot finish the calculation and return the digest until the last byte is received. When you are ready to finish the calculation and receive the digest, you invoke one of three overloaded `digest( )` methods:

```
public byte[] digest( )
public byte[] digest(byte[] input)
public int digest(byte[] output, int offset, int length)
   throws DigestException
```

The first `digest( )` method simply returns the digest as an array of bytes based on the data that was already passed in through `update( )`. For example:

```
byte[] result = sha.digest( );
```

The second digest( ) method receives one last chunk of data in the input array, then returns the digest. The third digest( ) method calculates the digest and places it in the array output beginning at offset and continuing for at most length bytes, then returns the number of bytes in the digest. If the digest has more than length bytes, this variant throws a DigestException. After you've called digest( ), the MessageDigest object is reset so it can be reused to calculate a new digest.

## Reusing Digests

Creating a new message digest with MessageDigest.getInstance( ) carries some overhead. Therefore, when calculating digests for many different streams with the same algorithm, you should reset the digest and reuse it. The reset( ) method accomplishes this:

```
public void reset( )
```

In practice, you rarely call reset( ) directly because the digest( ) method invokes the reset( ) method after it's through. Once you've reset a message digest, all information you had previously passed into it through update( ) is lost.

## Comparing Digests

It's not all that hard to loop through two byte arrays to see whether or not they're equal. Nonetheless, if you do have two MessageDigest objects, the MessageDigest class does provide the simple static method MessageDigest.isEqual( ) that does the work for you. As you certainly expect, this method returns true if the two byte arrays are byte-for-byte identical or false otherwise.

```
public static boolean isEqual(byte[] digest1, byte[] digest2)
```

A little surprisingly, MessageDigest does *not* override equals( ). Therefore, md1.equals(md2) returns true if and only if md1 and md2 are both references to the same MessageDigest object.

Example 12-2 uses this method to compare the byte arrays returned by two MD5 digests, one for an original web page and one for a mirror copy of the page. The URLs to compare are passed in from the command line. It would not be hard to expand this to a general program that automatically checked a list of mirror sites to determine whether they needed to be updated.

*Example 12-2. TrueMirror*

```java
import java.net.*;
import java.io.*;
import java.security.*;

public class TrueMirror {

  public static void main(String[] args)
    throws IOException, NoSuchAlgorithmException {
```

*Example 12-2. TrueMirror (continued)*

```
    if (args.length != 2) {
      System.err.println("Usage: java TrueMirror url1 url2");
      return;
    }

    URL source = new URL(args[0]);
    URL mirror = new URL(args[1]);
    byte[] sourceDigest = getDigestFromURL(source);
    byte[] mirrorDigest = getDigestFromURL(mirror);
    if (MessageDigest.isEqual(sourceDigest, mirrorDigest)) {
      System.out.println(mirror + " is up to date");
    }
    else {
      System.out.println(mirror + " needs to be updated");
    }
  }

  public static byte[] getDigestFromURL(URL u)
   throws IOException, NoSuchAlgorithmException {

    MessageDigest md5 = MessageDigest.getInstance("MD5");
    InputStream in = u.openStream();
    byte[] data = new byte[128];
    while (true) {
      int bytesRead = in.read(data);
      if (bytesRead < 0) { // end of stream
        break;
      }
      md5.update(data, 0, bytesRead);
    }
    return md5.digest();
  }
}
```

Here's a sample run:

```
$ java TrueMirror http://www.cafeaulait.org/ http://www.ibiblio.org/javafaq/
http://www.ibiblio.org/javafaq/ is up to date
```

## Accessor Methods

The MessageDigest class contains three getter methods that return information about the digest:

```
public final Provider getProvider()
public final String   getAlgorithm()
public final int      getDigestLength()
```

The getProvider() method returns a reference to the instance of java.security. Provider that provided this MessageDigest implementation. The getAlgorithm() method returns a string containing the name of the digest algorithm as given in

Table 12-1; for example, "SHA" or "MD2". Finally, getDigestLength( ) returns the length of the digest in bytes. Digest algorithms usually have fixed lengths. For instance, SHA-1 digests are always 20 bytes long. However, this method allows for the possibility of variable length digests. It returns 0 if the length of the digest is not yet available.

## Digest Streams

The MessageDigest class isn't particularly hard to use, as I hope Example 12-1 and Example 12-2 demonstrated. It's flexible and can calculate a digest for anything that can be converted into a byte array, such as a string, an array of floating-point numbers, or the contents of a text area. Nonetheless, the input data almost always comes from streams. Therefore, the java.security package contains an input stream and an output stream class that use MessageDigest to calculate a digest for the stream as it is read or written. These are DigestInputStream and DigestOutputStream.

### DigestInputStream

The DigestInputStream class is a subclass of FilterInputStream :

```
public class DigestInputStream extends FilterInputStream
```

DigestInputStream has all the usual methods of any input stream, like read( ), skip( ), and close( ). It overrides two read( ) methods to do its filtering. Clients use these methods exactly as they use the read( ) methods of other input streams.

DigestInputStream does not change the data it reads in any way. However, as each byte or group of bytes is read, it is fed as input to a MessageDigest object stored in the class as the protected digest field:

```
protected MessageDigest digest;
```

The digest field is normally set in the constructor:

```
public DigestInputStream(InputStream stream, MessageDigest digest)
```

For example:

```
URL u = new URL("http://java.sun.com");
DigestInputStream din = new DigestInputStream(u.openStream( ),
        MessageDigest.getInstance("SHA-256"));
```

The digest is not cloned inside the class. Only a reference to it is stored. Therefore, the message digest used inside the stream should only be used by the stream. Simultaneous or interleaved use by other objects will corrupt the digest.

The setMessageDigest( ) method changes the MessageDigest object used by the stream:

```
public void setMessageDigest(MessageDigest digest)
```

You can retrieve the message digest at any time by calling getMessageDigest( ):

```
public MessageDigest getMessageDigest()
```

After you invoke getMessageDigest( ), the digest field of the stream has received all the data read by the stream up to that point. However, it has not been finished. It is still necessary to invoke digest( ) to complete the calculation. For example:

```
MessageDigest md = dis.getMessageDigest();
md.digest();
```

On rare occasions, you may only want to digest part of a stream. You can turn digesting off at any point by passing false to the on( ) method:

```
public void on(boolean on)
```

You can turn digesting back on by passing true to on( ). When digest streams are created, they are on by default.

Finally, there's a toString( ) method, which is a little unusual in input streams. It simply returns "[Digest Input Stream]" plus the string representation of the digest.

```
public String toString()
```

The body of Example 12-1 could be rewritten to make use of a DigestInputStream like this:

```
URL u = new URL(args[0]);
InputStream in = u.openStream();
MessageDigest sha = MessageDigest.getInstance("SHA");
DigestInputStream din = new DigestInputStream(in, sha);
byte[] data = new byte[128];
while (true) {
  int bytesRead = din.read(data);
  if (bytesRead < 0) break;
}
MessageDigest md = din.getMessageDigest();
byte[] result = md.digest();

for (int i = 0; i < result.length; i++) {
  System.out.println(result[i]);
}
```

The main purpose of DigestInputStream is to be one of a chain of filters. Otherwise, it doesn't really make your work any easier. You still need to construct the MessageDigest object by invoking getInstance( ), pass it to the DigestInputStream( ) constructor, retrieve the MessageDigest object from the input stream, invoke its digest( ) method, and retrieve the digest data from that object. I would prefer the DigestInputStream to completely hide the MessageDigest object. You could pass the name of the digest algorithm to the constructor as a string rather than as an actual MessageDigest object. The digest would be made available only after the stream was closed, and then only through its data, not through the actual object.

# DigestOutputStream

The DigestOutputStream class is a subclass of FilterOutputStream that maintains a digest of all the bytes it has written:

```
public class DigestOutputStream extends FilterOutputStream
```

DigestOutputStream has all the usual methods of any output stream, like write( ), flush( ), and close( ). It overrides two write( ) methods to do its filtering, but they are used as they would be for any other output stream. DigestOutputStream does not change the data it writes in any way. However, as each byte or group of bytes is written, it is fed as input to a MessageDigest object stored in the class as the protected digest field:

```
protected MessageDigest digest;
```

This field is normally set in the constructor:

```
public DigestOutputStream(OutputStream out, MessageDigest digest)
```

For example:

```
FileOutputStream fout = new FileOutputStream("data.txt");
DigestOutputStream dout = new DigestOutputStream(fout,
            MessageDigest.getInstance("SHA"));
```

The constructor does not copy the MessageDigest object; it just stores a reference to it. Therefore, the message digest stored inside the stream should only be used by the stream. Interleaved use by other objects or simultaneous use by other threads will corrupt the digest. You can change the MessageDigest object used by the stream with the setMessageDigest( ) method:

```
public void setMessageDigest(MessageDigest digest)
```

You can retrieve the message digest at any time by calling getMessageDigest( ):

```
public MessageDigest getMessageDigest( )
```

After you invoke getMessageDigest( ), the digest field contains the digest of all the data written by the stream up to that point. However, it has not been finished. It is still necessary to invoke digest( ) to complete the calculation. For example:

```
MessageDigest md = dout.getMessageDigest( );
md.digest( );
```

On rare occasions, you may want to digest only part of a stream. For instance, you might want to calculate the digest of the body of an email message while ignoring the headers. You can turn digesting off at any point by passing false to the on( ) method:

```
public void on(boolean on)
```

You can turn digesting back on by passing true to on( ). When digest output streams are created, they are on by default.

Finally, there's a toString( ) method, which is a little unusual in output streams. It simply returns "[Digest Output Stream]" plus the string representation of the digest.

```
public String toString( )
```

Example 12-3 is a FileDigest class that reads data from a specified URL and copies it into a file on the local system. As the file is written, its SHA digest is calculated. When the file is closed, the digest is printed.

*Example 12-3. FileDigest*

```
import java.net.*;
import java.io.*;
import java.security.*;

public class FileDigest {

  public static void main(String[] args)
   throws IOException, NoSuchAlgorithmException {

    if (args.length != 2) {
      System.err.println("Usage: java FileDigest url filename");
      return;
    }

    URL u = new URL(args[0]);
    FileOutputStream out = new FileOutputStream(args[1]);
    copyFileWithDigest(u.openStream( ), out);
    out.close( );
  }

  public static void copyFileWithDigest(InputStream in, OutputStream out)
   throws IOException, NoSuchAlgorithmException {

    MessageDigest sha = MessageDigest.getInstance("SHA-512");
    DigestOutputStream dout = new DigestOutputStream(out, sha);
    byte[] data = new byte[128];
    while (true) {
      int bytesRead = in.read(data);
      if (bytesRead < 0) break;
      dout.write(data, 0, bytesRead);
    }
    dout.flush( );
    byte[] result = dout.getMessageDigest().digest( );
    for (int i = 0; i < result.length; i++) {
      System.out.print(result[i] + " ");
    }
    System.out.println( );
  }
}
```

A sample run looks like this:

```
% java FileDigest http://www.oreilly.com/ oreilly.html
10 -10 103 -27 -110 3 -2 -115 8 -112 13 19 25 76 -120 31 51 116 -94 -58
```

`DigestOutputStream` is useful when you need a digest in the middle of a chain of filter streams. For instance, you could write data onto a data output stream chained to a gzip output stream chained to a file output stream. When you had finished writing the data onto the data output stream, you could calculate the digest and write that directly onto the file output stream. When the data was read back in, you could use a digest input stream chained to a data input stream to check that the file had not been corrupted in the meantime. If the digest calculated by the digest input stream matched the digest stored in the file, you'd know the data was OK.

## Encryption Basics

In this section, we begin discussing cryptography. The packages, classes, and methods discussed in this and following sections are part of the Java Cryptography Extension (JCE). As a standard extension to Java, the JCE cryptography classes live in the `javax` package rather than the `java` package. Several third parties in other countries have published their own implementations of this API. In particular, the open source implementation from the Legion of the Bouncy Castle (*http://www.bouncycastle.org/*) is worth a look.

I frankly don't trust Sun not to have inserted backdoors into its software for the use of various governments. I recommend using the third-party libraries no matter where you are if you really care about your privacy.

There are many different kinds of codes and ciphers, both for digital and nondigital data. To be precise, a code encrypts data at word or higher levels. Ciphers encrypt data at the level of letters or, in the case of digital ciphers, bytes. Most ciphers replace each byte in the original, unencrypted data, called *plaintext*, with a different byte, thus producing encrypted data, called *ciphertext*. There are many different possible algorithms for determining how plaintext is transformed into ciphertext (encryption) and how the ciphertext is transformed back into plaintext (decryption).

## Keys

All the algorithms discussed here, and included in the JCE, are key-based. A key is a sequence of bytes used to parameterize the cipher. The same algorithm encrypts the same plaintext differently when a different key is used. Decryption also requires a key. Good algorithms make it effectively impossible to decrypt ciphertext without knowing the right key.

One common attack on cryptosystems is an exhaustive search through all possible keys. As a result, one popular measure of algorithmic security is key length. Shorter keys (56 bits and less) are definitely breakable by brute force search with specialized equipment. Keys of 112 bits are considered to have the minimum key length required for reasonable security. However, remember that a reasonable key length is only a necessary condition for security. Long key length is far from a sufficient condition. Long keys do not protect a weak algorithm or implementation.

## Secret Key Versus Public Key Algorithms

There are two primary kinds of ciphers: symmetric (secret key) ciphers and asymmetric (public key) ciphers. Symmetric ciphers such as AES use the same key to encrypt and decrypt the data. Symmetric ciphers rely on the secrecy of the key for security. Anybody who knows the key can both encrypt and decrypt data.

Asymmetric ciphers, also known as public key ciphers, use different keys for encryption and decryption. This makes the problem of key exchange relatively trivial. To allow people to send you encrypted messages, you simply send them your encryption (public) key. Even if the key is intercepted, this only allows the interceptor to send you encrypted messages. It does not allow them to decode encrypted messages intended for you. Furthermore, you can digitally sign messages by encrypting either a message or a hash code of the message with your private key, which may then be decrypted with your public key. Any message that can be successfully decrypted with your public key may be presumed to have come from you because only you could have encrypted it with your private key in the first place. (Of course, if someone steals your private key, all bets are off.) The most famous public key cipher is the RSA cipher, named after its inventors, Ronald L. Rivest, Adi Shamir, and Leonard M. Adleman. RSA has the particularly nice property that either key can be used for encryption or decryption.

## Block Versus Stream Ciphers

Encryption algorithms may also be divided into block and stream ciphers. A block cipher always encrypts a fixed number of bytes with each pass. For example, DES encrypts eight-byte blocks. If the data you're encrypting is not an integral multiple of the block size, the data must be padded with extra bytes to round up to the block size. Stream ciphers, by contrast, act on each bit or byte individually in the order it appears in the stream; padding is not required.

Block ciphers can operate in a variety of modes that use various algorithms to determine how the result of the encryption of one block of data influences the encryption of subsequent blocks. This ensures that identical blocks of plaintext do not produce identical blocks of ciphertext, a weakness code breakers could exploit. To ensure that messages that start with the same plaintext (for example, many email messages or form letters) don't also start with the same ciphertext (also a weakness code breakers can exploit), these modes require a nonsecret initialization vector, generally of the same size as a block, in order to begin the encoding. Initialization vectors are not secret and are generally passed in the clear with the encrypted data.

# Key Management

Storing keys securely is a difficult problem. If the key is stored in hardware like a smartcard, it can be stolen. If the key is stored in a file on a disk, the disk can be stolen. Many basic PC protection schemes are based on OS- or driver-level operations that refuse to mount the disk without the proper password, but simply using a new OS (or driver or custom hardware) allows the key or unencrypted data to be read off the disk.

Ideally, keys should not be stored anywhere except in a human being's memory. Human beings, however, have a hard time remembering arbitrary 56-bit keys such as 0x78A53666090BCC, much less more secure 64-, 112-, or 128-bit keys. Therefore, keys humans have to remember are generally stored as a string of text called a password. Even then, the password is vulnerable to a rubber hose attack. Truly secure systems like those used to protect bank vaults require separate passwords remembered by two or more individuals.

A text password is converted into the raw bits of the key according to some well-known, generally public, hash algorithm. The simplest such algorithm is to use the bytes of the password as the key, but this weakens the security because the bits are somewhat predictable. For instance, the bits 01110001 (q) are very likely to be followed by the bits 01110101 (u). The bits 01111111 (the nonprinting delete character) are unlikely to appear at all. Because of the less than random nature of text, passwords must be longer than the corresponding keys.

To make matters worse, humans like passwords that are common words or phrases, like "secret," "password," or "sex." Therefore, one of the most common attacks on password-based systems is to attempt decryption with every word in a dictionary. To make these sorts of attacks harder, passwords are commonly "salted": combined with a random number that's also stored in the ciphertext. Salting can increase the space that a dictionary-based attack must search by several orders of magnitude.

Humans also write passwords down, especially when they need to store many different passwords for different networks, computers, and web sites. These written passwords can then be stolen. The java.security.KeyStore class is a simple, password-protected digital lockbox for keys of all sorts. Keys can be stored in the key store, and only the password for the key store needs to be remembered.

 This discussion has been necessarily brief. A lot of interesting details have been skimmed over or omitted entirely. For the more complete story, see the Crypt Cabal's Cryptography FAQ at *http://www.faqs.org/faqs/cryptography-faq/* or *Java Security* by Scott Oaks (O'Reilly).

# The Cipher Class

The `javax.crypto.Cipher` class is a concrete class that encrypts arrays of bytes. The default implementation performs no encryption, but you'll never see this. You'll only receive subclasses that implement particular algorithms.

```
public class Cipher extends Object
```

The subclasses of `Cipher` that do real encryption are supplied by providers. Different providers can provide different sets of algorithms. For instance, an authoritarian government might only allow the installation of algorithms it knows how to crack, and create a provider that provided those algorithms and only those algorithms. A corporation might want to install algorithms that allow for key recovery in the event that an employee leaves the company or forgets their password.

JDK 1.3 and earlier only include the Sun provider that supplies no encryption schemes, though it does supply several digest algorithms. The JCE (which is bundled with Java 1.4 and later) adds one more provider, SunJCE, which provides DES, triple DES (DESede), and password-based encryption (PBE). Other vendors may bundle additional providers. For instance, Apple's Java 5 VM includes an Apple-specific provider that implements DES, Triple DES, AES, Blowfish, PBE, Diffie-Hellman, MD5, and SHA1. RSA's payware BSafe Crypto-J product has a security provider that implements the RSA, DES, DESede, RC2, RC4, and RC5 cipher algorithms. The open source JCE provider from the Legion of the Bouncy Castle supports AES, Blowfish, CAST5, CAST6, DES, Triple DES, IDEA, RC2, RC5, RC6, Rijndael, Skipjack, Twofish, and Serpent, among others.

Most providers include some unique algorithms. However, providers usually also include some algorithms already supplied by other providers. At compile time, you do not know which providers will be installed at runtime. Indeed, different people running your program are likely to have different providers available, especially if you ship internationally. Therefore, rather than using constructors, the `Cipher` class relies on two static `getInstance()` factory methods that return `Cipher` objects initialized to support particular transformations:

```
public static final Cipher getInstance(String transformation)
  throws NoSuchAlgorithmException, NoSuchPaddingException
public static final Cipher getInstance(String transformation, String provider)
  throws NoSuchAlgorithmException, NoSuchProviderException,
  NoSuchPaddingException
```

The first argument, `transformation`, is a string that names the algorithm, mode, and padding scheme to be used to encrypt or decrypt the data. Examples include "DES", "PBEWithMD5AndDES", and "DES/ECB/PKCS5Padding". The optional second argument to `getInstance()`, `provider`, names the preferred provider for the requested transformation. If more than one installed provider supports the transformation, the one named in the second argument is used. Otherwise, an implementation is selected from any available provider that supports the transformation. If you request a transformation from getInstance( ) that the provider does not support, a NoSuchAlgorithmException or NoSuchPaddingException is thrown. If you request a provider that is not installed, a NoSuchProviderException is thrown.

The transformation string always includes the name of a cryptographic algorithm: for example, DES. The standard names for common algorithms are listed in Table 12-2. Not all of these algorithms are guaranteed to be available.

Sun's JDK 1.4 only bundles DES, DESede, AES, Blowfish, PBEWithMD5AndDES, and PBEWithMD5AndTripleDES. JDK 1.5 added RC2, ARCFOUR, PBEWithSHA1AndDESede, and PBEWithSHA1AndRC2_40.

*Table 12-2. JCE standard algorithm names*

| Name | Algorithm |
| --- | --- |
| AES (a.k.a. Rijndael) | The U.S. Federal government's Advanced Encryption Standard as defined by NIST in FIPS 197 and invented by Joan Daemen and Vincent Rijmen; a symmetric 128-bit block cipher with keys of length 128, 192, or 256 bits; see *http://csrc.nist.gov/publications/fips/fips197/fips-197.pdf*. There are no known practical attacks on this algorithm, but a couple of theoretical attacks have been devised, and cryptographers are nervous that it may not be as strong as initially thought. |
| DES | The U.S. Federal government's Data Encryption Standard as defined by NIST in FIPS 46-1 and 46-2; a symmetric 64-bit block cipher that uses a 56-bit key; see *http://www.itl.nist.gov/ fipspubs/fip46-2.htm*. Given the small key space, this algorithm can be broken by brute force. |
| DESede | DES encryption-*decryption*-encryption; triple DES; like DES, a 64-bit symmetric block cipher. DES encryption with one 56-bit key is followed by decryption with a different 56-bit key, which is followed by encryption with the first 56-bit key, effectively providing a 112-bit key space. (However, a known weakness in the algorithm reduces the effective strength of the key to roughly 80 bits.) This is one of the slower algorithms in use. |
| PBEWithMD5 AndDES | Password-Based Encryption as defined in RSA Laboratories, "PKCS #5: Password-Based Encryption Standard," Version 1.5, Nov. 1993; based on DES; also requires a salt; see *http:// www.rsasecurity.com/rsalabs/node.asp?id=2127*. |
| PBEWithMD5 AndTripleDES | Password-Based Encryption as defined in RSA Laboratories, "PKCS #5: Password-Based Encryption Standard," version 1.5, Nov. 1993; based on Triple DES; also requires a salt and an initialization vector; see *http://www.rsasecurity.com/rsalabs/node.asp?id=2127*. |
| PBEWithSHA1AndDESede | Password-Based Encryption using triple DES encryption and SHA1 hashing; also requires a salt and an initialization vector. |
| PBEWithMD5AndTripleDES | Password-Based Encryption using triple DES encryption and MD5 hashing; also requires a salt and an initialization vector. |
| RSA | The Rivest, Shamir, and Adleman asymmetric cipher algorithm; RSA encryption as defined in the RSA Laboratories Technical Note PKCS#1, *http://www.rsasecurity.com/rsalabs/node. asp?id=2125*. It is possible that the NSA cannot penetrate this algorithm.[a] |
| IDEA | The International Data Encryption Algorithm developed and patented by Dr. X. Lai and Professor J. Massey of the Federal Institute of Technology in Zurich, Switzerland; a symmetrical 64-bit block cipher with a 128-bit key. The patent expires in 2010 in the U.S., 2011 in Europe. |
| RC2 | A variable key-size symmetric 64-bit block cipher designed by Ron Rivest as a drop-in replacement for DES. The NSA probably doesn't have much trouble breaking this one; see IETF RFC 2268, *http://www.faqs.org/rfcs/rfc2268.html*. |

Table 12-2. JCE standard algorithm names (continued)

| Name | Algorithm |
|------|-----------|
| ARCFOUR (a.k.a. RC4) | A weak symmetric stream cipher algorithm designed by Ron Rivest used in Netscape's Secure Sockets Layer (SSL), among other products. The name "RC4" is trademarked, so this algorithm is also referred to by the untrademarked name ARCFOUR. Used (and broken) in the Wireless Encryption Protocol (WEP). |
| Blowfish | An unpatented fast, free, symmetric, variable key length (32 to 448 bits) 64-bit block cipher designed by Bruce Schneier as a drop-in replacement for DES; see *http://www.schneier.com/blowfish.html*. |
| Twofish | An unpatented free, symmetric, variable key length (128, 192 or 256 bits) 128-bit block cipher designed by Bruce Schneier; see *http://www.schneier.com/twofish.html*. |
| Skipjack | A symmetric key block encryption algorithm designed by the NSA with 80-bit keys. Several as yet impractical attacks on the algorithm have been found. Regardless of the algorithm's strength, the key length is too short to inspire confidence. |
| Serpent | A symmetric variable key length (128, 192 or 256 bits) 128-bit block cipher designed by Ross Anderson, Eli Biham, and Lars Knudsen. It is notable for its highly parallelizable design. |

[a] I have a hunch (not necessarily shared by experts in the field) that RSA and similar algorithms will be broken someday by means much less computationally intensive than brute force search. RSA's strength rests on the difficulty of factoring a large number into two large primes. However, it is not known whether such factorization is fundamentally hard or whether we just don't yet know the right factoring algorithms. It seems obvious to me that there's a lot of structure in the prime numbers that has yet to be exploited or understood by number theorists. For instance, Goldbach's conjecture and the number of twin primes are still unsolved questions. Therefore, I would not be surprised if far more efficient factorization algorithms are discovered. Any such algorithm would severely reduce the strength of encryption schemes like RSA. Furthermore, there's been an explosion of interest and research in quantum computing, following the discovery that RSA would be much more easily cracked by a quantum computer than by a traditional one. This does not seem to be the case for public key encryption schemes based on something other than prime factorization, for instance, discrete logarithms or elliptic curves.

When faced with input longer than its block size, a block cipher must divide and possibly reorder that input into blocks of the appropriate size. The algorithm for doing this is called a *mode*. A mode name may be included in the transformation string separated from the algorithm by a slash. If a mode is not selected, the provider supplies a default. Modes apply to block ciphers in general and DES in particular, though other block ciphers like Blowfish may use some of these modes as well. The named modes in the JCE are listed in Table 12-3. All of these modes are supported by the JCE, but modes are algorithm-specific. If you try to use an unsupported mode or a mode that doesn't match the algorithm, a NoSuchAlgorithmException is thrown.

Table 12-3. Block cipher modes

| Name | Mode |
|------|------|
| ECB | Electronic CodeBook Mode; the 64-bit blocks are encrypted independently of each other and may also be decrypted independently of each other, so this mode is useful when you want random access to an encrypted file but in general is less secure than other modes. It does not require an initialization vector. See "DES Modes of Operation," National Institute of Standards and Technology Federal Information Processing Standards Publication 81, December 1980; *http://www.itl.nist.gov/fipspubs/fip81.htm* (NIST FIPS PUB 81). |
| CBC | Cipher Block Chaining Mode, as defined in NIST FIPS PUB 81; best choice for encrypting files; uses an initialization vector. |

*Table 12-3. Block cipher modes (continued)*

| Name | Mode |
|------|------|
| CFB | K-bit Cipher FeedBack Mode, as defined in NIST FIPS PUB 81; best choice for real-time encryption of streaming data such as network connections where each byte must be sent immediately rather than being buffered; uses an initialization vector. |
| OFB | K-bit Output FeedBack Mode, as defined in NIST FIPS PUB 81; designed so that a 1-bit error in the ciphertext only produces a 1-bit error in the plaintext; therefore, the best choice on noisy, error-prone channels; uses an initialization vector. |
| PCBC | Propagating Cipher Block Chaining, as used in pre-Version 5 Kerberos; similar to the more secure CBC mode used in Kerberos Version 5 and later; uses an initialization vector. |

If the algorithm is a block cipher like DES, the transformation string may include a padding scheme that adds extra bytes to the input to fill out the last block. The named padding schemes are shown in Table 12-4. Algorithms that use modes must generally also specify a padding scheme.

*Table 12-4. Padding schemes*

| Name | Scheme |
|------|--------|
| NoPadding | Do not add any padding bytes. |
| ZeroByte | Pad with zeros; insecure and not recommended. |
| PKCS5Padding | RSA Laboratories, "PKCS #5: Password-Based Encryption Standard," Version 1.5, Nov. 1993; see *http://www.rsasecurity.com/rsalabs/node.asp?id=2127*. |
| PKCS7Padding | RSA Laboratories, "PKCS #7: Cryptographic Message Syntax Standard," Version 1.5, Nov. 1993; see *http://www.rsasecurity.com/rsalabs/node.asp?id=2129*. |
| WithCTS | Ciphertext Stealing; really a variant mode of Cipher Block Chaining (CBC) that does not require any padding; requires at least one full block of data to operate. |
| SSL3Padding | A slight variation of PKCS5Padding used in Secure Sockets Layer (SSL); see "SSL Protocol Version 3.0, November 18, 1996, section 5.2.3.2 (CBC block cipher)" at *http://wp.netscape.com/eng/ssl3/ssl-toc.html*. |

Encrypting data with a Cipher object takes six steps:

1. Create the key for the cipher.
2. Retrieve the transformation you want to use with the Cipher.getInstance( ) factory method.
3. Initialize the cipher by passing Cipher.ENCRYPT_MODE and the key to the init( ) method.
4. Feed data to the update( ) method.
5. While there's more data, repeat step 4.
6. Invoke doFinal( ).

Steps 1 and 2 can be reversed, as is done in the flowchart for this process shown in Figure 12-2. Decryption is almost an identical process except that you pass Cipher.DECRYPT_MODE to init( ) instead of Cipher.ENCRYPT_MODE. The same engine can both encrypt and decrypt data with a given transformation.

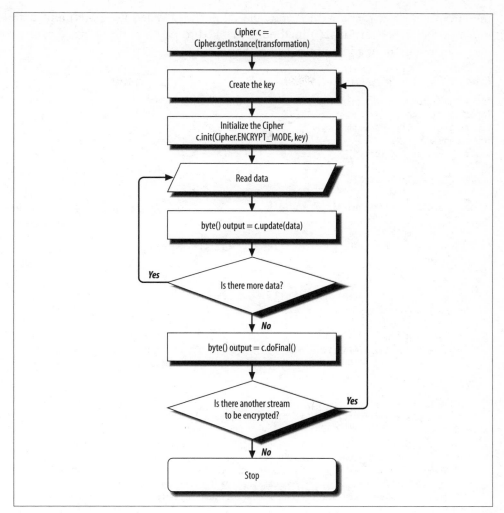

*Figure 12-2. Encrypting data*

Example 12-4 is a simple program that reads a filename and a password from the command line and encrypts the file with DES. The key is generated from the bytes of the password in a fairly predictable and insecure fashion. The cipher is initialized for encryption with the DES algorithm in CBC mode with PKCS5Padding and a random initialization vector. The initialization vector and its length are written at the start of the encrypted file so they'll be conveniently available for decryption.

Data is read from the file in 64-byte blocks. This happens to be an integral multiple of the 8-byte block size used by DES, but that's not necessary. The `Cipher` object buffers as necessary to handle nonintegral multiples of the block size. Each block of data is fed into the `update()` method to be encrypted. `update()` returns either encrypted data or `null` if it doesn't have enough data to fill out a block. If it returns the encrypted data, that's written into the output file. When no more input data remains, the cipher's doFinal( ) method is invoked to pad and flush any remaining data. Then both input and output files are closed.

*Example 12-4. FileEncryptor*

```
import java.io.*;
import java.security.*;
import java.security.spec.*;
import javax.crypto.*;
import javax.crypto.spec.*;

public class FileEncryptor {

  public static void main(String[] args) {

    if (args.length != 2) {
      System.err.println("Usage: java FileEncryptor filename password");
      return;
    }

    String filename = args[0];
    String password = args[1];

    if (password.length( ) < 8 ) {
      System.err.println("Password must be at least eight characters long");
    }

    try {
      FileInputStream fin = new FileInputStream(args[0]);
      FileOutputStream fout = new FileOutputStream(args[0] + ".des");

      // Create a key.
      byte[] desKeyData = password.getBytes( );
      DESKeySpec desKeySpec = new DESKeySpec(desKeyData);
      SecretKeyFactory keyFactory = SecretKeyFactory.getInstance("DES");
      SecretKey desKey = keyFactory.generateSecret(desKeySpec);

      // Use Data Encryption Standard.
      Cipher des = Cipher.getInstance("DES/CBC/PKCS5Padding");
      des.init(Cipher.ENCRYPT_MODE, desKey);

      // Write the initialization vector onto the output.
      byte[] iv = des.getIV( );
      DataOutputStream dout = new DataOutputStream(fout);
      dout.writeInt(iv.length);
      dout.write(iv);

      byte[] input = new byte[64];
      while (true) {
        int bytesRead = fin.read(input);
        if (bytesRead == -1) break;
        byte[] output = des.update(input, 0, bytesRead);
```

*Example 12-4. FileEncryptor (continued)*

```
      if (output != null) dout.write(output);
    }

    byte[] output = des.doFinal( );
    if (output != null) dout.write(output);
    fin.close( );
    dout.flush( );
    dout.close( );

  }
  catch (InvalidKeySpecException ex) {System.err.println(ex);}
  catch (InvalidKeyException ex) {System.err.println(ex);}
  catch (NoSuchAlgorithmException ex) {System.err.println(ex);}
  catch (NoSuchPaddingException ex) {System.err.println(ex);}
  catch (BadPaddingException ex) {System.err.println(ex);}
  catch (IllegalBlockSizeException ex) {System.err.println(ex);}
  catch (IOException ex) {System.err.println(ex);}
  }
}
```

Many different exceptions must be caught. Except for the usual IOException, they are all subclasses of java.security.GeneralSecurityException. You could save some space simply by catching that. For example:

```
      catch (GeneralSecurityException ex) {
          System.err.println(ex);
          ex.printStackTrace( );
      }
```

One exception I'll note in particular (because it threw me more than once while writing this chapter): if you should see a NoSuchAlgorithmException, it probably means you haven't properly installed a provider that supports your algorithm.

Decrypting a file is similar, as Example 12-5 shows. The name of the input and output files and the password are read from the command line. A DES key factory converts the password to a DES secret key. Both input and output files are opened in file streams, and a data input stream is chained to the input file. The main reason for this is to read the initialization vector. First, the integer size is read, and then the actual bytes of the vector. The resulting array is used to construct an IvParameterSpec object that is used along with the key to initialize the cipher. Once the cipher is initialized, the data is copied from input to output much as before.

*Example 12-5. FileDecryptor*

```
import java.io.*;
import java.security.*;
import java.security.spec.*;
import javax.crypto.*;
import javax.crypto.spec.*;

public class FileDecryptor {
```

*Example 12-5. FileDecryptor (continued)*

```java
public static void main(String[] args) {

  if (args.length != 3) {
    System.err.println("Usage: java FileDecryptor infile outfile password");
    return;
  }

  String infile = args[0];
  String outfile = args[1];
  String password = args[2];

  if (password.length( ) < 8 ) {
    System.err.println("Password must be at least eight characters long");
  }

  try {
    FileInputStream fin = new FileInputStream(infile);
    FileOutputStream fout = new FileOutputStream(outfile);

    // Create a key.
    byte[] desKeyData = password.getBytes( );
    DESKeySpec desKeySpec = new DESKeySpec(desKeyData);
    SecretKeyFactory keyFactory = SecretKeyFactory.getInstance("DES");
    SecretKey desKey = keyFactory.generateSecret(desKeySpec);

    // Read the initialization vector.
    DataInputStream din = new DataInputStream(fin);
    int ivSize = din.readInt( );
    byte[] iv = new byte[ivSize];
    din.readFully(iv);
    IvParameterSpec ivps = new IvParameterSpec(iv);

    // Use Data Encryption Standard.
    Cipher des = Cipher.getInstance("DES/CBC/PKCS5Padding");
    des.init(Cipher.DECRYPT_MODE, desKey, ivps);

    byte[] input = new byte[64];
    while (true) {
      int bytesRead = fin.read(input);
      if (bytesRead == -1) break;
      byte[] output = des.update(input, 0, bytesRead);
      if (output != null) fout.write(output);
    }

    byte[] output = des.doFinal( );
    if (output != null) fout.write(output);
    fin.close( );
    fout.flush( );
    fout.close( );
  }
  catch (GeneralSecurityException ex) {
    ex.printStackTrace( );
```

*Example 12-5. FileDecryptor (continued)*

```
    }
    catch (IOException ex) {System.err.println(ex);}
  }
}
```

Let's investigate some of the methods used in Example 12-4 and Example 12-5 in more detail.

# init( )

Before a `Cipher` object can encrypt or decrypt data, it needs four things:

- The mode to operate in (encryption or decryption; not a block cipher mode)
- A key
- Algorithm parameters, e.g., an initialization vector
- A source of randomness

The init( ) method prepares the cipher by providing these four quantities or reasonable defaults. There are six overloaded variants:

```
public final void init(int opmode, Key key) throws InvalidKeyException
public final void init(int opmode, Key key, SecureRandom random)
  throws InvalidKeyException
public final void init(int opmode, Key key, AlgorithmParameterSpec params)
  throws InvalidKeyException, InvalidAlgorithmParameterException
public final void init(int opmode, Key key, AlgorithmParameterSpec params,
  SecureRandom random) throws InvalidKeyException,
  InvalidAlgorithmParameterException
public final void init(int opmode, Key key, AlgorithmParameters params)
  throws InvalidKeyException, InvalidAlgorithmParameterException
public final void init(int opmode, Key key, AlgorithmParameters params,
  SecureRandom random) throws InvalidKeyException,
  InvalidAlgorithmParameterException
```

You can reuse a cipher object by invoking its init( ) method a second time. If you do, all previous information in the object is lost.

## Mode

The mode determines whether this cipher is used for encryption or decryption. The mode argument has two possible values, which are both mnemonic constants defined by the `Cipher` class: `Cipher.ENCRYPT_MODE` and `Cipher.DECRYPT_MODE`.

```
public static final int ENCRYPT_MODE
public static final int DECRYPT_MODE
```

## Key

The key is an instance of the `java.security.Key` interface. Symmetric ciphers like DES use the same key for both encryption and decryption. Asymmetric ciphers like

RSA use different keys for encryption or decryption. Keys generally depend on the cipher. For instance, an RSA key cannot be used to encrypt a DES file or vice versa. If the key you provide doesn't match the cipher's algorithm, an InvalidKeyException is thrown.

To create a key, you first use the bytes of the key to construct a KeySpec for the algorithm you're using. Key specs are instances of the java.security.spec.KeySpec interface. Algorithm-specific implementations in the java.security.spec package include EncodedKeySpec, X509EncodedKeySpec, KCS8EncodedKeySpec, DSAPrivateKeySpec, and DSAPublicKeySpec, RSAPrivateKeySpec, RSAPrivateCrtKeySpec, RSAMultiPrimePrivateCrtKeySpec, RSAPublicKeySpec, and X509EncodedKeySpec. Java 5 added ECPrivateKeySpec and ECPublicKeySpec for public key cryptography based on elliptic curves rather than prime factorization. The javax.crypto spec package provides a few more including DESKeySpec, DESedeKeySpec, DHPrivateKeySpec, DHPublicKeySpec, PBEKeySpec. For example, this code fragment creates a DESKeySpec object that can be used to encrypt or decrypt from a password string using the DES algorithm:

```
byte[] desKeyData = password.getBytes();
DESKeySpec desKeySpec = new DESKeySpec(desKeyData);
```

Once you've constructed a key specification from the raw bytes of the key, a key factory generates the actual key. A key factory is normally an instance of an algorithm-specific subclass of java.security.KeyFactory. It's retrieved by passing the name of the algorithm to the factory method javax.crypto.SecretKeyFactory.getInstance(). For example:

```
SecretKeyFactory keyFactory = SecretKeyFactory.getInstance("DES");
SecretKey desKey = keyFactory.generateSecret(desKeySpec);
```

Providers should supply the necessary key factories and spec classes for any algorithms they implement.

A few algorithms, most notably Blowfish, use raw bytes as a key without any further manipulations. In these cases there may not be a key factory for the algorithm. Instead, you simply use the key spec as the secret key. For example:

```
byte[] blowfishKeyData = password.getBytes();
SecretKeySpec blowfishKeySpec = new SecretKeySpec(blowfishKeyData,
                                                  "Blowfish");
Cipher blowfish = Cipher.getInstance("Blowfish/ECB/PKCS5Padding");
blowfish.init(Cipher.ENCRYPT_MODE, blowfishKeySpec);
```

Most of the examples in this book use very basic and not particularly secure passwords as keys. Stronger encryption requires more random keys. The javax.crypto.KeyGenerator class provides methods that generate random keys for any installed algorithm. For example:

```
KeyGenerator blowfishKeyGenerator = KeyGenerator.getInstance("Blowfish");
SecretKey blowfishKey = blowfishKeyGenerator.generateKey();
Cipher blowfish = Cipher.getInstance("Blowfish/ECB/PKCS5Padding");
blowfish.init(Cipher.ENCRYPT_MODE, blowfishKey);
```

Generating random keys opens up the issue of how one stores and transmits the secret keys. To my way of thinking, random key generation makes more sense in public key cryptography, where all keys that need to be transmitted can be transmitted in the clear.

### Algorithm parameters

The third possible argument to init( ) is a series of instructions for the cipher contained in an instance of the java.security.spec.AlgorithmParameterSpec interface or an instance of the java.security.AlgorithmParameters class. The AlgorithmParameterSpec interface declares no methods or constants. It's simply a marker for more specific subclasses that can provide additional, algorithm-dependent parameters for specific algorithms and modes (for instance, an initialization vector). If the algorithm parameters you provide don't fit the cipher's algorithm, an InvalidAlgorithmParameterException is thrown. The JCE provides several AlgorithmParameterSpec classes in the javax.crypto.spec package, including IVParameterSpec, which can set an initialization vector for modes that need it (CBC, CFB, and OFB), and PBEParameterSpec for password-based encryption.

### Source of randomness

The final possible argument to init( ) is a SecureRandom object. This argument is only used when in encryption mode. It is an instance of the java.security. SecureRandom class, a subclass of java.util.Random that uses a pseudo-random number algorithm based on the SHA-1 hash algorithm instead of java.util.Random's linear congruential formula. java.util.Random's random numbers aren't random enough for strong cryptography. In this book, I will simply accept the default source of randomness.

# update( )

Once the init( ) method has prepared the cipher for use, the update( ) method feeds data into it, encrypting or decrypting as it goes. This method has four overloaded variants. The first two return the encrypted or decrypted bytes:

```
public final byte[] update(byte[] input) throws IllegalStateException
public final byte[] update(byte[] input, int inputOffset, int inputLength)
    throws IllegalStateException
```

They may return null if you're using a block cipher and not enough data has been provided to fill a block. The input data to be encrypted or decrypted is passed in as an array of bytes. Optional offsets and lengths may be used to select a particular subarray to be processed. update( ) throws an IllegalStateException if the cipher has not been initialized or it has already been finished with doFinal( ). In either case, it's not prepared to accept data until init( ) is called.

The second two variants of update( ) store the output in a buffer byte array passed in as the fourth argument and return the number of bytes stored in the buffer:

```
public final int update(byte[] input, int inputOffset, int inputLength,
    byte[] output) throws IllegalStateException, ShortBufferException
public final int update(byte[] input, int inputOffset, int inputLength,
    byte[] output, int outputOffset) throws IllegalStateException,
    ShortBufferException
```

You can also provide an offset into the output array to specify where in the array data should be stored. An offset is useful when you want to repeatedly encrypt/decrypt data into the same array until the data is exhausted. You cannot, however, specify a length for the output data because it's up to the cipher to determine how many bytes of data it's willing to provide. The trick here is to make sure your output buffer is big enough to hold the processed output. Most of the time, the number of output bytes is close to the number of input bytes. However, block ciphers sometimes return fewer bytes on one call and more on the next. You can use the getOutputSize( ) method to determine an upper bound on the amount of data that will be returned if you were to pass in inputLength bytes of data:

```
public final int getOutputSize(int inputLength) throws IllegalStateException
```

If you don't do this and your output buffer is too small, update( ) throws a ShortBufferException. In this case, the cipher stores the data for the next call to update( ).

Java 5 added an update( ) method that reads from a ByteBuffer and writes into an output ByteBuffer:

```
public final int update(ByteBuffer input, ByteBuffer output)
    throws ShortBufferException, IllegalStateException,
    ReadOnlyBuffer Exception, IllegalArgumentException
```

Once you run out of data to feed to update( ), invoke doFinal( ). This signals the cipher that it should pad the data with extra bytes if necessary and encrypt or decrypt all remaining bytes.

## doFinal( )

The doFinal( ) method is responsible for reading one final array of data, wrapping that up with any data remaining in the cipher's internal buffer, adding any extra padding that might be necessary, and then returning the last chunk of encrypted or decrypted data. The simplest implementation of doFinal( ) takes no arguments and returns an array of bytes containing the encrypted or decrypted data. This is used to flush out any data that still remains in the cipher's buffer.

```
public final byte[] doFinal( )
    throws IllegalStateException, IllegalBlockSizeException, BadPaddingException
```

An IllegalStateException means that the cipher is not ready to be finished; it has not been initialized; it has been initialized but no data has been fed into it; or it has already been finished and not yet reinitialized. An `IllegalBlockSizeException` is thrown by encrypting block ciphers if no padding has been requested, and the total number of bytes fed into the cipher is not a multiple of the block size. A `BadPaddingException` is thrown by a decrypting cipher that does not find the padding it expects to see.

There are five overloaded variants of `doFinal()` that allow you to provide additional input data or to place the result in an output buffer you supply. These variants are:

```
public final int doFinal(byte[] output, int outputOffset)
 throws IllegalStateException, IllegalBlockSizeException,
 ShortBufferException, BadPaddingException
public final byte[] doFinal(byte[] input)
 throws IllegalStateException, IllegalBlockSizeException, BadPaddingException
public final byte[] doFinal(byte[] input, int inputOffset, int inputLength)
 throws IllegalStateException, IllegalBlockSizeException, BadPaddingException
public final int doFinal(byte[] input, int inputOffset, int inputLength,
 byte[] output) throws IllegalStateException, ShortBufferException,
 IllegalBlockSizeException, BadPaddingException
public final int doFinal(byte[] input, int inputOffset, int inputLength,
 byte[] output, int outputOffset) throws IllegalStateException,
 ShortBufferException, IllegalBlockSizeException, BadPaddingException
```

All of the arguments are essentially the same as they are for `update()`. `output` is a buffer where the cipher places the encrypted or decrypted data. `outputOffset` is the position in the output buffer where this data is placed. `input` is a byte array that contains the last chunk of data to be encrypted. `inputOffset` and `inputLength` select a subarray of input to be encrypted or decrypted.

## Accessor Methods

As well as the methods that actually perform the encryption, the `Cipher` class has several getter methods that provide various information about the cipher. The `getProvider()` method returns a reference to the `Provider` that's implementing this algorithm. This is an instance of a subclass of `java.security.Provider`.

```
public final Provider getProvider()
```

For block ciphers, `getBlockSize()`returns the number of bytes in a block. For non-block methods, it returns 0.

```
public final int getBlockSize()
```

The `getOutputSize()` method tells you how many bytes of output this cipher produces for a given number of bytes of input. You generally use this before calling `doFinal()` or `update()` to make sure you provide a large enough byte array for the output, given `inputLength` additional bytes of data.

```
public final int getOutputSize(int inputLen) throws IllegalStateException
```

The length returned is the maximum number of bytes that may be needed. In some cases, fewer bytes may actually be returned when doFinal() is called. An IllegalStateException is thrown if the cipher is not ready to accept more data.

The getIV() method returns a new byte array containing this cipher's initialization vector. It's useful when the system picks a random initialization vector and you need to find out what that vector is so you can pass it to the decryption program, perhaps by storing it with the encrypted data.

```
public final byte[] getIV()
```

getIV() returns null if the algorithm doesn't use initialization vectors or if the initialization vector isn't yet set.

# Cipher Streams

The Cipher class is the engine that powers encryption. Example 12-5 showed how this class could be used to encrypt and decrypt data read from a stream. The javax. crypto package also provides CipherInputStream and CipherOutputStream filter streams that use a Cipher object to encrypt or decrypt data passed through the stream. Like DigestInputStream and DigestOutputStream, they aren't a great deal of use in themselves. However, you can chain them in the middle of several other streams. For example, if you chain a GZIPOutputStream to a CipherOutputStream that is chained to a FileOutputStream, you can compress, encrypt, and write to a file, all with a single call to write(), as shown in Figure 12-3. Similarly, you might read from a URL with the input stream returned by openStream(), decrypt the data read with a CipherInputStream, check the decrypted data with a MessageDigestInputStream, and finally pass it all into an InputStreamReader for conversion from Latin-1 to Unicode. On the other side of the connection, a web server could read a file from its hard drive, write the file onto a socket with an output stream, calculate a digest with a DigestOutputStream, and encrypt the file with a CipherOutputStream.

*Figure 12-3. The CipherOutputStream in the middle of a chain of filters*

## CipherInputStream

CipherInputStream is a subclass of FilterInputStream.

```
public class CipherInputStream extends FilterInputStream
```

CipherInputStream has all the usual methods of any input stream, like read( ), skip( ), and close( ). It overrides seven of these methods to do its filtering. These methods are all invoked much as they would be for any other input stream. However, as the data is read, the stream's Cipher object either decrypts or encrypts the data. (Assuming your program wants to work with unencrypted data, as is most commonly the case, the cipher input stream will decrypt the data.)

A CipherInputStream object contains a Cipher object that's used to decrypt or encrypt all data read from the underlying stream before passing it to the eventual source. This Cipher object is set in the constructor. Like all filter stream constructors, this constructor takes another input stream as an argument:

```
public CipherInputStream(InputStream in, Cipher c)
```

The Cipher object c must be a properly initialized instance of javax.crypto.Cipher, most likely returned by Cipher.getInstance( ). This Cipher object must also have been initialized for either encryption or decryption with init( ) before being passed into the constructor. There is also a protected constructor that might be used by subclasses that want to implement their own, non-JCE-based encryption scheme:

```
protected CipherInputStream(InputStream in)
```

CipherInputStream overrides most methods declared in FilterInputStream. Each of these makes the necessary adjustments to handle encrypted data. For example, skip( ) skips the number of bytes after encryption or decryption, which is important if the ciphertext does not have the same length as the plaintext. The available( ) method also returns the number of bytes available after encryption or decryption. The markSupported( ) method returns false; you cannot mark and reset a cipher input stream, even if the underlying class supports marking and resetting. Allowing this would confuse many encryption algorithms. However, you can make a cipher input stream the underlying stream of another class like BufferedInputStream, which does support marking and resetting.

Strong encryption schemes have the distinct disadvantage that changing even a single bit in the data can render the entire file unrecoverable gibberish. Therefore, it's useful to combine encryption with a digest so you can tell whether a file has been modified. Example 12-6 uses CipherInputStream to DES-encrypt a file named on the command line, but that's not all. The ciphertext is also digested and the digest saved so corruption can be detected.

*Example 12-6. DigestEncryptor*

```
import java.io.*;
import java.security.*;
import java.security.spec.*;
import javax.crypto.*;
import javax.crypto.spec.*;

public class DigestEncryptor {
```

*Example 12-6. DigestEncryptor (continued)*

```
public static void main(String[] args)
 throws IOException, GeneralSecurityException {

  if (args.length != 2) {
    System.err.println("Usage: java DigestEncryptor filename password");
    return;
  }

  String filename = args[0];
  String password = args[1];

  if (password.length( ) < 8 ) {
    System.err.println("Password must be at least eight characters long");
  }

  FileInputStream fin = new FileInputStream(filename);
  FileOutputStream fout = new FileOutputStream(filename +".des");
  FileOutputStream digest = new FileOutputStream(filename + ".des.digest");

  // Create the key.
  byte[] desKeyData = password.getBytes( );
  DESKeySpec desKeySpec = new DESKeySpec(desKeyData);
  SecretKeyFactory keyFactory = SecretKeyFactory.getInstance("DES");
  SecretKey desKey = keyFactory.generateSecret(desKeySpec);

  // Use Data Encryption Standard.
  Cipher des = Cipher.getInstance("DES/ECB/PKCS5Padding");
  des.init(Cipher.ENCRYPT_MODE, desKey);
  CipherInputStream cin = new CipherInputStream(fin, des);

  // Use SHA digest algorithm.
  MessageDigest sha = MessageDigest.getInstance("SHA");
  DigestInputStream din = new DigestInputStream(cin, sha);

  byte[] input = new byte[64];
  while (true) {
    int bytesRead = din.read(input);
    if (bytesRead == -1) break;
    fout.write(input, 0, bytesRead);
  }

  digest.write(sha.digest( ));
  digest.close( );
  din.close( );
  fout.flush( );
  fout.close( );
 }
}
```

The file is read with a file input stream chained to a cipher input stream chained to a digest input stream. As the file is read, encrypted, and digested, it's written into an output file. After the file has been completely read, the digest is written into another file so it can later be compared with the first file. Because the cipher input stream appears before the digest input stream in the chain, the digest is of the ciphertext, not the plaintext. If you read the file with a file input stream chained to a digest input stream chained to a cipher input stream, you would digest the plaintext. In fact, you could even use a file input stream chained to a digest input stream chained to a cipher input stream chained to a second digest input stream to get digests of both plain- and ciphertext.

## CipherOutputStream

`CipherOutputStream` is a subclass of `FilterOutputStream`.

```
public class CipherOutputStream extends FilterOutputStream
```

Each `CipherOutputStream` object contains a `Cipher` object used to decrypt or encrypt all data passed as arguments to the `write()` method before writing it to the underlying stream. This `Cipher` object is set in the constructor. Like all filter stream constructors, this constructor takes another input stream as an argument:

```
public CipherOutputStream(OutputStream out, Cipher c)
```

The `Cipher` object used here must be a properly initialized instance of `javax.crypto.Cipher`, most likely returned by `Cipher.getInstance()`. The `Cipher` object c should be initialized for encryption or decryption by calling `init()` before being passed to the `CipherOutputStream()` constructor. There is also a protected constructor that might be used by subclasses that want to implement their own, non-JCE-based encryption scheme:

```
protected CipherOutputStream(OutputStream out)
```

`CipherOutputStream` has all the usual methods of any output stream, like `write()`, `flush()`, and `close()`. It overrides five of these methods to do its filtering. Clients use these methods the same way they use them in any output stream. Before the data is written, the stream's cipher either decrypts or encrypts the data. Each of these five methods makes the necessary adjustments to handle encrypted data. For example, the `flush()` method (which is invoked by the `close()` method as well) calls `doFinal()` on the `Cipher` object to make sure it has finished padding and encrypting all the data before it flushes the final data to the underlying stream.

There are no new methods in `CipherOutputStream` not declared in the superclass. Anything else you need to do, such as getting the cipher's initialization vector, must be handled by the `Cipher` object.

Example 12-7 uses `CipherOutputStream` to decrypt files encrypted by the `DigestEncryptor` of Example 12-6. A digest input stream chained to a file input stream checks the digest of the ciphertext as it's read from the file. If the digest does not match, an error message is printed. The file is still written into the output file, since—depending on the algorithm and mode used—it may be partially legible, especially if the error does not occur until relatively late in the encrypted data.

*Example 12-7. DigestDecryptor*

```java
import java.io.*;
import java.security.*;
import java.security.spec.*;
import javax.crypto.*;
import javax.crypto.spec.*;

public class DigestDecryptor {

  public static void main(String[] args)
    throws IOException, GeneralSecurityException {

    if (args.length != 3) {
      System.err.println("Usage: java DigestDecryptor infile outfile password");
      return;
    }

    String infile = args[0];
    String outfile = args[1];
    String password = args[2];

    if (password.length() < 8 ) {
      System.err.println("Password must be at least eight characters long");
    }

    FileInputStream fin = new FileInputStream(infile);
    FileOutputStream fout = new FileOutputStream(outfile);

    // Get the digest.
    FileInputStream digestIn = new FileInputStream(infile + ".digest");
    DataInputStream dataIn = new DataInputStream(digestIn);
    // SHA digests are always 20 bytes long.
    byte[] oldDigest = new byte[20];
    dataIn.readFully(oldDigest);
    dataIn.close();

    // Create a key.
    byte[] desKeyData = password.getBytes();
    DESKeySpec desKeySpec = new DESKeySpec(desKeyData);
    SecretKeyFactory keyFactory = SecretKeyFactory.getInstance("DES");
    SecretKey desKey = keyFactory.generateSecret(desKeySpec);

    // Use Data Encryption Standard.
    Cipher des = Cipher.getInstance("DES/ECB/PKCS5Padding");
    des.init(Cipher.DECRYPT_MODE, desKey);
    CipherOutputStream cout = new CipherOutputStream(fout, des);

    // Use SHA digest algorithm.
    MessageDigest sha = MessageDigest.getInstance("SHA");
    DigestInputStream din = new DigestInputStream(fin, sha);

    byte[] input = new byte[64];
    while (true) {
```

*Example 12-7. DigestDecryptor (continued)*

```
    int bytesRead = din.read(input);
    if (bytesRead == -1) break;
    cout.write(input, 0, bytesRead);
  }

  byte[] newDigest = sha.digest();
  if (!MessageDigest.isEqual(newDigest, oldDigest)) {
    System.out.println("Input file appears to be corrupt!");
  }

  din.close();
  cout.flush();
  cout.close();
  }
}
```

# File Viewer, Part 5

Handling a particular form of encryption in the FileDumper program is not hard. Handling the general case is not. It's not that decryption is difficult. In fact, it's quite easy. However, most encryption schemes require more than simply providing a key. You also need to know an assortment of algorithm parameters, like initialization vector, salt, iteration count, and more. Higher level protocols usually pass this information between the encryption program and the decryption program. The simplest protocol is to store the information unencrypted at the beginning of the encrypted file. You saw an example of this in the FileDecryptor and FileEncryptor programs. The FileEncryptor chose a random initialization vector and placed its length and the vector itself at the beginning of the encrypted file so the decryptor could easily find it.

For the next iteration of the FileDumper program, I am going to use the simplest available encryption scheme, DES in ECB mode with PKCS5Padding. Furthermore, the key is simply the first eight bytes of the password. This is probably the least secure algorithm discussed in this chapter. However, it doesn't require an initialization vector, salt, or other metainformation to be passed between the encryptor and the decryptor. Because of the nature of filter streams, it is relatively straightforward to add decryption services to the FileDumper program, assuming you know the format in which the encrypted data is stored. Generally, you'll want to decrypt a file before dumping it. This does not require a new dump filter. Instead, I simply pass the file through a cipher input stream before passing it to one of the dump filters.

When a file is both compressed and encrypted, compression is usually performed first. Therefore, we'll always decompress after decrypting. The reason is twofold. Since encryption schemes make data appear random, and compression works by taking advantage of redundancy in nonrandom data, it is difficult, if not impossible, to compress encrypted files. In fact, one quick test of how good an encryption scheme is to compress an encrypted file. If the file is compressible, it's virtually certain the encryption scheme is flawed and can be broken. Conversely, compressing files before encrypting them removes redundancy from the data that a code breaker can exploit and thereby may shore up some weaker algorithms. On the other hand, some algorithms have been broken by taking advantage of magic numbers and other known plaintext sequences that compression programs insert into the encrypted data. Thus, there's no guarantee that compressing files before encrypting them makes them harder to penetrate. The best option is simply to use the strongest encryption available.

We'll let the user set the password with the -password command-line switch. The next argument after -password is assumed to be the password. Example 12-8, FileDumper5, demonstrates.

*Example 12-8. FileDumper5*

```java
import java.io.*;
import java.util.zip.*;
import java.security.*;
import javax.crypto.*;
import javax.crypto.spec.*;
import com.elharo.io.*;

public class FileDumper5 {

  public static final int ASC   = 0;
  public static final int DEC   = 1;
  public static final int HEX   = 2;
  public static final int SHORT = 3;
  public static final int INT   = 4;
  public static final int LONG  = 5;
  public static final int FLOAT = 6;
  public static final int DOUBLE = 7;

  public static void main(String[] args) {

    if (args.length < 1) {
      System.err.println(
        "Usage: java FileDumper5 [-ahdsilfx] [-little] [-gzip|-deflated] "
        + "[-password password] file1...");
    }

    boolean bigEndian = true;
    int firstFile = 0;
    int mode = ASC;
    boolean deflated = false;
    boolean gzipped = false;
    String password = null;

    // Process command-line switches.
    for (firstFile = 0; firstFile < args.length; firstFile++) {
```

*Example 12-8. FileDumper5 (continued)*

```
          if (!args[firstFile].startsWith("-")) break;
          if (args[firstFile].equals("-h")) mode = HEX;
          else if (args[firstFile].equals("-d")) mode = DEC;
          else if (args[firstFile].equals("-s")) mode = SHORT;
          else if (args[firstFile].equals("-i")) mode = INT;
          else if (args[firstFile].equals("-l")) mode = LONG;
          else if (args[firstFile].equals("-f")) mode = FLOAT;
          else if (args[firstFile].equals("-x")) mode = DOUBLE;
          else if (args[firstFile].equals("-little")) bigEndian = false;
          else if (args[firstFile].equals("-deflated") && !gzipped) deflated = true;
          else if (args[firstFile].equals("-gzip") && !deflated) gzipped = true;
          else if (args[firstFile].equals("-password")) {
            password = args[firstFile+1];
            firstFile++;
          }
        }

      for (int i = firstFile; i < args.length; i++) {
        try {
          InputStream in = new FileInputStream(args[i]);
          dump(in, System.out, mode, bigEndian, deflated, gzipped, password);

          if (i < args.length-1) {  // more files to dump
            System.out.println();
            System.out.println("-------------------------------------");
            System.out.println();
          }
        }
        catch (IOException ex) {
          System.err.println(ex);
          ex.printStackTrace();
        }
      }
    }

  public static void dump(InputStream in, OutputStream out, int mode,
   boolean bigEndian, boolean deflated, boolean gzipped, String password)
   throws IOException {

    // The reference variable in may point to several different objects
    // within the space of the next few lines.
    if (password != null && password.length() > 0) {
      // Create a key.
      try {
        byte[] desKeyData = password.getBytes();
        DESKeySpec desKeySpec = new DESKeySpec(desKeyData);
        SecretKeyFactory keyFactory = SecretKeyFactory.getInstance("DES");
        SecretKey desKey = keyFactory.generateSecret(desKeySpec);

        // Use Data Encryption Standard.
        Cipher des = Cipher.getInstance("DES/ECB/PKCS5Padding");
        des.init(Cipher.DECRYPT_MODE, desKey);
```

*Example 12-8. FileDumper5 (continued)*

```
        in = new CipherInputStream(in, des);
      }
    catch (GeneralSecurityException ex) {
      throw new IOException(ex.getMessage( ));
    }
  }

  if (deflated) {
    in = new InflaterInputStream(in);
  }
  else if (gzipped) {
    in = new GZIPInputStream(in);
  }

  // could really pass to FileDumper3 at this point
  if (bigEndian) {
    DataInputStream din = new DataInputStream(in);
    switch (mode) {
      case HEX:
        in = new HexFilter(in);
        break;
      case DEC:
        in = new DecimalFilter(in);
        break;
      case INT:
        in = new IntFilter(din);
        break;
      case SHORT:
        in = new ShortFilter(din);
        break;
      case LONG:
        in = new LongFilter(din);
        break;
      case DOUBLE:
        in = new DoubleFilter(din);
        break;
      case FLOAT:
        in = new FloatFilter(din);
        break;
      default:
    }
  }
  else {
    LittleEndianInputStream lin = new LittleEndianInputStream(in);
    switch (mode) {
      case HEX:
        in = new HexFilter(in);
        break;
      case DEC:
        in = new DecimalFilter(in);
        break;
      case INT:
```

*Example 12-8. FileDumper5 (continued)*

```
          in = new LEIntFilter(lin);
          break;
        case SHORT:
          in = new LEShortFilter(lin);
          break;
        case LONG:
          in = new LELongFilter(lin);
          break;
        case DOUBLE:
          in = new LEDoubleFilter(lin);
          break;
        case FLOAT:
          in = new LEFloatFilter(lin);
          break;
        default:
      }
    }
    for (int c = in.read(); c != -1; c = in.read( )) {
      out.write(c);
    }
    in.close( );
  }
}
```

Note how little needed to change. I simply imported two more packages and added a command-line switch and about a dozen lines of code (which could easily have been half that) to build a Cipher object and add a cipher input stream to the chain. Other encryption schemes, like password-based encryption, would not be hard to support either. The main difficulty lies in deciding exactly how the key would be entered since not all algorithms have keys that map to passwords in a straightforward way. I leave that as an exercise for the reader.

# CHAPTER 13
# Object Serialization

The last several chapters have shown you how to read and write Java's fundamental data types (byte, int, String, etc.). However, there's been one glaring omission. Java is an object-oriented language, and yet aside from the special case of strings, you haven't seen any general-purpose methods for reading or writing objects.

Object serialization, first used in the context of Remote Method Invocation (RMI) and later for JavaBeans, addresses this need. The java.io.ObjectOutputStream class provides a writeObject( ) method you can use to write a Java object onto a stream. The java.io.ObjectInputStream class has a readObject( ) method that reads an object from a stream. ObjectInputStream and ObjectOutputStream implement the DataInput and DataOutput interfaces respectively so they can also write primitive data types such as ints, floats, and doubles, In this chapter you'll learn how to use these two classes to read and write objects as well as how to customize the format used for serialization.

## Reading and Writing Objects

Object serialization saves an object's state in a sequence of bytes so that the object can be reconstituted from those bytes at a later time. Serialization in Java was first developed for use in RMI. RMI allows an object in one virtual machine to invoke methods in an object in another virtual machine, possibly in a different computer on the other side of the planet, by sending arguments and return values across the Internet. This requires a way to convert those arguments and return values to and from byte streams. It's a trivial task for primitive data types, but you need to be able to convert objects as well. That's what object serialization provides.

Object serialization is also used in the JavaBeans component software architecture. Bean classes are loaded into visual builder tools such as NetBeans. The designer then customizes the beans by assigning fonts, sizes, text, and other properties to each bean and connects them together with events. For instance, a button bean generally has a label property that is encoded as a string of text. The designer can change this text.

Once the designer has assembled and customized the beans, the form containing all the beans must be saved. It's not enough to save the bean classes themselves; the customizations that have been applied to the beans must also be saved. That's where serialization comes in: it stores the bean as an object and thus includes any customizations, which are nothing more than the values of the bean's fields. The customized beans are stored in a *.ser* file, which is often placed inside a JAR archive. Thus, instead of having to write long init( ) methods that create and initialize many different components and objects, you can assemble the components in a visual tool, assign properties to them, save the whole group, and then load them back in.

Object serialization provides a predefined format you can use for saving files. For example, suppose you're writing a chess game with a Board class that stores the locations of all the pieces on the board. It's not particularly difficult to design a file format that includes the position of every piece on the board and write the code to write the current state of the board into a file. It is, however, time-consuming. With object serialization, you can write the entire board into a file with one method call. All you need to do to save a game is write the Board object onto an object output stream chained to a file output stream. To restore the game, read the Board object from an object input stream chained to a file input stream. I don't suggest using object serialization for all your file formats. For one thing, object serialization is slow and a performance bottleneck for large and complicated files. If you define your own format, you can save the minimum amount of information you need; serialization saves the entire object graph for the Board, including lots of things that aren't necessary to restore the state of the board. Furthermore, while it's quite easy to create simple systems based on object serialization in two or three lines of code, these simple systems tend to be unreliable, fragile, and insecure. Robust, reliable, secure serialization is a good deal more complex. Certainly, for small chores, though, object serialization provides a very convenient predefined file format.

# Object Streams

Objects are serialized by object output streams. They are deserialized by object input streams. These classes are instances of java.io.ObjectOutputStream and java.io. ObjectInputStream, respectively:

```
public class ObjectOutputStream extends OutputStream
  implements ObjectOutput, ObjectStreamConstants
public class ObjectInputStream extends InputStream
  implements ObjectInput, ObjectStreamConstants
```

The ObjectOutput interface is a subinterface of java.io.DataOutput that adds methods to write objects. The ObjectInput interface is a subinterface of java.io.DataInput that adds methods to read objects. By extending DataInput and DataOutput, ObjectInput and ObjectOutput guarantee that their implementers are able to read and write primitive types like int and double, as well as objects. Since an object may contain fields of primitive types, anything that has to read or write the state of an object also has to be able to read or write the primitive fields the object contains.

java.io.ObjectStreamConstants is an unimportant interface that merely declares mnemonic constants for "magic numbers" used in the object serialization file format. A major goal of the object stream classes is shielding client programmers from these sorts of details about the format used to serialize objects.

ObjectOutputStream and ObjectInputStream are filter streams, and thus they are chained to underlying streams in their constructors:

```
public ObjectOutputStream(OutputStream out) throws IOException
public ObjectInputStream(InputStream in) throws IOException
```

To write an object onto a stream, pass the object to the ObjectOutputStream's writeObject() method:

```
public final void writeObject(Object o) throws IOException
```

For example, this code fragment chains an ObjectOutputStream to a FileOutputStream and writes a java.awt.Point object into that file:

```
Point p = new Point(34, 22);
FileOutputStream fout = new FileOutputStream("point.ser");
ObjectOutputStream oout = new ObjectOutputStream(fout);
oout.writeObject(p);
oout.close();
```

Later, the object can be read back using the readObject() method of the ObjectInputStream class:

```
public final Object readObject()
   throws OptionalDataException, ClassNotFoundException, IOException
```

For example:

```
FileInputStream fin = new FileInputStream("point.ser");
ObjectInputStream oin = new ObjectInputStream(fin);
Object o = oin.readObject();
Point p = (Point) o;
oin.close();
```

The reconstituted Point has the same values as the original Point. Its $x$ is 34 and its $y$ is 22, just like the Point object that was written. However, since readObject() is only declared to return an Object, you usually need to cast the deserialized object to a more specific type.

Both writeObject() and readObject() throw IOException for all the usual reasons an I/O operation can fail (disk filling up, network connection being severed, etc.). There are also several object-serialization specific subclasses of IOException. For example, an InvalidClassException indicates that the data in the stream can't be matched to the corresponding class (for instance, because the version of the class that was serialized is not the same as the version of the class used in the VM deserializing the object). The readObject() method also throws a ClassNotFoundException if a definition for the class of the object read from the input stream is not available in the current VM.

# How Object Serialization Works

Objects possess state. This state is stored in the values of the nonstatic, nontransient fields of an object's class. Consider this TwoDPoint class:

```
public class TwoDPoint {
  public double x;
  public double y;
}
```

Every object of this class has a state defined by the values of the double fields x and y. If you know the values of those fields, you know the value of the TwoDPoint. Nothing changes if you add some methods to the class or make the fields private, as in Example 13-1.

*Example 13-1. The TwoDPoint class*

```
public class TwoDPoint {
  private double x;
  private double y;

  public TwoDPoint(double x, double y) {
    this.x = x;
    this.y = y;
  }

  public double getX() {
    return x;
  }

  public double getY() {
    return y;
  }

  public String toString() {
    return "[TwoDPoint:x=" + this.x + ", y=" + y +"]";
  }
}
```

The object state, the information stored in the fields, is still the same. If you know the values of x and y, you know everything there is to know about the state of the object. The methods only affect the actions an object can perform. They do not change what an object is.

Now suppose you wanted to save the state of a particular TwoDPoint object by writing a sequence of bytes onto a stream. This process is called *serialization* since the object is serialized into a sequence of bytes. You could add a writeState() method to your class that looked something like this:

```
public void writeState(OutputStream out) throws IOException {
    DataOutputStream dout = new DataOutputStream(out);
    dout.writeDouble(x);
    dout.writeDouble(y);
}
```

To restore the state of a Point object, you could add a readState() method like this:

```
public void readState(InputStream in) throws IOException {
    DataInputStream din = new DataInputStream(in);
    this.x = din.readDouble();
    this.y = din.readDouble();
}
```

Needless to say, this is a lot of work. You would have to define readState() and writeState() methods for every class whose instances you wanted to serialize. Furthermore, you would have to track where in the byte stream particular values were stored to make sure that you didn't accidentally read the y coordinate of one point as the x coordinate of the next. You'd also have to make sure you could serialize the object's superclasses if the superclass contained a relevant state. Classes composed of other classes would cause a lot of trouble since you'd need to serialize each object the first object contained, then each object those objects contained, then the objects those objects contained, and so forth. Finally, you'd need to avoid circular references that could put you in an infinite loop.

Fortunately, Sun's done all the work for you. Object streams can access all the non-static, nontransient fields of an object (including the private parts) and write them out in a well-specified format. All you have to do is chain object output streams to an underlying stream where you want the object to be written and call writeObject(); you do not have to add any new methods. Reading objects in from an object input stream is only slightly more complicated; in addition to reading the object from the stream, you also need to cast the object to the correct type.

## Performance

Serialization is often the easiest way to save the state of your program. You simply write out the objects you're using and read them back in when you're ready to restore the document. There is a downside, however. First of all, serialization is slow. If you can define a custom file format for your application's documents, using that format is almost certainly much faster than object serialization.

Second, serialization can slow or prevent garbage collection. Every time an object is written onto an object output stream, the stream holds onto a reference to the object. Then, if the same object is written onto the same stream again, it can be replaced with a reference to its first occurrence in the stream. However, this means that your program holds onto live references to the objects it has written until the stream is reset or closed—which means these objects won't be garbage-collected. The worst-case scenario is keeping a stream open as long as your program runs and writing every object created onto the stream. This prevents any objects from being garbage-collected.

The easy solution is to avoid keeping a running stream of the objects you create. Instead, save the entire state only when the entire state is available and then close the stream immediately.

If this isn't possible, you have the option to reset the stream by invoking its reset( ) method:

```
public void reset( ) throws IOException
```

reset( ) flushes the ObjectOutputStream object's internal cache of the objects it has already written so they can be garbage-collected. However, this also means that an object may be written onto the stream more than once, so use this method with caution.

## The Serializable Interface

Unlimited serialization would introduce security problems. For one thing, it allows unrestricted access to an object's private fields. By chaining an object output stream to a byte array output stream, a hacker can convert an object into a byte array. The byte array can be manipulated and modified without any access protection or security manager checks. Then the byte array can be reconstituted into a Java object by using it as the source of a byte array input stream.

Security isn't the only potential problem. Some objects exist only as long as the current program is running. A java.net.Socket object represents an active connection to a remote host. Suppose a socket is serialized to a file, and the program exits. Later the socket is deserialized from the file in a new program—but the connection it represents no longer exists. Similar problems arise with file descriptors, I/O streams, and many other classes.

For these and other reasons, Java does not allow instances of arbitrary classes to be serialized. You can only serialize instances of classes that implement the java.io. Serializable interface. By implementing this interface, a class indicates that it may be serialized without undue problems.

```
public interface Serializable
```

This interface does not declare any methods or fields; it is a marker interface that serves purely to indicate that a class may be serialized. However, subclasses of a class that implements a particular interface also implement that interface. Thus, many classes that do not explicitly declare that they implement Serializable are in fact serializable. For instance, java.awt.Component implements Serializable. Therefore, its direct and indirect subclasses, including `Button`, `Scrollbar`, `TextArea`, `List`, `Container`, `Panel`, `Applet`, and all Swing components may be serialized. `java.lang.Throwable` implements `Serializable`. Therefore, all exceptions and errors are serializable.

You can glean some general principles about what classes are and are not likely to be serializable. For instance, exceptions, errors, and other throwable objects are always serializable. Streams, readers and writers, and most other I/O classes are not serializable. AWT and Swing components, containers, and events are serializable, but event adapters, image filters, and AWT classes that abstract OS-dependent features are not. `java.beans` classes are not serializable. Type wrapper classes are serializable except for `Void`; most other `java.lang` classes are not. Reflection classes are not serializable. `java.math` classes are serializable. `URL` objects are serializable. `Socket`, `URLConnection`, and most other `java.net` classes are not. Container classes are serializable (though see the next section). Compression classes are not serializable. Nonstatic inner classes (including your own inner classes) are almost never serializable.

Overall, there are seven common reasons why a class may not be serializable:

1. It is too closely tied to native code (`java.util.zip.Deflater`).
2. The object's state depends on the internals of the virtual machine or the runtime environment and thus may change from run to run (`java.lang.Thread`, `java.io.InputStream`, `java.io.FileDescriptor`, `java.awt.PrintJob`).
3. Serializing it is a potential security risk (`java.lang.SecurityManager`, `java.security.MessageDigest`).
4. The class is mostly a holder for static methods without any real internal state (`java.beans.Beans`, `java.lang.Math`).
5. The class is a nonstatic inner class. Serialization just doesn't work well with nonstatic inner classes. (Static inner classes have no problem being serialized.)
6. The programmer who wrote the class simply didn't think about serialization.
7. An alternate serialization format is preferred in a particular context. (XOM node classes are not serializable because the proper serialization format for XML is XML.)

## Classes That Implement Serializable but Aren't

Just because a class *may* be serialized does not mean that it *can* be serialized. Several problems can prevent a class that implements `Serializable` from actually being serialized. Attempting to serialize such a class throws a `NotSerializableException`, a kind of `IOException`:

```
public class NotSerializableException extends ObjectStreamException
```

## Problem 1: References to nonserializable objects

The first common problem that prevents a serializable class from being serialized is that its graph contains objects that do not implement `Serializable`. The graph of an object is the collection of all objects that the object holds references to, and all the objects those objects hold references to, and all the objects those objects hold references to, and so on, until there are no more connected objects that haven't appeared in the collection. For an object to be serialized, all the objects it holds references to must also be serializable, and all the objects they hold references to must be serializable, and so on. For instance, consider this skeleton of a class:

```java
import java.applet.*;
import java.net.*;

public class NetworkApplet extends Applet {

  private Socket theConnection;
  //...
}
```

`NetworkApplet` extends `Applet`, which extends `Panel`, which extends `Container`, which extends `Component`, which implements `Serializable`. Thus, `NetworkApplet` should be serializable. However, `NetworkApplet` contains a reference to a `java.net.Socket` object. `Socket` is not a serializable class. Therefore, if you try to pass a `NetworkApplet` instance to `writeObject( )`, a `NotSerializableException` is thrown.

The situation is even worse for container classes like `HashMap` and `Vector`. Since serialization performs a deep copy to the output stream, storing even a single nonserializable class inside a container prevents it from being serialized. Since the objects stored in a container can vary from program to program or run to run, there's no sure-fire way to know whether or not a particular instance of a container class can be serialized, short of trying it.

## Problem 2: Missing a no-argument constructor in superclass

The second common problem that prevents a serializable class from being deserialized is that a superclass of the class is not serializable *and* does not contain a no-argument constructor. `java.lang.Object` does not implement `Serializable`, so all classes have at least one superclass that's not serializable. When an object is deserialized, the no-argument constructor of the closest superclass that does not implement `Serializable` is invoked to establish the state of the object's nonserializable superclasses. If that class does not have a no-argument constructor, the object cannot be deserialized. For example, consider the `java.io.ZipFile` class introduced in Chapter 10. It does not implement `Serializable`:

```java
public class ZipFile extends Object implements java.util.zip.ZipConstants
```

Furthermore, it has only these two constructors, both of which take arguments:

```java
public ZipFile(String filename) throws IOException
public ZipFile(File file) throws ZipException, IOException
```

Suppose you want to subclass it to allow the class to be serialized, as shown in Example 13-2.

*Example 13-2. A SerializableZipFileNot*

```
import java.io.*;
import java.util.zip.*;

public class SerializableZipFileNot extends ZipFile
 implements Serializable {

  public SerializableZipFileNot(String filename) throws IOException {
    super(filename);
  }

  public SerializableZipFileNot(File file) throws IOException {
    super(file);
  }

  public static void main(String[] args) {

    try {
      SerializableZipFileNot szf = new SerializableZipFileNot(args[0]);
      ByteArrayOutputStream bout = new ByteArrayOutputStream( );
      ObjectOutputStream oout = new ObjectOutputStream(bout);
      oout.writeObject(szf);
      oout.close( );
      System.out.println("Wrote object!");

      ByteArrayInputStream bin = new
       ByteArrayInputStream(bout.toByteArray( ));
      ObjectInputStream oin = new ObjectInputStream(bin);
      Object o = oin.readObject( );
      System.out.println("Read object!");
    }
    catch (Exception ex) {ex.printStackTrace( );}
  }
}
```

The main( ) method attempts to create an instance of this class, serialize it to a byte array output stream, and read it back in from a byte array input stream. However, here's what happens when you run it:

```
D:\JAVA> java SerializableZipFileNot test.zip
Wrote object!
java.io.InvalidClassException: java.util.zip.ZipFile; <init>
        at java.io.ObjectInputStream.inputObject(Compiled Code)
        at java.io.ObjectInputStream.readObject(ObjectInputStream.java:363)
        at java.io.ObjectInputStream.readObject(ObjectInputStream.java:226)
        at SerializableZipFileNot.main(SerializableZipFileNot.java:28)
```

Since the superclass, ZipFile, is not itself serializable and cannot be instantiated with a no-argument constructor, the subclass cannot be deserialized. It can be serialized, but that isn't much use unless you can get the object back again. Later, you'll see how to make a SerializableZipFile class that can be both written and read. However, to do this, you'll have to give up something else, notably the ZipFile type.

### Problem 3: Deliberate throwing of NotSerializableException

A few classes appear to be unserializable out of pure spite (though normally there's more reason to it than that). Sometimes it's necessary, for security or other reasons, to make a class or even a particular object not serializable, even though one of its superclasses does implement Serializable. Since a subclass can't unimplement an interface implemented in its superclass, the subclass may choose to deliberately throw a NotSerializableException when you attempt to serialize it. You'll see exactly how this is done shortly.

### Locating the offending object

When you encounter a class that you think should be serializable but isn't (and this happens all too frequently, often after you've spent two hours adjusting and customizing several dozen beans in a builder tool that now can't save your work), you'll need to locate the offending class. The detailMessage field of the NotSerializableException contains the name of the unserializable class. This can be retrieved with the getMessage( ) method of java.lang.Throwable or as part of the string returned by toString( ):

```
try {
  out.writeObject(unserializableObject);
}
catch (NotSerializableException ex) {
  System.err.println(ex.getMessage() + " could not be serialized");
}
```

It is not always obvious where the offending class sneaked in. For example, if you're trying to serialize a hash table that contains seven lists, each of which contains many different objects of different classes, a single nonserializable object in one of the lists causes a NotSerializableException. You'll need to walk through the object graph in a debugger to determine which object caused the problem.

### Making nonserializable fields transient

Once you've identified the problem object, the simplest solution to is to mark the field that contains the object transient. For example, we can mark the Socket field transient in the networking applet:

```
import java.applet.*;
import java.net.*;

public class NetworkApplet extends Applet {

  private transient Socket theConnection;  //...
}
```

The transient keyword tells the writeObject() method not to serialize the Socket object theConnection onto the underlying output stream. Instead, it's just skipped. When the object is deserialized, you still need to ensure that the state is consistent with what you expect. It may be enough to make sure theConnection is nonnull before accessing it.

# Versioning

When an object is written onto a stream, only the state of the object and the name of the object's class are stored; the byte codes for the object's class are not stored with the object. There's no guarantee that a serialized object will be deserialized into the same environment from which it was serialized. It's possible for the class definition to change between the time the object is written and the time it's read.

There are even more differences when methods, constructors, and static and transient fields are considered. Not all changes, however, prevent deserialization. For instance, the values of static fields aren't saved when an object is serialized. Therefore, you don't have to worry about adding or deleting a static field to or from a class. Similarly, serialization completely ignores the methods in a class, so changing method bodies or adding or removing methods does not affect serialization.

However, removing an instance field does affect serialization because deserializing an object saved by the earlier version of the class results in an attempt to set the value of a field that no longer exists.

## Compatible and Incompatible Changes

Changes to a class are divided into two groups: compatible changes and incompatible changes. Compatible changes are those that do not affect the serialization format of the object, like adding a method or deleting a static field. Incompatible changes are those that do prevent a previously serialized object from being restored. Examples include changing a class's superclass or changing the type of a field. As a general rule, any change that affects the signature of the class itself or its nontransient instance fields of a class is incompatible while any change that does not affect the signatures of the nontransient instance fields of a class is compatible. However, there are a couple of exceptions. The following changes are compatible:

- Most changes to constructors and methods, whether instance or static. Serialization doesn't touch the methods of a class. The exceptions are those methods directly involved in the serialization process, particularly writeObject() and readObject().

- All changes to static fields—changing their type, their names, adding or removing them, etc. Serialization ignores all static fields.

- All changes to transient fields—changing their type, their names, adding or removing them, etc. Serialization ignores all transient fields.

- Adding or removing an interface (except the Serializable interface) from a class. Interfaces say nothing about the instance fields of a class.

- Adding or removing inner classes.

- Changing the access specifiers of a field. Serialization does not respect access protection.

- Changing a field from static to nonstatic or transient to nontransient. This is the same as adding a field.

The following changes are incompatible and thus prevent deserialization of serialized objects:

- Changing the name of a class.

- Changing the type of an instance field.

- Changing the superclass of a class. This may affect the inherited state of an object.

- Changing the writeObject() or readObject() method (discussed later) in an incompatible fashion.

- Changing a class from Serializable to Externalizable (discussed later) or Externalizable to Serializable.

Finally, adding, removing, or changing the name of a nontransient instance field is incompatible by default. However, it can usually be made compatible with a small effort and an SUID.

## SUIDs

To help identify compatible or incompatible classes, each serializable class has a *stream unique identifier*, SUID for short. When Java deserializes an object, it compares the SUID of the class found in the stream to the SUID of the class with the same name in the local classpath. If they match, Java assumes the two versions of the class are compatible. If they don't match, Java assumes the class has changed in an incompatible way since the object was serialized and throws a java.io. InvalidClassException:

```
Exception in thread "main" java.io.InvalidClassException: Test;
  local class incompatible:
stream classdesc serialVersionUID = 5590355372728923878,
  local class serialVersionUID = -1390649424173445192
```

By default, the SUID is calculated by hashing together all the pieces of a class's interface: the signature of the class, the signatures of the nonprivate methods in the class, the signatures of the fields, and so on. If any of these change, the SUID changes. By default, this is fairly strict. Even compatible changes that don't affect the serialized format such as adding a public method can prevent a serialized object from being deserialized against the newer version of the class.

Sometimes a normally incompatible change can be made compatible. For instance, if you add a new int field to a class, it may be OK for deserialization of old instances of that class to just set the field to 0. If you remove a field from a class, it may be OK for deserialization of old instances to ignore the value stored for that field. Java will do this, but only if the SUIDs of the two versions of the class match.

To tell Java that it's OK to ignore removed fields and use default values for added fields, as well as telling it that other changes don't matter, you can specify the SUID for a class rather than allow it to be calculated automatically. The SUID you specify is a private final static long field named serialVersionUID:

```
public class UnicodeApplet extends Applet {

    private static final long serialVersionUID = 5913267123532863320L;
    // ...
```

As long as you keep the value of this field constant as you evolve the class, Java will serialize and deserialize old saved instances into new versions of the class and vice versa. However, it now becomes your responsibility to make sure that the old and new versions of the class are indeed compatible. For instance, if you change the name of a field, you'll need to write a little code to make sure the value for the old field gets put in the new field when deserializing. You can do this in the readObject( ) and writeObject( ) methods to be discussed shortly. If you can't maintain forward and backward compatibility with the serialization format, you must change the serialVersionUID field to keep Java from deserializing old instances into the new class version and vice versa.

The *serialver* tool, included with the JDK, calculates an SUID that fits the class. For example:

```
% serialver UnicodeApplet
UnicodeApplet: static final long serialVersionUID = 5913267123532863320L;
```

There's also a GUI interface available with the –show flag, as shown in Figure 13-1.

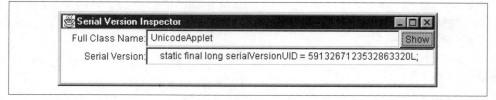

*Figure 13-1. The serialver GUI*

This generates the same hash code Java would calculate if no serialVersionUID field were present. However, unlike the default hash, you can continue using this same value as the class evolves.

You do not have to use the SUID values that *serialver* calculates. You can use your own version-numbering scheme. The simplest such scheme would be to give the first version of the class SUID 1, the next incompatible version SUID 2, and so forth. Whether you use a custom SUID or let *serialver* calculate one for you, you are responsible for deciding when a change to a class is compatible with serialization. The *serialver* tool does not necessarily generate the same SUID for two compatible but different classes.

# Customizing the Serialization Format

The default serialization procedure does not always produce the results you want. Most often, a nonserializable field like a Socket or a FileOutputStream needs to be excluded from serialization. Sometimes, a class may contain data in nonserializable fields like a Socket that you nonetheless want to save—for example, the host that the socket's connected to. Or perhaps a singleton object wants to verify that no other instance of itself exists in the virtual machine before it's reconstructed. Or perhaps an incompatible change to a class such as changing a Font field to three separate fields storing the font's name, style, and size can be made compatible with a little programmer-supplied logic. Or perhaps you want to compress a large array of image data before writing it to disk. For these or many other reasons, you can customize the serialization process.

The simplest way to customize serialization is to declare certain fields transient. The values of transient fields are not written onto the underlying output stream when an object in the class is serialized. However, this only goes as far as excluding certain information from serialization; it doesn't help you change the format that's used to store the data or take action on deserialization or ensure that no more than one instance of a singleton class is created.

For more control over the details of your class's serialization, you can provide custom readObject() and writeObject() methods. These are *private* methods that the virtual machine uses to read and write the data for your class. This gives you complete control over how data in your class is written onto the underlying stream but still uses standard serialization techniques for all fields of the object's superclasses.

If you need even more control over the superclasses and everything else, you can implement the java.io.Externalizable interface, a subinterface of java.io. Serializable. When serializing an externalizable object, the virtual machine does almost nothing except identify the class. The class itself is completely responsible for reading and writing its state and its superclass's state in whatever format it chooses.

## The readObject() and writeObject() Methods

By default, serialization takes place as previously described. When an object is passed to an ObjectOutput's writeObject() method, the ObjectOutput reads the data in the object and writes it onto the underlying output stream in a specified format. Data is written starting with the highest serializable superclass of the object and continuing down through the hierarchy. However, before the data of each class is written, the virtual machine checks to see if the class in question has methods with these two signatures:

```
private void writeObject(ObjectOutputStream out) throws IOException
private void readObject(ObjectInputStream in)
   throws IOException, ClassNotFoundException
```

(Actually, an ObjectOutput only checks to see if the object has a writeObject() method, and an ObjectInput only checks for a readObject() method, but it's rare to implement one of these methods without implementing the other.) If the appropriate method is present, it is invoked to serialize the fields of this class rather than writing them directly. The object stream still handles serialization for any superclass or subclass fields.

For example, let's return to the issue of making a SerializableZipFile. Previously it wasn't possible because the superclass, ZipFile, didn't have a no-argument constructor. In fact, because of this problem, no subclass of this class can be serializable. However, it is possible to use composition rather than inheritance to make our zip file serializable. Example 13-3 shows a SerializableZipFile class that does *not* extend java.util.zip.ZipFile. Instead, it stores a ZipFile object in a transient field in the class called zf. The zf field is initialized either in the constructor or in the readObject() method. Invocations of the normal ZipFile methods, like entries() or getInputStream(), are merely passed along to the ZipFile field zf.

*Example 13-3. SerializableZipFile*

```
import java.io.*;
import java.util.*;
import java.util.zip.*;

public class SerializableZipFile implements Serializable {

  private ZipFile zf;

  public SerializableZipFile(String filename) throws IOException {
    this.zf = new ZipFile(filename);
  }

  public SerializableZipFile(File file) throws IOException {
    this.zf = new ZipFile(file);
  }

  private void writeObject(ObjectOutputStream out) throws IOException {
    out.writeObject(zf.getName());
  }

  private void readObject(ObjectInputStream in)
   throws IOException, ClassNotFoundException {
```

*Example 13-3. SerializableZipFile (continued)*

```
    String filename = (String) in.readObject();
    zf = new ZipFile(filename);
  }

  public ZipEntry getEntry(String name) {
    return zf.getEntry(name);
  }

  public InputStream getInputStream(ZipEntry entry) throws IOException {
    return zf.getInputStream(entry);
  }

  public String getName() {
    return zf.getName();
  }

  public Enumeration entries() {
    return zf.entries();
  }

  public int size() {
    return zf.size();
  }

  public void close() throws IOException {
    zf.close();
  }

  public static void main(String[] args) {

    try {
      SerializableZipFile szf = new SerializableZipFile(args[0]);
      ByteArrayOutputStream bout = new ByteArrayOutputStream();
      ObjectOutputStream oout = new ObjectOutputStream(bout);
      oout.writeObject(szf);
      oout.close();
      System.out.println("Wrote object!");

      ByteArrayInputStream bin = new ByteArrayInputStream(bout.toByteArray());
      ObjectInputStream oin = new ObjectInputStream(bin);
      Object o = oin.readObject();
      System.out.println("Read object!");
    }
    catch (Exception ex) {ex.printStackTrace();}
  }
}
```

Let's look closer at the serialization parts of this program. What does it mean to serialize ZipFile? Internally, a ZipFile object is a filename and a long integer that serves as a native file descriptor to interface with the native zlib library. File descriptors have no state that would make sense across multiple runs of the same program or from one machine to the next. This is why ZipFile is not itself declared serializable.

However, if you know the filename, you can create a new ZipFile object that is the same for all practical purposes.

This is the approach Example 13-3 takes. To serialize an object, the writeObject( ) method writes the filename onto the output stream. The readObject( ) method reads this name back in and recreates the object. When readObject( ) is invoked, the virtual machine creates a new SerializableZipFile object out of thin air; no constructor is invoked. The zf field is set to null. Next, the private readObject( ) method of this object is called. The value of filename is read from the stream. Finally, a new ZipFile object is created from the filename and assigned to zf.

This scheme isn't perfect. In particular, the whole thing may come crashing down if the file that's referred to isn't present when the object is deserialized. This might happen if the file was deleted in between the time the object was written and the time it was read, for example. However, this will only result in an IOException, which the client programmer should be ready for in any case.

The main( ) method tests this scheme by creating a serializable zip file with a name passed in from the command line. Then the serializable zip file is serialized. Next the SerializableZipFile object is deserialized from the same byte array it was previously written into. Here's the result:

```
D:\JAVA>java SerializableZipFile test.zip
Wrote object!
Read object!
```

## The defaultWriteObject() and defaultReadObject( ) Methods

Sometimes rather than changing the format of an object that's serialized, all you want to do is add some additional information, perhaps something that isn't normally serialized, like a static field. In this case, you can use ObjectOutputStream's defaultWriteObject( ) method to write the state of the object and then use ObjectInputStream's defaultReadObject( ) method to read the state of the object. After this is done, you can perform any custom work you need to do on serialization or deserialization.

```
public final void defaultReadObject()
   throws IOException, ClassNotFoundException, NotActiveException
public final void defaultWriteObject() throws IOException
```

For example, let's suppose an application that would otherwise be serializable contains a Socket field. As well as this field, assume it contains more than a few other complex fields, so that serializing it by hand, while possible, would be onerous. It might look something like this:

```
public class NetworkWindow extends Frame implements Serializable {

   private Socket theSocket;

   // several dozen other fields and methods
}
```

You could make this class fully serializable by merely declaring theSocket transient:

```
private transient Socket theSocket;
```

Let's assume you actually do want to restore the state of the socket when the object is deserialized. In this case, you can use private readObject( ) and writeObject( ) methods as in the last section. You can use defaultReadObject( ) and defaultWriteObject( ) methods to handle all the normal, nontransient fields and then handle the socket specifically. For example:

```
private void writeObject(ObjectOutputStream out) throws IOException {

    out.defaultWriteObject( );
    out.writeObject(theSocket.getInetAddress( ));
    out.writeInt(theSocket.getPort( ));
}

private void readObject(ObjectInputStream in)
 throws IOException, ClassNotFoundException {

    in.defaultReadObject( );
    InetAddress ia = (InetAddress) in.readObject( );
    int thePort = in.readInt( );

    theSocket = new Socket(ia, thePort);
}
```

It isn't even necessary to know what the other fields are to make this work. The only extra work that has to be done is for the transient fields. This technique applies far beyond this one example. It can be used anytime when you're happy with the default behavior and merely want to do additional things on serialization or deserialization. For instance, it can be used to set the values of static fields or to execute additional code when deserialization is complete. For example, let's suppose you have a Die class that must have a value between 1 and 6, as shown in Example 13-4.

*Example 13-4. A six-sided die*

```
import java.util.*;
import java.io.*;

public class Die implements Serializable {

  private int face = 1;
  Random shooter = new Random( );

  public Die(int face) {
    if (face < 1 || face > 6) throw new IllegalArgumentException( );
    this.face = face;
  }

  public final int getFace( ) {
    return this.face;
  }
```

*Example 13-4. A six-sided die (continued)*

```
  public void setFace(int face) {
    if (face < 1 || face > 6) throw new IllegalArgumentException();
    this.face = face;
  }

  public int roll() {
    this.face = (Math.abs(shooter.nextInt()) % 6) + 1;
    return this.face;
  }
}
```

Obviously, this class, simple as it is, goes to a lot of trouble to ensure that the die always has a value between 1 and 6. Every method that can possibly set the value of the private field face carefully checks to make sure the value is between 1 and 6. However, serialization provides a back door through which the value of face can be changed. Default serialization uses neither constructors nor setter methods; it accesses the private field directly. Thus it's possible for someone to manually edit the bytes of a serialized Die object so that the value of the face field is greater than 6 or less than 1. To plug the hole, you can provide a readObject( ) method that performs the necessary check:

```
    private void readObject(ObjectInputStream in)
      throws IOException, ClassNotFoundException {
      in.defaultReadObject();
      if (face < 1 || face > 6) {
        throw new InvalidObjectException("Illegal die value: " + this.face);
      }
    }
```

In this example, the normal serialization format is perfectly acceptable, so that's completely handled by defaultReadObject( ). It's just that a little more work is required than merely restoring the fields of the object. If the deserialized object has an illegal value for face, an exception is thrown and the readObject( ) method in ObjectInputStream rethrows this exception instead of returning the object.

It's important to distinguish between this readObject( ) method, which is a private method in the Die class, and the public readObject( ) method in the ObjectInputStream class. The latter invokes the former.

## The writeReplace( ) Method

Sometimes rather than customizing its serialization format, a class simply wants to replace an instance of itself with a different object. For example, if you were distributing a serialized object for a class you didn't expect all recipients to have, you might replace it with a more common superclass. For instance, you might want to replace a quicktime.io.QTFile object with a java.io.File object because Windows systems usually don't have QuickTime for Java installed. The `writeReplace()` method enables this. The signature is normally like this:

```
private Object writeReplace() throws ObjectStreamException;
```

The access modifier may be public, protected, private, or not present. That doesn't matter. However, if a method with this signature is present when another class that has a reference to this object is writing this object as part of its own serialization strategy, it will write the object returned by this method rather than this object. Normally, the return type of this method is going to be an instance of this class or one of its subclasses. You can change this using the `readResolve()` method.

## The readResolve( ) Method

The `readResolve()` method allows you to read one object from a stream but replace it with a different object. The signature of the method is:

```
private Object readResolve() throws ObjectStreamException
```

As with `writeReplace()`, whether the access modifier is public, protected, or private doesn't matter. You can return any type you like from this method, but it has to be able to substitute for the type read from the stream in the appropriate place in the object graph.

The classic use case for `readResolve()` is maintaining the uniqueness of singleton or typesafe enum objects. For instance, consider a serializable singleton such as Example 13-5.

*Example 13-5. A Serializable Singleton class*

```java
import java.io.Serializable;

public class SerializableSingleton implements Serializable {

  public final static SerializableSingleton INSTANCE
    = new SerializableSingleton();

  private SerializableSingleton() {}

}
```

By serializing the instance of this class and then deserializing it, one can create a new instance despite the private constructor because serialization doesn't rely on constructors. To fix this, you have to make sure that whenever the class is deserialized, the new object is replaced by the genuine single instance. This is easy to accomplish by adding this `readResolve()` method:

```java
private Object readResolve(){
  return INSTANCE;
}
```

# serialPersistentFields

You can explicitly specify which fields should and should not be serialized by listing them in a serialPersistentFields array in a private static field in the class. If such a field is present, only fields included in the array are serialized. All others are treated as if they were transient. In other words, transient marks fields *not* to serialize while serialPersistentFields marks fields *to* serialize.

The components of the serialPersistentFields array are ObjectStreamField objects which are constructed using the name and the type of each field to serialize. For example, suppose you wanted the x-coordinate of a TwoDPoint to be serialized but not the y-coordinate. You could mark the y component transient like this:

```
public class TwoDPoint {
  private          double x;
  private transient double y;
  // ...
}
```

or you could place the x field and not the y field in the serialPersistentFields array like this:

```
private static final ObjectStreamField[] serialPersistentFields
  = {new ObjectStreamField("x", double.class)};
```

The first argument to the ObjectStreamField constructor is the name of the field. The second is the type of the field given as a Class object. This is normally a class literal such as BigDecimal.class, Frame.class, int.class, double.class, or double[].class.

The next trick is to use serialPersistentFields to declare fields that don't actually exist in the class. The writeObject() method then writes these phantom fields, and the readObject() method reads them back in. Typically this is done to maintain backward compatibility with old serialized versions after the implementation has changed. It's also important when different clients may have different versions of the library.

For example, suppose the TwoDPoint class was modified to use polar coordinates instead of Cartesian coordinates. That is, it might look like this:

```
public class TwoDPoint {
  private double radius;
  private double angle;
  // ...
}
```

The serialPersistentFields array could still declare the x and y fields, even though they're no longer present in the class:

```
private static final ObjectStreamField[] serialPersistentFields  = {
  new ObjectStreamField("x", double.class),
  new ObjectStreamField("y", double.class),
};
```

The writeObject( ) method converts the polar coordinates back to Cartesian coordinates and writes those fields. This is accomplished with the ObjectOutputStream's PutField object. (PutField is an inner class in ObjectOutputStream.) You get such an object by invoking the putFields( ) method on the ObjectOutputStream. (Confusingly, this method *gets* the PutField object. It does not *put* anything.) You add fields to the PutField object by passing the names and values to the put( ) method. Finally, you invoke the ObjectOutputStream's writeFields method to write the fields onto the output stream. For example, this writeObject( ) method converts polar coordinates into Cartesian coordinates and writes them out as the values of the x and y pseudo-fields:

```
private void writeObject(ObjectOutputStream out) throws IOException {
  // Convert to Cartesian coordinates
  ObjectOutputStream.PutField fields = out.putFields( );
  fields.put("x", radius * Math.cos(angle));
  fields.put("y", radius * Math.sin(angle));
  out.writeFields( );
}
```

The readObject( ) method reverses the procedure using an ObjectInputStream's GetField object. (GetField is an inner class in ObjectInputStream.) You retrieve the GetField object by invoking the readFields( ) method on the ObjectInputStream. You then read the fields by passing the names and default values to the get( ) method. (If the field is missing from the input stream, get( ) returns the default value instead.) Finally, you store the values of the pseudo-fields you read from the stream into the object's real fields after performing any necessary conversions. For example, this readObject( ) method reads Cartesian coordinates as the values of the x and y pseudo-fields and converts them into polar coordinates that it stores in the radius and angle fields:

```
private void readObject(ObjectInputStream in)
  throws ClassNotFoundException, IOException {
  ObjectInputStream.GetField fields = in.readFields( );
  double x = fields.get("x", 0.0);
  double y = fields.get("y", 0.0);

  // Convert to polar coordinates
  radius = Math.sqrt(x*x + y*y);
  angle = Math.atan2(y, x);
}
```

The advantage to using serialPersistentFields instead of merely customizing the readObject( ) and writeObject( ) methods is versioning. A class can be both forward and backward compatible as long as the SUIDs are the same, even if the old version did not have custom readObject( ) and writeObject( ) methods. If the old class had an explicit serialVersionUID field, just copy that into the new class. Otherwise, use the *serialver* tool on the old version of the class to determine its default SUID and then copy that value into the serialVersionUID field in the new version of the class.

The `PutField.put()` and `GetField.get()` methods are heavily over-loaded to support all the Java primitive data types as well as objects. For instance, the get( ) method has these nine variants:

```
public abstract boolean get(String name, boolean value)
   throws IOException
public abstract byte    get(String name, byte value)
   throws IOException
public abstract char    get(String name, char value)
   throws IOException
public abstract short   get(String name, short value)
   throws IOException
public abstract int     get(String name, int value)
   throws    IOException
public abstract long    get(String name, long value)
   throws IOException
public abstract float   get(String name, float value)
   throws IOException
public abstract double  get(String name, double value)
   throws IOException
public abstract Object  get(String name, Object value)
   throws IOException
```

The put( ) method is equally overloaded.

The object stream uses the type of the value argument to determine the type of the field. For instance, if the type of value is double, put( ) puts a double in the stream and get( ) looks for a double when read-ing the stream. The problem occurs when the type of the argument doesn't match the type of the field. For instance, I initially wrote my readObject( ) method like this:

```
double x = fields.get("x", 0);
double y = fields.get("y", 0);
```

I then proceeded to bang my head against the wall trying to figure out why Java kept throwing an `IllegalArgumentException` with the mes-sage "no such field". The problem was that the second argument to this method is an int, not a double. Therefore Java was trying to read a field named x (which I had) with a value of type int (which I didn't). Changing these lines to use a double literal fixed the problem:

```
double x = fields.get("x", 0.0);
double y = fields.get("y", 0.0);
```

About 99% of the time it's safe to use an int literal where a double is intended. This is one of the 1% of cases where it's not.

## Preventing Serialization

On occasion, you need to prevent a normally serializable subclass from being serial-ized. You can prevent an object from being serialized, even though it or one of its superclasses implements Serializable, by throwing a NotSerializableException from writeObject( ). NotSerializableException is a subclass of java.io. ObjectStreamException, which is itself a kind of IOException:

```
public class NotSerializableException extends ObjectStreamException
```

For example:

```
private void writeObject(ObjectOutputStream out) throws IOException {
  throw new NotSerializableException( );
}

private void readObject(ObjectInputStream in) throws IOException {
  throw new NotSerializableException( );
}
```

# Externalizable

Sometimes customization requires you to manipulate the values stored for the super-class of an object as well as for the object's class. In these cases, you should implement the java.io.Externalizable interface instead of Serializable. Externalizable is a subinterface of Serializable:

```
public interface Externalizable extends Serializable
```

This interface declares two methods, readExternal( ) and writeExternal( ):

```
public void writeExternal(ObjectOutput out) throws IOException
public void readExternal(ObjectInput in)
   throws IOException, ClassNotFoundException
```

The implementation of these methods is completely responsible for saving the object's state, including the state stored in its superclasses. This is the primary difference between implementing Externalizable and providing private readObject( ) and writeObject( ) methods. Since some of the superclass's state may be stored in private or package-accessible fields that are not visible to the Externalizable object, saving and restoring can be a tricky proposition. Furthermore, externalizable objects are responsible for tracking their own versions; the virtual machine assumes that whatever version of the externalizable class is available when the object is deserialized is the correct one. It does not check the serialVersionUID field as it does for merely serializable objects. If you want to check for different versions of the class, you must write your own code to do the checks.

For example, suppose you want a list that can be serialized no matter what it contains, one that will never throw a NotSerializableException even if it contains objects that aren't serializable. You can do this by creating a subclass of ArrayList that implements Externalizable, as in Example 13-5. The writeExternal( ) method uses instanceof to test whether each element is or is not serializable before writing it onto the output. If the element does not implement Serializable, writeExternal( ) writes null in its place.

The key criterion for being able to use Externalizable is that there are enough getter and setter methods to read and write all necessary fields in the superclasses. If this isn't the case, often your only recourse is to use the Decorator pattern to wrap a class to which you do have complete access around the original class. This was the tack taken in Example 13-6 for SerializableZipFile.

*Example 13-6. SerializableList*

```java
import java.util.*;
import java.io.*;
import java.net.*;

public class SerializableList extends ArrayList
 implements Externalizable {

  public void writeExternal(ObjectOutput out) throws IOException {

   out.writeInt(size());
   for (int i = 0; i < size(); i++) {
     if (get(i) instanceof Serializable) {
       out.writeObject(get(i));
     }
     else {
       out.writeObject(null);
     }
   }
  }

  public void readExternal(ObjectInput in)
   throws IOException, ClassNotFoundException {

   int elementCount = in.readInt();
   this.ensureCapacity(elementCount);
   for (int i = 0; i < elementCount; i++) {
     this.add(in.readObject());
   }
  }

  public static void main(String[] args) throws Exception {

    SerializableList list = new SerializableList();
    list.add("Element 1");
    list.add(new Integer(9));
    list.add(new URL("http://www.oreilly.com/"));

    // not Serializable
    list.add(new Socket("www.oreilly.com", 80));

    list.add("Element 5");
    list.add(new Integer(9));
    list.add(new URL("http://www.oreilly.com/"));

    ByteArrayOutputStream bout = new ByteArrayOutputStream();
    ObjectOutputStream temp = new ObjectOutputStream(bout);
    temp.writeObject(list);
    temp.close();

    ByteArrayInputStream bin = new ByteArrayInputStream(bout.toByteArray());
    ObjectInputStream oin = new ObjectInputStream(bin);
    List out = (List) oin.readObject();
```

*Example 13-6. SerializableList (continued)*

```
   Iterator iterator = out.iterator( );
   while (iterator.hasNext( )) {
     System.out.println(iterator.next( ));
   }
 }
}
```

One might quibble about the name; `ExternalizableList` may seem more accurate. However, from the perspective of a programmer using a class, it doesn't matter whether a class is serializable or externalizable. In either case, instances of the class are passed to the `writeObject( )` method of an object output stream or read by the `readObject( )` method of an object input stream. The difference between `Serializable` and `Externalizable` is hidden from the client.

The `writeExternal( )` method first writes the number of elements onto the stream using `writeInt( )`. It then loops through all the elements in the list, testing each one with `instanceof` to see whether or not it's serializable. If the element is serializable, it's written with `writeObject( )`; otherwise, `null` is written instead. The `readExternal( )` method reads in the data. First, it ensures capacity to the length of the list. It then adds each deserialized object (or null) to the list.

The `main( )` method tests the program by serializing and deserializing a `SerializableVector` that contains assorted serializable and nonserializable elements. Its output is:

```
D:\JAVA> java SerializableList
Element 1
9
http://www.oreilly.com/
null
Element 1
9
http://www.oreilly.com/
```

This isn't a perfect solution. The list may contain an object that implements `Serializable` but isn't serializable, for example, a hash table that contains a socket. However, this is probably the best you can do without more detailed knowledge of the classes of objects that will be written.

# Resolving Classes

The `readObject( )` method of `java.io.ObjectInputStream` only creates new objects from known classes in the local classpath. If a class for an object can't be found, `readObject( )` throws a `ClassNotFoundException`. It does not read the class data from the object stream. This is limiting for some things you might want to do, particularly RMI. Therefore, trusted subclasses of `ObjectInputStream` may be allowed to load classes from the stream or some other source like a URL. Specifically, a class is trusted if, and only if, it was loaded from the local classpath (that is, the `ClassLoader` object returned by `getClassLoader()` is `null`).

Two protected methods are involved. The first is the `annotateClass()` method of `ObjectOutputStream`:

```
protected void annotateClass(Class c) throws IOException
```

In `ObjectOutputStream`, this is a do-nothing method. A subclass of `ObjectOutputStream` can provide a different implementation that provides data for the class. For instance, this might be the byte code of the class itself or a URL where the class can be found.

Standard object input streams cannot read and resolve the class data written by `annotateClass()`. For each subclass of `ObjectOutputStream` that overrides `annotateClass()`, there will normally be a corresponding subclass of `ObjectInputStream` that implements the `resolveClass()` method:

```
protected Class resolveClass(ObjectStreamClass c)
   throws IOException, ClassNotFoundException
```

In `java.io.ObjectInputStream`, this is a do-nothing method. A subclass of `ObjectInputStream` can provide an implementation that loads a class based on the data read from the stream. For instance, if `annotateClass()` wrote byte code to the stream, the `resolveClass()` method would need to have a class loader that read the data from the stream. If `annotateClass()` wrote the URL of the class to the stream, the `resolveClass()` method would need a class loader that read the URL from the stream and downloaded the class from that URL.

The `resolveClass()` method is called exactly once for each class encountered in the stream (not just those written by `annotateClass()`). `resolveClass()` is responsible for knowing what sort of data needs to be read to reconstruct the class and for reading it from the input stream. `resolveClass()` should then load and return the class. If it can't do so, it should throw a `ClassNotFoundException`. If it returns a class, but that class's SUID does not match the SUID of the class in the stream, the runtime throws a `ClassNotFoundException`.

## Resolving Objects

Sometimes you may need to replace the objects read from the stream with other, alternative objects. Perhaps an old version of a program used `Franc` objects, but the new version of the program uses `Euro` objects. The `ObjectInputStream` can replace each `Franc` object read with the equivalent `Euro` object.

Only trusted subclasses of `ObjectInputStream` may replace objects. A class is only trusted if it was loaded from the local classpath. To make it possible for a trusted subclass to replace objects, first pass `true` to its `enableResolveObject()` method:

```
protected final boolean enableResolveObject(boolean enable)
   throws SecurityException
```

Generally, you do this in the constructor of any class that needs to replace objects. Once object replacement is enabled, whenever an object is read, it is passed to the ObjectInputStream subclass's resolveObject( ) method before readObject( ) returns:

```
protected Object resolveObject(Object o) throws IOException
```

The resolveObject( ) method may return the object itself (the default behavior) or return a different object. Resolving objects is a tricky business. The substituted object must be compatible with the use of the original object, or errors will soon surface as the program tries to invoke methods or access fields that don't exist. Most of the time, the replacing object is an instance of a subclass of the class of the replaced object. Another possibility is that the replacing object and the object it replaces are both instances of different subclasses of a common superclass or interface, where the original object was only used as an instance of that superclass or interface.

# Validation

It is not always enough to merely restore the state of a serialized object. You may need to verify that the value of a field still makes sense, you may need to notify another object that this object has come into existence, or you may need to have the entire graph of the object available before you can finish initializing it.

Most obviously, you may need to check the class invariants on an object you deserialize. In Java, class invariants are normally enforced by explicit code in setters and constructors that checks method preconditions as well as testing to see that no internal code can violate the invariants given that the preconditions hold. Object deserialization bypasses this careful infrastructure completely. There's absolutely nothing to stop someone from reaching right into the serialized bytes of your Clock object and setting the time to 13:00.

Certainly, this would be a nasty thing to do, but it's possible. Some may object that these sorts of shenanigans are also enabled by the Reflection API, particularly through the setAccessible( ) method. However, at least setAccessible( ) only functions from code running inside your own VM. If you're reading a serialized object some other system has passed to you or left sitting around on the disk, you have no idea what might have been done to it or why. You need to be wary of accepting arbitrary serialized objects from untrusted sources.

For example, suppose an application maintains a map of Person objects, each of which is identified primarily by its social security number. Let's further suppose that the application doesn't allow two Person objects with the same social security number to exist at the same time. You can use an ObjectInputValidation to check each Person object as its deserialized to make sure it doesn't duplicate the social security number of a person already in the map.

The ObjectInputStream's registerValidation() method specifies the ObjectInputValidation object that will be notified of the object after its entire graph has been reconstructed but before readObject() has returned it. This gives the validator an opportunity to make sure that the object doesn't violate any implicit assertions about the state of the system.

```
public void registerValidation(ObjectInputValidation oiv,
    int priority) throws NotActiveException, InvalidObjectException
```

This method is invoked inside the readObject() method of the object that needs to be validated. Every time the readObject() method is called to read an object, that object is registered with the stream as needing to be validated when the rest of the graph is available. Invoking the registerValidation() method from anywhere except the readObject() method throws a NotActiveException. The oiv argument is the object that implements the ObjectInputValidation interface and that will validate deserialized objects. Most of the time, this is the object that has the readObject() method; that is, objects tend to validate themselves. The priority argument determines the order in which objects will be validated if there's more than one registered ObjectInputValidation object for the class. Validators with higher priorities are invoked first.

The ObjectInputValidation interface declares a single method, validateObject():

```
public abstract void validateObject() throws InvalidObjectException
```

If the object is invalid, validateObject() throws an InvalidObjectException.

Example 13-7 demonstrates with a class that implements the previously described scheme for avoiding duplicate social security numbers.

*Example 13-7. Person*

```
import java.util.*;
import java.io.*;

public class Person implements Serializable, ObjectInputValidation {

  static Map thePeople = new HashMap();

  private String name;
  private String ss;

  public Person(String name, String ss) {
    this.name = name;
    this.ss = ss;
    thePeople.put(ss, name);
  }

  private void readObject(ObjectInputStream in)
   throws IOException, ClassNotFoundException {
    in.registerValidation(this, 5);
    in.defaultReadObject();
  }
```

*Example 13-7. Person (continued)*

```java
public void validateObject() throws InvalidObjectException {
  if (thePeople.containsKey(this.ss)) {
    throw new InvalidObjectException(this.name + " already exists");
  }
  else {
    thePeople.put(this.ss, this.name);
  }
}

public String toString() {
  return this.name + "\t" + this.ss;
}

public static void main(String[] args)
 throws IOException, ClassNotFoundException {

  Person p1 = new Person("Rusty", "123-45-5678");
  Person p2 = new Person("Beth",  "321-45-5678");
  Person p3 = new Person("David", "453-45-5678");
  Person p4 = new Person("David", "453-45-5678");

  Iterator iterator = thePeople.values().iterator();
  while (iterator.hasNext()) {
    System.out.println(iterator.next());
  }

  ByteArrayOutputStream bout = new ByteArrayOutputStream();
  ObjectOutputStream oout = new ObjectOutputStream(bout);
  oout.writeObject(p1);
  oout.writeObject(p2);
  oout.writeObject(p3);
  oout.writeObject(p4);
  oout.flush();
  oout.close();

  ByteArrayInputStream bin = new ByteArrayInputStream(bout.toByteArray());
  ObjectInputStream oin = new ObjectInputStream(bin);
  try {
    System.out.println(oin.readObject());
    System.out.println(oin.readObject());
    System.out.println(oin.readObject());
    System.out.println(oin.readObject());
  }
  catch (InvalidObjectException ex) {
    System.err.println(ex);
  }
  oin.close();

  // now empty the map and try again
  thePeople.clear();
  bin = new ByteArrayInputStream(bout.toByteArray());
  oin = new ObjectInputStream(bin);
```

*Example 13-7. Person (continued)*

```
    try {
      System.out.println(oin.readObject());
      System.out.println(oin.readObject());
      System.out.println(oin.readObject());
      System.out.println(oin.readObject());
    }
    catch (InvalidObjectException ex) {
      System.err.println(ex);
    }
    oin.close();

    iterator = thePeople.values().iterator();
    while (iterator.hasNext()) {
      System.out.println(iterator.next());
    }
  }
}
```

Here's the output:

```
Beth
Rusty
David
java.io.InvalidObjectException: Rusty already exists
Rusty     123-45-5678
Beth      321-45-5678
David     453-45-5678
Beth
Rusty
David
java.io.InvalidObjectException: David already exists
```

# Sealed Objects

The Java Cryptography Extension discussed in the last chapter provides a SealedObject class that can encrypt objects written onto an object output stream using any available cipher. Most of the time, I suspect, you'll either encrypt the entire object output stream by chaining it to a cipher output stream, or you won't encrypt anything at all. However, if there's some reason to encrypt only some of the objects you're writing to the stream, you can make them sealed objects.

The javax.crypto.SealedObject class wraps a serializable object in an encrypted digital lockbox. The sealed object is serializable so that it can be written onto object output streams and read from object input streams as normal. However, the object inside the sealed object can only be deserialized by someone who knows the key.

```
    public class SealedObject extends Object implements Serializable
```

The big advantage to using sealed objects rather than encrypting the entire output stream is that the sealed objects contain all necessary parameters for decryption (algorithm used, initialization vector, salt, iteration count). All the receiver of the sealed object needs to know is the key; there doesn't necessarily have to be any prior agreement about these other aspects of encryption.

You seal an object with the SealedObject() constructor. The constructor takes as arguments the object to be sealed, which must be serializable, and the properly initialized Cipher object with which to encrypt the object:

```
public SealedObject(Serializable object, Cipher c)
    throws IOException, IllegalBlockSizeException
```

Inside the constructor, the object is immediately serialized by an object output stream chained to a byte array output stream. The byte array is then stored in a private field that is encrypted using the Cipher object c. The cipher's algorithms and parameters are also stored. Thus, the state of the original object written onto the ultimate object output stream is the state of the object when it was sealed; subsequent changes it may undergo between being sealed and being written are not reflected in the sealed object. Since serialization takes place immediately inside the constructor, the constructor throws a NotSerializableException if the object argument cannot be serialized. It throws an IllegalBlockSizeException if c is a block cipher with no padding and the length of the serialized object's contents is not an integral multiple of the block size.

You unseal an object by first reading the sealed object from an object input stream and then invoking one of the three getObject() methods to return the original object. All of these methods require you to supply a key and an algorithm.

Example 13-8 is a very simple program that writes an encrypted java.awt.Point object into the file *point.des*. First a file output stream is opened to the file *point.des* and then chained to the ObjectOutputStream oin. As in the last chapter, a fixed DES key called desKey is built from a fixed array of bytes and used to construct a Cipher object called des. des is initialized in encryption mode with the key. Finally, both the des Cipher object and the Point object tdp are passed into the SealedObject() constructor to create a SealedObject so. Since SealedObject implements Serializable, this can be written on the ObjectOutputStream oout as any other serializable object. At this point, this program closes oout and exits. However, the same Cipher object des could be used to create more sealed objects from serializable objects, and these could also be written onto the stream if you had more objects to serialize.

*Example 13-8. SealedPoint*

```
import java.security.*;
import java.io.*;
import javax.crypto.*;
import javax.crypto.spec.*;
import java.awt.*;

public class SealedPoint {
```

*Example 13-8. SealedPoint (continued)*

```java
  public static void main(String[] args)
   throws GeneralSecurityException, IOException {

    Point tdp = new Point(32, 45);
    FileOutputStream fout = new FileOutputStream("point.des");
    ObjectOutputStream oout = new ObjectOutputStream(fout);

    // Create a key.
    byte[] desKeyData = {(byte) 0x90, (byte) 0x67, (byte) 0x3E, (byte) 0xE6,
                         (byte) 0x42, (byte) 0x15, (byte) 0x7A, (byte) 0xA3 };
    DESKeySpec desKeySpec = new DESKeySpec(desKeyData);
    SecretKeyFactory keyFactory = SecretKeyFactory.getInstance("DES");
    SecretKey desKey = keyFactory.generateSecret(desKeySpec);

    // Use Data Encryption Standard.
    Cipher des = Cipher.getInstance("DES/ECB/PKCS5Padding");
    des.init(Cipher.ENCRYPT_MODE, desKey);

    SealedObject so = new SealedObject(tdp, des);
    oout.writeObject(so);
    oout.close();
  }
}
```

Reading a sealed object from an object input stream is easy. You read it exactly as you read any other object from an object input stream. For example:

```java
    FileInputStream fin = new FileInputStream(filename);
    ObjectInputStream oin = new ObjectInputStream(fin);
    SealedObject so = (SealedObject) oin.readObject();
```

Once you've read the object, unsealing it to retrieve the original object is straightforward, provided you know the key. Three getObject( ) methods return the original object:

```java
    public final Object getObject(Key key) throws IOException,
      ClassNotFoundException, NoSuchAlgorithmException, InvalidKeyException
    public final Object getObject(Cipher c) throws IOException,
      ClassNotFoundException, IllegalBlockSizeException, BadPaddingException
    public final Object getObject(Key key, String provider) throws IOException,
      ClassNotFoundException, NoSuchAlgorithmException, NoSuchProviderException,
      InvalidKeyException
```

The first variant is the most useful since it only requires the key. It does not require you to create and initialize a Cipher object. You will need to know the algorithm in order to know what kind of key to create, but that information is available from the getAlgorithm( ) method:

```java
    public final String getAlgorithm( )
```

For example:

```java
    if (so.getAlgorithm( ).startsWith("DES")) {
      byte[] desKeyData = {(byte) 0x90, (byte) 0x67, (byte) 0x3E, (byte) 0xE6,
```

```
       (byte) 0x42, (byte) 0x15, (byte) 0x7A, (byte) 0xA3, };
    DESKeySpec desKeySpec = new DESKeySpec(desKeyData);
    SecretKeyFactory keyFactory = SecretKeyFactory.getInstance("DES");
    SecretKey desKey = keyFactory.generateSecret(desKeySpec);
    Object o = so.getObject(desKey);
  }
```

Example 13-9 reads the sealed object from the *point.des* file written by Example 13-8, unseals the object, and prints it on System.out.

*Example 13-9. UnsealPoint*

```java
import java.security.*;
import java.io.*;
import javax.crypto.*;
import javax.crypto.spec.*;
import java.awt.*;

public class UnsealPoint {

  public static void main(String[] args)
    throws IOException, GeneralSecurityException, ClassNotFoundException {

    FileInputStream fin = new FileInputStream("point.des");
    ObjectInputStream oin = new ObjectInputStream(fin);

    // Create a key.
    byte[] desKeyData = {(byte) 0x90, (byte) 0x67, (byte) 0x3E, (byte) 0xE6,
                         (byte) 0x42, (byte) 0x15, (byte) 0x7A, (byte) 0xA3 };
    DESKeySpec desKeySpec = new DESKeySpec(desKeyData);
    SecretKeyFactory keyFactory = SecretKeyFactory.getInstance("DES");
    SecretKey desKey = keyFactory.generateSecret(desKeySpec);

    SealedObject so = (SealedObject) oin.readObject();

    Point p = (Point) so.getObject(desKey);
    System.out.println(p);
    oin.close();
  }
}
```

# JavaDoc

Documenting the serialized form of a class is important when you need to interoperate with different implementations of the same API. For instance, the open source GNU Classpath library should be able to deserialize objects serialized by Sun's class library and vice versa, even though they share no code and indeed may have quite different private data. JavaDoc has three tags specifically to document the serialized form of a class: @serial, @serialField, and @serialData. The *javadoc* application reads these tags to generate a description of the serialization format of each Serializable class.

## @serial

An @serial tag should be attached to each nontransient instance field. The content of this tag should describe the meaning of the field and the any constraints on its values. For example, this is how you might document the x and y fields in the TwoDPoint class:

```
import java.io.Serializable;

public class TwoDPoint implements Serializable {

  /** @serial the X-coordinate of the point;
   *           any double value except NaN
   */
  private double x;

  /** @serial the Y-coordinate of the point;
   *           any double value except NaN
   */
  private double y;
//...
```

This is a major violation of data encapsulation, but then serialization pretty much always is. Of course, there's no rule that says an alternate implementation of this class has to use two double x and y fields. It could use BigDecimals or doubles expressing polar coordinates. However, for compatibility when serializing, it should be prepared to write two doubles expressing Cartesian coordinates. The serialized form ultimately becomes just another part of the class's published interface, albeit one you can ignore for most operations.

## @serialData

A class that customizes the serialization format by implementing writeObject() or writeExternal() should annotate those methods with an @serialData tag explaining in detail the format written. For example, the writeObject() method in SerializableZipFile could be documented like this:

```
/** @serialData the name of the file is written as a String.
 *              No other data is written.
 */
private void writeObject(ObjectOutputStream out) throws IOException {
  out.writeObject(zf.getName());
}
```

This example's quite simple. Of course, the more complex the custom serialization format, the longer and more complex the comment will be.

# @serialField

Finally, if you have a serialPersistentFields array, each ObjectStreamField component of the array should be documented by @serialField tag. This tag is followed by the name of the field, the type of the field, and the description of the field. For example, this comment documents a serialPersistentFields array for the TwoDPoint:

```
/**
 * @serialField x double the Cartesian x-coordinate; never NaN
 * @serialField y double the Cartesian y-coordinate; never NaN
 */
private static final ObjectStreamField[] serialPersistentFields = {
   new ObjectStreamField("x", double.class),
   new ObjectStreamField("y", double.class)
};
```

 If you're starting to get the idea that object serialization is more complex than you thought, you're probably right. Doing object serialization properly takes forethought, care, and effort. It is not just a simple matter of declaring that a class implements Serializable and writing objects onto streams. Doing object serialization wrong can lead to brittle code that breaks every time you make small changes to what look like private parts of a class. It can lock you into a data structure you'd really rather change.

That's not to say you shouldn't use object serialization. There are many cases where it fits well, and if you have one of those cases, by all means use it. However, don't use it lightly. Make sure a class really needs to be serializable before you type "implements Serializable." In particular, do not make your classes Serializable out of habit. It's best to default to unserializable classes. After all, you can always add serialization support later if you find a need for it. It's much harder to take away a feature, even one that's causing you pain, after other developers are relying on it.

# PART IV

# New I/O

# CHAPTER 14

# Buffers

Traditional synchronous I/O is designed for traditional applications. Such applications have the following characteristics:

- Files may be large but not huge. It's possible to read an entire file into memory.

- An application reads from or writes to only a few files or network connections at the same time, ideally using only one stream at a time.

- The application is sequential. It won't be able to do much until it's finished reading or writing a file.

As long as these characteristics hold, stream-based I/O is reasonably quick and operates fairly efficiently. However, if these prerequisites are violated, the standard I/O model begins to show some weaknesses. For example, web servers often need to service hundreds or thousands of connections simultaneously. Scientific, engineering, and multimedia applications often need to manipulate datasets that are gigabytes in size.

Java 1.4 introduced a new model for I/O that is designed more for these sorts of applications and less for the more traditional applications that don't have to do so much I/O. The classes that make up this new I/O library are all found in the java. nio package and its subpackages. The new I/O model does not replace traditional, stream-based I/O. Indeed, several parts of the new I/O API are based on streams. However, the new I/O model is much more efficient for certain types of I/O-bound applications.

Whereas the traditional I/O model is based on streams, the new I/O model is based on buffers and channels. A buffer is like an array (in some implementations it may in fact be an array) that holds the data to be read and written. However, unlike input and output streams—even buffered input and output streams—the same buffer can be used for both reading and writing. Input channels fill a buffer with data that output channels then drain. Rather than being a part of a channel, a buffer is a neutral meeting ground in which channels exchange data. Furthermore, because buffers are objects accessed via methods, they may not really be arrays. They can be implemented directly on top of memory or the disk for extremely fast, random access. For the right kind of application, the performance gains can be dramatic.

Different buffers have different element types, just as arrays do. For instance, there are byte buffers, int buffers, float buffers, and char buffers. The class library doesn't contain any string buffers or object buffers, but you could write these classes yourself if you found a need. The same basic operations apply to all these different kinds of buffers:

- Allocate the buffer.
- Put values in the buffer.
- Get values from the buffer.
- Flip the buffer.
- Clear the buffer.
- Rewind the buffer.
- Mark the buffer.
- Reset the buffer.
- Slice the buffer.
- Compact the buffer.
- Duplicate the buffer.

## Copying Files with Buffers

I'm going to begin with a simple example, copying one file to another file. The basic interface to the program looks like this:

```
$ java FileCopier original copy
```

Obviously this program could be written in a traditional way with streams, and that's going to be true of almost all the programs you use the new I/O (NIO) model to write. NIO doesn't make anything possible that was impossible before. However, if the files are large and the local operating system is sophisticated enough, the NIO version of FileCopier might just be faster than the traditional version.

The rough outline of the program is typical:

```
import java.io.*;
import java.nio.*;

public class NIOCopier {

  public static void main(String[] args) throws IOException {

    FileInputStream inFile = new FileInputStream(args[0]);
    FileOutputStream outFile = new FileOutputStream(args[1]);
```

```
      // copy files here...

      inFile.close();
      outFile.close();
    }
  }
```

However, rather than merely reading from the input stream and writing to the output stream, I'm going to do something a little different. First, I open channels to both files using the getChannel( ) methods in FileInputStream and FileOutputStream:

```
FileChannel inChannel = inFile.getChannel();
FileChannel outChannel = outFile.getChannel();
```

Next, I create a one-megabyte buffer with the static factory method ByteBuffer.allocate( ):

```
ByteBuffer buffer = ByteBuffer.allocate(1024*1024);
```

The input channel will fill this buffer with data from the original file and the output channel will drain data out of this buffer to store into the copy.

To read data, you pass the buffer to the input channel's read( ) method, much as you'd pass a byte array to an input stream's read( ) method:

```
inChannel.read(buffer);
```

The read( ) method returns the number of bytes it read. As with input streams, there's no guarantee that the read( ) method completely fills the buffer. It may read fewer bytes or no bytes at all. When the input data is exhausted, the read( ) method returns –1. Thus, you normally do something like this:

```
long bytesRead = inChannel.read(buffer);
if (bytesRead == -1) break;
```

Now the output channel needs to write the data in the buffer into the copy. Before it can do that, though, the buffer must be *flipped*:

```
buffer.flip();
```

Flipping a buffer converts it from input to output.

To write the data, you pass the buffer to the output channel's write( ) method:

```
outChannel.write(buffer);
```

However, this is not like an output stream's write(byte[]) method. That method is guaranteed to write every byte in the array to the target or throw an IOException if it can't. The output channel's write( ) method is more like the read( ) method. It will write some bytes, but perhaps not all, and perhaps even none. It returns the number of bytes written. You could loop repeatedly until all the bytes are written, like this:

```
long bytesWritten = 0;
while (bytesWritten < bytesRead){
  bytesWritten += outChannel.write(buffer);
}
```

However, there's a simpler way. The buffer object itself knows whether all the data has been written. The hasRemaining( ) method can check this:

```
while (buffer.hasRemaining( )) outChannel.write(buffer);
```

This code reads and writes at most one megabyte. To copy larger files, we have to wrap all this up in a loop:

```
while (true) {
  ByteBuffer buffer = ByteBuffer.allocate(1024*1024);
  int bytesRead = inChannel.read(buffer);
  if (bytesRead == -1) break;
  buffer.flip( );
  while (buffer.hasRemaining( )) outChannel.write(buffer);
}
```

Allocating a new buffer for each read is wasteful and inefficient; we should reuse the same buffer. Before we do that, though, we must restore the buffer to a fresh state by invoking its clear( ) method:

```
ByteBuffer buffer = ByteBuffer.allocate(1024*1024);
while (true) {
  int bytesRead = inChannel.read(buffer);
  if (bytesRead == -1) break;
  buffer.flip( );
  while (buffer.hasRemaining( )) outChannel.write(buffer);
  buffer.clear( );
}
```

Finally, both the input and output channels should be closed to release any native resources the channel object may be holding onto:

```
inChannel.close( );
outChannel.close( );
```

Example 14-1 demonstrates the complete program, after taking a couple of common small shortcuts in the code. Compare this to the equivalent program for copying with streams found in Example 4-2.

*Example 14-1. Copying files using NIO*

```
import java.io.*;
import java.nio.*;
import java.nio.channels.*;

public class NIOCopier {

  public static void main(String[] args) throws IOException {

    FileInputStream inFile = new FileInputStream(args[0]);
    FileOutputStream outFile = new FileOutputStream(args[1]);

    FileChannel inChannel = inFile.getChannel( );
    FileChannel outChannel = outFile.getChannel( );
```

*Example 14-1. Copying files using NIO (continued)*

```
    for (ByteBuffer buffer = ByteBuffer.allocate(1024*1024);
    inChannel.read(buffer) != -1;
    buffer.clear( )) {
      buffer.flip( );
      while (buffer.hasRemaining( )) outChannel.write(buffer);
    }

    inChannel.close( );
    outChannel.close( );
  }
}
```

In a very unscientific test, copying one large (4.3-GB) file on one platform (a dual 2.5-GHz PowerMac G5 running Mac OS X 10.4.1) using traditional I/O with buffered streams and an 8192-byte buffer took 305 seconds. Expanding and reducing the buffer size didn't shift the overall numbers more than 5% and if anything tended to increase the time to copy. (Using a one-megabyte buffer like Example 14-1's actually increased the time to over 23 minutes.) Using new I/O as implemented in Example 14-1 was about 16% faster, at 255 seconds. A straight Finder copy took 197 seconds. Using the Unix *cp* command actually took 312 seconds, so the Finder is doing some surprising optimizations under the hood.

What this suggests is that new I/O doesn't help a great deal for traditional file operations that move through the file from beginning to end. The new I/O API is clearly not a panacea for all I/O performance issues. You can expect to see the biggest improvements in two other areas:

- Network servers that talk to many clients simultaneously
- Repeated random access to parts of large files

# Creating Buffers

java.nio has seven basic buffer classes for the seven different primitive data types:

- ByteBuffer
- ShortBuffer
- IntBuffer
- CharBuffer
- FloatBuffer
- DoubleBuffer
- LongBuffer

All seven buffer classes have very similar APIs that differ primarily in the return types of their get methods and the argument types of their put methods. Of these seven classes, ByteBuffer is by far the most important. For instance, the read( ) and write( )

methods in FileChannel will only take a ByteBuffer as an argument. However, there are ways to create views of a ByteBuffer as one of the other types so you can still write ints or chars or doubles onto a channel that works only with bytes. The patterns are very similar to how a DataOutputStream enables you to write ints or chars or doubles onto a stream that expects to receive bytes.

You create new buffers primarily in two ways: by allocation and by wrapping. *Allocation* creates a new buffer backed by memory, whereas *wrapping* uses a buffer as an interface to an existing array.

Allocation is straightforward. Simply pass the desired capacity of the buffer to the static allocate( ) method in the class you want to instantiate. For example, this statement creates a new ByteBuffer with room for 1024 bytes:

```
ByteBuffer bBuffer = ByteBuffer.allocate(1024);
```

This statement creates a new IntBuffer with room for 500 ints:

```
IntBuffer iBuffer = IntBuffer.allocate(500);
```

Both of these will be backed by an array. That is, bBuffer contains a byte array of length 1024 and iBuffer contains an int array of length 500. You can retrieve references to these backing arrays using the array( ) methods:

```
int[]  iData = iBuffer.array( );
byte[] bData = bBuffer.array( );
```

If you already have data in an array, you can build a buffer around it using the wrap( ) methods. For example:

```
int[] data = {1, 3, 2, 4, 23, 53, -9, 67};
IntBuffer buffer = IntBuffer.wrap(data);
```

In both cases, the arrays are not copies. These are the actual internal arrays where the buffer holds its data. Changing the data in these arrays changes the buffer's contents too, and vice versa.

However, there is another option, and this is where things get very interesting. Not all buffers are backed by Java arrays. You can allocate an array directly using the allocateDirect( ) methods instead of allocate( ):

```
ByteBuffer directBuffer = ByteBuffer.allocateDirect(1024);
```

Direct buffers can also be created by memory mapping a file. In this case, a lot of I/O operations may be performed directly on the files without copying them to RAM first.

The API to a direct buffer is exactly the same as to an indirect buffer, aside from the factory method that creates it. However, internally the computer may use different optimization techniques. For instance, it may map the buffer directly into main memory instead of going through an intermediate Java array object. Furthermore, it will make extra efforts to store the data in a contiguous memory block.

Such tricks can dramatically improve performance for large buffers. However, allocating a direct buffer takes longer than allocating an indirect buffer, so direct buffers are likely to be at best a wash and at worst significantly slower for smaller buffers than the indirect, array-backed buffers. Furthermore, the exact implementation details for the direct buffers are highly platform dependent. On some platforms, direct buffers offer a huge performance boost. On others, performance ranges from about the same as with streams to substantially worse. If performance is your primary concern, be sure to measure carefully both before and after using direct buffers.

Should you later need to find out whether a particular buffer has been allocated directly or indirectly, the isDirect( ) method will tell you:

```
public abstract boolean isDirect( )
```

# Buffer Layout

The conceptual model of a buffer is a fixed-size array. For example, suppose we allocate an IntBuffer with a *capacity* of 8:

```
IntBuffer buffer = buffer.allocate(8);
```

Figure 14-1 is a graphical representation of this buffer that I'll use to demonstrate various points. The slots in the buffer are numbered like arrays, starting with zero and ending with one less than the total capacity of the buffer.

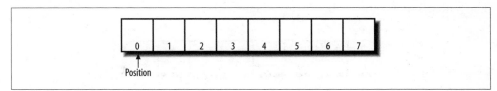

*Figure 14-1. An empty buffer with capacity 8*

A buffer's capacity is fixed when it is first created. Buffers do not expand or contract to fit the amount of data placed in them. Trying to put more data into a buffer than it has room for causes a BufferOverflowException. This is a runtime exception, since overflowing the buffer normally indicates a program bug.

As well as a list of indexed values, a buffer also contains a pointer into that list called the *position*. The position is the index of the next slot in the buffer that will be read or written. Its value is somewhere between zero and one less than the buffer's capacity. It is initially set to 0 and incremented as data is written to or read from the buffer. You can get the buffer's current position with the position( ) method:

```
public final int position( )
```

You can also change the buffer's position by passing the new position to this position( ) method:

```
public final Buffer position(int new Position)
```

However, most of the time you don't do this explicitly. Instead, the position is updated automatically as data is put into the buffer or retrieved from the buffer. For example, suppose we put the value 7 into the buffer in Figure 14-1:

```
buffer.put(7);
```

The int 7 is put in the buffer at position 0, and the position is incremented to 1, as shown in Figure 14-2.

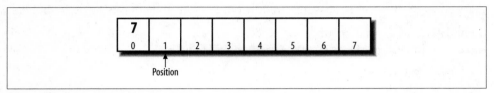

Figure 14-2. A buffer with position 1

 If the buffer were a more common ByteBuffer instead, you'd also need to cast the values put in the buffer, like so:

```
buffer.put((byte) 7);
```

Next, we'll put the value 65 in the buffer at position 1, so the position is incremented to 2:

```
buffer.put(65);
```

The buffer is now in the state shown in Figure 14-3.

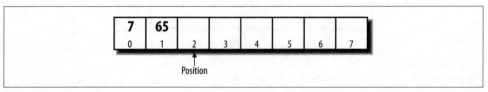

Figure 14-3. A buffer with position 2

We'll then put three more values in so the buffer is in the state shown in Figure 14-4:

```
buffer.put(-32);
buffer.put(116);
buffer.put(65);
```

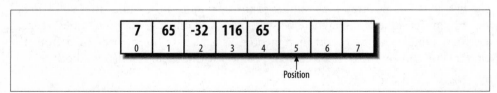

Figure 14-4. A buffer with position 5

I've left slots 5, 6, and 7 empty in the figure, but in reality they're filled with zeros, much as an array is initially filled with zeros.

Now it's time to read the data out of the buffer. There's a get( ) method that corresponds to the put( ) method. However, if we began getting from the current position, we'd read the zeros in slots 5, 6, and 7. Instead, first we *rewind* the buffer:

```
buffer.rewind( );
```

This doesn't change any of the data in the buffer, but it resets the position to 0, as shown in Figure 14-5.

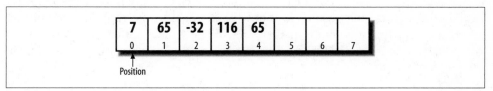

*Figure 14-5. A rewound buffer with position 0*

Now it's ready to be read. Call the get( ) method once to read the zeroth value from the buffer:

```
int i1 = buffer.get( );
```

Now the variable i1 has the value 7, and the position has advanced to 1. The buffer is in the state shown in Figure 14-6.

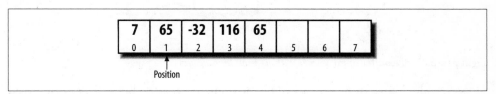

*Figure 14-6. After reading one value*

We can read the next values from the buffer the same way:

```
int i2 = buffer.get( );
int i3 = buffer.get( );
int i4 = buffer.get( );
int i5 = buffer.get( );
```

After this is done, the variable i2 has the value 65, i3 has the value –32, i4 has the value 116, and i5 has the value 65. The position has once again advanced to 5, as shown in Figure 14-7. It's important to note, however, that the data is still in the buffer. Unlike when writing data to a stream, the data hasn't vanished, even if we haven't stored what we read anywhere. It's possible to rewind the buffer and read it all again, any number of times. This capability turns out to be surprisingly useful.

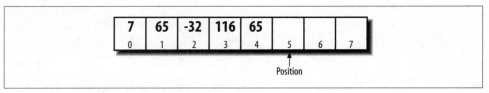

*Figure 14-7. The buffer after it's been drained*

We could read three more times from the buffer:

```
int i6 = buffer.get();
int i7 = buffer.get();
int i8 = buffer.get();
```

Again, although we never put anything in those slots, they are initialized to 0. After reading these bytes, the position will now be 8, equal to the capacity. Any further gets at this point without first rewinding the buffer will throw a BufferUnderflowException. This is a runtime exception that usually indicates a bug in the program.

## Limit

Besides position and capacity, each buffer also has a *limit* pointer. This is initially the same as the buffer's capacity. That is, a new, empty buffer with eight elements looks like Figure 14-8.

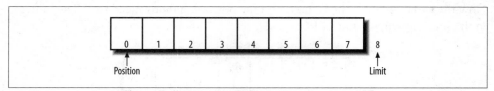

*Figure 14-8. A new buffer at position 0 with its limit equal to its capacity*

However, the limit can be set to a different value to keep the buffer from being read or written past a certain point. You can set the limit explicitly with this limit() method:

```
public final Buffer limit(int limit)
```

The no-args version returns the current limit:

```
public final int limit()
```

For example, you might initialize a buffer with a very large capacity, perhaps 2 MB, to make room for any possible data you might want to put there. You'd fill the buffer with as much data as you have. Then, before draining the data out of the buffer, you'd set the limit to the size of the data actually stored. For example, if you put five bytes in the buffer, you could set the limit to 5 and then reset the position back to 0:

```
buffer.limit(5);
buffer.position(0);
```

This would allow the process to retrieve elements 0 through 4 from the buffer, but if it tried to read elements 5 through 7, a BufferUnderflowException would be thrown. Before reading, you'd check that the position is less than the limit:

```
while (buffer.position() < buffer.limit()) buffer.get();
```

In practice, we don't manipulate the buffer quite so directly. Instead, we use the flip( ) and hasRemaining( ) methods:

```
public final Buffer flip()
public final boolean hasRemaining()
```

The flip( ) method sets the limit to the current position and then sets the position to 0. The hasRemaining( ) method returns true as long as the position is less than the limit. Using these two methods, we can make the code a little simpler and more generic:

```
buffer.flip();
while (buffer.hasRemaining()) buffer.get();
```

For example, suppose we put three bytes in the buffer from Figure 14-8, like this:

```
buffer.put(5);
buffer.put(23);
buffer.put(5);
```

Figure 14-9 shows the result.

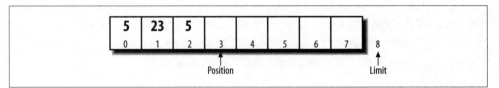

*Figure 14-9. A buffer at position 3 with capacity 8 and limit 8*

Before draining the data out of it, the buffer is flipped, like so:

```
buffer.flip();
```

This puts it in the state shown in Figure 14-10: the data is the same, but now the position is 0 and the limit is 3. As data is read out of the buffer, the position advances, but the limit stays the same.

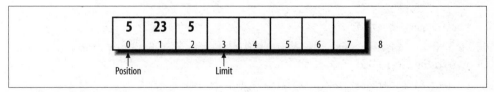

*Figure 14-10. A flipped buffer*

You read from the buffer only as long as the current position is less than the limit:

```
while (buffer.hasRemaining()) buffer.get();
```

After this loop completes, the buffer is in the state shown in Figure 14-11, with the limit equal to the position.

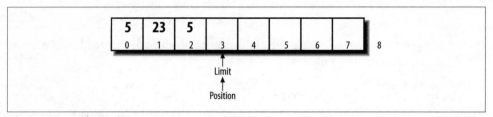

Figure 14-11. A flipped buffer with the limit equal to the position

# Bulk Put and Get

You've already seen the relative put and get methods, which insert or retrieve data at the current position. Bulk versions of these methods operate on arrays of the buffer's element type. For instance, ByteBuffer has these two bulk put methods:

```
public final ByteBuffer put(byte[] data)
public        ByteBuffer put(byte[] data, int offset, int length)
```

The first puts the entire contents of the array data into the buffer beginning at its current position. The position is incremented by the length of the array. The second puts only the sub-array of data beginning at offset and continuing for length bytes. These methods copy the array. Changing the data array after calling put( ) does not change the data in the buffer.

For example, this code fragment creates the buffer shown in Figure 14-12:

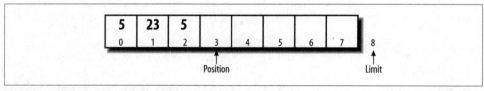

Figure 14-12. A byte buffer with position 3

```
ByteBuffer buffer = ByteBuffer.allocate(8);
buffer.put((byte) 5);
buffer.put((byte) 23);
buffer.put((byte) 5);
```

If we now put a byte array with length 4 in it, the position will move forward to 7, as shown in Figure 14-13:

```
byte[] data = {(byte) 67, (byte) -23, (byte) -5, (byte) 17};
buffer.put(data);
```

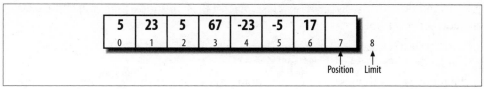

*Figure 14-13. A byte buffer with position 7*

From this point, we can put one more byte in the buffer, flip the buffer and drain it, clear the buffer and write eight more bytes, or do anything else we want. How the data was put in the buffer—whether with bulk or single methods, or relative or absolute methods—is irrelevant. All that matters is the state of the buffer.

Two corresponding bulk get methods copy bytes from the buffer starting at the current position into a provided array:

```
public ByteBuffer get(byte[] data)
public ByteBuffer get(byte[] data, int offset, int length)
```

Both methods update the position by the number of bytes returned.

For both put and get, the array must fit into the available space. If you try to put a larger array (or sub-array) into the buffer than it has space left for, put( ) throws a BufferOverflowException. If you try to get a larger array (or sub-array) than the buffer has data remaining, get( ) throws a BufferUnderflowException. In both cases, the buffer is left in its original state and no data is transferred.

Other buffers have these same methods. All that differs are the return and argument types. For instance, the IntBuffer class has these four methods:

```
public final IntBuffer put(int[] data)
public        IntBuffer put(int[] data, int offset, int length)
public        IntBuffer get(int[] data)
public        IntBuffer get(int[] data, int offset, int length)
```

DoubleBuffer has these four methods:

```
public final DoubleBuffer put(double[] data)
public        DoubleBuffer put(double[] data, int offset, int length)
public        DoubleBuffer get(double[] data)
public        DoubleBuffer get(double[] data, int offset, int length)
```

The other buffer classes are similar.

# Absolute Put and Get

The putters and getters you've seen so far have all been *relative*. That is, they put or got the data at the current position, and incremented the position accordingly. Some buffers also support *absolute* puts and gets. That is, they store or retrieve an element at a particular location in the buffer, irrespective of the position (though the limit and the capacity are still respected). For example, these are the absolute put( ) and get( ) methods for the `ByteBuffer` class. Each takes an index that is used instead of the current position:

```
public abstract ByteBuffer put(int index, byte b)
public abstract byte      get(int index)
```

If the index is less than zero or greater than or equal to the buffer's limit, these methods throw an `IndexOutOfBoundsException`. Otherwise, their use is straightforward. For example, this code fragment creates the holey buffer shown in Figure 14-14. Notice that these methods have no effect on the position or the limit:

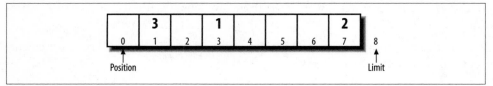

*Figure 14-14. A byte buffer that's been filled out of order*

```
ByteBuffer buffer = ByteBuffer.allocate(8);
buffer.put(3, (byte) 1);
buffer.put(7, (byte) 2);
buffer.put(1, (byte) 3);
```

The absolute methods for the other six buffer classes are similar, aside from the obvious type changes. For instance, these are the equivalent methods for `DoubleBuffer`:

```
public abstract DoubleBuffer put(int index, double x)
public abstract double        get(int index)
```

There are no absolute bulk get and put methods.

The absolute get and put operations are optional. Buffer objects are not guaranteed to support them. If a particular buffer object does not allow absolute gets or puts, and you attempt one anyway, the method will throw an `UnsupportedOperationException`. However, I've never encountered this in practice, and all buffers included with the JDK do support these methods.

As an example, suppose you've stored a GIF file into a `ByteBuffer` named `gifBuffer`, and you want to find the width and height of the image. The width is always found in the seventh and eighth bytes of the file (i.e., bytes 6 and 7, since the first byte is byte 0). The height is always found in the ninth and tenth bytes of the file. Both are unsigned little-endian shorts. We can read those values like this:

```
byte width1 = gifBuffer.get(6);
byte width2 = gifBuffer.get(7);
byte height1 = gifBuffer.get(8);
byte height2= gifBuffer.get(9);
int width = (width2 << 8) | width1;
int height = (height2 << 8) | height1;
```

The current position in the buffer is irrelevant. The width and the height are always found in bytes 6 to 9.

# Mark and Reset

Like input streams, buffers can be marked and reset using the mark( ) and reset( ) methods:

```
public final Buffer mark( )
public final Buffer reset( ) throws InvalidMarkException
```

Initially, the mark is unset. Invoking the buffer's mark( ) method places the mark at the buffer's current position. Resetting returns the position to the previous mark. Unlike with InputStream, there's no markSupported( ) method. All buffers support marking and resetting.

The mark is always less than or equal to the position and the limit. If either the limit or the position is set to a value less than the current mark, the mark is cleared. Resetting when there's no mark throws an InvalidMarkException.

# Compaction

Buffers are often used for sequential reading and writing. That is, first some data is read from a file, a network connection, or some other source and stored in the buffer. Next, data is drained from the buffer and written into a different file, network connection, or some other destination. However, the output that drains data from the buffer may not move as quickly as the input that fills the buffer. For instance, if data is being read from a file and written onto a network connection, input is likely to substantially outpace output.

To assist in such scenarios, many buffers can be *compacted* by invoking their compact( ) methods. This is the compact( ) method for ByteBuffer:

```
public abstract ByteBuffer compact( )
```

Each of the seven buffer classes has its own compact method that differs only in return type. For example, this is the compact method for DoubleBuffer:

```
public abstract DoubleBuffer compact( )
```

Compacting removes all the data from the buffer before the current position, then shifts the remaining data backwards in the buffer to the beginning. Finally, the limit is set to the capacity, and the position is set to the first empty space. For example, suppose we put five ints into a buffer, like this:

```
IntBuffer buffer = IntBuffer.allocate(8);
buffer.put(10).put(20).put(30).put(40).put(50);
```

The buffer is now in the state shown in Figure 14-15.

We now flip the buffer to prepare it for draining and read three ints from it using a bulk get:

```
buffer.flip( );
int[] data = new int[3]
buffer.get(data);
```

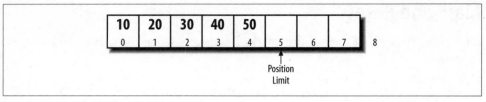

*Figure 14-15. A partially filled int buffer*

Now the buffer is in the state shown in Figure 14-16.

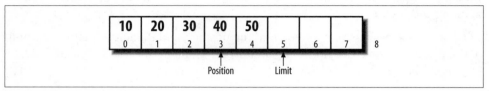

*Figure 14-16. The buffer when three ints have been read*

If we just want to continue draining from this point, we're good to go. However, if instead we now want to fill the buffer with more data, we have several problems. First, the position is set to 3, not 5. If we start putting now, we'll overwrite data that hasn't been processed. We could move the position to 5 and the limit to 8, but we'd still only have three empty slots left, and we may have more data than that. We could clear the buffer, but then we'd lose the unread data. Any manipulation of the position and the limit really isn't going to solve these problems. Instead, we call compact( ):

```
buffer.compact( );
```

This places the buffer in the state shown in Figure 14-17. As you can see, the two remaining ints are still available, and the position has been updated to allow as much data to be put in the buffer as possible without losing any unprocessed elements.

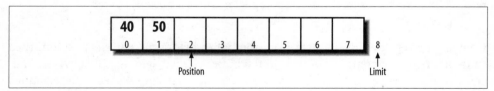

*Figure 14-17. A compacted buffer*

Example 14-2 demonstrates one possible use of the compact( ) method. This example copies a file, like the earlier Example 14-1. However, it uses only a single loop. One read and one write are performed in each pass through the loop. The flip( ) method makes the buffer ready for output and the compact( ) method makes it ready for input.

*Example 14-2. Copying files using NIO*

```java
import java.io.*;
import java.nio.*;
import java.nio.channels.*;

public class NIODuplicator {

  public static void main(String[] args) throws IOException {

    FileInputStream inFile = new FileInputStream(args[0]);
    FileOutputStream outFile = new FileOutputStream(args[1]);

    FileChannel inChannel = inFile.getChannel();
    FileChannel outChannel = outFile.getChannel();

    ByteBuffer buffer = ByteBuffer.allocate(1024*1024);
    int bytesRead = 0;
    while (bytesRead >= 0 || buffer.hasRemaining()) {
      if (bytesRead != -1) bytesRead = inChannel.read(buffer);
      buffer.flip();
      outChannel.write(buffer);
      buffer.compact();
    }

    inChannel.close();
    outChannel.close();
  }
}
```

If the output tends to block and the input doesn't, this program might be somewhat faster than Example 14-1, but then again, it might not be. As with any detailed performance analysis, actual results vary from one system and platform to the next. A better, more reliable solution to this problem would involve nonblocking I/O, which I'll take up in Chapter 16.

# Duplication

It is sometimes helpful to *duplicate* a buffer. A duplicate is not a copy or a clone. Rather, it is a new buffer object that has the same internal data as the original buffer, but an independent mark, limit, and position. Changes to the elements in the original buffer—that is, putting data in the buffer—affect the duplicate, and vice versa. However, getting data from one buffer, or flipping, resetting, rewinding, or clearing it, has no effect on the other. Duplicates are often useful when you want to pass the same fixed content to several different operations that run simultaneously or independently.

This is the duplicate method for ByteBuffer:

```java
public abstract ByteBuffer duplicate()
```

As usual, each of the seven buffer classes has its own duplicate method that differs primarily in return type. For example, this is the duplicate method for IntBuffer:

```
public abstract IntBuffer duplicate( )
```

When the duplicate is created, its position and mark are set to 0 and its limit is set to the capacity, regardless of the position, mark, and limit in the original buffer.

## Slicing

A *slice* is similar to a duplicate. However, rather than including a complete copy of the original's data, it includes only a subsequence. This subsequence begins at the original's position when the slice is made and continues until the original's limit. Because the data is shared, changes to the elements in the original buffer also change the slice, and vice versa. However, the position, limit, and mark in the slice are all independent of the position, limit, and mark in the original. The slice's capacity will be less than or equal to the original's capacity. Furthermore, they index differently. Position 5 in the original might be position 0 in the slice, in which case position 6 in the original is position 1 in the slice, position 7 is position 2, and so forth.

For example, suppose we put 8 multiples of 10 in an IntBuffer, like so:

```
IntBuffer original = IntBuffer.allocate(8);
original.put(10).put(20).put(30).put(40).put(50).put(60).put(70).put(80);
```

The original buffer is now in the state shown in Figure 14-18.

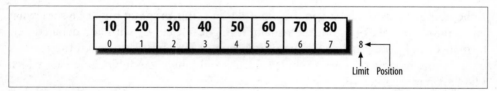

*Figure 14-18. A filled int buffer*

Now suppose we set the position to 4 and take a slice:

```
original.position(4);
IntBuffer slice = original.slice( );
```

Now we have two buffers, as shown in Figure 14-19. We can get from either one without changing the other. However, putting in the slice or putting in the original from position 4 on will affect the other buffer.

Slices are often useful for chopping headers off data. For example, a PNG image consists of an initial 8-byte signature (in hexadecimal), 0x89 0x50 0x4E 0x47 0x0D 0x0A 0x1A 0x0A, followed by three or more *chunks* of data. Each chunk consists of four parts:

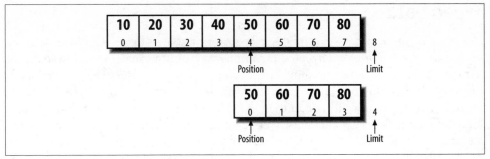

*Figure 14-19. A buffer and a slice of the buffer*

1. A 4-byte big-endian integer giving the length of the data in the chunk. Although unsigned, the value is between 0 and $2^{31}-1$.

2. A 4-byte ASCII signature such as IHDR or tIME identifying the type of the chunk.

3. The chunk data with the length given by field 1. This can be empty. (That is, its length can be 0.)

4. A 4-byte CRC checksum for the chunk. The checksum is calculated over fields 2 and 3; that is, the signature and the data but not the length.

Let us suppose that you have memory mapped the entire contents of a PNG image into a read-only buffer named pngBuffer. The first thing you might do is chop off the 8-byte signature, which is constant and therefore uninteresting. Slicing accomplishes this:

```
pngBuffer.position(8);
pngBuffer = buffer.slice();
```

You might then wish to create separate buffers for each individual chunk of the PNG image. These separate buffers can be implemented by slicing the buffer at the beginning of each chunk's data and then setting the limit of the slice to the end of the data. For example, this code fragment will map the first such chunk's data:

```
int i1 = buffer.get();
int i2 = buffer.get();
int i3 = buffer.get();
int i4 = buffer.get();
int size = i1 << 24 | i2 << 16 | i3 << 8 | i4
StringBuffer signature = new StringBuffer(4);
signature.append((char) buffer.get());
signature.append((char) buffer.get());
signature.append((char) buffer.get());
signature.append((char) buffer.get());
ByteBuffer firstChunkData = buffer.slice();
firstChunkData.limit(size);
```

Subsequent chunks can be sliced similarly.

# Typed Data

I/O is really about bytes—not ints, not text, not doubles—bytes. The bytes that are read and written can be interpreted in various ways, but as far as the filesystem, the network socket, or almost anything else knows, they're just bytes. The detailed interpretation is left up to the program that reads and writes those bytes. Thus, it shouldn't come as any surprise in the next chapter when you discover that different kinds of channels—TCP channels, UDP channels, file channels, and the like—deal almost exclusively with byte buffers and almost never with int buffers, char buffers, or anything else.

However, sometimes it's convenient to be able to pretend that I/O is about something else. If a program were dealing in ints, it would be nice to be able to read and write ints, not bytes. In traditional I/O, DataInputStream and DataOutputStream fill this gap. In new I/O, *view buffers* meet this need.

## View Buffers

The ByteBuffer class, and only the ByteBuffer class, can present a view of itself as a buffer of a different type: an IntBuffer, CharBuffer, ShortBuffer, LongBuffer, FloatBuffer, or DoubleBuffer. A view buffer is backed by a ByteBuffer. When you write an int such as 1,789,554 into the view buffer, the buffer writes the four bytes corresponding to that int into the underlying buffer. The encoding used is the same as that used by DataOutputStream, except for a possible byte order adjustment. The view buffer has a position, mark, limit, and capacity defined in terms of its type. The underlying ByteBuffer has a position, mark, limit, and capacity defined in terms of bytes. If the view buffer is an IntBuffer, the underlying ByteBuffer's position, mark, limit, and capacity will be four times the position, mark, limit, and capacity of the view buffer, because there are four bytes in an int. If the view buffer is a DoubleBuffer, the underlying ByteBuffer's position, mark, limit, and capacity will be eight times the position, mark, limit, and capacity of the view buffer, because there are eight bytes in a double. (If the buffer's size isn't an exact multiple of the view type's size, excess bytes at the end are ignored.)

Six methods in ByteBuffer create view buffers:

```
public abstract ShortBuffer  asShortBuffer()
public abstract IntBuffer    asIntBuffer()
public abstract LongBuffer   asLongBuffer()
public abstract FloatBuffer  asFloatBuffer()
public abstract DoubleBuffer asDoubleBuffer()
public abstract CharBuffer   asCharBuffer()
```

In Example 8-3, you saw how a DataOutputStream could write square roots in a file as doubles. Example 14-3 repeats this example using the new I/O API instead of streams. First, a ByteBuffer big enough to hold 1001 doubles is allocated. Next, a

DoubleBuffer is created as a view of the ByteBuffer. The double roots are put into this view buffer. Finally, the underlying ByteBuffer is written into the file.

*Example 14-3. Writing doubles with a view buffer*

```java
import java.io.*;
import java.nio.*;
import java.nio.channels.*;

public class RootsChannel {

  final static int SIZE_OF_DOUBLE = 8;
  final static int LENGTH = 1001;

  public static void main(String[] args) throws IOException {

    // Put 1001 roots into a ByteBuffer via a double view buffer
    ByteBuffer data = ByteBuffer.allocate(SIZE_OF_DOUBLE * LENGTH);
    DoubleBuffer roots = data.asDoubleBuffer();
    while (roots.hasRemaining()) {
      roots.put(Math.sqrt(roots.position()));
    }

    // Open a channel to the file where we'll store the data
    FileOutputStream fout = new FileOutputStream("roots.dat");
    FileChannel outChannel = fout.getChannel();
    outChannel.write(data);
    outChannel.close();
  }
}
```

Interestingly, the ByteBuffer in this example does not need to be flipped. Because the original buffer and the view buffer have separate positions and limits, writing data into the view buffer doesn't change the original's position; it only changes its data. When we're ready to write data from the original buffer onto the channel, the original buffer's position and limit still have their default values of 0 and the capacity, respectively.

## Put Type Methods

View buffers work as long as you want to write only one type of data (for example, all doubles, as in Example 14-4). However, very often files need to contain multiple types of data: doubles, ints, chars, and more. For instance, a PNG file contains unsigned integers, ASCII strings, and raw bytes. For this purpose, ByteBuffer has a series of put methods that take the other primitive types:

```java
public abstract ByteBuffer putChar(char c)
public abstract ByteBuffer putShort(short s)
public abstract ByteBuffer putInt(int i)
public abstract ByteBuffer putLong(long l)
public abstract ByteBuffer putFloat(float f)
public abstract ByteBuffer putDouble(double d)
```

The formats used to write these types are the same as for DataOutput (modulo byte order).

Each of these advances the position by the size of the corresponding type. For instance, putChar and putShort increment the position by 2, putInt and putFloat increment the position by 4, and putLong and putDouble increment the position by 8.

Of course, there are corresponding get methods:

```
public abstract char   getChar( )
public abstract short  getShort( )
public abstract int    getInt( )
public abstract long   getLong( )
public abstract float  getFloat( )
public abstract double getDouble( )
```

These all get from the current position. Each of these methods has an absolute variant that allows you to specify the position at which to put or get a value:

```
public abstract ByteBuffer putChar(int index , char c)
public abstract ByteBuffer putShort(int index , short s)
public abstract ByteBuffer putInt(int index , int i)
public abstract ByteBuffer putLong(int index , long l)
public abstract ByteBuffer putFloat(int index , float f)
public abstract ByteBuffer putDouble(int index , double d)
public abstract char       getChar(int index)
public abstract short      getShort(int index)
public abstract int        getInt(int index)
public abstract long       getLong(int index)
public abstract float      getFloat(int index)
public abstract double     getDouble(int index)
```

The earlier PNG example read the size of a data chunk by getting four bytes and then combining them into an int using the bitwise operators:

```
int i1 = buffer.get( );
int i2 = buffer.get( );
int i3 = buffer.get( );
int i4 = buffer.get( );
int size = i1 << 24 | i2 << 16 | i3 << 8 | i4
```

This can now be compressed into a single call to getInt( ):

```
int size = buffer.getInt( );
```

Be careful, though. These methods are not quite the same as the equivalent methods in CharBuffer, ShortBuffer, and so forth. The difference is that the index is into the byte range, not the double range. For example, consider this code fragment:

```
ByteBuffer buffer = buffer.allocate(8008);
for (int i = 0; i <= 1000; i++) {
  roots.putDouble(i, Math.sqrt(i));
}
```

It actually stores only 1,007 bytes in the buffer. Each double overwrites the seven low-order bytes of the previous double. The proper way to write this code is like this:

```
final int DOUBLE_SIZE = 8;
ByteBuffer buffer = buffer.allocate(1001 * DOUBLE_SIZE);
for (int i = 0; i <= 1000; i++) {
  roots.putDouble(i* DOUBLE_SIZE, Math.sqrt(i));
}
```

Despite these methods, a ByteBuffer still just stores bytes. It doesn't know which elements hold a piece of an int, which hold pieces of doubles, and which hold plain bytes. Your code is responsible for keeping track of the boundaries. If a buffer doesn't contain fixed types in fixed positions, you'll need to design some sort of meta-protocol using length and type codes to figure out where the relevant boundaries are.

Unlike DataOutputStream, there aren't any methods to write strings into a ByteBuffer. However, it's straightforward to write each char in the string. For example, this code writes the string "Laissez les bon temps roulez!" into a buffer:

```
String s = "Laissez les bon temps roulez!";
for (int i = 0; i < s.length(); i++) {
  buffer.putChar(s.charAt(i));
}
```

Alternately, you could create a CharBuffer view of the ByteBuffer, and then use the write(String) methods in CharBuffer:

```
CharBuffer cb = buffer.asCharBuffer();
cb.put("Laissez les bon temps roulez!");
```

In both cases it might be helpful to precede the string with its length, since buffers have no notions of boundaries between subsequent puts. For example:

```
String s = "Laissez les bon temps roulez!";
buffer.putInt(s.length());
CharBuffer cb = buffer.asCharBuffer();
cb.put(s);
```

Remember, the CharBuffer view starts at the position of the underlying buffer when the view was created. Here, this is immediately after the int containing the string's length.

## Byte Order

The DataInputStream and DataOutputStream classes in java.io only handle big-endian data. The buffers in new I/O are a little more flexible. By default, they're configured for big-endian data. However, they can be changed to little-endian if that's what you need. Usually, you need to specify byte order. For example, if you're reading or writing astronomy data in the FITS format, you have to use big-endian. It doesn't matter what platform you're on; FITS files are always big-endian.

Well, not quite always. The FITS spec says numbers are supposed to be big-endian, but you can in fact find FITS files and software that use little-endian representations. Either way, given a file in big- or little-endian format, you have to read it in the order it was written for the data to make sense, regardless of the native byte order of the host platform.

The order( ) method lets you specify the required byte order:

```
public final ByteBuffer order(ByteOrder order)
```

The current byte order is returned by the no-args version of the method:

```
public final ByteOrder order( )
```

ByteOrder has exactly two possible values:

```
ByteOrder.BIG_ENDIAN
ByteOrder.LITTLE_ENDIAN
```

Sometimes what you want is the native byte order of the host platform. The static ByteOrder.nativeOrder( ) method tells you this:

```
public static ByteOrder nativeOrder( )
```

## Read-Only Buffers

Buffers can be read-only. For example, a buffer that's backed by a file on a CD-ROM would be read-only. Buffers might also be read-only if they're memory mapped to a file you don't have write permission for, or to the input buffer on a network card. A CharBuffer that wraps a CharSequence is read-only. If you aren't sure whether you can write to a buffer, you can invoke isReadOnly( ) before attempting to do so:

```
public abstract boolean isReadOnly( )
```

Any attempt to store data into a read-only buffer throws a ReadOnlyBufferException. This is a runtime exception.

You can create a read-only buffer using the asReadOnly( ) method:

```
public abstract ByteBuffer asReadOnlyBuffer( )
```

As usual, there are variants of this for all the different types of buffers that differ only in return type. For example, this is DoubleBuffer's asReadOnly( ) method:

```
public abstract DoubleBuffer asReadOnlyBuffer( )
```

This is essentially a view buffer of the same type that doesn't allow puts. Its mark, limit, position, capacity, and content are initially the same as those of the buffer from which it was created. However, from this point forward, the limit, mark, and position can change independently of the underlying buffer.

For buffers created in this way, "read-only" is a bit of a misnomer. While you cannot put into such a buffer, you can still put values into the original underlying buffer, and any changes made in that way will immediately be reflected in the overlaid read-only buffer.

 There are no write-only buffers. All buffers can be read.

# CharBuffers

A CharBuffer works pretty much the same as an IntBuffer, a DoubleBuffer, a LongBuffer, and any of the other multibyte buffer types. That is, it has absolute and relative put methods that put chars; absolute and relative get methods that get chars; bulk put and get methods that put and get arrays of chars; and methods to flip, clear, rewind, and so forth. CharBuffer also has some convenience methods that operate on CharSequences (usually Strings, but also StringBuffers, StringBuilders, and so on). Furthermore, the CharBuffer class itself implements CharSequence, so you can pass it to methods such as Java 6's Normalizer.isNormalized( ), query it with regular expressions, and generally use it as you would any string.

A CharBuffer can be created in the three usual ways: by allocation, by wrapping a preexisting char[ ] array, or as a view of a ByteBuffer. A CharBuffer can also be created by wrapping a CharSequence:

```
public static CharBuffer wrap(CharSequence sequence)
```

or from a subsequence beginning at a certain offset and continuing to a certain point:

```
public static CharBuffer wrap(CharSequence sequence, int start, int end)
```

Because CharSequence is a read-only interface (i.e., it has no setter methods), the buffers created in this way are also read-only. You can get from them, but you can't put into them. Attempting to do so throws a ReadOnlyBufferException.

# Memory-Mapped I/O

About 12 years ago, I was a grad student working at the National Solar Observatory in Sunspot, New Mexico. The program I was working on involved three-dimensional Fourier transforms on four-dimensional data. We had taken snapshots of wind speeds in a particular three-dimensional chunk of the sun's photosphere, and my job was to try to make sense out of them. Our measurements covered an area of roughly 200 points by 100 points at 10 different depths over 100 time increments. This doesn't sound like a lot, but if you multiply it out, and figure we had a 4-byte float at each point, that's about 75 MB of data. To do the transforms we needed double that amount of memory. Every time I started running my naïve code to transform this monstrous set, everyone else's terminals slowed to a crawl as the disks began to thrash madly. Solaris was swapping everything in and out to try to find enough space to run my program. Within a couple of minutes, our normally friendly sysadmin would run down the hall yelling, "Rusty, what are you doing now?!"

In 2006 150 MB of working set size is no big deal, but back then it was a lot. Of course, the telescopes, spectrometers, charge-coupled detectors, and other tools have grown to match the capacity of today's computers, and grad students are now manipulating datasets that are gigabytes or more in size, still outpacing the growth of memory capacity.

Fortunately for the sysadmin's sanity and my continued employment, I soon discovered the magic of memory-mapped I/O. Instead of loading the arrays into memory, I just flipped one little switch in my program that told IDL (the programming language I was using at the time) to keep those particular arrays on disk and treat the disk as if it were a block of memory. This wasn't quite as fast as using real memory, but in this case the real memory wasn't there to be used anyway. It was all going out to disk sooner or later, and the only question was whether or not it went through Solaris's virtual memory system first. Memory-mapped I/O was like magic. My programs ran. In fact, they ran faster than they had before because the disks stopped thrashing, and the sysadmin stopped yelling at me because I was no longer overloading the server. Everyone was happy.

Memory-mapped I/O is not a solution to all problems. It really applies only when you have datasets that equal or exceed the available memory. However, in that event, it's a godsend. Programmers working in C, IDL, Fortran, and many other environments have been able to rely on memory-mapped I/O for a long time, and finally (as of 1.4) Java programmers can too.

## Creating Mapped Byte Buffers

The MappedByteBuffer class maps a file directly into a ByteBuffer. You operate on it using the same put( ), get( ), putInt( ), getInt( ), and other methods for operating on any other ByteBuffer. However, the puts and gets access the file directly without copying a lot of data to and from RAM.

Mapped byte buffers are created using the map( ) method in the FileChannel class:

```
public abstract MappedByteBuffer map(FileChannel.MapMode mode,
  long position, long size) throws IOException
```

Memory mapping can operate in three modes:

FileChannel.MapMode.READ_ONLY
> You can get data from the buffer but cannot change the data in the buffer.

FileChannel.MapMode.READ_WRITE
> You can both get data from and put data in the buffer.

FileChannel.MapMode.PRIVATE
> You can get data from and put data in the buffer. However, data you put is visible only through this buffer. The file itself is not changed.

For example, this code fragment maps the file *test.png* in read/write mode:

```
RandomAccessFile file = new RandomAccessFile("test.png", "rw");
FileChannel channel = file.getChannel();
ByteBuffer buffer = channel.map(
  FileChannel.MapMode.READ_WRITE, 0, file.length());
```

The position of the buffer is initially equal to 0 and the limit is initially equal to the buffer's capacity. The capacity is whatever value was passed for the third argument. These are not necessarily the same as the zero position in and the length of the file itself. You can and often do memory map just a portion of a large file, if you don't need the while thing. For instance, this code fragment maps the portion of a PNG file that follows the initial 8-byte signature:

```
ByteBuffer buffer = channel.map(FileChannel.MapMode.READ_WRITE,
  8, file.length()-8);
```

The initial position cannot be negative. That is, it cannot precede the beginning of the file. However, if the file is open for writing, the capacity can exceed the file's length. If so, the file will be expanded to the requested length.

The available modes depend on the underlying object from which the FileChannel was created. Random access files can be mapped in read-only or read/write modes. File input streams can be mapped in read-only mode. File output streams cannot be mapped at all. Normally, a RandomAccessFile is the source.

Java does not specify what happens if another process or even another part of the same program changes the file while it's mapped. The ByteBuffer object may or may not show the changes. If it does reflect those changes, the reflection may or may not be immediate. This will vary from one platform to the next.

## MappedByteBuffer Methods

Besides the methods common to all byte buffers, MappedByteBuffer has three methods of its own: force(), load(), and isLoaded().

The load() method attempts to load the entire buffer into main memory:

```
public final MappedByteBuffer load()
```

This may make access to the buffer faster, but then again it may not. If the data is larger than Java's heap size, this is likely to cause some page faults and disk thrashing. The isLoaded() method tells you whether a buffer is loaded:

```
public final boolean isLoaded()
```

Finally, if you've put data in a MappedByteBuffer, you should flush the buffer when you're done with it, just like an OutputStream. However, instead of a flush() method, you use the force() method:

```
public final MappedByteBuffer force()
```

As with flushing, this may not always be necessary. Data will eventually be written out from the buffer into the underlying file if the program doesn't crash. However, the force( ) method enables you to control when this happens and to make sure it does, at least for local filesystems. Java can't always immediately force network-mounted disks.

As a final example, let's consider how one might securely overwrite a file. The U.S. Department of Defense National Industrial Security Program Operating Manual 5220.22 (page 8-3-6) requires that the erasure of secret data be accomplished by overwriting each location with a 0 byte (0x00), its complement (0xFF), and then a random byte.

 Top-secret data requires a more secure approach, with at least seven passes, including some overwriting with particular bit patterns. The truly paranoid use 35 passes in random orders. However this example suffices to demonstrate the points relevant to NIO.

Beyond performing multiple passes over the data, improved security also requires carefully erasing the file's name and other metadata, as well as any virtual memory or other locations where copies of the file's contents may reside.

Example 14-4 maps the entire file to be erased into memory. It then writes zeros into the file, then ones, then random data produced by a java.util.SecureRandom object. After each run, the buffer is forced to make sure the data is actually written to the disk. Otherwise, only the last pass might be committed. Failing to force the data might leave magnetic patterns an adversary could analyze, even if the actual file contents were the same.

*Example 14-4. Erasing a file with a MappedByteBuffer*

```
import java.io.*;
import java.nio.*;
import java.nio.channels.*;
import java.security.SecureRandom;

public class SecureDelete {

  public static void main(String[] args) throws IOException {

    File file = new File(args[0]);
    if (file.exists()) {
      SecureRandom random = new SecureRandom( );
      RandomAccessFile raf = new RandomAccessFile(file, "rw");
      FileChannel channel = raf.getChannel( );
      MappedByteBuffer buffer
       = channel.map(FileChannel.MapMode.READ_WRITE, 0, raf.length( ));
      // overwrite with zeros
      while (buffer.hasRemaining( )) {
        buffer.put((byte) 0);
```

*Example 14-4. Erasing a file with a MappedByteBuffer (continued)*

```
    }
    buffer.force( );
    buffer.rewind( );
    // overwrite with ones
    while (buffer.hasRemaining( )) {
      buffer.put((byte) 0xFF);
    }
    buffer.force( );
    buffer.rewind( );
    // overwrite with random data; one byte at a time
    byte[] data = new byte[1];
    while (buffer.hasRemaining( )) {
      random.nextBytes(data);
      buffer.put(data[0]);
    }
    buffer.force( );
    file.delete( );
    }
  }
}
```

This program is not especially fast. On fairly impressive hardware, it could erase a little over 100K a second. Some improvement could be made by overwriting more than a byte at a time, but if you do this be careful that the final write doesn't write too much and cause a BufferOverflowException.

# CHAPTER 15

# Channels

The examples in the last chapter all read and wrote file channels. However, just as streams aren't limited to files, neither are channels. Like streams, channels can read and write network sockets, byte arrays, piped data from other threads, and more. The basic methods and patterns for reading and writing channels don't change from one data source to the next. You drain data from buffers when writing and fill buffers with data when reading. You can also transfer data directly from one channel to another. However, some things do change from one channel to the next. For instance, some channels are read-only and some are write-only. Some scatter data to multiple targets while some gather data from multiple sources. In this chapter, we take up the details of the various channel classes found in the java.nio.channels package.

## The Channel Interfaces

Much of the channel functionality is abstracted into a series of different interfaces. Interfaces are used rather than abstract classes because there's frequently a need to mix and match different components. Some channels can be read, some can be written, and some can be both read and written. Some channels are interruptible and some are not. Some channels scatter and some gather. In practice, these capabilities appear in almost any combination.

### Channel

The key superinterface is java.nio.channels.Channel. This interface defines the only two methods all channels implement, isOpen( ) and close( ):

```
public boolean isOpen( )
public void    close( ) throws IOException
```

That is, the only things you know you can do with any channel are find out whether or not it's open and close it. Given this limited functionality, it's rare to work with just a Channel variable instead of using a more detailed type.

# ReadableByteChannel and WritableByteChannel

The next most basic interfaces are ReadableByteChannel and WritableByteChannel, which are used for channels that read and write bytes, respectively. Some channels can both read and write, but most channels do one or the other. In theory, channels could work with ints, doubles, strings, and so on. In practice, though, it's always bytes.

ReadableByteChannel declares a single method that fills a ByteBuffer with data read from the channel:

```
public int read(ByteBuffer target) throws IOException
```

WritableByteChannel declares a single method that drains data from a ByteBuffer and writes it out to the channel:

```
public int write(ByteBuffer source) throws IOException
```

These are the two methods you saw used in the examples in the previous chapter. Each returns the number of bytes read or written, and each advances the position of the buffer argument by the same amount.

## ByteChannel

Channels that can both read and write sometimes implement the ByteChannel interface. This is simply a convenience interface that implements both ReadableByteChannel and WritableByteChannel. It does not declare any additional methods.

```
public interface ByteChannel extends ReadableByteChannel, WritableByteChannel
```

In the core library, this is implemented by SocketChannel, DatagramChannel, and FileChannel. Other channels implement one or the other.

## Exceptions

The read( ) and write( ) methods are declared to throw IOException, which they do for all the same reasons a stream might throw an IOException: the disk you're writing to fills up, the remote network server you're talking to crashes, your cat dislodges the Ethernet cable from the back of the computer, and so on.

You cannot write to or read from a closed channel; if you try, the method will throw a ClosedChannelException, a subclass of IOException. If the channel is closed by another thread while the write or read is in progress, AsynchronousCloseException, a subclass of ClosedChannelException, is thrown. If another thread interrupts the thread's read or write operation, ClosedByInterruptException, a subclass of AsynchronousCloseException, is thrown.

The read( ) and write( ) methods can also throw runtime exceptions, which usually result from logic errors in the program. The read( ) method throws a

NonReadableChannelException if you try to read from a channel that has been opened only for writing. (You'd think such a channel would not be an instance of ReadableByteChannel in the first place, but sometimes the strictures of API design require Java to act as if it were weakly typed, static type checking notwithstanding.) Similarly, the write( ) method throws a NonWritableChannelException if you try to write to a channel that was opened only for reading.

## Gathering and Scattering Channels

Most classes that implement ReadableByteChannel also implement its subinterface, ScatteringByteChannel. This interface adds two more read( ) methods that can use several buffers:

```
public long read(ByteBuffer[] dsts) throws IOException
public long read(ByteBuffer[] dsts, int offset, int length) throws IOException
```

After the first buffer fills up, data read from the channel is placed in the second buffer in dsts. After the second buffer fills up, data is then placed in the third buffer, and so on. The second method is the same except that it starts with the buffer at offset and continues through length buffers. That is, offset and length define the subset of buffers to use from the dsts array, not the offset and length inside each individual buffer.

Similarly, most classes that implement WritableByteChannel also implement its sub-interface, GatheringByteChannel. This interface adds two more write( ) methods that drain data from an array of buffers:

```
public long write(ByteBuffer[] srcs) throws IOException
public long write(ByteBuffer[] srcs, int offset, int length) throws IOException
```

After the first buffer empties, the channel starts draining the second buffer. After the second buffer is empty, data is drained from the third buffer, and so on. Again, the three-argument version is the same except that it starts draining the buffer at offset and continues through length buffers.

This is most useful when the data written to a channel consists of several distinct pieces. For instance, an HTTP server might store the HTTP header in one buffer and the HTTP body in another, then write both using a gathering write. If you're writing a file containing individual records, each record could be stored in a separate buffer.

These methods mostly throw the same exceptions for the same reasons as the non-gathering/scattering read( ) and write( ) methods do: IOException, ClosedChannelException, NonReadableChannelException, and so on. They can also throw an IndexOutofBoundsException if the offset or the length exceeds the bounds of the array.

As a very simple example, let's suppose you wish to concatenate several files, as you might with the Unix *cat* utility. You could map each input file into a ByteBuffer and write all the buffers into a new File, as Example 15-1 demonstrates.

*Example 15-1. Gathering channels*

```java
import java.io.*;
import java.nio.*;
import java.nio.channels.*;

public class NIOCat {

  public static void main(String[] args) throws IOException {

    if (args.length < 2) {
      System.err.println("Usage: java NIOCat inFile1 inFile2... outFile");
      return;
    }

    ByteBuffer[] buffers = new ByteBuffer[args.length-1];
    for (int i = 0; i < args.length-1; i++) {
      RandomAccessFile raf = new RandomAccessFile(args[i], "r");
      FileChannel channel = raf.getChannel();
      buffers[i] = channel.map(FileChannel.MapMode.READ_ONLY, 0, raf.length());
    }

    FileOutputStream outFile = new FileOutputStream(args[args.length-1]);
    FileChannel out = outFile.getChannel();
    out.write(buffers);
    out.close();
  }
}
```

Example 15-1 makes one dangerous assumption, though: it only works if the write( ) method writes every byte from every buffer. For file channels in blocking mode, this is likely the case and will be true most of the time. A gathering write tries to write all the bytes possible, and more often than not it will do so. However, some channels may be limited. For instance, a socket channel operating in nonblocking mode cannot write more bytes than the local TCP buffer will hold. A more robust solution would write continuously in a loop until none of the buffers had any remaining data:

```java
outer: while (true) {
  out.write(buffers);
  for (int i = 0; i < buffers.length; i++) {
    if (buffers[i].hasRemaining()) continue outer;
  }
  break;
}
```

Honestly, this is ugly, and on a nonblocking channel I'd be inclined to just write the buffers individually instead, like so:

```java
for (int i = 0; i < buffers.length; i++) {
  while (buffers[i].hasRemaining()) out.write(buffers[i]);
}
```

# File Channels

A java.nio.channels.FileChannel can potentially be both a GatheringByteChannel and a ScatteringByteChannel. That is, it implements both interfaces. Most of the time, however, each actual FileChannel object is either readable or writable, not both. FileChannels created by invoking the getChannel() method of a FileOutputStream are writable. FileChannels created by invoking the getChannel() method of a FileInputStream are readable. Invoking a write() method on a channel connected to a FileInputStream throws a NonWritableChannelException. Invoking a read() method on a channel connected to a FileOutputStream throws a NonReadableChannelException. Only a FileChannel created from a RandomAccessFile can be both read and written.

Besides reading and writing, file channels permit several other file-specific operations:

- Data can be transferred from the file to a channel, or from a channel to the file, without your code reading and writing each individual byte.

- The current position in the file can be changed. That is, you don't have to read or write a file from beginning to end, as with a stream. You can jump around in the file.

- File channels can be locked so that other processes cannot access them.

- File channels can be flushed to write data to an associated device.

## Transferring Data

Example 14-1 in the previous chapter showed you how to copy one file to another using two FileChannels and a ByteBuffer to hold the data as it is copied from the old file into the new one. You can simplify the operation by taking advantage of FileChannel's two transfer methods:

```
public abstract long transferFrom(
 ReadableByteChannel src, long position, long count)
 throws IOException
public abstract long transferTo(
 long position, long count,  WritableByteChannel target)
 throws IOException
```

The first method copies count bytes from the source channel into the file starting at position. The second method copies count bytes from the file onto the target channel starting at position.

Example 15-2 demonstrates using transferTo() to copy one file to another.

*Example 15-2. Transferring data between channels*

```java
import java.io.*;
import java.nio.channels.*;

public class NIOTransfer {

  public static void main(String[] args) throws IOException {

    FileInputStream inFile = new FileInputStream(args[0]);
    FileOutputStream outFile = new FileOutputStream(args[1]);

    FileChannel inChannel = inFile.getChannel();
    FileChannel outChannel = outFile.getChannel();

    inChannel.transferTo(0, inChannel.size(), outChannel);

    inChannel.close();
    outChannel.close();
  }
}
```

Neither the source nor the target channel has to be a file. These methods can also transfer data from a file to a network channel or from a network channel into a file. However, in this case, because both channels are files, the same program could be implemented using transferFrom( ) instead.

To do this, simply change inChannel.transferTo(0, inChannel.size( ), outChannel) to outChannel.transferFrom(inChannel, 0, inChannel.size( )).

Neither transferTo( ) nor transferFrom( ) is guaranteed to transfer as many bytes as requested. However, they're a little more reliable than the multibyte read( ) methods of InputStream. These methods will fail to transfer count bytes only if either the input channel doesn't have that many bytes or the output channel is nonblocking. Neither of those is the case here.

It's possible that this is just a shortcut for moving data from one channel to another through a buffer, as seen in Example 14-1. However, some platforms can transfer the bytes much more directly and quickly when using this method. Intermediate buffering might not be used. Thus, when moving data to and from files, you should use transferTo( ) or transferFrom( ) whenever possible. They should never be noticeably slower than manually managing the buffers, and sometimes they may be significantly faster.

## Random Access

Although files are often read by streams, files are not streams. Unlike a network socket, a file does not have to be read sequentially. The disk controller can easily reposition itself to read or write at any given position in a file, and file channels can take advantage of this capability.

Each file channel knows its current position within the file. This is measured in bytes and is returned by the position( ) function:

```
public abstract long position() throws ClosedChannelException, IOException
```

As data is read out of the file or written into the file, the position is updated automatically. However, you can also change the position manually using this overloaded position( ) method:

```
public abstract FileChannel position(long newPosition)
  throws IllegalArgumentException , ClosedChannelException, IOException
```

For example, this code fragment skips over the next 4K in the file:

```
channel.position(channel.position( )+4096);
```

You can position the file pointer past the end of the file. Trying to read from this position returns –1 to signal the end of the file. Of course, unlike with an InputStream, you can reposition the file pointer and reread from earlier in the file, despite having reached the end of it. Trying to write past the end of file automatically expands the file. The only things you can't do are read or write before the beginning of the file. Setting the position to a negative number throws an IllegalArgumentException.

If you set the file pointer past the end of the file and then start writing, the content of the file between the old end and the new position is system dependent. On some systems this region may be filled with random data that was left on the disk. In many circumstances this can be a security hole, since it may expose data that was meant to be deleted. Therefore, you really shouldn't do this unless you know you're going to go back later and fill in those bytes before closing the file.

You can check the size of the file with the size( ) method:

```
public abstract long size() throws IOException
```

There's no corresponding setter. You can expand a file only by writing more data at the desired end of the file. You can, however, shorten a file to a specified length using the truncate( ) method:

```
public abstract FileChannel truncate(long size) throws IOException
```

This method reduces the file to the specified size. Any bytes after that point are lost.

 The truncated bytes still exist on the disk, though, until some process overwrites them. Security-conscious applications may wish to overwrite them before truncating the data.

## Threading and Locking

Unlike streams, file channels are safe for access from multiple concurrent threads. Multiple threads can read from or write to the same FileChannel simultaneously. Reads that use absolute positions in the file could possibly be genuinely simultaneous. Writes and relative reads queue up behind each other. Operations block as necessary to keep the file in a well-defined state. Writes are not allowed to overlap.

Nonetheless, the ordering of writes from different threads can still be unpredictable. This may not matter for some use cases, such as a log file, where all that matters is that each write is atomic and the relative order of writes is unimportant. However, much of the time, more control is needed.

Applications sometimes need exclusive access to particular files. For instance, if two different word processors try to edit the same document at the same time, conflicts are almost inevitable. File channels allow Java applications to attempt to lock a given file or piece of a file for exclusive access. The attempt may not always succeed, of course. Another process may have locked the same file already, but at least you can ask. The method that asks is lock( ):

```
public final FileLock lock( ) throws IOException
```

This method blocks until it can get the lock on the file. If it can't get the lock on the file, it throws one of a variety of IOExceptions, depending on exactly why it can't get the lock. Besides the usual reasons (IOException, ClosedChannelException, etc.), it may also throw a FileLockInterruptionException if another thread interrupts this one while it's waiting for the lock.

On Windows, locks are mandatory and are enforced by the operating system. Once you've locked a file, no other program can access it (though another thread in the same VM can). Most of the time on Unix, though, locks are only advisory. That is, another process is supposed to check to see if the file is locked, and wait if it is. However, the operating system does not enforce this.

For some use cases, it's not necessary to lock the entire file. You can instead request a lock over only a piece of it, starting at a specified position and continuing for a certain number of bytes:

```
public abstract FileLock lock(long position, long size, boolean shared)
  throws IOException
```

The range bounded by position and size need not be contained within the file. You can lock regions that go beyond the end of the file or are even completely outside it. If so, the lock is retained if the file grows. If the file grows beyond the range you've locked, new content past the lock's boundary is not locked.

Some operating systems, including Windows and Unix, support *shared locks*. A shared lock allows multiple applications, all of which have the shared lock, to access the file. However, no one application can exclusively lock the file. If the third argument is true, lock( ) tries to get a shared lock. However, if the operating system doesn't support this functionality, it just waits for an exclusive lock instead. Shared locks are allowed only on readable files (i.e., you can't have a shared lock on a write-only channel). Unshared locks are allowed only on writable files (i.e., you can't have an unshared lock on a read-only channel).

Both lock( ) methods can wait for an indefinite amount of time. If you want to lock if possible but don't want to block the entire thread, use the tryLock( ) methods instead:

```
public final   FileLock tryLock( ) throws IOException
public abstract FileLock tryLock(long position, long size, boolean shared)
  throws IOException
```

These methods act the same as lock( ), except that they return immediately. If a file has already been locked, these two methods return null. If the file can't be locked for some other reason, these methods throw an IOException.

## FileLock

All four lock( ) and tryLock( ) methods return a FileLock object that represents the lock on the file. The primary purpose of this object is to release the lock when you're done with the file:

```
public abstract void release( ) throws IOException
```

A FileLock can also tell you whether it has locked at least part of a given range:

```
public final boolean overlaps(long position, long size)
```

This class also has a few getter methods that may occasionally be useful:

```
public final     FileChannel channel( )
public final     long        position( )
public final     long        size( )
public final     boolean     isShared( )
public abstract  boolean     isValid( )
```

They don't follow the usual Java naming conventions—almost nothing in the new I/O API does—but they are all basic getter methods. The channel( ) method returns the channel that locked the file. The position( ) method returns the byte index of the start of the locked range. The size( ) method returns the length of the locked range. The isShared( ) method returns true if the lock is shared and false otherwise; the isValid( ) method returns false if the lock has been released or the channel closed and true otherwise.

Example 15-3 demonstrates locking a file before copying data into it. The output channel needs an unshared lock because it's write-only, so we can use the simple no-args lock( ) method to lock it. The input channel needs a shared lock because it's read-only, so we have to use the three-args lock( ) method to lock it from the first byte of the file through the last byte of the file.

*Example 15-3. Copying locked files*

```
import java.io.*;
import java.nio.channels.*;
```

*Example 15-3. Copying locked files (continued)*

```java
public class LockingCopier {

  public static void main(String[] args) throws IOException {

    FileInputStream inFile = new FileInputStream(args[0]);
    FileOutputStream outFile = new FileOutputStream(args[1]);

    FileChannel inChannel = inFile.getChannel();
    FileChannel outChannel = outFile.getChannel();

    FileLock outLock = outChannel.lock();
    FileLock inLock  = inChannel.lock(0, inChannel.size(), true);

    inChannel.transferTo(0, inChannel.size(), outChannel);

    outLock.release();
    inLock.release();

    inChannel.close();
    outChannel.close();
  }
}
```

Technically, the lock release isn't necessary here. Closing the output channel also releases the locks on it. However, it's good form and it will definitely be necessary if you're not going to close the file immediately after finishing the operation for which you locked it in the first place.

## Flushing

Like file streams, file channels can be buffered. The actual implementation of the buffer is usually different, though. In particular, a file channel's buffering most likely reflects the caching of the native filesystem, while an OutputStream's buffer usually reflects operations inside the VM. However, the effect in both cases is the same.

To make sure that data is actually written to the disk, it may be necessary to flush it. The method that flushes a FileChannel is called force():

```java
public abstract void force(boolean metaData) throws IOException
```

The single argument specifies whether or not any file metadata changes (e.g., last modified time, name changes, and so on) should also be committed, in addition to the contents of the file.

For example, in Example 15-3, we could flush the output channel before releasing its lock and closing it like so:

```java
outChannel.force();
outLock.release();
outChannel.close();
```

Here are a couple of caveats about forcing:

- Forcing is only guaranteed to work on local files. Files on network-mounted disks such as NFS filesystems may or may not be forced.

- Only data written using the FileChannel methods is guaranteed to be forced. Data written using memory mapping may or may not be written out. For memory-mapped files, use the force( ) method in MappedByteBuffer instead, as shown in Chapter 14.

# Converting Between Streams and Channels

Channels are cool, but streams aren't going away. In many cases, especially with small amounts of data, streams are just faster. Other times, they're more convenient. And sometimes they're part of a legacy API. For instance, I've seen a lot of XML libraries for Java. I've even written one or two, but I've yet to encounter one that uses buffers and channels. They all have deep dependencies on streams. Thus, even when using channels, you will find cases where you also need to interact with stream-based I/O.

The java.nio.Channels class provides eight static utility methods for connecting channels to streams and vice versa. It can also connect channels to readers and writers. (We'll get to those in Chapter 20.)

## Converting Channels to Streams

The newInputStream( ) method converts any ReadableByteChannel, including FileChannels, into an InputStream:

```
public static InputStream newInputStream(ReadableByteChannel ch)
```

You can use the methods of the InputStream class to read from the channel. Most importantly, you can pass the InputStream object to another method that knows how to work with streams but doesn't know what to do with a channel. For example, suppose you discover that your XML processing is I/O bound and you need to speed up the filesystem access. You could try a FileChannel to do that:

```
XMLReader parser = XMLReaderFactory.createXMLReader( );
FileInputStream in = new FileInputStream("document.xml");
FileChannel channel = in.getChannel( );
```

Now say you want to pass this channel to the XML parser. However, the parser will accept only an InputStream, not a channel, so instead you do this:

```
in = Channels.newInputStream(channel);
parser.parse(in);
```

At this point you may be objecting. You started with an input stream. This was then turned into a channel. The channel was then turned back into an input stream. What has really been gained? The difference is that the raw I/O is now done with channels rather than streams. The original `FileInputStream` in is only used to create the channel. Its `read( )` methods are never called. The actual disk reading is done by native file channel code that should be quite fast. Of course, this is all hypothetical. Whether this strategy would really improve performance would have to be carefully measured on the particular systems where you planned to run the code.

Sometimes it's an `OutputStream` that's needed. In this case, the `Channels.newOutputStream( )` method serves to convert a `WritableByteChannel` into an `OutputStream`:

```
public static OutputStream newOutputStream(WritableByteChannel ch)
```

One advantage of these streams is that, unlike most streams, they are threadsafe. That is, these streams can be shared between multiple threads, and Java will ensure that the reads and writes are atomic and do not interrupt each other. This alone may be sufficient reason to use these methods instead of just creating the streams directly.

## Converting Streams to Channels

Sometimes you need to go the other direction, taking an existing stream and changing it into a channel. This isn't necessary for file channels or network channels, which have their own special channel classes. However, it may be necessary to use this approach to get channels from more obscure streams, such as a `GZipInputStream` or a `ProgressMonitorInputStream`, or you may have a class such as the Apache HTTP-Client's `InputStreamRequestEntity` that gives you a stream that you want to read or write using new I/O. There are two `newChannel( )` methods, depending on whether you want a `WritableByteChannel` for output or a `ReadableByteChannel` for input:

```
public static ReadableByteChannel newChannel(InputStream in)
public static WritableByteChannel newChannel(OutputStream out)
```

Example 15-4 shows how you might decompress a gzipped file by first decompressing it with a `GZipInputStream`, then converting this input stream into a `ReadableByteChannel`. Next, `System.out` is converted into a `WritableByteChannel`. Finally, the decompressed data is copied from one channel to another through an intermediate buffer.

*Example 15-4. Converting streams to channels*

```
import java.io.*;
import java.util.zip.*;
import java.nio.*;
import java.nio.channels.*;

public class NIOUnzipper {

  public static void main(String[] args) throws IOException {
```

*Example 15-4. Converting streams to channels (continued)*

```
      FileInputStream fin = new FileInputStream(args[0]);
      GZIPInputStream gzin = new GZIPInputStream(fin);
      ReadableByteChannel in = Channels.newChannel(gzin);

      WritableByteChannel out = Channels.newChannel(System.out);
      ByteBuffer buffer = ByteBuffer.allocate(65536);
      while (in.read(buffer) != -1) {
        buffer.flip( );
        out.write(buffer);
        buffer.clear( );
      }
   }
}
```

The while loop relies on Java's promise that every call to `write( )` will write all of the requested bytes. While not true of all writable byte channels, this is true of the ones returned by the `Channels.newChannel( )` method.

## Converting Channels to Readers and Writers

The `Channels` class also has four methods to convert between `WritableByteChannels` and `Writers` and `ReadableByteChannels` and `Readers`. We haven't talked about readers and writers yet; that discussion will start in Chapter 20, but in the meantime these methods aren't hard to understand. They work much the same as the methods that convert between streams and channels. However, channels are byte-based and readers and writers are char-based. Therefore, these methods also require you to provide a `CharsetEncoder` or `CharsetDecoder` object that will convert between bytes and Java chars. Alternatively, instead of providing an encoder or decoder, you can just give the name of the character set and let Java find the right encoder or decoder object:

```
   public static Reader newReader(ReadableByteChannel channel,
    String characterSetName)
   public static Writer newWriter(WritableByteChannel channel,
    String characterSetName)
```

Unlike the streams returned by `Channels.newInputStream( )` and `Channels.newOutputStream( )`, the readers and writers returned by `Channels.newReader( )` and `Channels.newWriter( )` are buffered. You can specify a minimum buffer capacity if you like:

```
   public static Reader newReader(ReadableByteChannel channel,
    CharsetDecoder decoder, int minimumBufferCapacity)
   public static Writer newWriter(WritableByteChannel channel,
    CharsetEncoder encoder, int minimumBufferCapacity)
```

We'll talk more about `CharsetEncoder` and `CharsetDecoder` in Chapter 19.

# Socket Channels

The SocketChannel class provides network input and output. With a few exceptions, most network protocols are read/write, and the same channel object is used for both reading and writing. However, you'll probably use different buffers for reading and writing.

SocketChannel implements both ScatteringByteChannel and GatheringByteChannel. You read or write it using the same methods and patterns you use to read or write a FileChannel. However, a few key differences between files and sockets are exposed at the level of the API:

- Sockets must be explicitly connected.
- Sockets can be disconnected.
- Sockets can be selected.
- Sockets support nonblocking I/O.

The last two points will be the subject of the next chapter. For now, let's explore the simple blocking style of socket I/O.

There are no constructors in the SocketChannel class. Instead, a new SocketChannel object is returned by one of the two static open( ) methods:

```
public static SocketChannel open( ) throws IOException
public static SocketChannel open(SocketAddress remote) throws IOException
```

For example, this statement creates a new SocketChannel that is not yet connected to anything:

```
SocketChannel channel = SocketChannel.open( );
```

To connect to a remote site, you pass a java.net.SocketAddress (in practice, a java.net.InetSocketAddress) for the remote site to the channel's connect( ) method:

```
public abstract boolean connect(SocketAddress remote) throws IOException
```

For example:

```
SocketAddress remote = new InetSocketAddress("www.google.com", 80);
channel.connect(remote);
```

To connect immediately, just pass the address directly to the open( ) method:

```
SocketAddress remote = new InetSocketAddress("www.google.com", 80);
SocketChannel channel = SocketChannel.open(remote);
```

However, as often as not, you're going to want to configure the channel after opening it but before connecting it.

You can check whether a channel is currently connected with the isConnected( ) method:

```
public abstract boolean isConnected( )
```

This returns true while the channel is connected and false at other times. Of course, the SocketChannel also inherits all the usual methods of any channel, such as isOpen( ) and close( ).

There are a few more methods in this class, but they're all related to nonblocking I/O, which I'll take up in the next chapter. In the meantime, this is all you need to write simple network clients. For instance, it's easy to write a program that downloads the data from any given *http* URL (including the HTTP response header) and stores it in a file. The procedure is:

1. Read the URL and the filename from the command line.

2. Open a FileChannel to the file.

3. Open a SocketChannel to the remote server.

4. Connect the channel.

5. Write the HTTP request header over the socket channel.

6. Transfer the response from the server into the file.

Example 15-5 demonstrates.

*Example 15-5. The HTTPGrab program*

```
import java.net.*;
import java.nio.*;
import java.nio.channels.*;
import java.io.*;

public class HTTPGrab {

  public static void main(String[] args) throws IOException {

    if (args.length != 2) {
      System.err.println("Usage: java HTTPGrab url filename");
      return;
    }

    URL u = new URL(args[0]);
    if (!u.getProtocol().equalsIgnoreCase("http")) {
      System.err.println("Sorry, " + u.getProtocol()
        + " is not supported");
      return;
    }

    String host = u.getHost();
    int port    = u.getPort();
    String file = u.getFile();
    if (file == null) file = "/";
    if (port <= 0) port = 80;

    SocketAddress remote = new InetSocketAddress(host, port);
    SocketChannel channel = SocketChannel.open(remote);
```

*Example 15-5. The HTTPGrab program (continued)*

```
    FileOutputStream out = new FileOutputStream(args[1]);
    FileChannel localFile = out.getChannel();

    String request = "GET " + file + " HTTP/1.1\r\n"
     + "User-Agent: HTTPGrab\r\n"
     + "Accept: text/*\r\n"
     + "Connection: close\r\n"
     + "Host: " + host + "\r\n"
     + "\r\n";

    ByteBuffer header = ByteBuffer.wrap(request.getBytes("US-ASCII"));
    channel.write(header);

    ByteBuffer buffer = ByteBuffer.allocate(8192);
    while (channel.read(buffer) != -1) {
      buffer.flip();
      localFile.write(buffer);
      buffer.clear();
    }

    localFile.close();
    channel.close();
  }
}
```

# Server Socket Channels

The ServerSocketChannel class is where NIO really begins to shine. One server thread using a ServerSocketChannel can manage many different clients. The key to this is nonblocking I/O, discussion of which I'll again defer to the next chapter. However, for the moment we can look at the basics of writing a server using the new I/O API. We'll add selectors in the next chapter.

The basic strategy for writing a server with the new I/O API is:

1. Open a ServerSocketChannel using the open( ) method.
2. Retrieve the channel's ServerSocket using the socket( ) method.
3. Bind the ServerSocket to a port.
4. Accept an incoming connection to get a socket channel.
5. Communicate over the SocketChannel.
6. Close the SocketChannel.
7. Go to step 4.

This is very similar to how a server written using traditional I/O works, except that you use buffers and channels instead of streams to communicate. You could move steps 5 and 6 into a separate thread to handle multiple connections simultaneously.

More likely, you'd use the nonblocking I/O introduced in the next chapter, but for the moment let's look at the simpler blocking approach.

There are no public constructors in the ServerSocketChannel class. Instead, a new ServerSocketChannel object is returned by the static open() method:

```
public static SocketChannel open() throws IOException
```

For example, this statement creates a new ServerSocketChannel that is not yet connected to anything:

```
ServerSocketChannel channel = ServerSocketChannel.open();
```

To start listening for incoming connections, you have to bind to the port. This is done not by the ServerSocketChannel itself, but rather by its associated java.net. ServerSocket object. This object is returned by the socket() method:

```
public abstract ServerSocket socket()
```

For example:

```
SocketAddress port = new InetSocketAddress(8000);
channel.socket().bind(port);
```

You can now begin accepting connections with the accept() method:

```
public abstract SocketChannel accept() throws IOException
```

This returns a SocketChannel object that you use to communicate with the remote client. The ServerSocketChannel class itself does not have any read() or write() methods.

Of course, ServerSocketChannel also inherits all the usual methods of any channel, such as isOpen() and close().

We're now ready to write a simple network server. Let's reproduce the Hello server from Example 5-4, but this time implement it with the new I/O API rather than the traditional stream-based APIs. Recall that this server responds to any client that connects with a message like:

```
Hello titan.oit.unc.edu/152.2.22.14 on port 50361
This is utopia.poly.edu/128.238.3.21 on port 2345
```

Neither the ServerSocketChannel class nor the SocketChannel class has methods to determine the IP address of either the local or the remote end of the connection. However, we can use the socket() methods to get this information from the associated Socket and ServerSocket objects. Example 15-6 demonstrates.

*Example 15-6. The new HelloServer program*

```
import java.net.*;
import java.io.*;
import java.nio.ByteBuffer;
import java.nio.channels.*;
```

*Example 15-6. The new HelloServer program (continued)*

```
public class NewIOHelloServer {

  public final static int PORT = 2345;

  public static void main(String[] args) throws IOException {

    ServerSocketChannel serverChannel = ServerSocketChannel.open( );
    SocketAddress port = new InetSocketAddress(PORT);
    serverChannel.socket( ).bind(port);

    while (true) {
      try {
        SocketChannel clientChannel = serverChannel.accept( );

        String response = "Hello "
         + clientChannel.socket().getInetAddress() + " on port "
         + clientChannel.socket().getPort() + "\r\n";
        response += "This is " + serverChannel.socket() + " on port "
         + serverChannel.socket().getLocalPort() + "\r\n";

        byte[] data = response.getBytes("UTF-8");
        ByteBuffer buffer = ByteBuffer.wrap(data);
        while (buffer.hasRemaining( )) clientChannel.write(buffer);
        clientChannel.close( );
      }
      catch (IOException ex) {
        // This is an error on one connection. Maybe the client crashed.
        // Maybe it broke the connection prematurely. Whatever happened,
        // it's not worth shutting down the server for.
      }
    } // end while
  } // end main
} // end NewIOHelloServer
```

Here's some typical output when connecting to this server with *telnet*:

```
$ telnet 192.168.254.100 2345
Trying 192.168.254.100...
Connected to 192.168.254.100.
Escape character is '^]'.
Hello /192.168.254.36 on port 4940
This is ServerSocket[addr=/0.0.0.0,localport=2345] on port 2345
Connection closed by foreign host.
```

To be honest, this is complete overkill for such a simple server. If there's any performance difference between the original stream-based example and this one, I'd expect the original to be faster. There's enough constant overhead in setting up the buffers and channels that speedups become apparent only for larger datasets, and likely then only if you're using nonblocking I/O. However, this example does enable me to demonstrate the relevant points.

# Datagram Channels

Data is sent across the Internet in unreliable packets called *IP datagrams*. More often than not, these packets are automatically reassembled into the correct sequence using a higher-level protocol called TCP. Lost and corrupted packets are retransmitted automatically. The end result is something that looks very much like a stream or a channel. Indeed, Java's interface to TCP data is through streams or channels (your choice).

However, some protocols, such as NFS, SIP, and DNS, can send data over UDP instead. UDP still detects and drops corrupted datagrams, but that's it. UDP does not guarantee that packets arrive in the order they were sent, or indeed that the packets arrive at all. UDP can be faster than TCP though, if you can live with or compensate for its unreliability.

UDP data arrives in raw packets of bytes. A packet does not necessarily have any relation to the previous packet or the next packet. You may get nothing for several seconds, or even minutes, and then suddenly have to deal with a few hundred packets. Packets arriving close together in time may be part of the same transmission, two transmissions, or several transmissions.

java.nio.channels includes a `DatagramChannel` class for UDP. This class does not have any public constructors. Instead, you create a new `DatagramChannel` object using the static open( ) method:

```
public static DatagramChannel open( ) throws IOException
```

For example:

```
DatagramChannel channel = DatagramChannel.open( );
```

This channel initially listens to and sends from an anonymous (system-selected) port. Servers that need to listen on a particular port can bind to that port through the channel's peer `DatagramSocket` object. This is returned by the socket( ) method:

```
public abstract DatagramSocket socket( )
```

For example, this code fragment binds a channel to port 4567:

```
SocketAddress address = new InetSocketAddress(4567);
DatagramSocket socket = channel.socket( );
socket.bind(address);
```

`DatagramChannel` has both read( ) and write( ) methods. That is, it implements both `ReadableByteChannel` and `WritableByteChannel`. It also implements `GatheringByteChannel` and `ScatteringByteChannel`. However, more often than not you read and write data with its two special methods, send( ) and receive( ), instead:

```
public abstract SocketAddress receive(ByteBuffer dst) throws IOException
public abstract int send(ByteBuffer src, SocketAddress target) throws IOException
```

UDP by its nature is connectionless. That is, a single UDP channel can send packets to and receive packets from multiple hosts. As a result, when sending, you need to specify the address of the system to which you're sending. When receiving, you'll probably want to know the address of the system from which the packet originated. Both are provided as java.net.SocketAddress objects. For example, this code fragment sends a UDP packet containing the byte 100 to the server at *time.nist.gov*:

```
ByteBuffer buffer = ByteBuffer.allocate(512);
buffer.put((byte) 100);
// Don't forget to flip the buffer or nothing will be sent
buffer.flip();
SocketAddress address = new InetSocketAddress("time.nist.gov", 37);
socket.send(buffer, address);
```

This code fragment receives a packet from some server and then prints the address of the originating host:

```
ByteBuffer receipt = ByteBuffer.allocate(8192);
SocketAddress sender = socket.receive(receipt)
System.out.println(address);
```

If the two code fragments are run in sequence, chances are the second fragment will print the same address that was used to send the first fragment. That is, the server will have responded with a UDP packet to the sender. However, that's not guaranteed. If for some reason a different system sent a UDP packet to this host and port at the right time, that packet would be received instead.

By default, both of these methods block. That is, they do not return until a UDP datagram has been sent or received. (We'll see how to change this in the next chapter.) For sending, this is normally not a problem as long as the network hardware is working. For receiving, it can be. Because UDP is unreliable, there's no warning if the server fails to respond or if its response is lost in transit. If the program does anything other than wait for incoming packets, you should either put the call to receive() in a separate thread or set the socket's SO_TIMEOUT. For instance, this statement sets the timeout to 3 seconds (3000 milliseconds):

```
channel.socket().setSoTimeout(3000);
```

If the specified time passes with no incoming packet, receive() throws a java.net. SocketTimeoutException, a subclass of IOException.

Furthermore, if a datagram arrives with more data than the buffer has space remaining, *the extra data is thrown away with no notification of the problem*. There is no BufferOverflowException or anything similar. UDP is unreliable, after all.

On the other hand, if you try to send more data from a buffer than can fit into a single datagram, the send() method sends nothing and returns 0. send() will not fragment the data into multiple UDP packets: it writes everything or nothing. You're probably okay up to 8K of data on a modern system, and you may be okay somewhat beyond that. However, 64K (indeed, a little less than that when space for IP headers and such is set aside) is the absolute maximum that can ever fit into one UDP datagram. If you have more than 8K or so of data, you should probably break it up into multiple calls to send() and design a higher-level protocol for reassembling and perhaps retransmitting them. You can use the ByteBuffer's limit( ) methods to set the limit no more than 8192 bytes ahead of the position before sending.

Like all channels, a datagram channel should be closed when you're done with it to free up the port and any other resources it may be using:

```
public void close( ) throws IOException
```

Closing an already closed channel has no effect. Attempting to send data to or receive data from a closed channel throws a ClosedChannelException. If you're uncertain whether a channel has been closed, check with isOpen( ):

```
public boolean isOpen( )
```

This returns false if the channel is closed, or true if it's open.

Example 15-7 is a complete program that both sends and receives some data over UDP. Specifically, it sends a request to the time server at *time.nist.gov*. It then receives a UDP datagram containing the number of seconds since midnight, January 1, 1900. Of course, with UDP, you're not guaranteed to get anything back, so it's important to set a timeout on the socket operation. Example 15-7 waits at most five seconds.

*Example 15-7. A UDP time client*

```
import java.io.IOException;
import java.net.*;
import java.nio.ByteBuffer;
import java.nio.channels.*;
import java.util.*;

public class UDPTimeClient {

  public static void main(String[] args) throws IOException {

    DatagramChannel channel = null;
    try {
      channel = DatagramChannel.open( );
      // port 0 selects any available port
      SocketAddress address = new InetSocketAddress(0);
      DatagramSocket socket = channel.socket( );
      socket.setSoTimeout(5000);
      socket.bind(address);

      SocketAddress server = new InetSocketAddress("time.nist.gov", 37);
      ByteBuffer buffer = ByteBuffer.allocate(8192);
      // time protocol always uses big-endian order
      buffer.order(ByteOrder.BIG_ENDIAN);
      // Must put at least one byte of data in the buffer;
      // it doesn't matter what it is.
      buffer.put((byte) 65);
      buffer.flip( );

      channel.send(buffer, server);
```

*Example 15-7. A UDP time client (continued)*

```
        buffer.clear( );
        buffer.put((byte) 0).put((byte) 0).put((byte) 0).put((byte) 0);
        channel.receive(buffer);
        buffer.flip( );
        long secondsSince1900 = buffer.getLong( );
        // The time protocol sets the epoch at 1900,
        // the java.util.Date class at 1970. This number
        // converts between them.
        long differenceBetweenEpochs = 2208988800L;

        long secondsSince1970
          = secondsSince1900 - differenceBetweenEpochs;
        long msSince1970 = secondsSince1970 * 1000;
        Date time = new Date(msSince1970);

        System.out.println(time);
      }
      catch (Exception ex) {
        System.err.println(ex);
        ex.printStackTrace( );
      }
      finally {
        if (channel != null) channel.close( );
      }
    }
}
```

The time protocol encodes the time as an unsigned big-endian 4-byte int. Java doesn't have any such data type. We could manually read the bytes and form a long from them. However, it's a little more obvious and informative to use the buffer class in a tricky way. Before receiving the data, I put four zeros in the buffer's first four positions. Then I receive the next four bytes from the server. A total of eight bytes, which is the desired value, can then be read as a signed long using getLong( ).

Here's the output from running the program, along with the output from the Unix *date* command for comparison:

```
$ date;java UDPTimeClient
Wed Oct 15 07:37:40 EDT 2005
Wed Oct 15 07:37:41 EDT 2005
```

The server-supplied time is only a second off from the time measured by the client computer's clock. The error is likely a combination of clock drift between the two systems and the time it takes for the UDP request and response to travel between my local computer in Brooklyn and the server in Boulder.

Unlike socket-based programs, there's not a huge amount of difference between the UDP server API and the UDP client API. Example 15-8 shows a UDP server implemented using these same classes and methods. Here, the server waits for a client to send a datagram rather than initiating the communication, but the methods and classes are all the same.

*Example 15-8. A UDP time server*

```java
import java.io.IOException;
import java.net.*;
import java.nio.*;
import java.nio.channels.*;
import java.util.*;

public class UDPTimeServer {

  public final static int DEFAULT_PORT = 37;

  public static void main(String[] args) throws IOException {

    int port = 37;

    if (args.length > 0) {
      try {
        port = Integer.parseInt(args[1]);
        if (port <= 0 || port > 65535) port = DEFAULT_PORT;;
      }
      catch (Exception ex){
      }
    }

    ByteBuffer in = ByteBuffer.allocate(8192);
    ByteBuffer out = ByteBuffer.allocate(8);
    out.order(ByteOrder.BIG_ENDIAN);
    SocketAddress address = new InetSocketAddress(port);
    DatagramChannel channel = DatagramChannel.open();
    DatagramSocket socket = channel.socket();
    socket.bind(address);
    System.err.println("bound to " + address);
    while (true) {
      try {
        in.clear();
        SocketAddress client = channel.receive(in);
        System.err.println(client);
        long secondsSince1900 = getTime();
        out.clear();
        out.putLong(secondsSince1900);
        out.flip();
        // skip over the first four bytes to make this an unsigned int
        out.position(4);
        channel.send(out, client);
      }
      catch (Exception ex) {
        System.err.println(ex);
      }
    }
  }

  private static long getTime() {
      long differenceBetweenEpochs = 2208988800L;
      Date now = new Date();
```

*Example 15-8. A UDP time server (continued)*

```
      long secondsSince1970 = now.getTime() / 1000;
      long secondsSince1900 = secondsSince1970 + differenceBetweenEpochs;
      return secondsSince1900;
  }
}
```

This program is blocking and synchronous. This is much less of a problem for UDP-based protocols than for TCP protocols. The unreliable, packet-based, connectionless nature of UDP means that the server at most has to wait for the local buffer to clear. It does not have to and does not wait for the client to be ready to receive data. There's much less opportunity for one client to get held up behind a slower client.

## Connecting

Unlike regular sockets and socket channels, datagram channels can normally send data to and receive data from any host. However, you can force a DatagramChannel to communicate with only one specified host using the connect( ) method:

```
public abstract DatagramChannel connect(SocketAddress remote)
 throws IOException
```

UDP is a connectionless protocol. Unlike the connect( ) method of SocketChannel, this method does not actually send or receive any packets across the network. Instead, it simply changes the datagram socket object so it will refuse to send packets to other hosts (i.e., throw an IllegalArgumentException) and ignore packets received from other hosts. Thus, this method returns fairly quickly and never blocks.

The isConnected( ) method returns true if the DatagramSocket is connected and false otherwise:

```
public abstract boolean isConnected( )
```

However, this just tells you whether the DatagramChannel is limited to one host. Unlike a SocketChannel, a DatagramChannel does not have to be connected to transmit or receive data.

Finally, there is a disconnect( ) method that breaks the connection:

```
public abstract DatagramChannel disconnect( ) throws IOException
```

This doesn't really close anything, because nothing was really open in the first place. It just allows the channel to once again send data to and receive data from multiple hosts.

## Reading

Besides the special-purpose receive( ) method, DatagramChannel has the usual three read( ) methods:

```
public abstract int  read(ByteBuffer dst) throws IOException
public final    long read(ByteBuffer[] dsts) throws IOException
```

```
public final   long read(ByteBuffer[] dsts, int offset, int length)
   throws IOException
```

However, these methods can be used only on connected channels. That is, before invoking one of these methods, you must invoke connect( ) to glue the channel to a particular remote host. This makes them more suitable for use with clients that know whom they'll be talking to than for servers that must accept input from multiple hosts at the same time.

Each of these three methods reads only a single datagram packet from the network. As much data from that datagram as possible is stored in the ByteBuffer. Each method returns the number of bytes read, or -1 if the channel has been closed. This method may return 0 for any of several reasons, including:

- The channel is nonblocking and no packet was ready.
- A datagram packet contained no data.
- The buffer is full.

As with the receive( ) method, if the datagram packet has more data than the ByteBuffer can hold, *the extra data is thrown away with no notification of the problem*. You do not receive a BufferOverflowException or anything similar.

## Writing

Naturally, DatagramChannel has the three write( ) methods common to all writable, scattering channels, which can be used instead of the send( ) method:

```
public abstract int  write(ByteBuffer src) throws IOException
public final   long write(ByteBuffer[] dsts) throws IOException
public final   long write(ByteBuffer[] dsts, int offset, int length)
   throws IOException
```

However, these methods can be used only on connected channels; otherwise, they don't know where to send the packet. Each of these methods sends a single datagram packet over the connection. None of these methods is guaranteed to write the complete contents of the buffer(s). If the value returned is less (or more) than the amount of data expected in the packet, you may have sent a corrupted packet. The protocol needs some way of recognizing and discarding such packets on the other end. Furthermore, in this case you'll probably want to retransmit the original packet from the beginning.

The write( ) method works best for simple protocols such as echo and chargen that accept more or less arbitrary data in more or less arbitrary order. However, to the extent that packet boundaries matter, the send( ) method is more reliable here since it always sends everything or nothing.

Example 15-9 revises the UDP time client program so that it first connects to the server. It sends a packet to the server using the write( ) method and gets the result back using the read( ) method.

*Example 15-9. A connected time client*

```java
import java.io.IOException;
import java.net.*;
import java.nio.ByteBuffer;
import java.nio.channels.*;
import java.util.*;

public class ConnectedTimeClient {

  public static void main(String[] args) throws IOException {

    DatagramChannel channel = DatagramChannel.open( );
    SocketAddress address = new InetSocketAddress(0);
    DatagramSocket socket = channel.socket( );
    socket.bind(address);

    SocketAddress server = new InetSocketAddress("time-a.nist.gov", 37);
    channel.connect(server);

    ByteBuffer buffer = ByteBuffer.allocate(8);
    buffer.order(ByteOrder.BIG_ENDIAN);
    // send a byte of data to the server
    buffer.put((byte) 0);
    buffer.flip( );
    channel.write(buffer);

    // get the buffer ready to receive data
    buffer.clear( );
    // fill the first four bytes with zeros
    buffer.putInt(0);
    channel.read(buffer);
    buffer.flip( );

    // convert seconds since 1900 to a java.util.Date
    long secondsSince1900 = buffer.getLong( );
    long differenceBetweenEpochs = 2208988800L;
    long secondsSince1970
      = secondsSince1900 - differenceBetweenEpochs;
    long msSince1970 = secondsSince1970 * 1000;
    Date time = new Date(msSince1970);

    System.out.println(time);
  }
}
```

This program is a little simpler than the previous version, mostly because it uses a connected channel. One other small change: this program calls `buffer.putInt(0)` to store zeros in the first four bytes of the buffer rather than putting the byte 0 four times.

# CHAPTER 16

# Nonblocking I/O

Nonblocking I/O is one of the most important features of the new I/O API. Traditional stream-based I/O is limited by the speed of whatever it is you're reading or writing: the disk, the network, and so on. Very often code has to sit and wait for the disk or network to respond. This is especially problematic if the program has many different things to do. For instance, a network server may need to service hundreds or thousands of simultaneous clients. It doesn't want one slow connection to hold back all the others.

The traditional approach to this problem is to place each connection in a separate thread. One hundred simultaneous connections require one hundred threads. However, although threads are lighter-weight than processes, they still have nontrivial overhead. It takes time to set up and tear down each thread, and each one uses a finite quantity of system resources. For instance, in some versions of Windows, each thread has a megabyte of stack space. Thus, if you try to spawn 2,000 threads on a system with only a gigabyte of memory, you're going to start swapping pretty badly (and that's not even accounting for all the memory that's needed for anything other than thread stacks). Thread pools improve the situation, perhaps allowing you to handle twice as many simultaneous connections as you could otherwise, but not to the point where you can simply ignore thread overhead.

Fortunately, the new buffer- and channel-based I/O comes to the rescue. In addition to the synchronous blocking I/O explored in the last two chapters, NIO also supports *nonblocking I/O*. In nonblocking I/O, one thread can manage many different connections. Rather than fully processing each one in turn, the thread asks the channels which one is ready to be read or written without blocking. It then reads or writes a channel that it knows in advance won't block. Then it repeats the process. On high-volume servers, this can easily more than triple the number of clients one system can handle.

Nonblocking I/O is primarily relevant to network connections. Pipe channels that move data between two threads also support nonblocking I/O. File channels don't support it at all because file access doesn't block nearly as often as network channels do, and most modern disk controllers can fill a CPU with data fast enough to keep it satisfied. Furthermore, it's uncommon for one program to read or write hundreds of files simultaneously. However, on network servers, this usage pattern is the rule, not the exception.

# Nonblocking I/O

Allow me to demonstrate with a very simple network server that might be used for testing routers and the like. The server accepts a connection from any client. It then sends that client a continuous stream of bytes beginning with 0 and continuing through 255, at which point it starts again with 0. The server never closes the connection; it waits for the client to close. You could use this to test the speed of the server's network connection. Example 16-1 implements this protocol using classic I/O plus threads.

*Example 16-1. DataStuffer implemented with classic I/O*

```
import java.net.*;
import java.io.*;

public class DataStuffer {

  private static byte[] data = new byte[256];

  public static void main(String[] args) throws IOException {

    int port = 9000;
    for (int i = 0; i < data.length; i++) data[i] = (byte) i;

    ServerSocket server = new ServerSocket(port);
    while (true) {
      Socket socket = server.accept();
      Thread stuffer = new StuffThread(socket);
      stuffer.start();
    }

  }

  private static class StuffThread extends Thread {

    private Socket socket;

    public StuffThread(Socket socket) {
      this.socket = socket;
    }

    public void run() {
      try {
        OutputStream out = new BufferedOutputStream(socket.getOutputStream());
        while (!socket.isClosed()) {
```

*Example 16-1. DataStuffer implemented with classic I/O (continued)*

```
        out.write(data);
      }
    }
    catch (IOException ex) {
      if (!socket.isClosed()) {
        try {
          socket.close();
        }
        catch (IOException e) {
          // Oh well. We tried.
        }
      }
    }
  }
 }
}
```

Using channels instead of streams, we can implement this entire program in one thread and support many more clients to boot. The initial process is as follows:

1. Open a ServerSocketChannel.
2. Put the channel in nonblocking mode.
3. Open a Selector.
4. Register the ServerSocketChannel with the Selector for accept operations.

To create a nonblocking channel, open the server socket in the usual way:

```
ServerSocketChannel server = ServerSocketChannel.open();
```

Then pass true to the configureBlocking() method to put it in nonblocking mode:

```
server.configureBlocking(false);
```

Next, create a Selector object:

```
Selector selector = Selector.open();
```

This object will be responsible for managing all the different channels and deciding which one is ready to be read or written. Initially, you just have one channel, the server socket channel. When you register each channel with the Selector, you have to specify the kinds of operations for which you're registering. There are four kinds, each represented by a named constant in the SelectionKey class:

SelectionKey.ACCEPT
:   Accept a connection from a client.

SelectionKey.CONNECT
:   Open a connection to a server.

SelectionKey.READ
:   Read data from a channel.

```
SelectionKey.WRITE
```
Write data to a channel.

The ServerSocketChannel needs to be registered for accepting connections:

```
server.register(selector, SelectionKey.OP_ACCEPT);
```

From this point, you enter an infinite loop that selects the ready channels:

```
while (true) {
  selector.select();
  Set readyKeys = selector.selectedKeys();
  // process each ready key...
}
```

Initially, the Selector is registered with only one key, so only one key can be selected. However, we're going to register the Selector with more keys inside the loop as connections are accepted. The keys themselves are processed in a finite loop, like this:

```
Iterator iterator = readyKeys.iterator();
while (iterator.hasNext()) {
  SelectionKey key = (SelectionKey) iterator.next();
  iterator.remove();
  // work with the key...
}
```

It's necessary to remove each key from the set of ready keys before processing it. Should the key become ready again in the future, it is included in the next set returned by readyKeys( ).

Different keys may be ready to do different things. Some are ready for reading, some for writing, and some for accepting. When processing a key, the first thing to do is figure out what it's ready for:

```
if (key.isAcceptable()) {
  // accept the connection and register the Selector
  // with the key for this connection...
}
else if (key.isWritable()) {
  // write to the connection...
}
```

This example doesn't need to read from the channel, but most applications do this as well.

The first possibility is that the Selector has found a channel ready to accept an incoming connection. In this case, we tell the server channel to accept the connection. This returns a SocketChannel that is then configured in nonblocking mode and registered with the same Selector. However, it's registered as being interested in write operations:

```
SocketChannel client = server.accept();
client.configureBlocking(false);
SelectionKey key2 = client.register(selector, SelectionKey.OP_WRITE);
```

The key also needs to know what data is being written to the channel and how much of it has already been written. This requires some sort of object that contains a reference to the actual data and an index into that data. For some servers, the data is a file or a stream of some kind. In this case, it's a constant byte array. In fact, the same byte array is written to all the different channels. However, different channels are at different positions in that array at different times, so we wrap a ByteBuffer around the array just for the use of this channel. As long as every connection treats its buffer as read-only, there won't be any conflicts. This buffer is then attached to the key:

```
ByteBuffer source = ByteBuffer.wrap(data);
key2.attach(source);
```

The other possibility is that the key is not ready for accepting. Instead, it's ready for writing. In this case, the key points to a previously opened SocketChannel. If so, we get the channel for the socket and write some data onto the channel:

```
SocketChannel client = (SocketChannel) key.channel();
ByteBuffer output = (ByteBuffer) key.attachment();
if (!output.hasRemaining()) output.rewind();
client.write(output);
```

Notice that the ByteBuffer that was attached to the key earlier when the channel was accepted is now retrieved.

This whole process is put together in two nested loops, as shown in Example 16-2.

*Example 16-2. DataStuffer implemented with nonblocking I/O*

```
import java.net.*;
import java.io.*;
import java.nio.*;
import java.nio.channels.*;
import java.util.*;

public class NewDataStuffer {

  private static byte[] data = new byte[255];

  public static void main(String[] args) throws IOException {

    for (int i = 0; i < data.length; i++) data[i] = (byte) i;

    ServerSocketChannel server = ServerSocketChannel.open();
    server.configureBlocking(false);

    server.socket().bind(new InetSocketAddress(9000));
    Selector selector = Selector.open();
    server.register(selector, SelectionKey.OP_ACCEPT);

    while (true) {
      selector.select();
      Set readyKeys = selector.selectedKeys();
      Iterator iterator = readyKeys.iterator();
```

*Example 16-2. DataStuffer implemented with nonblocking I/O (continued)*

```
      while (iterator.hasNext()) {
        SelectionKey key = (SelectionKey) iterator.next();
        iterator.remove();
        try {
          if (key.isAcceptable()) {
            SocketChannel client = server.accept();
            System.out.println("Accepted connection from " + client);
            client.configureBlocking(false);
            ByteBuffer source = ByteBuffer.wrap(data);
            SelectionKey key2 = client.register(selector, SelectionKey.OP_WRITE);
            key2.attach(source);
          }
          else if (key.isWritable()) {
            SocketChannel client = (SocketChannel) key.channel();
            ByteBuffer output = (ByteBuffer) key.attachment();
            if (!output.hasRemaining()) {
              output.rewind();
            }
            client.write(output);
          }
        }
        catch (IOException ex) {
          key.cancel();
          try {
            key.channel().close();
          }
          catch (IOException cex) {}
        }
      }
    }
  }
}
```

That, in a nutshell, is how a nonblocking server is written. Now that you've seen the big picture, let's drill down and look more closely at the individual classes involved in this system.

# Selectable Channels

By default, channels (and streams) block. That is, when you write to or read from the channel, the current thread stops until the writing or reading is complete. (The same is true for connecting and accepting connections, but I'm just going to say writing and reading from here on and let the connecting and accepting be understood.) In nonblocking mode, by contrast, the read or write happens as fast as the hardware allows. It doesn't take absolutely zero time, but it goes as quickly as it possibly can. If the thread has to wait for more data to arrive from the network, for an Ethernet card buffer to be released by some other process, or for some other relatively long-lasting operation, it instead returns having read or written only some or even none of the bytes it was asked to read or write. Your program needs to keep track of how many bytes have been read or written and try again with the bytes that haven't been read or written. If the program doesn't have anything else to do, it might as well operate in blocking mode. However, if the program does have something else it can do in the meantime—for instance, a network server might process a different connection— then this is worthwhile.

Not all channels support nonblocking I/O. Network channels do, but file channels don't. Those channels that do support nonblocking I/O are all subclasses of the java.nio.channels.SelectableChannel class.

All channels are created in blocking mode. To switch a channel to nonblocking mode, you pass false to the configureBlocking( ) method:

```
public abstract SelectableChannel configureBlocking(boolean block)
  throws IOException
```

This is normally the first thing you do after opening the channel. You can actually change a channel from blocking to nonblocking or vice versa later in its life if it's not currently associated with any Selectors, but this is unusual.

Once you've put a channel in nonblocking mode, you don't read or write it immediately. Instead, you register a Selector with the channel. You then ask the Selector if the channel is ready for reading or writing. If the Selector says, "Yes, the channel is ready," you go ahead and read it or write it. Otherwise, you do something else. (A little more accurately, you ask the Selector which of its channels are ready for some operation and you operate on the channels the Selector says are ready. You don't ask it about individual channels.)

The register( ) method registers a Selector with the channel:

```
public abstract SelectionKey register(Selector selector, int operations)
  throws ClosedChannelException
```

Each channel can be registered only once with any given Selector object. Otherwise, however, there is a many-to-many relationship between Selectors and channels. Each Selector normally monitors many different channels, and each channel may be registered with several different Selectors. The most common usage pattern, though, is that each channel registers only a single Selector.

The second argument specifies the operations for which the Selector should select. There are four: reading, writing, accepting, and connecting. Server socket channels normally register only for accepting. Socket channels register for any or all of the other three. These operations are represented as named constants in the SelectionKey class. These constants follow the usual powers of two pattern, so you can register for more than one operation using the bitwise or operator. For example, this statement registers a channel for both reading and writing:

```
channel.register(selector, SelectionKey.OP_READ | SelectionKey.OP_WRITE);
```

A second overloaded version of the register( ) method adds a third argument for an attachment:

```
public abstract SelectionKey register(
  Selector selector, int operations, Object attachment)
  throws ClosedChannelException
```

Neither the channel nor the Selector uses the attachment object, and it can be null. It's there for your own use. Most programs use it to store a ByteBuffer or other object that tracks the data being written to or read from the channel.

Both register( ) methods return a SelectionKey object that represents the unique connection between this channel and this Selector. More often than not, however, the return value is ignored. The Selector gives you back the key when you need it.

If you need to change the operations of interest (e.g., changing reading to writing, or read-only to read/write), you can call the register( ) method a second time. This also changes the attachment, but it does not change the key. The same key is always returned for a particular Selector/SelectableChannel pair. If the key has already been cancelled, reregistering throws a CancelledKeyException.

The register( ) and configureBlocking( ) methods are threadsafe, but they may block for a short period of time when used concurrently. You can also synchronize your own code on the same lock object, which is returned by the blockingLock( ) method:

```
public abstract Object blockingLock( )
```

Several getter methods correspond to the setter methods. The isBlocking( ) method returns true if a channel is in blocking mode and false otherwise:

```
public abstract boolean isBlocking( )
```

The isRegistered( ) method returns true if one or more Selectors are registered with this channel and false otherwise:

```
public abstract boolean isRegistered( )
```

The keyFor( ) method returns the SelectionKey corresponding to a particular Selector:

```
public abstract SelectionKey keyFor(Selector sel)
```

The validOps( ) method returns a combination of bit flags specifying which operations are and are not available to this channel:

```
public abstract int validOps( )
```

It's rare to need any of these. Most of the time your own code creates the SelectableChannel objects you use, and you know exactly what state they're in.

# Selectors

The `java.nio.channels.Selector` class is the crucial component of nonblocking I/O. It is the class that enables your program to determine which channels are ready to be accessed when. The only constructor is protected, and subclassing this class yourself would be unusual. Instead, you create a `Selector` by opening it with the static `Selector.open()` method:

```
public static Selector open() throws IOException
```

Each `Selector` may be registered with several `SelectableChannels`, as discussed in the last section. Registration is threadsafe and ongoing. You can register the `Selector` with various channels at any time.

When your program has a little time to do some work, you ask the `Selector` which of its channels are ready, that is, which channels can be read or written without blocking. You do this by invoking one of these three methods:

```
public abstract int selectNow() throws IOException
public abstract int select() throws IOException
public abstract int select(long timeout) throws IOException
```

All three methods return the number of keys whose readiness states were changed by this selection. Important: this is not necessarily the number of keys that are ready to be operated on! Extra keys may well have been ready before the selection and may still be ready. You rarely need to know how many keys' readiness states were changed by the selection, so the return values of these methods are generally ignored.

The `selectNow()` method is nonblocking, whereas the other two methods block. `selectNow()` returns immediately even if it can't select anything. The other two methods return only after they select some channel, the thread is interrupted, or the timeout expires. Even in nonblocking I/O, you tend to use blocking selects if there's nothing for the program to do except I/O. Example 16-2 is a case in point. However, if your program can do something useful even when no channel is ready, you might use `selectNow()` instead of `select()`.

After you've called one of these methods, the `selectedKeys()` method returns a `java.util.Set` containing keys for all the ready channels registered with this `Selector`:

```
public abstract Set selectedKeys()
```

The returned set contains zero or more `SelectionKey` objects. Like a lot of similar methods, Java 5 retrofits this method's signature with generics to make it a little more typesafe:

```
public abstract Set<SelectionKey> selectedKeys()
```

In both Java 1.4 and 5, you normally iterate though this `Set` using an `Iterator` and process each key in turn, as shown in Example 16-2. However, there are other patterns. For instance, you could reselect after processing one key:

```
while (true) {
  selector.select();
```

```
Set readyKeys = selector.selectedKeys();
Iterator iterator = readyKeys.iterator();
if (iterator.hasNext()) {
  SelectionKey key = (SelectionKey) iterator.next();
  iterator.remove();
  // process key...
}
}
```

Selectors may use native system resources. Once you're done with one, you should close it by invoking its close() method:

```
public abstract void close() throws IOException
```

Otherwise, your program may leak memory and other resources, though details vary by platform. Closing a Selector deregisters all its associated keys and wakes up any threads waiting on the select() methods. Any further attempts to use a closed Selector or one of its keys throws an exception. If you don't know whether a Selector is closed, you can check with the isOpen() method:

```
public abstract boolean isOpen()
```

 Technically, this checks to see only whether the Selector is open. In some rare cases, this method could return false because the Selector has been created but not yet opened. However, this is remotely plausible only if you're writing your own implementation of all these classes.

In a high-volume system, even the blocking select methods are likely to return very quickly. In a less stressful environment, though, select() can block a thread for some time. Another thread can wake up a thread blocked by a select() method by invoking the Selector's wakeup() method:

```
public abstract Selector wakeup()
```

You can actually wake up a Selector before it selects. In this case, the next call to select() returns immediately.

# Selection Keys

The java.nio.channels.SelectionKey class encapsulates the information about a channel registered with a Selector. Each SelectionKey object holds the following information:

- The channel
- The Selector
- An arbitrary object attachment, normally used to point to the data the channel is reading or writing
- The operations the channels is interested in performing
- The operations the channel is currently ready to perform without blocking (or, more accurately, was ready to perform when select() was last called)

Most of the methods in the SelectionKey class amount to setters and getters for this information. There's also one method that cancels the key.

The only constructor in SelectionKey is protected, but it's rare that you yourself extend this class. Instead, SelectionKey objects tend to be returned by the selectedKeys() method of Selector and the register() methods of SelectableChannel. The first thing you'll usually want to do with such a key is find out what its channel is ready to do: read, write, connect, or accept. The readyOps() method returns a group of bitwise flags inside an int indicating which operations are possible on this key's channel:

```
public abstract int readyOps()
```

The low-order four bits of the return value are 1 or 0, depending on whether the key's channel is ready for reading, writing, connecting, or accepting. The specific masks to use for the flags are stored in named constants:

```
public static final int OP_READ
public static final int OP_WRITE
public static final int OP_CONNECT
public static final int OP_ACCEPT
```

For example, this code fragment checks to see if the key is ready for reading:

```
if (key.readyOps() & SelectionKey.READ != 0) {
  // read from the key's channel...
}
```

However, it's usually more convenient to ask about each of the four operations individually with these four methods:

```
public final boolean isReadable()
public final boolean isWritable()
public final boolean isConnectable()
public final boolean isAcceptable()
```

If the channel is ready for reading, read it; if the channel is ready for writing, write it; and so on. Of course, you can simply ignore operations you aren't interested in performing. Example 16-2 didn't bother to check if the channel was ready for connecting or reading because it was never going to do either of those operations. However, in the most general case, a Selector is registered with multiple channels, some of which are used for reading, some for writing, and some for both. The Selector only tells you which channels are ready. It does not read or write or accept or connect itself.

The interestOps() methods set and get the operations the key's Selector is interested in performing:

```
public abstract int interestOps()
public abstract SelectionKey interestOps(int ops)
```

They use the same bitwise constants that readyOps( ) does. The no-args version tells you the operations for which this key will be tested. The one-arg version lets you change those operations, so you can change the Selector from checking for reading to checking for writing or vice versa, for example.

## Getters

The Selector returns a set of SelectionKeys to indicate which channels are ready. It does not return the channels themselves. To read or write (or accept or connect), you have to get the channel from its key using the channel( ) method:

```
public abstract SelectableChannel channel( )
```

You usually cast the result to a more specific subclass of SelectableChannel. In context, it's normally obvious what kind of channel is returned. For instance, if you've only registered socket channels with a Selector for reading, the channel( ) method of any key that is ready for reading returns a SocketChannel:

```
SocketChannel client = (SocketChannel) key.channel( );
```

There's no corresponding setter method. You cannot change the channel with which a key is associated. One channel may have multiple keys, but each key has only a single channel.

Less commonly, you might need to get the Selector given a key. That is what the selector( ) method does:

```
public abstract Selector selector( )
```

## Attachments

Because this is nonblocking I/O, it may not be possible to write or read as much data as you want with each call. For instance, when reading from a network, a thousand bytes might be waiting for you in the Ethernet card's buffer that can be read immediately. However, there could be megabytes of data yet to come. You need some sort of data structure where you can store the data you've read that keeps track of your place in the stream. Exactly what this data structure is depends on what you're trying to do. For instance, it might be a byte array, or a file, or a string. Often, this data structure is represented as some sort of java.nio.Buffer object. This is exactly what buffers are designed to do.

Whatever this data structure is, it is normally attached to the key using the attach( ) method (or the register( ) method in SelectableChannel) and retrieved from the key using the attachment( ) method:

```
public final Object attach(Object ob)
public final Object attachment( )
```

It would be more conventional to call these methods getAttachment( ) and setAttachment( ), but the people who designed the NIO API seem to have really disliked that common convention. It's used almost nowhere in the java.nio packages.

## Canceling

You can deregister a Selector from a channel by canceling its key with the cancel( ) method:

```
public abstract void cancel( )
```

This is not required as strongly as closing a stream is required. However, it can be a good idea if you're finished with a channel and do not want the Selector to monitor it any longer.

The isValid( ) method tells you whether or not the key is still meaningful:

```
public abstract boolean isValid( )
```

It returns true if the key's channel and Selector are both open and the key has not been cancelled.

# Pipe Channels

Pipe channels move data between two threads, one of which writes and one of which reads. The basic ideas are essentially the same as for piped streams. Data is written onto a Pipe.SinkChannel and then read from the connected Pipe.SourceChannel.

The details are about as simple as they can be. Pipe.SinkChannel is a subclass of AbstractSelectableChannel and implements WritableByteChannel and GatheringByteChannel:

```
public abstract static class Pipe.SinkChannel extends AbstractSelectableChannel
  implements WritableByteChannel, GatheringByteChannel
```

Pipe.SourceChannel is also a subclass of AbstractSelectableChannel and implements ReadableByteChannel and ScatteringByteChannel:

```
public abstract static class Pipe.SinkChannel extends AbstractSelectableChannel
  implements ReadableByteChannel, ScatteringByteChannel
```

Both are public inner classes in the java.nio.channels.Pipe class. Setting up a pipe between two threads is accomplished as follows:

1. Open a pipe with the static Pipe.open( ) method.

2. Get the SinkChannel from the pipe and pass it to the producing thread.

3. Get the SourceChannel from the pipe and pass it to the consuming thread.

4. The producing thread writes data onto the SinkChannel using the usual WritableByteChannel channel methods.

5. The consuming thread reads data from the SourceChannel using the usual ReadableByteChannel methods.

Of course, since this is multithreaded, steps 4 and 5 happen in parallel. If anything, this is a little simpler than using PipedInputStream and PipedOutputStream to do the same job. Furthermore, because both channels can be put into nonblocking mode, each thread can do other things if it's running ahead of its partner. The speeds of the two channels aren't locked together.

As an example of this, I'll reproduce the Fibonacci producers and consumers from Chapter 9, this time implemented with channels and buffers instead of streams. To make this a little more interesting, I'll do it with BigIntegers instead of plain ints, since Fibonacci numbers grow exponentially. This is going to require a protocol for recognizing number boundaries in the stream. The protocol I chose is that the producing thread first writes the number of integers it plans to write onto the stream as a 4-byte int. It then writes the length (in bytes) of each number as a 4-byte int, then writes the bytes that make up that number.

The consuming thread first reads the number of numbers to read. For each such number, it then reads the size of the number from the channel, reads exactly that many bytes from the channel, and converts that to a BigInteger. This does set a theoretical upper limit on the size of the numbers that can be calculated, but in practice you'd run out of heap space long before you hit that limit.

This program has three classes: FibonacciProducer and FibonacciConsumer, which are subclasses of Thread, and NewIOFibonacciDriver, which sets up and runs the threads. Example 16-3 shows the driver class. It opens a pipe and retrieves its source and sink channels, which it uses to construct FibonacciProducer and FibonacciConsumer objects. It then starts those two threads.

*Example 16-3. The NewIOFibonacciDriver class*

```
import java.io.IOException;
import java.nio.channels.*;

public class NewIOFibonacciDriver {

  public static void main (String[] args) throws IOException {
    Pipe pipe = Pipe.open();
    WritableByteChannel out = pipe.sink();
    ReadableByteChannel in = pipe.source();

    FibonacciProducer producer = new FibonacciProducer(out, 200);
    FibonacciConsumer consumer = new FibonacciConsumer(in);
    producer.start();
    consumer.start();
  }
}
```

Example 16-4 shows the `FibonacciProducer` class, a subclass of `Thread`. This class does not directly use a sink channel; it just writes data onto the channel it's given in its constructor. After it has finished writing the requested amount of numbers, the channel is closed.

*Example 16-4. The FibonacciProducer class*

```java
import java.io.IOException;
import java.math.BigInteger;
import java.nio.*;
import java.nio.channels.*;

public class FibonacciProducer extends Thread {

  private WritableByteChannel out;
  private int howMany;

  public FibonacciProducer(WritableByteChannel out, int howMany) {
    this.out = out;
    this.howMany = howMany;
  }

  public void run( ) {

    BigInteger low = BigInteger.ONE;
    BigInteger high = BigInteger.ONE;
    try {
      ByteBuffer buffer = ByteBuffer.allocate(4);
      buffer.putInt(this.howMany);
      buffer.flip( );
      while (buffer.hasRemaining( )) out.write(buffer);

      for (int i = 0; i < howMany; i++) {
        byte[] data = low.toByteArray( );
        // These numbers can become arbitrarily large, and they grow
        // exponentially so no fixed size buffer will suffice.
        buffer = ByteBuffer.allocate(4 + data.length);

        buffer.putInt(data.length);
        buffer.put(data);
        buffer.flip( );

        while (buffer.hasRemaining( )) out.write(buffer);

        // find the next number in the series
        BigInteger temp = high;
        high = high.add(low);
        low = temp;
      }
      out.close( );
      System.err.println("Closed");
    }
    catch (IOException ex) {
```

*Example 16-4. The FibonacciProducer class (continued)*

```
      System.err.println(ex);
    }
  }
}
```

Example 16-5 shows the `FibonacciConsumer` class. It could just as well have been called the `BigIntegerConsumer` class, since it doesn't know anything about Fibonacci numbers. Its `run( )` method merely reads the size of the `BigInteger` from the source channel, reads that many bytes, and converts those bytes into a `BigInteger`, which it then prints. It repeats this until the channel is exhausted.

*Example 16-5. The FibonacciConsumer class*

```java
import java.io.IOException;
import java.math.BigInteger;
import java.nio.channels.*;
import java.nio.*;

public class FibonacciConsumer extends Thread{

  private ReadableByteChannel in;

  public FibonacciConsumer(ReadableByteChannel in) {
    this.in = in;
  }

  public void run( ) {

    ByteBuffer sizeb = ByteBuffer.allocate(4);
    try {
      while (sizeb.hasRemaining( )) in.read(sizeb);
      sizeb.flip( );
      int howMany = sizeb.getInt( );
      sizeb.clear( );

      for (int i = 0; i < howMany; i++) {
        while (sizeb.hasRemaining( )) in.read(sizeb);
        sizeb.flip( );
        int length = sizeb.getInt( );
        sizeb.clear( );

        ByteBuffer data = ByteBuffer.allocate(length);
        while (data.hasRemaining( )) in.read(data);

        BigInteger result = new BigInteger(data.array( ));
        System.out.println(result);
      }
    }
    catch (IOException ex) {
      System.err.println(ex);
    }
```

*Example 16-5. The FibonacciConsumer class (continued)*

```
    finally {
      try {
        in.close( );
      }
      catch (Exception ex) {
        // We tried
      }
    }
  }
}
```

One thing that's a little unusual about this example is the use of two buffers to read the channel. This is necessary because the first buffer has to read the size of the second buffer. The first buffer can be reused. However, because the size of the numbers increases as we read further, new buffers are necessary to read the Fibonacci numbers themselves. It would probably be possible to contrive a way to reuse the same buffer repeatedly if it were too small for the numbers, but that seemed unnecessarily complex for no particular benefit.

There's not a lot of call for nonblocking mode in this example because the producer thread only writes and the consumer thread only reads, and both on only one channel. If either thread had something else to do it might make sense to use a Selector and put these channels into nonblocking mode.

# PART V

# The File System

# CHAPTER 17

# Working with Files

You've learned how to read and write data in files using file input streams, file output streams, and file channels, but that's not all there is to files. Files can be created, moved, renamed, copied, deleted, and otherwise manipulated without respect to their contents. Files are also often associated with metainformation that's not strictly part of the contents of the file, such as the time the file was created, the icon for the file, the permissions that determine which users can read or write to the file, and the name of the file.

While the view of the contents of a file as an ordered sequence of bytes used by file input and output streams is almost standard across platforms, the metainformation is not. The java.io.File class attempts to provide a platform-independent abstraction for common file operations and metainformation. Unfortunately, this class really shows its Unix roots. It works well on Unix, but at best adequately on Windows and the Macintosh (even Mac OS X). Coming up with something that genuinely works on all platforms is an extremely difficult problem.

File manipulation is thus one of the real difficulties of cross-platform Java programming. Before you can hope to write truly cross-platform code, you need a solid understanding of the filesystem basics on all the target platforms. This chapter tries to cover those basics for the major platforms that support Java: Unix/Linux, Windows/DOS, and the Mac. It then shows you how to write your file code so that it's as portable as possible.

## Understanding Files

As far as a Java program knows, a file is a sequential set of bytes stored on a random access medium such as a hard disk or CD. There is a first byte in the file, a second byte, and so on, until the end of the file. In this way, a file is similar to a stream. However, a program can jump around in a file, reading first one part of a file and then another. This isn't possible with a stream.

# Filenames

Every file has a name. The format of the filename is determined by the operating system. For example, in DOS and Windows 3.1, filenames are 8 ASCII characters long with a 3-letter extension. *README.TXT* is a valid DOS filename, but *Read me before you run this program or your hard drive will get trashed* is not. All ASCII characters from 32 up (that is, noncontrol characters), except for the 15 punctuation characters (+=/][":;,?*\<>|) and the space character, may be used in filenames. Filenames are case-insensitive (though generally rendered as all capitals). *README.TXT* and *readme.txt* are the same filename. A period may be used only as a separator between the 8-character name and the 3-letter extension. Furthermore, the complete path to the file, including the disk drive and all directories, may not exceed 80 characters in length.

On the other hand, *Read me before you run this program or your hard drive will get trashed* is a valid Win32 (Windows 95 and later) filename. On those systems filenames may contain up to 255 characters, though room also has to be left for the path to the file. The full pathname may not exceed 255 characters. Furthermore, Win32 systems allow any Unicode character with value 32 or above in filenames, except \/*<>: ?" and |. In particular, the +,;=][ characters, forbidden in DOS and Windows 3.1, are legal in Win32 filenames.

Win32 also makes short versions of the filename that conform to the DOS 8.3 format available to non-32-bit applications that don't understand the long filenames. Java understands the long filenames and uses them in preference to the short form.

*Read me before you run this program or your hard drive will get trashed* is not a valid Mac OS 9 filename because on Mac OS 9 file and directory names cannot be longer than 31 bytes. Volume names cannot be longer than 27 bytes. However, there's no fixed length to a full path name. The exact number of characters allowed in a name depends on the number of bytes per character used by the local encoding. *Read me or your HD will be trashed* only contains 27 bytes in most encodings and is thus a valid Macintosh file, directory, and volume name. Mac OS 9 filenames can contain slashes and backslashes (unlike Windows filenames) but may not contain colons. Otherwise, any ASCII characters, as well as 8-bit MacRoman characters like ® and π, can be used in a Mac filename.

Of course today most Mac users are running Mac OS X, which is a version of Unix. Just as Windows converts names to 8.3 filenames as necessary to support older applications, so too does Mac OS X convert really long filenames to shorter ones for older apps. Java programs running on Mac OS X only see the longer Unix style names.

Pretty much all modern Unix systems including Linux and Mac OS X allow at least 255 characters in a filename, and none of those 255 characters needs to be left for a path. Just about any ASCII character except the forward slash (/) and the null character (ASCII 0) are valid in a Unix filename. However, because Unix makes heavy use of a command line, filenames containing spaces, single quotation marks, double quotes, hyphens, or other characters interpreted by the Unix shell are often inconvenient. Underscores (which aren't interpreted by the Unix shell) are safe and often used in place of problematic characters (for example, *Read_me_or_your_HD_will_be_trashed.*)

Character sets are an issue for filenames too. Some Unixes use ISO 8859-1, some use ASCII only, and some use Unicode. Worse yet, the names of the files can change from one user to the next depending on how they've configured their locale. American Mac OS 9 filenames are given in the 8-bit MacRoman character set, but internationalized versions of the Mac OS use different character sets. Mac OS X uses Unicode throughout. However, some bugs in Apple's Java implementation prevent it from reading or writing files whose names contain characters from outside the Basic Multilingual Plane. Windows 95 and later, fortunately, use Unicode exclusively, and it pretty much works. However, the reliable lowest common denominator character set for filenames is still ASCII.

Case sensitivity is a problem too. *Readme.txt* and *README.TXT* are the same file on Mac OS 9 and Windows but represent two different files on Unix. Mac OS X is basically Unix, but in this respect it's actually more similar to Windows and the classic Mac OS. Mac OS X filenames are case insensitive. (Actually case sensitive filenames are an option when a disk is formatted, but the default that almost everyone uses is case insensitive.)

Handling different filename conventions is one of the difficulties of doing real cross-platform work. For best results:

- Use only printable ASCII characters, periods, and underscores in filenames.
- Avoid punctuation characters in filenames where possible, especially forward and back slashes.
- Never begin a filename with a period, a hyphen, or an @.
- Avoid extended character sets and accented characters like ü, ç, and é.
- Use mixed-case filenames (since they're easier to read), but do not assume case alone will distinguish between filenames.
- Try to keep your filenames to 32 characters or less.
- If a filename can be stored in a DOS-compatible 8.3 format without excessive effort, you might as well do so. However, Java itself assumes a system on which files have long names with four- and five-character extensions, so don't go out of your way to do this.

# File Attributes

Most operating systems also store a series of attributes describing each file. The exact attributes a file possesses are platform-dependent. For example, on Unix a file has an owner ID, a group ID, a modification time, and a series of read, write, and execute flags that determine who is allowed to do what with the file. If an operating system supports multiple types of filesystems (and most modern desktop and server operating systems do), the attributes of a file may vary depending on what kind of filesystem it resides on.

Many Mac files also have a type code and a creator code as well as a potentially unlimited number of attributes that determine whether a file is a bundle or not, is an alias or not, has a custom icon or not, and various other characteristics mostly unique to the Mac platform.

DOS filesystems store a file's last modification date, the actual size of the file, the number of allocation blocks the file occupies, and essentially boolean information about whether or not a file is hidden, read-only, a system file, or whether the file has been modified since it was last backed up.

Modern versions of Windows support multiple kinds of filesystems including FAT (the basic DOS-compatible filesystem) and NTFS (NT File System). Each of these filesystems supports a slightly different set of attributes. They all support a superset of the basic DOS file attributes, including creation time, modification time, access time, allocation size, file size, and whether the file is read-only, system, hidden, archive, or control.

Any cross-platform library like the java.io package is going to have trouble supporting all these attributes. Java can read a fairly broad cross-section of these possible attributes for which most platforms have some reasonable equivalent. It does not allow you easy access to platform-specific attributes, like Mac file types and creator codes, Windows' archive attributes, or Unix group IDs.

# Filename Extensions and File Types

Filename extensions often indicate the type of a file. For example, a file that ends with the four-letter extension *.java* is presumed to be a text file containing Java source code; a file ending in the five-letter extension *.class* is assumed to contain compiled Java byte code; a file ending in the 3-letter extension *.gif* is assumed to contain a GIF image.

What does your computer do when you double-click on the file *panther.gif*? If your computer is a Macintosh, it opens the file in the program that created the file. That's because the Mac stores a four-letter creator code for every file on the disk. Assuming the application associated with that creator code can be found (it can't always, though), the file *panther.gif* is opened in the creating program. On the other hand, if your computer is a Windows PC or a Unix workstation, the creating program is not necessarily opened. Instead, whichever program is registered as the viewer of .*gif* files is launched and used to view the file. In command-line environments, like the Unix shell, this isn't really an issue because you begin by specifying the program to run (that is, you type *xv panther.gif*, not simply *panther.gif*) but in GUI environments, the program that's opened may not be the program you want to use.

File extensions have the further disadvantage that they do not really guarantee the content type of their document and are an unreliable means of determining the type of a file. Users can easily change them. For example, the simple DOS command copy `HelloWorld.java HelloWorld.gif` causes a text file to be misinterpreted as a GIF image. Filename extensions are only as reliable as the user who assigned them. What's more, it's hard to distinguish between files that belong to different applications that have the same type. For instance, many users are surprised to discover that after installing Firefox, all their HTML files appear to belong to Firefox instead of Internet Explorer.

The Macintosh solved this problem over two decades ago. Almost every Mac file has a four-letter type code like "TEXT" and a four-letter creator code like "R*ch". Since each file has both a type code *and* a creator code, a Mac can distinguish between files that belong to different applications but have the same type. Installing Firefox doesn't mean that Firefox suddenly thinks it owns all your Internet Explorer documents. Software vendors register codes with Apple so that companies don't accidentally step on each other's toes. Since codes are almost never seen by end users, there's not a huge rush to snap up all the good ones like "TEXT" and "HTML". Overall, this is a pretty good system that's worked incredibly well for more than twenty years. Apple actually tried to get rid of it in favor of Unix/DOS style file extensions when they moved to Mac OS X, but backed down after massive outcries from developers and users alike. Neither Windows nor Unix has anything nearly as simple and trouble-free. However, because Windows and Unix have not adopted Mac-style type and creator codes, Java does not have any standard means for accessing them.

 The `com.apple.eio.FileManager` class included with Apple's port of the JDK 1.4 and 1.5 provides access to Mac-specific type and creator codes and other file attributes. Steve Roy's open source MRJAdapter library (*https://mrjadapter.dev.java.net/*) provides this for almost every version of Java Apple has ever shipped.

None of these solutions are perfect. On a Mac, you're likely to want to use Photoshop to create GIF files but Preview or Firefox to view them. Furthermore, it's relatively hard to say that you want all text files opened in BBEdit. On the other hand, the Windows solution is prone to user error; filename extensions are too exposed. For example, novice HTML coders often can't understand why their HTML files painstakingly crafted in Notepad open as plaintext in Internet Explorer. Notepad surreptitiously inserts a *.txt* extension on all the files it saves unless the filename is enclosed in double quote marks. For instance, a file saved as *HelloWorld.html* actually becomes *HelloWorld.html.txt* while a file saved as "HelloWorld.html" is saved with the expected name. Furthermore, filename extensions make it easy for a user to lie about the contents of a file, potentially confusing and crashing applications. (You can lie about a file type on a Mac too, but it takes a lot more work.) Finally, Windows provides absolutely no support for saying that you want one group of GIF images opened in Photoshop and another group opened in Paint.

Some algorithms can attempt to determine a file's type from its contents, though these are also error-prone. Many file formats begin with a particular *magic number* that uniquely identifies the format. For instance, all compiled Java class files begin with the number 0xCAFEBABE (in hexadecimal). If the first four bytes of a file aren't 0xCAFEBABE, it's definitely not a Java class file. Furthermore, barring deliberate fraud, there's only about a one in four billion chance that a random, non-Java file will begin with those four bytes. Unfortunately, only a few file formats require magic numbers. Text files, for instance, can begin with any four ASCII characters. You can apply some heuristics to identify such files. For example, a file of pure ASCII should not contain any bytes with values between 128 and 255 and should have a limited number of control characters with values less than 32. But such algorithms are complicated to devise and imperfect. Even if you are able to identify a file as ASCII text, how would you determine whether it contains Java source code or a letter to your mother? Worse yet, how could you tell whether it contains Java source code or C source code? It's not impossible, barring deliberately perverse files like a concatenation of a C program with a Java program, but it's difficult and often not worth your time.

# Directories and Paths

Modern operating systems organize files into hierarchical directories. Directories are also called folders, especially by Mac users. Each directory contains zero or more files or other directories. Like files, directories have names and attributes, though—depending on the operating system—those names and attributes may be different from the attributes allowed for files.

## Paths and Separators

To specify a file completely, you don't just give its name. You also give the directory the file lives in. Of course, that directory may itself be inside another directory, which may be in another directory, until you reach the *root* of the filesystem. The complete list of directories from the root to a specified file plus the name of the file itself is called the *absolute path* to the file. The exact syntax of absolute paths varies from system to system. Here are a few examples:

| DOS | C:\PUBLIC\HTML\JAVAFAQ\INDEX.HTM |
| Win32 | C:\public\html\javafaq\index.html |
| Mac OS 9 | Macintosh HD:public:html:javafaq:index.html |
| Unix/Linux/Mac OS X | /Volumes/Macintosh HD/public/html/javafaq/index.html |

All of these strings reference a file named *index.html* on the primary hard drive in the *javafaq* directory, which is itself in the *html* directory, which is in the *public* directory. One obvious difference is the file separator character. Unix (including Linux and Mac OS X) use a forward slash (/) to separate directories. DOS-based filesystems, including the variants of Windows and OS/2, use a backslash (\). Other platforms may use something completely different.

The separator used on a given system is available from the mnemonic constants `java.io.File.separator` and `java.io.File.separatorChar`. `File.separatorChar` is the first character of the string `File.separator`. All operating systems I'm familiar with use a single character separator string, so these two variables are essentially the same. The `File.separator` variable is set from the system property `file.separator`:

```
public static final String separator = System.getProperty("file.separator");
public static final char separatorChar = separator.charAt(0);
```

## System Properties

Several system properties provide full paths to directories according to the local filesystem conventions. The security manager permitting, you can use these to construct cross-platform filenames. Such properties include:

`java.home`
> The directory where Java is installed, e.g., */usr/local/java* on many Unix systems.

`java.class.path`
> The classpath contains many directories separated by the path separator character.

`user.home`
> The user's home directory.

`user.dir`
> The current working directory.

There are also two related mnemonic constants, `File.pathSeparator` and `File.pathSeparatorChar`. The path separator string is set from the system property `path.separator`. As with the separator character, `File.pathSeparatorChar` is the first character in `File.pathSeparator`.

```
public static final String pathSeparator
 = System.getProperty("path.separator");
public static final char pathSeparatorChar = pathSeparator.charAt(0);
```

The path separator is used to separate two files (generally with complete pathnames) in a list of paths such as a classpath. For example, with a separator of a slash and a path separator of a colon, my classpath looks like this:

```
.:/usr/local/java/lib:/home/users/elharo/:/home/users/elharo/JavaDis/
```

Now the bad news: although Java has a fairly powerful abstraction layer so that programmers don't need to hardcode explicit separators and path separators, few programmers actually use this. Many programmers simply assume that the file separator is a slash and the path separator is a colon and hardcode those constants as "/" and ":". Therefore, to avoid breaking all this third-party code, Java passes pathnames through a normalization phase that attempts to recognize the separator conventions and convert those to the conventions of the local platform.

You probably don't need to know about the encoding at this level of detail unless you're trying to manipulate filenames manually—for example, walking directories by looking for separator characters rather than calling getParent( ). The more you let Java do the work for you, the better off you'll be. As long as you use the methods of the File class rather than parsing pathnames as strings, the details should be transparent.

## Relative versus Absolute Paths

There are two ways to reference a file, relative and absolute. Absolute addressing gives a complete path to a file, starting with the disk or root of the filesystem and working its way down. *C:\PUBLIC\HTML\JAVAFAQ\INDEX.HTM*, *Macintosh HD: public:html:javafaq:index.htm*, and */public/html/javafaq/index.htm* are all examples of absolute paths. Relative addressing does not use a complete path to a file; instead, it specifies the path relative to the current working directory. A relative pathname may point to a file in the current working directory by giving its name alone; other times it may point to a file in a subdirectory of the current working directory by giving the name of the subdirectory and the name of the file, and it may point to the parent of the current working directory with the double period (..).

### Absolute paths

On Unix, all mounted disks, whether local or mounted over the network, are combined into a single virtual filesystem. The *root* of this filesystem is the directory called /. You generally do not need to concern yourself with which physical disk any particular directory resides on, as long as that disk has sufficient space. Absolute paths always begin with the root directory, /.

On Windows and Mac OS 9, there is no root directory. Each mounted disk partition or network server is a separate and independent filesystem. On Windows, these disks are assigned drive letters. A: is normally the floppy drive. B: is the second floppy drive (uncommon these days), C: is the primary boot disk. D: is often the CD-ROM, though it can be an additional hard disk or partition as well. E: through Z: can be used for further disks, partitions, or network servers. A full pathname begins with the drive letter where the file resides, e.g., *C:\PUBLIC\HTML\ JAVAFAQ\INDEX.HTM*.

Windows can also refer to remote machines on the network by specifying an additional level like this: *\\BIO\C\PUBLIC\HTML\JAVAFAQ\INDEX.HTM*. This path refers to a file called *INDEX.HTM* in the directory *JAVAFAQ* in the directory *HTML* in the directory *PUBLIC* on the *C* drive of the machine *BIO*.

For these reasons and more, absolute pathnames are a royal pain to work with across platforms. You should avoid hardcoding them in your programs whenever possible. Instead, you should calculate them at runtime from system properties and user input.

### Relative paths

The following are some examples of relative paths:

| | |
|---|---|
| Unix | *html/index.html* |
| DOS | *HTML\INDEX.HTM* |
| Win32 | *html\index.html* |
| Mac OS 9 | *:html:index.html* |
| Unix | *index.html* |
| DOS | *INDEX.HTM* |
| Win32 | *index.html* |
| Mac OS 9 | *index.html* |

Note that a filename in isolation constitutes a relative path on all platforms.

Generally, the running application identifies one directory as the current working directory. Relative pathnames are interpreted relative to the working directory. Normally, the current working directory is the directory in which the application was launched. For example, if you started your program from the command line in the */home/users/elharo* directory, a relative path of *classes/juggler.class* would point to a file with the absolute path */home/users/elharo/classes/juggler.class*. On the Macintosh, the current working directory is generally whichever one the application lives in.

The current working directory is fixed once a program starts running. Java provides no means to change it.

Because the current working directory is unpredictable, you should not hardcode relative pathnames into your application. A common solution is to distribute your program as a JAR archive, store the data files in the JAR file, and retrieve them with the various getResource( ), getResourceAsStream( ), and findResource( ) methods of `java.lang.Class` or `java.lang.ClassLoader`. This works irrespective of the current working directory as long as the JAR archive has been placed somewhere in the classpath.

# The File Class

Instances of the `java.io.File` class represent *filenames* on the local system, not actual files. Occasionally, this distinction is crucial. For instance, `File` objects can represent directories as well as files. Also, you cannot assume that a file exists just because you have a `File` object for a file.

```
public class File extends Object implements Serializable, Comparable
```

Although there are no guarantees that a file named by a `File` object actually exists, the `File` class does contain many methods for getting information about the attributes of a file and for manipulating those files. The `File` class attempts to account for system-dependent features like the file separator character and file attributes.

Each `File` object contains a single `String` field called `path` that contains either a relative or absolute path to the file, including the name of the file or directory itself:

```
private String path
```

Many methods in this class work solely by looking at this string. They do not necessarily look at any part of the filesystem.

## Constructing File Objects

The `java.io.File` class has three constructors. Each accepts some variation of a filename as an argument. This one is the simplest:

```
public File(String path)
```

The `path` argument should be either an absolute or relative path to the file in a format understood by the host operating system. For example, using Unix filename conventions:

```
File uf1 = new File("25.html");
File uf2 = new File("course/week2/25.html");
File uf3 = new File("/public/html/course/week2/25.html");
```

Much poorly written Java code implicitly assumes Unix filename conventions, and most VMs take this into account. Therefore, code that assumes Unix conventions is likely to produce reasonable results on most operating systems. Windows VMs generally allow you to use Windows conventions instead. For example:

```
File wf1 = new File("25.htm");
File wf2 = new File("course\\week2\\25.html");
File wf3 = new File("D:\\public\\html\\course\\week2\\25.htm");
```

The double backslashes are merely the escape sequence for the single backslash in a string literal. Otherwise, attempts to compile this code would generate an "Invalid escape character" error message. Remember that \t is a tab, \n a linefeed, and so on. Here, however, we need a backslash to simply be a backslash.

The second File constructor specifies an absolute or relative pathname and a filename:

```
public File(String directory, String filename)
```

For example:

```
File f2 = new File("course/week2", "25.html");
```

This produces a File object with the path field set to course/week2/25.html. The constructor is smart enough to handle the case of directories with and without trailing separators. The third constructor is identical to the second, except that the first argument is a File object instead of a string.

```
public File(File directory, String filename)
```

This third constructor is the most robust of the lot, provided the filename is only a filename like *readme.txt* and not a relative path like *cryptozip/readme.txt*. The reason is that this constructor guarantees the use of the local path separator character and is thus more platform-independent. You can use this to build a file structure that works on all platforms regardless of path separators or normalization routines. For example, suppose you want to build a File object that points to the file *com/elharo/io/StreamCopier.class*. The following four lines do this without reference to the file separator character:

```
File temp = new File("com");
temp = new File(temp, "elharo");
temp = new File(temp, "io");
File scfile = new File(temp, "StreamCopier.class");
```

None of these constructors throw any exceptions. All the constructor does is set the path field; Java never checks to see whether the file named by path actually exists or even whether the name passed to the constructor is a valid filename. For example, the following File object causes problems on Unix, OS/2, Mac OS 9, Mac OS X, and Windows, but you can still construct it:

```
File f = new File("-This is not a /nice\\ file:\r\nno it isn't");
```

Some methods in other classes also return File objects, most notably the java.awt. FileDialog and javax.swing.JFileChooser methods discussed in the next chapter. Using file dialogs or choosers to ask the user for a filename is preferable to hardcoding them or reading them from the command line because file dialogs properly handle cross-platform issues and the distinctions between relative and absolute paths.

One thing you may not have noticed about these constructors: since a File object does not represent a file as much as a filename, these constructors do not actually create files. To create a new file with Java, you can open a file output stream to the file or invoke the createNewFile( ) method.

In Java 1.2 and later, construction of a File object includes normalization. This process reads hardcoded pathnames and attempts to convert them to the conventions of the local platform. This improves compatibility with code that's making assumptions about filenames. For instance, if a Windows VM is asked to create a File object with the path */public/html/javafaq/course/week2/index.html*, it actually sets the path field to *\public\ html\ javafaq\ course\week2\ index.html*. The reverse process happens on Unix; backslashes are converted to forward slashes. Because it can only really normalize separators, not filesystem roots, this scheme works better for relative pathnames than absolute ones.

## Listing the Roots

The static File.listRoots( ) method returns an array containing the roots of the filesystem as File objects:

```
public static File[] listRoots()
```

On Unix, this array is likely to have length 1 and contain the single root /. On Windows, it probably contains all the drive letters mapped to one device or another, whether or not there's actually any media in the drive, e.g., A:\, C:\, D:\, E:\, F:\, G:\. If the security manager does not allow the program to read a particular root, that root is not included in the returned list. If the security manager does not allow the program to read any root, the returned list will have length zero. Do not assume the array returned by listRoots( ) necessarily has any members! null is returned if the list can't be determined at all. This is not the same thing as a zero-length array.

The list of roots may or may not contain drives that are mounted over the network. If the drive is mounted in such a fashion that it pretends to be a local drive, it probably will be in the list. If the filesystem does not look like a local drive, it probably won't appear in the list. For instance, on Windows, network drives mapped to letters appear, but drives with UNC pathnames do not. Example 17-1 is a very simple program to list the roots and print them.

*Example 17-1. RootLister*

```
import java.io.*;

public class RootLister {

  public static void main(String[] args) {
```

*Example 17-1. RootLister (continued)*

```
    File[] roots = File.listRoots();
    for (int i = 0; i < roots.length; i++) {
      System.out.println(roots[i]);
    }
  }
}
```

Here's the output produced by RootLister on my Windows NT system. A: is the floppy drive. This system doesn't have a second floppy, which would normally be B:. C:, D:, E:, and F: are all partitions of the primary hard drive that appear to be separate drives. G: is an external hard drive, and H: is the CD-ROM. I: is a Macintosh drive mounted over the LAN.

```
D:\JAVA\ioexamples\17>java RootLister
A:\
C:\
D:\
E:\
F:\
G:\
H:\
I:\
```

The output on Unix (including Mac OS X) is much simpler and is virtually guaranteed to look like this:

```
$ java RootLister
/
```

## Listing Information about a File

The File class contains many methods that return particular information about the file. Most of this information can be gleaned from the path field alone without accessing the filesystem. Therefore, most of these methods do not throw IOExceptions.

### Does the file exist? Is it a normal file? Is it a directory?

Since a File object does not necessarily correspond to a real file on the disk, the first question you'll probably want to ask is whether the file corresponding to the File object actually exists. This is especially important if you're relying on a user to type a filename rather than select it from a dialog because users routinely mistype filenames. The exists( ) method returns true if the file named in this file object's path field exists or false if it doesn't:

```
public boolean exists()
```

There are two other ways to ask this question. The isFile( ) method returns true if the file exists and is not a directory. On the other hand, the isDirectory( ) method returns true if the file exists and is a directory.

```
public boolean isFile( )
public boolean isDirectory( )
```

The isDirectory( ) method considers Unix symbolic links and Mac aliases to directories to be directories themselves; it does *not* consider Windows shortcuts to directories to be directories. All three of these methods throw a security exception if the security manager does not allow the specified file to be read. In fact, if the file couldn't be read if it did exist, isDirectory( ) throws an exception whether the file actually exists or not. Revealing whether certain files exist can be a security violation.

### Filename and path

The getName( ) method takes no arguments and returns the name of the file as a string:

```
public String getName( )
```

The name does not include any part of the directory in which the file lives. That is, you get back *index.html* instead of */public/html/javafaq/index.html*. If the file is a directory like */public/html/javafaq/*, only the last name is returned (*javafaq* in this example).

The getPath( ) method returns the complete path to the file:

```
public String getPath( )
```

This simply returns the path field. Therefore, the path is relative if the File object was constructed with a relative path and absolute if the File object was constructed with an absolute path. Furthermore, this method never throws IOExceptions. Consider Example 17-2. This simple program constructs two File objects, one with a relative path and one with an absolute path, and prints the name and path of each object.

*Example 17-2. Paths*

```
import java.io.*;

public class Paths {

  public static void main(String[] args) {

    File absolute = new File("/public/html/javafaq/index.html");
    File relative = new File("html/javafaq/index.html");

    System.out.println("absolute: ");
    System.out.println(absolute.getName( ));
    System.out.println(absolute.getPath( ));
```

*Example 17-2. Paths (continued)*

```
    System.out.println("relative: ");
    System.out.println(relative.getName( ));
    System.out.println(relative.getPath( ));
  }
}
```

When the program is run on Unix, here's the output:

```
$ java Paths
absolute:
index.html
/public/html/javafaq/index.html
relative:
index.html
html/javafaq/index.html
```

On Windows the output is a little different because the File constructor normalizes the file separator character to the backslash:

```
D:\JAVA\ioexamples\17>java Paths
absolute:
index.html
\public\html\javafaq\index.html
relative:
index.html
html\javafaq\index.html
```

## Absolute paths

The getAbsolutePath( ) method returns the complete path to the file starting from a filesystem root:

```
public String getAbsolutePath( )
```

Examples of absolute paths include */public/html/javafaq/index.html* and *D:\JAVA\ ioexamples\17* but not *html/javafaq/index.html* or *ioexamples\17*. If the File object's path field is already an absolute path, its value is returned. Otherwise, a separator character and the value of the path field are appended to the value of the system property user.dir, which refers to the current working directory. This method throws a security exception when run from untrusted code because untrusted code cannot normally read the user.dir property.

If you need to know whether a file is specified by a relative or absolute path, you can call isAbsolute( ):

```
public boolean isAbsolute( )
```

This does not throw any security exceptions because it does not need to go outside the class to determine whether or not a pathname is absolute. Instead, the check is performed by looking at the first few characters of the path field. On Unix, an absolute path begins with a /. On Windows or OS/2, an absolute path begins with a capital letter followed by a colon and a backslash, like C:\.

## Canonical paths

Exactly what a canonical path is, and how it differs from an absolute path, is system-dependent, but it tends to mean that the path is somehow more real than the absolute path. Typically, if the full path contains aliases, shortcuts, shadows, or symbolic links of some kind, the canonical path resolves those aliases to the actual directories they refer to. The canonical path is returned by the getCanonicalPath( ) method:

```
public String getCanonicalPath( ) throws IOException
```

For example, suppose */bin/perl* is a symbolic link to the real file at */usr/local/bin/perl*, and you construct a File object perlLink like this:

```
File perlLink = new File("/bin/perl");
```

perlLink.getAbsolutePath( ) returns */bin/perl*, but perlLink.getCanonicalPath( ) returns */usr/local/bin/perl*.

 getCanonicalPath( ) only resolves symbolic links. It does not resolve hard links. That is, it resolves links created with "ln -s file link" but not "ln file link."

getCanonicalPath( ) also removes relative references like the double period (..), which refers to the parent directory in paths. For instance, suppose the current working directory is */home/elharo/javaio/ioexamples/17*. Then you create a File object like this:

```
File f = new File("../11/index.html");
String absolutePath = f.getAbsolutePath( );
String canonicalPath = f.getCanonicalPath( );
```

absolutePath is now */home/elharo/javaio/ioexamples/17/../11/index.html*. However, canonicalPath is */home/elharo/javaio/ioexamples/11/index.html*.

On Windows, getCanonicalPath( ) normalizes the case of two paths so that *C:\ Documents\Books* and *C:\DOCUMENTS\BOOKS* are recognized as the same path. Mac OS X also normalizes the case. Other Unixes with case sensitive filesystems do not. Usually, the normalized form is whatever was initially provided for the file's name.

One use for canonical paths is to test whether two files are the same. You might need to do this if you're reading from an input file and writing to an output file. While it might occasionally be possible to read from and write to the same file, doing so always requires special care. For example, the FileCopier program from Example 4-2 in Chapter 4 failed when the source and destination were the same file. Now we can use canonical paths to correct that flaw by testing whether two files are the same before copying, as shown in Example 17-3. If the files are the same, no copy needs to take place.

*Example 17-3. Safe FileCopier*

```java
import java.io.*;

public class SafeFileCopier {

  public static void main(String[] args) throws IOException {
    if (args.length != 2) {
      System.err.println("Usage: java FileCopier infile outfile");
    }
    else copy(new File(args[0]), new File(args[1]));
  }

  public static void copy(File inFile, File outFile) throws IOException {

    if (inFile.getCanonicalPath().equals(outFile.getCanonicalPath())) {
      // inFile and outFile are the same;
      // hence no copying is required.
      return;
    }

    InputStream in = null;
    OutputStream out = null;

    try {
      in = new BufferedInputStream(new FileInputStream(inFile));
      out = new BufferedOutputStream(new FileOutputStream(outFile));
      for (int c = in.read(); c != -1; c = in.read()) {
        out.write(c);
      }
    }
    finally {
      if (in != null) in.close();
      if (out != null) out.close();
    }
  }
}
```

I could test the files themselves, but since a single file may have multiple paths through aliases or parent links, I'm still not guaranteed that the inFile and outFile aren't the same. But each file has exactly one unique canonical path, so if inFile's canonical path is not equal to outFile's canonical path, they can't possibly be the same file. Conversely, if inFile's canonical path is equal to outFile's canonical path, they must be the same file.

The getCanonicalFile( ) method acts just like getCanonicalPath( ), except that it returns a new File object instead of a string:

```java
public File getCanonicalFile() throws IOException
```

The File object returned has a path field that's the canonical path of the file. Both getCanonicalPath( ) and getCanonicalFile( ) can throw IOExceptions because both need to read the filesystem to resolve aliases, shadows, symbolic links, shortcuts, and parent directory references.

## Parents

The getParent() method returns a string containing everything before the last file separator in the path field:

```
public String getParent()
```

For example, if a File object's path field is */home/users/elharo/javaio/ioexamples/11/index.html*, getParent() returns /home/users/elharo/javaio/ioexamples/11. If a File object's path field is *11/index.html*, getParent() returns 11. If a File object's path field is *index.html*, getParent() returns null. Filesystem roots have no parent directories. For these files, getParent() returns null.

The getParentFile() method does the same thing, except that it returns the parent as a new File object instead of a string:

```
public File getParentFile()
```

## File attributes

The File class has several methods that return information about the file, such as its length, the time it was last modified, whether it's readable, whether it's writable, and whether it's hidden.

The canWrite() method indicates whether the program can write into the file referred to by this File object. The canRead() method indicates whether the program can read from the file.

```
public boolean canRead()
public boolean canWrite()
```

Both these methods perform two checks. The first check determines whether Java's security manager allows the file in question to be read or written; the second determines whether the operating system allows the file to be read or written. If Java's security manager disallows the access, a security exception is thrown. If the OS disallows the access, the method returns false but does not throw any exceptions. However, attempting to read from or write to such a file will almost certainly throw an IOException.

Java 6 adds a canExecute() method that tests whether the current application can execute the file represented by the File object:

```
public boolean canExecute() // Java 6
```

Like canRead() and canWrite(), this method does not merely check the execute bit. The question is whether the current program can launch the file (e.g., by Runtime's exec() methods).

The isHidden() method returns true if the file exists but is hidden; that is, it does not appear in normal displays or listings. It returns false if the file isn't hidden or doesn't exist.

```
public boolean isHidden()
```

Exactly how a file is hidden varies from platform to platform. On Unix, any file whose name begins with a period is hidden. On Windows, hidden files are identified by particular attributes. This method throws a security exception if the security manager doesn't allow the file to be read.

The `lastModified( )` method returns a `long` indicating the last time this file was modified:

```
public long lastModified( )
```

The time is the number of milliseconds since midnight, January 1, 1970, Greenwich Mean Time. However, in older VMs the conversion between this `long` and a real date is platform-dependent, so it's only useful for comparing the modification dates of different files, not for determining the absolute time a file was modified. This method throws a security exception if the security manager doesn't allow the file to be read. It returns 0 if the file doesn't exist or the last modified date can't be determined.

Finally, the `length( )` method returns the number of bytes in the file or 0 if the file does not exist:

```
public long length( )
```

This method throws a security exception if the security manager doesn't allow the file to be read.

### An example

Example 17-4 is a character-mode program that lists all the available information about files named on the command line. Names may be given as absolute or relative paths.

*Example 17-4. The FileSpy program*

```java
import java.io.*;
import java.util.*;

public class FileSpy {

  public static void main(String[] args) {

    for (int i = 0; i < args.length; i++) {
      File f = new File(args[i]);
      if (f.exists()) {
        System.out.println("Name: " + f.getName( ));
        System.out.println("Absolute path: " + f.getAbsolutePath( ));
        try {
          System.out.println("Canonical path: " + f.getCanonicalPath( ));
        }
        catch (IOException ex) {
          System.out.println("Could not determine the canonical path.");
        }
```

*Example 17-4. The FileSpy program (continued)*

```
        String parent = f.getParent( );
        if (parent != null) {
          System.out.println("Parent: " + f.getParent( ));
        }

        if (f.canWrite()) System.out.println(f.getName( ) + " is writable.");
        if (f.canRead()) System.out.println(f.getName( ) + " is readable.");

        if (f.isFile( )) {
          System.out.println(f.getName( ) + " is a file.");
        }
        else if (f.isDirectory( )) {
          System.out.println(f.getName( ) + " is a directory.");
        }
        else {
          System.out.println("What is this?");
        }

        if (f.isAbsolute( )) {
          System.out.println(f.getPath( ) + " is an absolute path.");
        }
        else {
          System.out.println(f.getPath( ) + " is not an absolute path.");
        }

        long lm = f.lastModified( );
        if (lm != 0) System.out.println("Last Modified at " + new Date(lm));

        long length = f.length( );
        if (length != 0) {
          System.out.println(f.getName( ) + " is " + length + " bytes long.");
        }
      }
      else {
        System.out.println("I'm sorry. I can't find the file " + args[i]);
      }
    }
  }
}
```

Here's the result of running FileSpy on itself:

```
D:\JAVA\ioexamples\17>java FileSpy FileSpy.java
Name: FileSpy.java
Absolute path: D:\JAVA\ioexamples\17\FileSpy.java
Canonical path: D:\Java\ioexamples\17\FileSpy.java
FileSpy.java is writable.
FileSpy.java is readable.
FileSpy.java is a file.
FileSpy.java is not an absolute path.
Last Modified at Fri Sep 11 15:11:24 PDT 1998
FileSpy.java is 1846 bytes long.
```

# Manipulating Files

The File class has methods to create, move, rename, and delete files. A method to copy files is a noticeable omission.

### Creating files

The createNewFile( ) method creates the file referenced by the File object:

```
public boolean createNewFile( )  throws IOException
```

This method checks to see whether the file exists and creates the file if it doesn't already exist. It returns true if the file was created and false if it wasn't created, either because it couldn't be created or because the file already existed. For example:

```
File f = new File("output.dat");
boolean success = f.createNewFile( );
if (success) {
  //...
}
else { //...
```

This method throws an IOException if an I/O error occurs. It throws a security exception if the security manager vetoes the creation of the file.

### Moving and renaming files

The renameTo( ) method changes the name of a file:

```
public boolean renameTo(File destination)
```

For example, to change the name of the file *src.txt* in the current working directory to *dst.txt*, you would write:

```
File src = new File("src.txt");
File dst = new File("dst.txt");
src.renameTo(dst);
```

If a file already exists with the destination name, the existing file may be overwritten or the rename may fail and return false. This varies from one platform and VM to another.

If the destination file is in a different directory than the source file, the renameTo( ) may move the source file from its original directory to the directory specified by the destination argument. For example, to move a file *src* to the directory */usr/tmp* on a Unix system without changing the file's name, do this:

```
File dest = new File("/usr/tmp/" + src.getName( ));
src.renameTo(dest);
```

However, this behavior is unreliable and platform-dependent. For instance, renameTo( ) moves files if, and only if, the directory structure specified in the dest File object already exists. I've also seen this code work on some Unix versions with some versions of the JDK and fail on others. It's best not to rely on this method for more than renaming a file in the same directory.

If src is successfully renamed, the method returns true. If the security manager doesn't allow the program to write to both the source file and the destination file, renameTo( ) throws a security exception. Otherwise, it returns false. Be sure to check this. Renaming is one of the more flaky areas of Java.

---

## Copying Files

There is no copy( ) method that merely copies a file to a new location without removing the original. However, you can open a file output stream to the copy, open a file input stream from the original file, and copy the data byte by byte from the original into the copy. For example, to copy the file src to the file dst:

```
FileInputStream  in  = new FileInputStream(src);
FileOutputStream out = new FileOutputStream(dst);
for (int c = in.read(); c != -1; c = in.read()) {
  out.write(c);
}
in.close( );
out.close( );
```

There are some serious problems with this code. First of all, it assumes that both src and dst refer to files, not directories. Second, it only copies the contents of the files. If the file is associated with metainformation or extra data, that data is lost.

---

### Deleting files

The delete( ) method removes files from the filesystem permanently:

```
public boolean delete( )
```

This method returns true if the file existed and was deleted. (You can't delete a file that doesn't exist.) If the security manager disallows this action, a security exception is thrown. Otherwise, delete( ) returns false.

### Changing file attributes

The setLastModified( ) method changes a file's last modified time:

```
public boolean setLastModified(long time)
```

The time argument is the number of milliseconds since midnight, GMT, January 1, 1970. This is converted to the format necessary for a particular platform's file modification times. If the platform does not support millisecond-accurate file modification times, the time is rounded to the nearest time the host platform does support. This method throws an IllegalArgumentException if time is negative; it throws a SecurityException if the security manager disallows write access to the file.

The setReadOnly( ) method marks the file so that writing to the file is disallowed:

```
public boolean setReadOnly( )
```

Java 6 adds several more methods for changing a file's attributes. You can mark a file readable, writable, or executable:

```
public boolean setReadable(boolean executable)    // Java 6
public boolean setWritable(boolean executable)    // Java 6
public boolean setExecutable(boolean executable) // Java 6
```

Passing true makes the file readable, writable, and executable by the file's owner; passing false does the opposite. Changing these attributes may not always be possible. These methods return true if the file now has the requested attribute value or false if it doesn't. These methods can also throw a SecurityException if the security manager disallows access to the file.

You can pass false as the second argument to these methods to indicate that the file should be readable, writable, and executable by everyone, not just the file's owner:

```
public boolean setReadable(boolean executable,   boolean ownerOnly)  // Java 6
public boolean setWritable(boolean executable,   boolean ownerOnly)  // Java 6
public boolean setExecutable(boolean executable, boolean ownerOnly)  // Java 6
```

Java has no concept of Unix group access, though.

## Temporary Files

The File class provides two methods that create temporary files that exist only as long as the program runs:

```
public static File createTempFile(String prefix, String suffix)
   throws IOException
public static File createTempFile(String prefix, String suffix,
   File directory) throws IOException
```

The createTempFile( ) methods create a file with a name that begins with the specified prefix and ends with the specified suffix. The prefix is a string used at the beginning of all temporary filenames; the suffix is appended to the end of all temporary filenames. The suffix may be null. If so, *.tmp* is used as the suffix. The same run of the same VM does not create two files with the same name. For example, consider this for loop:

```
for (int i=0; i < 10; i++) {
  File.createTempFile("mail", ".tem");
}
```

When run, it creates files named something like *mail30446.tem*, *mail30447.tem*, etc. through *mail30455.tem*.

By default, temporary files are placed in the directory named by the java.io.tmpdir property. On Unix, this is likely to be */tmp* or */var/tmp*. On Windows, it's probably *C:\temp* or *C:\Windows\Temp*. On Mac OS X, it's probably */private/tmp*. You can specify a different directory using the third argument to createTempFile( ). For instance, this code fragment creates a temporary file in the current working directory:

```
File cwd = new File(System.getProperty("user.dir"));
File temp = File.createTempFile("rus", ".tmp", cwd);
```

You often want to delete temporary files when your program exits. You can accomplish this by passing them to the deleteOnExit( ) method:

```
public void deleteOnExit( )
```

For example:

```
File temp = File.createTempFile("mail", ".tem");
temp.deleteOnExit( );
```

This method works on any File object, not just temporary files. Be careful because there's no good way to cancel a request to delete files.

Temporary files are useful when you need to operate on a file in place. You can do this in two passes. In the first pass, read from the file you're converting and write into the temporary file. In the second pass, read from the temporary file and write into the file you're converting. Here's an example:

```
File infile = new File(args[2]);
File outfile = new File(args[3]);
boolean usingTempFile = false;

if (infile.getCanonicalPath().equals(outfile.getCanonicalPath())) {
  outfile = File.createTempFile("temp", null);
  outfile.deleteOnExit( );
  usingTempFile = true;
}

// perform operations as normal, then close both files...
if (usingTempFile) {
  FileInputStream fin = new FileInputStream(outfile);
  FileOutputStream fout = new FileOutputStream(infile);
  for (int c = fin.read(); c != -1; c = fin.read()) {
    fout.write(c);
  }
  fin.close( );
  fout.close( );
}
```

## Checking for Free Space/Java 6

Java 6 adds three methods to inspect the amount of available and used space on a particular partition. A File object is used to choose the partition but otherwise it has no effect on the value returned. Two files on the same partition would give the same answers.

The getTotalSpace( ) method returns the size of the file's partition in bytes:

```
public long getTotalSpace( )
```

The getFreeSpace( ) method returns the total amount of empty space on the file's partition in bytes:

```
public long getFreeSpace( )
```

If the file does not exist, these methods return 0. They do not throw an exception. The number returned by this method is approximate. Depending on the nature of the filesystem, you may not be able to use all the bytes for a single file. For instance, some filesystems have maximum file sizes. The getUsableSpace( ) method makes a slightly better effort to find out how much space you can actually use.

```
public long getUsableSpace( )
```

It accounts for details like read-only filesystems that getFreeSpace( ) may not. However, the number it returns is still only approximate.

Even Java 6 doesn't have any reliable means to list all the partitions on a disk or to determine which partition you're on. If you happen to know the locations of files on each partition, these methods tell you how much space is left on each one. Normally, you have a single directory where a file will be saved and what you want to know is how much space is left on that directory's partition.

Example 17-5 is a simple program that lists the total, free, and usable space on the partition that contains the current working directory:

*Example 17-5. Listing available space on the current partition*

```java
import java.io.*;

public class CWDSpace {

  public static void main(String[] args) {

    File cwd = new File(".");
    System.out.println("Total space on current partition:  "
      + cwd.getTotalSpace() / (1024 * 1024) + " MB\t");
    System.out.println("Free space on current partition:  "
      + cwd.getFreeSpace() / (1024 * 1024) + " MB\t");
    System.out.println("Usable space on current partition:  "
      + cwd.getUsableSpace() / (1024 * 1024) + " MB");
  }
}
```

Here's the output when I ran this on my Linux box from a directory in the */home* partition:

```
$ java CWDSpace
Total space on current partition:  6053 MB
Free space on current partition:  2601 MB
Usable space on current partition:  2293 MB
```

If I had to save a large file in this directory, I could save around two gigabytes. Anything much larger and I'd have to free up some space first.

# Directories

A File object can represent a directory as easily as a file. Most of the File methods like getName( ), canWrite( ), and getPath( ) behave exactly the same for a directory as they do for a file. However, a couple of methods in the File class behave differently when they operate on directories than they do when operating on ordinary files.

The delete( ) method only works on empty directories. If a directory contains even one file, it can't easily be deleted. If you attempt to delete a nonempty directory, delete( ) fails and returns false. No exception is thrown.

The renameTo( ) method works on both empty and nonempty directories. However—whether a directory is empty or not—renameTo( ) can only rename it, not move it to a different directory. If you attempt to move a directory into another directory, renameTo( ) fails and returns false. No exception is thrown.

The File class also has several methods that just work with directories, not with regular files.

## Creating directories

The createNewFile( ) doesn't work for directories. For that purpose, the File class has a mkdir( ) method:

```
public boolean mkdir( )
```

The mkdir( ) method attempts to create a directory with the path specified in the path field. If the directory is created, the method returns true. For example:

```
File f = new File("tmp/");
f.mkdir( );
```

The trailing slash is optional, but it helps you to remember that you're dealing with a directory rather than a plain file. If the security manager does not allow the directory to be created, mkdir( ) throws a security exception. If the directory cannot be created for any other reason, mkdir( ) returns false. The mkdir( ) method only works for single directories. Trying to create a directory like *com/elharo/io/* with mkdir( ) only works if *com/elharo* already exists.

The mkdirs( ) method creates every directory in a path that doesn't already exist:

```
public boolean mkdirs( )
```

For example:

```
File f = new File("com/elharo/io/");
f.mkdirs( );
```

mkdirs( ) returns true if all directories in this path are created or already exist and false if only some or none of them are created. If mkdirs( ) returns false, you need to test each directory in the path to see whether it was created because the invocation could have been partially successful.

One reason mkdir( ) and mkdirs( ) may return false (fail to create a directory) is that a file already exists with the name the directory has. Neither mkdir( ) nor mkdirs( ) will overwrite an existing file or directory.

### Listing directories

The list( ) method returns an array of strings containing the names of each file in the directory referred to by the File object:

```
public String[] list( )
```

This method returns null if the File object doesn't point to a directory. It throws a security exception if the program isn't allowed to read the directory being listed. An alternative version of list( ) uses a FilenameFilter object (discussed later in the chapter) to restrict which files are included in the list:

```
public String[] list(FilenameFilter filter)
```

Example 17-6 is a simple character-mode program that recursively lists all the files in a directory, and all the files in directories in the directory, and all the files in directories in the directory, and so on. Files are indented two spaces for each level deep they are in the hierarchy.

*Example 17-6. The DirList program*

```
import java.io.*;
import java.util.*;

public class DirList {

  private File directory;
  private int indent = 2;
  private static List seen = new ArrayList( );

  public static void main(String[] args) throws IOException {
      DirList dl = new DirList(args[0]);
      dl.list( );
  }

  public DirList(String name) throws IOException {
    this(new File(name), 2);
  }

  public DirList(File f) throws IOException {
    this(f, 2);
  }
```

*Example 17-6. The DirList program (continued)*

```java
  public DirList(File directory, int indent) throws IOException {
    if (directory.isDirectory()) {
      this.directory = new File(directory.getCanonicalPath());
    }
    else {
      throw new IOException(directory.toString() + " is not a directory");
    }
    this.indent = indent;
    String spaces = "";
    for (int i = 0; i < indent-2; i++) spaces += " ";
    System.out.println(spaces + directory + File.separatorChar);
  }

  public void list() throws IOException {

    if (!seen.contains(this.directory)) {
      seen.add(this.directory);
      String[] files = directory.list();
      String spaces = "";
      for (int i = 0; i < indent; i++) spaces += " ";
      for (int i = 0; i < files.length; i++) {
        File f = new File(directory, files[i]);
        if (f.isFile()) {
          System.out.println(spaces + f.getName());
        }
        else { // it's another directory
          DirList dl = new DirList(f, indent + 2);
          dl.list();
        }
      }
    }
  }
}
```

Special care has to be taken to make sure this program doesn't get caught in an infinite recursion. If a directory contains an alias, shadow, shortcut, or symbolic link that points to one of its own parents, there's potential for infinite recursion. To avoid this possibility, all paths are converted to canonical paths in the constructor, and these paths are stored in the static list seen. A directory is listed only if it has not yet been traversed by this program.

### The listFiles( ) methods

The two list( ) methods return arrays of strings. The strings contain the names of files. You can use these to construct File objects. Java allows you to eliminate the intermediate step of creating File objects by providing two listFiles( ) methods that return arrays of File objects instead of arrays of strings.

```java
public File[] listFiles()
public File[] listFiles(FilenameFilter filter)
public File[] listFiles(FileFilter filter)
```

The no-argument variant of listFiles( ) simply returns an array of all the files in the given directory. The other two variants return the files that pass through their filters. File and filename filters will be discussed shortly.

## File URLs

File URLs locate a file on the local filesystem. (Very early web browsers used file URLs to refer to FTP sites. However, that usage has long since disappeared.) They have this basic form:

```
file://<host>/<path>
```

<host> should be the fully qualified domain name of the system on which the <path> is found, though if it's omitted, the local host is assumed. <path> is the hierarchical path to the file, using a forward slash as a directory separator (regardless of host filename conventions) and URL encoding of any special characters in filenames that would normally be encoded in a URL. Examples of file URLs include:

```
file:///C|/docs/JCE%201.2%20beta%201/guide/API_users_guide.html
file:///D:/JAVA/
file:///usr/local/java/docs/JCE%201.2%20beta%201/guide/API_users_guide.html
file:///D%7C/JAVA/
file:///Macintosh%20HD/Java/Cafe%20au%20%Lait/course/week4/01.5.html
file:/Users/elharo/Documents/books/Java%20IO%20 2/
```

Many web browsers allow other, nonstandard formats like:

```
file:///C|/jdk2beta4/docs/JCE 1.2 beta 1/guide/API_users_guide.html
file:///C:\jdk1.2beta4\docs\JCE 1.2 beta 1\guide\API_users_guide.html
file:/D:/Java/ioexamples/17/FileDialogApplet.html
file:/Users/elharo/Documents/books/Java IO 2/
```

Because of the differences between file and directory names from one computer to the next, the exact syntax of file URLs is unpredictable from platform to platform and web browser to web browser. The File class has a toURL( ) method that returns a file URL that's appropriate for the local platform:

```
public URL toURL( ) throws MalformedURLException
```

However, this method does not properly escape non-ASCII and non-URL-legal characters such as the space so it's been deprecated as of Java 1.4 and replaced by the toURI( ) method:

```
public URI toURI( )
```

toURI( ) isn't perfect, but it does a better job than toURL( ), and you should use it if it's available.

# Filename Filters

You often want to look for a particular kind of file—for example, text files. To do this, you need a FilenameFilter object that specifies which files you'll accept. FilenameFilter is an interface in the java.io package:

```
public interface FilenameFilter
```

This interface declares a single method, accept():

```
public abstract boolean accept(File directory, String name);
```

The directory argument is a File object pointing to a directory, and the name argument is the name of a file. The method should return true if a file with this name in this directory passes through the filter and false if it doesn't. Example 17-7 is a class that filters out everything that is not an HTML file.

*Example 17-7. HTMLFilter*

```
import java.io.*;

public class HTMLFilter implements FilenameFilter {

 public boolean accept(File directory, String name) {

   if (name.endsWith(".html")) return true;
   if (name.endsWith(".htm")) return true;
   return false;
 }
}
```

Files can be filtered using any criteria you like. An accept() method may test modification date, permissions, file size, and any attribute Java supports. This accept() method tests whether the file ends with *.html* and is in a directory where the program can read files:

```
public boolean accept(File directory, String name) {

  if (name.endsWith(".html") && directory.canRead()) {
    return true;
  }
  return false;
}
```

Filename filters are primarily intended for the use of file dialogs, which will be discussed in the next chapter. However, the listFiles() method can take a FilenameFilter as an argument:

```
public File[] listFiles(FilenameFilter filter)
```

This method assumes that the File object represents a directory. The array of File objects returned by listFiles() only contains those files that passed the filter. For example, the following lines of code list HTML files in the */public/html/javafaq* directory using the HTMLFilter of Example 17-7:

```
File dir = new File("/public/html/javafaq");
File[] htmlFiles = dir.listFiles(new HTMLFilter());
for (int i = 0; i < htmlFiles.length; i++) {
  System.out.println(htmlFiles[i]);
}
```

# File Filters

The FileFilter interface is very similar to FilenameFilter:

```
public abstract interface FileFilter
```

The accept( ) method of FileFilter takes a single File object as an argument, rather than two strings giving the directory and path:

```
public boolean accept(File pathname)
```

Example 17-8 is a filter that only passes HTML files. Its logic is essentially the same as the filter of Example 17-7.

*Example 17-8. HTMLFileFilter*

```
import java.io.*;

public class HTMLFileFilter implements FileFilter {

 public boolean accept(File pathname) {

   if (pathname.getName( ).endsWith(".html")) return true;
   if (pathname.getName( ).endsWith(".htm")) return true;
   return false;
 }
}
```

This class appears as an argument in one of the listFiles( ) methods of java.io. File:

```
public File[] listFiles(FileFilter filter)
```

Example 17-9 uses the HTMLFileFilter to list the HTML files in the current working directory.

*Example 17-9. List HTML files*

```
import java.io.*;

public class HTMLFiles {

  public static void main(String[] args) {

    File cwd = new File(System.getProperty("user.dir"));
    File[] htmlFiles = cwd.listFiles(new HTMLFileFilter());
```

*Example 17-9. List HTML files (continued)*

```
    for (int i = 0; i < htmlFiles.length; i++) {
      System.out.println(htmlFiles[i]);
    }
  }
}
```

# File Descriptors

As I've said several times so far, the existence of a `java.io.File` object doesn't imply the existence of the file it represents. A `java.io.FileDescriptor` object does, however, refer to an actual file:

```
public final class FileDescriptor extends Object
```

A `FileDescriptor` object is an abstraction of an underlying machine-specific structure that represents an open file. While file descriptors are very important for the underlying OS and filesystem, their only real use in Java is to guarantee that data that's been written to a stream is in fact committed to disk, that is, to synchronize between the program and the hardware.

In addition to open files, file descriptors can also represent open sockets. There are also three file descriptors for the console: `System.in`, `System.out`, and `System.err`. These are available as the three mnemonic constants `FileDescriptor.in`, `FileDescriptor.out`, and `FileDescriptor.err`:

```
public static final FileDescriptor in
public static final FileDescriptor out
public static final FileDescriptor err
```

Because file descriptors are very closely tied to the native operating system, you never construct your own file descriptors. Various methods in other classes that refer to open files or sockets may return them. Both the `FileInputStream` and `FileOutputStream` classes and the `RandomAccessFile` class have a `getFD()` method that returns the file descriptor associated with the open stream or file:

```
public final FileDescriptor getFD() throws IOException
```

Since file descriptors are only associated with *open* files and sockets, they become invalid as soon as the file or socket is closed. You can test whether a file descriptor is still valid with the `valid()` method:

```
public native boolean valid()
```

This returns true if the descriptor is still valid or `false` if it isn't.

The one real use to which a client programmer can put a file descriptor object is to sync a file. This is accomplished with the aptly named `sync()` method:

```
public native void sync() throws SyncFailedException
```

The sync( ) method forces the system buffers to write all the data they contain to the actual hardware. Generally, you'll want to flush the stream before syncing it. Flushing clears out Java's internal buffers. Syncing clears out the operating system's, device driver's, and hardware's buffers. If synchronization does not succeed, sync( ) throws a java.io.SyncFailedException, a subclass of IOException.

# Random-Access Files

File input and output streams require you to start reading or writing at the beginning of a file and then read or write the file in order, possibly skipping over some bytes or backing up but mostly moving from start to finish. Sometimes, however, you need to read parts of a file in a more or less random order, where the data near the beginning of the file isn't necessarily read before the data nearer the end. Other times you need to both read and write the same file. For example, in record-oriented applications like databases, the actual data may be indexed; you would use the index to determine where in the file to find the record you need to read or write. While you could do this by constantly opening and closing the file and skipping to the point where you needed to read, this is far from efficient. Writes are even worse since you would need to read and rewrite the entire file, even to change just one byte of data.

Random-access files can be read from or written to or both from a particular byte position in the file. A single random-access file can be both read and written. The position in the file where reads and writes start from is indicated by an integer called the file pointer. Each read or write advances the file pointer by the number of bytes read or written. Furthermore, the programmer can reposition the file pointer at different bytes in the file without closing the file.

In Java, random file access is performed through the java.io.RandomAccessFile class. This is *not* a subclass of java.io.File:

```
public class RandomAccessFile extends Object implements DataInput, DataOutput
```

Among other differences between File objects and RandomAccessFile objects, the RandomAccessFile constructors actually open the file in question and throw an IOException if it doesn't exist:

```
public RandomAccessFile(String filename, String mode) throws FileNotFoundException
public RandomAccessFile(File file, String mode) throws IOException
```

The first argument to the constructor is the file you want to access. The second argument is the mode for access. The mode can be "r" for read-only access or "rw", "rws", or "rwd" for read/write access. Java does not support write-only access. For example:

```
RandomAccessFile raf = new RandomAccessFile("29.html", "r");
```

The rw mode is regular buffered read-write access. Changes may not be immediately written to the file. This can lose data in the event of a system crash. In rws mode, Java writes all data to the disk immediately and is safer if slower. In rwd mode, Java writes all content immediately but may buffer changes to the file's metadata (its name, permissions, and so on).

An IllegalArgumentException is thrown if anything other than these four strings is specified as the mode. (In Java 1.3 and earlier, only "rw" and "r" were allowed.) A security exception is thrown if the security manager does not allow the requested file to be read. A security exception is also thrown if you request read/write access, but only read access is allowed. Security checks are made only when the object is constructed. It is assumed that the security manager's policy won't change while the program is running. Finally, an IOException is thrown if the operating system doesn't allow the file to be accessed or some other I/O problem occurs.

The getFilePointer( ) and seek( ) methods allow you to query and change the position in the file at which reads and writes occur. Attempts to seek (position the file pointer) past the end of the file just move the file pointer to the end of the file. Attempts to write from the end of the file extend the file.

```
public native long getFilePointer( ) throws IOException
public native void seek(long pos) throws IOException
```

Attempts to read from the end of the file throw an EOFException (a subclass of IOException). You can determine the length of the file with the length( ) method:

```
public native long length( ) throws IOException
```

The RandomAccessFile class implements both the DataInput and DataOutput interfaces. Therefore, reads and writes use methods exactly like the methods of the DataInputStream and DataOutputStream classes, such as read( ), readFully( ), readInt( ), writeInt( ), readBoolean( ), writeBoolean( ), and so on.

Finally, there are a few miscellaneous methods. The getFD( ) method simply returns the file descriptor for this file:

```
public final FileDescriptor getFD( ) throws IOException
```

The skipBytes( ) method attempts to reposition the file pointer *n* bytes further in the file from where it is now. It returns the number of bytes actually skipped, which may be less than *n*:

```
public int skipBytes(int n) throws IOException
```

The seek( ) method jumps to an absolute position in the file starting from 0, whereas skipBytes( ) moves *n* bytes past wherever the file pointer is now:

```
public void seek(long position) throws IOException
```

Finally, the close( ) method closes the file:

```
public native void close( ) throws IOException
```

Once the file is closed, it may not be read from, though a new RandomAccessFile object that refers to the same file can be created.

# General Techniques for Cross-Platform File Access Code

It's hard to write truly cross-platform file manipulation code. The NIO working group was supposed to fix this years ago. However, they spent so much time on channels and buffers that they never fulfilled their mandate to design a decent, platform-independent filesystem API. Now it looks like it's not going to make it into Java 6 either. Maybe we'll finally get one in Java 7. In the meantime, to help you achieve greater serenity and overall cross-platform nirvana, I've summarized some basic rules from this chapter to help you write file manipulation code that's robust across a multitude of platforms:

- Never, never, never hardcode pathnames in your application.
- Ask the user to name your files. If you must provide a name for a file, try to make it fit in an 8.3 DOS filename with only pure ASCII characters.
- Do not assume the file separator is "/" (or anything else). Use `File. separatorChar` instead.
- Do not parse pathnames to find directories. Use the methods of the `java.io.File` class instead.
- Do not use `renameTo( )` for anything except renaming a file. In particular, do not use it to move a file.
- Try to avoid moving and copying files from within Java programs if at all possible.
- Do not use . to refer to the current directory. Use `System.getProperty("user. dir")` instead.
- Do not use .. to refer to the parent directory. Use `getParent( )` instead.
- Place any data files your program requires in JAR archives rather than directly in the filesystem and load them as resources from the classpath.
- When in doubt, it never hurts to convert filenames to canonical form.
- Do not assume anything about filesystem conventions. Some platform somewhere will surprise you. (Have you tested your program on BeOS yet?)
- Test your code on as many different filesystems as you can get your hands on.

Despite all the problems I've pointed out, it is possible to write robust file access code that works across all platforms where Java runs, but doing so requires understanding, effort, and thought. You cannot simply write for Windows or Unix and hope things will work out for the best on other platforms. You must plan to handle a wide range of filesystems and filename conventions.

# CHAPTER 18

# File Dialogs and Choosers

Filenames are problematic, even if you don't have to worry about cross-platform idiosyncrasies. Users forget filenames, mistype them, can't remember the exact path to files they need, and more. The proper way to ask a user to select a file is to show them a list of the files in the current directory and ask them to select from that list. You also need to allow them to navigate between directories, insert and remove disks, mount network servers, and more.

Most graphical user interfaces provide standard widgets for selecting a file. In Java the platform's native file selector widget is exposed through the `java.awt.FileDialog` class. Like many native peer-based classes, however, `FileDialog` doesn't behave exactly the same on all platforms. Therefore, Swing provides a pure Java implementation of a file dialog, the `javax.swing.JFileChooser` class. `JFileChooser` has much more reliable though less native cross-platform behavior.

## File Dialogs

File dialogs are the standard open and save dialogs provided by the host GUI. Users use them to pick a directory and a name under which to save a file or to choose a file to open. The appearance varies from platform to platform, but the intent is the same. Figure 18-1 shows a standard Save dialog on the Mac; Figure 18-2 shows a standard open dialog on Linux.

`FileDialog` is a subclass of `java.awt.Dialog` that represents the native save and open dialog boxes:

```
public class FileDialog extends Dialog
```

A file dialog is almost completely implemented by a native peer. Your program doesn't add components to a file dialog or handle user interaction with event listeners. It just displays the dialog and retrieves the name and directory of the file the user chose after the dialog is dismissed.

To ask the user to select a file from a file dialog, perform these four steps:

Figure 18-1. The Mac's standard Save dialog

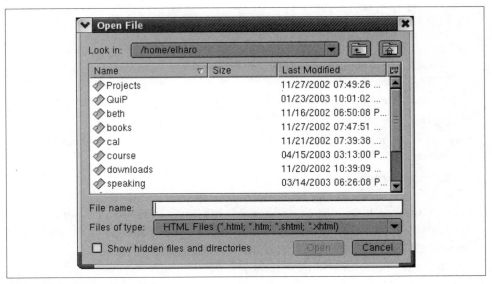

Figure 18-2. Gnome Open dialog

1. Construct a FileDialog object.
2. Set the default directory or file for the dialog (optional).
3. Make the dialog visible.

4. Get the name and directory of the file the user chose.

File dialogs are modal. While the file dialog is shown, input to the parent frame is blocked, as with the parent frame of any modal dialog. The parent frame is normally the window from whose menu bar File/Open was selected. The parent frame is always set in the constructor:

```
public FileDialog(Frame parent)
```

Starting in Java 5, you can use another Dialog as the parent if you prefer:

```
public FileDialog(Dialog parent) // Java 5
```

Each FileDialog usually has a title. This is the prompt string for the file dialog, such as "Open File" or "Save Message As". This is also set in the constructor:

```
public FileDialog(Frame parent, String title)
public FileDialog(Dialog parent, String title) // Java 5
```

Finally, each FileDialog is either in open mode or save mode. The default for the previous constructors is open mode. However, this can be specified with one of these two constructors:

```
public FileDialog(Frame parent, String title, int mode)
public FileDialog(Dialog parent, String title, int mode) // Java 5
```

The mode argument is one of the two mnemonic constants FileDialog.LOAD or FileDialog.SAVE:

```
public static final int LOAD = 0;
public static final int SAVE = 1;
```

A typical invocation of this constructor might look like this:

```
FileDialog fd = new FileDialog(framePointer,
  "Please choose the file to open:", FileDialog.LOAD);
```

In load mode, the user chooses an existing file. In save mode the user can either choose an existing file or create a new one.

Getter and setter methods allow the mode to be inspected and changed after the dialog is constructed:

```
public int  getMode( )
public void setMode(int mode)
```

To specify that the file dialog should appear with a particular directory opened or a particular file in that directory selected, you can invoke the setDirectory( ) and setFile( ) methods:

```
public void setDirectory(String directory)
public void setFile(String file)
```

For example:

```
fd.setDirectory("/etc");
fd.setFile("passwd");
```

You make the file dialog visible by invoking the file dialog's setVisible(true) method, just like any other window:

```
fd.setVisible(true);
```

As soon as the file dialog becomes visible, the calling thread stops and waits for the user to choose a file. The operating system takes over and handles user interaction until the user chooses a file or presses the Cancel button. At this point, the file dialog disappears from the screen, and normal program execution resumes.

Once the dialog has been dismissed, you can find out which file the user chose by using the file dialog's getDirectory( ) and getFile( ) methods:

```
public String getFile( )
public String getDirectory( )
```

For example:

```
FileDialog fd = new FileDialog(
    new Frame( ), "Please choose a file:", FileDialog.LOAD);
fd.setVisible(true);
File f = new File(fd.getDirectory(), fd.getFile( ));
```

If the user cancels the file dialog without selecting a file, getFile( ) and getDirectory( ) return null. You should be ready to handle this, or you'll bump into a NullPointerException in short order.

Example 18-1 is a program that presents an open file dialog to the user and writes the contents of the file she selected on System.out.

*Example 18-1. The FileTyper program*

```
import java.io.*;
import java.awt.*;

public class FileTyper {

  public static void main(String[] args) throws IOException {

    InputStream in = null;
    try {
      File f = getFile( );
      if (f == null) return;
      in = new FileInputStream(f);
      for (int c = in.read(); c != -1; c = in.read( )) {
        System.out.write(c);
      }
    }
    finally {
      if (in != null) in.close( );
    }

    // Work around annoying AWT non-daemon thread bug.
    System.exit(0);
  }
```

*Example 18-1. The FileTyper program (continued)*

```
  public static File getFile( ) {

    // dummy Frame, never shown
    Frame parent = new Frame( );
    FileDialog fd = new FileDialog(parent, "Please choose a file:",
      FileDialog.LOAD);
    fd.setVisible(true);

    // Program stops here until user selects a file or cancels.
    String dir = fd.getDirectory( );
    String file = fd.getFile( );

    // Clean up our windows, they won't be needed again.
    parent.dispose( );
    fd.dispose( );

    if (dir == null || file == null) { // user cancelled the dialog
      return null;
    }
    return new File(dir, file);
  }
}
```

File dialogs only allow the user to select ordinary files, never directories. To ask users to pick a directory, you have to ask them to choose a file in that directory and then call getDirectory( ). Better yet, you can use a JFileChooser (discussed in the next section) that does allow the user to choose a directory.

A filename filter can be attached to a file dialog via the dialog's setFilenameFilter( ) method:

```
  public void setFilenameFilter(FilenameFilter filter)
```

Once a file dialog's filename filter is set, it should only display files that pass through the filter. However, filename filters in file dialogs are only reliable on Unix (including Linux and Mac OS X). Windows is almost congenitally unable to support it because Windows' native file chooser dialog can only filter by file extension.

Example 18-2 demonstrates a simple filename filter that accepts files ending in *.text*, *.txt*, *.java*, *.jav*, *.html*, and *.htm*; all others are rejected.

*Example 18-2. TextFilter*

```
import java.io.*;

public class TextChooser implements FilenameFilter {

  public boolean accept(File dir, String name) {

    if (name.endsWith(".java")) return true;
    else if (name.endsWith(".jav")) return true;
    else if (name.endsWith(".html")) return true;
```

*Example 18-2. TextFilter (continued)*

```
    else if (name.endsWith(".htm")) return true;
    else if (name.endsWith(".txt")) return true;
    else if (name.endsWith(".text")) return true;
    return false;
  }
}
```

This program demonstrates one problem of relying on file extensions to determine file type. Many other file extensions indicate text files, for example, *.c, .cc, .pl, .f,* and many more. Furthermore, many text files, especially those on Macintoshes, have no extension at all. This program completely ignores all those files.

You do not necessarily have to write a new subclass for each different file filter. Example 18-3 demonstrates a class that can be configured with different lists of filename extensions. Every file with an extension in the list passes the filter. Others don't.

*Example 18-3. ExtensionFilenameFilter*

```
package com.elharo.io;

import java.awt.*;
import java.util.*;
import java.io.*;

public class ExtensionFilenameFilter implements FilenameFilter {

  ArrayList extensions = new ArrayList();

  public ExtensionFilenameFilter(String extension) {

    if (extension.indexOf('.') != -1) {
      extension = extension.substring(extension.lastIndexOf('.')+1);
    }
    extensions.add(extension);
  }

  public void addExtension(String extension) {

    if (extension.indexOf('.') != -1) {
      extension = extension.substring(extension.lastIndexOf('.')+1);
    }
    extensions.add(extension);
  }

  public boolean accept(File directory, String filename) {

    String extension = filename.substring(filename.lastIndexOf('.')+1);
    if (extensions.contains(extension)) {
      return true;
    }
```

*Example 18-3. ExtensionFilenameFilter (continued)*

```
    return false;
  }
}
```

This class is designed to filter files by extension. You configure which extensions pass the filter when you create the object or by calling addExtension( ). This avoids excessive proliferation of classes.

# JFileChooser

Swing provides a much more sophisticated and useful file chooser component written in pure Java, javax.swing.JFileChooser:

```
public class JFileChooser extends JComponent implements Accessible
```

JFileChooser is not an independent, free-standing window like FileDialog. Instead, it is a component you can add to your own frame, dialog, or other container or window. You can, however, ask the JFileChooser class to create a modal dialog just for your file chooser. Figure 18-3 shows a file chooser embedded in a JFrame window with the Metal look and feel. Of course, like all Swing components, the exact appearance depends on the current look and feel.

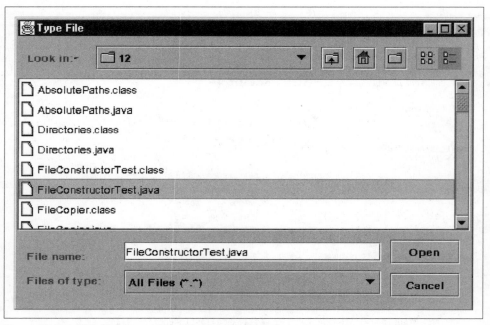

*Figure 18-3. A JFileChooser with the Metal look and feel*

For the most part, the file chooser works as you expect, especially if you're accustomed to Windows. (On Mac OS X, it's much more obviously a nonnative dialog, in fact, so much so that you're probably better off using a `java.awt.FileDialog` on that platform instead.) You select a file with the mouse. Double-clicking the filename or pressing the Open button returns the currently selected file. You can change which files are displayed by selecting different filters from the pop-up list of choosable file filters. All the components have tooltips to help users who are a little thrown by an unfamiliar look and feel.

The `JFileChooser` class relies on support from several classes in the `javax.swing.filechooser` package, including:

```
public abstract class FileFilter
public abstract class FileSystemView
public abstract class FileView
```

There are three basic steps for asking the user to choose a file with a `JFileChooser`:

1. Construct the file chooser.
2. Display the file chooser.
3. Get the files the user selected.

You can also set a lot of options for how files are displayed and chosen, which directory and file are selected when the file chooser first appears, which files are and are not shown in the choosers, and several other options. However, these three are your basic operations.

## Constructing File Choosers

The `JFileChooser` class has six constructors. These specify the initial directory and file that appear when the chooser is shown and the view of the filesystem:

```
public JFileChooser( )
public JFileChooser(String initialDirectoryPath)
public JFileChooser(File initialDirectory)
public JFileChooser(FileSystemView fileSystemView)
public JFileChooser(File initialDirectory, FileSystemView fileSystemView)
public JFileChooser(String initialDirectoryPath,
                    FileSystemView fileSystemView)
```

Most of the time the no-argument constructor is sufficient. The first time a particular `JFileChooser` object is shown, it brings up the user's home directory. If you'd like it to appear somewhere else, you can pass the directory to the constructor. For example, the following two lines construct a file chooser that appears with the Java home directory shown:

```
String javahome = System.getProperty("java.home");
JFileChooser chooser = new JFileChooser(javahome);
```

If you reuse the same JFileChooser object repeatedly by showing and hiding it, it initially displays the last directory where the user chose a file.

## Displaying File Choosers

Although JFileChooser is a component, not a window, you usually want to display a modal dialog containing a JFileChooser component that asks the user to save or open a file. Three methods do this without requiring you to construct a dialog or frame explicitly:

```
public int showOpenDialog(Component parent)
public int showSaveDialog(Component parent)
public int showDialog(Component parent, String approveButtonText)
```

You use all three methods the same way. The only difference is the text shown in the dialog's title bar and on its approve button. For showOpenDialog( ), it is usually the word *Open*, possibly translated for the local environment. For showSaveDialog( ), it is usually the word *Save*, possibly translated for the local environment, and for showDialog( ), it is whatever string is passed as the second argument.

All three methods display a modal dialog that blocks input to the dialog's parent and blocks the current thread until the user either selects a file or cancels the dialog. If the user does choose a file, both these methods return JFileChooser.APPROVE_OPTION. If the user does not choose a file, both these methods return JFileChooser.CANCEL_OPTION.

## Getting the User's Selection

If showOpenDialog( ) or showSaveDialog( ) returns JFileChooser.APPROVE_OPTION, the getSelectedFile( ) method returns a File object pointing to the file the user chose; otherwise, it returns null:

```
public File getSelectedFile( )
```

If the file chooser allows multiple selections, getSelectedFiles( ) returns an array of all the files the user chose:

```
public File[] getSelectedFiles( )
```

You can get a File object for the directory in which the selected file lives by calling getCurrentDirectory( ):

```
public File getCurrentDirectory( )
```

Example 18-4 is a program that uses JFileChooser to ask the user to select a file and then prints the file's contents on System.out. This example is essentially the same as Example 18-1, except that it uses JFileChooser instead of FileDialog.

*Example 18-4. JFileTyper*

```java
import java.io.*;
import java.lang.reflect.InvocationTargetException;
import javax.swing.*;

public class JFileTyper {

  public static void main(String[] args)
    throws InterruptedException, InvocationTargetException {

    SwingUtilities.invokeAndWait(
      new Runnable() {
        public void run() {
          JFileChooser fc = new JFileChooser();
          int result = fc.showOpenDialog(new JFrame());
          if (result == JFileChooser.APPROVE_OPTION) {
            InputStream in = null;
            try {
              File f = fc.getSelectedFile();
              if (f != null) { // Make sure the user didn't choose a directory.
                in = new FileInputStream(f);
                for (int c = in.read(); c != -1; c = in.read()) {
                  System.out.write(c);
                }
              }
              in.close();
            }
            catch (IOException e) {System.err.println(e);}
          }
          System.exit(0);
        }
      }
    );
  }
}
```

The dialogs shown by JFileChooser.showOpenDialog() and JFileChooser.showSaveDialog() are still Swing dialogs, and they are still subject to the usual constraints on Swing dialogs. One of those is that dialogs should only be shown from the AWT thread and then only by calling SwingUtilities.invokeLater(), SwingUtilities.invokeAndWait(), or the equivalent methods in EventQueue.

## Manipulating the JFileChooser

The JFileChooser class includes several methods to specify which files and directories are selected and displayed when the chooser is shown. These include:

```java
public void changeToParentDirectory()
public void rescanCurrentDirectory()
public void ensureFileIsVisible(File f)
```

The changeToParentDirectory( ) method simply displays the parent directory of the directory currently displayed; that is, it moves one level up in the directory hierarchy. The rescanCurrentDirectory( ) method refreshes the list of files shown. Use it when you have reason to believe a file may have been added to or deleted from the directory. ensureFileIsVisible( ) scrolls the list up or down until the specified file is shown.

Three methods allow you to specify which directory and file are selected in the file chooser:

```
public void setSelectedFile(File selectedFile)
public void setSelectedFiles(File[] selectedFiles)
public void setCurrentDirectory(File dir)
```

You can use these methods to point the user at a particular file. For instance, a Java source code editor might like to set the filename to the title of the class being edited plus the customary *.java* extension. Another common example: if the user opens a file, edits it, and selects Save As... from the File menu, it's customary to bring up the save dialog with the previous location of the file already selected. The user can change this if desired.

## Custom Dialogs

File choosers support three dialog types: open, save, and custom. The type is indicated by one of these three mnemonic constants:

```
FileChooser.OPEN_DIALOG
FileChooser.SAVE_DIALOG
FileChooser.CUSTOM_DIALOG
```

You set the type with the setDialogType( ) method or, less commonly, retrieve it with getDialogType( ):

```
public int  getDialogType( )
public void setDialogType(int dialogType)
```

If you use a custom dialog, you should also set the dialog title, the text of the approve button's label, the text of the approve button's tool tip, and the approve button mnemonic (shortcut key). Setting the approve button's text automatically sets the dialog to custom type. Five setter and four getter methods handle these tasks:

```
public void    setDialogTitle(String dialogTitle)
public String  getDialogTitle( )
public void    setApproveButtonToolTipText(String toolTipText)
public String  getApproveButtonToolTipText( )
public int     getApproveButtonMnemonic( )
public void    setApproveButtonMnemonic(int mnemonic)
public void    setApproveButtonMnemonic(char mnemonic)
public void    setApproveButtonText(String approveButtonText)
public String  getApproveButtonText( )
```

Use these methods sparingly. If you use them, you'll probably want to store the exact strings you use in a resource bundle so that your code is easily localizable.

When you're showing a custom dialog, you'll simply use the showDialog( ) method rather than showOpenDialog( ) or showSaveDialog( ) (since a custom dialog is neither):

```
public int showDialog(Component parent, String approveButtonText)
```

Suppose you want a file chooser that allows you to gzip files and exit when the user presses the Cancel button. You can set the Approve button text to "GZIP," the approve button tooltip to "Select a file, then press this button to gzip it," the approve button mnemonic to the letter "g" (for gzip), and the dialog title to "Please choose a file to gzip:," as Example 18-5 demonstrates. The chosen file is read from a file input stream and copied onto a file output stream chained to a gzip output stream that compresses the data. After both input and output streams are closed, the directory is rescanned so the compressed file appears in the list.

*Example 18-5. GUIGZipper*

```
import java.io.*;
import java.lang.reflect.InvocationTargetException;
import java.util.zip.*;
import javax.swing.*;

public class GUIGZipper {

  public final static String GZIP_SUFFIX = ".gz";

  public static void main(String[] args)
    throws InterruptedException, InvocationTargetException {

    SwingUtilities.invokeAndWait(
      new Runnable( ) {
        public void run( ) {
          JFrame parent = new JFrame( );
          JFileChooser fc = new JFileChooser( );
          fc.setDialogTitle("Please choose a file to gzip: ");
          fc.setApproveButtonMnemonic('g');

          while (true) {
            int result = fc.showDialog(parent,
              "Select a file, then press this button to gzip it");
            if (result == JFileChooser.APPROVE_OPTION) {
              try {
                File f = fc.getSelectedFile( );
                if (f == null) {
                  JOptionPane.showMessageDialog(parent,
                    "Can only gzip files, not directories");
                }
                else {
                  InputStream in = new FileInputStream(f);
                  FileOutputStream fout = new FileOutputStream(f.getAbsolutePath( )
```

*Example 18-5. GUIGZipper (continued)*

```
                    + GZIP_SUFFIX);
                OutputStream gzout = new GZIPOutputStream(fout);
                for (int c = in.read(); c != -1; c = in.read()) {
                  gzout.write(c);
                }
                // These next two should be in a finally block; but the multiple
                // nested try-catch blocks just got way too complicated for a
                //  simple example
                in.close();
                gzout.close();
              }
            }
            catch (IOException ex) {
              ex.printStackTrace();
            }
          }
          else {
            System.exit(0);
          } // end else
        } // end while
      }  // end run
    } // end Runnable
  ); // end invokeAndWait
  } // end main
} // end class
```

To be honest, this interface is a little funny (though not nearly as strange as Win-Zip). If I were really tasked with writing such an application, I probably wouldn't design it like this. At a minimum, the cancel button text needs to change to "Exit" or "Quit." There's no setCancelButtonText( ) method corresponding to setApproveButtonText( ). However, you can ask for no buttons at all by passing false to setControlButtonsAreShown( ):

```
public void setControlButtonsAreShown(boolean b)
```

This would enable you to manage the chooser through your own buttons in your own frame. However, some look and feels do not respect this setting and show the approve and cancel buttons whether you turn this property off or not.

If you do want to manage the file chooser more directly, the action listeners for your buttons need to control it. They can do this by calling the approveSelection( ) and cancelSelection( ) methods:

```
public void approveSelection()
public void cancelSelection()
```

These methods have the same effect as pushing the regular approve and cancel buttons.

# Filters

A FilenameFilter determines which files a file dialog shows to the user. The user cannot change this list. For instance, a user can't switch from displaying HTML files to displaying Java source code. However, a FileFilter in combination with a JFileChooser allows programmers to give users a choice about which files are filtered by providing users with a series of different file filters. By choosing a file filter from the pop-up menu in a file chooser dialog, the user can adjust which files are and are not shown. Figure 18-4 shows a file chooser that allows the user to select text files, all files, C and C++ files, Perl files, HTML files, or Java source code files.

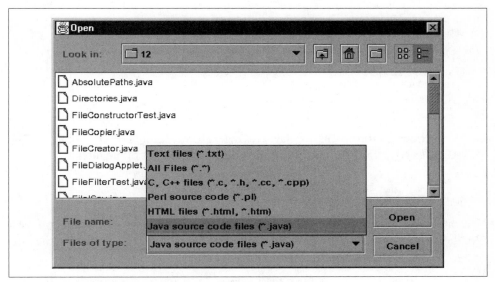

*Figure 18-4. The choosable file filters pop-up in a file chooser*

Annoyingly, these file filters are not instances of the java.io.FileFilter interface you're already familiar with. Instead, they're instances of a new abstract class in the javax.swing.filechooser package. Because of name conflicts with the java.io.FileFilter interface, any file that imports both packages has to use the fully qualified name.

```
public abstract class javax.swing.filechooser.FileFilter
```

This class declares two methods, both abstract:

```
public abstract boolean accept(File f);
public abstract String getDescription();
```

The accept() method returns true if the file passes the filter and should be displayed in the chooser or false if it shouldn't be. Unlike the accept() method in java.io.FilenameFilter, this accept() method is called to filter directories as well as files. Most filters accept all directories to allow the user to navigate between directories. The getDescription( ) method returns a string describing the filter to be shown to the user in the chooser's pop-up menu, for example, Text files (*.txt, *.text). Example 18-6 is a simple file filter that only passes Java source code files:

*Example 18-6. JavaFilter*

```java
import java.io.*;

public class JavaFilter extends javax.swing.filechooser.FileFilter {

  public boolean accept(File f) {
    if (f.getName().endsWith(".java")) return true;
    else if (f.getName().endsWith(".jav")) return true;
    else if (f.isDirectory()) return true;
    return false;
  }

  public String getDescription() {
    return "Java source code (*.java)";
  }
}
```

Each file chooser stores a list of javax.swing.filechooser.FileFilter objects. The JFileChooser class has methods for setting and getting the list of file filters:

```
public void       addChoosableFileFilter(FileFilter filter)
public boolean    removeChoosableFileFilter(FileFilter f)
public FileFilter[] getChoosableFileFilters()
```

You can add a file filter to the list with addChoosableFileFilter( ). You can remove a file filter from the list with removeChoosableFileFilter( ). You can retrieve the current list of file filters with getChoosableFileFilters( ).

At any given time, exactly one file filter is selected and active. In Figure 18-4, the Java filter is active. That one file filter is returned by the getFileFilter( ) method and can be changed by the setFileFilter( ) method:

```
public void setFileFilter(FileFilter filter)
public FileFilter getFileFilter()
```

By default, a JFileChooser object includes a file filter that accepts all files (*.*). A reference to this object is returned by the getAcceptAllFileFilter( ) method:

```
public FileFilter getAcceptAllFileFilter()
```

The resetChoosableFileFilters( ) method removes all file filters from the list, except the *.* filter:

```
public void resetChoosableFileFilters()
```

To remove the *.* filter from the list, pass false to setAcceptAllFileFilterUsed( ):

```
public void setAcceptAllFileFilterUsed(boolean b)
```

To remove a specific filter from the list, pass it to removeChoosableFileFilter( ):

```
public boolean removeChoosableFileFilter(FileFilter f)
```

Example 18-7 uses the `JavaFilter` class of Example 18-6 to set up a file chooser that passes Java source code files or all files.

*Example 18-7. JavaChooser*

```java
import java.io.*;
import java.lang.reflect.InvocationTargetException;
import javax.swing.*;

public class JavaChooser {

  public static void main(String[] args)
    throws InterruptedException, InvocationTargetException {

    SwingUtilities.invokeAndWait(
      new Runnable( ) {
        public void run( ) {
          JFileChooser fc = new JFileChooser( );
          fc.addChoosableFileFilter(new JavaFilter( ));
          int result = fc.showOpenDialog(new JFrame( ));
          if (result == JFileChooser.APPROVE_OPTION) {
            try {
              File f = fc.getSelectedFile( );
              if (f != null) {
                InputStream in = new FileInputStream(f);
                for (int c = in.read(); c != -1; c = in.read( )) {
                  System.out.write(c);
                }
                in.close( );
              }
            }
            catch (IOException ex) {System.err.println(ex);}
          }

          System.exit(0);
        } // end run
      } // end Runnable
    ); // end invokeAndWait
  } // end main
} // end class
```

You do not need to construct a new subclass of `FileFilter` to create a new filter. Often it's more convenient to encapsulate some algorithm in a subclass than to parameterize the algorithm in particular objects. For instance, Example 18-8 is an `ExtensionFilter` that extends `FileFilter`. It's similar to the `ExtensionFilenameFilter` of Example 18-3. However, this class also needs to store a description for each extension. Furthermore, the extensions are used one at a time, not all at once. This reflects the difference between `JFileChooser` and `FileDialog`.

*Example 18-8. ExtensionFilter*

```java
package com.elharo.swing.filechooser;

import java.io.*;
import javax.swing.filechooser.*;
import javax.swing.*;

public class ExtensionFilter extends javax.swing.filechooser.FileFilter {

  private String extension;
  private String description;

  public ExtensionFilter(String extension, String description) {

    if (extension.indexOf('.') == -1) {
      extension = "." + extension;
    }
    this.extension = extension;
    this.description = description;
  }

  public boolean accept(File f) {

    if (f.getName().endsWith(extension)) {
      return true;
    }
    else if (f.isDirectory()) {
      return true;
    }
    return false;
  }

  public String getDescription() {
    return this.description + "(*" + extension + ")";
  }
}
```

ExtensionFilter is used in several upcoming examples.

## Selecting Directories

FileDialog doesn't provide a good way to select directories instead of files. JFileChooser, by contrast, can have a selection mode that allows the user to select files, directories, or both. The selection mode is set by setFileSelectionMode() and returned by getFileSelectionMode():

```java
public void setFileSelectionMode(int mode)
public int  getFileSelectionMode()
```

The selection mode should be one of the three mnemonic constants JFileChooser.FILES_ONLY, JFileChooser.DIRECTORIES_ONLY, or JFileChooser.FILES_AND_DIRECTORIES:

```
public static final int FILES_ONLY = 0;
public static final int DIRECTORIES_ONLY = 1;
public static final int FILES_AND_DIRECTORIES = 2;
```

For example:

```
JFileChooser fc = new JFileChooser();
fc.setFileSelectionMode(JFileChooser.DIRECTORIES_ONLY);
```

The isFileSelectionEnabled( ) method returns true if the selection mode allows files to be selected—that is, the selection mode is either FILES_ONLY or FILES_AND_DIRECTORIES.

```
public boolean isFileSelectionEnabled( )
```

The isDirectorySelectionEnabled( ) method returns true if the selection mode allows directories to be selected—that is, the selection mode is either DIRECTORIES_ONLY or FILES_AND_DIRECTORIES.

```
public boolean isDirectorySelectionEnabled( )
```

Example 18-9 is a simple program that lets the user pick a directory from the file chooser. The contents of that directory are then listed.

*Example 18-9. DirectoryChooser*

```
import java.io.*;
import java.lang.reflect.InvocationTargetException;
import javax.swing.*;

public class DirectoryLister {

  public static void main(String[] args)
    throws InterruptedException, InvocationTargetException {

    SwingUtilities.invokeAndWait(
      new Runnable( ) {
        public void run( ) {
          JFileChooser fc = new JFileChooser();
          fc.setFileSelectionMode(JFileChooser.DIRECTORIES_ONLY);

          int result = fc.showOpenDialog(new JFrame());
          if (result == JFileChooser.APPROVE_OPTION) {
            File dir = fc.getSelectedFile();
            String[] contents = dir.list();
            for (int i = 0; i < contents.length; i++) {
              System.out.println(contents[i]);
            }
          }
          System.exit(0);
```

*Example 18-9. DirectoryChooser (continued)*

```
        }
      }
    );
  }
}
```

## Multiple Selections

JFileChooser also enables you to allow users to choose more than one file. Just pass true to setMultiSelectionEnabled( ):

```
public void setMultiSelectionEnabled(boolean b)
```

Typically, the user shift-clicks or command-clicks on the different files he wants to select.

The isMultiSelectionEnabled( ) method returns true if the file chooser allows multiple files to be selected at one time or false otherwise:

```
public boolean isMultiSelectionEnabled( )
```

## Hidden Files

Most operating systems have ways of hiding a file. By default, hidden files are not shown in file choosers. However, you can change this by passing false to the setFileHidingEnabled( ) method. You can check whether or not hidden files are shown with the isFileHidingEnabled( ) method:

```
public boolean isFileHidingEnabled( )
public void     setFileHidingEnabled(boolean b)
```

## File Views

The file view determines how information about files is interpreted and displayed to the user. For instance, you can use a file view to display names but not extensions, icons for files, last-modified dates of files, file sizes, and more. In general, the more information you choose to display in the file chooser, the slower the choosers are to appear and the longer it takes to switch directories. This information is encapsulated in a javax.swing.filechooser.FileView object. This class has five methods:

```
public String  getName(File f)
public String  getDescription(File f)
public String  getTypeDescription(File f)
public Icon    getIcon(File f)
public boolean isTraversable(File f)
```

You can get the current view with the getFileView( ) method:

```
public FileView getFileView( )
```

Most of the time the default file view is enough. However, you can write your own subclass of `FileView` that implements all five of these methods and install it in the file chooser with `setFileView( )`:

```
public void setFileView(fileView)
```

The `getName( )` method should return the name of the file to be displayed to the user. The `getDescription( )` method returns a short description of the file, generally not shown to the user. `getTypeDescription( )` should return a short description of the general kind of file, also generally not shown to the user. The `getIcon( )` method returns a `javax.swing.ImageIcon` object for the type of file, which is generally shown to the user to the left of the filename. Finally, `isTraversable( )` should return `Boolean.TRUE` for directories the user can enter and `Boolean.FALSE` for a directory the user can't open. Example 18-10 is a `FileView` class that describes compressed files.

*Example 18-10. CompressedFileView*

```java
import java.io.*;
import javax.swing.*;
import javax.swing.filechooser.*;

public class CompressedFileView extends FileView {

  ImageIcon zipIcon = new ImageIcon("images/zipIcon.gif");
  ImageIcon gzipIcon = new ImageIcon("images/gzipIcon.gif");
  ImageIcon deflateIcon = new ImageIcon("images/deflateIcon.gif");

  public String getName(File f) {
    return f.getName( );
  }

  public String getTypeDescription(File f) {

    if (f.getName( ).endsWith(".zip")) return "Zip archive";
    if (f.getName( ).endsWith(".gz")) return "Gzipped file";
    if (f.getName( ).endsWith(".dfl")) return "Deflated file";
    return null;
  }

  public Icon getIcon(File f) {

    if (f.getName( ).endsWith(".zip")) return zipIcon;
    if (f.getName( ).endsWith(".gz")) return gzipIcon;
    if (f.getName( ).endsWith(".dfl")) return deflateIcon;
    return null;
  }

  public String getDescription(File f) {
    return null;
  }

  public Boolean isTraversable(File f) {
```

*Example 18-10. CompressedFileView (continued)*

```
    return null;
  }
}
```

Two methods in this class, getDescription( ) and isTraversable( ), always return null. The other three methods can return null if they don't recognize the file's extension. Returning null in this context means that the look and feel should figure out the details for itself. Using this class is easy once you've written it. Simply pass an instance of it to the file chooser's setFileView( ) method like this:

```
    fc.setFileView(new CompressedFileView( ));
```

You also need to make sure that the GIF files *images/zipIcon.gif*, *images/gzipIcon.gif*, and *images/deflateIcon.gif* exist in the current working directory. In practice, it would probably be more reliable to place these files in a JAR archive and load them from there using System.getResource( ).

## FileSystem Views

javax.swing.FileSystemView is an abstract class that connects the filesystem abstraction the programmer works with to the GUI abstraction an end user works with. For instance, on Windows, the File class shows a multiply rooted filesystem: *C:*, *D:*, etc. However, a file chooser shows a single root that is actually the *C:\Documents and Settings\Username\Desktop* directory. FileSystemView represents this user's view of the filesystem rather than the programmer's view of the File class.

The details depend on the platform. For example, the FileSystemView has to tell which files are hidden and which aren't. On Unix, a file whose name begins with a period is hidden. On Windows, it's not. The getFileSystemView( ) method returns a FileSystemView object configured for the local system:

```
    public FileSystemView getFileSystemView( )
```

This class is mostly designed for the internal use of Swing and JFileChooser. However, it contains some generally useful methods, even if your application has no GUI at all. It's sometimes worth creating a JFileChooser just to get a FileSystemView:

```
    JFileChooser chooser = new JFileChooser( );
    FileSystemView view = chooser.getFileSystemView( );
```

However, this launches the AWT thread with the usual consequences, so you may not want to use it in a non-GUI application.

Once you have such an object, you can learn a lot of details about files and the filesystem that the regular java.io.File class won't tell you. This is not the intended use of this class, and it's definitely a hack, but it is useful. For example, the isRoot( ) method tells you whether a given file appears to be the root of the filesystem to a user:

```
    public boolean isRoot(File f)
```

On Windows, this returns true for real roots such as *C:\* but also returns true for the user's *Desktop* folder.

The isTraversable( ) method returns Boolean.TRUE if the user can enter the directory and Boolean.FALSE if she can't:

```
public Boolean isTraversable(File f)
```

 I have no idea why this method returns a java.lang.Boolean object instead of a boolean primitive, but that's what it does.

The isHidden( ) method returns true if the file is not normally shown to the user or false if it is normally shown:

```
public boolean isHiddenFile(File f)
```

The getFiles( ) method returns an array of the files within a directory. The second argument controls whether or not hidden files are included in the list:

```
public File[] getFiles(File dir, boolean useFileHiding)
```

The getSystemDisplayName( ) method returns the name of the file as it should be shown to the user.

```
public String getSystemDisplayName(File f)
```

Mostly this is the same as the filename. However, occasionally it's something different. For example, on Windows, the name of the primary hard disk is *C:\*, but the display name is *Local Disk (C:)*.

The getSystemTypeDescription( ) method returns a short description of the file you might also want to show to the user:

```
public String getSystemTypeDescription(File f)
```

The getSystemIcon( ) method returns the file's icon that would typically be shown in the GUI shell:

```
public Icon getSystemIcon(File f)
```

The isParent( ) method returns true if the GUI shows the folder as the parent of the specified file:

```
public boolean isParent(File folder, File file)
```

Again, think of the Desktop on Windows whose parent is really the *C:\Documents and Settings\Username* folder but which appears to be the parent of everything else, including all the disks and network mounts.

The getParentDirectory( ) method returns the apparent parent directory of a specified file:

```
public File getParentDirectory(File dir)
```

For example, on Windows the parent of the *C:\* directory is *My Computer*. (Of course, this isn't the real name of the directory. That's usually something incomprehensible like *::{20D04FE0-3AEA-1069-A2D8-08002B30309D}*)

The getChild( ) method is the reverse of this:

```
public File getChild(File parent, String fileName)
```

This method returns a File object for an apparent child of a specified directory. Almost all the time this is the same File object you'd get with the usual constructors. However, there are a few special cases where the GUI shows the parent and child somewhere other than where they actually are. In this case, getChild( ) returns the actual location of the child.

The isFileSystemRoot( ) method returns true if the file is the root of a filesystem or false if it isn't:

```
public boolean isFileSystemRoot(File f)
```

For instance, on Windows, *C:\*, *D:\*, and the like are treated as roots.

The isFileSystem( ) method returns true if the specified file appears to the user as a file or folder:

```
public boolean isFileSystem(File f)
```

It returns false if the file is one of the special files such as the Desktop on Windows that is shown differently in the GUI than in the filesystem.

The isDrive( ) method returns true if the file represents an entire disk. This usually means it has a special disk icon of some kind in the GUI shell.

```
public boolean isDrive(File dir)
```

On Windows, this returns true for *A:\*, *B:\*, *C:\*, and so on and false for pretty much everything else. On Mac OS X, this method is more or less broken and can't be relied on.

The isFloppyDrive( ) method returns true if the file represents a floppy disk:

```
public boolean isFloppyDrive(File dir)
```

On Windows, this is normally true of the *A:\* and *B:\* directories.

The isComputerNode( ) method returns true if and only the file represents an entire computer:

```
public boolean isComputerNode(File dir)
```

This is normally true of any mounted network servers and false of all other directories.

Example 18-11 is a simple class that calls FileSystemView to list various information about a file as it might appear to a user.

*Example 18-11. User-level file info*

```java
import java.io.*;

import javax.swing.JFileChooser;
import javax.swing.filechooser.*;

public class GUIFileSpy {

  public static void main(String[] args) {
    File f = new File(args[0]);
    JFileChooser chooser = new JFileChooser();
    FileSystemView view = chooser.getFileSystemView();

    String name = view.getSystemDisplayName(f);
    if (view.isHiddenFile(f)) System.out.println(name + " is hidden.");
    if (view.isRoot(f)) System.out.println(name + " is a root.");
    if (view.isTraversable(f).booleanValue()) {
      System.out.println(name + " is traversable.");
    }
    System.out.println("The parent of " + name + " is "
     + view.getParentDirectory(f));
    if (view.isFileSystem(f)) System.out.println(name + " is a regular file.");
    if (view.isFileSystemRoot(f)) System.out.println(name + " is the root.");
    if (view.isComputerNode(f)) System.out.println(name + " is the computer.");
    if (view.isDrive(f)) System.out.println(name + " is a disk.");
    if (view.isFloppyDrive(f)) System.out.println(name + " is a floppy disk.");
  }
}
```

Here's the output when run on the Mac OS X Desktop folder:

```
Desktop is traversable.
The parent of Desktop is /Users/elharo
Desktop is a regular file.
```

Here's the output when run on the Windows Desktop folder:

```
Desktop is a root.
Desktop is traversable.
The parent of Desktop is C:\Documents and Settings\Administrator
Desktop is a regular file.
```

Compare this output to that from the FileSpy class in Example 17-4. That class listed information about a file as a Java program sees it. This class lists information about the file as an end user sees it. The information is related, but is not the same.

Three methods create files in a specified directory. The createNewFolder() method makes a new directory:

```java
public abstract File createNewFolder(File containingDir) throws IOException
```

Typically, this uses whatever name is common for new directories on the host platform, *untitled folder, untitled folder 2, untitled folder 3*, etc. on the Mac; *New Folder, New Folder (2)*, etc. on Windows. (Actually, the current Mac VM gets this wrong. It uses the names *NewFolder, NewFolder.1*, etc.)

You can also create a file. However, for this you have to provide a name as well as a directory, or a full path to the file:

```
public File createFileObject(File dir, String filename)
public File createFileObject(String path)
```

However, these two methods only create the File object. If the corresponding file does not already exist, these methods do not create it. To create the file, you have to invoke createNewFile( ) on the File object these methods return.

Several methods return information about the entire filesystem rather a particular file. The getRoots( ) method returns an array containing all the filesystem roots:

```
public File[] getRoots( )
```

This is not the same as File.listRoots( ). The getRoots( ) method returns the apparent root while File.listRoots( ) returns the actual roots. For example, on Windows getRoots( ) typically returns a length one array containing *C:\Documents and Setting\ Administrator\Desktop*. On the same system, File.listRoots( )returns a longer array containing *A:\*, *C:\*, *D:\*, and all other mapped drive letters.

The getHomeDirectory( ) method returns the user's home directory:

```
public File getHomeDirectory( )
```

This is an alternative to System.getProperty("user.home").

The getDefaultDirectory( ) method returns the directory that the file chooser lists by default unless told otherwise:

```
public File getDefaultDirectory( )
```

On most platforms, the default directory is either the user's home directory or the current working directory. Example 18-12 is a simple class that calls FileSystemView to list various information about the local filesystem as it might appear to a user.

*Example 18-12. Filesystem info*

```
import java.io.*;
import javax.swing.JFileChooser;
import javax.swing.filechooser.*;

public class FileSystemViewer {

  public static void main(String[] args) {

    JFileChooser chooser = new JFileChooser( );
    FileSystemView view = chooser.getFileSystemView( );

    System.out.println("The home directory is " + view.getHomeDirectory( ));
    System.out.println("The default directory is " + view.getDefaultDirectory( ));
    System.out.println("The roots of this filesystem are: ");
```

*Example 18-12. Filesystem info (continued)*

```
    File[] roots = view.getRoots( );
    for (int i = 0; i < roots.length; i++) {
      System.out.println("  " + roots[i]);
    }
  }
}
```

Here's the output when run on Windows while logged in as Administrator:

```
The home directory is C:\Documents and Settings\Administrator\Desktop
The default directory is C:\Documents and Settings\Administrator\My Documents
The roots of this filesystem are:
  C:\Documents and Settings\Administrator\Desktop
```

# Handling Events

FileDialog is difficult to work with because of its synchronous nature. When a file dialog is shown, it blocks execution of the calling thread and all input to the parent frame. A raw JFileChooser, by contrast (*not* a JFileChooser embedded in a modal dialog by showOpenDialog( ), showSaveDialog( ), or showDialog( )), is asynchronous. It follows the standard AWT event model and can fire action and property change events.

### Action events

When the user hits the Approve button, the chooser fires an action event with the action command JFileChooser.APPROVE_SELECTION. When the user hits the Cancel button, the chooser fires an action event with the action command JFileChooser. CANCEL_SELECTION.

```
public static final String CANCEL_SELECTION  = "CancelSelection";
public static final String APPROVE_SELECTION = "ApproveSelection";
```

You register and remove action listeners with the file chooser in the usual fashion using addActionListener( ) and removeActionListener( ):

```
public void addActionListener(ActionListener l)
public void removeActionListener(ActionListener l)
```

The approveSelection( ) and cancelSelection( ) methods are called by the user interface when the user hits the Approve or Cancel button, respectively. You can call them yourself if you're driving the selection directly:

```
public void approveSelection( )
public void cancelSelection( )
```

Each of these methods fires an action event to all the registered action listeners by invoking the fireActionPerformed( ) method:

```
protected void fireActionPerformed(String command)
```

### Property change events

When the state of a file chooser changes, the file chooser fires a property change event (an instance of java.beans.PropertyChangeEvent). Property changes are triggered by file selections, changing directories, hitting the Approve or Cancel button, and many more actions. The event fired has its own name property set to one of the following constants in the JFileChooser class:

```
public static final String CANCEL_SELECTION = "CancelSelection";
public static final String APPROVE_SELECTION = "ApproveSelection";
public static final String APPROVE_BUTTON_TEXT_CHANGED_PROPERTY =
    "ApproveButtonTextChangedProperty";
public static final String APPROVE_BUTTON_TOOL_TIP_TEXT_CHANGED_PROPERTY =
    "ApproveButtonToolTipTextChangedProperty";
public static final String APPROVE_BUTTON_MNEMONIC_CHANGED_PROPERTY =
    "ApproveButtonMnemonicChangedProperty";
public static final String DIRECTORY_CHANGED_PROPERTY = "directoryChanged";
public static final String SELECTED_FILE_CHANGED_PROPERTY =
    "ApproveSelection";
public static final String MULTI_SELECTION_ENABLED_CHANGED_PROPERTY =
    "fileFilterChanged";
public static final String FILE_SYSTEM_VIEW_CHANGED_PROPERTY =
    "FileSystemViewChanged";
public static final String FILE_VIEW_CHANGED_PROPERTY = "fileViewChanged";
public static final String FILE_HIDING_CHANGED_PROPERTY =
    "FileHidingChanged";
public static final String FILE_FILTER_CHANGED_PROPERTY =
    "fileFilterChanged";
public static final String FILE_SELECTION_MODE_CHANGED_PROPERTY =
    "fileSelectionChanged";
public static final String ACCESSORY_CHANGED_PROPERTY =
    "AccessoryChangedProperty";
public static final String DIALOG_TYPE_CHANGED_PROPERTY =
    "DialogTypeChangedProperty";
public static final String CHOOSABLE_FILE_FILTER_CHANGED_PROPERTY =
    "ChoosableFileFilterChangedProperty";
```

You listen for and respond to property change events through an instance of the java.beans.PropertyChangeListener interface. This interface declares a single method, propertyChange( ). However, it's relatively rare to use a property change listener with a file chooser. Most of the time, you don't need to do anything as a result of a state change in the file chooser. You might want to respond to a property change event fired by a file chooser if you're using an accessory to preview the selected file. In this case, you'll watch for changes in the SELECTED_FILE_CHANGED_PROPERTY, as demonstrated in the next section.

## Accessory

An accessory is an optional component you can add to the JFileChooser. The most common use of an accessory is to show a preview of the file. For example, a file chooser for selecting an image file might provide an accessory that shows a thumb-nail of the picture. The setAccessory( ) method adds an accessory to the file chooser while the getAccessory( ) method returns a reference to it:

```
public JComponent getAccessory( )
public void setAccessory(JComponent newAccessory)
```

A JFileChooser object can have at most one accessory and does not need to have any.

Example 18-13 is a chooser that uses a JTextArea as an accessory to show the first few lines of the selected text file. This TextFilePreview class extends JTextArea so that it can easily display text. It implements the PropertyChangeListener interface so that it can be notified through its propertyChange( ) method when the user changes the selected file and the preview needs to be changed. The loadText( ) method reads in the first few hundred bytes of the selected file and stores that data in the preview field. Finally, the main( ) method tests this class by displaying a file chooser with this accessory. Figure 18-5 shows the result.

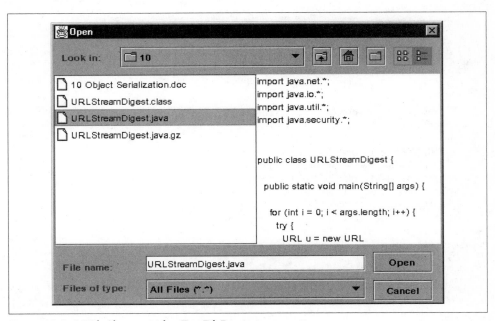

*Figure 18-5. A JFileChooser with a TextFilePreview accessory*

*Example 18-13. TextFilePreview*

```
import javax.swing.*;
import java.beans.*;
import java.io.*;
import java.lang.reflect.InvocationTargetException;
import java.awt.*;

public class TextFilePreview extends JTextArea
 implements PropertyChangeListener {
```

*Example 18-13. TextFilePreview (continued)*

```java
  private File selectedFile = null;
  private String preview = "";
  private int previewLength = 250;

  public TextFilePreview(JFileChooser fc) {
    super(10, 20);
    this.setEditable(false);
    this.setPreferredSize(new Dimension(150, 150));
    this.setLineWrap(true);
    fc.addPropertyChangeListener(this);
  }

  private void loadText( ) {

    if (selectedFile != null) {
      try {
        FileInputStream fin = new FileInputStream(selectedFile);
        byte[] data = new byte[previewLength];
        int bytesRead = 0;
        for (int i = 0; i < previewLength; i++) {
          int b = fin.read( );
          if (b == -1) break;
          bytesRead++;
          data[i] = (byte) b;
        }
        preview = new String(data, 0, bytesRead);
        fin.close( );
      }
      catch (IOException ex) {
        // File preview is not an essential operation so
        // we'll simply ignore the exception and return.
      }
    }
  }

  public void propertyChange(PropertyChangeEvent evt) {

    if (evt.getPropertyName( ).equals(
     JFileChooser.SELECTED_FILE_CHANGED_PROPERTY)) {
      selectedFile = (File) evt.getNewValue( );
      if(isShowing( )) {
        loadText( );
        this.setText(preview);
      }
    }
  }

  public static void main(String[] args)
    throws InterruptedException, InvocationTargetException {

    SwingUtilities.invokeAndWait(
      new Runnable( ) {
```

*Example 18-13. TextFilePreview (continued)*

```java
    public void run( ) {
      JFileChooser fc = new JFileChooser( );
      fc.setAccessory(new TextFilePreview(fc));
      int result = fc.showOpenDialog(new JFrame( ));
      if (result == JFileChooser.APPROVE_OPTION) {
        try {
          File f = fc.getSelectedFile( );
          if (f != null) {
            InputStream in = new FileInputStream(f);
            for (int c = in.read( ); c != -1; c = in.read( )) {
              System.out.write(c);
            }
            in.close( );
          }
        }
        catch (IOException ex) {System.err.println(ex);}
      }
      System.exit(0);
    } // end run
  } // end Runnable
); // end invokeAndWait
  }
}
```

# File Viewer, Part 6

We now have the tools needed to put a graphical user interface onto the FileViewer application we've been developing. The back end doesn't need to change at all. It's still based on the same filter streams we've used for the last several chapters. However, instead of reading filenames from the command line, we can get them from a file chooser. Instead of dumping the files on System.out, we can display them in a text area. And instead of relying on the user remembering a lot of confusing command-line switches, we can provide simple radio buttons for the user to choose from. This has the added advantage of making it easy to repeatedly interpret the same file according to different filters.

Figure 18-6 shows the finished application. This gives you some idea of what the code is aiming at. Initially, I started with a pencil-and-paper sketch, but I'll spare you my inartistic renderings. The single JFrame window is organized with a border layout. The west panel contains various controls for determining how the data is interpreted. The east panel contains the JFileChooser used to select the file. Notice that the Approve button has been customized to say "View File" rather than "Open". Ideally, I'd like to make the Cancel button say "Quit" instead, but the JFileChooser class doesn't allow you to do that without using resource bundles, a subject I would prefer to leave for another book. The south panel contains a scroll pane. Inside the scroll pane is a streamed text area.

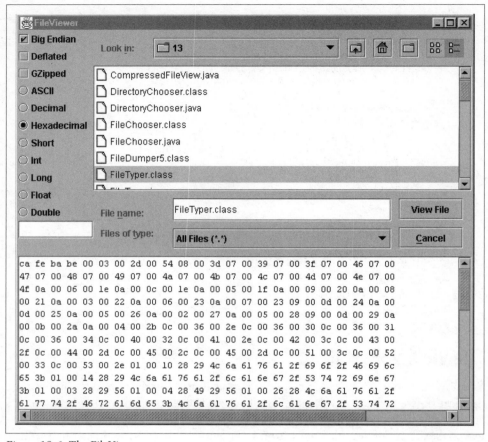

*Figure 18-6. The FileViewer*

Let's begin the exegesis of the code where I began writing it, with the user interface. The main driver class is FileViewer, shown in Example 18-14. This class extends JFrame. Its constructor doesn't do a lot. Most of the work is relegated to the init() method, which sets up the user interface composed of the three parts previously described and centers the whole frame on the primary display.

*Example 18-14. FileViewer*

```
import javax.swing.*;
import java.io.*;
import java.awt.*;
import java.awt.event.*;
import com.elharo.io.ui.JStreamedTextArea;

public class FileViewer extends JFrame implements ActionListener {

  private JFileChooser chooser = new JFileChooser();
  private JStreamedTextArea theView = new JStreamedTextArea();
  private ModePanel mp = new ModePanel();
```

*Example 18-14. FileViewer (continued)*

```java
public FileViewer( ) {
  super("FileViewer");
}

public void init( ) {
  chooser.setApproveButtonText("View File");
  chooser.setApproveButtonMnemonic('V');
  chooser.addActionListener(this);

  this.getContentPane( ).add(BorderLayout.CENTER, chooser);
  JScrollPane sp = new JScrollPane(theView);
  sp.setPreferredSize(new Dimension(640, 400));
  this.getContentPane( ).add(BorderLayout.SOUTH, sp);
  this.getContentPane( ).add(BorderLayout.WEST, mp);
  this.pack( );

  // Center on display.
  Dimension display = getToolkit().getScreenSize( );
  Dimension bounds = this.getSize( );

  int x = (display.width - bounds.width)/2;
  int y = (display.height - bounds.height)/2;
  if (x < 0) x = 10;
  if (y < 0) y = 15;
  this.setLocation(x, y);
}

public void actionPerformed(ActionEvent evt) {

  if (evt.getActionCommand( ).equals(JFileChooser.APPROVE_SELECTION)) {
    File f = chooser.getSelectedFile( );
    if (f != null) {
      theView.reset( );
      try {
        InputStream in = new FileInputStream(f);
        in = new ProgressMonitorInputStream(this, "Reading...", in);
        OutputStream out = theView.getOutputStream( );
        FileDumper5.dump(in, out, mp.getMode( ), mp.isBigEndian( ),
         mp.isDeflated( ), mp.isGZipped( ), mp.getPassword( ));
      }
      catch (IOException ex) {
        JOptionPane.showMessageDialog(this, ex.getMessage( ),
          "I/O Error", JOptionPane.ERROR_MESSAGE);
      }
    }
  }
  else if (evt.getActionCommand( ).equals(JFileChooser.CANCEL_SELECTION)) {
    this.setVisible(false);
    this.dispose( );
  }
}
```

*Example 18-14. FileViewer (continued)*

```java
  public static void main(String[] args) {
    FileViewer viewer = new FileViewer();
    viewer.init();
    // This is a single window application
    viewer.setDefaultCloseOperation(JFrame.EXIT_ON_CLOSE);
    viewer.setVisible(true);
  }
}
```

FileViewer implements the ActionListener interface. However, the action events that its actionPerformed() method responds to are fired by the file chooser, indicating that the user pressed the View File button.

When the user presses the View File button, the mode panel is read to determine exactly how the file is to be interpreted. These parameters and the selected file are fed to the static FileDumper5.dumpFile() method from Chapter 12.

The next new class in this application is the ModePanel, shown in Example 18-15. This class provides a simple user interface to allow the user to specify the format the file is in, whether and how it's compressed, and the password, if any. This part of the GUI is completely contained inside this class. Other methods that need access to this information can query the ModePanel for it through any of several public getter methods. They do not need to concern themselves with the internal details of the ModePanel GUI.

*Example 18-15. ModePanel*

```java
import java.awt.*;
import javax.swing.*;

public class ModePanel extends JPanel {

private JCheckBox bigEndian = new JCheckBox("Big Endian", true);
  private JCheckBox deflated = new JCheckBox("Deflated", false);
  private JCheckBox gzipped   = new JCheckBox("GZipped", false);

  private ButtonGroup  dataTypes    = new ButtonGroup();
  private JRadioButton asciiRadio   = new JRadioButton("ASCII");
  private JRadioButton decimalRadio = new JRadioButton("Decimal");
  private JRadioButton hexRadio     = new JRadioButton("Hexadecimal");
  private JRadioButton shortRadio   = new JRadioButton("Short");
  private JRadioButton intRadio     = new JRadioButton("Int");
  private JRadioButton longRadio    = new JRadioButton("Long");
  private JRadioButton floatRadio   = new JRadioButton("Float");
  private JRadioButton doubleRadio  = new JRadioButton("Double");

  private JTextField password = new JPasswordField();

  public ModePanel() {
```

*Example 18-15. ModePanel (continued)*

```
    this.setLayout(new GridLayout(13, 1));
    this.add(bigEndian);
    this.add(deflated);
    this.add(gzipped);

    this.add(asciiRadio);
    asciiRadio.setSelected(true);
    this.add(decimalRadio);
    this.add(hexRadio);
    this.add(shortRadio);
    this.add(intRadio);
    this.add(longRadio);
    this.add(floatRadio);
    this.add(doubleRadio);

    dataTypes.add(asciiRadio);
    dataTypes.add(decimalRadio);
    dataTypes.add(hexRadio);
    dataTypes.add(shortRadio);
    dataTypes.add(intRadio);
    dataTypes.add(longRadio);
    dataTypes.add(floatRadio);
    dataTypes.add(doubleRadio);

    this.add(password);
  }

  public boolean isBigEndian() {
    return bigEndian.isSelected();
  }

  public boolean isDeflated() {
    return deflated.isSelected();
  }

  public boolean isGZipped() {
    return gzipped.isSelected();
  }

  public int getMode() {

    if (asciiRadio.isSelected()) return FileDumper6.ASC;
    else if (decimalRadio.isSelected()) return FileDumper6.DEC;
    else if (hexRadio.isSelected()) return FileDumper6.HEX;
    else if (shortRadio.isSelected()) return FileDumper6.SHORT;
    else if (intRadio.isSelected()) return FileDumper6.INT;
    else if (longRadio.isSelected()) return FileDumper6.LONG;
    else if (floatRadio.isSelected()) return FileDumper6.FLOAT;
    else if (doubleRadio.isSelected()) return FileDumper6.DOUBLE;
    else return FileDumper6.ASC;
  }
```

*Example 18-15. ModePanel (continued)*

```
  public String getPassword( ) {
    return password.getText( );
  }
}
```

And there you have it: a graphical file viewer application. The I/O code hasn't changed at all, but the resulting application is much easier to use. One final piece remains before we can say the file viewer is complete. Chapter 20 adds support for many additional text encodings besides the ASCII used here.

# PART VI

# Text

# CHAPTER 19

# Character Sets and Unicode

We live on a planet on which many languages are spoken. I can walk out my front door in Brooklyn and hear people conversing in English, French, Creole, Hebrew, Arabic, Spanish, and languages I don't even recognize. The Internet is even more diverse than Brooklyn. A local doctor's office that sets up a storefront on the Web to sell vitamins may soon find itself shipping to customers whose native languages are Chinese, Gujarati, Turkish, German, Portuguese, or something else. There's no such thing as a local business on the Internet.

However, the first computers and the first programming languages were mostly designed by English-speaking programmers in countries where English was the native language. These programmers designed character sets that worked well for English text, though not much else. The preeminent such set is ASCII. Since ASCII is a 7-bit character set, each ASCII character can be represented as a single byte, signed or unsigned. Thus, it's natural for ASCII-based programming languages, such as C, to equate the character data type with the byte data type. In these languages, the same operations that read and write bytes also read and write characters.

Unfortunately, ASCII is inadequate for almost all non-English languages. It contains no cedillas, umlauts, betas, thorns, or any of the other thousands of non-English characters used around the world. Fairly shortly after the development of ASCII there was an explosion of extended character sets, each of which encoded the basic ASCII characters plus the additional characters needed for another language, such as Greek, Turkish, Arabic, Chinese, Japanese, or Russian. Many of these character sets are still used today, and much existing data is encoded in them.

However, these character sets are still inadequate for many needs. For one thing, most assume that you only want to encode English plus one other language. This makes it difficult for a Russian classicist to write a commentary on an ancient Greek text, for example. Furthermore, documents are limited by their character sets. Email sent from Morocco may become illegible in India if the sender is using an Arabic character set but the recipient is using Devanagari.

The Unicode character set is the end result of an ongoing international effort to create a single character set that everyone can use. Unicode supports the characters needed for English, Arabic, Cyrillic, Greek, Devanagari, and many other languages. Unicode isn't perfect—there are some omissions and redundancies—but it is the most comprehensive character set yet devised for all the languages of planet Earth.

Java adopts Unicode as its native character set. Java chars and strings are Unicode (more specifically, the UTF-16 encoding of the Unicode character set). However, since there's also a lot of non-Unicode legacy text in the world, in a dizzying array of encodings, Java provides classes to read and write text in those encodings as well.

## The Unicode Character Set

The Unicode character set maps characters to integer code points. For instance, the Latin letter A is assigned the code point 65. The Greek letter Σ is assigned the code point 931. The musical symbol 𝄢 is assigned the code point 119,074. Unicode has room for over one million characters, which is enough to hold every character from all the world's scripts. The current version of Unicode (4.1) defines 97,655 different characters from many languages, including English, Russian, Arabic, Hebrew, Greek, Korean, Chinese, Japanese, and Sanskrit.

The first 128 Unicode characters (characters 0 through 127) are identical to the ASCII character set. The ASCII space is 32; therefore, 32 is the Unicode space. The ASCII exclamation point is 33, so 33 is the Unicode exclamation point, and so on. Table A-1 in Appendix A shows this character set. The next 128 Unicode characters (characters 128 through 255) have the same values as the equivalent characters in the Latin-1 character set defined by ISO standard 8859-1. Latin-1, a slight variation of which is used by Windows, adds the various accented characters, umlauts, cedillas, upside-down question marks, and other characters needed to write text in most Western European languages. Table A-2 shows these characters. The first 128 characters in Latin-1 are identical to the ASCII character set.

Unicode is divided into blocks. For example, characters 0 through 127 are the Basic Latin block and contain ASCII. Characters 128 through 255 are the Latin Extended-A block and contain the upper 128 characters of the Latin-1 character set. Characters 9984 through 10,175 are the Dingbats block and contain the characters in the popular Zapf Dingbats font. Characters 19,968 through 40,959 are the unified Chinese-Japanese-Korean ideograph block.

 For complete lists of all the Unicode characters and associated glyphs, the canonical reference is *The Unicode Standard, Version 4.0* by the Unicode Consortium (ISBN 0-321-18578-1). Online versions of the character tables can be found at *http://unicode.org/charts/*.

Although internally Java can handle full Unicode data (code points are just numbers, after all), not all Java environments can display all Unicode characters. The biggest problem is the lack of fonts. Few computers have fonts for all the scripts Java supports. Even computers that possess the necessary fonts can't install a lot of them because of their size. A normal, 8-bit outline font ranges from about 30–60K. A Unicode font that omits the Han ideographs will be about 10 times that size. A Unicode font that includes the full range of Han ideographs will occupy between 5 and 7 MB. Furthermore, text display algorithms based on English often break down when faced with right-to-left languages like Hebrew and Arabic, vertical languages like the traditional Chinese used in Taiwan, or context-sensitive languages like Arabic.

# UTF-16

The integers to which Unicode maps characters can be encoded in a variety of ways. The simplest approach is to write each integer as a normal big-endian 4-byte int. This encoding scheme is called UCS-4. However, it's rather inefficient because the vast majority of characters seen in practice have code points less than 65,535, and in English text most are less than 127.

In practice, most Unicode text is encoded in either UTF-16 or UTF-8. UTF-16 uses two bytes for characters with code points less than or equal to 65,535 and four bytes for characters with code points greater than 65,535. It comes in both big-endian and little-endian formats. The endianness is normally indicated by an initial byte order mark. That is, the first character in the file is the zero-width nonbreaking space, code point 65,279. In big-endian UTF-16, this is the two bytes 0xFEFF (in hexadecimal). In little-endian UTF-16, this is the reverse, 0xFFFE.

UTF-16 encodes characters with code points from 0 to 65,535 (the Basic Multilingual Plane, or BMP for short) as 2-byte unsigned ints. Characters from beyond the BMP are encoded as surrogate pairs made up of four bytes: first a high surrogate, then a low surrogate. The Java char data type is really a big-endian UTF-16 code point, not a Unicode character, though the difference is significant only for characters from outside the BMP.

To see how this works, consider a character from outside the BMP in a typical UCS-4 (4-byte) big-endian representation. This is composed of four bytes of eight bits each. I will label the bits as x0 through x31:

| x31 | x30 | x29 | x28 | x27 | x26 | x25 | x24 |
| --- | --- | --- | --- | --- | --- | --- | --- |
| x23 | x22 | x21 | x20 | x19 | x18 | x17 | x16 |
| x15 | x14 | x13 | x12 | x11 | x10 | x9 | x8 |
| x7 | x6 | x5 | x4 | x3 | x2 | x1 | x0 |

In reality, the high-order byte is always 0. The first three bits of the second byte are also always 0, so these don't need to be encoded. Only bits x0 through x20 need to be encoded. These are encoded in four bytes, like this:

| | | | | | | | |
|---|---|---|---|---|---|---|---|
| 1 | 1 | 0 | 1 | 1 | 0 | $w_1$ | $w_2$ |
| $w_3$ | $w_4$ | $x_{15}$ | $x_{14}$ | $x_{13}$ | $x_{12}$ | $x_{11}$ | $x_{10}$ |
| 1 | 1 | 0 | 1 | 1 | 1 | $x_9$ | $x_8$ |
| $x_7$ | $x_6$ | $x_5$ | $x_4$ | $x_3$ | $x_2$ | $x_1$ | $x_0$ |

Here, $w_1w_2w_3w_4$ is the 4-bit number formed by subtracting 1 from the 5-bit number $x_{20}x_{19}x_{18}x_{17}x_{16}$. There are simple, efficient algorithms for breaking up non-BMP characters into these surrogate pairs and recomposing them. Most of the time you'll let the Reader and Writer classes do this for you automatically. The main thing you need to remember is that a Java char is really a UTF-16 code point, and while 99% of the time this is the same as one Unicode character, there are cases where it takes two chars to make a single character.

# UTF-8

UTF-8 is the preferred encoding of Unicode for most scenarios that don't require fast random indexing into a string. It has a number of nice characteristics, including robustness and compactness compared to other Unicode encodings.

UTF-8 encodes the ASCII characters in a single byte, characters between 128 and 2,047 in two bytes, other characters in the BMP in three bytes, and characters from outside the BMP in four bytes. Java *.class* files use UTF-8 to store string literals, identifiers, and other text data in compiled byte code.

To better understand UTF-8, consider a typical Unicode character from the Basic Multilingual Plane as a sequence of 16 bits:

| | | | | | | | |
|---|---|---|---|---|---|---|---|
| $x_{15}$ | $x_{14}$ | $x_{13}$ | $x_{12}$ | $x_{11}$ | $x_{10}$ | $x_9$ | $x_8$ |
| $x_7$ | $x_6$ | $x_5$ | $x_4$ | $x_3$ | $x_2$ | $x_1$ | $x_0$ |

Each ASCII character (each character between 0 and 127) has its upper nine bits equal to 0:

| | | | | | | | |
|---|---|---|---|---|---|---|---|
| 0 | 0 | 0 | 0 | 0 | 0 | 0 | 0 |
| 0 | $x_6$ | $x_5$ | $x_4$ | $x_3$ | $x_2$ | $x_1$ | $x_0$ |

Therefore, it's easy to encode an ASCII character as a single byte. Just drop the high-order byte:

| | | | | | | | |
|---|---|---|---|---|---|---|---|
| 0 | $x_6$ | $x_5$ | $x_4$ | $x_3$ | $x_2$ | $x_1$ | $x_0$ |

Now consider characters between 128 and 2,047. These all have their top five bits equal to 0, as shown here:

| | | | | | | | |
|---|---|---|---|---|---|---|---|
| 0 | 0 | 0 | 0 | 0 | x10 | x9 | x8 |
| x7 | x6 | x5 | x4 | x3 | x2 | x1 | x0 |

These characters are encoded into two bytes, but not in the most obvious fashion. The 11 significant bits of the character are broken up like this:

| | | | | | | | |
|---|---|---|---|---|---|---|---|
| 1 | 1 | 0 | x10 | x9 | x8 | x7 | x6 |
| 1 | 0 | x5 | x4 | x3 | x2 | x1 | x0 |

Neither of the bytes that make up this number begins with a 0 bit. Thus, you can distinguish between bytes that are part of a 2-byte character and bytes that represent 1-byte characters (which all begin with 0).

The remaining characters in the BMP have values between 2,048 and 65,535. Any or all of the bits in these characters may take on the value of either 0 or 1. Thus, they are encoded in three bytes, like this:

| | | | | | | | |
|---|---|---|---|---|---|---|---|
| 1 | 1 | 1 | 0 | x15 | x14 | x13 | x12 |
| 1 | 0 | x11 | x10 | x9 | x8 | x7 | x6 |
| 1 | 0 | x5 | x4 | x3 | x2 | x1 | x0 |

Within this scheme, any byte beginning with a 0 bit must be a 1-byte ASCII character between 1 and 127. Any byte beginning with the three bits 110 must be the first byte of a 2-byte character. Any byte beginning with the four bits 1110 must be the first byte of a 3-byte character. Finally, any byte beginning with the two bits 10 must be the second or third byte of a multibyte character.

The `DataOutputStream` class provides a `writeUTF()` method that encodes a string in a slight variation of UTF-8. It first writes the number of encoded bytes in the string (as an unsigned short), followed by the UTF-8-encoded format of the string:

```
public final void writeUTF(String s) throws IOException
```

The `DataInputStream` class provides two corresponding `readUTF()` methods to read such a string from its underlying input stream:

```
public final String readUTF() throws IOException
public static final String readUTF(DataInput in) throws IOException
```

Each of these first reads a 2-byte unsigned short that tells it how many more bytes to read. These bytes are then read and decoded into a Java Unicode string. An `EOFException` is thrown if the stream ends before all the expected bytes have been read. If the bytes read cannot be interpreted as a valid UTF-8 string, a `UTFDataFormatException` is thrown.

However, `DataInputStream` and `DataOutputStream` diverge from the official UTF-8 format in one respect: they encode the null character (0x00) in two bytes rather than one. This makes it slightly easier for C code that expects null-terminated strings to parse Java *.class* files. On the other hand, it makes the data written by `writeUTF( )` incompatible with most other libraries. The `Reader` and `Writer` classes discussed in the next chapter read and write true UTF-8 with 1-byte nulls, and these should be preferred for almost all use cases other than parsing Java byte code.

## Other Encodings

Unicode support is growing, but there will doubtless be legacy data in other encodings that must be read for centuries to come. Such encodings include ASCII and Latin-1, as well as less common encoding schemes such as EBCDIC and MacRoman. There are multiple encodings in use for Arabic, Turkish, Hebrew, Greek, Cyrillic, Chinese, Japanese, Korean, and many other languages and scripts. The `Reader` and `Writer` classes allow you to read and write data in these different character sets. The `String` class also has a number of methods that convert between different encodings (though a `String` object itself is always represented in Unicode).

Modern desktop and server Java environments are pretty well guaranteed to have these six character sets available:

- US-ASCII
- ISO-8859-1
- UTF-8
- UTF-16BE
- UTF-16LE
- UTF-16

All other encodings are optional and may not be supported in any given VM. Most VMs will have many more encodings as well, but only these six are almost certain to be present. They're likely to be more interoperable, not just with Java but with other programs written in other languages. Some VMs, especially on Windows, omit some of the more obscure or larger encodings to save space. J2ME VMs will likely include many fewer to save space, and they don't have the `java.nio.charsets` package at all.

If you've installed Sun's JRE/JDK, a basic set of encodings is included in the standard *rt.jar* file along with all the other classes from the Java class library. There may also be a *charsets.jar* file that includes several dozen additional encodings, such as MacRoman and SJIS.

# Converting Between Byte Arrays and Strings

I/O is about bytes. Disks and networks understand bytes, not characters. Nonetheless, much actual programming is modeled in terms of characters and text. When reading in data, it's generally necessary to convert the bytes into characters. When writing out data, it's necessary to convert the characters into bytes. The Reader and Writer classes can perform the conversions implicitly, which is normally the simplest approach when you only need to work on text. However, when working with mixed formats such as FITS, GIF, or XOP that contain both text and binary data, it's normally necessary to explicitly convert the text to or from bytes in some encoding.

## The String Class

The java.lang.String class has several constructors that form a string from a byte array and several methods that return a byte array corresponding to a given string. There's no unique way to do this. There are multiple encodings of characters into bytes. Anytime a string is converted to bytes or vice versa, that conversion happens according to a certain encoding. The same string can produce different byte arrays when converted into different encodings.

Six constructors form a new String object from a byte array:

```
public String(byte[] ascii, int highByte)
public String(byte[] ascii, int highByte, int offset, int length)
public String(byte[] data, String encoding)
  throws UnsupportedEncodingException
public String(byte[] data, int offset, int length, String encoding)
  throws UnsupportedEncodingException
public String(byte[] data)
public String(byte[] data, int offset, int length)
```

The first two constructors, the ones with the highByte argument, are leftovers from Java 1.0 that are deprecated in Java 1.1 and later. These two constructors do not accurately translate non-Latin-1 character sets into Unicode. Instead, they read each byte in the ascii array as the low-order byte of a 2-byte character and fill in the high-order byte with the highByte argument. For example:

```
byte[] isoLatin1 = new byte[256];
for (int i = 0; i < 256; i++) isoLatin1[i] = (byte) i;
String s = new String(isoLatin1, 0);
```

Frankly, this is a kludge. It's deprecated for good reason. This scheme works quite well for Latin-1 data with a high byte of 0. However, it's extremely difficult to use for character sets where different characters need to have different high bytes, and it's completely unworkable for character sets like MacRoman that also need to adjust bits in the low-order byte to conform to Unicode. The only approach that genuinely works for the broad range of character sets Java programs may be asked to handle is table lookup. Each supported character encoding requires a table mapping characters in the set to Unicode characters. These tables are hidden inside the sun.io package, but they are present, and they are how the next four constructors translate from various encodings to Unicode.

The third and fourth constructors allow the client programmer to specify not only the byte data but also the encoding table to be used when converting these bytes to Unicode chars. The third constructor converts the entire array from the specified encoding into Unicode. The fourth one converts only the specified subarray of data starting at offset and continuing for length bytes. Otherwise, they're identical. The first argument is the data to be converted. The final argument is the encoding scheme to be used to perform the conversion. For example:

```
byte[] isoLatin1 = new byte[256];
for (int i = 0; i < 256; i++) isoLatin1[i] = (byte) i;
String s = new String(isoLatin1, "8859_1");
```

The fifth and sixth constructors are similar to the third and fourth. However, they always use the host platform's default encoding, as specified by the system property file.encoding. If this is ISO 8859-1, you may write:

```
byte[] isoLatin1 = new byte[256];
for (int i = 0; i < 256; i++) isoLatin1[i] = (byte) i;
String s = new String(isoLatin1);
```

This code fragment produces different results on platforms with different default encodings.

The three getBytes( ) methods go the other direction, converting the Unicode string into an array of bytes in a particular encoding:

```
public void getBytes(int srcBegin, int srcEnd, byte[] dst, int dstBegin)
public byte[] getBytes( )
public byte[] getBytes(String encoding) throws UnsupportedEncodingException
```

Once again, the first method is deprecated. The byte array it returns contains only the low-order bytes of the 2-byte characters in the string (starting at srcBegin and continuing through srcEnd). This works well enough for ASCII and Latin-1 but fails miserably for pretty much all other character sets. The no-arg getBytes( ) method properly converts the Unicode characters in the string into a byte array in the platform's default encoding—assuming a full conversion is possible (and it isn't always; you cannot, for example, convert a string of Chinese ideographs into Latin-1). The byte array returned contains the converted characters. The third and final getBytes( ) method specifies the encoding to be used to make the conversion. For example, this statement converts the Greek word ανδροσ (man) into its byte equivalent using the MacGreek encoding:

```
byte[] man = "ανδροσ".getBytes("MacGreek");
```

This method throws an UnsupportedEncodingException if the Java virtual machine does not supply the requested encoding.

# The Charset Class

Char-to-byte conversion through the String class is relatively indirect and not always as efficient as one would like. In Java 1.4, the java.nio.charsets package provides classes for efficient conversion of large chunks of text to and from any encoding Java supports. This is in fact a more direct interface to the character conversion code that's used by the String class and has been present in the JDK since Java 1.1.

Charset is an abstract class that represents a character set such as US-ASCII, ISO-8859-1, or SJIS. Each Charset object defines a mapping between the characters in that set and some subset of Unicode. The mapping is sometimes implemented algorithmically, sometimes as simple table lookup, and sometimes as a combination of both, but the details need not concern you. The Charset abstraction hides all this.

## Retrieving Charset objects

The one constructor in the Charset class is protected:

```
protected Charset(String canonicalName,String[] aliases)
```

While you might invoke this if adding support for an encoding Java doesn't support out of the box, that usage is rare. Much more commonly, you'll call the Charset. forName( ) factory method to ask Java for one of the encodings it supports:

```
public static Charset forName(String charsetName)
  throws IllegalCharsetNameException, UnsupportedCharsetException
```

For example, this statement requests the Charset object for the Big5 encoding for Chinese:

```
Charset big5 = Charset.forName("Big5");
```

Character set names are case insensitive. Charset.forName("BIG5") returns the same Charset object as Charset.forName("Big5").

If the local JDK supports the requested encoding, Charset.forName( ) returns a Charset object. Otherwise, it throws an UnsupportedCharsetException. This is a runtime exception, so you don't need to explicitly handle it as long as you're confident the runtime contains the requested character set. Charset.forName( ) may also throw an IllegalCharsetNameException if the name contains spaces, non-ASCII characters, or punctuation marks other than the hyphen, period, colon, and underscore.

Java 5 adds one more way to get a Charset. The static Charset.defaultCharset( ) method returns the current system's default character set:

```
public static Charset defaultCharset( )
```

This code prints the name of the platform's default character set:

```
System.out.println(Charset.defaultCharset( ));
```

When I tested this, the default on Mac OS X was MacRoman, on Windows it was windows-1252, and on Linux it was UTF-8. These were all U.S.-localized systems.

Systems localized for other countries, especially outside Western Europe and the Americas, would probably show something different.

## Character set info

The static `Charset.isSupported()` method checks whether an encoding is available in the current VM:

```
public static boolean isSupported(String charsetName)
```

For example, if you wanted to use Big5 if possible but fall back to UTF-8 if it wasn't, you might write code like this:

```
Charset cs;
if (Charset.isSupported("Big5") cs = Charset.forName("Big5");
else cs = Charset.forName("UTF-8");
```

The static `Charset.availableCharsets()` method enables you to inquire which character sets are installed in the local VM:

```
public static SortedMap availableCharsets()
```

The keys in the returned method are the character set names. The values are the Charset objects themselves. In Java 5, a genericized signature makes this more explicit:

```
public static SortedMap <String, Charset> availableCharsets()
```

Example 19-1 is a simple program to list all the available character sets:

*Example 19-1. List available character sets*

```
import java.nio.charset.*;
import java.util.*;

class CharsetLister {

  public static void main(String[] args) {
    Map charsets = Charset.availableCharsets();
    Iterator iterator = charsets.keySet().iterator();
    while (iterator.hasNext()) {
      System.out.println(iterator.next());
    }
  }
}
```

When run on the Apple Java VM 1.4, it found 64 character sets, including the following:

```
$ java CharsetLister
Big5
Big5-HKSCS
EUC-JP
EUC-KR
GB18030
```

```
GBK
ISO-2022-JP
ISO-2022-KR
ISO-8859-1
ISO-8859-13
ISO-8859-15
ISO-8859-2
...
x-MS950-HKSCS
x-mswin-936
x-windows-949
x-windows-950
```

The Java 5 VM has 85 more. Character set availability varies from one VM vendor and version to the next. In general, I recommend sticking to UTF-8 if at all possible for new data. UTF-8 should always be supported. Legacy protocols, formats, and data may require occasional use of US-ASCII, ISO-8859-1, or other encodings, but new text data should be encoded in UTF-8.

Many character sets are commonly known by more than one name. For instance, UTF-8 is also referred to as UTF8 and unicode-1-1-utf-8. The names shown in the program's output are the canonical names of the character sets. The `name( )` instance method returns the canonical name of a given `Charset` object:

```
public String name( )
```

The `aliases( )` method returns all the aliases for a given character set, not including its canonical name:

```
public final Set aliases( )
```

The values in the set are strings. In Java 5, a genericized signature makes this more explicit:

```
public final Set<String> aliases( )
```

Character sets may also have display names that can be localized and may contain non-ASCII characters:

```
public String displayName( )
```

The display name is usually the same as the canonical name, but specific implementations may instead return a localized value that can contain spaces and non-ASCII characters. The display name is meant for showing to people, not for looking up character sets.

For interoperability, character set names and aliases should be registered with the Internet Assigned Number Authority (IANA) and listed in the registry at *http://www.iana.org/assignments/character-sets*. The `isRegistered( )` method returns true if the character set has been so registered:

```
public final boolean isRegistered( )
```

Many of the character sets shipped with the JDK have not been registered. You may need to use these character sets to decode existing data, but you should not generate any new data in an unregistered character set.

Example 19-3 is a slightly more complex program that lists all the available character sets by their display names, canonical names, and aliases.

*Example 19-2. List different names for character sets*

```
import java.nio.charset.*;
import java.util.*;

class AliasLister {

  public static void main(String[] args) {
    Map charsets = Charset.availableCharsets();
    Iterator iterator = charsets.values().iterator();
    while (iterator.hasNext()) {
      Charset cs = (Charset) iterator.next();
      System.out.print(cs.displayName());
      if (cs.isRegistered()) {
        System.out.print(" (registered): ");
      }
      else {
        System.out.print(" (unregistered): ");
      }
      System.out.print(cs.name() );
      Iterator names = cs.aliases().iterator();
      while (names.hasNext()) {
        System.out.print(", ");
        System.out.print(names.next());
      }
      System.out.println();
    }
  }
}
```

Here's a sample of the output from the Apple Java VM 1.4:

```
$ java AliasLister
Big5 (registered): Big5, csBig5
Big5-HKSCS (registered): Big5-HKSCS, big5-hkscs, Big5_HKSCS, big5hkscs
EUC-JP (registered): EUC-JP, eucjis, x-eucjp, csEUCPkdFmtjapanese, eucjp,
Extended_UNIX_Code_Packed_Format_for_Japanese, x-euc-jp, euc_jp
EUC-KR (registered): EUC-KR, ksc5601, 5601, ksc5601_1987, ksc_5601, ksc5601-1987,
euc_kr, ks_c_5601-1987, euckr, csEUCKR
GB18030 (registered): GB18030, gb18030-2000
...
x-MS950-HKSCS (unregistered): x-MS950-HKSCS, MS950_HKSCS
x-mswin-936 (unregistered): x-mswin-936, ms936, ms_936
x-windows-949 (unregistered): x-windows-949, windows949, ms_949, ms949
x-windows-950 (unregistered): x-windows-950, windows-950, ms950
```

## Encoding and decoding

Of course, the primary purpose of a `Charset` object is to encode and decode text. The `encode()` and `decode()` methods do this:

```
public final CharBuffer decode(ByteBuffer buffer)
public final ByteBuffer encode(CharBuffer buffer)
public final ByteBuffer encode(String s)
```

You can encode either a `String` or a `CharBuffer`. Decoding operates on a `ByteBuffer` and produces a `CharBuffer`. These methods do not throw exceptions. If they encounter a character they cannot convert, they replace it with the replacement character (normally a question mark).

All character sets support decoding, and most but not all support encoding. The `canEncode()` method returns `true` if the `Charset` supports encoding and `false` if it doesn't:

```
public boolean canEncode()
```

A few special sets automatically detect the encoding of an incoming stream and set the decoder appropriately. In the VM I use, there are exactly two such nonencoding charsets: csISO2022CN and JISAutoDetect. If you try to encode text with a `Charset` that does not support encoding, the `encode()` method throws an `UnsupportedOperationException`.

Example 19-5 is a simple program that reads a stream in one encoding and writes it out in another encoding. A `Charset` object converts between the two encodings. The user interface implemented in the `main()` method simply reads the names of the encodings to convert to and from the command-line arguments. Input is read from `System.in` and written to `System.out`, mostly because I didn't want to spend a lot of lines parsing command-line arguments. However, the `convert()` method is more general and can operate on any streams you pass in.

*Example 19-3. Converting encodings*

```java
import java.io.*;
import java.nio.charset.*;
import java.nio.*;
import java.nio.channels.*;

public class Recoder {

  public static void main(String[] args) {

    if (args.length != 2) {
      System.err.println(
        "Usage: java Recoder inputEncoding outputEncoding <inFile >outFile");
      return;
    }

    try {
```

*Example 19-3. Converting encodings (continued)*

```
        Charset inputEncoding = Charset.forName(args[0]);
        Charset outputEncoding = Charset.forName(args[1]);
        convert(inputEncoding, outputEncoding, System.in, System.out);
      }
      catch (UnsupportedCharsetException ex) {
        System.err.println(ex.getCharsetName() + " is not supported by this VM.");
      }
      catch (IllegalCharsetNameException  ex) {
        System.err.println(
          "Usage: java Recoder inputEncoding outputEncoding <inFile >outFile");
      }
      catch (IOException ex) {
        System.err.println(ex.getMessage());
      }
    }

  private static void convert(Charset inputEncoding, Charset outputEncoding,
   InputStream inStream, OutputStream outStream) throws IOException {

    ReadableByteChannel in = Channels.newChannel(inStream);
    WritableByteChannel out = Channels.newChannel(outStream);

    for (ByteBuffer inBuffer = ByteBuffer.allocate(4096);
     in.read(inBuffer) != -1;
     inBuffer.clear()) {

      inBuffer.flip();
      CharBuffer cBuffer = inputEncoding.decode(inBuffer);
      ByteBuffer outBuffer = outputEncoding.encode(cBuffer);
      while (outBuffer.hasRemaining()) out.write(outBuffer);
    }
  }
}
```

The convert() method wraps a channel around the InputStream and another channel around the OutputStream. Data is read from the input channel into a ByteBuffer. Next, this buffer is flipped and decoded into a CharBuffer using the input Charset. That CharBuffer is then reencoded into a new ByteBuffer using the output encoding. Finally, this byte buffer is written onto the output channel.

Example 19-5 is simple, but it has one inobvious bug. What if the input data in the buffer does not contain a complete multibyte character? That is, what if it reads in only the first byte of a 2-byte or longer character? In this case, that character is replaced by the replacement character (usually a question mark). However, suppose you have a long stream that requires multiple reads from the channel into the buffer—that is, say the entire stream can't fit into the buffer at once. Or suppose the channel is nonblocking and the first couple of bytes of a 3- or 4-byte character have arrived, but the last bytes haven't. In other words, suppose the data in the buffer is malformed, even though the stream itself isn't. The encode() method does not leave anything in the buffer. It will drain the buffer completely and use replacement characters at the end if necessary. This has the potential to corrupt good data, and it can be a very hard bug to diagnose because 99% of the time you're not going to hit the fencepost condition that triggers the bug. (One way to make it a little more likely to show up is to reduce the size of the buffer to something quite small, even three or four bytes.)

You can avoid this problem by using a CharsetDecoder object directly to fill the buffer with data repeatedly, and decode it only once all the data has been placed in the buffer.

# CharsetEncoder and CharsetDecoder

The decode( ) and encode( ) methods suffice for most simple use cases (as do the String constructors and the getBytes( ) method). However, for more sophisticated needs, you may wish to use an explicit CharsetEncoder or CharsetDecoder. These aren't as simple as the previous methods, but they allow greater customization. For example, you can configure them to throw an exception if they encounter an unencodable character rather than replacing it with a question mark. Let's address the encoder first. The decoder is similar, except it runs in the opposite direction.

### Encoding

The constructor in the CharsetEncoder class is protected. Encoders are created by first getting a Charset object for the encoding and then invoking its newEncoder( ) method:

```
public abstract CharsetEncoder newEncoder( )
  throws UnupportedOperationException
```

This method throws an UnupportedOperationException if this is one of those uncommon character sets that does not support encoding. For example:

```
Charset utf8 = Charset.forName("UTF-8");
CharsetEncoder encoder = utf8.newEncoder( );
```

The encoder encodes bytes from a CharBuffer into a ByteBuffer:

```
public final CoderResult encode(CharBuffer in, ByteBuffer out,
  boolean endOfInput)
```

encode( ) reads as much data as possible from the CharBuffer and writes the encoded bytes into the ByteBuffer. You normally call this method repeatedly, passing in more data each time. All but the last time, you pass false as the final argument, indicating that this is not the end of the input data. The last time you call encode( ), you pass true. (If necessary, you can encode until there are no bytes remaining while passing false and then encode zero bytes while passing true, but you do need to pass true the last and only the last time you call the method.) Finally, you invoke the flush( ) method to write any last bytes that need to be written. The output buffer can then be flipped and drained somewhere else.

For example, this method converts a string into a ByteBuffer containing the UTF-8 encoding of the string:

```
public static ByteBuffer convertToUTF8(String s) {
  CharBuffer input = CharBuffer.wrap(s);
  Charset utf8 = Charset.forName("UTF-8");
  CharsetEncoder encoder = utf8.newEncoder( );
  ByteBuffer output = ByteBuffer.allocate(s.length( )*3);
  while (input.hasRemaining( )) {
    encoder.encode(input, output, false);
  }
  encoder.encode(input, output, true);
  encoder.flush(output);
  output.flip( );
  return output;
}
```

In UTF-8, each char in the string is encoded into at most three bytes in the output array, so there's no possibility of underflow or overflow. However, there is a small chance of the data being malformed if surrogate characters are used incorrectly in the input string. Java doesn't check for this. To check for it (and you should, or this code could get caught in an infinite loop), you need to inspect the return value from encode( ). The return value is a CoderResult object that has five methods to tell you what happened:

```
public boolean isError( )
public boolean isUnderflow( )
public boolean isOverflow( )
public boolean isMalformed( )
public boolean isUnmappable( )
```

(There's no result for success. If the encoding succeeded, these five methods each return false.) Inspecting the result, and throwing an error if the encoding failed for any reason, the convertToUTF8( ) method now becomes this:

```
public static ByteBuffer convertToUTF8(String s) throws IOException {
  CharBuffer input = CharBuffer.wrap(s);
  Charset utf8 = Charset.forName("UTF-8");
  CharsetEncoder encoder = utf8.newEncoder( );
  ByteBuffer output = ByteBuffer.allocate(s.length( )*3);
  while (input.hasRemaining( )) {
    CoderResult result = encoder.encode(input, output, false);
    if (result.isError( )) throw new IOException("Could not encode " + s);
  }
  encoder.encode(input, output, true);
  encoder.flush(output);
  output.flip( );
  return output;
}
```

CharsetEncoder also has a convenience method that encodes all the remaining text in a character buffer and returns a ByteBuffer of the necessary size:

```
public final ByteBuffer encode(CharBuffer in) throws CharacterCodingException
```

This avoids problems with underflow and overflow. However, if the data is malformed or a character cannot be converted into the output character set, it may throw a CharacterCodingException. (This is configurable with the onMalformedInput( ) and onUnmappableCharacter( ) methods.)

You can use a single CharsetEncoder object to encode multiple buffers in sequence. If you do this, you will need to call the reset( ) method between buffers:

```
public final CharsetEncoder reset( )
```

This returns the same CharsetEncoder object to enable method invocation chaining.

### Decoding

The CharsetDecoder class is almost a mirror image of CharsetEncoder. It converts from bytes to characters rather than from characters to bytes. The constructor in the CharsetDecoder class is protected too. Instead, an encoder for a character is created by first getting a Charset object for the encoding and then invoking its newDecoder( ) method:

```
Charset utf8 = Charset.forName("UTF-8");
CharsetDecoder decoder = utf8.newDecoder( );
```

The decoder decodes bytes from a ByteBuffer into a CharBuffer:

```
public final CoderResult decode(ByteBuffer in, CharBuffer out, boolean endOfInput)
```

As much data as possible is read from the ByteBuffer, converted into chars, and written into the CharBuffer. You call this method repeatedly, passing in more data each time. All but the last time, you pass false as the final argument. The last time you call decode( ), pass true. Finally, invoke the flush( ) method to clear any last state. At this point, the final data is flushed into the output buffer, which can be flipped and drained somewhere else. For example, this method converts a byte array containing UTF-8 text into a string:

```
public static String convertFromUTF8(byte[] data) throws IOException {
  ByteBuffer input = ByteBuffer.wrap(data);
  Charset utf8 = Charset.forName("UTF-8");
  CharsetDecoder decoder = utf8.newDecoder( );
  CharBuffer output = CharBuffer.allocate(data.length);
  while (input.hasRemaining( )) {
    CoderResult result = decoder.decode(input, output, false);
    if (result.isError()) throw new IOException( );
  }
  decoder.decode(input, output, true);
  decoder.flush(output);
  output.flip( );
  return output.toString( );
}
```

CharsetDecoder also has a convenience method that decodes all the remaining data in a byte buffer and returns a CharBuffer of the necessary size:

```
public final CharBuffer decode(ByteBuffer in) throws CharacterCodingException
```

This avoids problems with underflow and overflow. However, if the data is malformed or a character cannot be converted into the output character set, it may throw a `CharacterCodingException`. (This is configurable with the `onMalformedInput()` and `onUnmappableCharacter()` methods.)

You can reuse a single `CharsetDecoder` object to decode multiple buffers in sequence. If you do this, you will need to call the `reset()` method between buffers:

```
public final CharsetDecoder reset()
```

## Error handling

Each call to `encode()` or `decode()` returns a `CoderResult` object. This object tells you whether the encoding succeeded, and, if so, how many bytes were encoded. Normally, all you care about is whether the encoding succeeded or not. This is revealed by the `isError()` method:

```
public boolean isError()
```

However, if you care about why the encoding failed, several more methods in `CoderResult` reveal the reason. Encoding can fail because there were insufficient characters to encode into bytes:

```
public boolean isUnderflow()
```

This might happen if only the first half of a surrogate pair were supplied at the end of the input buffer.

Encoding or decoding can fail because there are too many characters to encode into the output buffer:

```
public boolean isOverflow()
```

Decoding can fail because the data is malformed in some way:

```
public boolean isMalformed()
```

For instance, this might happen in UTF-8 if the bytes of a multibyte character were shuffled.

Encoding can fail because the character you're trying to encode is unmappable:

```
public boolean isUnmappable()
```

For instance, this would happen if you were trying to encode the Greek letter $\alpha$ using the ISO-8859-1 character set because this character set does not contain the letter $\alpha$.

Some charsets may also tell you the length of the bad data that caused the encoding or decoding to fail:

```
public int length() throws UnsupportedOperationException
```

However, not all will, and this method may throw an `UnsupportedOperationException`.

The whole idea of returning a special object to specify the error is a little strange for Java. This is exactly what exceptions were designed to replace. If you like, you can cause the CoderResult to throw an equivalent exception instead, using the throwException() method:

```
public void throwException() throws CharacterCodingException
```

Depending on the type of the error, this throws a BufferUnderflowException, BufferOverflowException, MalformedInputException, or UnmappableCharacterException. For example:

```
CoderResult result = decoder.decode(input, output, false);
if (result.isError()) result.throwException();
```

Sometimes you want to throw the exception and then stop reading or writing. For example, this would be appropriate if you were feeding data to an XML parser. However, if you're in the less draconian world of HTML, you might want to just keep on trucking. To loosen up this way, you can set the action for malformed input and/or unmappable characters to CodingErrorAction.IGNORE or CodingErrorAction.REPLACE with onUnmappableCharacter() and onMalformedInput():

```
public final CharsetEncoder onMalformedInput(CodingErrorAction action)
public final CharsetEncoder onUnmappableCharacter(CodingErrorAction action)
```

Ignoring simply drops bad data while replacing changes the bad data to a specified replacement character (usually the question mark, by default). There's no separate method for overflow and underflow errors. They count as malformed input. For example, these statements tell a CharsetEncoder to drop malformed input and to replace unmappable characters:

```
encoder.onMalformedInput(CodingErrorAction.IGNORE);
encoder.onUnmappableCharacter(CodingErrorAction.REPLACE);
```

You can also set the action to CodingErrorAction.REPORT. This is usually the default and simply indicates that the encoder or decoder should return an error in a CoderResult or throw a CharacterCodingException.

The replaceWith() method changes the replacement bytes the encoder uses when it encounters an unmappable character while operating in replace mode:

```
public final CharsetEncoder replaceWith(byte[] replacement)
  throws IllegalArgumentException
```

Not all byte sequences are legal here. The replacement array must contain characters allowed in the encoding. If not, this method throws an IllegalArgumentException.

There's also a getter method for this value:

```
public final byte[] replacement()
```

The CharsetDecoder class has similar methods, except that it uses a string replacement value instead of a byte replacement value:

```
public final CharsetDecoder replaceWith(String newReplacement)
public final String replacement()
```

## Measurement

A CharsetEncoder can estimate the number of bytes that will be required for each char that's encoded:

```
public final float averageBytesPerChar( )
```

This may be exact for some encodings, but for variable-width encodings such as UTF-8 it's only approximate. Java estimates UTF-8 as averaging 1.1 bytes per character, but the exact ratio can vary widely from one string to the next.

A CharsetEncoder can also tell you the theoretical maximum number of bytes that will be needed for each character:

```
public final float maxBytesPerChar( )
```

Both of these values can be useful in choosing the size of the ByteBuffer to encode into.

## Encodability

Encoders have the useful ability to tell whether or not a particular character, string, or character sequence can be encoded in a given encoding:

```
public boolean canEncode(char c)
public boolean canEncode(CharSequence cs)
```

For example, this is very useful for XML serializers writing non-Unicode encodings. These need to know whether any given string can be written directly or needs to be escaped with a numeric character reference such as   or  . Serializers that operate in Java 1.3 and earlier have to either use undocumented classes in the sun packages, use really ugly hacks where they first convert the bytes into a string and then look to see if a replacement character was used, or implement their own lookup tables for all this data. In Java 1.4 and later, by contrast, serializers can just create an appropriate encoder and then call canEncode( ).

# CHAPTER 20

# Readers and Writers

You're probably going to experience a little déjà vu in this chapter. The java.io. Writer class is modeled on the java.io.OutputStream class. The java.io.Reader class is modeled on the java.io.InputStream class. The names and signatures of the methods of the Reader and Writer classes are similar (sometimes identical) to the names and signatures of the methods of the InputStream and OutputStream classes. The patterns these classes follow are similar as well. Filtered input and output streams are chained to other streams in their constructors. Filtered readers and writers are chained to other readers and writers in their constructors. InputStream and OutputStream are abstract superclasses that identify common functionality in the concrete subclasses. Likewise, Reader and Writer are abstract superclasses that identify common functionality in the concrete subclasses. The difference between readers and writers and input and output streams is that streams are fundamentally byte-based while readers and writers are fundamentally character-based. Where an input stream reads a byte, a reader reads a character. Where an output stream writes a byte, a writer writes a character.

While bytes are a more or less universal concept, characters are not. As you learned in the last chapter, the same character can be encoded differently in different character sets, and different character sets include different characters. Characters can even have different sizes in different character sets. For example, ASCII and Latin-1 use 1-byte characters. UTF-8 uses characters of varying width between one and four bytes.

A language that supports international text must separate the reading and writing of raw bytes from the reading and writing of characters. Classes that read characters must be able to parse a variety of character encodings, not just ASCII, and translate them into the language's native character set. Classes that write characters must be able to translate the language's native character set into a variety of formats and write those. In Java, this task is performed by the InputStreamReader and OutputStreamWriter classes.

# The java.io.Writer Class

The Writer class is abstract, just like OutputStream is abstract. You won't have any pure instances of Writer that are not also instances of some concrete subclass of Writer. However, many of the subclasses of Writer differ primarily in the targets of the text they write, just as many concrete subclasses of OutputStream differ only in the targets of the data they write. Most of the time you don't care about the difference between FileOutputStream and ByteArrayOutputStream. Similarly, most of the time you won't care about the difference between FileWriter and StringWriter. You'll just use the methods of the common superclass, java.io.Writer.

You use a writer almost exactly like you use an output stream. Rather than writing bytes, you write chars. The write( ) method writes a subarray from the char array text starting at offset and continuing for length characters:

```
public abstract void write(char[] text, int offset, int length)
    throws IOException
```

For example, given some Writer object w, you can write the string Testing 1-2-3 like this:

```
char[] test = {'T', 'e', 's', 't', 'i', 'n', 'g', ' ',
               '1', '-', '2', '-', '3'};
w.write(test, 0, test.length);
```

This method is abstract. Concrete subclasses that convert chars into bytes according to a specified encoding and write those bytes onto an underlying stream must override this method. An IOException may be thrown if the underlying stream's write( ) method throws an IOException. You can also write a single character, an entire array of characters, a string, or a substring:

```
public void write(int c) throws IOException
public void write(char[] text) throws IOException
public void write(String s) throws IOException
public void write(String s, int offset, int length) throws IOException
```

The default implementations of these four methods convert their first argument into an array of chars and pass that to write(char[] text, int offset, int length). Specific subclasses may provide more efficient implementations of these methods.

 This is one of the few instances where the general structure of the Writer and the OutputStream classes diverge, though not in a very significant way. In OutputStream, the fundamental, abstract method that must be overridden by subclasses is the write( ) method that writes a single byte. OutputStream's multibyte write( ) methods are implemented in terms of the single-byte write( ) method whereas Writer's single-character write( ) method is implemented in terms of a multicharacter write( ) method.

Beginning in Java 5, the `Writer` class implements the `Appendable` interface. This gives it three more methods:

```
public Writer append(char c) throws IOException  // Java 5
public Writer append(CharSequence sequence)throws IOException // Java 5
public Writer append(CharSequence sequence,int start,int end)// Java 5
  throws IOException
```

The `append(char)` method behaves the same as `write(char)` with the single difference that it returns this `Writer` object to allow method invocation chaining. The other two methods behave the same as the equivalent `write(String)` and `write(String, int, int)` methods. However, they accept any class that implements `CharSequence`, not just `String`.

Like output streams, writers may be buffered. To force the write to take place, call `flush( )`:

```
public abstract void flush() throws IOException
```

The `close( )` method closes the writer and releases any resources associated with it:

```
public abstract void close() throws IOException
```

This flushes the writer and closes the underlying output stream.

 In Java 5, `Writer` implements `Flushable` and `Closeable`. However, it still has these two methods in 1.4 and earlier.

# The OutputStreamWriter Class

`java.io.Writer` is an abstract class. Its most basic concrete subclass is `OutputStreamWriter`:

```
public class OutputStreamWriter extends Writer
```

Its constructor connects a character writer to an underlying output stream:

```
public OutputStreamWriter(OutputStream out)
public OutputStreamWriter(OutputStream out, String encoding) throws
  UnsupportedEncodingException
```

The first constructor configures the writer to encode text in the platform's default encoding. The second constructor specifies an encoding. For example, this code attaches an `OutputStreamWriter` to `System.out` with the default encoding:

```
OutputStreamWriter osw = new OutputStreamWriter(System.out);
```

On U.S. and Western European systems, the default encoding is usually Cp1252 on Windows, ISO 8859-1 (Latin-1) on Unix and Linux, and MacRoman on Macs. More recent Linuxes may use UTF-8 everywhere. Whatever the default is, you can read it from the system property `file.encoding`:

```
String defaultEncoding = System.getProperty("file.encoding");
```

On the other hand, if you want to write a file encoded in ISO 8859-7 (ASCII plus Greek) you'd have to do this:

```
FileOutputStream fos = new FileOutputStream("greek.txt");
OutputStreamWriter greekWriter = new OutputStreamWriter(fos, "8859_7");
```

You should almost never use the default encoding. It's likely to cause problems as files are moved between platforms and countries, especially if the document format contains no means of indicating the encoding. If the file format does not specify a different encoding, choose UTF-8:

```
FileOutputStream fos = new FileOutputStream("data.txt");
OutputStreamWriter utfWriter = new OutputStreamWriter(fos, "UTF-8");
```

There are reasons to pick other encodings, especially when dealing with legacy software and formats that mandate something else. However, unless specified otherwise, you should choose UTF-8. It has the best mix of interoperability, robustness, compactness, and script support.

The write( ) methods convert characters to bytes according to the specified character encoding and write those bytes onto the underlying output stream:

```
public void write(int c) throws IOException
public void write(char[] text, int offset, int length) throws IOException
public void write(String s, int offset, int length) throws IOException
```

Once the Writer is constructed, writing the characters is easy:

```
String  arete = "\u03B1\u03C1\u03B5\u03C4\u03B7";
greekWriter.write(arete, 0, arete.length( ));
```

The String variable arete contains the Unicode-escaped encoding of αρετη, the Greek word for excellence. The second line writes this word in the ISO 8859-7 character set. In this encoding, these five Unicode characters (10 bytes) become the five bytes 225, 241, 229, 244, 231. You don't have to worry about exactly how this conversion is performed. You just have to construct the writer, write the string, and let Java do the grunt work of figuring out which Unicode characters map to which 8859-7 characters.

Unicode is a fairly large character set. Most other character sets don't have all the characters in Unicode. Writing a character that doesn't exist in the current character set produces a substitution character, usually a question mark.

The getEncoding( ) method returns a string containing the name of the encoding used by this writer:

```
public String getEncoding( )
```

Example 20-1 loops through every nonsurrogate, defined character in the Basic Multilingual Plane (BMP) and writes each one into the file given on the command line, using the specified character encoding. If no character encoding is specified, the platform's default encoding is used. If no file is specified, System.out is used.

---

*Example 20-1. Printing all the BMP characters*

```java
import java.io.*;

public class UnicodeBMPTable {

  public static void main(String[] args) throws IOException {
    // Use platform default with a fallback to Latin-1 if necessary
    String encoding = System.getProperty("file.encoding", "ISO-8859-1");
    String lineSeparator = System.getProperty("line.separator", "\r\n");

    OutputStream target = System.out;
    if (args.length > 0) target = new FileOutputStream(args[0]);
    if (args.length > 1) encoding = args[1];

    OutputStreamWriter out = null;
    try {
      out = new OutputStreamWriter(target, encoding);
    }
    catch (UnsupportedEncodingException ex) {
      // use platform default encoding
      out = new OutputStreamWriter(target);
    }

    try {
      for (int i = Character.MIN_VALUE; i <= Character.MAX_VALUE; i++) {
        // Skip undefined code points; these are not characters
        if (!Character.isDefined(i)) continue;

        char c = (char) i;
        // Surrogates are not full characters so skip them;
        // this requires Java 5
        if (Character.isHighSurrogate(c) || Character.isLowSurrogate(c)) continue;

        out.write(i + ":\t" + c + lineSeparator);
      }
    }
    finally {
      out.close( );
    }
  }
}
```

Here's a sample of the file this program writes when the MacRoman encoding is specified:

```
213:    Ō
214:    Ö
215:    ?
216:    Ø
217:    Ù
218:    Ú
219:    Û
220:    Ü
```

```
221:    ?
222:    ?
223:    ß
224:    à
```

MacRoman is a one byte encoding so it can only hold about 256 different characters. The remaining characters are all replaced by the substitution character, a question mark. Unicode characters 215, 221, and 222 just don't exist in this character set.

# The java.io.Reader Class

You use a reader almost exactly as you use an input stream. Rather than reading bytes, you read characters. The basic read( ) method reads a specified number of characters from the underlying input stream into an array starting at a given offset:

```
public abstract int read(char[] text, int offset, int length)
    throws IOException
```

This read( ) method returns the number of characters actually read. As with input streams reading bytes, there may not be as many characters available as you requested. Also like the read( ) method of an input stream, it returns −1 when it detects the end of the data.

This read( ) method is abstract. Concrete subclasses that read bytes from some source must override this method. An IOException may be thrown if the underlying stream's read( ) method throws an IOException or an encoding error is detected.

You can also fill an array with characters using this method:

```
public int read(char[] text) throws IOException
```

This is equivalent to invoking read(text, 0, text.length). Thus, it also returns the number of characters read and throws an IOException when the underlying stream throws an IOException or when an encoding error is detected. The following method reads a single character and returns it:

```
public int read( ) throws IOException
```

Although an int is returned, this int is always between 0 and 65,535 and may be cast to a char without losing information. All three read( ) methods block until some input is available, an I/O error occurs, or the end of the stream is reached.

In Java 5, Reader implements the java.lang.Readable interface which requires the ability to read directly into a CharBuffer starting at the buffer's current position:

```
public int read(CharBuffer target) // Java 5
    throws IOException, NullPointerException, ReadOnlyBufferException
```

Like the other read( ) methods, this method returns the number of characters read, or −1 on end of stream.

You can skip a certain number of characters. This method also blocks until some characters are available. It returns the number of characters skipped or −1 if the end of stream is reached.

```
public long skip(long n) throws IOException
```

The ready( ) method returns true if the reader is ready to be read from or false if it isn't. Generally, this means the underlying stream has available data.

```
public boolean ready( ) throws IOException
```

This is not quite the same as InputStream's available( ) method. available( ) returns an int specifying how many bytes are available to be read. However, it's not always possible to tell how many characters are available in a stream without actually reading them, particularly with encodings that use characters of different widths (such as UTF-8, where a character may be one, two, three, or four bytes long).

Like input streams, some readers support marking and resetting, and some don't. The markSupported( ) method returns true if the Reader supports marking and resetting or false if it doesn't.

```
public boolean markSupported( )
public void mark(int readAheadLimit) throws IOException
public void reset( ) throws IOException
```

The close( ) method closes the Reader and releases any resources the reader held:

```
public abstract void close( ) throws IOException
```

# The InputStreamReader Class

The most important concrete subclass of Reader is InputStreamReader:

```
public class InputStreamReader extends Reader
```

The constructor connects a character reader to an underlying input stream:

```
public InputStreamReader(InputStream in)
public InputStreamReader(InputStream in, String encoding)
 throws UnsupportedEncodingException
```

The first constructor uses the platform's default encoding, as given by the system property file.encoding. The second one uses the specified encoding. For example, to attach an InputStreamReader to System.in with the default encoding:

```
InputStreamReader isr = new InputStreamReader(System.in);
```

If you want to read a file encoded in Latin-5 (ASCII plus Turkish, as specified by ISO 8859-9), you might do this:

```
FileInputStream fin = new FileInputStream("turkish.txt");
InputStreamReader isr = new InputStreamReader(fin, "8859_9");
```

In Java 1.4 and later, you can specify the encoding as a Charset or CharsetDecoder object instead:

```
public InputStreamReader(InputStream in, Charset encoding)  // Java 1.4
public InputStreamReader(InputStream in, CharsetDecoder decoder)  // Java 1.4
```

The read( ) methods read bytes from an underlying input stream and convert those bytes to characters according to the specified encoding:

```
public int read( ) throws IOException
public int read(char[] text, int offset, int length) throws IOException
public int read(CharBuffer target) // Java 5
   throws IOException, NullPointerException, ReadOnlyBufferException
```

The getEncoding( ) method returns a string containing the name of the encoding used by this reader:

```
public String getEncoding( )
```

The remaining two methods just override methods from java.io.Reader but behave identically from the perspective of the programmer:

```
public boolean ready( ) throws IOException
public void    close( ) throws IOException
```

The close( ) method does close the underlying input stream.

InputStreamReader does not itself support marking and resetting, though it can be chained to a reader that does.

Example 20-2 uses an InputStreamReader to read a file in a user-specified encoding. The FileConverter reads the name of the input file, the name of the output file, the input encoding, and the output encoding. Characters that are not available in the output character set are replaced by the substitution character.

*Example 20-2. CharacterSetConverter*

```
import java.io.*;

public class StreamRecoder {

  public static void main(String[] args) {

    if (args.length < 2) {
      System.err.println(
       "Usage: java StreamRecoder "
        + "infile_encoding outfile_encoding infile outfile");
      return;
    }

    InputStreamReader isr = null;
    OutputStreamWriter osw = null;
    try {
      File infile = new File(args[2]);
      File outfile = new File(args[3]);
```

*Example 20-2. CharacterSetConverter (continued)*

```java
    if (outfile.exists()
      && infile.getCanonicalPath().equals(outfile.getCanonicalPath())) {
      System.err.println("Can't convert file in place");
      return;
    }

    FileInputStream fin = new FileInputStream(infile);
    FileOutputStream fout = new FileOutputStream(outfile);
    isr = new InputStreamReader(fin, args[0]);
    osw = new OutputStreamWriter(fout, args[1]);

    while (true) {
      int c = isr.read();
      if (c == -1) break;  // end of stream
      osw.write(c);
    }
    osw.close();
    isr.close();
  }
  catch (IOException ex) {
    System.err.println(ex);
    ex.printStackTrace();
  }
  finally {
    if (isr != null) {
      try {
        isr.close();
      } catch (IOException ex) {
        ex.printStackTrace();
      }
    }
    if (osw != null) {
      try {
        osw.close();
      }
      catch (IOException ex) {
        ex.printStackTrace();
      }
    }
  }
 }
}
```

Since this is just a simple example, I haven't put a lot of effort into the user interface. A more realistic command-line interface would provide a set of flags and sensible defaults. Even better would be a graphical user interface. I'll demonstrate that at the end of the chapter, when we return to the file viewer program.

Example 20-2 is very similar to the Recoder class in Example 19-3 in the previous chapter. However, that class accessed the CharsetEncoder and CharsetDecoder more directly. This is a higher level approach that hides a lot of the implementation detail, which makes it much simpler and easier to understand. Most of the time in streaming situations, it's going to be a lot easier to use `InputStreamReader` and/or `OutputStreamWriter` than `Charset` or `CharsetEncoder`/`CharsetDecoder`. `Charset`, `CharsetEncoder`, and `CharsetDecoder` fit better when you have one large block of text or bytes to encode or decode rather than an ongoing stream. `Charset`, `CharsetEncoder`, and `CharsetDecoder` also offer a few more configuration options, especially for handling encoding errors in the input data. However, usually the way `InputStreamReader` and `OutputStreamWriter` handle this (replacing each malformed byte with the default substitution character) is fine.

## Encoding Heuristics

There's no 100% guaranteed way to determine the encoding of an arbitrary file or stream. However, you can make some reasonable guesses that are likely to be more correct than not.

Unicode files are especially easy to detect because most such files begin with a byte order mark. This is the Unicode zero-width nonbreaking space character that has code point 0xFEFF. The byte-swapped character 0xFFFE is never a legal Unicode character. Furthermore the single bytes 0xFF and 0XFE are uncommon in most single-byte encodings like Latin-1 and MacRoman, unlikely to occur in sequence, and unlikely to occur at the beginning of a stream. Therefore, a stream that begins with the two bytes 0XFF and 0xFE in that order is almost certainly encoded in big-endian UTF-16. A stream that starts with the opposite order (0XFE and 0xFF) is almost certainly encoded in little-endian UTF-16.

In UTF-8, the zero-width nonbreaking space is represented by the three bytes 0xEF 0xBB 0xBF, always in that order. Thus, any file that begins with these three bytes is almost certainly UTF-8. However, not all UTF-8 files begin with a byte order mark, but UTF-8 is a very picky standard, and it's unlikely that any non-UTF-8 file will accidentally parse correctly as UTF-8. If you think a file might be UTF-8, try reading a few hundred characters as UTF-8. If there are no exceptions, chances are very good it is UTF-8.

Some other encodings of Unicode such as UTF-32 can be also be detected by inspecting the byte order mark. However, these are mostly of theoretical interest. I've never encountered one in the wild.

If a file isn't Unicode, life is tougher. Most single-byte character sets are supersets of ASCII, so even if you guess wrong, the majority of the text is likely to come through unchanged. Latin-1 misread as MacRoman or vice versa isn't pretty. However, it is intelligible in most cases.

If you have some idea of the file type, there may be other ways to guess the encoding. For instance, all XML documents that are not written in Unicode must begin with an XML declaration that includes an encoding declaration:

```
<?xml version="1.0" encoding="SJIS"?>
```

Other than Unicode and EBCDIC, most character sets are supersets of ASCII so you can assume the encoding is ASCII, read far enough in the stream to find the encoding declaration, then back up and reread the document with the correct encoding. To detect Unicode, look for a byte order mark. To detect EBCDIC-encoded XML, look for the initial four bytes 0x4C 0x6F 0xA7 0x94 in that order. This is "<?xm" in all EBCDIC variants.

HTML is similar. You treat the file as ASCII or EBCDIC just long enough to read the encoding meta tag:

```
<meta http-equiv="content-type" content="text/html; charset=sjis" />
```

However unlike XML, HTML is case-insensitive, so you also need to look for variants like this:

```
<META Http-equiv="content-type" Content="text/html; charset=sjis" />
```

Either way, once you've found the meta element, you back up and start over once you know the encoding. (mark( ) and reset( ) are very helpful here.)

Sometimes there's metadata outside the file or stream that can help you. For instance, HTTP servers normally send a Content-type header that may include a charset parameter like this one:

```
Content-type: text/html; charset=sjis
```

If there's no explicit parameter, the protocol may give you enough information. For instance, HTTP specifies that all text/* documents are assumed to be Latin-1 (ISO-8859-1) unless explicitly specified otherwise.

Following these rules along with a smattering of local knowledge will probably suffice most of the time. If it's not enough, there are still more sophisticated tricks you can try. For instance, you can spellcheck a document in a variety of encodings and see which one generates the fewest errors for words containing non-ASCII characters. Of course, this requires you to know or make a reasonable guess at the language. That too can be done based on the stream contents if necessary. Honestly, though, very few programs need to make this level of effort.

# Character Array Readers and Writers

The ByteArrayInputStream and ByteArrayOutputStream classes use stream methods to read and write arrays of bytes. The CharArrayReader and CharArrayWriter classes use Reader and Writer methods to read and write arrays of chars. Since char arrays are purely internal to Java, this is one of the few uses of readers and writers where you don't need to concern yourself with conversions between different encodings. If you want to read arrays of text encoded in some non-Unicode encoding, you should chain a `ByteArrayInputStream` to an `InputStreamReader` instead. Similarly, to write text into a byte array in a non-Unicode encoding, just chain an `OutputStreamWriter` to a `ByteArrayOutputStream`.

## The CharArrayWriter Class

A `CharArrayWriter` maintains an internal array of chars into which successive characters are written. The array is expanded as needed. This array is stored in a protected field called buf:

```
protected char[] buf
```

The no-argument constructor creates a `CharArrayWriter` object with a 32-character buffer. This is on the small side, so you can expand it with the second constructor:

```
public CharArrayWriter()
public CharArrayWriter(int initialSize)
```

The write() methods write their characters into the buffer. If there's insufficient space in buf to hold the characters, it's expanded to at least the amount necessary to hold the extra text.

The buffer can be read in several ways. The writeTo() method copies the text in the buffer onto another Writer object:

```
public void writeTo(Writer out) throws IOException
```

The toCharArray() method returns a copy of the text in the buffer:

```
public char[] toCharArray()
```

Changes to the copy do not affect the `CharArrayWriter`'s internal data and vice versa.

The toString() method returns a string initialized from the characters stored in the buffer:

```
public String toString()
```

The size() method returns the number of characters currently stored in the buffer:

```
public int size()
```

Finally, the reset() method empties the buffer so that the writer can be reused for new data:

```
public void reset()
```

However, the internal buffer is not freed and still occupies memory. It will only be garbage collected when the writer itself is.

There is a close( ) method, but it's a no-op. In fact, you can continue writing to a CharArrayWriter after it's been closed. This should probably be classified as a bug.

For example, the following code fragment fills a char array with the Unicode Basic Multilingual Plane:

```
CharArrayWriter caw = new CharArrayWriter(65536);
for (int i = 0; i < 65536; i++) {
  caw.write(i);
}
caw.close( );
char[] unicode = caw.toCharArray( );
```

## The CharArrayReader Class

A CharArrayReader uses an array of chars as the underlying source of text to read. It is one of the few readers that does not have an underlying input stream; it has an underlying char array instead. This array is set in the constructor. Either an entire array may be used or a specified subarray beginning at offset and continuing for length characters:

```
public CharArrayReader(char[] text)
public CharArrayReader(char[] text, int offset, int length)
```

The CharArrayReader class stores a reference to the text array in a protected field called buf. A separate copy is not made. Modifying this array from outside the class can violate data encapsulation and potentially cause thread synchronization problems. The reader also stores the current position in the array (the index of the next array component that will be returned by read( )), the number of chars in the array, and the current mark, if any.

```
protected char[] buf
protected int     pos
protected int     count
protected int     markedPos
```

The read( ) methods read text from the buf array, updating the pos field as they do so. These methods behave like any other reader's read( ) methods. If the end of the array is reached, they return −1.

CharArrayReaders support marking and resetting to the limit of the length of the array. markSupported( ) returns true. mark( ) marks the current position in the stream by setting markedPos equal to pos. The readAheadLimit argument is for compatibility; its value is ignored. The reset( ) method sets pos equal to markedPos.

Finally, the close( ) method sets buf to null so that the array can be garbage collected. Attempts to read from a CharArrayReader after it's been closed throw IOExceptions.

# String Readers and Writers

The `java.io.StringReader` and `java.io.StringWriter` classes allow programmers to use `Reader` and `Writer` methods to read and write strings. Like `char` arrays, Java strings are composed of pure Unicode characters. Therefore, they're good sources of data for readers and good targets for writers. This is the other common case where readers and writers don't need to convert between different encodings.

## String Writers

This class would more accurately be called `StringBufferWriter`, but `StringWriter` is more poetic. A `StringWriter` maintains an internal `StringBuffer` to which it appends characters. This buffer can easily be converted to a string as necessary. `StringWriter` has a no-args constructor:

```
public StringWriter( )
```

There is also a constructor that allows you to specify the initial size of the internal string buffer. This isn't too important because string buffers (and, by extension, string writers) are expanded as necessary. Still, if you can estimate the size of the string in advance, it's more efficient to select a size big enough to hold all characters that will be written:

```
public StringWriter(int initialSize)
```

The `StringWriter` class has the usual collection of `write( )` methods, all of which just append their data to the `StringBuffer`.

There are `flush( )` and `close( )` methods, but both have empty method bodies, as string writers operate completely internal to Java and do not require flushing or closing. You can continue to write to a `StringWriter` even after it's been closed. This should probably be classified as a bug, and I don't recommend that you write code that relies on this behavior.

There are two ways to get the current contents of the `StringWriter`'s internal buffer. The `toString( )` method returns it as a new `String` object while the `getBuffer( )` method returns the actual buffer:

```
public String toString( )
public StringBuffer getBuffer( )
```

Strings are immutable, but changes to the buffer object returned by `getBuffer( )` change the state of the `StringWriter`.

The following code fragment creates a string containing the printable ASCII character set:

```
StringWriter sw = new StringWriter(128);
for (int i = 32; i < 127; i++) {
  sw.write(i);
}
String ascii = sw.toString( );
```

# String Readers

A `StringReader` uses the methods of the `Reader` class to get characters from a string. This is useful when you want to process each character in a string in sequential order. This class replaces the deprecated `StringBufferInputStream` class:

```
public class StringReader extends Reader
```

The single constructor sets the string that's the source of data for this reader:

```
public StringReader(String s)
```

Since string objects are immutable, the data in the string may not be changed after the `StringReader` is constructed.

Of course, the class has the usual read( ) methods, all of which read as many characters as requested from the string. These methods return −1 if the end of the string has been reached. They throw an `IOException` if the reader has been closed.

The ready( ) method returns true. Strings are always ready to be read.

String readers support marking and resetting to the limit of the string's length. markSupported( ) returns true. mark( ) marks the current position in the stream. (The readAheadLimit argument is for compatibility only; its value is ignored.) The reset( ) method moves backward in the string to the marked position.

Finally, the close( ) method sets the internal string data to null. Attempts to read from a `StringReader` after it's been closed throw IOExceptions.

Here's a simple method that uses `StringReader` to break a string into its separate characters and print them:

```java
public static void printCharacters(String s) {

    StringReader sr = new StringReader(s);
    try {
      int c;
      while ((c = sr.read()) != -1) {
        System.out.println((char) c);
      }
    }
    catch (IOException ex) {
      // should not happen; StringReaders do not throw exceptions
    }
    return;
  }
```

Admittedly, this is a contrived example. If you really needed to do this, you could just loop through the string itself using its charAt( ) method.

# Reading and Writing Files

You've already learned how to chain an `OutputStreamWriter` to a `FileOutputStream` and an `InputStreamReader` to a `FileInputStream`. Although this isn't hard, Java provides two simple utility classes that take care of the details, `java.io.FileWriter` and `java.io.FileReader`.

## FileWriter

The `FileWriter` class is a subclass of `OutputStreamWriter` that writes text files using the platform's default character encoding and buffer size. If you need to change these values, construct an `OutputStreamWriter` on a `FileOutputStream` instead.

```
public class FileWriter extends OutputStreamWriter
```

This class has four constructors:

```
public FileWriter(String fileName) throws IOException
public FileWriter(String fileName, boolean append) throws IOException
public FileWriter(File file) throws IOException
public FileWriter(FileDescriptor fd)
```

The first constructor opens a file and positions the file pointer at the beginning of the file. Any text in the file is overwritten. For example:

```
FileWriter fw = new FileWriter("36.html");
```

The second constructor allows you to specify that new text is appended to the existing contents of the file rather than overwriting it by setting the second argument to true. For example:

```
FileWriter fw = new FileWriter("36.html", true);
```

The third and fourth constructors use a `File` object and a `FileDescriptor`, respectively, instead of a filename to identify the file to be written to. Any preexisting contents in a file so opened are overwritten.

You use the standard `Writer` methods like `write( )`, `flush( )`, and `close( )` to write the text in the file.

## FileReader

The `FileReader` class is a subclass of `InputStreamReader` that reads text files using the platform's default character encoding. If you need to change the encoding, construct an `InputStreamReader` chained to a `FileInputStream` instead.

```
public class FileReader extends InputStreamReader
```

This class has three constructors that differ only in how the file to be read is specified:

```
public FileReader(String fileName) throws FileNotFoundException
public FileReader(File file) throws FileNotFoundException
public FileReader(FileDescriptor fd)
```

Only the constructors are declared in this class. You use the standard Reader methods like read( ), ready( ), and close( ) to read the text in the file.

FileReader and FileWriter always use the local default encoding for converting characters to and from bytes. This is rarely what you want. You should almost always specify the encoding explicitly, or perhaps autodetect it. FileReader and FileWriter are a minor convenience at most. Instead of using them, you can easily chain an InputStreamReader to a FileInputStream or an OutputStreamWriter to a FileOutputStream. Even if you know you want the default encoding, you're better off requesting it explicitly to make your intention clear.

# Buffered Readers and Writers

Input and output can be time-consuming operations. It's often quicker to read or write text in large chunks rather than in many separate smaller pieces, even when you only process the text in the smaller pieces. The java.io.BufferedReader and java.io.BufferedWriter classes provide internal character buffers. Text that's written to a buffered writer is stored in the internal buffer and only written to the underlying writer when the buffer fills up or is flushed. Likewise, reading text from a buffered reader may cause more characters to be read than were requested; the extra characters are stored in an internal buffer. Future reads first access characters from the internal buffer and only access the underlying reader when the buffer is emptied.

Even if the underlying stream is buffered, it still pays to buffer the reader or writer too. Many character conversions can be done more quickly in blocks than they can on individual characters, irrespective of I/O speed. That is, for maximum performance use a BufferedReader *and* a BufferedInputStream or a BufferedWriter *and* a BufferedOutputStream.

## Buffering Writes

The java.io.BufferedWriter class is a subclass of java.io.Writer that you chain to another Writer class to buffer characters. This allows more efficient writing of text.

```
public class BufferedWriter extends Writer
```

There are two constructors. One has a default buffer size (8192 characters); the other lets you specify the buffer size:

```
public BufferedWriter(Writer out)
public BufferedWriter(Writer out, int size)
```

For example:

```
BufferedWriter bw = new BufferedWriter(new FileWriter("37.html"));
```

BufferedWriter overrides most of its superclass's methods, but all changes are purely internal. write( ), flush( ), close( ), etc. are all used exactly as they are for any writer object.

There is one new method in this class, newLine( ). This method writes a platform-dependent line terminator string: \n on Unix, \r on the Mac, \r\n on Windows. The value of this string is taken from the system property line.separator.

```
public String newLine( ) throws IOException
```

 Do not use the newLine( ) method if you're writing network code such as an HTTP server. Instead, explicitly write the carriage return/line-feed pair. Most network protocols specify a \r\n line separator, regardless of host-platform conventions.

Example 20-3 is a revised version of Example 20-1 that uses a BufferedWriter to increase efficiency and handle platform-dependent line separators.

*Example 20-3. BufferedUnicodeTable*

```
import java.io.*;

public class BufferedBMPTable {

  public static void main(String[] args) throws IOException {
    // Use platform default with a fallback to Latin-1 if necessary
    String encoding = System.getProperty("file.encoding", "ISO-8859-1");
    String lineSeparator = System.getProperty("line.separator", "\r\n");

    OutputStream target = System.out;
    if (args.length > 0) target = new FileOutputStream(args[0]);
    if (args.length > 1) encoding = args[1];

    BufferedWriter out = null;
    try {
      out = new BufferedWriter(new OutputStreamWriter(target, encoding));
    }
    catch (UnsupportedEncodingException ex) { // platform default encoding
      out = new BufferedWriter(new OutputStreamWriter(target));
    }

    try {
      for (int i = Character.MIN_VALUE; i <= Character.MAX_VALUE; i++) {
```

*Example 20-3. BufferedUnicodeTable (continued)*

```
        if (!Character.isDefined(i)) continue;
        char c = (char) i;
        if (Character.isHighSurrogate(c) || Character.isLowSurrogate(c)) continue;

        out.write(i + ":\t" + c);
        out.newLine();
      }
    }
    finally {
      out.close();
    }
  }
}
```

This is actually not the fastest you can go. BufferedWriter is internally synchronized. Each call to one of its methods is atomic. If two threads try to write onto the same BufferedWriter at the same time, one of them blocks. This prevents the threads from corrupting the data. However, this synchronization has a performance cost, even when only one thread has access to the writer. You can often improve performance by replacing the stock BufferedWriter from java.io with an unsynchronized version such as shown in Example 20-4. When you don't need to worry about synchronization, this version can increase speed by 30–50%, though as always exact performance gains are likely to vary from one VM to the next.

*Example 20-4. UnsynchronizedBufferedWriter*

```
package com.elharo.io;

import java.io.*;

public class UnsynchronizedBufferedWriter extends Writer {

  private final static int CAPACITY = 8192;

  private char[]  buffer = new char[CAPACITY];
  private int     position = 0;
  private Writer  out;
  private boolean closed = false;

  public UnsynchronizedBufferedWriter(Writer out) {
    this.out = out;
  }

  public void write(char[] text, int offset, int length) throws IOException {
    checkClosed();
    while (length > 0) {
      int n = Math.min(CAPACITY - position, length);
      System.arraycopy(text, offset, buffer, position, n);
      position += n;
      offset += n;
```

*Example 20-4. UnsynchronizedBufferedWriter (continued)*

```java
        length -= n;
        if (position >= CAPACITY) flushInternal( );
    }
}

public void write(String s) throws IOException {
    write(s, 0, s.length( ));
}

public void write(String s, int offset, int length) throws IOException {
    checkClosed( );
    while (length > 0) {
        int n = Math.min(CAPACITY - position, length);
        s.getChars(offset, offset + n, buffer, position);
        position += n;
        offset += n;
        length -= n;
        if (position >= CAPACITY) flushInternal( );
    }
}

public void write(int c) throws IOException {
    checkClosed( );
    if (position >= CAPACITY) flushInternal( );
    buffer[position] = (char) c;
    position++;
}

public void flush( ) throws IOException {
    flushInternal( );
    out.flush( );
}

private void flushInternal( ) throws IOException {
    if (position != 0) {
        out.write(buffer, 0, position);
        position = 0;
    }
}

public void close( ) throws IOException {
    closed = true;
    this.flush( );
    out.close( );
}

private void checkClosed( ) throws IOException {
    if (closed) throw new IOException("Writer is closed");
}
}
```

All characters are first written into an internal byte array of length 8192. Only when that buffer fills up is it flushed to the underlying writer. The java.io.BufferedWriter class is organized very much like this, except that it also has a number of synchronized blocks to permit threadsafe usage.

## Buffering Reads

BufferedReader is a subclass of Reader that is chained to another Reader class to buffer input. This allows more efficient reading of characters and lines.

```
public class BufferedReader extends Reader
```

For example:

```
BufferedReader br = new BufferedReader(new FileReader("37.html"));
```

There are two constructors. One has a default buffer size (8192 characters); the other requires the programmer to specify the buffer size:

```
public BufferedReader(Reader in, int buffer_size)
public BufferedReader(Reader in)
```

In a BufferedReader, the two multicharacter read( ) methods try to completely fill the specified array or subarray of text by reading repeatedly from the underlying reader. They return only when the requested number of characters have been read, the end of the data is reached, or the underlying reader would block. This is not the case for most readers which attempt only one read from the underlying data source before returning.

BufferedReader does support marking and resetting, at least up to the length of the buffer. Another reason to use a BufferedReader is to enable marking and resetting on a reader that otherwise wouldn't support it, such as an InputStreamReader.

Besides buffering, BufferedReader is notable for its readLine( ) method that allows you to read text a line at a time. This replaces the common but deprecated readLine( ) method in DataInputStream.

```
public String readLine( ) throws IOException
```

This method returns a string that contains a line of text from a text file. \r, \n, and \r\n are assumed to be line breaks and are not included in the returned string. This method is often used when reading user input from System.in since most platforms only send the user's input to the running program after the user has typed a full line (that is, hit the Enter key).

 readLine( ) can hang if the last character of the stream is not a carriage return or a linefeed and the sender does not close the stream. This problem tends to arise on network connections where the client or server keeps a socket open for a response after sending its data. For this reason, readLine( ) should not be used in network programming.

Example 20-5 uses a `BufferedReader` and `readLine()` to read all files named on the command line, line by line, and copy them to `System.out`. In essence it implements the Unix *cat* or the DOS *type* utility.

*Example 20-5. The cat program*

```java
import java.io.*;

class Cat {

  public static void main (String[] args) {
    String thisLine;
    for (int i=0; i < args.length; i++) {
      try {
        BufferedReader br = new BufferedReader(new FileReader(args[i]));
        while ((thisLine = br.readLine()) != null) {
          System.out.println(thisLine);
        } // end while
      } // end try
      catch (IOException ex) {System.err.println(ex);}
    } // end for
  } // end main
}
```

## Line Numbering

`LineNumberReader` is a subclass of `BufferedReader` that keeps track of which line it's currently reading. It also has methods to get and set the line number. This class replaces the deprecated `LineNumberInputStream` class.

```java
public class LineNumberReader extends BufferedReader
```

This class has two constructors. Both chain this reader to an underlying reader; the second also sets the size of the buffer.

```java
public LineNumberReader(Reader in)
public LineNumberReader(Reader in, int size)
```

`LineNumberReader` has all the methods of `BufferedReader`, including `readLine()`. These are overridden to keep track of the line number. The behavior of these methods is not changed.

`LineNumberReader` also introduces two methods for inspecting and changing the line number:

```java
public int getLineNumber()
public void setLineNumber(int lineNumber)
```

The `setLineNumber()` method does not change the line that you're reading in the file. It just changes the value `getLineNumber()` returns. For example, it would allow you to start counting from −5 if you knew there were six lines of header data, and you wanted line 1 to be the first line of the body text.

Example 20-6 uses a LineNumberReader and readLine( ) to read all files named on the command line, line by line, and copy them to System.out, prefixing each line with its line number.

*Example 20-6. The LineCat Program*

```java
import java.io.*;

class LineCat {

  public static void main (String[] args) {
    String thisLine;
    for (int i=0; i < args.length; i++) {
      try {
        LineNumberReader br = new LineNumberReader(new FileReader(args[i]));
        while ((thisLine = br.readLine()) != null) {
          System.out.println(br.getLineNumber() + ": " + thisLine);
        } // end while
      } // end try
      catch (IOException ex) {System.err.println(ex);}
    } // end for
  } // end main
}
```

# Print Writers

The java.io.PrintWriter class is a subclass of java.io.Writer that contains the familiar print( ) and println( ) methods from System.out and other instances of PrintStream. In Java 5 and later, it also has all the format( ) and printf( ) methods introduced in Chapter 7. It's deliberately similar to the java.io.PrintStream class.

The main difference between PrintStream and PrintWriter is that PrintWriter handles multiple-byte and other non-Latin-1 character sets properly. The other, more minor difference is that automatic flushing is performed only when println( ) is invoked, not every time a newline character is seen. Sun would probably like to deprecate PrintStream and use PrintWriter instead, but that would break too much existing code. (In fact, Sun did deprecate the PrintStream( ) constructors in Java 1.1, but they undeprecated them in 1.2.)

There are four constructors in this class:

```java
public PrintWriter(Writer out)
public PrintWriter(Writer out, boolean autoFlush)
public PrintWriter(OutputStream out)
public PrintWriter(OutputStream out, boolean autoFlush)
```

The PrintWriter can send text either to an output stream or to another writer. If autoFlush is set to true, the PrintWriter is flushed every time println( ) is invoked.

The PrintWriter class implements the abstract write( ) method from java.io.Writer and overrides five other methods:

```
public void write(int c)
public void write(char[] text)
public void write(String s)
public void write(String s, int offset, int length)
public void flush( )
public void close( )
```

These methods are used almost identically to their equivalents in any other Writer class. The one difference is that none of them throw IOExceptions; in fact, no method in the PrintWriter class ever throws an IOException. If the underlying output stream or writer throws an IOException, it's caught inside PrintWriter and an error flag is set. Read the status of this flag with the checkError( ) method:

```
public boolean checkError( )
```

Since checkError( ) returns a boolean, it only tells you that an I/O error has occurred; it does not tell you what that error was. Furthermore, once an error has occurred, checkError( ) always returns true—there is no way to reset it so you can test for later errors.

The main advantages of the PrintWriter class are the 9-way overloaded print( ) method and the 10-way overloaded println( ) method. Any Java object, variable, or literal can be printed by passing it to a print( ) or println( ) method. The println( ) method follows its argument with a platform-dependent line separator (such as \r\n) and then flushes the output if autoFlush is enabled. The print( ) method does not. Otherwise, these methods are the same.

```
public void print(boolean b)
public void print(char c)
public void print(int i)
public void print(long l)
public void print(float f)
public void print(double d)
public void print(char[] text)
public void print(String s)
public void print(Object o)
public void println( )
public void println(boolean b)
public void println(char c)
public void println(int i)
public void println(long l)
public void println(float f)
public void println(double d)
public void println(char[] text)
public void println(String s)
public void println(Object o)
```

You should never use println( ), either the PrintWriter or the PrintStream version, in networking code. Most network protocols like HTTP expect to see a carriage return/linefeed pair as the line separator character. If you use `println( )`, your network programs may run on Windows, but they'll have problems on most other platforms. Furthermore, these problems can be hard to diagnose because some servers and clients are more forgiving of improper line-ending conventions than others.

Java 5 adds two `format( )` and two `printf( )` methods:

```
public PrintWriter printf(String format, Object... args)
  throws IllegalFormatException, NullPointerException
public PrintWriter printf(Locale l, String format, Object... args)
  throws IllegalFormatException, NullPointerException
public PrintWriter format(String format, Object... args)
  throws IllegalFormatException, NullPointerException
public PrintWriter format(Locale l, String format, Object... args)
  throws IllegalFormatException, NullPointerException
```

These methods have the same behavior as the similarly named methods in the `PrintStream` class discussed in Chapter 7.

# Piped Readers and Writers

Piped readers and writers do for character streams what piped input and output streams do for byte streams: they allow two threads to communicate. Character output from one thread becomes character input for the other thread:

```
public class PipedWriter extends Writer
public class PipedReader extends Reader
```

The `PipedWriter` class has two constructors. The first constructs an unconnected `PipedWriter` object. The second constructs one that's connected to the `PipedReader` object sink:

```
public PipedWriter( )
public PipedWriter(PipedReader sink) throws IOException
```

The `PipedReader` class also has two constructors. Again, the first constructor creates an unconnected `PipedReader` object. The second constructs one that's connected to the `PipedWriter` object source:

```
public PipedReader( )
public PipedReader(PipedWriter source) throws IOException
```

Piped readers and writers are normally created in pairs. The piped writer becomes the underlying source for the piped reader. This is one of the few cases where a reader does not have an underlying input stream. For example:

```
PipedWriter pw = new PipedWriter( );
PipedReader pr = new PipedReader(pw);
```

This simple example is a little deceptive because these lines of code will normally be in different methods and perhaps even different classes. Some mechanism must be established to pass a reference to the `PipedWriter` into the thread that handles the

PipedReader, or you can create them in the same thread and pass a reference to the connected stream into a separate thread.

Alternatively, you can start with a PipedReader and then wrap it with a PipedWriter:

```
PipedReader pr = new PipedReader();
PipedWriter pw = new PipedWriter(pr);
```

Or you can create them both unconnected and use one or the other's connect( ) method to link them:

```
public void connect(PipedReader sink) throws IOException
public void connect(PipedWriter source) throws IOException
```

PipedWriter's connect( ) method takes as an argument the PipedReader to connect to. PipedReader's connect( ) argument takes as an argument the PipedWriter to connect to:

```
PipedReader pr = new PipedReader();
PipedWriter pw = new PipedWriter();
pr.connect(pw);
```

or:

```
PipedReader pr = new PipedReader();
PipedWriter pw = new PipedWriter();
pw.connect(pr);
```

Neither a PipedWriter nor a PipedReader can be connected to more than one reader or writer. Attempts to do so throw IOExceptions. Furthermore, once connected, a PipedWriter/PipedReader pair may not be disconnected. Otherwise, these classes have the usual read( ), write( ), flush( ), close( ), and ready( ) methods like all reader and writer classes.

When characters are written on the PipedWriter, that text becomes available as input to be read by the connected PipedReader. If a PipedReader tries to read characters, but its connected PipedWriter hasn't yet provided it with any, the PipedReader blocks.

Closing either a PipedReader or a PipedWriter also closes the reader or writer it's connected to.

# Filtered Readers and Writers

The java.io.FilterReader and java.io.FilterWriter classes are abstract classes that read characters and filter them in some way before passing the text along. You can imagine a FilterReader that converts all characters to uppercase.

```
public abstract class FilterReader extends Reader
public abstract class FilterWriter extends Writer
```

Although FilterReader and FilterWriter are modeled after java.io. FilterInputStream and java.io.FilterOutputStream, they are much less commonly used than those classes. There are no concrete subclasses of `FilterWriter` in the java packages and only one concrete subclass of `FilterReader` (`PushbackReader`). These classes exist so you can write your own filters.

## The FilterReader Class

`FilterReader` has a single constructor, which is protected:

```
protected FilterReader(Reader in)
```

The `in` argument is the `Reader` to which this filter is chained. This reference is stored in a protected field called `in` from which text for this filter is read and is `null` after the filter has been closed.

```
protected Reader in
```

Since `FilterReader` is an abstract class, only subclasses can be instantiated. Therefore, it doesn't matter that the constructor is protected since it may only be invoked from subclass constructors.

`FilterReader` provides the usual collection of `read()`, `skip()`, `ready()`, `markSupported()`, `mark()`, `reset()`, and `close()` methods. These all simply invoke the equivalent method in the `in` field with the same arguments. For example, the `skip()` method works like this:

```
public long skip(long n) throws IOException {
    return in.skip(n);
}
```

Each subclass usually overrides at least these two `read()` methods to perform the filtering:

```
public int read() throws IOException
public int read(char[] text, int offset, int length) throws IOException
```

In `FilterReader`, neither method invokes the other. You must override each of them, even if it's only to call the other one.

Java source code can include Unicode escapes for characters not available in the current character set. An escape sequence is a \u followed by the four-hexadecimal-digit equivalent of the Unicode character. As an example, I'll write a `FilterReader` subclass that reads a \u-escaped file and converts it to pure Unicode. This is a much trickier problem than it first appears. First, there's not a fixed ratio between the number of bytes and number of chars. Most of the time one byte is one char, but some of the time five bytes are one char. The second difficulty is ensuring that \u09EF is recognized as Unicode escape while \\u09EF is not. In other words, only a u preceded by an odd number of slashes is a valid Unicode escape. A u preceded by an even number of slashes should be passed along unchanged. Example 20-7 shows a solution.

*Example 20-7. SourceReader*

```java
package com.elharo.io;

import java.io.*;

public class SourceReader extends FilterReader {

  public SourceReader(Reader in) {
    super(in);
  }

  private int buffer = -1;

  public int read() throws IOException {

    if (this.buffer != -1) {
      int c = this.buffer;
      this.buffer = -1;
      return c;
    }

    int c = in.read();
    if (c != '\\') return c;

    int next = in.read();
    if (next != 'u' ) { // This is not a Unicode escape
      this.buffer = next;
      return c;
    }

    // Read next 4 hex digits
    // If the next four chars do not make a valid hex digit
    // this is not a valid .java file.
    StringBuffer sb = new StringBuffer();
    sb.append((char) in.read());
    sb.append((char) in.read());
    sb.append((char) in.read());
    sb.append((char) in.read());
    String hex = sb.toString();
    try {
      return Integer.valueOf(hex, 16).intValue();
    }
    catch (NumberFormatException ex) {
      throw new IOException("Bad Unicode escape: \\u" + hex);
    }
  }


  private boolean endOfStream = false;

  public int read(char[] text, int offset, int length) throws IOException {

    if (endOfStream) return -1;
    int numRead = 0;
```

*Example 20-7. SourceReader (continued)*

```
    for (int i = offset; i < offset+length; i++) {
      int temp = this.read( );
      if (temp == -1) {
        this.endOfStream = true;
        break;
      }
      text[i] = (char) temp;
      numRead++;
    }
    return numRead;

  }

  public long skip(long n) throws IOException {
    char[] c = new char[(int) n];
    int numSkipped = this.read(c);
    return numSkipped;

  }
}
```

## The FilterWriter Class

The FilterWriter class has a single constructor and no other unique methods:

```
    protected FilterWriter(Writer out)
```

The out argument is the writer to which this filter is chained. This reference is stored in a protected field called out to which text sent through this filter is written.

```
    protected Writer out
```

Since FilterWriter is an abstract class, only subclasses may be instantiated. Therefore, it doesn't matter that the constructor is protected since it may only be invoked from subclass constructors anyway. FilterWriter provides the usual collection of write( ), close( ), and flush( ) methods. These all simply invoke the equivalent method in the out field with the same arguments. For example, the close( ) method works like this:

```
    public void close( ) throws IOException {
      out.close( );
    }
```

Each subclass has to override at least these three write( ) methods to perform the filtering:

```
    public void write(int c) throws IOException
    public void write(char[] text, int offset, int length) throws IOException
    public void write(String s, int offset, int length) throws IOException
```

In FilterWriter, these methods do not invoke each other. You must override each of them, even if it's only to call one of the other two.

There are no subclasses of FilterWriter in the core API. Example 20-8, SourceWriter, is an example of a FilterWriter that converts Unicode text to \u-escaped ASCII. The big question is what to do if the input text contains an unes-caped backslash. The simplest and most robust solution is to replace it with \u005C, the Unicode escape for the backslash itself.

*Example 20-8. SourceWriter*

```
package com.elharo.io;

import java.io.*;

public class SourceWriter extends FilterWriter {

  public SourceWriter(Writer out) {
    super(out);
  }

  public void write(char[] text, int offset, int length) throws IOException {
    for (int i = offset; i < offset+length; i++) {
      this.write(text[i]);
    }
  }

  public void write(String s, int offset, int length) throws IOException {
    for (int i = offset; i < offset+length; i++) {
      this.write(s.charAt(i));
    }
  }

  public void write(int c) throws IOException {

    // We have to escape the backslashes below.
    if (c == '\\') out.write("\\u005C");
    else if (c < 128) out.write(c);
    else {
      String s = Integer.toHexString(c);
      // Pad with leading zeroes if necessary.
      if (c < 256) s = "00" + s;
      else if (c < 4096) s = "0" + s;
      out.write("\\u");
      out.write(s);
    }
  }
}
```

## PushbackReader

The PushbackReader class is a filter that provides a pushback buffer around a given reader. This allows a program to "unread" the last character it read. It's similar to PushbackInputStream discussed in Chapter 6, but instead of pushing back bytes, it

---

pushes back chars. Both PushbackReader and BufferedReader use buffers, but only PushbackReader allows unreading and only BufferedReader allows marking and resetting. The first difference is that pushing back characters allows you to unread characters after the fact. Marking and resetting requires you to mark in advance the location you want to reset to. The second difference is that you can push back a character that was never on the stream in the first place. Marking and resetting only allows you to reread the same characters, not add new characters to the stream.

PushbackReader has two constructors, both of which take an underlying reader as an argument. The first uses a one-character pushback buffer; the second sets the pushback buffer to a specified size:

```
public PushbackReader(Reader in)
public PushbackReader(Reader in, int size)
```

The PushbackReader class has the usual collection of read( ) methods. These methods first try to read the requested characters from the pushback buffer and only read from the underlying reader if the pushback buffer is empty or has too few characters.

PushbackReader also has ready( ), markSupported( ), and close( ) methods. The ready( ) and close( ) methods merely invoke the ready( ) and close( ) methods of the underlying reader. The markSupported( ) method returns false; pushback readers do not support marking and resetting.

Three unread( ) methods push back specific characters. The first pushes back the character c, the second pushes back the text array, and the third pushes back the subarray of text beginning at offset and continuing for length chars.

```
public void unread(int c) throws IOException
public void unread(char[] text) throws IOException
public void unread(char[] text, int offset, int length) throws IOException
```

The unread characters aren't necessarily the same as the characters that were read. The client programmer can insert text as the stream is read. The number of characters you can push back onto the stream is limited by the size of the buffer set in the constructor. Attempts to unread more characters than can fit in the buffer throw an IOException. An IOException is also thrown if you try to unread a closed reader; once a PushbackReader has been closed, it can be neither read nor unread.

# File Viewer Finis

As a final example of working with readers and writers, we return for the last time to the FileDumper application last seen in Chapter 18. At that point, we had a GUI program that allowed any file to be opened and interpreted in one of several formats, including ASCII, decimal, hexadecimal, short, regular, and long integers in both big- and little-endian formats, floating point, and double-precision floating point.

In this section, we expand the program to read many different text formats besides ASCII. The user interface must be adjusted to allow a binary choice of whether the file contains text or numeric data. If a user chooses text, a reader reads the file instead of an input stream. We also need a way for the user to pick the text encoding (e.g., MacRoman, Latin-1, Unicode, etc). Since there are several dozen text encodings, the best choice is a list box. All of this can be integrated into the mode panel. Figure 20-1 shows the revised TextModePanel class. The code is given in Example 20-9. I've added two new public methods, isText( ) and getEncoding( ). The rest of the changes are fairly minor ones to set up the GUI.

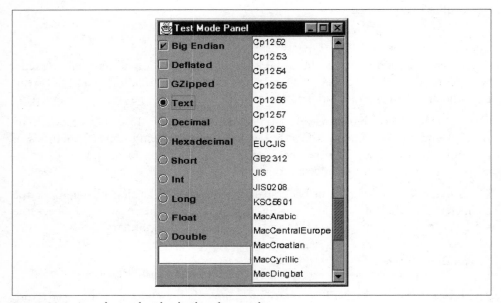

*Figure 20-1. A mode panel with a list box for encodings*

*Example 20-9. TextModePanel*

```java
import java.awt.*;
import javax.swing.*;
import java.nio.charset.*;
import java.util.*;

public class TextModePanel extends JPanel {

private JCheckBox bigEndian = new JCheckBox("Big Endian", true);
private JCheckBox deflated  = new JCheckBox("Deflated", false);
private JCheckBox gzipped    = new JCheckBox("GZipped", false);

private ButtonGroup dataTypes       = new ButtonGroup();
private JRadioButton asciiRadio   = new JRadioButton("Text");
private JRadioButton decimalRadio = new JRadioButton("Decimal");
private JRadioButton hexRadio     = new JRadioButton("Hexadecimal");
```

*Example 20-9. TextModePanel (continued)*

```
prviate JRadioButton shortRadio    = new JRadioButton("Short");
private JRadioButton intRadio      = new JRadioButton("Int");
private JRadioButton longRadio     = new JRadioButton("Long");
private JRadioButton floatRadio    = new JRadioButton("Float");
private JRadioButton doubleRadio   = new JRadioButton("Double");

private JTextField password = new JPasswordField();
private JList encodings = new JList();

  public TextModePanel() {
    Map charsets = Charset.availableCharsets();
    encodings.setListData(charsets.keySet().toArray());

    this.setLayout(new GridLayout(1, 2));

    JPanel left = new JPanel();
    JScrollPane right = new JScrollPane(encodings);
    left.setLayout(new GridLayout(13, 1));
    left.add(bigEndian);
    left.add(deflated);
    left.add(gzipped);

    left.add(asciiRadio);
    asciiRadio.setSelected(true);
    left.add(decimalRadio);
    left.add(hexRadio);
    left.add(shortRadio);
    left.add(intRadio);
    left.add(longRadio);
    left.add(floatRadio);
    left.add(doubleRadio);

    dataTypes.add(asciiRadio);
    dataTypes.add(decimalRadio);
    dataTypes.add(hexRadio);
    dataTypes.add(shortRadio);
    dataTypes.add(intRadio);
    dataTypes.add(longRadio);
    dataTypes.add(floatRadio);
    dataTypes.add(doubleRadio);

    left.add(password);
    this.add(left);
    this.add(right);
  }

  public boolean isBigEndian() {
    return bigEndian.isSelected();
  }

  public boolean isDeflated() {
    return deflated.isSelected();
```

*Example 20-9. TextModePanel (continued)*

```
  }

  public boolean isGZipped( ) {
    return gzipped.isSelected( );
  }

  public boolean isText( ) {
    if (this.getMode( ) == FileDumper6.ASC) return true;
    return false;
  }

  public String getEncoding( ) {
    return (String) encodings.getSelectedValue( );
  }

  public int getMode( ) {
    if (asciiRadio.isSelected( )) return FileDumper6.ASC;
    else if (decimalRadio.isSelected( )) return FileDumper6.DEC;
    else if (hexRadio.isSelected( )) return FileDumper6.HEX;
    else if (shortRadio.isSelected( )) return FileDumper6.SHORT;
    else if (intRadio.isSelected( )) return FileDumper6.INT;
    else if (longRadio.isSelected( )) return FileDumper6.LONG;
    else if (floatRadio.isSelected( )) return FileDumper6.FLOAT;
    else if (doubleRadio.isSelected( )) return FileDumper6.DOUBLE;
    else return FileDumper6.ASC;
  }

  public String getPassword( ) {
    return password.getText( );
  }
}
```

Next we should fix an unrecognized bug in the earlier program. It used an OutputStream to stream data into the text area. It converted the bytes to chars simply by casting them as if they were Latin-1. This works for the simple ASCII output needed to represent numbers, but the whole point of this chapter has been that this hack just doesn't work for more realistic text that can include content from many different languages. Thus we need to revise the JStreamedTextArea to stream to a Writer rather than an OutputStream. If anything, this is more straightforward. Example 20-10 demonstrates.

*Example 20-10. The JWritableTextArea*

```
package com.elharo.io.ui;

import javax.swing.*;
import java.awt.Font;
import java.io.*;

public class JWritableTextArea extends JTextArea {
```

*Example 20-10. The JWritableTextArea (continued)*

```java
  private Writer writer = new BufferedWriter(new TextAreaWriter());

  public JWritableTextArea() {
    this("", 0, 0);
  }

  public JWritableTextArea(String text) {
    this(text, 0, 0);
  }

  public JWritableTextArea(int rows, int columns) {
    this("", rows, columns);
  }

  public JWritableTextArea(String text, int rows, int columns) {
    super(text, rows, columns);
    setFont(new Font("Monospaced", Font.PLAIN, 12));
    setEditable(false);
  }

  public Writer getWriter() {
    return writer;
  }

  public void reset() {
    this.setText("");
    writer = new BufferedWriter(new TextAreaWriter());
  }

  private class TextAreaWriter extends Writer {

    private boolean closed = false;

    public void close() {
      closed = true;
    }

    public void write(char[] text, int offset, int length) throws IOException {
      if (closed) throw new IOException("Write to closed stream");
      JWritableTextArea.this.append(new String(text, offset, length));
    }

    public void flush() {}
  }
}
```

Next we need to expand the FileDumper class to read and write text in a variety of encodings. This is straightforward and only requires one new overloaded dump( ) method, as shown in Example 20-11.

*Example 20-11. FileDumper6*

```java
import java.io.*;
import java.util.zip.*;
import java.security.*;
import javax.crypto.*;
import javax.crypto.spec.*;
import com.elharo.io.*;

public class FileDumper6 {

  public static final int ASC    = 0;
  public static final int DEC    = 1;
  public static final int HEX    = 2;
  public static final int SHORT  = 3;
  public static final int INT    = 4;
  public static final int LONG   = 5;
  public static final int FLOAT  = 6;
  public static final int DOUBLE = 7;

  public static void dump(InputStream in, Writer out, int mode,
   boolean bigEndian, boolean deflated, boolean gzipped, String password)
   throws IOException {

    // The reference variable in may point to several different objects
    // within the space of the next few lines.
    if (password != null && !password.equals("")) {
      // Create a key.
      try {
        byte[] desKeyData = password.getBytes( );
        DESKeySpec desKeySpec = new DESKeySpec(desKeyData);
        SecretKeyFactory keyFactory = SecretKeyFactory.getInstance("DES");
        SecretKey desKey = keyFactory.generateSecret(desKeySpec);

        // Use Data Encryption Standard.
        Cipher des = Cipher.getInstance("DES/ECB/PKCS5Padding");
        des.init(Cipher.DECRYPT_MODE, desKey);

        in = new CipherInputStream(in, des);
      }
      catch (GeneralSecurityException ex) {
        throw new IOException(ex.getMessage( ));
      }
    }

    if (deflated) {
      in = new InflaterInputStream(in);
    }
    else if (gzipped) {
      in = new GZIPInputStream(in);
    }

    if (bigEndian) {
      DataInputStream din = new DataInputStream(in);
      switch (mode) {
```

*Example 20-11. FileDumper6 (continued)*

```
          case HEX:
            in = new HexFilter(in);
            break;
          case DEC:
            in = new DecimalFilter(in);
            break;
          case INT:
            in = new IntFilter(din);
            break;
          case SHORT:
            in = new ShortFilter(din);
            break;
          case LONG:
            in = new LongFilter(din);
            break;
          case DOUBLE:
            in = new DoubleFilter(din);
            break;
          case FLOAT:
            in = new FloatFilter(din);
            break;
          default:
        }
      }
      else {
        LittleEndianInputStream lin = new LittleEndianInputStream(in);
        switch (mode) {
          case HEX:
            in = new HexFilter(in);
            break;
          case DEC:
            in = new DecimalFilter(in);
            break;
          case INT:
            in = new LEIntFilter(lin);
            break;
          case SHORT:
            in = new LEShortFilter(lin);
            break;
          case LONG:
            in = new LELongFilter(lin);
            break;
          case DOUBLE:
            in = new LEDoubleFilter(lin);
            break;
          case FLOAT:
            in = new LEFloatFilter(lin);
            break;
          default:
        }
      }
      for (int c = in.read(); c != -1; c = in.read()) {
        out.write(c);
```

*Example 20-11. FileDumper6 (continued)*

```
    }
    in.close();
  }

  public static void dump(InputStream in, Writer out,
   String inputEncoding, String outputEncoding, boolean deflated,
   boolean gzipped, String password) throws IOException {

    if (inputEncoding == null || inputEncoding.equals("")) {
      inputEncoding = "US-ASCII";
    }

    if (outputEncoding == null || outputEncoding.equals("")) {
      outputEncoding = System.getProperty("file.encoding", "8859_1");
    }

    // Note that the reference variable in
    // may point to several different objects
    // within the space of the next few lines.
    if (password != null && !password.equals("")) {
      try {
        // Create a key.
        byte[] desKeyData = password.getBytes();
        DESKeySpec desKeySpec = new DESKeySpec(desKeyData);
        SecretKeyFactory keyFactory = SecretKeyFactory.getInstance("DES");
        SecretKey desKey = keyFactory.generateSecret(desKeySpec);

        // Use Data Encryption Standard.
        Cipher des = Cipher.getInstance("DES/ECB/PKCS5Padding");
        des.init(Cipher.DECRYPT_MODE, desKey);
        in = new CipherInputStream(in, des);
      }
      catch (GeneralSecurityException ex) {
        throw new IOException(ex.getMessage());
      }
    }

    if (deflated) {
      in = new InflaterInputStream(in);
    }
    else if (gzipped) {
      in = new GZIPInputStream(in);
    }

    InputStreamReader isr = new InputStreamReader(in, inputEncoding);

    int c;
    while ((c = isr.read()) != -1) {
      out.write(c);
    }
  }
}
```

There's one new method in this class. An overloaded variant of dump( ) can be invoked to dump a text file in a particular encoding. This method accepts an input encoding string and an output encoding string as arguments. These are used to form readers and writers that interpret the bytes read from the file and written onto the output stream. Output encoding is optional. If it's omitted, the platform's default encoding is used.

The FileViewer2 class is straightforward. Aside from using a TextModePanel instead of a ModePanel, the only change it really requires is in the actionPerformed( ) method. Here you have to test whether the format is text or numeric and select the dump( ) method accordingly. Example 20-12 illustrates.

*Example 20-12. FileViewer2*

```java
import javax.swing.*;
import java.io.*;
import com.elharo.io.ui.*;
import java.awt.*;
import java.awt.event.*;

public class FileViewer2 extends JFrame implements ActionListener {

  JFileChooser chooser = new JFileChooser();
  JWritableTextArea theView = new JWritableTextArea();
  TextModePanel mp = new TextModePanel();

  public FileViewer2() {
    super("FileViewer");
  }

  public void init() {
    chooser.setApproveButtonText("View File");
    chooser.setApproveButtonMnemonic('V');
    chooser.addActionListener(this);

    this.getContentPane().add(BorderLayout.EAST, chooser);
    JScrollPane sp = new JScrollPane(theView);
    sp.setPreferredSize(new Dimension(640, 400));
    this.getContentPane().add(BorderLayout.SOUTH, sp);
    this.getContentPane().add(BorderLayout.WEST, mp);
    this.pack();

    // Center on display
    Dimension display = getToolkit().getScreenSize();
    Dimension bounds = this.getSize();
    int x = (display.width - bounds.width)/2;
    int y = (display.height - bounds.height)/2;
    if (x < 0) x = 10;
    if (y < 0) y = 15;
```

*Example 20-12. FileViewer2 (continued)*

```java
    this.setLocation(x, y);
  }

  public void actionPerformed(ActionEvent evt) {

    if (evt.getActionCommand( ).equals(JFileChooser.APPROVE_SELECTION)) {
      File f = chooser.getSelectedFile( );
      if (f != null) {
        theView.reset( );
        try {
          InputStream in = new FileInputStream(f);
          // This program was really slow until I buffered the stream.
          in = new BufferedInputStream(in);
          in = new ProgressMonitorInputStream(this, "Reading...", in);
          if (!mp.isText( )) {
            FileDumper6.dump(in, theView.getWriter( ), mp.getMode( ),
                             mp.isBigEndian( ),
              mp.isDeflated( ), mp.isGZipped( ), mp.getPassword( ));
          }
          else {
            FileDumper6.dump(in, theView.getWriter( ), mp.getEncoding( ), null,
              mp.isDeflated( ), mp.isGZipped( ), mp.getPassword( ));
          }
        }
        catch (IOException ex) {
          JOptionPane.showMessageDialog(this, ex.getMessage( ),
            "I/O Error", JOptionPane.ERROR_MESSAGE);
        }
      }
    }
    else if (evt.getActionCommand( ).equals(JFileChooser.CANCEL_SELECTION)) {
      this.setVisible(false);
      this.dispose( );
      // This is a single window application
      System.exit(0);
    }
  }

  public static void main(String[] args) {
    FileViewer2 viewer = new FileViewer2( );
    viewer.init( );
    viewer.setDefaultCloseOperation(JFrame.EXIT_ON_CLOSE);
    viewer.setVisible(true);
  }
}
```

Figure 20-2 shows the completed FileViewer application displaying a file full of Unicode text.

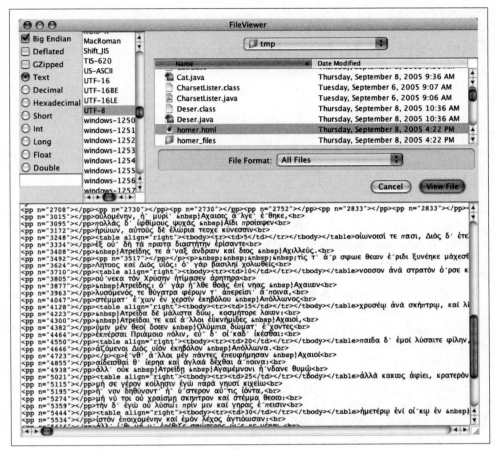

*Figure 20-2. The final FileViewer application*

This completes this program, at least as far as it will be taken in this book. You could certainly extend it further. For example, it would be a nice touch to add support for various image formats and perhaps even formatted text like HTML files. However, this would take us too far afield from the topic of this book, so I leave further improvements as exercises for the motivated reader.

# CHAPTER 21
# Formatted I/O with java.text

Java 1.4 and earlier have no equivalent of printf( ). Even Java 6 has no equivalent of scanf( ). Part of the reason is that Java didn't support the variable-length argument lists on which these functions depend until Java 5. However, the real reason Java didn't have equivalents to C's formatted I/O routines is a difference in philosophy. C's printf( ), scanf( ), and related functions combine number formatting and parsing with I/O in an inflexible manner. Java separates number formatting and I/O into separate packages and by so doing produces a much more general and powerful system.

 Of course, starting in version 5, Java does have variable-length argument lists and printf( ), as you saw in Chapter 7 (though scanf( ) is still missing). The printf( ) functionality introduced in Java 5 is really just a thin layer on top of the classes discussed in this chapter. To be honest, I'm not convinced this is an improvement.

More than one programmer has attempted to recreate printf( ) and scanf( ) in Java. However, overloading the + signs for string concatenation is easily as effective, probably more so, since it doesn't share the problems of mismatched argument lists. For example, which is clearer to you? This:

```
System.out.printf("%s worked %d hours at $%d per/hour for a total of %d dollars.\n",
    hours, salary, hours*salary);
```

or this:

```
System.out.println(employee + " worked " + hours + " hours at $" + salary
    + "per/hour for a total of $" + hours*salary);
```

I'd argue that the second is clearer. Among other advantages, it avoids problems with mismatched format strings and argument lists. (Did you notice that an argument is missing from the previous printf( ) statement?) On the flip side, the format string approach is a little less prone to missing spaces. (Did you notice that the println( )

statement would print pay scales as "$5.35per/hour" rather than "$5.35 per/hour"?) However, this is only a cosmetic problem and is easily fixed.

The real advantage of the printf( )/scanf( ) family of functions is not the format string. It's number formatting:

```
printf(
"%s worked %4.1d hours at $%6.2d per/hour for a total of %8.2d dollars.\n",
 employee, hours, salary, hours*salary);
```

Java's been able to format numbers like this since version 1.1. However, it's done so with the java.text.NumberFormat class rather than with embedded control codes in format strings.

# The Old Way

Traditional computer languages have combined input of text with the parsing of numeric strings. For example, to read a decimal number into the variable x, programmers are accustomed to writing C code like this:

```
scanf("%d", &x);
```

In C++, that line would become:

```
cin >> x;
```

In Pascal:

```
READLN (X);
```

In Fortran:

```
READ 2, X
   2 FORMAT (F5.1)
```

Similarly, formatting numeric strings for output tends to be mixed up with writing the string to the screen. For instance, consider the simple task of writing the double variable salary with two decimal digits of precision. In C, you'd write this:

```
printf("%.2d", salary);
```

In C++:

```
cout.precision(2);
cout << salary;
```

In Fortran:

```
PRINT 20, SALARY
   20 FORMAT(F10.2)
```

This conflation of basic input and output with number formatting is so ingrained in many programmers that we rarely stop to think whether it actually makes sense. What, precisely, does the formatting of numbers as text strings have to do with input and output? It's certainly true that you often need to format numbers to print numbers on the console, but you also need to format numbers to write data in files, to include numbers in text fields and text areas, and to send data across the network. What makes the console so special that it has to have a group of number-formatting routines all to itself? In C, the printf( ) and scanf( ) functions are supplemented by fprintf( ) and fscanf( ) for formatted I/O to files and by sprintf( ) and sscanf( ) for formatted I/O to strings. Perhaps the conflation of I/O with number formatting is really a relic of a time when command-line interfaces were a lot more important than they are today, and it's simply that nobody thought to challenge this assumption, at least until Java. When you think about it, there's no fundamental connection between converting a binary number like 11010100110110100100011101011011 to a text string like " -7.500E+12" and writing that string onto an output stream. These are two different operations, and in Java they're handled by separate classes. Input and output are handled by all the streams and readers and writers I've been discussing while number formatting is handled by a few NumberFormat classes from the java.text package I'll introduce in this chapter.

In Java you don't say, "Print the double variable salary 12 places wide with three decimal places of precision." Instead, you say "First, make a string from the double variable salary 12 places wide with three decimal places of precision. Then print that string." Similarly, when doing input, you first read the string, then convert it to a number. You don't read the number directly. This really isn't very different from the programs you're used to writing in other languages; it adds a step, but the benefit is enhanced flexibility, particularly in regard to internationalization. It's easy to add new NumberFormat classes and locales that handle different kinds of formatting.

In this chapter, we'll explore how to use the java.text.NumberFormat and java.text. DecimalFormat classes to format integers and floating-point numbers. You'll also learn how the java.util.Locale class lets you select number formats matched to different languages, cultures, and countries. There's more in the java.text package I won't cover. In particular, java.text includes classes for formatting dates, and sorting and collating text. These classes can also be customized to different locales. The date formats in particular work very similarly to the number formats discussed in this chapter and should be easy to pick up from the API documentation once you understand NumberFormat.

## Choosing a Locale

Number formats are dependent on the *locale*, that is, the country/language/culture group of the local operating system. Most English-speaking Americans are accustomed to use a period as a decimal point, a comma to separate every three orders of magnitude, a dollar sign for currency, and numbers in base 10 that read from left to right. In this locale, Bill Gates's personal fortune, in Microsoft stock alone as of September 12, 2006, is represented as $27,075,657,331. However, in Egypt this number could be written as $ ٢٧,٠٧٥,٦٥٧,٣٣١.

The primary difference here is that Egyptians use a different set of glyphs for the digits 0 through 9. For example, in Egypt zero is a • and the glyph ٦ means two. There are other differences in how Arabic and English treat numbers, and these vary from country to country. In most of the rest of North Africa, this number would be $27,075,657,331 as it is in the U.S. These are just two different scripts; there are several dozen more to go!

Java encapsulates many of the common differences between language/script/culture/country combinations in a loosely defined group called a *locale*. There's really no better word for it. You can't just rely on language or country or culture alone. Many languages are shared between countries (English is only the most obvious example) but with subtle differences in how they are used in different places: Do commas and periods belong inside or outside of quotation marks? Is green a color or a colour? Many countries have no clearly dominant tongue: Is Canada an English- or a French-speaking nation? Switzerland has four official languages. Almost all countries have significant minority populations with their own languages. The New York City public school system has to hire teachers fluent in over 100 different languages.

Locales are identified by a language and an optional country and variant which are supplied to the constructors in java.util.Locale:

```
public Locale(String languageCode, String countryCode)
public Locale(String languageCode, String countryCode, String variantCode)
```

The language is specified by a case insensitive two-letter ISO-639 language code such as EN for English or FR for French. The country is specified by a case insensitive two-letter ISO-3166 country code such as US for the United States or TT for Trinidad and Tobago. You can also pass the empty string to request a locale for a language independent of location. Finally, the variant can be pretty much anything. For example, you can ask for the locale for generic, standard French as spoken in France, French in the U.S., or French in the U.S. in New Orleans:

```
Locale french = new Locale("fr", "");
Locale parisian = new Locale("fr", "FR");
Locale french-US = new Locale("fr", "US");
Locale creoleFrench = new Locale("fr", "US", "NO");
```

There's no guarantee that the VM supports any of these, though the first two are likely available. The variant code for New Orleans in the last line is completely nonstandard, but legal. When encountering this locale, Java will almost certainly fall back to a generic French locale. In fact, it will probably fall back to that for the fr-US locale too. However, the fr-FR locale will probably be recognized and won't be quite the same as the fr-CA locale for Canadian French. The exact set of locales varies from one Java version and VM vendor to the next. However, these days the total number of available locales is usually well over a hundred.

The Locale class does include about twenty named constants for the most economically significant locales:

```
Locale.ENGLISH
Locale.FRENCH
Locale.GERMAN
Locale.ITALIAN
Locale.JAPANESE
Locale.KOREAN
Locale.CHINESE
Locale.SIMPLIFIED_CHINESE
Locale.TRADITIONAL_CHINESE
Locale.FRANCE
Locale.GERMANY
Locale.ITALY
Locale.JAPAN
Locale.KOREA
Locale.CHINA
Locale.PRC
Locale.TAIWAN
Locale.UK
Locale.US
Locale.CANADA
Locale.CANADA_FRENCH
```

However, not every available locale has such a constant.

## Number Formats

To print a formatted number in Java, perform these two steps:

1. Format the number as a string.
2. Print the string.

Simple, right? Of course, this is a little like the old recipe for rabbit stew:

1. Catch a rabbit.
2. Boil rabbit in pot with vegetables and spices.

Obviously, step 1 is the tricky part. Fortunately, formatting numbers as strings is somewhat easier than catching a rabbit. The key class that formats numbers as strings is java.text.NumberFormat. This is an abstract subclass of java.text.Format.

```
public abstract class NumberFormat extends Format implements Cloneable
```

Concrete subclasses such as java.text.DecimalFormat implement formatting policies for particular kinds of numbers. The static NumberFormat.getAvailableLocales() method returns a list of all installed locales that provide number formats. (There may be a few locales that only provide date or text formats, not number formats.)

```
public static Locale[] getAvailableLocales()
```

You can request a `NumberFormat` object for the default locale of the host computer or for a locale using the static `NumberFormat.getInstance()` method. For example:

```
NumberFormat myFormat = NumberFormat.getInstance();
NumberFormat canadaFormat = NumberFormat.getInstance(Locale.CANADA);
Locale turkey = new Locale("tr", "");
NumberFormat turkishFormat = NumberFormat.getInstance(turkey);
```

The number format returned by `NumberFormat.getInstance()` should do a reasonable job of formatting most numbers. However, there's at least a theoretical possibility that the instance returned will format numbers as currencies or percentages. Therefore, it wouldn't hurt to use `NumberFormat.getNumberInstance()` instead:

```
public static final NumberFormat getNumberInstance()
public static NumberFormat getNumberInstance(Locale inLocale)
```

For example:

```
NumberFormat myFormat = NumberFormat.getNumberInstance();
NumberFormat canadaFormat = NumberFormat.getNumberInstance(Locale.CANADA);
```

## Formatting Numbers

A `NumberFormat` object converts integers and floating-point numbers into formatted strings using one of five overloaded `format()` methods:

```
public final String format(long number)
public final String format(double number)
public abstract StringBuffer format(long number, StringBuffer toAppendTo,
   FieldPosition pos)
public abstract StringBuffer format(double number, StringBuffer toAppendTo,
   FieldPosition pos)
public final StringBuffer format(Object number, StringBuffer toAppendTo,
   FieldPosition pos)
```

These methods all return a string or a string buffer form of the number argument using the format's default formatting rules. These rules specify:

- Maximum and minimum integer width
- Maximum and minimum fraction width (precision, number of decimal places)
- Whether or not digits are grouped (e.g., 2,109,356 versus 2109356)

For any given number format, these rules can be quite complex. For instance, they may or may not take into account different digit characters, exponential or scientific notation, Roman numerals, or more. By creating new subclasses of `NumberFormat`, you can specify arbitrarily complex rules for converting binary numbers into strings. Regardless of exactly how a number format formats numbers, they are all manipulated the same way.

The last three `format()` methods append the string to the specified `StringBuffer` `toAppendTo`. They then return that modified string buffer. They use a `java.text.` `FieldPosition` object to provide information to the client programmer about where the different parts of the number fall. This will be discussed later. The final `format()` method formats instances of the numeric type wrapper classes, that is, `java.lang.Double`, `java.lang.Float`, `java.lang.Long`, `java.lang.Integer`, `java.lang.Short`, `java.lang.Character`, and `java.lang.Byte`. Some (but not all) `NumberFormat` objects may be able to format other kinds of numbers, like `java.math.BigDecimal` and `java.math.BigInteger` as well.

Example 21-1 is about the simplest use of `NumberFormat` imaginable. It uses the default number format for the default locale to print multiples of π. For comparison, both the formatted and unformatted numbers are printed.

*Example 21-1. Multiples of pi*

```java
import java.text.*;

public class FormatTest {

  public static void main(String[] args) {

    NumberFormat nf = NumberFormat.getInstance();
    for (double x = Math.PI; x < 100000; x *= 10) {
      String formattedNumber = nf.format(x);
      System.out.println(formattedNumber + "\t" + x);
    }
  }
}
```

On my U.S. English system, the results look like this:

```
3.141       3.14159265358979
31.415      31.4159265358979
314.159     314.159265358979
3,141.592   3141.5926535897897
31,415.926  31415.926535897896
```

The formatted numbers don't use a ridiculous number of decimal places and group the integer part with commas when it becomes large. Of course, the exact formatting depends on the default locale. For instance, when I changed the locale to French, I got this output:

```
3,141       3.14159265358979
31,415      31.4159265358979
314,159     314.159265358979
3 141,592   3141.5926535897897
31 415,926  31415.926535897896
```

The French locale uses a decimal comma instead of a decimal point and separates every three digits in the integer part with a space. This may be confusing to an American, but seems perfectly normal to a Parisian. One of the advantages of number formats is that by using the default number format for the system, much of your program is automatically localized. No extra code is required to do the right thing on French systems, on Canadian systems, on Japanese systems, and so on. However, if you know you want output in a particular locale, regardless of what the locale is on the current system, just pass the locale you desire to the getInstance( ) method. For instance, this requests a French NumberFormat:

```
NumberFormat format = NumberFormat.getInstance(Locale.FRENCH);
```

If no such format is installed, you'll end up with the default locale anyway, but if a French locale is available you can now use it.

## Specifying Precision

Number formats have both a maximum and a minimum number of integer and fraction digits. For instance, in the number 31.415, there are two integer digits and three fraction digits. If the maximum number of digits in a part is less than the number actually present, the number is truncated (integer part) or rounded (fraction part). If the minimum is greater than the number of digits actually present, extra zeros are added to the beginning of the integer part or the end of the fraction part. For example, with a minimum of three integer digits and a maximum of two fraction digits, 31.415 would be formatted as 031.42.

You specify the minimum and maximum of each type you want in each number using these four methods:

```
public void setMaximumIntegerDigits(int newValue)
public void setMinimumIntegerDigits(int newValue)
public void setMaximumFractionDigits(int newValue)
public void setMinimumFractionDigits(int newValue)
```

For example, to specify that myFormat should format numbers with at least 10 digits before the decimal point and at most 3 digits after, you would type:

```
myFormat.setMinimumIntegerDigits(10);
myFormat.setMaximumFractionDigits(3);
```

Setting the minimum digits guarantees that those digits will be printed, filled with zeros if necessary. Setting the maximum digits allows the digits to be printed if they're nonzero or a place-holding zero (i.e., not the leftmost or rightmost digit). Leftmost and rightmost zeros will only be printed if necessary to fill the minimum number of digits. If you try to set a maximum below a minimum or a minimum above a maximum, the last one set takes precedence. Java raises the maximum to meet the minimum or lowers the minimum to meet the maximum.

Specifying the number of digits is useful when printing many columns of numbers in a tabular format to the console or in a monospaced font. Example 21-2 prints a three-column table of the angles between 0 and 360 degrees in degrees, radians and grads without any formatting.

*Example 21-2. UglyTable*

```java
public class UglyTable {

  public static void main(String[] args) {

    System.out.println("Degrees \tRadians \tGrads");
    for (double degrees = 0.0; degrees < 360.0; degrees++) {
      double radians = Math.PI * degrees / 180.0;
      double grads = 400 * degrees / 360;
      System.out.println(degrees + "\t" + radians + "\t" + grads);
    }
  }
}
```

Its output looks like this (not very pretty):

```
300.0 5.2359877559829835 333.3333333333333
301.0 5.253441048502927 334.44444444444446
302.0 5.27089434102287 335.55555555555554
303.0 5.288347633542813 336.6666666666667
304.0 5.305800926062757 337.77777777777777
305.0 5.3232542185827 338.8888888888889
306.0 5.340707511102643 340.0
```

Example 21-3 prints the same table with each number formatted to at least three integer digits and exactly two fraction digits (both minimum and maximum set to 2).

*Example 21-3. PrettyTable*

```java
import java.text.*;

public class PrettyTable {

  public static void main(String[] args) {

    System.out.println("Degrees Radians Grads");
    NumberFormat myFormat = NumberFormat.getInstance( );
    myFormat.setMinimumIntegerDigits(3);
    myFormat.setMaximumFractionDigits(2);
    myFormat.setMinimumFractionDigits(2);
    for (double degrees = 0.0; degrees < 360.0; degrees++) {
      String radianString = myFormat.format(Math.PI * degrees / 180.0);
      String gradString = myFormat.format(400 * degrees / 360);
      String degreeString = myFormat.format(degrees);
      System.out.println(degreeString + "  " + radianString
       + "  " + gradString);
    }
  }
}
```

Its output looks like this (much nicer):

```
300.00   005.23  333.33
301.00   005.25  334.44
```

```
302.00   005.27   335.55
303.00   005.28   336.66
304.00   005.30   337.77
305.00   005.32   338.88
306.00   005.34   340.00
...
```

Note that the extra integer digits are padded with zeros rather than spaces. You'll learn how to fix that shortly.

There are getMinimumIntegerDigits( ) and getMaximumIntegerDigits( ) methods that let you inspect the minimum and maximum number of digits provided by any number format, including the default:

```
public int getMaximumIntegerDigits( )
public int getMinimumIntegerDigits( )
public int getMaximumFractionDigits( )
public int getMinimumFractionDigits( )
```

## Grouping

How big is 299792500? You can't easily tell because the number is hard to read. It's obviously a pretty big number, but at a glance you don't know whether it's in the ballpark of 3 million, 30 million, 300 million, or 3 billion. On the other hand, if it's written as 299,792,500, it's a lot more obvious that the number is about 300 million. The commas group different parts of the number. By counting the groups, you get a quick idea of the number's order of magnitude.

Like other aspects of text formatting, different locales use different grouping conventions. In Belgium, Denmark, Holland, Spain, and Germany, a period groups thousands, and a comma is used as the "decimal point." Thus, the U.S. number 2,365,335.32 is equivalent to the Danish/Dutch number 2.365.335,32. Finnish uses an English-style decimal point but separates characters with a space rather than a comma. Thus, 2,365,335.32 is, in Finnish, 2 365 335.32. France, Sweden, and Norway also separate thousands with spaces but use a decimal comma: 2 365 335,32. Francophone Canada follows France's convention, but Canadian Anglophones use the American-British convention. And in Switzerland, an apostrophe separates thousands in all four of its official languages: 2'365'335.32

Most number formats support grouping, and some use it by default. You may inquire whether a particular NumberFormat uses grouping with the isGroupingUsed( ) method:

```
public boolean isGroupingUsed( )
```

This method returns true if the format groups numbers or false if it doesn't. You can turn grouping on or off for a number format with the setGroupingUsed( ) method:

```
public void setGroupingUsed(boolean groupNumbers)
```

Passing true turns grouping on. Passing false turns it off. You'll usually want to use grouping in strings that will be read by human beings and not use grouping in strings that will be parsed by computers.

## Currency Formats

It's not hard to tack on a dollar sign before a decimal number with two digits of precision. The NumberFormat class does a little more, handling international currencies with relative ease. For money, you can request the default locale's currency formatter with the static NumberFormat.getCurrencyInstance( ) method:

```
public static final NumberFormat getCurrencyInstance( )
```

To get a currency formatter for a different locale, pass the locale to NumberFormat. getCurrencyInstance( ):

```
public static NumberFormat getCurrencyInstance(Locale inLocale)
```

Example 21-4 calculates the annual earnings of a worker making minimum wage in U.S. dollars. A currency format returned by NumberFormat. getCurrencyInstance(Locale.ENGLISH) formats the monetary quantities.

*Example 21-4. Currency Formats*

```
import java.text.*;
import java.util.*;

public class MinimumWage {

  public static void main(String[] args) {

    NumberFormat dollarFormat = NumberFormat.getCurrencyInstance(Locale.ENGLISH);
    double minimumWage = 5.15;

    System.out.println("The minimum wage is "
     + dollarFormat.format(minimumWage));
    System.out.println("A worker earning minimum wage and working for forty");
    System.out.println("hours a week, 52 weeks a year, would earn "
     + dollarFormat.format(40*52*minimumWage));
  }
}
```

This program prints:

```
The minimum wage is $5.15
A worker earning minimum wage and working for forty
hours a week, 52 weeks a year, would earn $10,712.00
```

Notice how nicely the numbers are formatted. Nowhere did I add dollar signs, say that I wanted exactly two numbers after the decimal point, or say that I wanted to separate the thousands with commas. The NumberFormat class took care of that.

There are limits to how far currency formatting goes. Currency formats may change the currency sign in different locales, but they won't convert values (between U.S. and Canadian dollars or between U.S. dollars and British pounds, for example). Since conversion rates float from day to day and minute to minute, that's a bit much to ask of a fixed class. If you want to do this, you need to provide some source of the conversion rate information, either from user input or pulled off the network.

## Percent Formats

Number formats can also handle percentages in a variety of international formats. In grammar school you learned that a number followed by a percent sign is really one-hundredth of its apparent value. Thus, 50% is really decimal 0.5, 100% is 1.0, 10% is 0.1, and so on. Percent formats allow you to use the actual decimal values in your code but print out the hundred-times larger percent values in the output. You request the default locale's percentage formatter with the static method NumberFormat.getPercentInstance( ):

```
public static final NumberFormat getPercentInstance( )
```

To get a percentage formatter for a different locale, pass the locale to NumberFormat.getPercentInstance( ):

```
public static NumberFormat getPercentInstance(Locale inLocale)
```

Example 21-5 prints a table of percents between 1% and 100%. Notice that doubles are used in the code, but integral percents appear in the output.

*Example 21-5. PercentTable*

```
import java.text.*;
import java.util.*;

public class PercentTable {

  public static void main(String[] args) {
    NumberFormat percentFormat = NumberFormat.getPercentInstance(Locale.ENGLISH);
    for (double d = 0.0; d <= 1.0; d += 0.005) {
      System.out.println(percentFormat.format(d));
    }
  }
}
```

Here's some of the output:

```
0%
0%
1%
1%
2%
2%
3%
```

```
3%
4%
4%
...
```

Notice that all percentage values are rounded to the nearest whole percent. This could be a problem if you need to format something like a tax rate. There is no 0.5% or 8.25% such as you might need when describing sales tax. To include fractional percents, call setMinimumFractionDigits() and setMaximumFractionDigits(). For example:

```
NumberFormat percentFormat = NumberFormat.getPercentInstance(Locale.ENGLISH);
percentFormat.setMaximumFractionDigits(2);
```

# Specifying Width with FieldPosition

The Java core API does not include any classes that pad numbers with spaces like the traditional I/O APIs in Fortran, C, and other languages. Part of the reason is that it's no longer a valid assumption that all output is written in a monospaced font on a VT-100 terminal. Therefore, spaces are insufficient to line up numbers in tables. Ideally, if you're writing tabular data in a GUI, you can use a real table component such as javax.swing.JTable. If that's not possible, you can measure the width of the string using a FontMetrics object and offset the position at which you draw the string. And if you are outputting to a terminal or a monospaced font, you can manually prefix the string with the right number of spaces.

The java.text.FieldPosition class separates strings into their component parts, called *fields*. (This is another unfortunate example of an overloaded term. These fields have nothing to do with the fields of a Java class.) For example, a typical date string can be separated into 18 fields including era, year, month, day, date, hour, minute, second, and so on. Of course, not all of these may be present in any given string. For example, 2006 CE includes only a year and an era field. The different fields that can be parsed are represented as public final static int fields (there's that annoying overloading again) in the corresponding format class. The java.text. DateFormat class defines these kinds of fields as mnemonic constants:

```
public static final int ERA_FIELD
public static final int YEAR_FIELD
public static final int MONTH_FIELD
public static final int DATE_FIELD
public static final int HOUR_OF_DAY1_FIELD
public static final int HOUR_OF_DAY0_FIELD
public static final int MINUTE_FIELD
public static final int SECOND_FIELD
public static final int MILLISECOND_FIELD
public static final int DAY_OF_WEEK_FIELD
public static final int DAY_OF_YEAR_FIELD
public static final int DAY_OF_WEEK_IN_MONTH_FIELD
public static final int WEEK_OF_YEAR_FIELD
```

```
public static final int WEEK_OF_MONTH_FIELD
public static final int AM_PM_FIELD
public static final int HOUR1_FIELD
public static final int HOUR0_FIELD
public static final int TIMEZONE_FIELD
```

Number formats are a little simpler. They are divided into only two fields, the integer field and the fraction field. These are represented by the mnemonic constants `NumberFormat.INTEGER_FIELD` and `NumberFormat.FRACTION_FIELD`:

```
public static final int INTEGER_FIELD
public static final int FRACTION_FIELD
```

The integer field is everything before the decimal point. The fraction field is everything after the decimal point. For instance, the string "-156.32" has an integer field of "-156" and a fraction field of "32".

The `java.text.FieldPosition` class identifies the boundaries of each field in the numeric string. You can then manually add the right number of monospaced characters or pixels to align the decimal points in a column of numbers. You create a `FieldPosition` object by passing one of these numeric constants into the `FieldPosition()` constructor:

```
public FieldPosition(int field)
```

For example, to get the integer field:

```
FieldPosition fp = new FieldPosition(NumberFormat.INTEGER_FIELD);
```

There's a `getField()` method that returns this constant:

```
public int getField()
```

Next you pass this object into one of the `format()` methods that takes a `FieldPosition` object as an argument:

```
NumberFormat nf = NumberFormat().getNumberInstance();
StringBuffer sb = nf.format(2.71828, new StringBuffer(), fp);
```

When `format()` returns, the `FieldPosition` object contains the start and end index of the field in the string. These methods return those items:

```
public int getBeginIndex()
public int getEndIndex()
```

You can subtract `getBeginIndex()` from `getEndIndex()` to find the number of characters in the field. If you're working with a monospaced font, this may be all you need to know. If you're working with a proportionally spaced font, you'll probably use `java.awt.FontMetrics` to measure the exact width of the field instead. Example 21-6 shows how to work in a monospaced font. This is essentially another version of the angle table. Now a `FieldPosition` object is used to figure out how many spaces to add to the front of the string; the `getSpaces()` method is simply used to build a string with a certain number of spaces.

*Example 21-6. PrettierTable*

```java
import java.text.*;

public class PrettierTable {

  public static void main(String[] args) {

    NumberFormat myFormat = NumberFormat.getNumberInstance();
    FieldPosition fp = new FieldPosition(NumberFormat.INTEGER_FIELD);
    myFormat.setMaximumIntegerDigits(3);
    myFormat.setMaximumFractionDigits(2);
    myFormat.setMinimumFractionDigits(2);

    System.out.println("Degrees  Radians  Grads");
    for (double degrees = 0.0; degrees < 360.0; degrees++) {
      String radianString = myFormat.format(
      radianString = getSpaces(3 - fp.getEndIndex()) + radianString;
      String gradString = myFormat.format(
      gradString = getSpaces(3 - fp.getEndIndex()) + gradString;
      String degreeString = myFormat.format(
          degrees, new StringBuffer(), fp).toString();
      degreeString = getSpaces(3 - fp.getEndIndex()) + degreeString;
      System.out.println(degreeString + "  " + radianString + "  " + gradString);
    }
  }

  public static String getSpaces(int n) {

    StringBuffer sb = new StringBuffer(n);
    for (int i = 0; i < n; i++) sb.append(' ');
    return sb.toString();
  }
}
```

Here's some sample output. Notice the alignment of the decimal points:

```
$ java PrettierTable
Degrees  Radians  Grads
   0.00    0.00    0.00
   1.00    0.02    1.11
   2.00    0.03    2.22
   3.00    0.05    3.33
   4.00    0.07    4.44
   5.00    0.09    5.56
   6.00    0.10    6.67
   7.00    0.12    7.78
   8.00    0.14    8.89
   9.00    0.16   10.00
  10.00    0.17   11.11
  11.00    0.19   12.22
  12.00    0.21   13.33
  13.00    0.23   14.44
```

This technique only works with monospaced fonts. In GUI environments, you'll need to work with pixels instead of characters. Instead of prefixing a string with spaces, you adjust the position where the pen starts drawing each string. The getBeginIndex( ) and getEndIndex( ) methods, along with substring( ) in java.lang. String can be used to get the actual field, and the stringWidth( ) method in the java. awt.FontMetrics class can tell you how wide the field is.

Example 21-7 is yet another variant of the angle table. This one draws the angles in an applet. Figure 21-1 shows a screenshot of the running applet. This technique works equally well in a panel, frame, scroll pane, canvas, or other drawing environment with a paint( ) method.

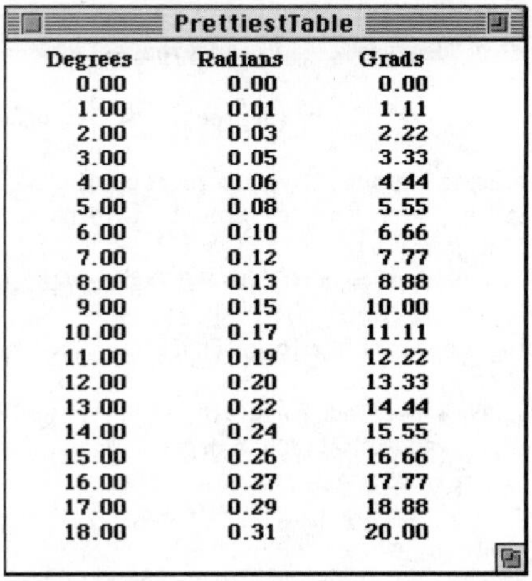

| PrettiestTable | | |
|---|---|---|
| **Degrees** | **Radians** | **Grads** |
| 0.00 | 0.00 | 0.00 |
| 1.00 | 0.01 | 1.11 |
| 2.00 | 0.03 | 2.22 |
| 3.00 | 0.05 | 3.33 |
| 4.00 | 0.06 | 4.44 |
| 5.00 | 0.08 | 5.55 |
| 6.00 | 0.10 | 6.66 |
| 7.00 | 0.12 | 7.77 |
| 8.00 | 0.13 | 8.88 |
| 9.00 | 0.15 | 10.00 |
| 10.00 | 0.17 | 11.11 |
| 11.00 | 0.19 | 12.22 |
| 12.00 | 0.20 | 13.33 |
| 13.00 | 0.22 | 14.44 |
| 14.00 | 0.24 | 15.55 |
| 15.00 | 0.26 | 16.66 |
| 16.00 | 0.27 | 17.77 |
| 17.00 | 0.29 | 18.88 |
| 18.00 | 0.31 | 20.00 |

Figure 21-1. The PrettiestTable applet

Example 21-7. PrettiestTable

```java
import java.text.*;
import java.applet.*;
import java.awt.*;

public class PrettiestTable extends Applet {

  NumberFormat myFormat = NumberFormat.getNumberInstance( );
  FieldPosition fp = new FieldPosition(NumberFormat.INTEGER_FIELD);

  public void init( ) {
    this.setFont(new Font("Serif", Font.BOLD, 12));
    myFormat.setMaximumIntegerDigits(3);
    myFormat.setMaximumFractionDigits(2);
    myFormat.setMinimumFractionDigits(2);
  }

  public void paint(Graphics g) {
```

*Example 21-7. PrettiestTable (continued)*

```
      FontMetrics fm = this.getFontMetrics(this.getFont()) ;
      int xmargin = 5;
      int lineHeight = fm.getMaxAscent() + fm.getMaxDescent();
      int y = lineHeight;
      int x = xmargin;
      int desiredPixelWidth = 3 * fm.getMaxAdvance();
      int fieldWidth = 6 * fm.getMaxAdvance();
      int headerWidth = fm.stringWidth("Degrees");
      g.drawString("Degrees", x + (fieldWidth - headerWidth)/2, y);
      headerWidth = fm.stringWidth("Radians");
      g.drawString("Radians", x + fieldWidth + (fieldWidth - headerWidth)/2, y);
      headerWidth = fm.stringWidth("Grads");
      g.drawString("Grads", x + 2*fieldWidth + (fieldWidth - headerWidth)/2, y);

      for (double degrees = 0.0; degrees < 360.0; degrees++) {
        y += lineHeight;
        String degreeString = myFormat.format(degrees, new StringBuffer(),
           fp).toString();
        String intPart = degreeString.substring(0, fp.getEndIndex());
        g.drawString(degreeString, xmargin + desiredPixelWidth
           - fm.stringWidth(intPart), y);
        String radianString = myFormat.format(Math.PI*degrees/180.0,
           new StringBuffer(), fp).toString();
        intPart = radianString.substring(0, fp.getEndIndex());
        g.drawString(radianString,
            xmargin + fieldWidth + desiredPixelWidth - fm.stringWidth(intPart), y);
        String gradString = myFormat.format(400 * degrees / 360,
           new StringBuffer(), fp).toString();
        intPart = gradString.substring(0, fp.getEndIndex());
        g.drawString(gradString,
           xmargin + 2*fieldWidth + desiredPixelWidth - fm.stringWidth(intPart), y);
      }
    }
  }
}
```

# Parsing Input

Number formats also handle input. When used for input, a number format converts a string in the appropriate format to a binary number, achieving more flexible conversions than you can get with the methods in the type wrapper classes (like Integer. parseInt()). For instance, a percent format parse() method can interpret 57% as 0.57 instead of 57. A currency format can read (12.45) as −12.45.

There are three parse() methods in the NumberFormat class. All do roughly the same thing:

```
public Number parse(String text) throws ParseException
public abstract Number parse(String text, ParsePosition parsePosition)
public final Object parseObject(String source, ParsePosition parsePosition)
```

The first parse( ) method attempts to parse a number from the given text. If the text represents an integer, it's returned as an instance of java.lang.Long. Otherwise, it's returned as an instance of java.lang.Double. If a string contains multiple numbers, only the first one is returned. For instance, if you parse "32 meters" you'll get the number 32 back. Java throws away everything after the number finishes. If the text cannot be interpreted as a number in the given format, a ParseException is thrown.

The second parse( ) method specifies where in the text parsing starts. The position is given by a ParsePosition object. This is a little more complicated than using a simple int but does have the advantage of allowing one to read successive numbers from the same string. The third parse( ) method merely invokes the second. It's declared to return Object rather than Number so that it can override the method of the same signature in java.text.Format. If you know you're working with a NumberFormat rather than a DateFormat or some other nonnumeric format, there's no reason to use it.

The java.text.ParsePosition class has one constructor and two public methods:

```
public ParsePosition(int index)
public int  getIndex( )
public void setIndex(int index)
```

This whole class is just a wrapper around a position, which is set by the constructor and the setIndex( ) method and returned by the getIndex( ) method. As a NumberFormat parses a string, it updates the associated ParsePosition's index. Thus, when passed into a parse( ) method, the ParsePosition contains the index where parsing will begin. When the parse( ) method returns, the ParsePosition contains the index immediately after the last character parsed. If parsing fails, the parse position is unchanged.

Some number formats can only read integers, not floating-point numbers. The isParseIntegerOnly( ) method returns true if this is the case or false otherwise.

```
public boolean isParseIntegerOnly( )
public void    setParseIntegerOnly(boolean value)
```

The setParseInteger( ) method lets you specify that the format should only parse integers. If a decimal point is encountered, parsing should stop.

Example 21-8 is a simple program of the sort that's common in CS 101 courses. The assignment is to write a program that reads a number entered from the command line and prints its square root. Successive numbers are read until a negative number is entered, at which point the program halts. Although this is a very basic exercise, it's relatively complex in Java because Java separates string parsing from basic I/O. Nonetheless, while it may not be suitable for the first week's homework, students should be able to handle it by the end of the semester.

*Example 21-8. RootFinder*

```java
import java.text.*;
import java.io.*;

public class RootFinder {

  public static void main(String[] args) {

    Number input = null;

    try {
      BufferedReader br = new BufferedReader(new InputStreamReader(System.in));
      NumberFormat nf = NumberFormat.getInstance( );
      while (true) {
        System.out.println("Enter a number (-1 to quit): ");
        String s = br.readLine( );
        try {
          input = nf.parse(s);
        }
        catch (ParseException ex) {
          System.out.println(s + " is not a number I understand.");
          continue;
        }
        double d = input.doubleValue( );
        if (d < 0) break;
        double root = Math.sqrt(d);
        System.out.println("The square root of " + s + " is " + root);
      }
    }
    catch (IOException ex) {System.err.println(ex);}
  }
}
```

Here's a sample run:

```
$ java RootFinder
Enter a number (-1 to quit):
87
The square root of 87 is 9.327379053088816
Enter a number (-1 to quit):
3.151592
The square root of 3.151592 is 1.7752723734683644
Enter a number (-1 to quit):
2,345,678
The square root of 2,345,678 is 1531.5606419596973
Enter a number (-1 to quit):
2.998E+8
The square root of 2.998E+8 is 1.7314733610425546
Enter a number (-1 to quit):
299800000
The square root of 299800000 is 17314.733610425545
Enter a number (-1 to quit):
0.0
The square root of 0.0 is 0.0
```

```
Enter a number (-1 to quit):
four
four is not a number I understand.
Enter a number (-1 to quit):
4
The square root of 4 is 2.0
Enter a number (-1 to quit):
(12)
(12) is not a number I understand.
Enter a number (-1 to quit):
-1
```

These results tell you a few things about Java's default number format in the locale where I ran it (U.S. English). First, it doesn't understand exponential notation. The square root of 2.998E+8 is not 1.7314733610425546; it's 1.7314733610425546E+4. The number format parsed up to the first character it didn't recognize (E) and stopped, thus returning the square root of 2.998 instead. You can also see that this number format doesn't understand negative numbers represented by parentheses or words like "four." On the other hand, it can parse numbers with thousands separators like 2,345,678. This is more than the I/O libraries in most other languages can do. With the appropriate, nondefault number format, Java could parse (12), four, and 2.998E+8 as well.

# Decimal Formats

The `java.text.DecimalFormat` class provides even more control over how floating-point numbers are formatted:

```
public class DecimalFormat extends NumberFormat
```

Most number formats are in fact decimal formats. Generally, you can simply cast any number format to a decimal format, like this:

```
DecimalFormat df = (DecimalFormat) NumberFormat.getCurrencyInstance( );
```

At least in theory, you might encounter a nondecimal format. Therefore, you should use instanceof to test whether or not you've got a DecimalFormat:

```
NumberFormat nf = NumberFormat.getCurrencyInstance( );
if (nf instanceof DecimalFormat) {
  DecimalFormat df = (DecimalFormat) NumberFormat.getCurrencyInstance( );
  //...
}
```

Alternatively, you can place the cast and associated operations in a try/catch block that catches ClassCastExceptions:

```
try {
  DecimalFormat df = (DecimalFormat) NumberFormat.getCurrencyInstance( );
  //...
}
catch (ClassCastException ex) {System.err.println(ex);}
```

## Decimal Format Patterns

Every `DecimalFormat` object has a pattern that describes how numbers are formatted and a list of symbols that describes with which characters they're formatted. This allows the single `DecimalFormat` class to be parameterized so that it can handle many different formats for different kinds of numbers in many locales. The pattern is given as an ASCII string. The symbols are provided by a `DecimalFormatSymbols` object. These are accessed and manipulated through the following six methods:

```
public DecimalFormatSymbols getDecimalFormatSymbols( )
public void setDecimalFormatSymbols(DecimalFormatSymbols newSymbols)
public String toPattern( )
public String toLocalizedPattern( )
public void applyPattern(String pattern)
public void applyLocalizedPattern(String pattern)
```

The decimal format symbols specify the characters or strings used for the zero digit, the grouping separator, the decimal sign, the percent sign, the mille percent sign, infinity (IEEE 754 Inf), not a number (IEEE 754 NaN), and the minus sign. In American English these are 0, ,, ., %, ‰, Inf, NaN, and -, respectively. They may be other things in different locales.

The pattern specifies whether leading and trailing zeros are printed, whether the fractional part of the number is printed, the number of digits in a group (three in American English), and the leading and trailing suffixes for negative and positive numbers.

For instance, `#,##0.###` is the decimal format pattern for U.S. English and most other non-Arabic-speaking locales. The notable exceptions are the Arabic-speaking countries and Macedonia. The primary difference between locales comes in the decimal format symbols, not the pattern. The currency formats have more variation because most countries have their own currencies with their own unique symbols.

The # mark means any digit character except a leading or trailing zero. The comma is the grouping separator, the period is the decimal point separator, and the 0 is a digit that will be printed even if it's a nonsignificant zero. Interpret this pattern as follows:

1. The integer part contains as many digits as necessary.

2. These are separated every three digits with the grouping separator.

3. If the integer part is zero, there is a single zero before the decimal separator.

4. Up to three digits are printed after the decimal separator. However, they are not printed if they are trailing zeros.

5. No separate pattern is included for negative numbers. Therefore, they will be printed the same as a positive number but prefixed with a minus sign.

You can apply your own patterns to support different formats. For example, the pattern `0.00000000E0` specifies a number will be formatted in exponential notation with exactly one digit before the decimal separator and exactly eight digits after the decimal separator.

It's relatively painful to work with this grammar directly. Fortunately, there are methods that allow you to get and set the values of these individual pieces directly, and I recommend that you use them:

```
public String  getPositivePrefix( )
public void    setPositivePrefix(String newValue)
public String  getPositiveSuffix( )
public void    setPositiveSuffix(String newValue)
public String  getNegativePrefix( )
public void    setNegativePrefix(String newValue)
public String  getNegativeSuffix( )
public void    setNegativeSuffix(String newValue)
public int     getMultiplier( )
public void    setMultiplier(int newValue)
public int     getGroupingSize( )
public void    setGroupingSize(int newValue)
public boolean isDecimalSeparatorAlwaysShown( )
public void    setDecimalSeparatorAlwaysShown(boolean newValue)
```

The positive prefix is the string prefixed to positive numbers. Most of the time, this is the empty string, but in some circumstances you might want to use a plus sign (+). In currency formats, the positive prefix is often set to the currency sign, like $ or £, depending on the locale. You can also set a positive suffix; that is, a string that is appended to all positive numbers. This is used to attach the percent sign to percentage formats. The negative prefix is the minus sign (-). However, in accounting and other financial applications it may be an open parenthesis instead. In these applications, there's also a negative suffix, generally a closing parenthesis. Thus, -12 might be formatted as (12).

The multiplier is an integer by which the number is multiplied before being formatted. This is commonly used in percent formats. This allows a number like 0.85 to be formatted as 85% instead of 0.85%. 1, 100, and 1000 are the only common values of this number. Grouping size is the number of digits between grouping separators, commas in English. This is how 75365 becomes 75,365. Most locales, including English, break every three digits; a few break every four, formatting 75365 as 7,5365. Finally, you can specify whether or not the decimal separator (decimal point) is shown in numbers without fractional parts. By default, a number like 1999 does not have a decimal point. However, there are situations (C source code, for example) where the difference between 1999 and 1999. is significant.

You also have access to the following methods, inherited from java.text. NumberFormat, which allow you to set and get the minimum and maximum number of integer and fraction digits and control whether or not grouping is used at all. These work just as well with decimal formats as they do with regular number formats:

```
public boolean isGroupingUsed( )
public void    setGroupingUsed(boolean useGrouping)
public int     getMaximumIntegerDigits( )
public void    setMaximumIntegerDigits(int maxDigits)
public int     getMinimumIntegerDigits( )
```

```
public void    setMinimumIntegerDigits(int minDigits)
public int     getMaximumFractionDigits()
public void    setMaximumFractionDigits(int maxDigits)
public int     getMinimumFractionDigits()
public void    setMinimumFractionDigits(int minDigits)
```

## DecimalFormatSymbols

Each DecimalFormat object has a DecimalFormatSymbols object that contains a list of the different symbols used by decimal number formats in a particular locale. The decimal format symbols specify the characters or strings used for the zero digit, the grouping separator, the decimal sign, the percent sign, the mille percent sign, infinity (IEEE 754 Inf), not a number (IEEE 754 NaN), and the minus sign. DecimalFormatSymbols has two constructors, but they're rarely used:

```
public DecimalFormatSymbols()
public DecimalFormatSymbols(Locale locale)
```

Instead, the DecimalFormatSymbols object is retrieved from a particular DecimalFormat object using its getDecimalFormatSymbols() method:

```
public DecimalFormatSymbols getDecimalFormatSymbols()
```

If you create your own DecimalFormatSymbols object, perhaps for a locale Java doesn't support, you can make a DecimalFormat use it by passing it to DecimalFormat's setDecimalFormatSymbols() method:

```
public void setDecimalFormatSymbols(DecimalFormatSymbols newSymbols)
```

The DecimalFormatSymbols class contains mostly getter and setter methods for inspecting and setting the values of the different symbols:

```
public char   getZeroDigit()
public void    setZeroDigit(char zeroDigit)
public char   getGroupingSeparator()
public void    setGroupingSeparator(char groupingSeparator)
public char   getDecimalSeparator()
public void    setDecimalSeparator(char decimalSeparator)
public char   getMonetaryDecimalSeparator()
public void    setMonetaryDecimalSeparator(char decimalSeparator)
public char   getPercent()
public void    setPercent(char percent)
public char   getPerMill()
public void    setPerMill(char perMill)
public String getInfinity()
public void    setInfinity(String infinity)
public String getNaN()
public void    setNaN(String NaN)
public char   getMinusSign()
public void    setMinusSign(char minusSign)
```

The zero digit is the character used for zero. This is 0 in most Western languages but is different in Arabic and a few other locales. The grouping separator is the character used to split groups; a comma is used in the U.S., but a period is used in some other countries that use a comma as the decimal separator. The decimal separator is a decimal point (a period) in English but a comma in some other locales. Most of the time regular numbers and money numbers use the same decimal separator, but in a few cases they're different. (Pre-Euro Portugal is one case.) The monetary separator specifies the decimal separator for currency formats. The percent and per mille characters are % and ‰ in English, occasionally other things in other locales. The infinity and not-a-number strings are rarely changed. They're Inf and NaN as specified by IEEE 754, generally even in non-English languages like German, where the word for infinity is Unbegrenztheit and "not a number" translates as "nicht eine Zahl." Finally, the minus sign is the default character used for negative numbers that do not have a specific prefix. It's a hyphen (-) in English. This character is not used if the associated pattern has set a negative prefix.

In Java 1.2 and later, there are methods to get and set the currency symbol and code:

```
public String    getCurrencySymbol()
public void      setCurrencySymbol(String symbol)
public String    getInternationalCurrencySymbol()
public void      setInternationalCurrencySymbol(String code)
public Currency  getCurrency() // Java 1.4
public void      setCurrency(Currency currency) // Java 1.4
```

The currency symbol is the actual currency character(s) that prefix a monetary value such as $, €, or £. The currency symbol is the ISO 4217 three-letter ASCII code for that currency such as USD, EUR, or GBP. The Currency object is a Java 1.4 typesafe enum that encapsulates the available currencies. These three values should be in sync. Setting the currency or the currency symbol will also set the other two properties to corresponding values. For example, changing the international currency symbol to EUR, changes the currency symbol to €. You don't have to explicitly call setCurrencySymbol() and setCurrency(). The reverse procedure does not work, however. Changing the currency symbol does not change the currency and the international currency symbol.

## Constructing Decimal Formats with Patterns and Symbols

Most of the time, you use the factory methods in NumberFormat to get DecimalFormat instances. However, there are three public DecimalFormat constructors you can use to create DecimalFormat instances directly:

```
public DecimalFormat()
public DecimalFormat(String pattern)
public DecimalFormat(String pattern, DecimalFormatSymbols symbols)
```

The no-argument constructor creates a decimal format that uses the default pattern and symbols for the default locale. The second constructor creates a decimal format that uses the specified pattern and the default symbols for the default locale. The third constructor creates a decimal format that uses the specified pattern and the specified symbols for the default locale. These are useful for special cases that aren't handled by the default patterns and symbols.

# PART VII

# Devices

# CHAPTER 22

# The Java Communications API

This chapter covers the Java Communications API, a standard extension that can send data to and receive data from RS-232 serial ports and IEEE 1284-parallel ports. This allows Java programs to talk to essentially any device connected to a serial or parallel port, like a printer, a scanner, a modem, a tape backup unit, and so on. The Communications API operates at a very low level. It only understands how to send and receive bytes to these ports. It does not understand anything about what these bytes mean. Doing useful work generally requires not only understanding the Java Communications API (which is actually quite simple) but also the protocols spoken by the devices connected to the ports (which can be almost arbitrarily complex).

## The Architecture of the Java Communications API

Because the Java Communications API is a standard extension, it is not installed by default with the JDK. You have to download it from *http://java.sun.com/products/javacomm/* and install it separately. The current version is 3.0. However. this is only available for Linux and Solaris. Version 2.0 was also available on Windows. However, Sun recently retired that version. At the time of this writing you can find it at *http://javashoplm.sun.com/ECom/docs/Welcome.jsp?StoreId=22&PartDetailId=7235-javacomm-2.0-spec-oth-JSpec&SiteId=JSC&TransactionId=noreg*  but I wouldn't count on that URL lasting forever. If you can find a copy, the difference between 2.0 and 3.0 is not huge (with the exception of Windows support), just a couple of extra methods here and there.

 There are a couple of third-party implementations of the Java Communications API for the Mac. However, since it's been almost ten years since any Macs shipped with serial ports and no Mac has ever had a parallel port, this probably isn't too big a deal. These days attaching a serial port device to a Mac requires a USB adapter or PCI card.

The Java Communications API contains a single package, javax.comm, which holds a baker's dozen of classes, exceptions, and interfaces. Because the Comm API is a standard extension, the javax prefix is used instead of the java prefix. The Comm API also includes a DLL or shared library containing the native code to communicate with the ports, and a few driver classes in the com.sun.comm package that mostly handle the vagaries of Unix or Wintel ports. Other vendors may need to muck around with these if they're porting the Comm API to another platform (e.g., the Mac or Pocket PC), but as a user of the API, you'll only concern yourself with the documented classes in javax.comm.

javax.comm is divided into high-level and low-level classes. High-level classes are responsible for controlling access to and ownership of the communication ports and performing basic I/O. The CommPortIdentifier class lets you find and open the ports available on a system. The CommPort class provides input and output streams connected to the ports. Low-level classes—SerialPort and ParallelPort, for example—manage interaction with particular kinds of ports and help you read and write the control wires on the ports. They also provide event-based notification of changes to the state of the port.

# Identifying Ports

The CommPortIdentifier class is the controller for the ports on a system. It has methods that list the available ports, figure out which program owns them, take control of a port, and open a port so you can perform I/O with it. The actual I/O, stream-based or otherwise, is performed through an instance of CommPort that represents the port in question. The purpose of CommPortIdentifier is to mediate between different programs, objects, or threads that want to use the same port.

## Finding the Ports

Before you can use a port, you need an identifier for the port. Because the possible port identifiers are closely tied to the physical ports on the system, you cannot simply construct an arbitrary CommPortIdentifier object. Instead, you use one of several static methods in CommPortIdentifier that find the right port. These include:

```
public static Enumeration getPortIdentifiers( )
public static CommPortIdentifier getPortIdentifier(String portName)
            throws NoSuchPortException
public static CommPortIdentifier getPortIdentifier(CommPort port)
            throws NoSuchPortException
```

The most general of these is CommPortIdentifier.getPortIdentifiers( ), which returns a java.util.Enumeration containing one CommPortIdentifier for each of the ports on the system. Example 22-1 uses this method to list all the ports on the system.

*Example 22-1. PortLister*

```
import javax.comm.*;
import java.util.*;

public class PortLister {

  public static void main(String[] args) {
    Enumeration e = CommPortIdentifier.getPortIdentifiers();
    while (e.hasMoreElements()) {
      System.out.println((CommPortIdentifier) e.nextElement());
    }
  }
}
```

To compile this and the other programs in this chapter, you need the JAR file containing the API. In Sun's implementation, this file is named *comm.jar*. For example,

```
$ javac -classpath .:jar/comm.jar PortLister.java
```

To run the program, you'll need the native libraries and a *javax.comm.properties* file. The native libraries are found in the *lib* directory. To link to these on Linux or Solaris, you need to add the *lib* directory to the LD_LIBRARY_PATH environment variable like so:

```
$ export LD_LIBRARY_PATH=lib
```

If $LD_LIBRARY_PATH has already been defined, you need to redefine it like this instead:

```
$ export LD_LIBRARY_PATH=lib:$ LD_LIBRARY_PATH
```

This assumes the *lib* directory is found in the current working directory. Otherwise, specify the complete path to where it is found.

Finally, you'll need to place the *javax.comm.properties* file in your classpath. Confusingly, Sun distributes this file in the *docs* directory. If your serial and parallel ports are not in the usual locations, or you have extra ports, customize this file to tell Java where they are.

Here's the output I got when I ran PortLister on my fairly stock Wintel PC:

```
D:\JAVA\22\>java PortLister
javax.comm.CommPortIdentifier@be3c9581
javax.comm.CommPortIdentifier@be209581
javax.comm.CommPortIdentifier@be489581
javax.comm.CommPortIdentifier@be4c9581
```

This shows you that my system has four ports, though it doesn't tell you what those ports are. Of course, the output varies depending on how many serial and parallel ports the system possesses. I also ran PortLister on the same hardware but this time running Linux and here's the output:

```
$ java -classpath .:jar/comm.jar PortLister
javax.comm.CommPortIdentifier@19f953d
javax.comm.CommPortIdentifier@1fee6fc
```

Surprisingly, only two ports were found now. The problem is that the default *javax.comm.properties* file specifies the serial ports at */dev/ttyS0* and */dev/ttyS1* and the parallel ports at */dev/parport0* and */dev/parport1*. However, the version of Debian I'm running maps the parallel ports to */dev/par0* and */dev/par1*. After I edited the *javax.comm.properties* file to recognize this, Java found all four ports:

```
$ java -classpath .:jar/comm.jar PortLister
javax.comm.CommPortIdentifier@19f953d
javax.comm.CommPortIdentifier@1fee6fc
javax.comm.CommPortIdentifier@1eed786
javax.comm.CommPortIdentifier@187aeca
```

Clearly, a better toString( ) method is needed. (CommPortIdentifier merely inherits java.lang.Object's toString( ) method.) You'll see how to work around this in the next section.

You can also get a CommPortIdentifier by using the static method getPortIdentifier( ) to request a port identifier, either by name or by the actual port object. The latter assumes that you already have a reference to the relevant port, which usually isn't the case. The former allows you to choose from Windows names like "COM1" and "LPT2" or Unix names like "Serial A" and "Serial B." The exact format of a name is highly platform- and implementation-dependent. If you ask for a port that doesn't exist, a NoSuchPortException is thrown. Example 22-2 looks for serial and parallel ports by starting with COM1 and LPT1 and counting up until one is missing. Be warned that this code is highly platform-dependent and probably won't work on Unix or the Mac.

*Example 22-2. NamedPortLister*

```
import javax.comm.*;

public class NamedPortLister {

  public static void main(String[] args) {

    // List serial (COM) ports.
    try {
      int portNumber = 1;
      while (true) {
        CommPortIdentifier.getPortIdentifier("COM" + portNumber);
        System.out.println("COM" + portNumber);
        portNumber++;
      }
    }
    catch (NoSuchPortException ex) {
      // Break out of loop.
    }

    // List parallel (LPT) ports.
    try {
      int portNumber = 1;
```

*Example 22-2. NamedPortLister (continued)*

```
    while (true) {
      CommPortIdentifier.getPortIdentifier("LPT" + portNumber);
      System.out.println("LPT" + portNumber);
      portNumber++;
    }
  }
  catch (NoSuchPortException ex) {
    // Break out of loop.
  }
 }
}
```

Once again, here's the output from a stock Wintel box:

```
D:\JAVA\22>java NamedPortLister
COM1
COM2
LPT1
LPT2
```

Now you can see that I have two serial and two parallel ports. However, this same program wouldn't find any ports on a Unix box because Unix uses different port names.

## Getting Information about a Port

Once you have a CommPortIdentifier, you can discover information about the port by calling several accessor methods. These include:

```
public String  getName( )
public int     getPortType( )
public String  getCurrentOwner( )
public boolean isCurrentlyOwned( )
```

The getName( ) method returns the platform-dependent name of the port, such as "COM1" (Windows) or "Serial A" (Solaris). The getPortType( ) method returns one of the two mnemonic constants CommPortIdentifier.PORT_SERIAL or CommPortIdentifier.PORT_PARALLEL:

```
public static final int PORT_SERIAL = 1;
public static final int PORT_PARALLEL = 2;
```

The isCurrentlyOwned( ) method returns true if some other Java process, thread, or application currently has control of the port. It returns false otherwise. If a port is owned by another Java program, the getCurrentOwner( ) returns the name supplied by the program that owns it; otherwise, it returns null. This isn't too useful because it doesn't handle the much more likely case that a non-Java program like Dial-Up Networking or PPP is using the port. Example 22-3 is a revision of the PortLister in Example 22-1 that uses these four accessor methods to provide information about each port rather than relying on the inherited toString( ) method.

*Example 22-3. PrettyPortLister*

```java
import javax.comm.*;
import java.util.*;

public class PrettyPortLister {

  public static void main(String[] args) {

    Enumeration e = CommPortIdentifier.getPortIdentifiers();
    while (e.hasMoreElements()) {
      CommPortIdentifier com = (CommPortIdentifier) e.nextElement();
      System.out.print(com.getName());

      switch(com.getPortType()) {
        case CommPortIdentifier.PORT_SERIAL:
          System.out.print(", a serial port, ");
          break;
        case CommPortIdentifier.PORT_PARALLEL:
          System.out.print(", a parallel port, ");
          break;
        default:
          System.out.print(" , a port of unknown type, ");
          break;
      }
      if (com.isCurrentlyOwned()) {
        System.out.println("is currently owned by "
        + com.getCurrentOwner() + ".");
      }
      else {
        System.out.println("is not currently owned.");
      }
    }
  }
}
```

Here's the output when run on a stock Wintel box:

```
D:\JAVA\22>java PrettyPrintLister
COM1, a serial port, is not currently owned.
COM2, a serial port, is not currently owned.
LPT1, a parallel port, is not currently owned.
LPT2, a parallel port, is not currently owned.
```

This output originally confused me because I expected one of the COM ports to be occupied by the Dial-Up Networking PPP connection on the internal modem (COM2). However, the isCurrentlyOwned( ) method only notices other Java programs in the same VM occupying ports. To detect whether a non-Java program is controlling a port, you must try to open the port and watch for PortInUseExceptions, as discussed in the next section.

# Opening Ports

Before you can read from or write to a port, you have to open it. Opening a port gives your application exclusive access to the port until you give it up or the program ends. (Two different programs should not send data to the same modem at the same time, after all.) Opening a port is not guaranteed to succeed. If another program (Java or otherwise) is using the port, a `PortInUseException` will be thrown when you try to open the port. Surprisingly, this is not a subclass of `IOException`.

```
public class PortInUseException extends Exception
```

`CommPortIdentifier` has two open( ) methods; they each return a `CommPort` object you can use to read data from and write data to the port. The first variant takes two arguments, a name and a timeout value:

```
public CommPort open(String name, int timeout) throws PortInUseException
```

The name argument is a name for the program that wants to use the port and is returned by getCurrentOwner( ) while the port is in use. The `timeout` argument is the maximum number of milliseconds this method blocks while waiting for the port to become available. If the operation does not complete within that time, a `PortInUseException` is thrown. Example 22-4 is a variation of the `PortLister` program that attempts to open each unowned port.

*Example 22-4. PortOpener*

```java
import javax.comm.*;
import java.util.*;

public class PortOpener {

  public static void main(String[] args) {

    Enumeration thePorts = CommPortIdentifier.getPortIdentifiers();
    while (thePorts.hasMoreElements()) {
      CommPortIdentifier com = (CommPortIdentifier) thePorts.nextElement();
      System.out.print(com.getName());

      switch(com.getPortType()) {
        case CommPortIdentifier.PORT_SERIAL:
          System.out.print(", a serial port, ");
          break;
        case CommPortIdentifier.PORT_PARALLEL:
          System.out.print(", a parallel port, ");
          break;
        default:
          System.out.print(" , a port of unknown type, ");
          break;
      }
      try {
        CommPort thePort  = com.open("PortOpener", 10);
        System.out.println("is not currently owned.");
```

*Example 22-4. PortOpener (continued)*

```
      thePort.close( );
    }
    catch (PortInUseException ex) {
      String owner = com.getCurrentOwner( );
      if (owner == null) owner = "unknown";
      System.out.println("is currently owned by " + owner + ".");
    }
  }
 }
}
```

Here's the output:

```
D:\JAVA\22>java PortOpener
COM1, a serial port, is not currently owned.
COM2, a serial port, is currently owned by Port currently not owned.
LPT1, a parallel port, is not currently owned.
LPT2, a parallel port, is currently owned by Port currently not owned.
```

In this example, you see that COM2 is occupied, though by a non-Java program that did not register its name. You also see that LPT2 is occupied, which was something of a surprise to me—I didn't think I was using any parallel ports.

On Linux, the results were a little different:

```
elharo@cafe:~/comm$ java -classpath .:jar/comm.jar PortOpener
/dev/ttyS0, a serial port,

Exception in thread "main" java.lang.RuntimeException:
  Error opening "/dev/ttyS0"
  Permission denied
        at com.sun.comm.LinuxDriver.getCommPort(LinuxDriver.java:66)
        at javax.comm.CommPortIdentifier.open(CommPortIdentifier.java:368)
        at PortOpener.main(PortOpener.java:27)
```

Linux and Unix often require root access to open ports. Since I didn't have it, they threw a rather nasty RuntimeException. This really should be an IOException or a SecurityException. After I su'd to root, I was able to run the program as expected and open the ports:

```
# /opt/java/j2sdk1.4.2_04/bin/java -classpath .:jar/comm.jar PortOpener
/dev/ttyS0, a serial port, is not currently owned.
/dev/ttyS1, a serial port, is not currently owned.
/dev/par0, a parallel port, is not currently owned.
/dev/par1, a parallel port,

Exception in thread "main" java.lang.RuntimeException:
  Error opening"/dev/par1"
  No such device or address
        at com.sun.comm.LinuxDriver.getCommPort(LinuxDriver.java:66)
        at javax.comm.CommPortIdentifier.open(CommPortIdentifier.java:368)
        at PortOpener.main(PortOpener.java:27)
```

That final exception came because this hardware only had one parallel port, even though there were entries for more in the */dev* directory.

The second open( ) method takes a file descriptor as an argument:

```
public CommPort open(FileDescriptor fd) throws UnsupportedCommOperationException
```

This may be useful on operating systems like Unix, where all devices, serial ports included, are treated as files. On all other platforms, this method throws an UnsupportedCommOperationException:

```
public class UnsupportedCommOperationException extends Exception
```

There is no corresponding close( ) method in the CommPortIdentifier class. The necessary close( ) method is included in the CommPort class itself. You should close all ports you've opened when you're through with them.

# Communicating with a Device on a Port

The open( ) method of the CommPortIdentifier class returns a CommPort object. The CommPort class has methods for getting input and output streams from a port and for closing the port. There are also a number of driver-dependent methods for adjusting the properties of the port.

## Communicating with a Port

There are five basic steps to communicating with a port:

1. Open the port using the open( ) method of CommPortIdentifier. If the port is available, this returns a CommPort object. Otherwise, it throws a PortInUseException.
2. Get the port's output stream using the getOutputStream( ) method of CommPort.
3. Get the port's input stream using the getInputStream( ) method of CommPort.
4. Read and write data onto those streams as desired.
5. Close the port using the close( ) method of CommPort.

Steps 2 through 4 are new. However, they're not particularly complex. Once the connection has been established, you simply use the normal methods of any input or output stream to read and write data. The getInputStream( ) and getOutputStream( ) methods of CommPort are similar to the methods of the same name in the java.net. URL class. The primary difference is that with ports, you're completely responsible for understanding and handling the data that's sent to you. There are no content or protocol handlers that perform any manipulation of the data. If the device attached to the port requires a complicated protocol—for example, a fax modem—you'll have to handle the protocol manually.

```
public abstract InputStream  getInputStream( ) throws IOException
public abstract OutputStream getOutputStream( ) throws IOException
```

Some ports are unidirectional. In other words, the port hardware only supports writing or reading, not both. For instance, early PC parallel ports allowed the computer to send data to the printer but could only send a small number of precisely defined signals back to the computer. This was fine for a printer, but it meant that the parallel port wasn't useful for a device like a CD-ROM or a Zip drive. If the port you've opened doesn't allow writing, getOutputStream() returns null. If the port doesn't allow reading, getInputStream() returns null.

Example 22-5 is a simple character-mode program that allows you to type back and forth with a port. If a modem is attached to the port, you can use it as an extremely rudimentary terminal emulator. Two separate threads handle input and output so that input doesn't get blocked waiting for output and vice versa.

*Example 22-5. PortTyper*

```java
import javax.comm.*;
import java.util.*;
import java.io.*;

public class PortTyper {

  public static void main(String[] args) {

    if (args.length < 1) {
      System.out.println("Usage: java PortTyper portName");
      return;
    }

    try {
      CommPortIdentifier com = CommPortIdentifier.getPortIdentifier(args[0]);
      CommPort thePort  = com.open("PortOpener", 10);
      CopyThread input = new CopyThread(System.in, thePort.getOutputStream());
      CopyThread output = new CopyThread(thePort.getInputStream(), System.out);
      input.start();
      output.start();
    }
    catch (Exception ex) {System.out.println(ex);}
  }
}

class CopyThread extends Thread {

  private InputStream theInput;
  private OutputStream theOutput;

  CopyThread(InputStream in) {
    this(in, System.out);
  }

  CopyThread(OutputStream out) {
    this(System.in, out);
  }
```

*Example 22-5. PortTyper (continued)*

```
  CopyThread(InputStream in, OutputStream out) {
    theInput = in;
    theOutput = out;
  }

  public void run( ) {

    try {
      byte[] buffer = new byte[256];
      while (true) {
        int bytesRead = theInput.read(buffer);
        if (bytesRead == -1) break;
        theOutput.write(buffer, 0, bytesRead);
      }
    }
    catch (IOException ex) {System.err.println(ex);}
  }
}
```

Here's a sample session where I used this program to connect to my ISP. After I logged out, the incoming line rang three times, which you also see:

```
D:\JAVA\22java PortTyper COM2
at&f
at&f

OK
atdt 321-1444
atdt 321-1444

CONNECT 9600/ARQ
Welcome to Cloud 9 Internet!

If you're already a user, please login below.
To sign up for an account, type 'new', with no password.

If you have trouble logging in, please call (914)696-4000.

login: elharo
elharo
Password: **********

Password: **********

Last login: Thu May 28 18:26:14 from 168.100.253.71
Copyright (c) 1980, 1983, 1986, 1988, 1990, 1991, 1993, 1994
        The Regents of the University of California.  All rights reserved.

FreeBSD 2.2.6-RELEASE (EARL-GREY) #0: Tue May 19 10:39:36 EDT 1998

You have new mail.
> logout
logo
```

```
Connection closed.

NO CARRIER

RING

RING

RING
```

This program would have been state of the art in 1978. These days, it's rather crude, and you'd have to do a lot of work to develop it further. For one thing, local echo mode should be turned off in the modem so that you don't see duplicates of everything you type. (Even my password originally appeared on the screen in clear text. I replaced it with asterisks manually.) And no effort at all is made to perform terminal emulation of any sort. Furthermore, there's no way to exit the program and close the port. Terminating it with a Ctrl-C forces abnormal execution that fails to release control of the port. Nonetheless, it's amazing just how quick and easy it is to write a program that communicates with a simple serial port device. Communicating with a basic daisy-wheel printer would be no harder.

## Port Properties

The CommPort class has a number of driver-dependent methods for adjusting the properties of the port. These properties are mostly generic characteristics such as buffer size that can be implemented in software. More specific properties of a particular type of port, like the baud rate of a serial port or the mode of the parallel port, must be set using a more specific subclass, like SerialPort or ParallelPort.

The five generic properties are receive threshold, timeout value, receive framing byte, input buffer size, and output buffer size:

- The receive threshold specifies the number of bytes that must be available before a call to read( ) returns.

- The receive timeout specifies the number of milliseconds that must pass before a call to read( ) returns.

- If receive framing is enabled, and the port does not have any data ready, read( ) returns a supplied dummy byte rather than blocking. Receive framing is disabled by default.

- The input buffer size requests a certain size buffer for input from serial port. If the buffer fills up, the read( ) method returns. This value is only a suggestion, and implementations are free to ignore it.

- The output buffer size requests a certain size buffer for output to the serial port. This is important because it's easy for a fast program to write data faster than the port can send it out. Buffer overruns are a common problem, especially on older PCs with slower serial ports. This value is only a suggestion, and implementations are free to ignore it.

Together, the receive threshold and the receive timeout determine exactly how long the input stream will wait for incoming data. For instance, if the receive threshold is set to 5, read( ) won't return until at least 5 bytes are available. If the receive timeout is set to 10 milliseconds, read( ) will wait 10 milliseconds before returning. However, if data becomes available before 10 milliseconds are up, read( ) returns immediately. For example, if the receive threshold is set to 5 bytes *and* the receive timeout is set to 10 milliseconds, read( ) will wait until either 10 milliseconds pass *or* 5 bytes are available before returning. Finally, if receive framing is enabled, all reads return immediately, regardless of the other values. However, you need to check each read and discard any dummy bytes in the input stream.

Each of these properties has four methods: one enables the property, one disables it, one checks whether the property is enabled, and one returns the current value. For instance, the receive threshold is adjusted by these four methods:

```
public abstract void    enableReceiveThreshold(int size)
   throws UnsupportedCommOperationException
public abstract void    disableReceiveThreshold( )
public abstract boolean isReceiveThresholdEnabled( )
public abstract int     getReceiveThreshold( )
```

The other three properties follow the same naming conventions. These four methods adjust the receive timeout:

```
public abstract void    enableReceiveTimeout(int ms)
   throws UnsupportedCommOperationException
public abstract void    disableReceiveTimeout( )
public abstract boolean isReceiveTimeoutEnabled( )
public abstract int     getReceiveTimeout( )
```

These four methods adjust the receive framing property:

```
public abstract void    enableReceiveFraming(int dummyByte)
   throws UnsupportedCommOperationException
public abstract void    disableReceiveFraming( )
public abstract boolean isReceiveFramingEnabled( )
public abstract int     getReceiveFramingByte( )
```

These four methods adjust the input and output buffer sizes:

```
public abstract void setInputBufferSize(int size)
public abstract int  getInputBufferSize( )
public abstract void setOutputBufferSize(int size)
public abstract int  getOutputBufferSize( )
```

All drivers must support input and output buffers, so there are no isInputBufferEnabled( ) or disableOutputBuffer( ) methods. However, other than the input and output buffer sizes, drivers are not required to support these properties. If a driver does not support the given property, attempting to enable it throws an UnsupportedCommOperationException. You can determine whether or not a driver supports a property by trying to enable it and seeing whether an exception is thrown. Example 22-6 uses this scheme to test the properties for the ports of the host system.

*Example 22-6. PortTester*

```java
import javax.comm.*;
import java.util.*;

public class PortTester {

  public static void main(String[] args) {

    Enumeration thePorts = CommPortIdentifier.getPortIdentifiers();
    while (thePorts.hasMoreElements()) {
      CommPortIdentifier com = (CommPortIdentifier) thePorts.nextElement();
      System.out.print(com.getName());

      switch(com.getPortType()) {
        case CommPortIdentifier.PORT_SERIAL:
          System.out.println(", a serial port: ");
          break;
        case CommPortIdentifier.PORT_PARALLEL:
          System.out.println(", a parallel port: ");
          break;
        default:
          System.out.println(" , a port of unknown type: ");
          break;
      }

      try {
        CommPort thePort = com.open("Port Tester", 20);
        testProperties(thePort);
        thePort.close();
      }
      catch (PortInUseException ex) {
        System.out.println("Port in use, can't test properties");
      }
      System.out.println();
    }
  }

  public static void testProperties(CommPort thePort) {

    try {
      thePort.enableReceiveThreshold(10);
      System.out.println("Receive threshold supported");
    }
    catch (UnsupportedCommOperationException ex) {
      System.out.println("Receive threshold not supported");
    }

    try {
      thePort.enableReceiveTimeout(10);
      System.out.println("Receive timeout not supported");
    }
    catch (UnsupportedCommOperationException e) {
      System.out.println("Receive timeout not supported");
```

*Example 22-6. PortTester (continued)*

```
  }

  try {
    thePort.enableReceiveFraming(10);
    System.out.println("Receive framing supported");
  }
  catch (UnsupportedCommOperationException e) {
    System.out.println("Receive framing not supported");
  }
 }
}
```

Here's the results for both serial and parallel ports from a Windows NT box running the Comm API 2.0:

```
D:\JAVA\22>java PortTester
COM1, a serial port:
Receive threshold supported
Receive timeout supported
Receive framing supported

COM2, a serial port:
Port in use, can't test properties

LPT1, a parallel port:
Receive threshold supported
Receive timeout supported
Receive framing supported

LPT2, a parallel port:
Port in use, can't test properties
```

# Serial Ports

The SerialPort class is an abstract subclass of CommPort that provides various methods and constants useful for working with RS-232 serial ports and devices. The main purposes of the class are to allow the programmer to inspect, adjust, and monitor changes in the settings of the serial port. Simple input and output is accomplished with the methods of the superclass, CommPort. SerialPort has a public constructor, but that shouldn't be used by applications. Instead, you should call the open() method of a CommPortIdentifier that maps to the port you want to communicate with, then cast the result to SerialPort. For example:

```
CommPortIdentifier cpi = CommPortIdentifier.getPortIdentifier("COM2");
  if (cpi.getType() == CommPortIdentifier.PORT_SERIAL) {
    try {
      SerialPort modem = (SerialPort) cpi.open();
    }
    catch (PortInUseException ex) {}
  }
```

Methods in the SerialPort class fall into roughly three categories:

- Methods that return the state of the port
- Methods that set the state of the port
- Methods that listen for the changes in the state of the port

## Control Functions

At the lowest level, wires are analog, not digital. Issues, like timing, noise, and the fundamentally analog nature of electronics have to be considered. Therefore, there's a host of layered protocols so that the receiving end can recognize when data is being sent, whether the data was received correctly, and more.

Serial communication uses some very basic, simple protocols. Sending between 3 and 15 volts across the serial cable for a number of nanoseconds inversely proportional to the baud rate of the connection is a zero bit. Sending between –3 and –15 volts for the same amount of time is a one bit. (Sending between 3 and –3 volts is a hardware error.)

These bits are grouped into serial data units, SDUs for short. Common SDU lengths are 8 (used for binary data) and 7 (used for basic ASCII text). Most modern devices use eight data bits per SDU. However, some older devices use seven, six, or even five data bits per SDU. Once an SDU is begun, the rest of the SDU follows in close order. However, there may be gaps of indeterminate length between SDUs.

One of the problems faced by asynchronous serial devices is determining SDU boundaries. If a modem receives eight data bits, how is it to tell whether that's an entire SDU or the last four bits of one SDU and the first four bits of another, especially if the connection has some noise and isn't particularly reliable? To assist with this, each SDU is preceded by a single start bit that's always 0, and followed by between one and two stop bits. Stop bits last longer than data bits so they can always be identified.

In addition to the data and the start and stop bits, an SDU may have a parity bit. Parity is a very simple error detection scheme that can detect (but not correct) single bit errors in an SDU. There are two basic parity schemes. Even parity adds an extra one bit to the end of the SDU if there are an even number of one bits in the data. Odd parity adds an extra one bit to the end of the SDU if there are an odd number of one bits in the data.[*] No parity simply omits the parity bit. The combination of data bits, parity scheme, and stop bits is abbreviated in forms like 8N1 or 7E1. 8N1 means a connection uses eight data bits, no parity, and one stop bit; 7E1 means seven data bits, even parity, and one stop bit. Virtually all modern systems use 8N1.

---

[*] There are two more parity schemes you may hear about. Mark parity always adds a one bit for the parity; space parity always adds a zero bit. These convey no useful information and are almost never used.

---

The baud rate is the number of times per second the state of the communication channel changes. This is *not* the same as bits per second. Modern modems send multiple bits per baud. Most U.S. phone lines, configured primarily for voice calls, have a maximum baud rate of 3200. Modems that send higher bit rates send multiple bits with each baud. A 28,800 bps modem is a 3200 baud modem with nine states, for example.

The Java Communications API lets you set all of these parameters, including baud rate, data bits, stop bits, and parity. They should all be familiar to anyone who's struggled with modem init strings and terminal software in the bad old days before the Internet separated connectivity from content. Four methods in the SerialPort class return the values of these settings. They are:

```
public abstract int getBaudRate()
public abstract int getDataBits()
public abstract int getStopBits()
public abstract int getParity()
```

A little surprisingly, you can't set these values independently. Instead, all four values (baud, data bits, stop bits, and parity) are set at once with the setSerialPortParams() method:

```
public abstract void setSerialPortParams(int baud, int dataBits, int
    stopBits, int parity) throws UnsupportedCommOperationException
```

If the requested values are not supported by the driver (e.g., a 240,000 baud connection), an UnsupportedCommOperationException is thrown. Except for the baud rate, these arguments should be one of several mnemonic constants in the SerialPort class:

```
SerialPort.DATABITS_5      // 5 data bits per byte
SerialPort.DATABITS_6      // 6 data bits per byte
SerialPort.DATABITS_7      // 7 data bits per byte
SerialPort.DATABITS_8      // 8 data bits per byte
SerialPort.STOPBITS_1      // 1 stop bit
SerialPort.STOPBITS_2      // 2 stop bits
SerialPort.STOPBITS_1_5    // 1.5 stop bits*
SerialPort.PARITY_NONE     // no parity
SerialPort.PARITY_ODD      // odd parity
SerialPort.PARITY_EVEN     // even parity
```

## Flow Control

Serial ports and the devices connected to them need a protocol to determine when the port is sending and the device is receiving, when the device is sending and the

---

\* If one and a half stop bits sounds a little funny to you, just remember that serial communications is ultimately an analog procedure, digital abstractions like bits not withstanding. A bit on a serial line is simply a raised or lowered voltage for a given unit of time. One and a half stop bits is simply a raised or lowered voltage for 150% of the normal time used to transfer a bit.

port is receiving, and how to switch between the two states. The two most common protocols are XON/XOFF and RTS/CTS. They are not mutually exclusive, though it's rare to use both at the same time, and nothing is gained by doing so. XON/XOFF is a software-based protocol; it sends special characters down the communication line to tell the other end when to stop and start sending. RTS/CTS is implemented in hardware and requires a special hardware handshaking cable that supports it. Almost all modern hardware, including all modems faster than 2400 bps, support hardware flow control.

The Java Communications API contains two methods to get and set the flow-control protocol:

```
public abstract int  getFlowControlMode( )
public abstract void setFlowControlMode(int protocol)
   throws UnsupportedCommOperationException
```

The int returned by getFlowControlMode( ) and the argument passed to setFlowControlMode( ) should be a bitwise OR of the following constants:

```
SerialPort.FLOWCONTROL_NONE          // no flow control
SerialPort.FLOWCONTROL_RTSCTS_IN     // RTS/CTS for input
SerialPort.FLOWCONTROL_RTSCTS_OUT    // RTS/CTS for output
SerialPort.FLOWCONTROL_XONXOFF_IN    // XON/XOFF for input
SerialPort.FLOWCONTROL_XONXOFF_OUT   // XON/XOFF for output
```

To set the flow control of the SerialPort object com1 to RTS/CTS for both input and output, you would write:

```
com1.setFlowControlMode(SerialPort.FLOWCONTROL_RTSCTS_IN
                     | SerialPort.FLOWCONTROL_RTSCTS_OUT);
```

## Control Wires

A serial port sends data one bit at a time, but it actually uses eight wires to do it. One wire is used for sending, one for receiving, and the other six for various control information. One or two more pins are connected to ground. Modern serial ports generally come in a nine-pin configuration that reflects this, though most modems and some PCs and terminals use a 25-pin connector. Table 22-1 shows the "pin-outs" of the standard 9-pin serial port you're likely to find on the back of a PC. Table 22-2 shows the "pin-outs" of the standard 25-pin serial port you're likely to find on a modem.

*Table 22-1. 9-Pin serial port pin-outs*

| Pin | Name | Code | Direction |
| --- | --- | --- | --- |
| 1 | Carrier Detect | CD | Device Computer |
| 2 | Receive Data | RD | Device Computer |
| 3 | Transmit Data | TD | Computer Device |
| 4 | Data Terminal Ready | DTR | Computer Device |

*Table 22-1. 9-Pin serial port pin-outs (continued)*

| Pin | Name | Code | Direction |
|---|---|---|---|
| 5 | Signal Ground | GND | |
| 6 | Data Set Ready | DSR | Device Computer |
| 7 | Request To Send | RTS | Computer Device |
| 8 | Clear To Send | CTS | Device Computer |
| 9 | Ring Indicator | RI | Device Computer |

*Table 22-2. 25-pin serial port pin-outs*

| Pin | Name | Code | Direction |
|---|---|---|---|
| 1 | Chassis ground | | |
| 2 | Transmit Data | TD | Computer Device |
| 3 | Receive Data | RD | Device Computer |
| 4 | Request To Send | RTS | Computer Device |
| 5 | Clear To Send | CTS | Device Computer |
| 6 | Data Set Ready | DSR | Device Computer |
| 7 | Signal Ground | GND | |
| 8 | Carrier Detect | CD | Device Computer |
| 20 | Data Terminal Ready | DTR | Computer Device |
| 22 | Ring Indicator | RI | Device Computer |

The 15 extra pins on the 25-pin port are generally not connected to anything; Java does not provide methods for manipulating them even if they are.

On a straight DB-25-to-DB-25 connection, about the simplest connection imaginable, used on some early PCs and Unix workstations, the serial cable that connects the PC to the modem runs wires between the corresponding pins. That is, the CD pin is connected to the CD pin, the TD pin is connected to the TD pin, and so forth. Figure 22-1 shows the connection from a PC DB-25 serial port to a DB-25 modem.

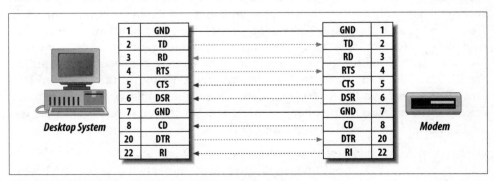

*Figure 22-1. PC DB-25 serial port to a DB-25 modem*

The computer and the modem communicate with each other by raising or lowering voltages on these lines. Each line is one-way. A device reads from or writes to that line but never both. The computer sends data to the modem across the TD line. The modem sends data to the computer across the RD line. The computer tells the modem it's ready to send by raising the voltage on the RTS line. The modem says it's OK for the PC to send using the CTS line. The modem indicates to the computer it's ready using the DSR line and that it's detected a carrier by using the DCD line. If the modem loses the carrier signal (i.e., the phone hangs up), it lowers the voltage on the DCD line. Finally, the computer indicates it's ready by raising the voltage on the DTR line.

These cables can get a little more complicated as different kinds of ports get connected. However, the main reason for the complexity is that not all ports put the same pins in the same positions. For example, Figure 22-2 shows a standard DB-9 PC port connected to a standard DB-25 modem port. It looks hairier, but if you look closer, you'll see that all that happened was that the pins swapped positions, taking their connections with them. The TD pin is still connected to the TD pin, the RD pin is still connected to the RD pin, and so forth. The only changes are the numbers of the pins and the omission of one ground pin from the DB-9 port.

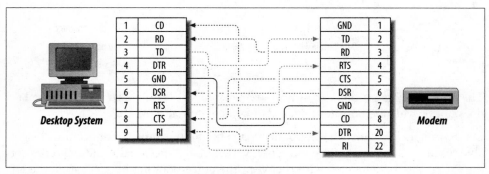

*Figure 22-2. PC DB-9 serial port to a DB-25 modem*

A standard modem cable connects the same pin on one end of the wire to the corresponding pin on the other end of the wire (e.g., DTR to DTR), as shown in Figure 22-1 and Figure 22-2. Cables for connecting other kinds of devices often deliberately cross or split wires. For instance, a null modem cable, shown in Figure 22-3 and used for direct connections between PCs, connects the TD pins to the RD pins, the RTS pin to the CTS pin, and the DTR pin to the DCD and DSR pins. This allows two PCs to communicate using a communications program and a direct serial connection without any modem. This is why not all serial cables are created equal, and the cable that works for one device may not work for another.

Data is sent from computer to device across the TD line and from device to computer across the RD line. You access these lines through the output and input streams returned by CommPort's getOutputStream( ) and getInputStream( ) methods.

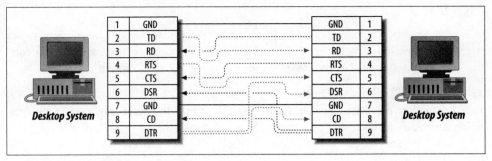

*Figure 22-3. PC null modem cable*

You do not directly manipulate these pins. The ground pins only maintain a common reference voltage between the devices. No program ever sends voltage over these lines. This leaves six pins to read or write. These are:

- DTR
- RTS
- CTS
- DSR
- RI
- CD

Each of these has an effectively boolean value: true if it's showing voltage relative to ground or false if it isn't. The SerialPort class provides methods to read the current state of all these pins. It provides methods to write to those pins that would normally be written to by the computer end of the connection.

### DTR

Data Terminal Ready, DTR, means the computer is ready to send or receive data. CR, Computer Ready, would be more likely true nowadays, but the RS-232 standard was developed in the days of dumb terminals, when personal computers were still an oddity.

```
public abstract void    setDTR(boolean dtr)
public abstract boolean isDTR( )
```

### RTS

Request To Send, RTS, is one-half of hardware handshaking. The computer raises voltage on the RTS line to tell the modem it's waiting to send.

```
public abstract void    setRTS(boolean rts)
public abstract boolean isRTS( )
```

## CTS

Clear To Send, CTS, is the other half of hardware handshaking. The modem raises the voltage on this wire to tell the computer that it's ready to receive data. It drops the voltage when it's no longer ready to receive data.

```
public abstract boolean isCTS( )
```

You cannot set the Clear To Send wire directly. Only the serial device can tell you when it is ready to receive. You cannot force it to be ready.

## DSR

The modem raises the voltage on the DSR line, Data Set Ready, to indicate that it's turned on and operating. This line is also read-only.

```
public abstract boolean isDSR( )
```

## RI

The modem raises the voltage on the RI wire, Ring Indicator, to tell the computer that the phone is ringing.

```
public abstract boolean isRI( )
```

You cannot set the Ring Indicator bit directly. This is used only for one-way communication from the device back to the computer, not for the computer to send information to the device. (In other words, the computer can't tell the modem the phone is ringing.)

## CD

The modem uses the CD wire, Carrier Detect, to tell the computer that it has successfully negotiated the low-level modem protocols with the modem on the other end of the connection.

```
public abstract boolean isCD( )
```

You cannot set the Carrier Detect bit directly. This is also a one-way communication from the device back to the computer.

# Serial Port Events

The examples so far all depend on the computer taking the initiative. The computer tells the modem when to dial, the printer when to print, and so on. By analogy with network programming, this is client-based. However, there's another model for port programs, the server-based program. Just as an Internet server waits for an incoming connection, a program can wait for incoming faxes through a fax modem, incoming BBS connections through a modem, notifications of impending shutdown from an uninterruptible power supply, paper-empty messages from a printer on a parallel port, and more. However, unlike the abstract network ports of Chapter 5, computers have no concept of binding to a serial port. Although you can check the various pins used to send information from a modem or other serial port device to the computer whenever you want to, it's more convenient to do it asynchronously.

Incoming port access relies on an event-based model. When the runtime detects a change in state at a monitored serial port, it fires a serial port event to the registered serial port listener.

## SerialPortEventListener

There are three steps to respond to serial port events:

1. Implement the SerialPortEventListener interface.
2. Register your SerialPortEventListener object with the SerialPort object representing the serial port you want to monitor.
3. Tell the SerialPort object the types of events you want to be notified of.

**Step 1.** As you might guess, you listen for serial port events with a SerialPortEventListener:

```
public interface SerialPortEventListener extends EventListener
```

This interface declares a single method, serialEvent( ):

```
public abstract void serialEvent(SerialPortEvent spe)
```

Inside this method, the getEventType( ) method of SerialPortEvent determines exactly what caused the serial port event and responds appropriately.

**Step 2.** Once you've constructed a SerialPortEventListener, you pass it to the SerialPort object's addEventListener( ) method:

```
public abstract void addEventListener(SerialPortEventListener listener)
    throws TooManyListenersException
```

You are limited to one event listener per port. Adding a second event listener throws a java.util.TooManyListenersException. If this is a problem, you can install an intermediate event listener directly with the SerialPort object. This listener could keep a list of other SerialPortEventListener objects and dispatch the events it receives to the other event listeners.

Should you need to, you can remove a listener from the port with the SerialPort object's removeEventListener( ) method. This method takes no arguments because there's never more than one event listener registered directly with the port.

```
public abstract void removeEventListener( )
```

**Step 3.** In many circumstances, you may not be interested in some or all of these events. By default, none of these events are fired unless you first enable them with one of the 10 notify methods in `SerialPort`:

```
public abstract void notifyOnDataAvailable(boolean enable)
public abstract void notifyOnOutputEmpty(boolean enable)
public abstract void notifyOnCTS(boolean enable)
public abstract void notifyOnDSR(boolean enable)
public abstract void notifyOnRingIndicator(boolean enable)
public abstract void notifyOnCarrierDetect(boolean enable)
public abstract void notifyOnOverrunError(boolean enable)
public abstract void notifyOnParityError(boolean enable)
public abstract void notifyOnFramingError(boolean enable)
public abstract void notifyOnBreakInterrupt(boolean enable)
```

By default, no events are fired when the serial port's state changes. If you pass true to any of these methods, the VM fires a serial port event when the matching state changes.

### SerialPortEvent

The VM creates and fires serial port events to indicate a change on one of the standard serial port lines. The `SerialPortEvent` class declares these three public methods:

```
public int     getEventType( )
public boolean getNewValue( )
public boolean getOldValue( )
```

The getEventType( ) method returns a named constant from the `SerialPortEvent` class that specifies what caused the event to be fired. There are 10 possibilities:

```
SerialPortEvent.DATA_AVAILABLE      // Data has arrived at the port.
SerialPortEvent.OUTPUT_BUFFER_EMPTY // Output buffer on the port is empty.
SerialPortEvent.CTS                 // The Clear To Send pin has changed state.
SerialPortEvent.DSR                 // The Data Set Ready pin has changed state.
SerialPortEvent.RI                  // The Ring Indicator pin has changed state.
SerialPortEvent.CD                  // The Carrier Detect pin has changed state.
SerialPortEvent.OE                  // An overrun error occurred.
SerialPortEvent.PE                  // A parity error occurred.
SerialPortEvent.FE                  // A framing error occurred.
SerialPortEvent.BI                  // A break interrupt was detected.
```

`SerialPortEvent.DATA_AVAILABLE` and `SerialPortEvent.OUTPUT_BUFFER_EMPTY` are enough information all by themselves. The other eight possible types, however, represent a boolean change from one state to another, from on to off or off to on. Therefore, there are also getNewValue( ) and getOldValue( ) methods to tell you what the state of the pin was before and after the event:

```
public boolean getNewValue( )
public boolean getOldValue( )
```

Example 22-7 activates the Ring Indicator and prints a message on System.out when the modem tells the computer the phone is ringing.

---

*Example 22-7. PhoneListener*

```
import javax.comm.*;
import java.util.TooManyListenersException;

public class PhoneListener implements SerialPortEventListener {

  public static void main(String[] args) {

    String portName = "COM1";
    if (args.length > 0) portName = args[0];

    PhoneListener pl = new PhoneListener();

    try {
      CommPortIdentifier cpi = CommPortIdentifier.getPortIdentifier(portName);
      if (cpi.getPortType() == CommPortIdentifier.PORT_SERIAL) {
        SerialPort modem = (SerialPort) cpi.open("Phone Listener", 1000);
        modem.notifyOnRingIndicator(true);
        modem.addEventListener(pl);
      }
    }
    catch (NoSuchPortException ex) {
      System.err.println("Usage: java PhoneListener port_name");
    }
    catch (TooManyListenersException ex) {
      // shouldn't happen in this example
    }
    catch (PortInUseException ex) {System.err.println(ex);}
  }

  public void serialEvent(SerialPortEvent evt) {

    System.err.println(evt.getEventType());
    if (evt.getEventType() == SerialPortEvent.RI) {
      System.out.println("The phone is ringing");
    }
  }
}
```

# Parallel Ports

Parallel ports are most common on PCs. Many Sun workstations from the Sparc V on also have them. However, Macs do not have them nor do many non-x86 workstations. Parallel ports are sometimes called printer ports because their original purpose was to support printers. The names of the parallel ports—"LPT1," "LPT2," etc.—stand for "line printer," reflecting this usage. Nowadays, parallel ports are also used for Zip drives, tape drives, and various other devices. However, parallel ports are still largely limited by their original goal of providing a simple connector for printers. A parallel port sends data eight bits at a time on eight wires. These bits are sent at the same time in parallel, hence the name. The original parallel ports only allowed data to flow one way, from the PC to the printer. The printer could only respond by sending a few standard messages on other wires. Each return wire corresponded to a particular message, like "Out of paper" or "Printer busy." Modern parallel ports allow full, bidirectional communication.

The ParallelPort class is a concrete subclass of CommPort that provides various methods and constants useful for working with parallel ports and devices. The main purposes of the class are to allow the programmer to inspect, adjust, and monitor changes in the settings of the parallel port. Simple input and output are accomplished with the methods of the superclass, CommPort. ParallelPort has a single public constructor, but that shouldn't be used by applications. Instead, you should simply call the open( ) method of a CommPortIdentifier that maps to the port you want to communicate with and then cast it to ParallelPort:

```
CommPortIdentifier cpi = CommPortIdentifier.getPortIdentifier("LPT2");
if (cpi.getType( ) == CommPortIdentifier.PORT_PARALLEL) {
  try {
    ParallelPort printer = (ParallelPort) cpi.open ( );
  }
  catch (PortInUseException ex) {
    System.err.println(ex);
  }
}
```

Methods in the ParallelPort class fall into roughly four categories:

- Methods that adjust the port mode
- Methods to control the port
- Methods to inspect the state of the port
- Methods that listen for changes in the state of the port

## Parallel Port Modes

Like most other computer hardware, parallel ports have evolved over the last two decades. Modern parallel ports support bidirectional communication and other features never envisioned for the original parallel port that was only supposed to send data to a daisy-wheel printer. However, older peripherals may not work with newer parallel ports, so they can, if necessary, be downgraded to any of several various compatibility modes. All of these are available as named int constants in the ParallelPort class:

```
ParallelPort.LPT_MODE_ANY     // Use the most advanced mode possible.
ParallelPort.LPT_MODE_SPP     // Original lineprinter mode. Unidirectional
                              // transfer from PC to printer. Most compatible
                              // with older peripherals.
ParallelPort.LPT_MODE_PS2     // Byte at a time, bidirectional mode as
                              // introduced in the IBM PS/2 family.
ParallelPort.LPT_MODE_EPP     // Extended parallel port.
ParallelPort.LPT_MODE_ECP     // Enhanced capabilities port.
```

```
ParallelPort.LPT_MODE_NIBBLE // Nibble (4 bits, half a byte) at a time mode,
                             // bidirectional, used by some Hewlett Packard
                             // equipment.
```

The mode the parallel port uses is returned by the getMode( ) method and set by passing the appropriate constant to the setMode( ) method:

```
public abstract int getMode( )
public abstract int setMode(int mode) throws UnsupportedCommOperationException
```

Attempts to set the port to an unsupported mode throw an Unsupported-CommOperationException .

## Controlling the Parallel Port

Data is sent to the parallel port and its attached device using the output stream returned by the CommPort class's getOutputStream( ) method. You can interrupt this data by sending the appropriate signals out the parallel port to the printer. The suspend( ) and restart( ) methods send these signals:

```
public abstract void restart( )
public abstract void suspend( )
```

These methods are generally interpreted as stopping and restarting printing. You normally suspend and restart printing if the printer reports an error. These methods do not automatically start a print job over from the beginning. You are still responsible for sending the printer whatever data it needs to print from whatever point it was printing or from the point where you want to restart printing.

## Checking the State of the Port

The original parallel port allowed printers to send only a few predefined messages. Each message was sent by raising the voltage on a specific wire connecting the port to the printer. These messages are always sent from the printer to the CPU, never in the other direction. Therefore, Java only allows you to check the state of each of these pins, not to set them. The methods are:

```
public abstract boolean isPaperOut( )
public abstract boolean isPrinterBusy( )
public abstract boolean isPrinterSelected( )
public abstract boolean isPrinterTimedOut( )
public abstract boolean isPrinterError( )
```

Each of these methods returns true if the matching wire is showing voltage relative to ground or false if it isn't.

There is also a getOutputBufferFree( ) method that returns the number of bytes currently available in the parallel port's output buffer—in other words, the number of bytes you can write before the buffer fills up:

```
public abstract int getOutputBufferFree( )
```

# Parallel Port Events

Although you can check the various pins used to send information from a printer to the computer whenever you want to, it's more convenient to do it asynchronously. The model used for notification is the same one used for JavaBeans, the AWT, and serial port events: when the runtime detects a change in state at a monitored parallel port, it fires a parallel port event to the registered parallel port listener. A parallel port event signals some sort of activity on the parallel port, either an error or an empty output buffer.

## Parallel Port Event Listeners

There are three steps to respond to parallel port events:

1. Implement the `ParallelPortEventListener` interface.
2. Register your `ParallelPortEventListener` object with the `ParallelPort` object representing the parallel port you want to monitor.
3. Tell the parallel port the types of events you want to be notified of.

This is the same pattern as a `SerialPortEventListener`.

**Step 1.** As you would probably guess, you listen for parallel port events with a `ParallelPortEventListener`:

```
public interface ParallelPortEventListener extends EventListener
```

This interface declares a single method, `parallelEvent( )`:

```
public abstract void parallelEvent(ParallelPortEvent ppe)
```

Inside this method, you generally use the `getEventType( )` method of `Parallel-PortEvent` to determine exactly what caused the parallel port event:

```
public int getEventType( )
```

This should return `ParallelPortEvent.PAR_EV_BUFFER` to signal an empty output buffer or `ParallelPortEvent.PAR_EV_ERROR` to signal some other sort of error.

**Step 2.** Once you've constructed a `ParallelPortEventListener`, you need to pass it to the `ParallelPort` object's `addEventListener( )` method:

```
public abstract void addEventListener(ParallelPortEventListener listener)
  throws TooManyListenersException
```

You are limited to one event listener per port. Attempting to add a second event listener throws a `java.util.TooManyListenersException`.

Should you need to, you can remove a listener from the port with the `ParallelPort` object's `removeEventListener( )` method:

```
public abstract void removeEventListener( )
```

This method takes no arguments because there's never more than one event listener registered directly with the port.

**Step 3.** In many circumstances, you may not be interested in both of these events. By default, neither of these events is fired unless you first enable them with the right notify method in `ParallelPort`:

```
public abstract void notifyOnError(boolean notify)
public abstract void notifyOnBuffer(boolean notify)
```

By default, no events are fired when the parallel port's state changes. However, if you pass true to either of these methods, it fires a parallel port event when the matching state changes.

### ParallelPortEvent

Parallel port events are represented by instances of the `ParallelPortEvent` class, a subclass of `java.util.EventObject`:

```
public class ParallelPortEvent extends EventObject
```

The `getEventType()` method returns a named constant from the `ParallelPortEvent` class that specifies what caused the event to be fired. There are two possibilities: an error and an empty output buffer. Each parallel port event has an eventType field; its value should be one of these mnemonic constants:

```
ParallelPortEvent.PAR_EV_ERROR   // An error occurred on the port.
ParallelPortEvent.PAR_EV_BUFFER  // The output buffer is empty.
```

These represent a change from one state to another, from on to off or off to on. Therefore, there are also getNewValue() and getOldValue() methods to tell you the state of the pin before and after the event:

```
public boolean getNewValue()
public boolean getOldValue()
```

# CHAPTER 23

# USB

RS-232 serial ports are one of the oldest I/O technologies still in use today. They really haven't changed a lot in the last 20 years. RS-232 serial ports work reliably and work well, but a 20-year-old technology designed for 300-baud modems, daisy-wheel printers, and 16-bit processors with 4.77-MHz clock rates doesn't suffice for digital video, DVD burners, and optical mice. Consequently, more modern computers have switched to a different serial protocol known as *Universal Serial Bus* (USB).

Hardware-wise, USB is much faster and thus better suited for the data transfer needs of today's more bandwidth-hungry devices. USB also uses a different connector that's much easier to plug in and unplug and less susceptible to bent pins and broken ports. USB cables carry power as well as data, so small USB devices that don't draw a lot of current don't need separate power cords. However, to a Java programmer there are two key differences:

1. Many different devices can be connected to the same USB port. Indeed, up to 127 different devices may be daisy chained to a single USB controller.

2. Data is sent to and received from USB devices in individual *I/O request packets* (IRPs). The stream classes are not used.

This makes communicating with USB devices more complex than reading and writing the streams from the single device on a serial port.

There are several extant versions of USB. The basic architecture and APIs are the same regardless of version. As a software developer or end user, the primary difference is speed. USB 1.0 and 1.1 support low-speed 1.5-Mbps connections and full-speed 12 Mbps connections.* USB 2.0 adds support for high-speed 480-Mbps connections. High-speed devices can normally fall back to full speed when attached to a USB 1.1 hub or controller. Furthermore, not all USB 2.0 devices are high speed. My typing speed is 30 words per minute at best. A low-speed USB keyboard is more than adequate.

---

* That's megabits per second, Mbps, not megabytes per second, MBps.

USB communication is not a standard part of the JDK. It is available as a standard extension in the javax.usb package. IBM has published an open source implementation of this API for Linux that can be downloaded from *http://javax-usb.org*. While, like most things Java, this API is at least theoretically platform independent, currently this is the only available implementation. It has not yet been ported to the Mac, Windows, or other platforms.

The Java USB API is a very low-level API that closely mirrors the actual USB hardware and protocols. It involves a lot of bit-twiddling and byte manipulation. A number of higher-level protocols, such as the Human Interface Device (HID) class and the Mass Storage Driver, sit on top of the raw USB API. The Java USB API does not support these higher-level protocols. They can be implemented on top of the low-level USB API Java does support, but this is a decidedly nontrivial undertaking.

 It's worth noting that many USB devices are already available to Java through native system drivers. Java treats a mouse connected via USB the same as it does one plugged in through the serial port or wirelessly with Bluetooth. A digital camera looks like any other mounted filesystem. The Java Printing API works the same whether the printer is connected via Ethernet, parallel cable, or USB. However, if you want to talk to a device that's a little different, that isn't just another kind of mouse or filesystem or printer, you'll need to use the Java USB API. For instance, Java does not have an API for controlling scanners. However, if the scanner is connected via USB, the USB API enables you to send the scanner commands and receive data from it. (This is much more important for custom laboratory equipment than it is for typical off-the-shelf consumer products.)

## USB Architecture

A USB-enabled computer has one or more *USB controllers*. The controller is attached to the *root hub*. Devices, including other hubs, are also attached to the root hub. Additional devices and hubs can be attached to these hubs in a tree topology. The devices can be quite diverse and typically include mice, keyboards, digital cameras, CD burners, microphones, speakers, iPods, and more. Devices are divided into separately addressable *functions*. Most devices have only one function, but some may have more than one. For instance, the Epson Stylus CX5200 is both a printer and a scanner.

Functions are connected to the host controller through unidirectional *pipes*. Each function can support up to 32 pipes, 16 going into the host controller and 16 coming out of the host controller. The pipes in each direction are numbered from 0 to 15. However, most functions don't use all their pipes. The zero pipe in both directions is reserved for the controller to manage the bus topology. You can often ignore this pipe and just use pipes 1 to 15. Data is transferred across the pipes in packets sized as powers of two: 8 bytes, 16 bytes, 32 bytes, 64 bytes, and so on. The number of pipes and the sizes of the packets vary from one device to another.

There are four kinds of transfers:

*Control*
Commands that control and configure the USB device and bus.

*Isochronous*
Fast data transfers at a guaranteed speed that may lose data.

*Interrupt*
Requests from the device to the host. The host periodically polls each device to see if it has any of these ready to go.

*Bulk*
Reliable transfers that guarantee all bytes are transferred but do not guarantee the speed.

The type of transfer used depends on the needs of the device. For instance, mice and keyboards mostly use interrupt transfers, microphones and speakers mostly use isochronous transfers, and CD burners and PDAs mostly use bulk transfers.

USB has special device classes for certain common device types, including:

- Human interface devices, such as keyboards and mice
- Mass storage devices, such as hard drives, iPods, and PDAs
- Communications devices, such as telephones, modems, and network adapters
- Printer devices

More often than not, these devices are exposed to Java through some other abstraction. For example, a USB hard drive can be accessed through the `FileInputStream`, `FileOutputStream`, and `File` classes like any other hard drive. Most of the time you don't know or care that the files are on a USB hard drive instead of an IDE or ATA hard drive. The USB APIs are for talking to the weird devices that don't have standard classes, such as uninterruptible power supplies (UPSs) or laboratory data acquisition hardware. Later in this chapter, we'll demonstrate communicating with a USB-enabled temperature probe.

# Finding Devices

Many different devices can be connected to a single computer through one USB port. The computer's built-in USB hub provides power for about four not particularly power-hungry devices. However, additional powered hubs can be daisy chained to enable a single system to have up to 127 different USB devices (though some of these devices must be hubs). This means the first question a programmer will ask is which devices are on the bus where.

Enumerating the currently attached USB devices is not hard. In fact, it's considerably easier than enumerating the mounted disks. Most applications begin by using the static `UsbHostManager.getUsbServices()` method to return a `UsbServices` object:

```
UsbServices services = UsbHostManager.getUsbServices();
```

This method can throw a `SecurityException` if the program is not allowed to access the USB port. It can also throw a more specific `UsbException` if there's any sort of problem on the USB bus that prevents the query.

You then ask this object to give you the root `UsbHub`:

```
UsbHub root = services.getRootUsbHub();
```

Now you can ask the hub for a list of all the devices connected to it:

```
List devices = root.getAttachedUsbDevices();
```

Each object in this list is an instance of the `javax.usb.UsbDevice` interface. This interface provides various methods for sending data to and receiving data from the device. I'll have more to say about those shortly. However, for now I'll just need one method from this interface: `isUsbHub()`, to tell if the device is itself another USB hub. Using these methods, Example 23-1 demonstrates a simple program that lists all the USB devices attached to a computer.

*Example 23-1. Enumerating attached USB devices*

```
import java.util.*;
import javax.usb.*;

public class USBLister {

  public static void main(String[] args) throws UsbException {
    UsbServices services = UsbHostManager.getUsbServices();
    UsbHub root = services.getRootUsbHub();
    listDevices(root);
  }

  public static void listDevices(UsbHub hub) {
    List devices = hub.getAttachedUsbDevices();
    Iterator iterator = devices.iterator();
    while (iterator.hasNext()) {
      UsbDevice device = (UsbDevice) iterator.next();
      System.out.println(device);
      if (device.isUsbHub()) {
        listDevices((UsbHub) device);
      }
    }
  }
}
```

To compile this and any other program that uses the Java USB API, you'll need the JAR file containing the API. You can download this and the other files you'll need from *http://javax-usb.org*. This file is named *jsr80-1.0.0.jar*. (The USB API was defined in Java Specification Request 80.) When you compile *USBLister.java*, you'll need to include *jsr80-1.0.0.jar* in the classpath:

```
$ javac -classpath jsr80-1.0.0.jar USBLister.java
```

To run it, you'll need four more files in addition to *jsr80-1.0.0.jar*: the reference implementation JAR, a platform-specific JAR, a native library, and a *javax.usb. properties* file. These can be downloaded from the same location. The JARs are installed in the classpath like any other JARs. The native library is currently distributed with the name *libJavaxUsb-1.0.0.so*, but you'll need to rename it to *libJavaxUsb. so* before it will work. For example, on Linux the directory containing *libJavaxUsb-1.0.0.so* must be included in the LD_LIBRARY_PATH environment variable:

```
$ export LD_LIBRARY_PATH=/where/you/put/libJavaxUsb.so
```

If LD_LIBRARY_PATH has already been defined, you need to redefine it like this instead:

```
$ export LD_LIBRARY_PATH=/where/you/put/libJavaxUsb.so:$ LD_LIBRARY_PATH
```

Note that this variable points to the parent directory, not to the *libJavaxUsb.so* file itself. For instance, I put *libJavaxUsb.so* in */home/elharo/jsr80*, so I set the library path like this:

```
$ export LD_LIBRARY_PATH=/home/elharo/jsr80
```

Running on my Linux box, here's what I saw:

```
$ java -cp jsr80-1.0.0.jar:.:jsr80_ri-1.0.0.jar:jsr80_linux-1.0.0.jar USBLister
$
```

After I remembered my Linux box was a server and didn't have any USB devices connected, I plugged my digital camera into my desktop workstation, which already had a USB mouse, and tried running Example 23-1 there. The results were exactly the same. It turns out that this program requires root access to talk to the USB ports at such a low level. So I *su*'d to root, set root's LD_LIBRARY_PATH environment variable, and ran it again. This time it found the devices:

```
# java -cp jsr80-1.0.0.jar:.:jsr80_ri-1.0.0.jar:jsr80_linux-1.0.0.jar USBLister
com.ibm.jusb.UsbHubImp@ec16a4
com.ibm.jusb.UsbDeviceImp@1c29ab2
com.ibm.jusb.UsbHubImp@13a328f
com.ibm.jusb.UsbDeviceImp@1cd8669
```

## Controlling Devices

Data is written to and read from USB devices in IRPs. More complex devices send IRPs in either bulk transfer, isochronous, or interrupt mode. However, the simplest low-speed devices operate with just the control channel and send a special kind of control IRP. Before we delve into the details of talking over other kinds of channels, let's go over preparing and submitting IRPs over the control channel.

Four methods in the `UsbDevice` send control IRPs to a device:

```
public void syncSubmit(UsbControlIrp irp)
  throws UsbException, IllegalArgumentException, UsbDisconnectedException
public void asyncSubmit(UsbControlIrp irp)
  throws UsbException, IllegalArgumentException, UsbDisconnectedException
public void syncSubmit(List list)
  throws UsbException, IllegalArgumentException, UsbDisconnectedException
public void asyncSubmit(List list)
  throws UsbException, IllegalArgumentException, UsbDisconnectedException
```

The choice of method depends on whether you want to send the IRPs in blocking or nonblocking mode, and how many you want to send. The `syncSubmit()` methods submit the IRPs and wait for the device to respond. The `asyncSubmit()` methods submit the IRPs and return immediately. You can submit either one IRP at a time, or a list of IRPs to be used in sequence.

Each IRP has a header and a data buffer. In Java, the data buffer appears to be a byte array. If you're writing to the device, you'll set the header, put the information you want to send in the IRP's data buffer, and submit it. If you're reading data from the device, you'll set the header, put an empty array in the data buffer, submit a packet, wait for the device to put some data in the buffer, and then read the values out of the array.

These methods each throw a `UsbDisconnectedException` if the device you're sending to has been removed from the bus. This is a runtime exception, so you don't have to catch it, but you probably should anyway since it's an external condition beyond the control of your program.

These methods can all throw a `UsbException` if the bus is having trouble and can't respond quickly or correctly. This can be caused by a misbehaving device, an overloaded bus without enough bandwidth for all the connected devices, an underpowered bus, or any of several other reasons. This is a checked exception, so you have to catch it or declare that you throw it. These methods also throw an `IllegalArgumentException` if you pass a malformed IRP to one of them.

For each control IRP you must provide five pieces of information:

bmRequestType

A 1-byte bitmap that classifies the request as follows:

- Bit 7 is the direction of the packet: 0 for host to device, 1 for device to host.

- Bits 5–6 are a 2-bit little-endian int that specifies the type of the control packet: 0 for standard, 1 for class, and 2 for vendor (3 is unused at the current time).

- Bits 0–4 are a 5-bit int indicating the recipient for which the packet is intended: 0 is a device, 1 is an interface, 2 is an endpoint, 3 is "other," and all other values are reserved. (We'll get to devices, interfaces, and endpoints shortly.)

bRequest

A 1-byte request code. The USB spec outlines standard request codes—for instance, the value 3 sets a feature—as well as device-specific request codes. For example, in HID devices, request code 2 means get the idle rate and request code 3 means set the idle rate. (The idle rate is the amount of time that the device waits before repeating data if nothing has changed.)

wValue

A 2-byte little-endian short whose meaning depends on the request.

wIndex

Also a 2-byte little-endian short whose meaning depends on the request. However, this one points to the actual data found elsewhere in the packet.

data

A byte array containing the content of this request (output) or a buffer into which the device places its response (input). You can also set an offset and a length to select a slice of this array.

IRPs sent over the control channel are represented by instances of the `UsbControlIrp` interface. You can implement this interface yourself if you like, or you can construct an instance of the `javax.usb.util.DefaultUsbControlIrp` class, but it's normally simplest to ask the `UsbDevice` to create a control IRP for you with its `createUsbControlIrp()` method. This factory method requires you to specify the first four values:

```
public UsbControlIrp createUsbControlIrp(byte bmRequestType, byte bRequest,
  short wValue, short wIndex)
```

The data array is then supplied using the `setData()` methods inherited from the superinterface, `UsbIrp`. If you're sending data to the device, you'll put the data in the array before setting it. If you're reading data from the device, you'll put an empty array in the device and then read the data the device put in the IRP from that same array.

## Describing Devices

Each USB device provides a hierarchy of descriptive information about the device and its capabilities. Each device has one or more configurations (though in practice most devices have just one configuration). Each configuration has one or more interfaces. Each interface has one or more endpoints, and each endpoint has exactly one pipe. Each level in this expanding hierarchy is represented by a different interface in the `javax.usb` package, which provides different information about the device. Figure 23-1 summarizes.

To get to the pipe that actually allows you to perform I/O, you need to start at the top and work your way down. That is, first you find the device. You ask the device to give you the active configuration, then you ask the configuration to give you the

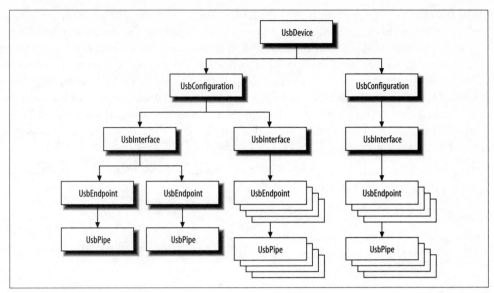

*Figure 23-1. The device hierarchy*

interfaces. Next, you choose an interface and ask it for its endpoints. Finally, you ask the endpoint for its pipe, and you then submit IRPs to this pipe to read or write data.

Thus, before writing software to talk to any particular device, you'll need to know its configurations, interfaces, and endpoints. In an ideal world, this information would be provided in the device's technical documentation. However, the vast majority of devices don't have any decent technical documentation, so it's fortunate that the USB specification requires devices to tell you how they're organized when asked politely.

> Some devices don't correctly follow the USB specification. In particular, many devices that only suck power from the USB port, such as reading lamps and cell phone chargers, do not respond to any USB commands. Aside from their power drain, they're effectively invisible to the USB bus.

## UsbDevice

The UsbDevice interface sits at the top of the hierarchy. This interface declares three getter methods that query the attached devices for information about their serial numbers, manufacturers, and names:

```
public String getSerialNumberString( )
 throws UsbException, UnsupportedEncodingException, UsbDisconnectedException
public String getManufacturerString( )
 throws UsbException, UnsupportedEncodingException, UsbDisconnectedException
public String getProductString( )
 throws UsbException, UnsupportedEncodingException, UsbDisconnectedException
```

All three methods may return null if the device does not provide the requested information. To get this information, the object needs to talk to the device—it does not cache the information the first time it talks to the device—so various exceptions can occur. A UsbDisconnectedException is thrown if the device you're querying has been removed from the bus. A UsbException is also thrown if the bus is having trouble. These methods are also declared to throw an UnsupportedEncodingException, which is a checked exception, so you have to handle it. However, this really shouldn't happen. USB strings are little-endian UTF-16, and this encoding is supposed to be supported by all Java VMs.

Example 23-2 expands on Example 23-1 by using these three methods to print more information about each attached device.

*Example 23-2. Enumerating attached USB devices*

```
import java.io.UnsupportedEncodingException;
import java.util.*;
import javax.usb.*;

public class PrettyUSBDeviceLister {

  public static void main(String[] args)
   throws UsbException, UnsupportedEncodingException {
    UsbServices services = UsbHostManager.getUsbServices();
    UsbHub root = services.getRootUsbHub();
    listDevices(root);
  }

  public static void listDevices(UsbHub hub)
   throws UnsupportedEncodingException, UsbException {
    List devices = hub.getAttachedUsbDevices();
    Iterator iterator = devices.iterator();
    while (iterator.hasNext()) {
      UsbDevice device = (UsbDevice) iterator.next();
      System.out.println(device.getProductString());
      System.out.println(device.getSerialNumberString());
      System.out.println(device.getManufacturerString());
      System.out.println();
      if (device.isUsbHub()) {
        listDevices((UsbHub) device);
      }
    }
  }
}
```

Here's the output I got by running this program as root on my Linux workstation:

```
# java -cp jsr80-1.0.0.jar:.:jsr80_ri-1.0.0.jar PrettyUSBDeviceLister
Silicon Integrated Systems [SiS] USB 1.0 Controller
0000:00:02.2
Linux 2.6.10-5-386 ohci_hcd
```

```
USB-PS/2 Optical Mouse
null
Logitech

Silicon Integrated Systems [SiS] USB 1.0 Controller (#2)
0000:00:02.3
Linux 2.6.10-5-386 ohci_hcd

DMC-FZ5
null
Panasonic
```

Now you can see that this computer has two USB hubs from Silicon Integrated Systems. A Logitech optical mouse with no serial number is attached to the first hub. A Panasonic DMC-FZ5 camera, also with no serial number, is plugged into the second hub. Interestingly, the manufacturer string for the controllers appears to be usurped by the native operating system (Linux, in this case) rather than coming from the devices themselves.

Devices may contain custom strings beyond these three standard strings. All the strings in a device are indexed by numbers from 0 to 255. (Few, if any, devices have all 256 entries in their tables, though.) You can enumerate the strings with the getString( ) method:

```
public String getString(byte index) throws UsbStallException, UsbException,
  UnsupportedEncodingException, UsbDisconnectedException
```

If you ask for a string index that's not in the table, getString( ) returns null. If you exceed the bounds of the table, getString( ) throws a UsbStallException, a subclass of UsbException that usually indicates that a device cannot perform the requested operation.

Example 23-3 is a program to dump the string tables of all currently attached devices.

*Example 23-3. Listing all device strings*

```
import java.io.UnsupportedEncodingException;
import java.util.*;
import javax.usb.*;

public class USBStringLister {

  public static void main(String[] args)
   throws UsbException, UnsupportedEncodingException {
    UsbServices services = UsbHostManager.getUsbServices();
    UsbHub root = services.getRootUsbHub();
    listDevices(root);
  }

  public static void listDevices(UsbHub hub)
   throws UnsupportedEncodingException, UsbException {
```

*Example 23-3. Listing all device strings (continued)*

```
    List devices = hub.getAttachedUsbDevices( );
    Iterator iterator = devices.iterator( );
    while (iterator.hasNext( )) {
      UsbDevice device = (UsbDevice) iterator.next( );
      listStrings(device);
      if (device.isUsbHub( )) {
        listDevices((UsbHub) device);
      }
    }
  }

  public static void listStrings(UsbDevice device)
   throws UnsupportedEncodingException, UsbException {

    for (int i = 0; i <= 255; i++) {
      try {
        String s = device.getString((byte) i);
        System.out.println(" " + i + ":\t" + s);
      }
      catch (UsbStallException ex) {
        // We've reached the end of the table for this device.
        break;
      }
    }
    System.out.println( );
  }
}
```

When run on my usual test system, this program found only the same strings previously exposed as the manufacturer, product, and serial number:

```
# java -cp jsr80_ri-1.0.0.jar:jsr80-1.0.0.jar:.:jsr80_linux-1.0.0.jar USBStringLister
  0:  null
  1:  0000:00:02.2
  2:  Silicon Integrated Systems [SiS] USB 1.0 Controller
  3:  Linux 2.6.10-5-386 ohci_hcd
  4:  null
  5:  null
  ...
  127: null

  0:  null
  1:  Logitech
  2:  USB-PS/2 Optical Mouse

  0:  null
  1:  0000:00:02.3
  2:  Silicon Integrated Systems [SiS] USB 1.0 Controller (#2)
  3:  Linux 2.6.10-5-386 ohci_hcd
  4:  null
  5:  null
  ...
  127: null
```

What else can we tell about the hubs and devices? First of all, there are several versions of USB: 1.0, 1.1, and 2.0. USB 1.x operates at a maximum speed of 12 Mbps. USB 2.0 can operate at up to 480 Mbps. However, not all USB 2.0 devices actually need to transfer that much data. For instance, 12 Mbps is more than enough for a mouse or a keyboard (though not nearly enough for a DVD burner).

USB devices operate at either 1.5 Mbps (low speed), 12 Mbps (full speed), or 480 Mbps (high speed, USB 2.0 only). Higher-speed devices can generally throttle back to lower speeds as necessary, but with a corresponding loss of performance. The getSpeed( ) method tells you the speed at which a given device operates:

```
public java.lang.Object getSpeed( )
```

The object it returns is one of these three constants:

- `UsbConst.DEVICE_SPEED_UNKNOWN`
- `UsbConst.DEVICE_SPEED_LOW`
- `UsbConst.DEVICE_SPEED_FULL`

 The Java USB API only officially supports USB 1.1, so there's no `UsbConst.DEVICE_SPEED_HIGH` constant for 480-Mbps devices. Such USB 2.0 devices do work with the Java USB API, but they'll return `UsbConst.DEVICE_SPEED_FULL` as their speed.

The getParentUsbPort( ) method returns the port to which the device is connected on the hub:

```
public UsbPort getParentUsbPort( ) throws UsbDisconnectedException
```

The isUsbPort( ) method returns true if the device is a hub or false if it isn't:

```
public boolean isUsbHub( )
```

## UsbDeviceDescriptor

For more detailed and technical information about a device, you can request its device descriptor:

```
public UsbDeviceDescriptor getUsbDeviceDescriptor( )
```

The UsbDeviceDescriptor interface is very closely tied to the USB hardware and tends to return information whose interpretation requires reading the USB specification (available at *http://www.usb.org/developers/docs/*). First, three methods get the indexes of the manufacturer, product, and serial number strings in the string table:

```
public byte iManufacturer( )
public byte iProduct( )
public byte iSerialNumber( )
```

The getSerialNumberString( ), getManufacturerString( ), and getProductString( ) methods in UsbDevice are convenience methods that basically do something like this:

```
public String getProductString( ) throws UsbException,
 UnsupportedEncodingexception {
  byte index = getUsbDeviceDescriptor( ).iProduct( );
  return getString(index);
}
```

These strings are meant for display to end users. Computers recognize devices by vendor ID and product ID:

```
public short idVendor( )
public short idProduct( )
```

The USB Implementers Forum assigns vendor IDs, after the payment of the appropriate four-figure fees. The vendors then choose the product IDs. For example, Hewlett-Packard's assigned vendor ID is 0x03f0. The product ID for HP's DeskJet 895c printer is 0x0004. The vendor ID for the DeskJet 880c is the same, but its product ID is 0x0104. Some vendors don't bother to change product IDs if two devices are similar enough to be supported by the same software and drivers. For example, the HP DeskJet 970c also has the product ID 0x104, same as the DeskJet 880c.

USB devices are organized into device classes. These classes are quite broad. For instance, the Human Interface Device class covers mice, keyboards, UPSs, and quite a bit more. What unifies the devices in a class is that they have similar data transfer requirements and can use the same basic drivers. For example, audio devices use isochronous transfers, and HID devices use control and interrupt transfers.

Classes are further subdivided into subclasses. Devices in a class or subclass speak a certain protocol. Each of these three—class, subclass, and protocol—is represented by an unsigned byte code. The next three methods return the device's USB class, subclass, and protocol codes:

```
public byte bDeviceClass( )
public byte bDeviceSubClass( )
public byte bDeviceProtocol( )
```

The USB Implementers Forum maintains a list of device class codes (currently available at *http://www.usb.org/developers/defined_class/*). Table 23-1 lists some common device class codes.

*Table 23-1. USB device class codes*

| Class code | Meaning |
| --- | --- |
| 0 | Class information at the interface level |
| 2 | Communications devices: fax machines, phones, modems, etc. |
| 9 | USB hubs |
| 220 | Diagnostic devices |

Table 23-1. USB device class codes (continued)

| Class code | Meaning |
| --- | --- |
| 224 | Wireless adapters |
| 239 | Miscellaneous |
| 255 | Vendor specific |

Subclass and protocol codes depend on the class. For example, in class 224, a subclass of 1 indicates a radiofrequency controller and a protocol of 1 indicates that the controller uses Bluetooth. In class 224, a subclass of 1 indicates a reprogrammable diagnostic device, and in this subclass protocol 1 indicates USB2 diagnostics.

Not all devices have class codes at this level, though. For instance, HID and mass storage devices don't. That is, the class code of an HID device such as a mouse or a mass storage device such as a hard drive is 0.

The bcdDevice( ) method returns the device's release number:

```
public short bcdDevice( )
```

The short returned is not really a short. Rather, it's the two bytes of a *binary-coded decimal* (BCD) number. The high-order byte is a number between 0 and 255 that represents the major version. The low-order byte is divided into two nibbles. The top nibble represents the minor version and the low-order nibble represents the revision. For instance, Version 2.5.7 would be encoded as the byte 00000010 (2) followed by the nibble 0101 (5) followed by the nibble 0111 (7).

The bcdUSB( ) method returns the version of the USB specification the device adheres to, again encoded as a BCD:

```
public short bcdUSB( )
```

For example, Version 1.1 of the USB spec is a 1 byte, followed by a 1 nibble, followed by a 0 nibble; that is, 00000001 0001 0000 in binary or 272 in decimal. In other words, 1.1 is the same as 1.1.0. Version 2.0 is a 2 byte followed by a 0 byte; that is, 00000010 00000000 in binary or 512 in decimal.

The bMaxPacketSize0( ) method returns the maximum packet size for endpoint 0, the control channel endpoint:

```
public byte bMaxPacketSize0( )
```

This value should always be 8, 16, 32, or 64 because these are the only packet sizes the USB spec allows on the control channel.

The bNumConfigurations( ) method returns the number of different configurations the device has:

```
public byte bNumConfigurations( )
```

It's a very rare device that has more than one configuration.

Example 23-4 is a program that uses this interface to describe the devices attached to the USB controller. It also demonstrates how to decode binary-coded decimal strings.

*Example 23-4. Listing all device strings*

```
import java.io.UnsupportedEncodingException;
import java.util.*;
import javax.usb.*;

public class USBDeviceDescriber {

  public static void main(String[] args)
   throws UsbException, UnsupportedEncodingException {
    UsbServices services = UsbHostManager.getUsbServices();
    UsbHub root = services.getRootUsbHub();
    listDevices(root);
  }

  public static void listDevices(UsbHub hub)
   throws UnsupportedEncodingException, UsbException {
    List devices = hub.getAttachedUsbDevices();
    Iterator iterator = devices.iterator();
    while (iterator.hasNext()) {
      UsbDevice device = (UsbDevice) iterator.next();
      describe(device);
      if (device.isUsbHub()) {
        listDevices((UsbHub) device);
      }
    }
  }

  public static void describe(UsbDevice device)
   throws UnsupportedEncodingException, UsbException {
    UsbDeviceDescriptor descriptor = device.getUsbDeviceDescriptor();
    byte manufacturerCode = descriptor.iManufacturer();
    System.out.println("Manufacturer index: " + manufacturerCode);
    System.out.println("Manufacturer string: "
     + device.getString(manufacturerCode));
    byte productCode = descriptor.iProduct();
    System.out.println("Product index: " + productCode);
    System.out.println("Product string: " + device.getString(productCode));
    byte serialCode = descriptor.iSerialNumber();
    System.out.println("Serial number index: " + serialCode);
    System.out.println("Serial Number string: " + device.getString(serialCode));

    System.out.println("Vendor ID: 0x"
     + Integer.toHexString(descriptor.idVendor()));
    System.out.println("Product ID: 0x"
     + Integer.toHexString(descriptor.idProduct()));
    System.out.println("Class: " + descriptor.bDeviceClass());
    System.out.println("Subclass: " + descriptor.bDeviceSubClass());
    System.out.println("Protocol: " + descriptor.bDeviceProtocol());
```

*Example 23-4. Listing all device strings (continued)*

```
    System.out.println("Device version: " + decodeBCD(descriptor.bcdDevice()));
    System.out.println("USB version: " + decodeBCD(descriptor.bcdUSB()));
    System.out.println("Maximum control packet size: "
     + descriptor.bMaxPacketSize0());
    System.out.println("Number of configurations: "
     + descriptor.bNumConfigurations());

    System.out.println();
  }

  public static String decodeBCD(short bcd) {
    int upper = (0xFF00 & bcd) >> 8;
    int middle = (0xF0 & bcd) >> 4;
    int lower = 0x0F & bcd;
    return upper + "." + middle + "." + lower;
  }
}
```

For example, here's the description this program prints for my Lumix FZ-5 camera:

```
Manufacturer index: 1
Manufacturer string: Panasonic
Product index: 2
Product string: DMC-FZ5
Serial number index: 0
Serial Number string: null
Vendor ID: 0x4da
Product ID: 0x2372
Class: 0
Subclass: 0
Protocol: 0
Device version: 0.1.0
USB version: 1.1.0
Maximum control packet size: 8
Number of configurations: 1
```

This device has one configuration, it supports USB 1.1, and the camera itself is only Version 0.1. Its class is 0, which means we'll have to look at the interface to figure out what class it really is.

## USB Configurations

Each USB device has at least one and possibly several *configurations*. The configuration specifies how much power the device uses, how many interfaces the device has, and whether the device draws power from the USB bus or has its own power supply. Since some devices have more than one possible configuration—for instance, both self powered and bus powered—the UsbDevice interface has several methods to find out which configurations are available and determine which is currently active. In practice, though, most devices have only one configuration.

The getUsbConfigurations( ) method returns a list of all possible configurations for a given device:

```
public List getUsbConfigurations()
```

The objects in this list are instances of the UsbConfiguration interface. There will be at least one.

Each configuration is identified by a byte value between 1 and 255. The getUsbConfiguration( ) method returns a specific configuration:

```
public UsbConfiguration getUsbConfiguration(byte number)
```

This method returns null if the device does not have the requested configuration. 0 stands for the unconfigured state.

The containsUsbConfiguration( ) method returns true if the device has the requested configuration or false if it doesn't:

```
public boolean containsUsbConfiguration(byte number)
```

The getActiveUsbConfigurationNumber( ) returns the index of the device's current configuration:

```
public byte getActiveUsbConfigurationNumber()
```

It returns 0 if the device is unconfigured.

The getActiveUsbConfiguration( ) method returns the current configuration:

```
public UsbConfiguration getActiveUsbConfiguration()
```

It returns null if the device is unconfigured.

The isConfigured( ) method returns true if a device is configured or false if it isn't:

```
public boolean isConfigured()
```

In practice, I've never seen an unconfigured device when working with Java. I suspect either the device autoconfigures itself, or the operating system does this before Java ever sees it.

Example 23-5 is an example method for enumerating all the configurations of a device, as well as identifying the active configuration and its number.

*Example 23-5. Listing device configurations*

```
public static void listConfigs(UsbDevice device)
 throws UsbDisconnectedException, UsbException {
  try {
    if (device.isConfigured()) {
      System.out.println(device.getProductString() + " is configured.");
      System.out.println("The active configuration is "
       + device.getActiveUsbConfiguration());
      System.out.println("The active configuration is number "
       + device.getActiveUsbConfigurationNumber());
    }
```

*Example 23-5. Listing device configurations (continued)*

```
    else {
      System.out.println(device.getProductString() + " is not configured.");
    }
  }
  catch (UnsupportedEncodingException ex) {
    throw new RuntimeException("This really shouldn't happen");
  }
  System.out.println("Available configurations include: ");
  List configs = device.getUsbConfigurations();
  Iterator iterator = configs.iterator();
  while (iterator.hasNext()) {
    UsbConfiguration config = (UsbConfiguration) iterator.next();
    System.out.println("  " + config);
  }
}
```

The typical output from this method looks like this:

```
USB-PS/2 Optical Mouse is configured.
The active configuration is com.ibm.jusb.UsbConfigurationImp@1027b4d
The active configuration is number 1
Available configurations include:
 com.ibm.jusb.UsbConfigurationImp@1027b4d
```

## UsbConfigurationDescriptor

You can find out more details about the configuration, such as whether it supports remote wakeup and whether or not the device is bus powered, using the UsbConfiguration and UsbConfigurationDescriptor interfaces. The getUsbConfigurationDescriptor() method in UsbConfiguration returns a UsbConfigurationDescriptor object:

```
public UsbConfigurationDescriptor getUsbConfigurationDescriptor()
```

This interface has five getter methods that describe the device as it operates in that particular configuration. The simplest of these is bMaxPower():

```
public byte bMaxPower()
```

This method returns an unsigned byte between 0 and 255. (b stands for byte.) That is, −1 is 255, −2 is 254, and so forth.

 The javax.usb.util.UsbUtil class has a static unsignedInt() method that converts a signed byte in the range −128 to 127 to an unsigned int in the range 0 to 255.

This number is *half* the number of milliamps the device draws at maximum usage. In other words, convert the return value to an unsigned int and double it to get the number of milliamps the device draws. For example, given a `UsbConfiguration` object `config`, this code fragment prints the device's maximum power draw:

```
UsbConfigurationDescriptor descriptor = config.getUsbConfigurationDescriptor();
byte power = descriptor.bMaxPower();
int milliamps = 2 * UsbUtil.unsignedInt(power);
System.out.println("Max power draw: " + milliamps + "mA");
```

It turns out my wired optical mouse can draw up to 98 milliamps (mA), and my global positioning system (GPS) receiver can draw a hefty 200 mA. On the other hand, USB devices are supposed to go to sleep after three milliseconds of inactivity, in which state they're not supposed to draw more than 500 microamps (half a milliamp) from the bus. Thus, `bMaxPower()` returns the maximum draw, not what a device pulls all the time. A bus can normally supply about half an amp, and a single device is allowed to draw up to the full 500 mA from the bus, if it's available. However, buses have limits, especially on already low-powered devices such as PDAs and laptops running on battery power. In these situations, a much more conservative 100-mA maximum is a good idea. (My 200-mA GPS receiver is quite greedy.) Even at that level, a device may need its own battery or power cord if many devices are on the bus. In practice, quite a few devices exceed the power maximums (especially devices such as USB-powered lights and cell phone chargers that just suck power without actually doing anything else).

Anyway, enough hardware. What about the other methods? The `bNumInterfaces()` method returns the number of interfaces this configuration has. Most devices have one interface.

```
public byte bNumInterfaces()
```

As with `bMaxPower()`, this value should be interpreted as an unsigned byte between 0 and 255. (Honestly, this API is exposing far more of the hardware implementation details than it should. Just because the USB device returns an unsigned byte does not mean the API can't or shouldn't return an int.)

The `bConfigurationValue()` method returns the index of this configuration:

```
public byte bConfigurationValue()
```

This is the value you'd use to request this configuration by sending the appropriate control IRP to the device.

The `iConfiguration()` method returns the index of the string descriptor describing this configuration in the device's string table:

```
public byte iConfiguration()
```

The `bmAttributes()` method returns a single byte containing two bit flags:

```
public byte bmAttributes()
```

The fifth bit (counting from 0) is on if the device supports remote wakeup, and off if it doesn't. (Remote wakeup means the device can wake up a suspended host if it has something to tell it.) The sixth bit is on if the device has its own power source (though it might still draw some power from the bus), and off if it doesn't. The other six bits are not used in USB 2.0 and earlier.

# UsbInterface

Besides printing out information about configurations, the main thing you'll want to do with a configuration is get the interfaces to the USB device. The getUsbInterfaces( ) method returns a list of all the interfaces for that configuration:

```
public List getUsbInterfaces( )
```

The objects in this list are instances of the UsbInterface interface. There will be at least one, and a multifunction device may have more than one. For example, a combination printer/scanner/copier could use one interface for each of those three tasks, all of which could be active simultaneously. However, most simple devices have exactly one interface per configuration.

Each USB interface is identified by a byte value between 0 and 255. The first interface will be 0, the second 1, the third 2, and so on. (All the devices I have handy start and stop with 0.) The getUsbInterface( ) method returns a specific interface:

```
public UsbConfiguration getUsbInterface(byte number)
```

This method returns null if the configuration does not have the requested interface.

The containsUsbInterface( ) method returns true if the configuration has the requested interface and false if it doesn't:

```
public boolean containsUsbConfiguration(byte number)
```

The UsbInterface interface itself has methods to control the interface. Specifically, it has methods to:

- Inspect and change the settings of the interface.
- Determine which setting is active.
- Claim and release the interface.
- Get the endpoints for the interface.

## Settings

Each interface may have alternate *settings*, also represented as UsbInterface objects. Only one such setting for an interface is active at a time (though several different interfaces may be active simultaneously). The isActive( ) method returns true if this UsbInterface object is the active setting and false if it isn't:

```
public boolean isActive( )
```

The getNumSettings( ) method tells you how many different settings the interface has. This will normally be one or two:

```
public int getNumSettings( )
```

Settings are numbered sequentially, starting at zero. Zero is the default setting. You can look up settings by their numbers using getSetting( ):

```
public UsbInterface getSetting(byte number)
```

This method returns null if there is no setting with the specified number. The containsSetting( ) method checks whether a numbered setting exists on this interface:

```
public boolean containsSetting(byte number)
```

The getSettings( ) method returns a list of all the settings for this interface:

```
public List getSettings( )
```

The objects in this list are UsbInterface objects.

Finally, you can request the active setting or its number specifically using these two methods:

```
public UsbInterface getActiveSetting( ) throws UsbNotActiveException
public byte getActiveSettingNumber( ) throws UsbNotActiveException
```

This is important because only the active setting can be claimed and used for I/O operations. This method throws a UsbNotActiveException if the configuration to which this setting belongs is not active. That is, you can get an active setting only from an active configuration.

To change the active setting, you use the setInterface( ) method in the javax.usb.util.StandardRequest class.

### Claiming

Before writing to or reading from the active interface, it is necessary to *claim* it so that your program has exclusive access to it. This is similar to locking a file to prevent reading or writing while your program is working with it.

```
public void claim( ) throws UsbClaimException, UsbException,
   UsbNotActiveException, UsbDisconnectedException
```

If another program has already claimed this device, this method throws a UsbClaimException. In that case, the other program will need to release it before you can go any further. For example, you may be able to see the system's mouse or keyboard, but you probably won't be able to control it unless you can convince the operating system to give it up.

In practice, this almost always happens. That is, the operating system grabs the device before Java has a chance to claim it and your program fails with a UsbClaimException. In this case, you'll need to force the claim. I don't know why this couldn't be done with a simple Boolean, but it can't. Instead, you need to supply an instance of the UsbInterfacePolicy interface that returns true from forceClaim( ). It's easiest to do this with an anonymous inner class:

```
theInterface.claim(new UsbInterfacePolicy() {
  public boolean forceClaim(UsbInterface usbInterface) {
    return true;
  }
});
```

This step is not guaranteed to succeed, but it worked for me. If it fails there's not much else you can do, although you might try uninstalling or quitting any other running programs that try to grab the USB device before you see it.

The isClaimed( ) method checks whether a device is already claimed:

```
public boolean isClaimed( )
```

When you're done with a device, you should give up your claim with the release( ) method:

```
public void release( ) throws UsbClaimException, UsbException,
  UsbNotActiveException, UsbDisconnectedException
```

You'll need to close any pipes you've opened to the device before releasing it.

## UsbInterfaceDescriptor

The UsbInterfaceDescriptor interface offers more details about the interface. The getUsbInterfaceDescriptor( ) method in UsbInterface returns a UsbInterfaceDescriptor object:

```
public UsbInterfaceDescriptor getUsbInterfaceDescriptor( )
```

This interface has seven methods that describe the interface in that particular setting. Three of these return the numeric identifiers for the interface's class, subclass, and protocol:

```
public byte bInterfaceClass( )
public byte bInterfaceSubClass( )
public byte bInterfaceProtocol
```

When the bDeviceClass is zero in the device descriptor (i.e., the value returned by bDeviceClass( ) in UsbDeviceDescriptor), you look at these three values to determine the device's class, subclass, and protocol.

The other information in this descriptor is rarely needed. bInterfaceNumber( ) returns this setting's number amongst its alternate settings:

```
public byte bInterfaceNumber( )
```

bAlternateSetting( ) returns the number of this interface's current alternate setting:

```
public byte bAlternateSetting( )
```

iInterface( ) returns the index of a string in the string table that provides a human-readable description of this interface:

```
public byte iInterface ( )
```

This method returns 0 if there is no such string.

bNumEndpoints( ) returns the number of endpoints this interface has, not counting endpoint 0:

```
public byte bNumEndpoints( )
```

## UsbEndpoints

Tired yet? Don't worry. We're almost done. Interfaces have endpoints. Full- and high-speed devices can have up to 16 endpoints (8 in each direction). Low-speed devices have only two, one in each direction. Each endpoint is a memory buffer where incoming or outgoing data is put. For data flowing from the host to the device (input to the device, output from the host), the host places the data in the endpoint, and the device's microprocessor is interrupted to work on the data. When data is moving from the device to the host, the device's microprocessor puts the data into the endpoint and waits for the host to collect it.

The getUsbEndpoints( ) method in UsbInterface returns a list of all the non-control endpoints of that interface:

```
public List getUsbEndpoints( )
```

The objects in this list are instances of the UsbEndpoint interface. Some devices only have control endpoints; for these devices, this method returns an empty list.

Each non-control endpoint has an address between 1 and 255. These addresses do not necessarily start at 1, though. Some of my devices with only one or two non-control endpoints have endpoint addresses such as 129 and 130. The getUsbEndpoint( ) method returns a specific endpoint:

```
public UsbConfiguration getUsbEndPoint(byte number)
```

This method returns null if the configuration does not have the requested endpoint.

 Endpoint 0 is reserved for the control channel. This is accessed through the UsbDevice and UsbControlIrp interfaces rather than UsbEndpoint and UsbPipe.

The containsUsbEndpoint( ) method returns true if the interface has the requested endpoint and false if it doesn't:

```
public boolean containsUsbEndpoint(byte number)
```

The UsbEndpoint interface itself has methods to query the endpoint for its type (control, bulk, interrupt, or isochronous); direction (in or out); parent interface; and descriptor. The getUsbInterface( ) method returns the parent interface of this endpoint:

```
public UsbInterface getUsbInterface( )
```

The getDirection( ) method tells you whether data is going into the device through this endpoint or coming out of the device:

```
public byte getDirection( )
```

The return value should be either UsbConst.ENDPOINT_DIRECTION_IN or UsbConst. ENDPOINT_DIRECTION_OUT. This is from the perspective of the host. That is, *in* is into the host and out from the device, and *out* is out from the host and into the device.

The getType( ) method tells you whether the endpoint is for control, bulk, interrupt, or isochronous transfers:

```
public byte getType( )
```

The return value should be one of these four constants:

- UsbConst.ENDPOINT_TYPE_CONTROL
- UsbConst.ENDPOINT_TYPE_BULK
- UsbConst.ENDPOINT_TYPE_INTERRUPT
- UsbConst.ENDPOINT_TYPE_ISOCHRONOUS

Finally, the getUsbEndpointDescriptor( ) method returns a UsbEndpointDescriptor for the endpoint:

```
public UsbEndpointDescriptor getUsbEndpointDescriptor( )
```

This interface has four getter methods to find out the maximum packet size for this endpoint, the actual endpoint address, the bmAttributes, and the bInterval:

```
package javax.usb;

public interface UsbEndpointDescriptor {
  public byte bEndpointAddress( );
  public byte bmAttributes( );
  public short wMaxPacketSize( );
  public byte bInterval( );
}
```

The bmAttributes determine whether this is a control, bulk, interrupt, or isochronous endpoint (though it's easier to use getType( ) in UsbEndpoint). The bInterval is the amount of time that elapses between successive polls of the endpoint. It applies only to isochronous endpoints (for which it should always be 1) and interrupt endpoints. For high-speed bulk and control out endpoints, bInterval specifies the maximum *NAK rate*. NAK is the signal a device sends when it can't accept a packet it previously told the host it would be able to accept. It has no particular meaning for low- and full-speed control and bulk endpoints or high-speed bulk and control in endpoints. The units vary depending on the device speed. For low-speed devices, this measures milliseconds. For full-speed devices, it measures eighths of a millisecond (125 microseconds). For high-speed devices, the measure is exponential rather than linear.

The code in Example 23-6 collects all the endpoints from a `UsbInterface` and prints various details about them.

*Example 23-6. Enumerating device endpoints*

```
public static void listEndpoints(UsbInterface theInterface) {
  List endpoints = theInterface.getUsbEndpoints( );
  System.out.println(endpoints.size( ) + " endpoints");
  Iterator iterator = endpoints.iterator( );
  while (iterator.hasNext( )) {
    UsbEndpoint endpoint = (UsbEndpoint) iterator.next( );
    listEndpointInfo(endpoint);
  }
}

public static void listEndpointInfo(UsbEndpoint endpoint) {
  int direction = endpoint.getDirection( );
  int type = endpoint.getType( );
  if (direction == UsbConst.ENDPOINT_DIRECTION_OUT) {
    System.out.println("Out endpoint");
  }
  else {
    System.out.println("In endpoint");
  }

  switch(type) {
    case UsbConst.ENDPOINT_TYPE_CONTROL:
    System.out.println("Control endpoint");
    break;
    case UsbConst.ENDPOINT_TYPE_BULK:
    System.out.println("Bulk endpoint");
    break;
    case UsbConst.ENDPOINT_TYPE_INTERRUPT:
    System.out.println("Interrupt endpoint");
    break;
    case UsbConst.ENDPOINT_TYPE_ISOCHRONOUS:
    System.out.println("Isochronous endpoint");
    break;
    default:
    System.out.println("Unrecognized type");
  }

  UsbEndpointDescriptor descriptor = endpoint.getUsbEndpointDescriptor( );
  System.out.println("Endpoint address: "
   + UsbUtil.unsignedInt(descriptor.bEndpointAddress( )));
  System.out.println("Maximum packet size: "
   + UsbUtil.unsignedInt(descriptor.wMaxPacketSize( )) + " bytes");

  // The meaning of bInterval depends on the speed of the device
  // and the type of the endpoint
  double interval = UsbUtil.unsignedInt(descriptor.bInterval( ));
  UsbDevice device
   = endpoint.getUsbInterface().getUsbConfiguration().getUsbDevice( );
```

*Example 23-6. Enumerating device endpoints (continued)*

```java
boolean highSpeed = false;
if (device.getSpeed() == UsbConst.DEVICE_SPEED_FULL) {
  interval = interval * 0.125;
}
else if (device.getSpeed() == UsbConst.DEVICE_SPEED_LOW) {
  interval = interval * 1;
}
else { // might be a high-speed device
  highSpeed = true;
  interval = Math.pow(2, interval-1) * 0.125;
}

if (type == UsbConst.ENDPOINT_TYPE_INTERRUPT
 || type == UsbConst.ENDPOINT_TYPE_ISOCHRONOUS) {
  System.out.println("Maximum latency: " + interval + "ms");
}
else if (highSpeed
 && endpoint.getDirection() == UsbConst.ENDPOINT_DIRECTION_OUT) {
System.out.println("Maximum NAK rate: " + interval + "ms");
}
// bInterval means nothing for control endpoints
}
```

Here are the results of using this on a Go!Temp probe, a typical interrupt-based device:

```
1 endpoints
In endpoint
Interrupt endpoint
Endpoint address: 129
Maximum packet size: 8 bytes
Maximum latency: 10.0ms
```

This device has a single interrupt endpoint for input. It also has two control endpoints, but these aren't listed here.

And here are the results for my Panasonic Lumix camera, a typical mass storage device:

```
2 endpoints
Out endpoint
Bulk endpoint
Endpoint address: 1
Maximum packet size: 64 bytes
In endpoint
Bulk endpoint
Endpoint address: 130
Maximum packet size: 64 bytes
```

You can see that it has two endpoints, both bulk, one for input and one for output. It also has two control endpoints, but these aren't listed here. They're managed at a lower level.

# Pipes

The absolute last piece where you finally get to send some non-control data is the USB pipe. This is represented by an instance of the `UsbPipe` interface. The `getUsbPipe()` method in `UsbEndpoint` returns the single pipe associated with that endpoint:

```
public UsbPipe getUsbPipe()
```

USB I/O is packet-based like UDP, not stream-based like TCP. You do not get an `InputStream` or an `OutputStream` from a pipe. Instead, you send or receive IRPs. In Java, IRPs are represented by the `javax.usb.UsbIrp` class. This is a wrapper around a byte array containing the actual data sent to or received from the device.

You cannot send arbitrarily large byte arrays to a device. A low-speed device can accept at most eight bytes in each packet. A full-speed device can accept up to 1,023 bytes. A high-speed device can accept up to 1,024 bytes per packet.

This can be further restricted depending on the type of transfer: low-speed control transfers always use 8-byte packets; high-speed control transfers use 8-, 16-, 32-, or 64-byte packets; and full-speed control transfers always use 64-byte packets.

Writing to an output pipe to move data from the host to the device follows these steps:

1. Open the pipe by calling the `open()` method.
2. Stuff a data array into a `UsbIrp`.
3. Send the IRP down the pipe, either synchronously with `syncSubmit()` or asynchronously with `asyncSubmit()`.
4. Close the pipe with the `close()` method.

Steps 2 and 3 may be repeated as many times as desired.

Reading from an input pipe to collect data from the device for the host follows these steps:

1. Open the pipe by calling the `open()` method.
2. Create a new empty `UsbIrp` to hold data received from the device.
3. Put an IRP on the pipe to receive the data from the device either synchronously with `syncSubmit()` or asynchronously with `asyncSubmit()`.
4. Read the data out of the IRP you created in step 2.
5. Close the pipe with the `close()` method.

Steps 2 through 4 can be repeated as many times as necessary. A completed IRP can be reused provided you call `setComplete(false)` on each IRP before you resubmit it.

Before you can write to a pipe, you must open it by invoking the `open()` method:

```
public void open() throws UsbException, UsbNotActiveException,
    UsbNotClaimedException, UsbDisconnectedException
```

---

The interface the pipe belongs to must be both active and claimed. Otherwise, this method throws a UsbNotActiveException or a UsbNotClaimedException, respectively.

You send the IRPs to the device either synchronously (blocking) or asynchronously (nonblocking):

```
public void syncSubmit(UsbIrp irp) throws UsbException, UsbNotActiveException,
 IllegalArgumentException, UsbDisconnectedException
public void asyncSubmit(UsbIrp irp) throws UsbException, UsbNotActiveException,
 UsbNotOpenException, IllegalArgumentException, UsbDisconnectedException
```

You can also submit a list of IRPs to be used in sequence:

```
public void syncSubmit(List list) throws UsbException, UsbNotActiveException,
 UsbNotOpenException, IllegalArgumentException, UsbDisconnectedException
public void asyncSubmit(List list) throws UsbException, UsbNotSctiveException,
 UsbNotOpenException, IllegalArgumentException, UsbDisconnectedException
```

 To keep data flowing at a brisk pace, you'll normally want to make sure enough IRPs are available for any incoming data. Streaming applications such as audio recording or anything that transfers large data buffers should submit multiple buffers in a block.

Finally, you can just submit the data array and let the pipe build the IRP for you. This is probably the simplest approach:

```
public void syncSubmit(byte[] data) throws UsbException, UsbNotActiveException,
 UsbNotOpenException, IllegalArgumentException, UsbDisconnectedException
public void asyncSubmit(byte[] data) throws UsbException, UsbNotActiveException,
 UsbNotOpenException, IllegalArgumentException, UsbDisconnectedException
```

However, this does not give you all the options working with an actual UsbIrp object does.

All six variants throw a UsbNotOpenException if the pipe has not yet been opened. All six throw an IllegalArgumentException if the IRP or list of IRPs is not properly prepared for the pipe.

When you're finished with a pipe you should close it. This takes three steps:

1. Cancel all pending submissions.
2. Close the pipe.
3. Release the interface you claimed.

For example:

```
pipe.abortAllSubmissions();
pipe.close();
theInterface.release();
```

It seems to be necessary to call abortAllSubmissions() even if you don't have any pending submissions. I'm not sure why, but when I skipped this step, I always got a UsbException with the message "Cannot close pipe with pending submissions."

# IRPs

Whether reading or writing, the first thing you need to do is create an IRP. IRPs are instances of the UsbIrp interface. You can implement this interface directly or instantiate the javax.usb.util.DefaultUsbIrp class, but it's normally simpler to use the createUsbIrp( ) factory method in the UsbPipe class:

```
public UsbIrp createUsbIrp( )
```

For an IRP created by this method, you only have to set the data storage array using setData( ):

```
public void setData(byte[] data);
public void setData(byte[] data, int offset, int length);
```

The size of the array should match the endpoint's maximum packet size:

```
int maxPacketSize = endpoint.getUsbEndpointDescriptor().wMaxPacketSize( );
byte[] buffer = new byte[maxPacketSize];
UsbIrp irp = pipe.createUsbIrp( );
irp.setData(buffer);
```

The offset is set to 0 and the length is the size of the data array. If you would prefer to use one larger array to support multiple IRPs, you can set the offset and the length appropriately to select slices of the array for each IRP, either in the constructor or with the setOffset( ) and setLength( ) methods:

```
public void setOffset(int offset);
public void setLength(int length);
```

For example:

```
int maxPacketSize = endpoint.getUsbEndpointDescriptor().wMaxPacketSize( );
byte[] buffer = new byte[8192];
UsbIrp irp1 = pipe.createUsbIrp( );
irp1.setData(buffer);
irp1.setOffset(0);
irp1.setLength(maxPacketSize);
UsbIrp irp2 = pipe.createUsbIrp( );
irp2.setData(buffer);
irp2.setOffset(maxPacketSize);
irp1.setLength(maxPacketSize);
UsbIrp irp3 = pipe.createUsbIrp( );
irp3.setData(buffer);
irp3.setOffset(3*maxPacketSize);
irp3.setLength(maxPacketSize);
```

Because packets tend to be so small, you'll often need to stuff your content into multiple successive IRPs. However, the last one won't always have exactly the amount of data needed to fill a packet. Most devices recognize a shorter than expected packet as indicating the end of the data. You can use the setActualLength( ) method to specify that only a subset of the normal data array contains real data:

```
public void setActualLength(int length);
```

This is not the same as selecting a subarray with setLength( ). The entire array is still sent; it's just that the actual IRP is modified so that the device knows not to consider some of it. If it happens that the data does exactly fill an integral number of IRPs, you may need to send a zero-length packet to tell the device that no more data is forthcoming. Details are device and protocol dependent.

Conversely, when receiving a packet, you may not get back quite as many bytes as you expected. The getActualLength( ) method tells you how many bytes the device actually sent:

```
public int getActualLength( );
```

If this is less than the length of the data array or subarray, the device has finished sending data. By default, most devices allow these short packets. However, a few devices require all IRPs to be full. If you're dealing with such a device, set the short packet policy to false:

```
public boolean getAcceptShortPacket( );
public void setAcceptShortPacket(boolean accept);
```

It's also possible that a problem has occurred on the bus or in the device and the data is not necessarily good. If so, the IRP is flagged with an exception. You can check for this condition with the isUsbException( ) method and retrieve the actual exception with getUsbException( ):

```
public boolean isUsbException( );
public UsbException getUsbException( );
public void setUsbException(UsbException usbException);
```

Yes, this is a very weird way of handling errors—not very Java-like at all.

Before you read data out of an IRP you submitted asynchronously, you need to check that it's *complete*; that is, that the device is finished with it. You do this with the isComplete( ) method:

```
public boolean isComplete( );
```

Alternatively, you can block until an IRP is complete with the waitUntilComplete( ) methods:

```
public void waitUntilComplete( );
public void waitUntilComplete(long timeout);
```

The first blocks indefinitely; the second blocks for a specified number of milliseconds. Neither approach is necessary for IRPs submitted synchronously, since that method always blocks as soon as the IRP is submitted.

You can also set the completion state of an IRP:

```
public void setComplete(boolean complete);
public void complete( );
```

As you'll see in the next example, this is useful if you want to reuse the same UsbIrp object since it allows you to uncomplete an IRP by passing false to setComplete( ).

# Temperature Sensor Example

As an example that puts all this together, I'm going to demonstrate a program that talks to the simplest off-the-shelf USB device I could find, a Vernier Go!Temp thermometer. This device, shown in Figure 23-2, is a laboratory sensor used in primary and secondary schools. More complex devices use the same basic USB principles but have more complicated protocols to control them. This device has the advantage of being simple and relatively cheap. All you have to do is plug it in and then read the data it sends back over the interrupt pipe.

*Figure 23-2. The Vernier Go!Temp next to a non-USB thermometer*

When writing software to communicate with a specific device, you have to determine the vendor and product ID in order to find the device. Fortunately, Example 23-4, `USBDeviceDescriber`, lists exactly this information. After plugging in the probe and running Example 23-4, we find that the vendor ID for Vernier is 0x08F7 and the product ID is 0x2. Let's store these in named constants:

```
public final static int VERNIER_VENDOR_ID = 0x08F7;
public final static int GOTEMP_PRODUCT_ID = 2;
```

These are the same for all devices of this type. Each probe also has a unique serial number that varies from one instrument to the next, but you don't need it.

The first thing the program needs to do is search the bus for the device with this ID. How this is done is very similar to some of the earlier examples: recursively traverse the USB tree looking for a device with the right vendor and product ID, and when it's found, return it, or return null if no such device is attached. Example 23-7 lists the program code.

*Example 23-7. Locating a device*

```
private static UsbDevice findProbe() throws UsbException {
  UsbServices services = UsbHostManager.getUsbServices();
  UsbHub root = services.getRootUsbHub();
  return searchDevices(root);
}

private static UsbDevice searchDevices(UsbHub hub)
 throws UsbException, IOException {
 List devices = hub.getAttachedUsbDevices();
 Iterator iterator = devices.iterator();
 while (iterator.hasNext()) {
   UsbDevice device = (UsbDevice) iterator.next();
   UsbDeviceDescriptor descriptor = device.getUsbDeviceDescriptor();
   int manufacturerCode = descriptor.idVendor();
   int productCode = descriptor.idProduct();

   if (manufacturerCode == VERNIER_VENDOR_ID
    && productCode == GOTEMP_PRODUCT_ID) {
     return device;
   }
   else if (device.isUsbHub()) {
     UsbDevice found = searchDevices((UsbHub) device);
     if (found != null) return found;
   }
 }
 return null; // didn't find it
}
```

This code assumes there's only one such probe on the bus. It would be simple enough to extend it to handle multiple probes, but for now I kept it simple by choosing the first one found and ignoring any subsequent devices.

The Go!Temp has a single configuration, a single interface, and a single input pipe from the device to the host that sends the temperature data. The next step is to find the single interface and claim it. From the device, we get the active configuration. From the configuration, we get the single interface:

```
UsbConfiguration config = probe.getActiveUsbConfiguration();
UsbInterface theInterface = (UsbInterface) config.getUsbInterfaces().get(0);
```

The interface number on this device should always be 0, so you could ask for it by number instead:

```
UsbInterface theInterface = config.getUsbInterface((byte) 0);
```

Now that we have the interface, we need to claim it. As usual, simple claiming does not work because the operating system has already grabbed hold of the device. We have to force the claim, like so:

```
theInterface.claim(new UsbInterfacePolicy() {
  public boolean forceClaim(UsbInterface usbInterface) {
    return true;
  }
});
```

Once the interface is claimed, we can ask it for its endpoint. For this device, there should be only one:

```
UsbEndpoint endpoint = (UsbEndpoint) theInterface.getUsbEndpoints().get(0);
```

In general, at this point you would check whether the endpoint was an in or out endpoint. However, as the Go!Temp has only a single in endpoint, we can skip that check.

The endpoint has a single pipe:

```
UsbPipe pipe = endpoint.getUsbPipe();
```

Normally here you'd check whether you have a control, bulk, isochronous, or interrupt pipe. Again, the Go!Temp probe is so simple that you know what you've got without asking: an interrupt pipe.

Now it's time to read from the pipe. First, create an IRP:

```
UsbIrp irp = pipe.createUsbIrp();
```

You can use any implementation of the UsbIrp interface here, but it's best to let the pipe object do it so it can optimize the IRP for the pipe.

The IRP should probably come with an appropriately sized data array. However, it doesn't, so make one and stuff it. For this device I happen to know that eight bytes is the right size:

```
byte[] input = new byte[8];
irp.setData(input);
```

If you don't know the size in advance, you can ask the UsbEndpointDescriptor for its wMaxPacketSize. If you send an incorrectly sized IRP, you'll get a UsbBabbleException when you submit it.

Next, we open the pipe and submit the IRP to the pipe. For this program we might as well submit synchronously, since we don't have anything else to do until the device responds:

```
pipe.open();
pipe.syncSubmit(irp);
```

When this method returns, the array is filled with binary data. There are no particular rules for how this data is interpreted. That's up to the device manufacturer. In this case, the Go!Temp stores the number of measurements it's taken as an unsigned integer in the first byte, a rolling sequence counter in the second byte, and 2-byte little-endian shorts in the last six spaces in this array. These shorts are the temperature measurements in 1/128ths of a degree Celsius. That looks suspiciously like a number chosen for convenience in binary arithmetic. I doubt the instrument is accurate beyond a tenth of a degree or so. In any case, dividing these shorts by 128 gives the temperature in degrees Celsius. This code finds the first temperature measurement returned:

```
int result = UsbUtil.toShort(data[3], data[2]);
double degreesCelsius = result / 128.0;
```

If the device has had time to make two measurements, the second temperature is in data[5] and data[4]. If it's had time to make three, the third is in data[7] and data[6]. You have to check the first byte to see how many measurements it took. Subsequent measurements require additional IRPs to be submitted.

FYI, I figured out how to interpret the data sent back by reading the C source code for a Linux device driver for the Go!Temp. I have no idea how the Linux hackers figured that out. They certainly didn't read the technical documentation, because there isn't any.

In practice, one of the hardest parts of writing software to interface with USB devices is getting quality documentation for the messages the devices send and receive. Reverse engineering with an expensive USB protocol analyzer is too often necessary. Some devices—mice, keyboards, mass storage devices, and the like—have fairly standard interfaces. Ironically, these are precisely the devices you don't need to write your own USB code to support.

To finish up, we wrap this in a loop that continuously reads from the pipe and prints the results to System.out. The loop can reuse the same IRP as long as it calls setComplete(false) on each pass and is careful not to read vestigial data from previous runs if the IRP is not completely refilled each time. I also added a little code to check whether the probe was being operated outside its advertised temperature range (−10˚C to 110˚C). Example 23-8 demonstrates.

*Example 23-8. Reading temperatures from a Go!Temp probe*

```
import java.util.*;
import javax.usb.*;
import javax.usb.util.*;
import java.io.*;

public class Thermometer {

  public final static int VERNIER_VENDOR_ID = 0x8F7;
  public final static int GOTEMP_PRODUCT_ID = 2;
```

*Example 23-8. Reading temperatures from a Go!Temp probe (continued)*

```java
  public static void main(String[] args) throws UsbException, IOException {
    UsbDevice probe = findProbe();
    if (probe == null) {
      System.err.println("No Go!Temp probe attached.");
      return;
    }

    UsbConfiguration config = probe.getActiveUsbConfiguration();
    UsbInterface theInterface = config.getUsbInterface((byte) 0);
    theInterface.claim(new UsbInterfacePolicy() {
      public boolean forceClaim(UsbInterface usbInterface) {
        return true;
      }
    });

    UsbEndpoint endpoint = (UsbEndpoint) theInterface.getUsbEndpoints().get(0);
    UsbPipe pipe = endpoint.getUsbPipe();

    // set up the IRP
    UsbIrp irp = pipe.createUsbIrp();
    byte[] data = new byte[8];
    irp.setData(data);
    pipe.open();

    outer: while (true) {
      pipe.syncSubmit(irp);
      int numberOfMeasurements = data[0];
      for (int i = 0; i < numberOfMeasurements; i++) {
        int result = UsbUtil.toShort(data[2*i+3], data[2*i+2]);
        int sequenceNumber = UsbUtil.unsignedInt(data[1]);
        double temperature = result / 128.0;
        if (temperature > 110.0) {
          System.err.println("Maximum accurate temperature exceeded.");
          break outer;
        }
        else if (temperature < -10) {
          System.err.println("Minimum accurate temperature exceeded.");
          break outer;
        }
        System.out.println("Measurement " + sequenceNumber + ": "
          + temperature + "°C");
      }
     // get ready to reuse IRP
     irp.setComplete(false);
    }
    pipe.abortAllSubmissions();
    pipe.close();
    theInterface.release();
  }

  private static UsbDevice findProbe() throws UsbException, IOException {
    UsbServices services = UsbHostManager.getUsbServices();
```

*Example 23-8. Reading temperatures from a Go!Temp probe (continued)*

```
    UsbHub root = services.getRootUsbHub( );
    return searchDevices(root);
  }

  private static UsbDevice searchDevices(UsbHub hub)
   throws UsbException, IOException {
   List devices = hub.getAttachedUsbDevices( );
   Iterator iterator = devices.iterator( );
   while (iterator.hasNext( )) {
     UsbDevice device = (UsbDevice) iterator.next( );
     UsbDeviceDescriptor descriptor = device.getUsbDeviceDescriptor( );
     int manufacturerCode = descriptor.idVendor( );
     int productCode = descriptor.idProduct( );

     if (manufacturerCode == VERNIER_VENDOR_ID
      && productCode == GOTEMP_PRODUCT_ID) {
       return device;
     }
     else if (device.isUsbHub( )) {
       UsbDevice found = searchDevices((UsbHub) device);
       if (found != null) return found;
     }
   }
   return null; // didn't find it
  }
}
```

Here's some output from when I ran it. The probe started collecting data just sitting on my desk, but then I dunked it in ice water. You can see it started with three measurements in one packet at room temperature. However, because the program was running faster than the probe could retrieve the temperature, each subsequent packet contained only a single measurement. Initially, the temperature was slowly rising, but as soon as I dunked it in the ice water it began dropping rapidly, stabilizing at around 6°C. If I let the ice melt and left the program running for an hour or so, it would heat back up to room temperature.

```
# java -classpath jsr80_ri-1.0.0.jar:jsr80-1.0.0.jar:.:jsr80_linux-1.0.0.jar Probe
Measurement 247: 18.9375 °C
Measurement 248: 18.9375 °C
Measurement 249: 18.9375 °C
Measurement 250: 18.9375 °C
Measurement 251: 18.9375 °C
Measurement 252: 18.9375 °C
Measurement 253: 18.9375 °C
Measurement 254: 18.9375 °C
Measurement 255: 19.0 °C
Measurement 0: 19.0625 °C
Measurement 1: 16.0625 °C
Measurement 2: 13.6875 °C
Measurement 3: 12.1875 °C
Measurement 4: 11.1875 °C
```

```
Measurement 5: 10.5 °C
Measurement 6: 10.0 °C
Measurement 7: 9.625 °C
Measurement 8: 9.25 °C
Measurement 9: 8.9375 °C
Measurement 10: 8.625 °C
Measurement 11: 8.375 °C
Measurement 12: 8.1875 °C
Measurement 13: 8.0 °C
Measurement 14: 7.8125 °C
Measurement 15: 7.6875 °C
Measurement 16: 7.5 °C
Measurement 17: 7.375 °C
Measurement 18: 7.25 °C
Measurement 19: 7.125 °C
Measurement 20: 7.0625 °C
Measurement 21: 6.9375 °C
Measurement 22: 6.875 °C
Measurement 23: 6.75 °C
Measurement 24: 6.6875 °C
Measurement 25: 6.625 °C
Measurement 26: 6.5625 °C
Measurement 27: 6.5 °C
Measurement 28: 6.5 °C
Measurement 29: 6.4375 °C
Measurement 30: 6.375 °C
Measurement 31: 6.375 °C
Measurement 32: 6.3125 °C
Measurement 33: 6.3125 °C
Measurement 34: 6.25 °C
Measurement 35: 6.25 °C
Measurement 36: 6.25 °C
Measurement 37: 6.1875 °C
Measurement 38: 6.1875 °C
```

Example 23-8 reads continuously. It should provide the user with a way to quit the program. When it does so, the program should release the device.

## Hot Plugging

The javax.usb.event.UsbServicesListener interface can notify your program whenever a USB device—even one you've never seen before—is plugged into or unplugged from the bus. This interface has two callback methods. usbDeviceAttached( ) is called when a device is plugged in, and usbDeviceDetached( ) is called when a device is unplugged (or turned off, which amounts to the same thing):

```
package javax.usb.event;

public interface UsbServicesListener extends java.util.EventListener {
```

```
    public void usbDeviceAttached(UsbServicesEvent event);
    public void usbDeviceDetached(UsbServicesEvent event);

}
```

Each of these methods receives a UsbServicesEvent object as an argument. This interface has a getUsbDevice( ) method that returns the device that was connected or disconnected:

```
    public UsbDevice getUsbDevice( )
```

Example 23-9 is a simple implementation of this interface that prints the manufacturer string and other info for each device added to or removed from the bus.

*Example 23-9. A listener for USB devices plugged in and unplugged*

```
import javax.usb.*;
import javax.usb.event.*;

public class HotplugListener implements UsbServicesListener {

  public void usbDeviceAttached(UsbServicesEvent event) {
    UsbDevice device = event.getUsbDevice( );
    System.out.println(getDeviceInfo(device) + " was added to the bus.");
  }

  public void usbDeviceDetached(UsbServicesEvent event) {
    UsbDevice device = event.getUsbDevice( );
    System.out.println(getDeviceInfo(device) + " was removed from the bus.");
  }

  private static String getDeviceInfo(UsbDevice device) {
    try {
      String product = device.getProductString( );
      String serial = device.getSerialNumberString( );
      if (product == null) return "Unknown USB device";
      if (serial != null) return product + " " + serial;
      else return product;
    }
    catch (Exception ex) {
    }
    return "Unknown USB device";
  }
}
```

You register your listeners with a javax.usb.UsbServices object using the customary add and remove methods:

```
    public void addUsbServicesListener(UsbServicesListener listener)
    public void removeUsbServicesListener(UsbServicesListener listener)
```

This object then calls back to your listener to notify it of devices added and removed.

Example 23-10 is a simple program that uses the listener in Example 23-9 to notify the user when devices are plugged in and unplugged.

*Example 23-10. A program that tells the user when USB devices are plugged in and unplugged*

```java
import javax.usb.*;
import javax.usb.event.*;

public class Hotplugger {

  public static void main(String[] args)
    throws UsbException, InterruptedException {
    UsbServices services = UsbHostManager.getUsbServices();
    services.addUsbServicesListener(new HotplugListener());
    // Keep this program from exiting immediately
    Thread.sleep(500000);
  }
}
```

Here's the output as I repeatedly connected and disconnected a couple of different devices from the bus:

```
Silicon Integrated Systems [SiS] USB 1.0 Controller 0000:00:02.2
was added to the bus.
USB-PS/2 Optical Mouse was added to the bus.
Silicon Integrated Systems [SiS] USB 1.0 Controller (#2) 0000:00:02.3
was added to the bus.
Unknown device was added to the bus.
Unknown device was removed from the bus.
Unknown device was added to the bus.
Unknown device was removed from the bus.
Unknown device was added to the bus.
Unknown device was removed from the bus.
DMC-FZ5 was added to the bus.
Unknown device was removed from the bus.
DMC-FZ5 was added to the bus.
```

Interestingly, when the program starts, usbDeviceAttached() is called once for each already attached device, including each of the USB controllers. You'll also notice that you can't get much info when a device is detached. All the usual methods—getProductString(), getSerialNumberString(), etc.—require the device to be connected to work. Otherwise, they throw an exception. However, the same object is returned when the device is detached as when it is attached, so you can load up all the information the first time, store it somewhere, and then retrieve it locally when the device is detached. Example 23-11 uses a HashMap to do this.

*Example 23-11. A USB listener that remembers devices*

```java
import javax.usb.*;
import javax.usb.event.*;
import java.util.*;

public class ImprovedHotplugListener implements UsbServicesListener {

  private Map devices = new HashMap();
```

*Example 23-11. A USB listener that remembers devices (continued)*

```java
  public void usbDeviceAttached(UsbServicesEvent event) {
    UsbDevice device = event.getUsbDevice( );
    String deviceInfo = getDeviceInfo(device);
    devices.put(device, deviceInfo);
    System.out.println(deviceInfo + " was added to the bus.");
  }

  public void usbDeviceDetached(UsbServicesEvent event) {
    UsbDevice device = event.getUsbDevice( );
    String deviceInfo = (String) devices.get(device);
    System.out.println(deviceInfo + " was removed from the bus.");
  }

  private static String getDeviceInfo(UsbDevice device) {
    try {
      String product = device.getProductString( );
      String serial = device.getSerialNumberString( );
      if (product == null) return "Unknown USB device";
      if (serial != null) return product + " " + serial;
      else return product;
    }
    catch (Exception ex) {
    }
    return "Unknown USB device";
  }
}
```

This only goes so far. The Java USB API does not recognize devices that are plugged in again: it creates a new UsbDevice object for a reconnected device.

# CHAPTER 24

# The J2ME Generic Connection Framework

While Windows running on X86 processors still commands more than 90% of the desktop market and more than half of the server space, the embedded device market is far more diverse. The small device ecosystem contains hundreds of different processors and dozens of operating systems. To some extent this is a reflection of the diversity of the devices themselves. There's not all that much difference between a laptop and a desktop and a blade server. They're pretty much all rectangular boxes with the same basic hardware, give or take a couple of ports. By contrast, embedded devices cover everything from cell phones to PDAs to watches to car ignition systems to hotel door locks to televisions to jewelry—very different devices with very different needs. A CPU and operating system that work well for an iPod may be completely unsuitable for the hard real-time requirements of avionics controls. Still, even among similar devices such as cell phones, the market is far more diverse than it is in personal computers.

Java's platform agnosticism makes it an obvious choice for the diverse embedded marketplace. It offers developers the hope of writing one piece of code that can run more or less reliably on many different vendors' hardware. The fit is not always perfect, but it's better than anything that has come before.

There are over two and a half billion Java-enabled devices on the planet today, and about 75% of those are embedded devices. These devices vary widely in capability. On the high end, an iPod might have a 60-GB hard drive and dual 100-MHz CPUs. On the low end, a hotel door lock might have no disk space, a few kilobytes of memory, and an 8-bit 1-MHz processor. In between, a cheap cell phone might have 300K of memory and a 30-MHz processor. Weak battery power and inadequate heat dissipation exacerbate these limits. While it might be possible to put a 1-GHz processor in a cell phone, you couldn't power it for more than a few minutes without running out of juice and burning a hole in the user's pocket.

Even at the high end, embedded devices are very limited compared to modern PCs. In particular, the memory requirements can be extremely tight. While desktop and server programmers stopped worrying about memory footprint years ago, embedded programmers still find themselves making gut-wrenching choices between functionality and features. Every extra byte carries a cost that must be weighed. Every class must be considered for the trade-off between programmer convenience and end user space. For instance, to a micro-programmer the Java habit of creating a new class for every tiny variation of an exception seems extremely wasteful.

Simply put, Java 2 Standard Edition (J2SE) is too big for most small devices. The sheer number of classes in the Java class library can be an obstacle to embedding standard Java. Consequently, Sun, Nokia, Motorola, and others have defined a different, incompatible version of Java tailored to the needs of small devices, called Java 2 Micro Edition (J2ME). In fact, they've defined several variants and versions for devices of different sizes and capabilities. At the very bottom is the Connected Limited Device Configuration (CLDC) 1.0. This platform is designed for battery-powered, intermittently connected devices with as little 160K of memory, most of which has to be used by the VM itself. The Connected Device Configuration (CDC) is targeted at slightly larger devices such as PDAs and settop boxes. These devices have at least 2 MB of memory and faster and more reliable network connectivity. The Mobile Information Device Profile (MIDP) adds features on top of a basic CLDC or CDC implementation, with an emphasis on user interface classes. The different profiles provide different subsets of and additions to the standard Java class library.

This is not the Java you know and love. The language is the same, but the library is quite different. In particular, it is much smaller and comes with greatly restricted functionality. Most programs are implemented as MIDlets rather than standalone applications with main( ) methods. Most interestingly for the purposes of this book, the I/O classes in J2ME are not just cut-back versions of the classes available in the standard java.io package. Instead, they are a completely different set of classes in the javax.microedition.io package, which is not available in regular Java. This is called the Generic Connection Framework (GCF).

The GCF offers two interfaces, five exceptions, and 11 classes from java.io. More specifically, it includes:

- The InputStream and OutputStream abstract classes
- The ByteArrayInputStream and ByteArrayOutputStream classes
- The DataInputStream and DataOutputStream classes
- The DataInput and DataOutput interfaces
- The PrintStream class
- The Reader and Writer abstract classes
- The InputStreamReader and OutputStreamWriter classes
- IOException and four subclasses: EOFException, InterruptedIOException, UnsupportedEncodingException, and UTFDataFormatException

However, that's all. Other classes from `java.io` and `java.net` are completely absent, and even the included classes are set up differently than they are in regular desktop Java, to avoid an explosion of classes for each different kind of stream.

These classes may not have all the methods you're accustomed to, either. For instance, in CLDC 1.0, `DataInput` and `DataInputStream` are missing `readLine()`, `readFloat()`, and `readDouble()`. `DataOutput` and `DataOutputStream` are missing `writeFloat()` and `writeDouble()`. `DataOutputStream` is also missing `size()`. `PrintStream` is missing all the methods that print doubles and floats. CLDC 1.1 devices contain the floating-point methods, though they're still missing the deprecated methods, such as `readLine()`. The `Reader` and `Writer` classes are complete, but they don't support all the encodings desktop Java versions do.

The CDC does provide a full implementation of `java.io` and `java.net` at the level of Java 1.3 for CDC 1.0.1 and 1.4 for CDC 1.1 (`java.nio` is still omitted). It also includes the Generic Connection Framework.

# The Generic Connection Framework

The Generic Connection Framework is the standard means of performing I/O, especially network I/O, in all profiles of J2ME. It is available in the CLDC, the MIDP, the Information Module Profile (IMP), and all CDC-derived profiles, including the Foundation Profile, the Personal Basis Profile, and the Personal Profile. As a result, I'm not going to worry a lot about exactly which profile you're using. For our purposes, they're equivalent.

What's not equivalent are the kinds of I/O the different devices support. Most embedded devices don't have filesystems, but some of the larger ones, such as the iPod, do. Some devices have no network access at all; some have full, unrestricted IP stacks; and some have access to some sort of proprietary network. Devices can have serial ports, parallel ports, USB ports, FireWire ports, and/or Bluetooth capabilities. Much like streams, the GCF is designed to allow particular devices to support all the different forms of I/O the devices have, but none of the ones they don't. This rules out classes like `URL`, `Socket`, `FileInputStream`, and `UsbDevice` that are closely tied to one particular kind of I/O service. No one wants to waste precious space on a `FileInputStream` class for a device that doesn't have a filesystem.

The GCF is based on an abstract `Connection` interface, which supports two basic kinds of connections: packet and stream. Packet connections are used for UDP and Bluetooth L2CAP. Stream connections are used for TCP, files, serial ports, and Bluetooth RFCOMM. Streams are read and written using the regular `InputStream` and `OutputStream` classes.

Reading input using the GCF follows these three steps:

1. Pass the URL of the resource you want to read to the static `Connector.openInputStream( )` method. This returns an `InputStream` object.

2. Read from the `InputStream` in the usual way.

3. Close the `InputStream` when you're done.

For example, this code fragment opens a connection to Google:

```
InputStream in  = Connector.openInputStream("http://www.google.com/");
// read from in like you would any other InputStream...
in.close( );
```

Output is similar, except you open an `OutputStream` instead of an `InputStream`:

```
OutputStream out = Connector.openOutputStream("socket://ftp.example.com:8979");
// write to out as you would any other OutputStream...
out.close( );
```

So far this looks a lot like the `URL` class, but with three key differences:

- Behind the scenes, this does not involve the heavyweight protocol handler mechanism that supports `URL`, `URLConnection`, `HttpURLConnection`, and associated classes.

- The `Connector` class in any particular environment may recognize nonstandard URLs that represent sockets, Bluetooth connections, serial ports, and more.

- The `Connector` class may not recognize standard URL schemes including *file* and *http* if the local device does not support them.

For example, if you wanted to open a socket to Google to read the headers of the page instead of just the body, you would use the nonstandard socket protocol, like this:

```
InputStream in = Connector.openInputStream("socket://www.google.com:80/");
// read from in like you would any other InputStream...
in.close( );
```

As in applets, access to the network is restricted to signed, trusted MIDlets. Untrusted MIDlets prompt the user for authorization before each potentially dangerous operation.

Example 24-1 shows a simple MIDlet program that displays the current time. It does this by connecting to the National Institute of Standards time server in Boulder, Colorado on the daytime port (13) and displaying the result. The daytime protocol sends a one-line ASCII string that is easy to display on most small MIDP 1.0 devices.

*Example 24-1. A MIDlet daytime client*

```
import javax.microedition.midlet.*;
import javax.microedition.lcdui.*;
import javax.microedition.io.*;
import java.io.*;
```

*Example 24-1. A MIDlet daytime client (continued)*

```java
public class Daytime extends MIDlet {

  public Daytime( ) {

    Form form = new Form("Network Time");
    InputStream in = null;
    try {
      in = Connector.openInputStream("socket://time-a.nist.gov:13");
      StringBuffer sb = new StringBuffer( );
      for (int c = in.read( ); c != -1; c = in.read( )) {
        sb.append((char) c);
      }
      form.append(sb.toString( ));
    }
    catch (IOException ex) {
      form.append(ex.getMessage( ));
    }
    finally {
      try {
        if (in != null) in.close( );
      }
      catch (IOException ex) { /* Oh well. We tried.*/ }
    }

    Display.getDisplay(this).setCurrent(form);
  }

  public void startApp( ) {}
  public void pauseApp( ) {}
  public void destroyApp(boolean unconditional) {}
}
```

Figure 24-1 shows this program displaying in the J2ME emulator bundled with the Sun Java Wireless Toolkit. When running this MIDlet, the phone prompts the user to allow the network connection. These prompts can be eliminated, but normally only if you can cut a deal with the phone company. Cell phones tend to be locked-down devices that do not allow arbitrary hacking.

 Note the lack of a main( ) method. A MIDlet is conceptually more like an applet than an application. It cannot be compiled and run like a typical standalone Java application. I'm assuming here you know how to compile and run MIDlets. If not, you can consult any number of good books on the topic, including *J2ME in a Nutshell* by Kim Topley (O'Reilly).

The socket protocol used here is available on some, but not all, MIDP devices. It is not turned on in the emulator by default. To enable it, set the Java system property com.sun.midp.io.enable_extra_protocols to true. You can do this with the -D

---

*Figure 24-1. The daytime MIDlet*

command-line option or by editing the *$(MIDP_HOME)/lib/internal.config* file, where the emulator reads its configuration information.

## The Connector Class

The Connector class contains all the static utility methods needed to open connections, regardless of what kinds of connections they are. You've already seen the openInputStream( ) and openOutputStream( ) methods:

```
public static InputStream openInputStream(String url)
  throws ConnectionNotFoundException, IOException, IllegalArgumentException
public static OutputStream openOutputStream(String url)
  throws ConnectionNotFoundException, IOException, IllegalArgumentException
```

These methods throw an IllegalArgumentException if the URL is malformed, a ConnectionNotFoundException (a subclass of IOException) if the remote is unreachable or the protocol is not supported, and an IOException if the stream can't be opened for any other reason.

Other methods open DataInputStreams and DataOutputStreams instead:

```
public static DataInputStream openDataInputStream(String url)
 throws ConnectionNotFoundException, IOException, IllegalArgumentException
public static DataOutputStream openDataOutputStream(String url)
 throws ConnectionNotFoundException, IOException, IllegalArgumentException
```

However, these four are the only kinds of streams you have. There are no object streams, piped streams, cipher streams, or any other kinds of filter streams in J2ME. Indeed, there's no FilterInputStream or FilterOutputStream class at all. In J2ME, DataInputStream and DataOutputStream extend InputStream and OutputStream directly:

```
public class DataInputStream extends InputStream implements DataInput
public class DataOutputStream extends OutputStream implements DataOutput
```

Another difference worth noting: the DataInputStream class has removed the deprecated readLine( ) method. In CLDC 1.0, readFloat( ) and readDouble( ) are also omitted, though these are present in CLDC 1.1 and CDC devices.

Instead of requesting a stream directly, you can ask the connector for a Connection object using one of its three open( ) methods:

```
public static Connection open(String url) throws IOException
public static Connection open(String url, int mode) throws IOException
public static Connection open(String url, int mode, boolean timeouts)
 throws IOException
```

There are two kinds of Connections: InputConnections and OutputConnections. The InputConnection interface has openInputStream( ) and openDataInputStream( ) methods. The OutputConnection interface has openOutputStream( ) and openDataOutputStream( ) methods. Once you have a connection, you'll have to cast it to one of these types to use it. For example, this code fragment opens a connection to Google and reads from it:

```
Connection conn  = Connector.open("http://www.google.com/");
InputConnection input = (InputConnection) c;
InputStream in = input.openInputStream( );
// read from in like you would any other InputStream...
conn.close( );
```

Some, though not all, objects implement both InputConnection and OutputConnection. Some objects implement only one or the other. If you know which you want, pass the appropriate constant (Connector.READ, Connector.WRITE, or Connector.READ_WRITE) to the open( ) method. For example, this line opens a read-only connection to Google:

```
Connection c  = Connector.open("http://www.google.com/", Connector.READ);
```

If a mode the protocol does not support is passed, open( ) throws an IllegalArgumentException.

Your final option is to pass true for the third argument. This indicates that the program is ready to handle timeouts and that the connection should throw a java.io.InterruptedIOException if the connection times out. (In practice, this doesn't have a lot of effect. While theoretically a connection might hang forever without this, in practice some exception is likely to be thrown sometime. It just won't be an InterruptedIOException.)

None of this is very different from just calling openInputStream( ) or openOutputStream( ) and working with that stream. What, then, is the point of open( )? If you know what kind of connection you're opening (file, HTTP, socket, etc.)—and you normally do know this—you can cast the returned InputConnection or OutputConnection to a more specific type: ContentConnection, HttpConnection, SocketConnection, and so on. Then you can use the extra methods of these classes to do interesting things.

# ContentConnection

Most connections are stream connections. StreamConnection is a convenience interface that implements both InputConnection and OutputConnection:

```
public interface StreamConnection extends InputConnection, OutputConnection
```

StreamConnection declares no additional methods of its own, just the five it inherits from its superinterfaces: openInputStream( ), openOutputStream( ), openDataInputStream( ), openDataOutputStream( ), and close( ).

Most stream connections are also instances of its subinterface, ContentConnection:

```
public interface ContentConnection extends StreamConnection
```

ContentConnection does add three methods for getting the length, content encoding, and MIME media type of the content in the stream:

```
public String getType( )
public String getEncoding( )
public long   getLength( )
```

getType( ) usually returns a MIME media type such as text/html or application/xml. However, it may return null if the content type can't be determined.

The getEncoding( ) method returns a string indicating which (if any) additional encodings have been applied to the content. For instance, if the content has been gzipped, it returns the string "gzip". This method is mostly meant for HTTP, where it returns the value of the Content-encoding header. In most other protocols, it will likely return null.

Finally, getLength( ) returns the length of the content in bytes. For HTTP, this is the value in the Content-length header. It returns –1 if the content length is not known.

These three methods are mostly designed for HTTP, but they can sometimes work for file streams or other kinds of streams as well. Example 24-2 is a simple MIDlet that displays this information for a user-supplied URL.

*Example 24-2. A MIDlet for showing the type and length of data*

```java
import javax.microedition.midlet.*;
import javax.microedition.lcdui.*;
import javax.microedition.io.*;
import java.io.IOException;

public class ContentInfo extends MIDlet implements CommandListener {

  private Display display;
  private TextBox textBox;

  public void startApp() {
    display = Display.getDisplay(this);

    if (textBox == null) {
      textBox = new TextBox("URL", "http://", 255, TextField.URL);
    }
    display.setCurrent(textBox);

    Command getInfo = new Command("Get Info", Command.OK, 10);
    textBox.addCommand(getInfo);
    textBox.setCommandListener(this);
  }

  public void commandAction(Command command, Displayable displayable) {
    // Network operations should not run in this same thread
    Thread t = new Thread(
      new Runnable() {
        public void run() {
          display.setCurrent(getInfo());
        }
      }
    );
    t.start();
  }

  private Form getInfo() {

    Form form = new Form("Content Info");
    ContentConnection conn = null;
    try {
      conn = (ContentConnection) Connector.open(textBox.getString());
      String type = conn.getType();
      String encoding = conn.getEncoding();
      long length = conn.getLength();

      form.append("Media type: " + type + "\r\n");
      if (encoding != null) form.append("Encoding: " + encoding + "\r\n");
      form.append("Length: " + String.valueOf(length));
    }
    catch (IOException ex) {
      form.append(ex.getMessage());
    }
    finally {
```

```
    try {
      if (conn != null) conn.close( );
    }
    catch (IOException ex) { /* Oh well. we tried.*/ }
  }
  return form;
}

public void pauseApp( ) {}
public void destroyApp(boolean unconditional) {}
}
```

When the MIDlet starts up, it displays a text box in which the user can enter a URL. Once the user enters the URL and activates the Get Info command, the MIDlet changes display to a form showing the content info. It does this in a separate thread to avoid a potential deadlock condition. The getInfo( ) method reads the URL from the text box and connects to it (after checking with the user to make sure the connection is allowed). It then displays the media type, content length, and content encoding (if any). Figure 24-2 shows this program in a J2ME emulator.

# Files

The most basic kind of StreamConnection is a javax.microedition.io.file. FileConnection:

```
    public interface FileConnection extends StreamConnection
```

In J2ME, the FileConnection class takes the place of java.io.File in J2SE. Thus, as well as methods to open streams, it has methods to get information about the file. Do be careful here. Every warning in Chapter 17 about cross-platform file access goes triple for J2ME. Some small device filesystems look like Windows, but many more look like DOS, right down to a maximum 8.3 filename. Others look like Unix (in fact, some are Unix), and still others look nothing like any common desktop operating system.

FileConnection is not a standard part of any J2ME profile, but devices that have filesystems are likely to include it. Filesystems include not only built-in filesystems on internal hard drives and flash memory, but also various types of removable memory, such as SmartMedia cards, CompactFlash cards, or Sony memory sticks. For instance, you'll find FileConnection on Nokia phones that implement the S60 Platform 2nd Edition or later, including the N80, N92, and N71. If you're not developing for a specific platform with known capabilities, you can check for its presence by testing the microedition.io.file.FileConnection.version system property:

```
    if (System.getproperty("microedition.io.file.FileConnection.version")
     != null) {
      // file connections are available
    }
```

File Tools Help

NOKIA

**Content Info**

Media type: text/html
Length: –1

not an actual product

NOKIA

*Figure 24-2. The content info MIDlet*

This property is set only on platforms where you can open a FileConnection.

To open a FileConnection, just use a standard file URL such as *file:///C:/Nokia/Images/Image(007).jpg*. Some devices also define virtual filesystem roots that don't expose the entire filesystem, such as */Images*. For example, on many recent Nokia phones, this statement opens the file at *file:///C:/Nokia/Images/Image(007).jpg*:

```
InputStream in
  = Connector.openInputStream("file:///Images/Image(007).jpg ");
```

As in applets, access to the filesystem is restricted to signed, trusted MIDlets. Untrusted MIDlets prompt the user for authorization before reading or writing files. Even trusted MIDlets are normally prevented from accessing or even seeing certain sensitive parts of the filesystem, such as Record Management System (RMS) databases or operating system files. For instance, a Linux-based PDA shouldn't allow access to /vmlinuz, and a MIDlet shouldn't need it. MIDlets are meant for basic user-level programs, after all, not device drivers and system software.

If you want to do more than just read from or write to the file, open a connection and cast it to FileConnection rather than opening an input or output stream directly:

```
FileConnnection fc = (FileConnection) Connector.open(
  "file:///Volumes/Birds/Contacts/ipod_created_instructions.vcf ");;
```

You can then call FileConnnection's openInputStream( ), openOutputStream( ), openDataInputStream( ), and openDataOutputStream( ) methods to get the streams you use to read and write:

```
public static InputStream openInputStream(String url)
 throws IOException, IllegalModeException, SecurityException
public static OutputStream openOutputStream(String url)
 throws IOException, IllegalModeException, SecurityException
public static DataInputStream openDataInputStream(String url)
 throws IOException, IllegalModeException, SecurityException
public static DataOutputStream openDataOutputStream(String url)
 throws IOException, IllegalModeException, SecurityException
```

Each FileConnection can have only one InputStream and one OutputStream open at a time, though you can open a new stream after closing the old one. Unlike sockets, closing the associated stream does not close the FileConnection. To close a FileConnection, you must explicitly call the connection's close( ) method.

A SecurityException is thrown if the user vetoes the file access. An IllegalModeException is thrown if the connection was opened in write-only mode. These are runtime exceptions. A checked IOException is thrown if anything else goes wrong.

Usually, you begin writing at the beginning of a file and overwrite any existing data in the file. FileConnection does not support random access. However, it adds one extra method that enables you to start writing at a specified position in the file rather than at the beginning:

```
public OutputStream openOutputStream(long byteOffset) throws IOException,
  IllegalArgumentException, IllegalModeException, SecurityException
```

You can also cut off the end of the file, truncating it to a certain length in bytes:

```
public void truncate(long byteOffset) throws IOException,
  IllegalArgumentException, IllegalModeException, ConnectionClosedException
```

In both cases, the byteOffset must be nonnegative, or an IllegalArgumentException is thrown.

As with `java.io.File`, having a `FileConnection` object does not guarantee that the file actually exists. Thus, before trying to read or write to a file, you should first check whether the file exists:

```
public boolean exists() throws IllegalModeException, SecurityException,
  ConnectionClosedException
```

You should also check whether the file is a really a file, or if it's a directory. `exists()` returns true in both cases, but the `isDirectory()` method tells you. It returns `true` if the file exists and is a directory or `false` otherwise:

```
public boolean isDirectory() throws SecurityException,
  IllegalModeException, ConnectionClosedException
```

If a file does not exist, you can use the `create()` method to create it:

```
public void create() throws IOException, IllegalModeException,
  SecurityException, ConnectionClosedException
```

For example, this code tries to create the file *newfile.txt* in the directory *CFCard* if it doesn't already exist:

```
FileConnection fc = (FileConnection) Connector.open("file:///CFCard/newfile.txt");
if (!fc.exists()) fc.create();
```

Unlike with `java.io.FileOutputStream`, merely opening an `OutputStream` to a file with `FileConnection` is not sufficient to create it. You must explicitly call `create()` before opening an `OutputStream` with `FileConnection`.

To create a directory, use the `mkdir()` method instead:

```
public void mkdir() throws IOException, IllegalModeException,
  SecurityException, ConnectionClosedException
```

You can also change the name of an existing file or directory using the `rename()` method:

```
public void rename(String newName) throws IOException,
  NullPointerException, IllegalArgumentException, IllegalModeException,
  SecurityException, ConnectionClosedException
```

The new name must not contain any slashes, or an `IllegalArgumentException` is thrown. Unlike the `rename()` method in `java.io.File`, this method never moves a file to a different directory. `FileConnection` has no methods to move or copy a file. This method also has the side effect of closing all currently open streams to the file, though the connections to the file remain open.

You can delete a file or directory, permissions permitting of course, with the `delete()` method:

```
public void delete() throws IOException, IllegalModeException,
  SecurityException, ConnectionClosedException
```

The `getName()` method takes no arguments and returns the name of the file as a string:

```
public String getName()
```

The name does not include any part of the directory in which the file lives. That is, you get back something like *index.html* instead of */public/html/javafaq/index.html*. If the file is a directory, the name ends with a forward slash (/).

The getPath() method returns an absolute path to the file's parent directory, as initially provided in the file URL:

```
public String getPath()
```

For example, if the URL was *file:///a/b/c/d.jpg*, getPath() would return /a/b/c/. If the URL was *file:///a/b/c/*, getPath() would return /a/b/. Forward slashes are always used, even on FAT and other DOS/Windows filesystems. The full absolute path to the file is getPath() + getFile().

Root directories are treated specially. For a root directory, getPath() always returns the empty string.

Finally, the getURL() method returns the complete file URL that was used to open the FileConnection:

```
public String getURL()
```

## File attributes

The FileConnection class has several methods that return information about the file, such as its length, the time it was last modified, whether it's readable, whether it's writable, and whether it's hidden.

The canWrite() method indicates whether the program can write into the file referred to by this FileConnection object, while the canRead() method indicates whether the program can read from the file:

```
public boolean canRead() throws SecurityException,
 ConnectionClosedException IllegalModeException,
public boolean canWrite() throws SecurityException,
 IllegalModeException, ConnectionClosedException
```

You can sometimes change the readability of a file using the setReadable() method or the writability using setWritable():

```
public boolean setReadable(boolean readable) throws  IOException,
 SecurityException, IllegalModeException, ConnectionClosedException
public boolean setWritable(boolean writable) throws IOException,
 SecurityException, IllegalModeException, ConnectionClosedException
```

More often than not, though, if a file isn't already readable or writable, you can't make it so; trying to do it anyway simply results in one exception or another.

The isOpen() method returns true if the file is open and false if it isn't:

```
public boolean isOpen() throws SecurityException,
 IllegalModeException, ConnectionClosedException
```

The isHidden( ) method returns true if the file exists but is hidden:

```
public boolean isHidden( ) throws SecurityException,
  IllegalModeException, ConnectionClosedException
```

Exactly what "hidden" means varies from one platform to the next, but you probably shouldn't show a hidden file to the user by default. isHidden( ) returns false if the file isn't hidden or doesn't exist.

You can hide a file by passing true to setHidden( ) or unhide it by passing false:

```
public void setHidden(boolean hidden) throws IOException,
  IllegalModeException, SecurityException, ConnectionClosedException
```

The lastModified( ) method returns a long indicating the last time this file was modified:

```
public long lastModified( ) throws SecurityException,
  IllegalModeException, ConnectionClosedException
```

The time is the number of milliseconds since midnight, January 1, 1970, Greenwich Mean Time. lastModified( ) returns 0 if for any reason the last modified date can't be determined.

The fileSize( ) method returns the number of bytes in the file:

```
public long fileSize( ) throws IOException,
  IllegalModeException, SecurityException, ConnectionClosedException
```

fileSize( ) returns –1 if the file doesn't exist or can't be read. It throws an IOException if you invoke it on a directory. However, the directorySize( ) method returns the sum of the sizes of all the files in the directory:

```
public long directorySize(boolean includeSubDirs) throws IOException,
  IllegalModeException, SecurityException, ConnectionClosedException
```

If includeSubDirs is true, this sum includes the sizes of all files in all subdirectories, applied recursively. Otherwise, it just returns the cumulative size of the files directly contained in this directory. Invoking directorySize( ) on a FileConnection object that represents a file throws an IOException.

Finally, you can use the totalSize( ), usedSize( ), and availableSize( ) methods to determine the size in bytes of the filesystem where this FileConnection object is found, the number of bytes used on the filesystem, and the number of free bytes, respectively:

```
public long totalSize( ) throws  IllegalModeException,
  SecurityException, ConnectionClosedException
public long availableSize( ) throws  IllegalModeException,
  SecurityException, ConnectionClosedException
public long usedSize( ) throws  IllegalModeException,
  SecurityException, ConnectionClosedException
```

The numbers returned for used and available space are estimates and may not be perfectly accurate.

### Listing directories

The list( ) method returns an enumeration of strings containing the names of each nonhidden file in the directory referred to by the FileConnection object:

```
public Enumeration list( ) throws IOException,
  IllegalModeException, SecurityException, ConnectionClosedException
```

This method throws an IOException if the FileConnection object doesn't point to an accessible directory. It throws a SecurityException if the program isn't allowed to read the directory being listed. An overloaded version of list( ) can optionally display hidden files and filter the files displayed:

```
public Enumeration list(String filter, boolean includeHidden)
  throws IOException, IllegalModeException, SecurityException,
  ConnectionClosedException
```

J2ME has no FileFilters or FilenameFilters. Instead, the filter is a simple string pattern for the files to be displayed. The asterisk (*) is a wildcard. For instance, the pattern "*.jpg" finds all files whose names end with *.jpg*. To find all JPEG files, you'd pass "*.jpg" as the first argument and true as the second argument:

```
fc.list("*.jpg", true);
```

Mostly, this all mirrors what you've already seen in the java.io.File class. However, FileConnection does have one unique ability File doesn't. The setFileConnection( ) method changes this object so it points to another file:

```
public void setFileConnection(String fileName) throws IOException,
  IllegalArgumentException, NullPointerException,
  SecurityException, ConnectionClosedException
```

This method is intended for directory traversal, and it has a number of prerequisites. The current FileConnection must point to a directory, not a file. Also, you can set the FileConnection only to a file or directory in the same directory, or to the parent directory (..).

## Filesystem Listeners

The FileSystemRegistry class and the FileSystemListener interface enable a J2ME program to learn about new filesystems as they're mounted or unmounted. This is important because many embedded devices still use removable media such as smart cards and memory sticks. On some devices, those may be the only filesystems a MIDlet can see.

The FileSystemListener interface declares a single method, rootChanged( ):

```
public void rootChanged(int state, String rootName)
```

The first argument is either FileSystemListener.ROOT_ADDED or FileSystemListener.
ROOT_REMOVED. Such listeners are added to or removed from the FileSystemRegistry
class using these two static methods:

```
public static boolean addFileSystemListener(FileSystemListener listener)
 throws SecurityException, NullPointerException
public static boolean removeFileSystemListener(FileSystemListener listener)
 throws NullPointerException
```

You can also use FileSystemRegistry to enumerate all the currently mounted filesystem roots, with the listRoots( ) method:

```
public static Enumeration listRoots() throws SecurityException
```

These roots are the logical roots exposed to the client program, not necessarily the
real roots of the filesystem. Normally, the true root or roots are inaccessible for security reasons. Thus, even Unix-based devices may have several logical roots.

Example 24-3 demonstrates a simple program that recursively lists all the files in a
directory, and all the files in directories in the directory, and so on. Files are indented
two spaces for each level deep they are in the hierarchy.

*Example 24-3. The DirLister MIDlet*

```
import java.io.*;
import java.util.*;
import javax.microedition.io.*;
import javax.microedition.midlet.*;
import javax.microedition.io.file.*;
import javax.microedition.lcdui.*;

public class DirLister extends MIDlet {

  private int level = 0;

  public void startApp( ) {
    Form form = new Form("File Roots");
    Enumeration roots = FileSystemRegistry.listRoots( );
    while (roots.hasMoreElements( )) {
      Object next = roots.nextElement( );
      String url = "file:///" + next;
      System.out.println(url);
      try {
        FileConnection connection = (FileConnection) Connector.open(url);
        getInfo(connection, form);
      }
      catch (IOException ex) {
        form.append(ex.getMessage( ) +"\n");
      }
    }
    Display.getDisplay(this).setCurrent(form);
  }

  public void pauseApp( ) {}
```

*Example 24-3. The DirLister MIDlet (continued)*

```
  public void destroyApp(boolean condition) {
    notifyDestroyed();
  }

  private void getInfo(FileConnection connection, Form form) throws IOException {
    if (connection.isDirectory()) form.append("------\n");
    for (int i = 0; i < level; i++) form.append(" ");
    form.append(connection.getPath() + connection.getName() + "\n");
    if (connection.isDirectory()) {
      level++;
      Enumeration list = connection.list();
      String path =  connection.getPath() + connection.getName();
      while (list.hasMoreElements()) {
        Object next = list.nextElement();
        String url = "file://" + path + next ;
        try {
          FileConnection child = (FileConnection) Connector.open(url);
          getInfo(child, form);
        }
        catch (Exception ex) {
          form.append(ex.getMessage() +"\n");
        }
      }
      level--;
    }
  }
}
```

Figure 24-3 shows this MIDlet running in the J2ME Wireless Toolkit Emulator. You can see that there are two roots on this system, *CFCard1* and *CFCard2*. *CFCard1* contains three directories, *movs*, *pix*, and *snds*. *movs* and *snds* are empty, but *pix* contains two files, *_dukeok2.png* and *_dukeok8.png*. *CFCard2* contains only a single file, *secrets.txt*.

# HTTP

Some of the most interesting opportunities for small mobile devices involve web services in one form or another. For instance, a bidder could use her mobile phone to keep tabs on an auction through the eBay SOAP API, or a commuter could browse his weblog subscriptions on a wireless PDA on the train ride to work. Of course, this requires the devices to support HTTP, and many do.

To download data from a web server, simply use the Connector or InputConnection class to open a regular HTTP URL:

```
InputConnection connection = (InputConnection) Connector.open(
  "http://www.google.com/search?q=xom");
```

The specific InputConnection returned is an HttpConnection:

```
public interface HttpConnection extends ContentConnection
```

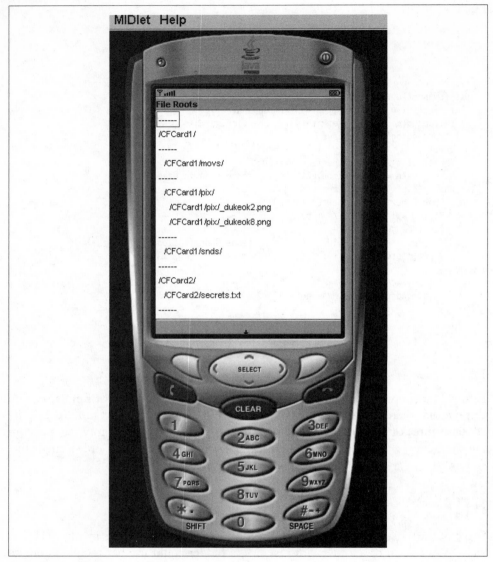

*Figure 24-3. The DirLister MIDlet*

It may also be an `HttpsConnection`, but that's a subinterface of `HttpConnection` that you normally use polymorphically as an instance of the superclass:

```
public interface HttpsConnection extends HttpConnection
```

In J2ME, `HttpConnection` fills in for several J2SE classes, including `URL`, `URLConnection`, and `HttpURLConnection`. Some of its methods are familiar from those classes, with occasionally subtle differences.

Of course, `HttpConnection` has the usual `openInputStream()`, `openOutputStream()`, `openDataInputStream()`, `openDataOutputStream()`, and `close()` methods common to any `StreamConnection`. It also has the `getEncoding()`, `getLength()`, and `getType()` methods of any `ContentConnection`. For basic uses such as downloading the latest sports scores or stock quotes, this is enough. However, more complex interactive applications will want to cast the `Connection` object returned by `Connector.open()` to `HttpConnection` so that they can use its additional methods. This is especially important if you want to send data back to the server via POST as well as simply GETting data from the server.

At any given time, a connection object is in one of three states:

- Setup (not yet connected)
- Connected
- Closed

When the object is first created, it is unconnected. At this point, you can call `setRequestMethod()` and `setRequestProperty()` to configure the HTTP header that is sent to the server.

There is no explicit `connect()` method. Instead, the connection is made and the header sent as soon as you invoke one of the methods that needs to read data from or send data to the server. These include obvious methods, such as `openInputStream()` and `openOutputStream()`, as well as methods that read from the HTTP header, such as `getHeaderField()` and `getLastModified()`.

Finally, the connection can be closed with the `close()` method. At this point, you can no longer read from the connection.

Which methods work depends on the connection's state. For instance, you can't use a method that sets a property in the HTTP request header after the connection has already been opened and the header sent. Nor can you reopen a closed connection. Calling the wrong method at the wrong time generally throws an `IOException`.

## Getter Methods

Every `Connection` object begins with a URL. However, the `HttpConnection` interface adds several methods that split that URL into its component parts. Generally speaking, URLs are composed of five pieces:

- The scheme, also known as the protocol
- The authority
- The path
- The fragment identifier, also known as the ref
- The query string

For example, in the URL *http://www.example.com:8000/foo/bar/index.html?hl=en&q=test#p3*, the scheme is *http*, the authority is *www.example.com:8000*, the path is */foo/bar/index.html*. the fragment identifier is *p3*, and the query string is *hl=en&q=test*. The authority is often subdivided into a host and a port, and the port is often omitted.

However, not all URLs have all these pieces. For instance, the URL *http://www.faqs.org/rfcs/rfc3986.html* has a scheme, an authority, and a path but no fragment identifier and no query string.

Five public methods provide read-only access to these parts of a URL: getFile( ), getHost( ), getPort( ), getProtocol( ), getRef( ), and getQuery( ).

The getProtocol( ) method returns a String containing the scheme of the URL. For example, this fragment sets the protocol variable to "http":

```
HttpInputConnection connection = (HttpInputConnection)
  Connector.open("http://www.google.com/");
String protocol = connection.getProtocol();
```

In practice, this value is always "http" or "https", because no other URL scheme creates an HttpConnection object.

The getHost( ) method returns a String containing the hostname of the URL. For example, in this case, the host is *www.google.com*:

```
HttpInputConnection connection =
  (HttpInputConnection) Connector.open("http://www.google.com:80/");
String host = connection.getProtocol();
```

The getPort( ) method returns the port number specified in the URL as an int. If no port was specified in the URL, getPort( ) returns 80 for HTTP and 443 for HTTPS.

The getFile( ) method returns a String that contains the path portion of a URL, not including the fragment identifier or query string. For example, here the path is */Top/News/*:

```
HttpInputConnection connection =
  (HttpInputConnection) Connector.open("http://www.google.com/Top/News/");
String path = connection.getFile();
```

If the URL does not have a path part, this method returns null.

The getRef( ) method returns the fragment identifier. If the URL doesn't have a fragment identifier, it returns null. In the following code, getRef( ) returns the string aw2:

```
InputConnection connection = Connector.open(
  "http://www.google.com/search?hl=en&lr=&q=test#aw2");
String fragment = connection.getRef();
```

The getQuery( ) method returns the query string. If the URL doesn't have a query string, it returns null. In the following code, getQuery( ) returns the string hl=en&lr=&q=test:

```
InputConnection connection = Connector.open(
 "http://www.google.com/search?hl=en&lr=&q=test#aw2");
String query = connection.getQuery( ));
```

## Configuring the HTTP Request Header

An HTTP request header precedes each request a browser sends to a server. For GET and HEAD requests, this is the only content. POST requests are followed by the body of the request. A typical GET request sent by HttpConnection looks like this:

```
GET /blog/feed HTTP/1.1
Host: www.elharo.com
Content-length: 0
```

For simple GET requests, the default header HttpConnection sends is fine. However, to POST data to a web server, you'll need to change the method using setRequestMethod( ):

```
public void setRequestMethod(String method) throws IOException
```

You then use the connection's output stream to write the data.

 DELETE, PUT, and other methods are not supported. This is a major hassle for implementing RESTful systems like the Atom Publishing Protocol (APP) that depend critically on PUT and DELETE.

The following code fragment connects to the service at *http://www.example.org/cgi/postquery* and submits the query string *color=blue&n=7*. This is written onto the body of the HTTP request:

```
HttpConnection connection = null;
try {
  connection = (HttpConnection) Connector.open(
   "http://www.example.org/cgi/postquery");
  connection.setRequestMethod("POST");
  DataOutputStream out = connection.openDataOutputStream( );
  out.writeUTF("color=blue&n=7");
  out.flush( );
  InputStream in = connection.openInputStream( );
  // read and process the response...
}
catch (Exception ex) {
  // handle exception...
}
finally {
  try {
```

```
    if (connection != null) connection.close();
  }
  catch (IOException ex) { /* Oh well. We tried.*/ }
}
```

Even if you're just using GET, you may need to modify the HTTP header to supply
cookies, specify the languages the user prefers to read, or indicate how fresh a cached
copy is. This is done with the setRequestProperty( ) method:

```
public void    setRequestProperty(String key, String value)
  throws IOException
public String getRequestProperty(String key)
```

For example, this request sets the Accept header to indicate that XML is preferred
but HTML is accepted:

```
conn.setRequestProperty("Accept", "application/xml; text/xml; text/html");
```

There can be at most one header with any given key. Adding a second header with
the same name changes the value rather than adding a new value. It is the client's
responsibility to make sure that the strings passed here satisfy the requirements for
HTTP headers (e.g., no line breaks in the name or value). The HttpConnection class
does not check for illegal values.

## Reading the HTTP Response Header

HTTP servers provide a substantial amount of information in the header that precedes each response. For example, here's a typical HTTP header returned by an
Apache web server:

```
HTTP/1.1 200 OK
Date: Sun, 04 Dec 2005 16:15:16 GMT
Server: Apache/2.0.55 (Unix) mod_ssl/2.0.55 OpenSSL/0.9.7d PHP/5.0.5
X-Powered-By: PHP/5.0.5
Last-Modified: Sat, 03 Dec 2005 21:32:30 GMT
ETag: "f8dd0d8d4d24dc754b6a8aeab63ea0ac"
X-Pingback: http://www.elharo.com/blog/xmlrpc.php
Transfer-Encoding: chunked
Content-Type: text/xml; charset=UTF-8
```

There's a lot of information there. In general, an HTTP header may include the content type of the requested document, the length of the document in bytes, the character set in which the content is encoded, the current date and time, the date the
content expires, the date the content was last modified, cookies, Etags, and more.
However, the information depends on the server. Some servers send all this information for each request, others send only some information, and a few don't send anything. The methods discussed in this section allow you to query an HttpConnection to
find out what metadata the server provided.

The zeroth line of the response header is the *status line*. In this example, that's:

```
HTTP/1.1 200 OK
```

This consists of the HTTP version (HTTP/1.1), the response code (200), and the response message (OK). The getResponseCode( ) and getResponseMessage( ) methods return the response code and the response message:

```
public int    getResponseCode() throws IOException
public String getResponseMessage() throws IOException
```

These methods throw an IOException if the connection to the server failed.

Codes between 200 and 299 indicate success, codes between 300 and 399 indicate redirection, codes between 400 and 499 indicate a client error, and codes between 500 and 599 indicate a server error. The HttpConnection class provides named constants for many of these codes, such as HttpConnection.HTTP_OK (200) and HttpConnection.HTTP_NOT_FOUND (404).

After the status line, the remainder of the header contains name/value pairs. The various getHeaderFieldKey( ) methods return the names of the fields, and the getHeaderField( ) methods return their values. You can iterate through these starting at zero:

```
public String getHeaderField(int n) throws IOException
public String getHeaderFieldKey(int n) throws IOException
```

If you know the name of the field you're looking for, you can ask for it directly:

```
public String getHeaderField(String name) throws IOException
```

If no such field is present in the response header, this method returns null.

Some fields have obvious interpretations as integers (Content-length, Age) or dates (Retry-after, Last-modified). These two methods read the string value of the named field and convert it to the desired type:

```
public int  getHeaderFieldInt(String name, int default) throws IOException
public long getHeaderFieldDate(String name, long default) throws IOException
```

If the field is not present in the header or a conversion error occurs, these methods return the second argument instead.

Three convenience methods read particularly common and useful headers (the date the document was sent, the expiration date, and the last modified time):

```
public long getDate() throws IOException
public long getExpiration() throws IOException
public long getLastModified() throws IOException
```

Each returns a long measuring milliseconds since midnight, January 1, 1970. You can convert this value to a java.util.Date. For example:

```
Date documentSent = new Date(connection.getDate());
```

This is the time the document was sent as seen from the server. It often won't match the time on the client. If the HTTP header does not include the corresponding field, these methods return 0.

Example 24-4 displays the complete headers from a user-specified URL. The startApp( ) method asks the user for a URL using a TextBox widget. Once the user enters one and activates the corresponding command, getInfo( ) spawns threads that connect to the server, download the headers, and display them. Networking, which may block, should not be done in the command thread. Doing so can deadlock the MIDlet (and in fact did in one of my tests before I added the separate thread).

*Example 24-4. Display the HTTP response header*

```java
import java.io.IOException;
import javax.microedition.io.*;
import javax.microedition.lcdui.*;
import javax.microedition.midlet.*;

public class HTTPInfo extends MIDlet implements CommandListener {

  private Display display;
  private TextBox textBox;

  private Form getInfo(String url) {
    Form form = new Form("HTTP Info");
    HttpConnection connection = null;
    try {
        connection = (HttpConnection) Connector.open(url);
        connection.setRequestMethod("HEAD");
        for (int i = 0; ; i++) {
            String key = connection.getHeaderFieldKey(i);
            String value = connection.getHeaderField(i);
            if (value == null) break;
            if (key != null) form.append(key + ": " + value + "\n");
            else form.append("***" + value + "\n");;
        }
    }
    catch (Exception ex) {
        form.append(ex.getMessage( ) +"\n");
    }
    finally {
      try {
        if (connection != null) connection.close( );
      }
      catch (IOException ex) { /* Oh well. we tried.*/ }
    }

    return form;
  }

  public void startApp( ) {
    display = Display.getDisplay(this);

    if (textBox == null) {
      textBox = new TextBox("URL", "http://", 255, TextField.URL);
```

*Example 24-4. Display the HTTP response header (continued)*

```
    }
    display.setCurrent(textBox);

    Command getInfo = new Command("HTTP Headers", Command.OK, 10);
    textBox.addCommand(getInfo);
    textBox.setCommandListener(this);
  }

  public void commandAction(Command command, Displayable displayable) {
    Thread t = new Thread (
      new Runnable() {
        public void run() {
          display.setCurrent(getInfo(textBox.getString()));
        }
      }
    );
    t.start();
  }

  protected void pauseApp() {}
  protected void destroyApp(boolean unconditional) {}
}
```

Figure 24-4 shows the headers from *http://www.google.com*. The content type of the file at *http://www.google.com* is text/html. No content encoding was used, but the transfer encoding was chunked. A cookie that expires more than three decades in the future was fed to the phone. The server is Google Web Server 2.1. (Google uses its own custom web server to support its very high-volume site.)

# Serial I/O

Serial ports are older technology. However, they're still found on a lot of equipment that might want to run or communicate with J2ME devices, such as multimeters, GPS receivers, printers, ham radios, and more. Furthermore, sometimes other less standard ports are made to look like serial ports to the operating system. For instance, some i-mate smart phones have an SDIO port that's mapped to a virtual serial port on COM7. IRDA infrared devices are also often treated as RS-232 serial ports.

MIDP 2.0 includes a CommConnection subinterface of StreamConnection suitable for talking to devices hooked up to serial ports. It is actually quite a bit easier to use than the Java Communications API discussed in Chapter 22.

```
    public interface CommConnection extends StreamConnection
```

Not all small devices have serial ports, so not all support CommConnection even if they support MIDP 2.0. You can test for the presence of CommConnection by checking the

*Figure 24-4. The header MIDlet*

microedition.commports system property. If it is nonnull, comm connections are supported:

```
if (System.getProperty("microedition.commports") != null) {
  //...
}
```

There's no standard form for a serial port URL, so one was invented. The scheme is *comm*, followed by the port number, followed by any parameters. For example, these are all serial port URLs:

- *comm:1*
- *comm:1;baudrate=9600*
- *comm:7;baudrate=19200;parity=even;autorts=on;blocking=off;bit_value=7*
- *comm:irda;baudrate=19200*

The host device defines the logical port names that follow the scheme. More often than not, these are just simple numbers: 1 for COMM port 1, 2 for COMM port 2, and so on. However, some devices may use more descriptive names. Sometimes COM1, COM2, and so forth are used for genuine RS-232 ports while IR1, IR2, and so on are used for IRDA ports. The microedition.commports system property contains a comma-separated list of all the identifiers valid for the current host.

The name/value parameters that follow the port name are just the standard serial port options discussed previously in Chapter 22. Table 24-1 summarizes them.

*Table 24-1. Serial port URL parameters*

| Parameter | Default | Description | Values |
| --- | --- | --- | --- |
| baudrate | Device dependent | Port speed in bits per second. | 300 to 238400 |
| bitsperchar | 8 | Bits per character. | 7 or 8 |
| stopbits | 1 | Stop bits per character. | 1 or 2 |
| parity | none | An extra bit in each byte used as a simple error-detection mechanism. | odd, even, or none |
| blocking | on | Wait for a full buffer when reading. | on or off |
| autocts | on | Wait for the CTS line to be on before writing. | on or off |
| autorts | on | Ask for permission to send by turning on the RTS line before writing; normally used in conjunction with autocts. | on or off |

To open a connection to a serial port–attached external device, just pass a URL configured with the necessary parameters to the usual Connector.open( ) method. For example, this opens a connection to the device attached to serial port 0 with a 9,600-baud rate:

```
Connection conn = Connector.open("comm:0;baudrate=9600");
```

Mostly, you just use the input streams and output streams returned by openInputStream( ) and openOutputStream( ) to talk to serial ports. CommConnection adds only two methods beyond those defined in StreamConnection, getBaudRate( ) and setBaudRate( ):

```
public int getBaudRate( )
public int setBaudRate(int baudrate)
```

If the URL did not specify a baud rate, getBaudRate( ) lets you determine the default speed for the device. setBaudRate( ) lets you change this speed. Not all speeds are available for any given device. If you try to set an unsupported speed, setBaudRate( ) may throw an exception, or it may pick a supported speed instead.

## Sockets

SocketConnection is a basic StreamConnection for network communications. It works much like HttpConnection. However, it has no particular understanding of HTTP or any other protocol. It just opens a standard TCP socket to a specified host and relies on your code to tell it what to do with the input and output from that host.

Socket URLs look like this:

```
socket://server.example.com:13
```

This indicates a TCP connection to *server.example.com* on port 13.

Opening SocketConnection is straightforward and works much like opening any other sort of connection:

```
Connection connection = Connector.open("socket://rama.poly.edu:13");
```

If you don't need to set any special socket options, you can use one of the four open stream methods, and proceed as you would with any other connection. Example 24-1 used the socket protocol.

Most of the time that's all you need. However, SocketConnection does have six unique methods of its own. To use these, you must first cast the connection object returned by open( ) to SocketConnection:

```
SocketConnection socket = (SocketConnection) connection;
```

## Getters

First, there are four getter methods that return the address and port of the remote and local hosts the socket connects:

```
public String getAddress( ) throws IOException
public int    getPort( ) throws IOException
public int    getLocalPort( ) throws IOException
public String getLocalAddress( ) throws IOException
```

J2ME doesn't include the InetAddress class, so the host addresses are all returned as strings like "192.168.254.100" or "FEDC::DC:0:7076:10". There's no method to get the hostname, because devices where J2ME runs are unlikely to have hostnames.

These methods all throw an IOException if the socket has been closed.

## Socket Options

J2ME devices often have different network characteristics than typical desktop and server systems. They may have very limited, unreliable, or sporadic bandwidth. As a result, it may be important to change socket options to better fit the characteristics of the network. The getSocketOption( ) and setSocketOption( ) methods enable this:

```
public void setSocketOption(byte option, int value)
  throws IllegalArgumentException, IOException
public int getSocketOption(byte option)
  throws IllegalArgumentException, IOException
```

Socket options must be set before the socket is connected; that is, before you ask a connection for its input or output stream.

J2ME recognizes five socket options, each referenced as a named constant in the SocketConnection class:

SocketConnection.DELAY
> Nonzero to enable Nagle's algorithm; zero to disable Nagle's algorithm

SocketConnection.LINGER
> Number of seconds to wait before closing a connection with pending data to write

SocketConnection.KEEPALIVE
> Nonzero to enable keepalive; zero to disable keepalive

SocketConnection.SNDBUF
> Size in bytes of the send buffer

SocketConnection.RCVBUF
> Size in bytes of the receive buffer

Picking an option not in this list throws an IllegalArgumentException.

# Server Sockets

While PDAs, cell phones, and MP3 players are more likely to act as clients than servers, the opposite is true for refrigerators, laboratory sensors, hotel door locks, and similar embedded devices. The natural mode of operation for these devices is to run a server providing their current status information that interested clients can query. The ServerSocketConnection class meets these needs.

Server socket URLs look like *socket://:13*. All you have to specify is the port to listen on (13, in this example).

The fundamental operation of a server socket is to listen for and accept incoming connections. Server sockets themselves do not send or receive data. The ServerSocketConnection class does not extend StreamConnection, and you cannot use

Connector's open stream methods to open one. You must open the connection and cast it to ServerSocketConnection:

```
ServerSocketConnection server
  = (ServerSocketConnection) Connector.open("socket://:37");
```

Next, you invoke the acceptAndOpen( ) method to receive an incoming connection:

```
public StreamConnection acceptAndOpen( ) throws IOException
```

You can then use the methods of StreamConnection to communicate with the remote client.

The acceptAndOpen( ) method blocks while waiting for incoming connections. You probably want to put it in a separate thread.

Example 24-5 demonstrates with a simple J2ME time server. The time protocol responds to each incoming connection by sending it the current time at the server. The time is measured in seconds since midnight, January 1, 1900. It is represented as a 4-byte big-endian unsigned int. Java doesn't have unsigned data types, so the program has to do the calculations using longs and then select the low-order four bytes of the resulting number manually. There's no local interface here. The startApp( ) method spawns a thread that constantly listens for incoming connections, responds to each one, and then closes the connections.

*Example 24-5. A J2ME time server client using the ServerSocketConnection class*

```
import javax.microedition.midlet.*;
import javax.microedition.io.*;
import java.io.*;
import java.util.Date;

public class TCPTimeServer extends MIDlet {

  private ServerSocketConnection server;
  // The time protocol sets the epoch at 1900,
  // the java Date class at 1970. This number
  // converts between them.
  private long differenceBetweenEpochs = 2208988800L;

  protected void startApp( ) {
    try {
      server = (ServerSocketConnection) Connector.open("socket://:37");
      Runnable r = new Runnable( ) {
        public void run( ) {
          while (true) {
            try {
              StreamConnection conn = server.acceptAndOpen( );
              Date now = new Date( );
              long msSince1970 = now.getTime( );
              long secondsSince1900 = msSince1970/1000L + differenceBetweenEpochs;
              DataOutputStream out = conn.openDataOutputStream( );
              // write the low-order four bytes
```

```
                out.write( (int) ((secondsSince1900 >>> 24) & 0xFFL));
                out.write( (int) ((secondsSince1900 >>> 16) & 0xFFL));
                out.write( (int) ((secondsSince1900 >>> 8) & 0xFFL));
                out.write( (int) (secondsSince1900 & 0xFFL));
                out.close( );
              }
              catch (IOException ex) {
              }
            }
          }
        };
        Thread t = new Thread(r);
        t.start( );
      }
      catch (IOException ex) {
        // not much we can do about this here
      }
    }

    protected void pauseApp( ) {}

    protected void destroyApp(boolean unconditional) {
      try {
        server.close( );
      }
      catch (IOException ex) {
        // We tried
      }
    }
}
```

You can omit the port in the connector URL. That is, *socket://*: is an acceptable URL to open a server socket. If you omit the port, Java picks any available port to start listening on. You can find out which port it chose with the getLocalPort( ) method:

```
public int getLocalPort( ) throws IOException
```

You can also find out the local IP address using the getLocalAddress( ) method:

```
public String getLocalAddress( ) throws IOException
```

# Datagrams

The connections we've talked about up to now have all been stream connections. However, just as in J2SE, UDP is a notable exception. UDP, whether implemented through standard I/O or the Generic Connection Framework, just isn't suited to a stream metaphor. In GCF, UDP is handled through the DatagramConnection and Datagram classes. These take the place of DatagramSocket and DatagramPacket in J2SE. Like the socket protocol, support for UDP and the datagram protocol is optional. Some devices support it; some don't.

## Datagram URLs

Datagram URLs take two forms. Client URLs for sending data look like this:

```
datagram://server.example.com:2546
```

This indicates a UDP connection to *server.example.com* on port 2546.

Datagram server URLs for receiving data look like this:

```
datagram://:2546
```

This indicates a server listening for incoming UDP datagrams on port 2546. Datagram URLs do not have any path or parameters. In theory, other schemes could be used to support different kinds of datagrams, such as raw IP or USB datagrams. However, I'm unaware of any such implementations.

Opening a DatagramConnection is straightforward and works much like opening any other sort of connection:

```
Connection connection = Connector.open("datagram://rama.poly.edu:13");
```

This method will throw a ConnectionNotFoundException if the device does not support UDP.

You cannot use Connector.openInputStream( ) and Connector.openOutputStream( ) methods with datagram URLs because these protocols don't support streaming. For the same reason, the connection returned by open( ) is neither an input nor an output connection. Instead, it should be cast to DatagramConnection:

```
DatagramConnection dgramConnection = (DatagramConnection) connection;
```

The DatagramConnection interface provides methods for creating new datagrams and for sending and receiving datagrams:

```
public void send(Datagram dgram) throws IOException
public void receive(Datagram dgram) throws IOException
public Datagram newDatagram(int size) throws IOException
public Datagram newDatagram(int size, String address) throws IOException
public Datagram newDatagram(byte[] buffer, int size) throws IOException
public Datagram newDatagram(byte[] buffer, int size, String address)
  throws IOException
```

It also has two methods that return the maximum and expected length of each datagram:

```
public int getMaximumLength( ) throws IOException
public int getNominalLength( ) throws IOException
```

To send datagrams to a server:

1. Open a connection with a datagram URL such as *datagram://server.example.com:13*.

2. Cast the connection object to DatagramConnection.

3. Pass the data to send, the length of the data, and the address to `newDatagram( )`. Check `getMaximumLength( )` to make sure you don't overflow the datagram.

4. Pass the resulting `Datagram` object to the `send( )` method.

To receive datagrams sent by a server:

1. Open a connection with a datagram URL such as *datagram://:13*.

2. Cast the connection object to `DatagramConnection`.

3. Pass the length of the data to receive to `newDatagram( )`.

4. Pass the resulting `Datagram` object to the `receive( )` method. This method blocks until some data is received.

5. Read the content received out of the `Datagram`.

In both server and client mode, datagrams are represented by instances of the `Datagram` interface summarized below. This interface includes methods for putting data in a datagram to send and getting data out of a received datagram. Besides the ones listed here, it has all the methods of `DataInput` and `DataOutput`, such as `readInt( )`, `writeInt( )`, `readChar( )`, `writeChar( )`, and so forth.

```
public interface Datagram extends DataInput, DataOutput {

    public String  getAddress( )
    public byte[]  getData( )
    public int     getLength( )
    public int     getOffset( )
    public void    setAddress(String address) throws IOException
    public void    setAddress(Datagram reference)
    public void    setLength(int lenght)
    public void    setData(byte[] buffer, int offset, int length)
    public void    reset( )

}
```

Example 24-6 is a UDP time client. This needs to function as both a sender and a receiver. First it sends a packet of data to the server at *time-a.nist.gov* on port 37. (The contents of this packet don't matter.) The server responds with the current time represented as a 4-byte unsigned big-endian integer. Of course, since UDP is unreliable, there's no guarantee the server response will arrive. Consequently, I set a timer that grabs the time from the local clock and shuts down the MIDlet if no response is received within 60 seconds.

*Example 24-6. A J2ME UDP time client*

```
import java.io.IOException;
import java.util.*;
import javax.microedition.io.*;
import javax.microedition.lcdui.*;
import javax.microedition.midlet.*;

public class TimeClient extends MIDlet {
```

*Example 24-6. A J2ME UDP time client (continued)*

```java
private Form form;
private final String server = "datagram://time-a.nist.gov:37";

public TimeClient( ) {
  form = new Form("TimeClient");
  form.append("The time is\n");
  Display.getDisplay(this).setCurrent(form);
}

protected void startApp( ) {
  Timer timer = new Timer( );
  TimerTask task = new TimerTask( ) {
    public void run( ) {
      form.append(new Date().toString( ));
      destroyApp(true);
      TimeClient.this.notifyDestroyed( );
    }
  };
  timer.schedule(task, 60000); // 60 seconds from now

  byte[] ping = {(byte) 50}; // any byte will do
  DatagramConnection connection = null;
  try {
    connection = (DatagramConnection) Connector.open(server);
    Datagram dgram = connection.newDatagram(ping, ping.length);
    Datagram response = connection.newDatagram(4);

    connection.send(dgram);
    connection.receive(response);
    byte[] result = response.getData( );

    if (result.length != 4) {
      form.append("Unrecognized response format");
      return;
    }

    long differenceBetweenEpochs = 2208988800L;
    long secondsSince1900 = 0;
    for (int i = 0; i < 4; i++) {
      secondsSince1900 = (secondsSince1900 << 8) | (result[i] & 0x000000FF);
    }

    long secondsSince1970 = secondsSince1900 - differenceBetweenEpochs;
    long msSince1970 = secondsSince1970 * 1000;
    Date time = new Date(msSince1970);
    form.append(time.toString( ) + "\n");

  }
  catch (IOException ex) {
    Alert alert = new Alert("UDP Error");
    alert.setTimeout(Alert.FOREVER);
    alert.setString(ex.getMessage( ));
```

*Example 24-6. A J2ME UDP time client (continued)*

```
    Display.getDisplay(this).setCurrent(alert, form);
  }
  finally {
    timer.cancel();
    try {
      if (connection != null) connection.close();
    }
    catch (IOException ex) {
    }
  }
}

protected void pauseApp() {}
protected void destroyApp(boolean unconditional) {}
}
```

If you have trouble getting this program to show the time, make sure your firewall is not blocking UDP traffic or try using a time server on your local subnet instead.

A server is no harder to implement. The primary difference is that it simply waits for incoming packets and then responds to each one immediately. It doesn't need to worry about timeouts. Example 24-7 demonstrates.

 Because this example listens on a port below 1024, it may need root privileges to run on Unix-derived systems such as Linux and Mac OS X, even in an emulator. It should run without trouble on most actual MIDP devices and Windows.

*Example 24-7. A J2ME UDP time server*

```
import java.io.IOException;
import java.util.Date;

import javax.microedition.io.*;
import javax.microedition.lcdui.Alert;
import javax.microedition.lcdui.Display;
import javax.microedition.midlet.*;

public class TimeServer extends MIDlet {

  protected void startApp() {
    DatagramConnection connection;
    try {
      connection = (DatagramConnection) Connector.open("datagram://:37");
      Datagram incoming = connection.newDatagram(128);
      Datagram response = connection.newDatagram(4);
      while (true) {
        try {
          connection.receive(incoming);
          response.reset();
          response.setAddress(incoming);
```

*Example 24-7. A J2ME UDP time server (continued)*

```
        response.setData(getTime( ), 0, 4);
        connection.send(response);
        incoming.reset( );
      }
      catch (IOException ex) {
        // As long as it's just an error on this one connection
        // we can ignore it
      }
    }
  }
  catch (IOException ex) {
    // If we can't open the channel, put up an Alert
    Alert alert = new Alert("UDP Error");
    alert.setTimeout(Alert.FOREVER);
    alert.setString("Could not connect to port 37. Needs root privileges?");
    Display.getDisplay(this).setCurrent(alert);
  }
}

private byte[] getTime( ) {

  byte[] result = new byte[4];
  Date now = new Date( );

  // The time protocol uses an unsigned 4-byte int, so we have
  // to do all the arithmetic with longs and then extract the
  // four low-order bytes
  long secondsSince1970 = now.getTime( )/1000;
  long differenceBetweenEpochs = 2208988800L;
  long secondsSince1900 = differenceBetweenEpochs + secondsSince1970;
  result[0] = (byte) ((secondsSince1900 & 0xFF000000) >>> 24);
  result[1] = (byte) ((secondsSince1900 & 0xFF0000) >>> 16);
  result[2] = (byte) ((secondsSince1900 & 0xFF00) >>> 8);
  result[3] = (byte) (secondsSince1900 & 0xFF);

  return result;
}

protected void pauseApp( ) {}
protected void destroyApp(boolean unconditional)  {}
}
```

This example is perhaps not as artificial as it might seem at first glance. I could easily see adding a time server to a digital clock or a smart appliance that includes a clock, such as a microwave. It could then provide time services to other devices on the LAN. This would be a very nice use for J2ME.

# CHAPTER 25

# Bluetooth

Nothing's so dated as yesterday's futurism. In 1993, naming a high-tech magazine "Wired" must have seemed really hip. Today, "wired" devices are yesterday's tech. No one wants a mess like the one in Figure 25-1, but everyone's got one...although slowly that's starting to change. Network, speaker, microphone, mouse, and keyboard connections are already going wireless. Disks, cameras, and monitors will follow soon. By the end of this decade, most systems should have a power cord and nothing more. By 2020, even the power cord might vanish. It's obvious the future belongs to wireless. After all, every cable you can remove from your system is one less leash tethering you to your desk. 802.11 is *de rigueur* for notebooks and increasingly common in desktops. Cell phones let us communicate from anywhere. Infrared gave rise to the clicker and freed us from commercials. Bluetooth is rapidly becoming the preferred way to connect computers to low-bandwidth peripherals like keyboards, mice, and remote controls.

## The Bluetooth Protocol

Bluetooth connects devices wirelessly in ranges of 1 to 100 meters, depending on power. There are several versions of Bluetooth: 1.0, 1.1, 1.2, and 2.0. (The Java API for accessing a Bluetooth device is the same regardless of version.) Bluetooth 1.0, 1.1, and 1.2 devices can reach speeds of 723 kilobits per second. Version 2.0 accelerates this to 2.1 megabits per second. In other words, Bluetooth is fast enough for network devices, but not fast enough for disk drives and monitors.

Because Bluetooth is wireless, it is less secure than wired alternatives such as USB connections (which themselves aren't as secure as is often thought). With the right equipment, it's possible to sniff Bluetooth communications one isn't meant to access. To prevent this, pairs of devices may require a shared secret passkey and may encrypt data passed back and forth between them. However, many devices don't bother to do this.

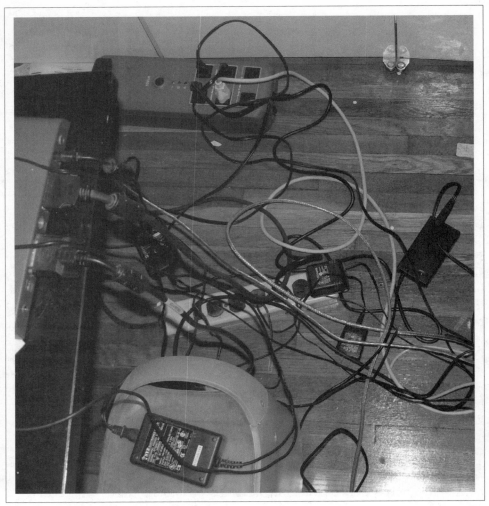

*Figure 25-1. A typical wired system*

Each Bluetooth controller can talk to up to seven different Bluetooth devices in a "master/slave" configuration. Among the eight devices, each device takes a turn at being the master while the other seven are slaves, in rotating order. The master is responsible for picking frequencies on which to communicate and deciding when to change them. The group of devices, one master and up to seven slaves, is called a *piconet*. In the future, it may be possible for piconets to be joined in larger *scatter-nets*. However, this is not yet possible.

Each Bluetooth device has a fixed 6-byte address, such as 00-13-c2-00-0d-23 or 00-0a-95-09-5a-59. Theoretically this address is unique, but conflicting addresses have shipped in real products. Each device also has a more human-friendly name, such as "elharo's mouse" or "WACOM pen tablet." Users and manufacturers can change the names, and name conflicts are possible.

Every device also has a 3-byte class identifier that is divided into four parts, as shown in Figure 25-2:

- The first two bits are always 0.
- The next six bits are a little-endian int for the minor device class.
- The next five bits are a little-endian int for the major device class.
- The final 11 bits are flags identifying the type of the device. For instance, if bit 22 is 1, it's a telephony device. If it's 0, it isn't.

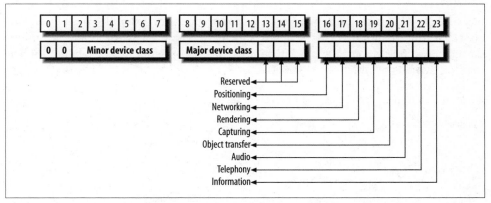

*Figure 25-2. Bluetooth class identifier layout, in big-endian form as seen by Java*

The currently defined major device class codes are shown in Table 25-1. Note that the numbers given are as Java reports them. Bits 8–12 define the major class. However, rather than interpreting this as a 5-bit number, Java represents it as a 13-bit number in which the low-order eight bits are always 0. (If you prefer, you can think of this as a 32-bit number in which all bits except 8–12 are 0.)

 Other Bluetooth APIs in other languages can and do provide different representations of the bit patterns in the class identifier shown in Figure 25-2. For instance, the Apple System Profiler presents major device classes as numbers from 0 to 31 (5-bit unsigned ints) instead of numbers from 0 to 7936. The following tables are valid for the Java Bluetooth API. They may not be valid in other environments.

*Table 25-1. Bluetooth major device classes*

| Decimal | Hexadecimal | Device type |
|---------|-------------|-------------|
| 0 | 0x0000 | Miscellaneous devices |
| 256 | 0x0100 | Computers and PDAs |
| 512 | 0x0200 | Phones, including modems and faxes |

Table 25-1. Bluetooth major device classes (continued)

| Decimal | Hexadecimal | Device type |
|---------|-------------|-------------|
| 768 | 0x0300 | LAN adapters, routers, and network access points |
| 1024 | 0x0400 | Audio/video devices (headsets, speakers, televisions, DVRs, etc.) |
| 1280 | 0x0500 | Input peripherals (mice, joysticks, keyboards, graphics tablets, etc.) |
| 1536 | 0x0600 | Imaging devices (printers, scanners, cameras, monitors, etc.) |
| 1792 | 0x0700 | Wearable devices |
| 2048 | 0x0800 | Toys |
| 7936 | 0x1F00 | Uncategorized: anything for which the Bluetooth Special Interest Group (SIG) has not yet defined a standardized code (e.g., GPS locators or laboratory probes) |

Minor device class codes depend on the major code. For example, the peripherals class has the 10 minor device classes shown in Table 25-2. Although the minor device class code is logically a 6-bit number, Java represents it as a 1-byte number, the first two bits of which are always 0.

Table 25-2. Bluetooth peripheral minor device classes

| Decimal | Hexadecimal | Type |
|---------|-------------|------|
| 0 | 0x00 | Uncategorized |
| 4 | 0x04 | Joystick |
| 8 | 0x08 | Gamepad |
| 12 | 0x0C | Remote control |
| 16 | 0x10 | Sensing device |
| 20 | 0x14 | Digitizer tablet |
| 24 | 0x18 | Card reader |
| 64 | 0x40 | Keyboard |
| 128 | 0x80 | Pointing device (mouse, trackball, etc.) |
| 192 | 0xC0 | Keyboard/mouse combination (0x80 | 0x40) |

While each device has exactly one major class and exactly one minor class, a device may support multiple *services*. For instance, a combination cell phone/PDA might be both a telephony device and an object transfer device. Table 25-3 lists the service classes and their associated bit fields. Each service a device supports is indicated a by a single bit in the class identifier. Java reports this as a 24-bit number in which the first 13 bits are always 0.

Table 25-3. Bluetooth service classes

| Bit | Decimal | Hexadecimal | Service class |
|-----|---------|-------------|---------------|
| 13 | 8192 | 0x2000 | Reserved |
| 14 | 16384 | 0x4000 | Reserved |

*Table 25-3. Bluetooth service classes (continued)*

| Bit | Decimal | Hexadecimal | Service class |
|-----|---------|-------------|---------------|
| 15 | 32768 | 0x8000 | Reserved |
| 16 | 65536 | 0x10000 | Positioning |
| 17 | 131072 | 0x20000 | Networking |
| 18 | 262144 | 0x40000 | Rendering |
| 19 | 524288 | 0x80000 | Capturing |
| 20 | 1048576 | 0x100000 | Object Transfer |
| 21 | 2097152 | 0x200000 | Audio |
| 22 | 4194304 | 0x400000 | Telephony |
| 23 | 8388608 | 0x800000 | Information |

For example, a GPS-enabled cell phone would have the major class 0x0200 and the minor class 0x04 and would support the positioning (0x10000) and telephony (0x400000) services. Therefore, its class ID would be 0x0200 | 0x04 | 0x10000 | 0x400000, or 0x410204.

Many devices support one or more standard *profiles* that offer particular types of services. These include the Serial Port Profile for streaming connections, the Basic Printing, Video Conferencing, File Transfer, Cordless Telephony, Fax, and Personal Area Network Profiles, and several dozen more.

Each profile communicates using a specified *protocol*. The lowest-level protocol is a packet-based protocol called the Logical Link Control and Adaptation Protocol (L2CAP). This is analogous to IP in the TCP stack. That is, other higher-level protocols are built on top of L2CAP and provide additional services. For instance, the RFCOMM protocol assembles L2CAP packets into input and output streams. If L2CAP is like IP, RFCOMM is like TCP. The Object Exchange (OBEX) protocol is a still higher-level protocol for exchanging binary data over RFCOMM. Stretching the analogy to the breaking point, if L2CAP is IP and RFCOMM is TCP, OBEX is HTTP. Different profiles and devices can plug into this stack wherever they find convenient, as shown in Figure 25-3. The Java Bluetooth API supports all three. There are also several additional protocols the Java Bluetooth API does not support, such as Bluetooth Network Encapsulation (BNEP) and the A/V Control Protocol.

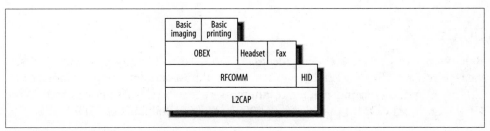

*Figure 25-3. Bluetooth protocol stack*

# The Java Bluetooth API

The Java Bluetooth API is designed to run in J2ME environments: cell phones, PDAs, and the like. In particular, it requires the Connected Limited Device Configuration (CLDC) with at least 512K of memory available to Java. It also requires vendor support. Currently, almost all the devices that support the Java Bluetooth API are mobile phones. At the time of this writing, they include the Motorola A1000; several Nokia phones, including the 6260; the Sony Ericsson P900, P908, and P910; and the Siemens S65, S66, and SK65.

The Java Bluetooth API supports four (out of a couple of dozen) Bluetooth profiles:

*Generic Access Profile (GAP)*
> Supplies the bare minimum of functionality all other services require

*Service Discovery Application Profile (SDAP)*
> Enables clients to find out which services the device supports

*Serial Port Profile (SPP)*
> Uses the RFCOMM protocol to emulate an RS-232 serial port

*Generic Object Exchange Profile (GOEP)*
> Uses OBEX to transfer data such as contact databases, pictures, and phone logs between devices

These primarily enable networking use cases such as uploading pictures from camera phones and downloading games to phones. The Java Bluetooth API doesn't support any of the other profiles, such as the Advanced Audio Distribution Profile or the Basic Printing Profile. However, many of these services may be available through other APIs and the host operating system.

> In many cases, Java doesn't care whether a device is connected via Bluetooth, USB, the network, or something else. Java treats a Bluetooth mouse or keyboard the same as it does one plugged into the serial port or a USB hub. A Bluetooth LAN adapter can be accessed via the Generic Connection Framework (GCF). A Bluetooth printer may be accessible through the Java Printing API. Direct Bluetooth connections are usually necessary only for relatively special-purpose devices, like GPS receivers and laboratory thermometers that don't have existing Java drivers.

## UUIDs

Bluetooth uses *Universal Unique Identifiers* (UUIDs) to identify protocols and service classes. A UUID is a 128-bit number that is almost certainly unique among other 128-bit numbers, barring deliberate attempts to create clashes. For example, the UUID for the RFCOMM protocol is 0x0000000300001000800000805F9B34FB.

---

Because space is at a premium in many Bluetooth devices, many services are identified with only 16 or 32 bits rather than the full 128 a UUID requires. For example, the 16-bit UUID for the RFCOMM protocol is 0x0003. The Bluetooth specification converts these shortened UUIDs into full 128-bit UUIDs by starting with the 16-byte base address 0000-0000-0000-1000-8000-0080-5F9B-34FB (in hexadecimal) and then replacing the third and fourth bytes with the two bytes of the 16-bit UUID.

The `javax.bluetooth.UUID` class recognizes all three widths of UUID (16-bit, 32-bit, and 128-bit) and can convert between them as necessary. Most methods in the Bluetooth API that take a UUID as an argument expect to see it in the form of a UUID object rather than a string or a number.

 Java 5 added a `java.util.UUID` class that conflicts with this class. Normally, Bluetooth applications should use only `javax.bluetooth.UUID`. If it's necessary to use both types in the same class, be sure to use fully qualified package names for both.

To create a Bluetooth-savvy UUID, just use one of these two constructors:

```
public UUID(long uuidValue)
public UUID(String uuidValue, boolean shortUUID)
```

The first constructor is used for the 16- and 32-bit short forms of UUIDs. A `long` is ironically not long enough (at 64 bits) for a full 128-bit UUID, so just pass a `String` argument containing its hexadecimal form to the second constructor instead and pass `false` for the second argument. Pass `true` for the second argument if the first argument uses the short form.

Other than these constructors, this UUID class merely defines the usual `equals( )`, `hashCode( )`, and `toString( )` methods, which are used to properly compare the short and long UUIDs.

## The Bluetooth Control Center

One of the least well-defined parts of the Java Bluetooth API is the Bluetooth Control Center (BCC). The BCC is a class, program (possibly native), default set of properties, or *something* that enables the user, vendor, or developer to:

- Specify security preferences.
- List previously known remote Bluetooth devices.
- List trusted remote Bluetooth devices.
- Pair two devices.
- Authorize connection requests.

Some BCCs offer additional functionality, such as changing the Bluetooth device name, setting timeouts, resetting devices, initializing the stack, and listing the services on the local device.

The Java Bluetooth API specification deliberately doesn't say much about what the BCC really is. It varies from one implementation to the next. It can even be a fixed set of unchangeable defaults compiled into the implementation-specific code.

## Initialization

There are many different implementations of the Java Bluetooth API from many different vendors. Atinav has one. Rococo has one. Blue Cove has an open source implementation, and there are others. Some run on PDAs and cell phones. Some run on standard desktop hardware. They are available for a variety of operating systems, including Linux, Windows, Mac OS X, Palm OS, PocketPC, and Symbian OS. While working on this chapter, I mostly used Avetana GMBH's implementation from *http://www.avetana-gmbh.de/avetana-gmbh/produkte/jsr82.eng.xml*. An open source version of this stack for Linux can be found at *http://sourceforge.net/projects/avetanabt/*.

Some of these implementations require initialization before any of the classes and methods discussed in this chapter will work. This initialization is normally done once in any given program. For example, if you're using Atinav's aveLink BT SDK for Java, you have to place the following static initializer block in the class that starts the application:

```
static {
  BCC.setPortNumber("COM1");
  BCC.setBaudRate(57600);
  BCC.setConnectable(true);
  BCC.setDiscoverable(DiscoveryAgent.GIAC);
}
```

In this implementation, BCC is the class that represents the Bluetooth Control Center. However, this part varies from one implementation to the next. You'll need to consult the documentation for your implementation. (One of the nice features of the Avetana implementation is that it's self-initializing. No explicit initialization is required.) This means most code you write will have at least some platform-dependent details.

## The Local Device

Most systems you're likely to encounter have at most one Bluetooth controller. This is represented by the singleton class `javax.bluetooth.LocalDevice`:

```
public class LocalDevice extends java.lang.Object
```

The static `LocalDevice.getLocalDevice()` method returns the single `LocalDevice` object that represents the host controller:

```
public static LocalDevice getLocalDevice() throws BluetoothStateException
```

This method never returns `null`. If the local system does not have a Bluetooth device, or if the Bluetooth hardware cannot be initialized, this method throws a `BluetoothStateException`, a subclass of `IOException`.

The `LocalDevice` class has a number of getter methods to query the controller and two methods for making the device discoverable (or not) and updating the device's service records.

The `getBluetoothAddress()` method returns a `String` containing the 6-byte Bluetooth address of the controller:

```
public String getBluetoothAddress()
```

The address is a string of 12 hex digits, such as 000D930D11B3. This isn't very nice for display to the end user, so there's also a `getFriendlyName()` method that returns a more human-legible name:

```
public String getFriendlyAddress()
```

Example 25-1 is a simple program that uses these two methods to list information about the host system.

*Example 25-1. Talking to the Bluetooth controller*

```
import javax.bluetooth.*;

public class BluetoothTest {

  public static void main(String[] args) throws Exception {
    LocalDevice device = LocalDevice.getLocalDevice();
    System.out.print(device.getFriendlyName() + " at ");
    System.out.print(device.getBluetoothAddress());
    System.exit(0);
  }
}
```

Loading the Bluetooth libraries sometimes spawns a nondaemon thread, so it's necessary to call `System.exit()` to force the program to quit (much the same as when using AWT classes).

Example 25-1 won't run with just the standard JDK. You'll need to have a JSR 82 implementation in your classpath. For example, here's how I compile and run this program on my PowerMac G5:

```
$ javac -classpath .:avetanaBluetooth.jar  BluetoothTest.java
$ java -classpath .:avetanaBluetooth.jar  BluetoothTest
avetanaBluetooth version 1.3.1
Local name eliza
Local address 00-0d-93-0d-11-b3
```

```
Device class 0
Possibilities array 3F
License-ID 1498
eliza at 000D930D11B3
```

The first six lines are just random junk the particular JSR 82 implementation I'm using spews. The last line is the actual output from the program. In upcoming examples, I'll omit Avetana's initialization info.

 A word to library vendors everywhere: libraries should never talk to the end user unless the client application tells them to, whether via System.out, a GUI, or any other mechanism. The client application should have complete control of the computer's interaction with the end user.

## Properties

LocalDevice's getProperty( ) method returns a named Bluetooth property:

```
public static String getProperty(String property)
```

These 10 properties are defined in all devices:

bluetooth.api.version
> The version of the Java API for Bluetooth wireless technology (currently 1.0)

bluetooth.master.switch
> Whether slaves and masters can exchange roles (either true or false)

bluetooth.sd.attr.retrievable.max
> The maximum number of service attributes in each service record

bluetooth.connected.devices.max
> The maximum number of simultaneously connected devices

bluetooth.l2cap.receiveMTU.max
> The maximum receive MTU size in L2CAP

bluetooth.sd.trans.max
> The maximum number of simultaneous service discovery transactions

bluetooth.connected.inquiry.scan
> Whether inquiry scanning is allowed during connection (either true or false)

bluetooth.connected.page.scan
> Whether page scanning is allowed during connection (either true or false)

bluetooth.connected.inquiry
> Whether inquiry is allowed during connection (either true or false)

bluetooth.connected.page
> Whether a connection can be established to a device that is already connected to another device (either true or false)

If this were primarily a J2SE API, each of these values might well be a separate method call. However, since space is at premium in the J2ME environments for which the Java Bluetooth API was designed, it pays to compress them all into one method. This approach is also more extensible, since particular JSR 82 implementations may define additional properties as well.

Example 25-2 is a simple program that prints the values of the 10 standard properties of the local system.

*Example 25-2. Listing the properties of the local device*

```
import javax.bluetooth.*;

public class BluetoothProperties {

  public static void main(String[] args) throws Exception {
    LocalDevice device  = LocalDevice.getLocalDevice( );
    System.out.println("API version: "
     + device.getProperty("bluetooth.api.version"));
    System.out.println("bluetooth.master.switch: "
     + device.getProperty("bluetooth.master.switch"));
    System.out.println("Maximum number of service attributes: "
     + device.getProperty("bluetooth.sd.attr.retrievable.max"));
    System.out.println("Maximum number of connected devices: "
     + device.getProperty("bluetooth.connected.devices.max"));
    System.out.println("Maximum receive MTU size in L2CAP: "
     + device.getProperty("bluetooth.l2cap.receiveMTU.max"));
    System.out.println(
     "Maximum number of simultaneous service discovery transactions: "
     + device.getProperty("bluetooth.sd.trans.max"));
    System.out.println("Inquiry scanning allowed during connection: "
     + device.getProperty("bluetooth.connected.inquiry.scan"));
    System.out.println("Page scanning allowed during connection: "
     + device.getProperty("bluetooth.connected.page.scan"));
    System.out.println("Inquiry allowed during connection: "
     + device.getProperty("bluetooth.connected.inquiry"));
    System.out.println("Page allowed during connection: "
     + device.getProperty("bluetooth.connected.page"));
    System.exit(0);
  }
}
```

Here's the output from running this on my PowerMac G5 using the Avetana implementation:

```
API version: 1.0
bluetooth.master.switch: true
Maximum number of service attributes: null
Maximum number of connected devices: 1
Maximum receive MTU size in L2CAP: null
Maximum number of simultaneous service discovery transactions: 1
Inquiry scanning allowed during connection: false
Page scanning allowed during connection: false
```

```
Inquiry allowed during connection: false
Page allowed during connection: false
```

It looks like the Avetana implementation fails to recognize the `bluetooth.sd.attr.`
`retrievable.max` and `bluetooth.l2cap.receiveMTU.max` properties. It recognizes the
rest.

## Device Class

The `getDeviceClass( )` method tells you what kind of Bluetooth device the program
is running on:

```
public DeviceClass getDeviceClass( )
```

The information is encapsulated in a `DeviceClass` object. This class has three getter
methods to describe the major class, minor class, and service classes:

```
public int getMajorDeviceClass( )
public int getMinorDeviceClass( )
public int getServiceClasses( )
```

These methods all return ints. The values of these ints are defined by the Bluetooth
specification. Table 25-1 listed the currently defined major device classes, but more
classes may be added in the future. Each device has exactly one major and one minor
class. However, it can have several service classes, in which case the constants for
each such class are combined with the bitwise or operator.

## Discoverability

Bluetooth devices may be *discoverable*. A discoverable device can be *paired* with
another Bluetooth device so that the two can exchange data. For security reasons,
devices often have personal identification numbers (PINs) that have to be entered
from the discovering device in order to connect to the discovered device. This makes
it harder for an unauthorized person to extract information from your Bluetooth
devices.

The `getDiscoverable( )` method returns an int indicating whether and how a device
is discoverable:

```
public int getDiscoverable( )
```

The return value can be:

`DiscoveryAgent.NOT_DISCOVERABLE`
  Device cannot be discovered by a remote device

`DiscoveryAgent.GIAC`
  Device can be discovered by any remote device

`DiscoveryAgent.LIAC`
  Device can be discovered by other LIAC devices for a limited period of time
  (more on LIAC in a moment)

Some devices may allow you to make them discoverable or not discoverable by passing the appropriate mode to the setDiscoverable( ) method:

```
public boolean setDiscoverable(int mode) throws BluetoothStateException
```

This method returns true if the device state was set as requested or false if it wasn't. It throws an IllegalArgumentException if you pass an illegal state. It throws a BluetoothStateException if the device is in a state that cannot be changed right now.

## Discovering Devices

Of course, there's only so much you can do with just the local device. Soon you're going to want to find out what other devices are out there. This is the purpose of the DiscoveryAgent class. There is one DiscoveryAgent per LocalDevice, and since there's exactly one LocalDevice, there's exactly one DiscoveryAgent. This is retrieved by the getDiscoveryAgent( ) method in LocalDevice:

```
public DiscoveryAgent getDiscoveryAgent()
```

For example:

```
DiscoveryAgent agent = LocalDevice.getLocalDevice().getDiscoveryAgent();
```

The startInquiry( ) method scans the airwaves for discoverable remote devices:

```
public boolean startInquiry(int accessCode, DiscoveryListener listener)
    throws BluetoothStateException
```

This search can take about a minute. To avoid blocking and tying up the user interface or other important operations, this scan can run asynchronously. When the local device finds a remote device, it tells the DiscoveryListener passed as the second argument.

The first argument, accessCode, controls the type of the inquiry. It is either DiscoveryAgent.GIAC (General/Unlimited Inquiry Access Code) or DiscoveryAgent. LIAC (Limited Dedicated Inquiry Access Code). Most of the time, you should use DiscoveryAgent.GIAC. Some implementations do not support LIAC mode.

You can prematurely terminate an inquiry by passing the listener to the cancelInquiry( ) method:

```
public boolean cancelInquiry(DiscoveryListener listener)
```

The retrieveDevices( ) method returns a list of the Bluetooth devices the agent already knows about (that is, it does not find any newly added devices):

```
public RemoteDevice[] retrieveDevices(int option)
```

The option argument should be DiscoveryAgent.CACHED or DiscoveryAgent.PREKNOWN. Cached devices are those discovered in previous inquiries. Preknown devices are specially configured before the application starts up. If none of the requested devices exists, this method returns null. If any devices are preknown or cached, retrieving them is quite a bit faster than launching a new inquiry over the air.

The DiscoveryListener interface has four callback methods that are invoked to signal a device. It actually supports two kinds of searches, one for devices and one for services. Which methods are called back depends on what type of search it is.

The deviceDiscovered( ) method is called when the search uncovers a new device:

```
public void deviceDiscovered(RemoteDevice btDevice, DeviceClass cod)
```

When the agent has given up on finding new devices, it calls inquiryCompleted( ):

```
public void inquiryCompleted(int discoveryType)
```

The discoveryType argument indicates how the search completed. It is one of three constants: DiscoveryListener.INQUIRY_COMPLETED, DiscoveryListener.INQUIRY_TERMINATED, or DiscoveryListener.INQUIRY_ERROR.

The servicesDiscovered( ) method is called when the search uncovers one or more new services on a device:

```
public void servicesDiscovered(int transactionID, ServiceRecord[] serviceRecord)
```

The transactionID argument identifies the search that found the service. The service records provide details about what the device can do and how it operates.

When the agent has given up on finding new services, it calls serviceSearchCompleted( ):

```
public void serviceSearchCompleted(int transactionID, int responseCode)
```

This search has five possible responses:

- DiscoveryListener.SERVICE_SEARCH_COMPLETED
- DiscoveryListener.SERVICE_SEARCH_TERMINATED
- DiscoveryListener.SERVICE_SEARCH_ERROR
- DiscoveryListener.SERVICE_SEARCH_NO_RECORDS
- DiscoveryListener.SERVICE_SEARCH_DEVICE_NOT_REACHABLE

However, a search started by startInquiry( ) won't find any services just yet, so you can implement these methods as do-nothings if you're looking for devices. Once you've found a remote device, you can search it for services. I'll have more to say about that shortly.

Example 25-3 is a simple program that searches for and enumerates all the Bluetooth devices it can find. For each device, it prints the name; the address; the major, minor, and service classes; and the combined 3-byte class identifier, printed in both hexadecimal and binary. This information is useful when you're first trying to figure out how to talk to an undocumented device.

*Example 25-3. Finding Bluetooth devices*

```java
import java.io.IOException;
import javax.bluetooth.*;

public class BluetoothSearch implements DiscoveryListener {

  private DiscoveryAgent agent;

  public static void main(String[] args) throws Exception {
    BluetoothSearch search = new BluetoothSearch( );
    search.agent = LocalDevice.getLocalDevice().getDiscoveryAgent( );
    search.agent.startInquiry(DiscoveryAgent.GIAC, search);
  }

  public void deviceDiscovered(RemoteDevice device, DeviceClass type) {
    int major = type.getMajorDeviceClass( );
    int minor = type.getMinorDeviceClass( );
    int services = type.getServiceClasses( );
    int classIdentifier = major | minor | services;
    try {
      System.out.println("Found " + device.getFriendlyName(false)
        + " at " + device.getBluetoothAddress( ));
    }
    catch (IOException ex) {
      System.out.println("Found unnamed device "
        + " at " + device.getBluetoothAddress( ));
    }
    System.out.println("  Major class: 0x" + Integer.toHexString(major));
    System.out.println("  Minor class: 0x" + Integer.toHexString(minor));
    System.out.println("  Service classes: 0x" + Integer.toHexString(services));
    System.out.println("  Class identifier: 0x"
     + Integer.toHexString(classIdentifier));
    System.out.println("  Class identifier: "
     + Integer.toBinaryString(classIdentifier));
  }

  public void inquiryCompleted(int discoveryType) {

    switch (discoveryType) {
      case DiscoveryListener.INQUIRY_TERMINATED:
        System.out.println("Search cancelled");
        break;
      case DiscoveryListener.INQUIRY_ERROR:
        System.out.println("Bluetooth error");
        break;
      case DiscoveryListener.INQUIRY_COMPLETED:
        System.out.println("Device search complete");;
        break;
      default:
        System.out.println("Unanticipated result: " + discoveryType);
    }

    System.exit(0);
```

*Example 25-3. Finding Bluetooth devices (continued)*

```
    }

    // This search is only looking for devices and won't discover any services,
    // but we have to implement these methods to fulfill the interface
    public void servicesDiscovered(int transactionID, ServiceRecord[] record) {}
    public void serviceSearchCompleted(int transactionID, int arg1) {}
}
```

For this program to find a device, the device must be turned on, be in discoverable mode, and not already have been grabbed by the host operating system. Otherwise, you may not see it. Here's the output from running this on my PowerMac G5:

```
$ java -classpath .:avetanaBluetooth.jar  BluetoothSearch
Found WACOM Pen Tablet at 0013C2000D23
Major class: 0x500
  Minor class: 0x80
  Service classes: 0x1
  Class identifier: 0x581
  Class identifier: 10110000001
Found elharo's mouse at 000A95095A59
  Major class: 0x500
  Minor class: 0x80
  Service classes: 0x1
  Class identifier: 0x581
  Class identifier: 10110000001
Found Earthmate Blue Logger GPS at 00904B2A88D6
  Major class: 0x1f00
  Minor class: 0x0
  Service classes: 0x0
  Class identifier: 0x1f00
  Class identifier: 1111100000000
Found elharo's keyboard at 000A953AFB0B
  Major class: 0x500
  Minor class: 0x40
  Service classes: 0x1
  Class identifier: 0x541
  Class identifier: 10101000001
Device search complete
```

From this we can see that this system has four devices in discoverable mode: a mouse, an Earthmate Blue Logger GPS unit, a WACOM tablet, and an unspecified keyboard. The keyboard and the mouse have the same major class but different minor classes. The graphics tablet and the mouse have the same major, minor, and service classes. The GPS unit has the uncategorized major class 0x1F00, since the Bluetooth SIG hasn't gotten around to defining an appropriate major class for this sort of device.

# Remote Devices

The `RemoteDevice` class represents a Bluetooth device with a certain address. Such devices may or may not be accessible at any given time. They are remote, so they can crash, move, be turned off, run out of battery power, or otherwise disappear from view independently of the local system. There is one protected constructor in this class:

```
protected RemoteDevice(String address)
```

However, it is not normally used. Instead, you discover devices as explained in the previous section. If you already have an open connection to the device you want to query, you can use the static `RemoteDevice.getRemoteDevice()` method to retrieve the `RemoteDevice` object representing the actual device:

```
public static RemoteDevice getRemoteDevice(Connection conn) throws IOException
```

You've now found the remote devices. What are you going to do with them? Of course, this depends on the type of the device. The `RemoteDevice` class tells you this. Although `LocalDevice` and `RemoteDevice` do not have a common superclass, they do share many methods that do pretty much the same thing. There is, however, one crucial difference: queries to the remote device go out over the air whereas queries to the local device stay within the system. This means remote queries are slower, less secure, and less reliable than local queries.

The `getBluetoothAddress()` method returns a `String` containing the 12-hex-digit Bluetooth address of the controller:

```
public final String getBluetoothAddress()
```

The `getFriendlyName()` method returns a more human-legible name:

```
public String getFriendlyName() throws IOException
```

Bluetooth connections can be authorized, authenticated, and/or encrypted, though not all devices support all these options. The latter is particularly uncommon because of the CPU cost of high-quality encryption. Nonetheless, the `RemoteDevice` class provides methods to inquire whether any particular connection is authorized, authenticated, or encrypted and to request such services.

A device is *authenticated* if it has successfully exchanged a 128-bit key with the host. Normally this requires entering the same PIN code on both the host and the device. The host or device may randomly generate a key and corresponding PIN and ask you to enter it on the other end of the connection. Java programs use the Bluetooth Control Center to do this. The `isAuthenticated()` method returns `true` if the device is authenticated and `false` if it isn't:

```
public boolean isAuthenticated()
```

The `authenticate()` method attempts to authenticate a device by exchanging the secret key derived from the shared PIN code:

```
public boolean authenticate() throws IOException
```

This method returns true if authentication succeeds and false if it doesn't. It throws an IOException if there's no current connection between the local and the remote device. Authentication needs to be performed only once per device. After a device has successfully authenticated, all further connections are automatically authenticated.

A device is *authorized* if the user has given permission for this remote device to use the local service. The isAuthorized( ) method returns true if the device is authorized and false if it isn't:

```
public boolean isAuthorized( )
```

The authorize( ) method asks the user to authorize the device for a particular connection:

```
public boolean authorize(Connection conn) throws IOException
```

This method returns true if authorization succeeds and false if it doesn't. It throws an IOException if there's no current connection between the local and remote devices. Authentication is a prerequisite for authorization. Before authorizing, this device attempts to authenticate itself.

Some devices can be permanently authorized. Such devices are called *trusted*. Java programs use the Bluetooth Control Center to identify a device as trusted. The isTrustedDevice( ) returns true if the device is trusted and false if it isn't:

```
public boolean isTrustedDevice( )
```

Finally, a few devices support encrypted communication. The isEncrypted( ) method returns true if the device encrypts connections and false if it doesn't:

```
public boolean isAuthenticated( )
```

The encrypt( ) method instructs a device to turn encryption on or off:

```
public boolean encrypt(Connection conn, boolean on) throws IOException
```

This method returns true if the device is now in encrypted mode and false if it isn't.

# Service Records

Each Bluetooth device supports one or more services, such as basic printing or generic telephony. Each service is identified by a UUID—sometimes a custom one, sometimes a standardized one. For example, the UUID for the basic printing service is 0x1122. (Normally, these are written using their short forms rather than the full 128-bit forms.)

Devices publish service records to tell other devices how to communicate with them. The Bluetooth specification lays out the exact structure and meaning of a service record in excruciating detail, but as usual Java encapsulates this in a much easier-to-use interface, javax.bluetooth.ServiceRecord.

A service record is essentially an indexed list of attributes. Attributes do not have names, only values. Given a ServiceRecord object, the getAttributeIDs( ) method returns an array of all the IDs of the attributes in the service record:

```
public int[] getAttributeIDs( )
```

You can then iterate through this list, passing each ID in turn to the getAttributeValue( ) method to retrieve each attribute:

```
public DataElement getAttributeValue(int attrID)
```

## The DataElement Class

Bluetooth attributes can have a variety of types, such as string, UUID, boolean, URL, sequence, null, and several signed and unsigned integer types. Java represents each of these as a DataElement object. These types, and the Java types they map to, are summarized in Table 25-4.

*Table 25-4. Bluetooth attribute types*

| Bluetooth type | Java type | Java constant |
| --- | --- | --- |
| NULL | null | DataElement.NULL |
| U_INT_1 | 1-byte unsigned long from 0 to 255 | DataElement.U_INT_1 |
| U_INT_2 | 2-byte unsigned long from 0 to 65,535 | DataElement.U_INT_2 |
| U_INT_4 | 4-byte unsigned long from 0 to 4,294,967,296 | DataElement.U_INT_4 |
| U_INT_8 | 8-byte byte[] array | DataElement.U_INT_8 |
| U_INT_16 | 16-byte byte[] array | DataElement.U_INT_16 |
| INT_1 | 1-byte signed long from −128 to 127 | DataElement.INT_1 |
| INT_2 | 2-byte signed long from −32,768 to 32,767 | DataElement.INT_2 |
| INT_4 | 4-byte signed long from −2,147,483,647 to 2,147,483,647 | DataElement.INT_4 |
| INT_8 | 8-byte unsigned long from $-2^{63}$ to $2^{63}-1$ | DataElement.INT_8 |
| INT_16 | 16-byte byte[] array | DataElement.INT_16 |
| URL | java.lang.String | DataElement.URL |
| UUID | javax.bluetooth.UUID | DataElement.UUID |
| BOOL | boolean | DataElement.BOOL |
| STRING | java.lang.String | DataElement.STRING |
| DATSEQ | java.util.Enumeration | DataElement.DATSEQ |
| DATALT | java.util.Enumeration | DataElement.DATALT |

Most of these types do not map precisely onto Java primitive types, so the Java Bluetooth API encapsulates them all in the javax.bluetooth.DataElement class. This class has three methods to read the value out of a DataElement as a long, boolean, or Object:

```
public long    getLong( )
public boolean getBoolean( )
public Object  getValue( )
```

The getDataType( ) method tells you the Bluetooth type of the DataElement object:

```
public int getDataType( )
```

The return value is one of the named constants found in the third column of Table 25-4. Once you know the type of value to expect, you can use one of the three getter methods to return the value as the corresponding Java object or primitive type. If you try to get a mismatched type—for example, an INT_4 as a boolean or a URL as a long—these methods throw a ClassCastException.

Data elements can also wrap two list types. DATSEQ is an ordered sequence of values. DATALT is a list of values from which any one should be chosen. For either of these two types, getValue( ) returns a java.util.Enumeration. In this case, the getSize( ) method returns the number of items in that enumeration:

```
public int getSize( )
```

The addElement( ) method appends a new item of one of the 18 Bluetooth types to a DATSEQ or DATALT:

```
public void addElement(DataElement element)
```

The insertElementAt( ) method inserts a new data element into the specified position in a DATSEQ or DATALT:

```
public void insertElement(DataElement element, int position)
```

The removeElement( ) removes the first occurrence of the specified new data element from the DATSEQ or DATALT:

```
public void removeElement(DataElement element)
```

The same element may appear in the list more than once. These methods all throw a ClassCastException if you attempt to use them on a DataElement that does not represent a DATALT or DATSEQ.

## Finding Service Records

Like the remote devices themselves, the service records for a device are obtained via the DiscoveryAgent class. The simplest way to find a known service is to ask for it by UUID using the selectService( ) method:

```
public String selectService(UUID uuid, int security, boolean master)
  throws BluetoothStateException
```

This returns a connection string with the URL used to connect to the service, such as:

```
btspp://00904B2A88D6:1;authenticate=false;encrypt=false;master=false
```

The security argument is usually one of these three named constants, depending on what combination of authentication and encryption you desire:

- ServiceRecord.NOAUTHENTICATE_NOENCRYPT
- ServiceRecord.AUTHENTICATE_NOENCRYPT
- ServiceRecord.AUTHENTICATE_ENCRYPT

Finally, the master argument is true if the client insists on being the master of the connection and false if it can act as the master or the slave.

For example, suppose you want to find a basic printing service. The UUID for this is 0x1122, so this code fragment locates one if there's one to be found:

```
UUID printingID = new UUID(0x1122);
String url = agent.selectService(
 printingID, ServiceRecord.AUTHENTICATE_NOENCRYPT, false);
```

If it can't locate the requested service, it returns null.

What if there's more than one available device that supports the relevant service? In this case, the results are implementation dependent, but usually one or another is returned. (The Avetana stack actually throws a custom checked exception here, which is not conformant with the specification.)

The searchServices( ) method asks a specific device what services it supports:

```
public int searchServices(int[] attrSet, UUID[] uuidSet, RemoteDevice device,
 DiscoveryListener listener) throws BluetoothStateException
```

This approach is somewhat more reliable if you might have more than one device that offers a given service. The uuidSet argument contains the UUIDs for all the protocols you're looking for. Table 25-5 lists the UUIDs (in 2-byte form) of the services you can request. The attrSet argument contains the list of attributes (in addition to the default attributes) whose information should be provided. device is the specific device to query for services, and listener is the listener to tell about any services that are found. The method returns an ID you can use if you later need to cancel the search, which you can do with the following method:

```
public boolean cancelServiceSearch(int transID)
```

 This method does not work in the Avetana stack. That product cannot cancel an ongoing search.

*Table 25-5. Bluetooth service UUIDs*

| Name | UUID | Protocol |
| --- | --- | --- |
| SDP | 0x0001 | Service Discovery Protocol |
| UDP | 0x0002 | UDP/IP |
| RFCOMM | 0x0003 | Serial port emulation |
| TCP | 0x0004 | Telephony Control Protocol |

*Table 25-5. Bluetooth service UUIDs (continued)*

| Name | UUID | Protocol |
|---|---|---|
| TCS-BIN | 0x0005 | Telephony Control Service |
| TCS-AT | 0x0006 | Modems (i.e., AT command sequences) |
| OBEX | 0x0008 | Object Exchange protocol |
| IP | 0x0009 | Internet Protocol |
| FTP | 0x000A | Bluetooth File Transfer Protocol; based on OBEX; not the same as the usual Internet FTP protocol |
| HTTP | 0x000C | Web |
| WSP | 0x000E | Wireless Session Protocol |
| BNEP | 0x000F | Bluetooth Network Encapsulation Protocol |
| UPNP | 0x0010 | Universal Plug and Play |
| HIDP | 0x0011 | Human Interface Device Profile (same as the USB HID, but over Bluetooth instead of USB) |
| HardcopyControlChannel | 0x0012 | Wireless printing control channel (device to printer) |
| HardcopyDataChannel | 0x0014 | Wireless printing data channel (data being printed) |
| HardcopyNotification | 0x0016 | Wireless printing notification channel (printer to device) |
| AVCTP | 0x0017 | Audio/Video Control Transport Protocol, Bluetooth SIG |
| AVDTP | 0x0019 | Audio/Video Distribution Transport Protocol, Bluetooth SIG |
| CMTP | 0x001B | Common ISDN API (CAPI) Message Transport Protocol |
| UDI_C-Plane | 0x001D | Unrestricted Digital Information Profile |
| L2CAP | 0x0100 | Logical Link Control and Adaptation Protocol |

Table 25-6 lists some of the attributes you can request. The first five—
ServiceRecordHandle, ServiceClassIDList, ServiceRecordState, ServiceID, and
ProtocolDescriptorList—are always returned. The others need to be specifically
requested.

*Table 25-6. Bluetooth service attribute IDs*

| Name | ID | Type |
|---|---|---|
| ServiceRecordHandle | 0x0000 | 4-byte unsigned integer |
| ServiceClassIDList | 0x0001 | DATSEQ of UUIDs |
| ServiceRecordState | 0x0002 | 4-byte unsigned integer |
| ServiceID | 0x0003 | UUID |
| ProtocolDescriptorList | 0x0004 | DATSEQ of DATSEQ of UUID and optional parameters |
| BrowseGroupList | 0x0005 | DATSEQ of UUIDs |
| LanguageBasedAttributeIDList | 0x0006 | DATSEQ of DATSEQ triples |
| ServiceInfoTimeToLive | 0x0007 | 4-byte unsigned integer |
| ServiceAvailability | 0x0008 | 1-byte unsigned integer |
| BluetoothProfileDescriptorList | 0x0009 | DATSEQ of DATSEQ pairs |

*Table 25-6. Bluetooth service attribute IDs (continued)*

| Name | ID | Type |
|------|-----|------|
| DocumentationURL | 0x000A | URL |
| ClientExecutableURL | 0x000B | URL |
| IconURL | 0x000C | URL |
| VersionNumberList | 0x0200 | DATSEQ of 2-byte unsigned integers |
| ServiceDatabaseState | 0x0201 | 4-byte unsigned integer |

Some of these IDs may vary depending on the profile. For instance, 0x0301 means "external network" in the Cordless Telephony Profile but "supported data stores" in the Synchronization Profile.

## The ServiceRecord Interface

The ServiceRecord interface provides a number of setter and getter methods for inspecting and updating service records. By far the most important thing you'll need from a ServiceRecord object is the connection string. This is the URL you'll use to open a connection to the device:

```
public String getConnectionURL(int requiredSecurity, boolean mustBeMaster)
```

The security argument is one of these three named constants, depending on what combination of authentication and encryption you desire:

- ServiceRecord.NOAUTHENTICATE_NOENCRYPT
- ServiceRecord.AUTHENTICATE_NOENCRYPT
- ServiceRecord.AUTHENTICATE_ENCRYPT

The master argument is true if the client insists on being the master of the connection or false if it can act as the master or the slave.

The value you get back is a complete GCF Bluetooth URL, such as:

```
btspp://00904B2A88D6:1;authenticate=false;encrypt=false;master=false
```

Once you have the URL, you can talk to the device using the methods of the last chapter.

You can add or remove parameters from the URL using substring operations. For instance, you could change the above URL to:

```
btspp://00904B2A88D6:1;authenticate=false;encrypt=false;master=true
```

However, getConnectionURL() is the only way to get the necessary protocol, address, and channel for the device.

The getAttributeIDs() method returns an array of the IDs of all the attributes this service possesses:

```
public int[] getAttributeIDs()
```

You can retrieve one of these attributes with the getAttributeValue( ) method:

```
public DataElement getAttributeValue(int attrID)
```

This returns a DataElement object that wraps the Bluetooth object in a Java class, as described in Table 25-4.

Example 25-4 is a program that searches for all L2CAP (UUID 0x0100) services. When it finds one, it lists its URL. Notice that you have to explicitly start a search for each device's services. That is, Example 25-4 first starts a search for devices as previously seen in Example 25-3. When a device is found, it searches that device for services using searchServices( ). For each service, it requests all attributes that might be present.

*Example 25-4. Finding all L2CAP services*

```java
import java.io.IOException;
import javax.bluetooth.*;

public class BluetoothServicesSearch implements DiscoveryListener {

  private DiscoveryAgent agent;
  private final static UUID L2CAP = new UUID(0x0100);

  public static void main(String[] args) throws Exception {
    BluetoothServicesSearch search = new BluetoothServicesSearch( );
    search.agent = LocalDevice.getLocalDevice().getDiscoveryAgent( );
    search.agent.startInquiry(DiscoveryAgent.GIAC, search);
  }

  public void deviceDiscovered(RemoteDevice device, DeviceClass type) {
    try {
      System.out.println("Found " + device.getFriendlyName(false)
      + " at " + device.getBluetoothAddress( ));
    }
    catch (IOException ex) {
      System.out.println("Found unnamed device "
      + " at " + device.getBluetoothAddress( ));
    }
    searchServices(device);
  }

  public final static int SERVICE_RECORD_HANDLE              = 0X0000;
  public final static int SERVICE_CLASSID_LIST               = 0X0001;
  public final static int SERVICE_RECORD_STATE               = 0X0002;
  public final static int SERVICE_ID                         = 0X0003;
  public final static int PROTOCOL_DESCRIPTOR_LIST           = 0X0004;
  public final static int BROWSE_GROUP_LIST                  = 0X0005;
  public final static int LANGUAGE_BASED_ATTRIBUTE_ID_LIST   = 0X0006;
  public final static int SERVICE_INFO_TIME_TO_LIVE          = 0X0007;
  public final static int SERVICE_AVAILABILITY               = 0X0008;
  public final static int BLUETOOTH_PROFILE_DESCRIPTOR_LIST  = 0X0009;
  public final static int DOCUMENTATION_URL                  = 0X000A;
```

*Example 25-4. Finding all L2CAP services (continued)*

```java
public final static int CLIENT_EXECUTABLE_URL            = 0X000B;
public final static int ICON_URL                          = 0X000C;
public final static int VERSION_NUMBER_LIST               = 0X0200;
public final static int SERVICE_DATABASE_STATE            = 0X0201;

private void searchServices(RemoteDevice device) {

  UUID[] searchList = {L2CAP};
  int[] attributes = {SERVICE_RECORD_HANDLE, SERVICE_CLASSID_LIST,
                      SERVICE_RECORD_STATE, SERVICE_ID,
                      PROTOCOL_DESCRIPTOR_LIST, BROWSE_GROUP_LIST,
                      LANGUAGE_BASED_ATTRIBUTE_ID_LIST,
                      SERVICE_INFO_TIME_TO_LIVE, SERVICE_AVAILABILITY,
                      BLUETOOTH_PROFILE_DESCRIPTOR_LIST, DOCUMENTATION_URL,
                      CLIENT_EXECUTABLE_URL, ICON_URL, VERSION_NUMBER_LIST,
                      SERVICE_DATABASE_STATE};
  try {
    System.out.println("Searching " + device.getBluetoothAddress()
      + " for services");
    int trans = this.agent.searchServices(attributes, searchList, device, this);
    System.out.println("Service Search " + trans + " started");
  }
  catch (BluetoothStateException ex) {
    System.out.println( "BluetoothStateException: " + ex.getMessage() );
  }

}

public void servicesDiscovered(int transactionID, ServiceRecord[] record) {
  for (int i = 0; i < record.length; i++) {
    System.out.println("Found service " + record[i].getConnectionURL(
      ServiceRecord.NOAUTHENTICATE_NOENCRYPT, false));
  }
}

public void serviceSearchCompleted(int transactionID, int responseCode) {

  switch (responseCode) {
    case DiscoveryListener.SERVICE_SEARCH_DEVICE_NOT_REACHABLE:
     System.out.println("Could not find device on search " + transactionID);
     break;
    case DiscoveryListener.SERVICE_SEARCH_ERROR:
     System.out.println("Error searching device on search " + transactionID);
     break;
    case DiscoveryListener.SERVICE_SEARCH_NO_RECORDS:
     System.out.println("No service records on device on search "
      + transactionID);
     break;
    case DiscoveryListener.SERVICE_SEARCH_TERMINATED:
     System.out.println("User cancelled search " + transactionID);
     break;
    case DiscoveryListener.SERVICE_SEARCH_COMPLETED:
```

*Example 25-4. Finding all L2CAP services (continued)*

```
      System.out.println("Service search " + transactionID + " complete");
      break;
    default:
      System.out.println("Unexpected response code " + responseCode
      + " from search " + transactionID);
    }
  }

  public void inquiryCompleted(int transactionID) {
    System.out.println("Device search " + transactionID + " complete");
  }
}
```

Most other Bluetooth protocols are built on top of L2CAP, so this program will probably find all the accessible devices. Here's what I got when I ran it on my system after making sure all devices were discoverable:

```
Found Earthmate Blue Logger GPS at 00904B2A88D6
Searching 00904B2A88D6 for services
Service Search 1 started
Found service btspp://00904B2A88D6:1;authenticate=false;encrypt=false;master=false
Service search 1 complete
Found elharo's mouse at 000A95095A59
Searching 000A95095A59 for services
Service Search 2 started
Found service btl2cap://000A95095A59:11;authenticate=false;encrypt=false;master=false
Found service btl2cap://000A95095A59:1;authenticate=false;encrypt=false;master=false
Service search 2 complete
Found WACOM Pen Tablet at 0013C2000D23
Searching 0013C2000D23 for services
Service Search 3 started
Found service btl2cap://0013C2000D23:11;authenticate=false;encrypt=false;master=false
Found service btl2cap://0013C2000D23:1;authenticate=false;encrypt=false;master=false
Service search 3 complete
Device search 0 complete
```

You can see there are three devices on this system: a GPS unit, a pen tablet, and a mouse. The GPS unit has a single serial port (RFCOMM) connection, which we'll make use of in the next section. The mouse and the graphics tablet each have two L2CAP URLs, one for the control channel and one for the interrupt channel. This is the common pattern for HID devices.

More often, you'll want to look for a particular service with a particular UUID. This normally happens asynchronously, but there's a maximum number of searches you can run at once. (The exact number varies from device to device but can be read from the `bluetooth.sd.trans.max` property.) Consequently, you need to keep track of the searches and cancel the ongoing searches when you've found what you're looking for. Example 25-5 demonstrates. The static `BluetoothServiceFinder.getConnectionURL( )` method finds a service with a specified UUID. We'll use this class again shortly.

*Example 25-5. A utility class to find a specified service*

```java
import javax.bluetooth.*;
import java.util.Vector;

public class BluetoothServiceFinder implements DiscoveryListener {

  public static String getConnectionURL(String uuid)
   throws BluetoothStateException {
    BluetoothServiceFinder finder
     = new BluetoothServiceFinder(BluetoothReceiver.UUID);
    return finder.getFirstURL();
  }

  private DiscoveryAgent agent;
  private int            serviceSearchCount;
  private ServiceRecord  record;
  // I'd rather use ArrayList, but Vector is more
  // commonly available in J2ME environments
  private Vector         devices = new Vector();
  private String         uuid;

  // Every search has an ID that allows it to be cancelled.
  // We need to store these so we can tell when all searches
  // are complete.
  private int[] transactions;

  private BluetoothServiceFinder(String serviceUUID)
   throws BluetoothStateException {
    this.uuid = serviceUUID;
    agent = LocalDevice.getLocalDevice().getDiscoveryAgent();
    int maxSimultaneousSearches = Integer.parseInt(
     LocalDevice.getProperty("bluetooth.sd.trans.max"));
    transactions = new int[maxSimultaneousSearches];
    // We need to initialize the transactions list with illegal
    // values. According to spec, the transaction ID is supposed to be
    // positive, and thus nonzero. However, several implementations
    // get this wrong and use zero as a transaction ID.
    for (int i = 0; i < maxSimultaneousSearches; i++) {
      transactions[i] = -1;
    }
  }

  private void addTransaction(int transactionID) {
    for (int i = 0; i < transactions.length; i++) {
      if (transactions[i] == -1) {
        transactions[i] = transactionID;
        return;
      }
    }
  }

  private void removeTransaction(int transactionID) {
    for (int i = 0; i < transactions.length; i++) {
      if (transactions[i] == transactionID) {
```

*Example 25-5. A utility class to find a specified service (continued)*

```
          transactions[i] = -1;
          return;
       }
    }
 }

 private boolean searchServices(RemoteDevice[] devices) {
   UUID[] searchList = { new UUID(uuid, false) };
   for (int i = 0; i < devices.length; i++) {
     if (record != null) {
       return true;
     }
     try {
       // don't care about attributes
       int transactionID = agent.searchServices(null, searchList, devices[i],
        this);
       addTransaction(transactionID);
     }
     catch (BluetoothStateException ex) {
     }

     synchronized (this) {
       serviceSearchCount++;
       if (serviceSearchCount == transactions.length) {
         try {
           this.wait();
         }
         catch (InterruptedException ex) {
           // continue
         }
       }
     }
   }

   while (serviceSearchCount > 0) { // unfinished searches
     synchronized (this) {
       try {
         this.wait();
       }
       catch (InterruptedException ex) {
         // continue
       }
     }
   }
   if (record != null) return true;
   else return false;
 }

 private String getFirstURL() {
   try {
     agent.startInquiry(DiscoveryAgent.GIAC, this);
     synchronized (this) {
       try {
```

*Example 25-5. A utility class to find a specified service (continued)*

```
          this.wait();
        }
        catch (InterruptedException ex) {
        }
      }
    }
    catch (BluetoothStateException ex) {
      System.out.println("No devices in range");
    }

    if (devices.size() > 0) {
      RemoteDevice[] remotes = new RemoteDevice[devices.size()];
      devices.copyInto(remotes);
      if (searchServices(remotes)) {
        return record.getConnectionURL(
          ServiceRecord.NOAUTHENTICATE_NOENCRYPT, false);
      }
    }
    return null;
  }

  // DiscoveryListener methods
  public void deviceDiscovered(RemoteDevice device, DeviceClass type) {
    devices.addElement(device);
  }

  public void serviceSearchCompleted(int transactionID, int responseCode) {
    removeTransaction(transactionID);
    serviceSearchCount--;
    synchronized (this) {
      this.notifyAll();
    }
  }

  public void servicesDiscovered(int transactionID, ServiceRecord[] records) {
    if (record == null) {
      record = records[0];
      for (int i = 0; i < transactions.length; i++) {
        if (transactions[i] != -1) {
          agent.cancelServiceSearch(transactions[i]);
        }
      }
    }
  }

  public void inquiryCompleted(int discType) {
    synchronized (this) {
      this.notifyAll();
    }
  }
}
```

# Talking to Devices

Bluetooth devices are talked to via the Generic Connection Framework. If you know the address of the device you're going to talk to, you may not even need to use any of the other classes in this chapter. Bluetooth URLs for the GCF look like this:

```
btspp://00904B2A88D6:1;authenticate=false;encrypt=false;master=false
btspp://localhost:3B9FA89520078C303355AAA694238F07;authenticate=true;encrypt=true
btspp://localhost:102030405060708090A1B1C1D1E100;name=SPPEx
btl2cap://localhost:3B9FA89520078C303355AAA694238F08;name=Aserv
btspp://localhost:3B9FA89520078C303355AAA694238F08
btgoep://0050C000321B:12
btgoep://localhost:3B9FA89520078C303355AAA694238F08
```

The URLs that begin with btspp are for devices that use the Bluetooth Serial Port Profile. These are streaming connections. URLs that begin with btl2cap are for devices that use the Bluetooth L2CAP protocol to exchange packetized data. Some higher-level protocols, such as RFCOMM, are built on top of L2CAP. Some devices use it more directly as well. URLs with the scheme btgoep are for devices that use the OBEX protocol to exchange binary data. For example, OBEX is used to synchronize contact lists between desktop computers and cell phones by exchanging binary representations of those lists.

The GCF can act as either a server or a client. The URLs that contain the word localhost are for servers. That is, they wait for incoming connections and respond to them. The URLs that don't contain the word localhost are for clients. They initiate connections to the specified Bluetooth address. For a server, the long string of hex digits is the UUID of the service. For a client, it's the address of the device you're talking to.

The address is sometimes followed by a colon and a channel number. This is analogous to a port in TCP protocols; that is, it is an extra number attached to each packet to help sort out which service on a given device a stream or packet is intended for. It has no particular meaning; devices that use only a single channel normally omit it.

Finally, up to five name=value optional parameters can configure the connection:

name
> For server URLs only, the value for the service name attribute in the service record

master
> true if this client must act as the master device; false if it can be a slave

encrypt
> true if the connection is to be encrypted; false if it isn't

authorize
> true if the connection is to be authorized; false if it isn't

authenticate
> true if the connection is to be authenticated; false if it isn't

Not all combinations are possible. For instance, you cannot have authenticate=false and encrypt=true.

As with USB devices or serial port devices, the details of communication are device dependent. Some devices share protocols. For example, one Bluetooth mouse is pretty much the same as another. You don't need different drivers for each brand. A Bluetooth modem can more or less use the raw Bluetooth Serial Port Protocol along with the customary Hayes command set. For less standard devices, you'll need to read the technical documentation (if any), communicate with the device vendors (if they'll talk to you), or reverse engineer the protocols the devices speak. A Bluetooth protocol analyzer that can sniff packets from the air is invaluable.

## RFCOMM Clients

RFCOMM devices are some of the simplest Bluetooth devices out there. Each has an output stream and an input stream. You write commands onto the output stream and read responses from the input stream. Some devices use a lockstep protocol (one command, one response). Others are asynchronous, and some don't even require any commands.

I'm going to demonstrate talking to the DeLorme Earthmate Blue Logger GPS receiver shown in Figure 25-4. Unlike some fancier and larger GPS units, it doesn't have an LCD display. Its input is limited to a single button and its output to a couple of LEDs. This device just sends a constant stream of GPS data to whoever's interested in listening.

*Figure 25-4. The DeLorme Earthmate Blue Logger*

The Blue Logger formats data in the industry-standard NMEA 183 protocol supported by most GPS devices. This protocol outputs real-time position, velocity, and time information in line-by-line ASCII text that looks like this:

```
7.8524,W,1,07,1.1,27.2,M,-34.3,M,30.0,0000*46
$GPRMC,204449.378,A,4040.2990,N,07357.8524,W,0.00,184.22,300106,,*14
$GPVTG,184.22,T,,M,0.00,N,0.0,K*6D
$GPGGA,204450.378,4040.2986,N,07357.8523,W,1,07,1.1,28.6,M,-34.3,M,30.0,0000*45
$GPGSA,A,3,10,06,05,07,04,30,02,,,,,,2.2,1.1,1.9*3A
$GPGSV,3,1,09,10,67,234,44,02,64,054,43,07,34,154,37,04,33,083,31*78
$GPGSV,3,2,09,30,24,271,37,06,21,313,32,05,21,242,41,13,19,043,21*78
$GPGSV,3,3,09,29,13,175,00*4A
$GPRMC,204450.378,A,4040.2986,N,07357.8523,W,0.00,184.22,300106,,*1C
$GPVTG,184.22,T,,M,0.00,N,0.0,K*6D
$GPGGA,204451.378,4040.2982,N,07357.8522,W,1,07,1.1,29.5,M,-34.3,M,30.0,0000*43
$GPRMC,204451.378,A,4040.2982,N,07357.8522,W,0.00,184.22,300106,,*18
```

 The NMEA 0183 specification (*http://www.nmea.org/pub/0183/*) is published by the National Marine Electronics Association, which is stuck in the bad old days of pay-to-play specifications. You can buy the spec from them for $340 (and at that price, you don't even get overnight shipping!). It is not available online. You can read more about NMEA in the NMEA FAQ at *http://vancouver-webpages.com/ peter/nmeafaq.txt*.

In NMEA terminology, each line of text is called a *sentence*. The sentence begins with a dollar sign and ends with a carriage return linefeed pair. Sentences should contain no more than 82 characters (including the carriage return linefeed pair). Each sentence is self-contained and independent of the other sentences. Standard GPS sentences all begin with GP.

 The first sentence in the above output looks suspect. It does not begin with a $ and an NMEA code. In fact, what's happened is that the program has hooked into the device in the middle of a sentence. NMEA devices normally send promiscuously and continuously, without considering whether anyone is listening. You should simply discard any line you receive that does not begin with a dollar sign. Similarly, if you want only some of the data, you just wait until it shows up in the output stream and ignore any sentences that aren't relevant to you.

Vendor-specific sentences begin with the letter P and a three-letter manufacturer code. For instance, Garmin-specific sentences all begin with PGRM. The next three letters determine the type of the sentence. I've seen the Blue Logger send four sentences:

GPGGA

Fix information. Essentially everything needed to determine a three-dimensional location and the accuracy thereof.

GPRMC

Recommended minimum data. This is basic time and position information.

GPVTG

Vector track and speed over ground. This includes the speed in both knots and kilometers per hour, as well as the direction of travel relative to true north and magnetic north.

GPGSA

General satellite data. This tells you which of the 28 GPS satellites the unit can currently see and how well it can see them.

A couple of dozen more sentences are emitted by various other GPS devices. For basic applications, the most interesting (and simplest) data is found in the GPRMC sentences. These give you the time, status, latitude, longitude, speed, angle, date, magnetic variation, and a checksum, in that order. Consider this GPRMC line:

```
$GPRMC,204449.378,A,4040.2990,N,07357.8524,W,0.00,184.22,300106,,*14
```

Within a sentence, commas separate the individual fields. The second field, 204449.378, is the time. Specifically, it is 20:44:49.378 seconds UTC; that is, 49.378 seconds after 8:44 PM, Greenwich Mean Time.

The third field, containing the letter A, is the status. This should be either A for Active or V for Void. Active units have found the GPS satellites. Void ones are not currently receiving GPS information, usually due to interference from buildings, canyons, and trees, and thus cannot be relied on.

4040.2990 is the latitude. Specifically, it is 40° 40.2990'. Four-digit accuracy is not guaranteed, and it may not even be reported by some units. My tests suggest that a hundredth of a minute is about the best accuracy you can hope for, and that may vary depending on your location and satellite positions. The next field, the single letter N, says that this is North latitude. Similarly, the next two fields, 07357.8524,W, indicate that this is 73° 57.8524' West longitude.

The next field is the speed in *knots*. (Remember, this protocol was designed for boats, which still haven't converted to sensible metric units.) In this case, the GPS reading was taken from a fixed location, so the speed is 0.00. The next field, with the value 184.22, is the angle of movement direction relative to true north. For a fixed location, this doesn't mean a lot.

The next field, with the value 300106, is the date in the format DDMMYY. This date is January 30, 2006. Yes, there's a looming Y2K/Y2100 problem here. Most software assumes that 90–99 map to 1990–1999 and 00–89 map to 2000–2089. One hopes that this will be fixed sometime in the next 83 years.

The GPS satellites themselves don't have a specific Y2K/Y2100 problem. Instead, they use atomic clocks accurate to within a microsecond. These clocks count time elapsed since midnight, January 6, 1980, GMT. They roll over every 1,024 weeks. The first such rollover happened on August 22, 1999. The next will happen on April 7, 2019. It's just the NMEA text format that is limited to two digits for the year.

The next field is empty in this example. If it were present it would include the magnetic variation, in the form 003.1,W.

The last field contains a checksum. This sum is formed by taking the bitwise exclusive or of all the bytes in the line between the $ and *, exclusive (that is, the $ and the * are not included when calculating the checksum).

 Yes, I'm skipping over a lot of technical detail here. People get PhDs in this stuff. Mapping is a lot more involved than your seventh-grade social studies teacher told you.

You can control some (not all) GPS receivers by writing similar sentences over the connection's output stream. For example, this enables you to download the track logs, upload waypoints and routes, or turn off the device. However, this is all completely proprietary. Every device family has its own sentences for doing this, and some features, such as uploading maps, are completely undocumented and may even be actively hidden. Details vary from one device to the next. Sad to say, most GPS vendors have yet to catch the open source bug. For the time being, if you want to send data to a GPS unit, whether over Bluetooth, USB, or a classic serial port, you first have to reverse engineer the protocol it speaks. For many devices it may be the case that an open source Linux driver already exists in some other language, such as Python or C. Although a straight port may not be possible, this is often enough to show you what commands you need to send.

The NMEA protocol is actually designed for devices that have serial ports, but that's where the Bluetooth Serial Port Profile comes into play. You can pretend that the device is a serial port device (though you will have to use the Generic Connection Framework instead of the Java Communications API).

The first step is hardware: make sure the device is turned on, discoverable, and in range. Details vary from device to device, but to turn on the Blue Logger and make it discoverable you just hold down its one button until it starts flashing blue. You can use your system's usual Bluetooth control panel to make sure that the host's Bluetooth controller is turned on and can see the device. However, don't actually pair with the device. If you have previously paired with it, you'll need to delete the pairing first so that it can be seen by Java.

The second step is to find the device. This is a little tricky. You'd normally search by major class, minor class, and service classes. However, there's no standard class for GPS devices. In such a case, the major class is set to 0x1FFF (i.e., five 1 bits in the major device class part of the class ID), and the minor class and service class bits are all 0s. Because this is a catch-all class ID for any unclassified device, there's no guarantee that the first one you find with that ID is actually a Blue Logger. Instead, we'll look for the friendly name "Earthmate Blue Logger." To be honest, this approach makes me a little nervous, but it seems to work. Example 25-6 demonstrates.

*Example 25-6. Finding the first Blue Logger in range*

```java
import java.io.IOException;
import javax.bluetooth.*;

public class BlueLoggerFinder implements DiscoveryListener {

  private DiscoveryAgent agent;
  private RemoteDevice device;

  public static RemoteDevice find()
   throws BluetoothStateException {
    BlueLoggerFinder search = new BlueLoggerFinder();
    search.agent = LocalDevice.getLocalDevice().getDiscoveryAgent();
    search.agent.startInquiry(DiscoveryAgent.GIAC, search);
    // wait for inquiry to finish
    synchronized(search){
      try {
        search.wait();
      }
      catch (InterruptedException ex) {
        // continue
      }
    }
    return search.device;
  }

  public void deviceDiscovered(RemoteDevice device, DeviceClass type) {
    int major = type.getMajorDeviceClass();
    try {
      if (device.getFriendlyName(false).startsWith("Earthmate Blue Logger")) {
        this.device = device;
        // stop looking for other devices
        agent.cancelInquiry(this);
        // wake up the main thread
        synchronized(this){
          this.notify();
        }
      }
    }
    catch (IOException ex) {
      // hopefully this isn't the device we're looking for
    }
  }

  public void inquiryCompleted(int discoveryType) {}

  // This search is only looking for devices and won't discover any services,
  // but we have to implement these methods to fulfill the interface
  public void servicesDiscovered(int transactionID, ServiceRecord[] record) {}
  public void serviceSearchCompleted(int transactionID, int arg1) {}
}
```

The BlueLogger.find( ) method returns a RemoteDevice object for the first operating Blue Logger it sees. If it can't find one, it returns null. What you need from this object is the unique address of that particular Blue Logger as returned by the getBluetoothAddress( ) method. Once you have this address you can form the necessary URL to pass to the Generic Connection Framework. For example:

```
btspp://00904B2A88D6:1;authenticate=false;encrypt=false;master=false
```

Once you have the URL, you can talk to the device. This is actually quite simple. As shown in the last chapter, open a connection to the URL and get an InputStream from the connection:

```
StreamConnection conn = (StreamConnection) Connector.open(url);
InputStream in = conn.openInputStream( );
```

This stream feeds you as much NMEA data as you want. Read this stream line by line. Look at the first six characters of each line. If they are $GPRMC, parse the line into individual components. Otherwise, ignore it and read the next line.

The easiest way to parse a comma-delimited line of this nature is to split the string along the commas. This is a little easier than parsing comma-delimited text normally is, because there's no possibility of a field containing the delimiter character or a line break.

Example 25-7 puts this together in a complete program that finds a Blue Logger and prints the time and location to System.out. Of course, this requires a desktop environment that has a console to write to. In a J2ME program, you'd have to adjust the program to output the content using javax.microedition.lcdui, as described in Chapter 24.

*Example 25-7. A Blue Logger client that monitors current position and time*

```
import java.io.*;
import javax.bluetooth.*;
import javax.microedition.io.*;

public class BluetoothTracker {

  public static void main(String[] args) throws IOException {

    RemoteDevice logger = BlueLoggerFinder.findBlueLogger( );
    String address = logger.getBluetoothAddress( );
    String url = "btspp://" + address
     + ":1;authenticate=false;encrypt=false;master=false";
    StreamConnection conn = (StreamConnection) Connector.open(url);
    InputStream in  = conn.openInputStream( );
    BufferedReader reader = new BufferedReader(
                         new InputStreamReader(in, "US-ASCII"));
    try {
      while (true) {
        String s = reader.readLine( );
        if (s == null) break;
```

```
        if (s.startsWith("$GPRMC,")) {
            String[] fields = s.split(",");
            String time = getTime(fields[1]);
            String latitude = getPosition(fields[3], fields[4]);
            String longitude = getPosition(fields[5], fields[6]);
            String date = getDate(fields[9]);
            System.out.println(time + "\t" + date + "\t"
             + latitude + "\t" + longitude);
        }
      }
    }
    catch (IOException ex) {
      // device turned off or out of range
    }
    reader.close( );

  }

  private static String getDate(String ddmmyy) {
    String year = "20" + ddmmyy.substring(4);
    String month = ddmmyy.substring(2, 4);
    String day = ddmmyy.substring(0, 2);
    return month + "-" + day + "-" + year;
  }

  // I'm not sure how robust this code is. There could well be some
  // StringIndexOutOfBoundsExceptions waiting to trip up the unwary.
  // I have not tested it at every possible location on the planet.
  private static String getPosition(String number, String direction) {
    // need to handle two-digit and three-digit longitudes
    int point = number.indexOf('.');
    String degrees = number.substring(0, point-2);
    String minutes = number.substring(degrees.length( ), point);
    String seconds = String.valueOf(
     Double.parseDouble(number.substring(point)) * 60);

    return degrees + "°" + minutes + "'" + seconds + "\"" + direction;
  }

  private static String getTime(String in) {
    String hours = in.substring(0, 2);
    String minutes = in.substring(2, 4);
    String seconds = in.substring(4, 6);
    return hours + ":" + minutes + ":" + seconds;
  }
}
```

Here's some typical output:

```
20:42:05  01-30-2006    40°40'17.832"N  073°57'51.378"W
20:42:06  01-30-2006    40°40'17.844"N  073°57'51.312"W
20:42:07  01-30-2006    40°40'17.855999999999998"N    073°57'51.234"W
20:42:08  01-30-2006    40°40'17.874"N  073°57'51.162"W
```

```
20:42:09   01-30-2006    40°40'17.898"N   073°57'51.096000000000004"W
20:42:10   01-30-2006    40°40'17.922"N   073°57'51.036"W
20:42:11   01-30-2006    40°40'17.945999999999998"N    073°57'50.994"W
20:42:12   01-30-2006    40°40'17.976"N   073°57'50.958000000000006"W
20:42:13   01-30-2006    40°40'18.006"N   073°57'50.946"W
20:42:14   01-30-2006    40°40'18.03"N    073°57'50.952"W
20:42:15   01-30-2006    40°40'18.048000000000002"N    073°57'50.976"W
20:42:16   01-30-2006    40°40'18.06"N    073°57'51.03"W
20:42:17   01-30-2006    40°40'18.06"N    073°57'51.096000000000004"W
20:42:18   01-30-2006    40°40'18.06"N    073°57'51.150000000000006"W
20:42:19   01-30-2006    40°40'18.066"N   073°57'51.192"W
20:42:20   01-30-2006    40°40'18.084"N   073°57'51.21"W
20:42:21   01-30-2006    40°40'18.108"N   073°57'51.19799999999999"W
20:42:22   01-30-2006    40°40'18.132"N   073°57'51.168"W
20:42:23   01-30-2006    40°40'18.162000000000003"N    073°57'51.126"W
20:42:24   01-30-2006    40°40'18.186"N   073°57'51.09"W
20:42:25   01-30-2006    40°40'18.21"N    073°57'51.048"W
```

The difference from one reading to the next is attributable to jitter in the GPS. It's not accurate to more than a meter at best anyway. At this location, one second of latitude is roughly 30 meters, and a second of longitude is roughly 24 meters, so this works out to about 1.5-meter accuracy for latitude and about 10-meter accuracy for longitude. That's acceptable error for many applications.

I cut this off early because I wasn't really moving when I took these readings. If you were driving or running with a PDA, it would produce somewhat more variable output. (I don't own a car, and running through the streets of Brooklyn carrying a laptop in one hand and a GPS receiver in the other did not strike me as a wise thing to try.) You could also easily set up a program to log the data once a minute or once every tenth of a mile. The device sends continuously, but you're free to ignore most of the readings.

## L2CAP Devices

L2CAP devices are a little more complex. The details of finding one, determining its URL, and opening a connection to it are essentially the same as they are for RFCOMM. However, L2CAP is based on packets rather than streams: instead of reading and writing streams, you send and receive packets. This is much like the difference between TCP and UDP on IP networks.

When given a btl2cap URL, Connector.open( ) returns an L2CAPConnection object. For example:

```
L2CAPConnection conn = (L2CAPConnection) Connector.open(
  "btl2cap:// 3B9FA89520078C303355AAA694238F08 ;ReceiveMTU=512;TransmitMTU=512");
```

This interface has methods to determine the Maximum Transmit Unit (MTU), tell whether the connection is ready to receive packets, and send and receive packets.

The MTU is normally set by the ReceiveMTU and TransmitMTU parameters when you first open the connection. This is the maximum number of bytes you can put in each packet. Wireless connections are much less reliable and normally use smaller packet sizes than wired connections. You can check the MTU size with these two methods:

```
public int getTransmitMTU( ) throws IOException
public int getReceiveMTU( )  throws IOException
```

Once you know the transmit MTU, you can send up to that amount of data at once using the send( ) method:

```
public void send(byte[] data) throws IOException
```

If you try to send more than the MTU, the extra data is discarded without warning.

To receive data coming in off the air, you pass a byte array to the receive( ) method:

```
public int receive(byte[] buffer) throws IOException
```

Data is placed in the array starting with the first component. This method blocks until data arrives off the air. To avoid that, you can first check with ready( ) before calling receive( ):

```
public boolean ready( ) throws IOException
```

ready( ) returns true if and only if receive( ) can read a packet without blocking.

I'll demonstrate this protocol with a dual example. First, I'll show a server that receives and prints out lines of ASCII text. Then I'll add a client that sends packets of ASCII text to the server. In this example, my code is controlling both ends of the connection on two different systems, so I can define any protocol I like on top of L2CAP. I'll keep it about as simple as imaginable, but this should still demonstrate the basic techniques for talking between two systems. Run this in both directions, and you'd have a basic chat program.

The server listens on the local host, so first you need a service URL. You need to pick a UUID for this. I used the java.util.UUID class in Java 5 to generate a random one. The UUID it gave me was 7140b25b-7bd7-41d6-a3ad-0426002febcd. You'll also need a name. L2CAPExampleServer works as well as any. With these two pieces in place, the local URL for the service is:

```
btl2cap://localhost:7140b25b7bd741d6a3ad0426002febcd;name=L2CAPExampleServer
```

Use GCF's Connector class to open a connection to this URL. This returns an L2CAPConnectionNotifier object, but you'll need to cast it to restore the type:

```
Connection conn = Connector.open(
  "btl2cap://localhost: 7140b25b7bd741d6a3ad0426002febcd;name=L2CAPExampleServer");
L2CAPConnectionNotifier notifier = (L2CAPConnectionNotifier) conn;
```

You now accept an incoming connection much like you would for a TCP server socket, except that for Bluetooth the method is called acceptAndOpen( ) instead of merely accept( ):

```
L2CAPConnection client = notifier.acceptAndOpen( );
```

You then receive packets from the connection and put them into a buffer. Size the buffer to match the client's maximum transmission size:

```
byte[] buffer = new byte[client.getTransmitMTU( )];
```

Most protocols define some packet that indicates the end of the transaction. I'll use a packet that contains a single null. Example 25-8 receives packets and copies them onto System.out until such a packet is seen.

*Example 25-8. A very simple L2CAP server*

```
import java.io.IOException;
import javax.bluetooth.*;
import javax.microedition.io.*;

public class BluetoothReceiver {

  public final static String UUID = "7140b25b7bd741d6a3ad0426002febcd";

  public static void main(String[] args) {
    try {
      LocalDevice device = LocalDevice.getLocalDevice( );
      // make sure other devices can find us
      device.setDiscoverable(DiscoveryAgent.GIAC);
      String url = "btl2cap://localhost:" + UUID + ";name=L2CAPExampleServer";

      L2CAPConnectionNotifier notifier
       = (L2CAPConnectionNotifier) Connector.open(url);
      L2CAPConnection client = notifier.acceptAndOpen( );
      byte[] buffer = new byte[client.getTransmitMTU( )];
      while (true) {
        int received = client.receive(buffer);
        if (received == 1 && buffer[0] == 0) {
          System.out.println("Exiting");
          break;
        }
        System.out.write(buffer, 0, received);
      }

    }
    catch (BluetoothStateException ex) {
      System.err.println("Could not initialize Bluetooth."
      + " Please make sure Bluetooth is turned on.");
    }
    catch (IOException ex) {
      System.err.println("Could not start server");
    }
    System.exit(0);
  }
}
```

Obviously, this program handles only one connection at a time, but it would not be hard to extend it to handle multiple simultaneous connections by spawning a thread for each. Because the maximum number of Bluetooth devices in one piconet is eight, you don't have to worry excessively about the sort of scaling issues that led to the new I/O API for network sockets.

Now let's look at the client. The first step is to discover a service with the specified UUID. Example 25-4 does this as long as we give it the necessary UUID. Of course, it would also be possible to have it return a list of all the URLs for each device with the requested service, but a single URL is all we need for the moment.

 If you have trouble getting this program to work, make sure the server is discoverable. It may also help to verify that you can establish a Bluetooth connection between the client and the server for some other purpose, such as file transfer.

From there, we simply read each line read from the console into a byte array and send it over the air to the server. As is customary for console applications, if the user types a period on a line by itself, this is interpreted as the signal to stop sending and exit the program. The trickiest bit is making sure that the user can't send a line longer than the transmit MTU. If that's attempted, we have to split the data into multiple packets. Example 25-9 demonstrates.

*Example 25-9. A very simple L2CAP client*

```java
import java.io.*;
import javax.bluetooth.*;
import javax.microedition.io.*;

public class BluetoothTransmitter {

  public static void main(String[] args) {

    try {
      String url = BluetoothServiceFinder.getConnectionURL(BluetoothReceiver.UUID);
      if (url == null) {
        System.out.println("No receiver in range");
        return;
      }
      System.out.println("Connecting to " + url);
      L2CAPConnection conn = (L2CAPConnection) Connector.open(url);
      int mtu = conn.getTransmitMTU(); // maximum packet length we can send
      // use safe???
      BufferedReader reader = new BufferedReader(
       new InputStreamReader(System.in));

      while (true) {
        String line = reader.readLine();
        if (".".equals(line)) {
          byte[] end = {0};
          conn.send(end);
          break;
```

*Example 25-9. A very simple L2CAP client (continued)*

```
      }
      line += "\r\n";
      // now we need to make sure this fits into the MTU
      byte[][] packets = segment(line, mtu);
      for (int i = 0; i < packets.length; i++) {
        conn.send(packets[i]);
      }
    }


  }
  catch (IOException ex) {
    ex.printStackTrace( );
  }
  System.exit(0);
}

private static byte[][] segment(String line, int mtu) {

  int numPackets = (line.length( )-1)/mtu + 1;
  byte[][] packets = new byte[numPackets][mtu];
  try {
    byte[] data = line.getBytes("UTF-8");
    // the last packet will normally not fill a complete MTU
    for (int i = 0; i < numPackets-1; i++) {
      System.arraycopy(data, i*mtu, packets[i], 0, mtu );
    }
    System.arraycopy(data, (numPackets-1)*mtu, packets[numPackets-1],
     0, data.length - ((numPackets-1)*mtu) );
    return packets;
  }
  catch (UnsupportedEncodingException ex) {
    throw new RuntimeException("Broken VM does not support UTF-8");
  }
 }
}
```

This combination of three classes allows one-way communication from the client to the server. Extending it to enable full bidirectional chat is not especially difficult, though, and is left as an exercise for the reader. (I'm not sure how useful such a chat program would be, since Bluetooth's reliable range is limited to about 10 meters, but I can think of a few uses for such short-range communications.)

# PART VIII

# Appendix

# Character Sets

The first 128 Unicode characters—that is, characters 0 through 127—are identical to the ASCII character set. 32 is the ASCII space; therefore, 32 is the Unicode space. 33 is the ASCII exclamation point; therefore, 33 is the Unicode exclamation point, and so on. Table A-1 lists this character set.

*Table A-1. The first 128 Unicode characters and the ASCII character set*

| Code | Character | Code | Character | Code | Character | Code | Character |
|---|---|---|---|---|---|---|---|
| 0 | NUL (null) | 32 | space | 64 | @ | 96 | ` |
| 1 | SOH (start of header) | 33 | ! | 65 | A | 97 | a |
| 2 | STX (start of text) | 34 | " | 66 | B | 98 | b |
| 3 | ETX (end of text) | 35 | # | 67 | C | 99 | c |
| 4 | EOT (end of transmission) | 36 | $ | 68 | D | 100 | d |
| 5 | ENQ (enquiry) | 37 | % | 69 | E | 101 | e |
| 6 | ACK (acknowledge) | 38 | & | 70 | F | 102 | f |
| 7 | BEL (bell) | 39 | ` | 71 | G | 103 | g |
| 8 | BS (backspace) | 40 | ( | 72 | H | 104 | h |
| 9 | TAB (tab) | 41 | ) | 73 | I | 105 | i |
| 10 | LF (linefeed) | 42 | * | 74 | J | 106 | j |
| 11 | VTB (vertical tab) | 43 | + | 75 | K | 107 | k |
| 12 | FF (formfeed) | 44 | , | 76 | L | 108 | l |
| 13 | CR (carriage return) | 45 | - | 77 | M | 109 | m |
| 14 | SO (shift out) | 46 | . | 78 | N | 110 | n |
| 15 | SI (shift in) | 47 | / | 79 | O | 111 | o |
| 16 | DLE (data link escape) | 48 | 0 | 80 | P | 112 | p |
| 17 | DC1 (device control 1, XON) | 49 | 1 | 81 | Q | 113 | q |
| 18 | DC2 (device control 2) | 50 | 2 | 82 | R | 114 | r |
| 19 | DC3 (device control 3, XOFF) | 51 | 3 | 83 | S | 115 | s |

| Code | Character | Code | Character | Code | Character | Code | Character |
|------|-----------|------|-----------|------|-----------|------|-----------|
| 20 | DC4 (device control 4) | 52 | 4 | 84 | T | 116 | t |
| 21 | NAK (negative acknowledge) | 53 | 5 | 85 | U | 117 | u |
| 22 | SYN (synchronous idle) | 54 | 6 | 86 | V | 118 | v |
| 23 | ETB (end of transmission block) | 55 | 7 | 87 | W | 119 | w |
| 24 | CAN (cancel) | 56 | 8 | 88 | X | 120 | x |
| 25 | EM (end of medium) | 57 | 9 | 89 | Y | 121 | y |
| 26 | SUB (substitute) | 58 | : | 90 | Z | 122 | z |
| 27 | ESC (escape) | 59 | ; | 91 | [ | 123 | { |
| 28 | IS4 (file separator) | 60 | < | 92 | \ | 124 | \| |
| 29 | IS3 (group separator) | 61 | = | 93 | ] | 125 | } |
| 30 | IS2 (record separator) | 62 | > | 94 | ^ | 126 | ~ |
| 31 | is1 (unit separator) | 63 | ? | 95 | _ | 127 | del (delete) |

In the first column, characters 0 through 31 are referred to as control characters because they're traditionally entered by holding down the control key and a letter key (on at least some dumb terminals). For instance, Ctrl-H is often ASCII 8, backspace. Ctrl-S is often mapped to ASCII 19, DC3, or XOFF. Ctrl-Q is often mapped to ASCII 17, DC1, or XON. Generally, each control character is entered by pressing the Control key and the printable character whose ASCII value is the ASCII value of the character you want plus 64 (or 96, if you count from the capitals). Character 127, delete, is also a control character.

The common abbreviation for the character is given first, followed by its common meaning. Some of these codes are pretty much obsolete. For instance, I'm not aware of any modern system that actually uses characters 28 through 31 as file, group, record, and unit separators. Those control codes that are still used often have different meanings on different platforms. For example, character 10, the linefeed, originally meant move the platen on the printer up one line, while character 13, the carriage return, meant return the print-head to the beginning of the line. On paperbased teletype terminals, this could be used to position the print-head anywhere on a page and perhaps overtype characters that had already been typed. This no longer makes sense in an era of glass terminals and GUIs, so linefeed has come to mean a generic end-of-line character.

The next 128 Unicode characters—that is, 128 through 255—have the same values as the equivalent characters in the Latin-1 character set defined in ISO standard 8859-1. Latin-1, a slight variation of which is used by Windows, adds the various accented characters, umlauts, cedillas, upside-down question marks, and other characters needed to write text in most Western European languages. shows these characters. The first 128 characters in Latin-1 are the ASCII characters shown in Table A-2.

*Table A-2. Unicode characters between 128 and 255, also the second half of the ISO 8859-1 Latin-1 character set*

| Code | Character | Code | Character | Code | Character | Code | Character |
|------|-----------|------|-----------|------|-----------|------|-----------|
| 128 | PAD (padding character) | 160 | non-breaking space | 192 | À | 224 | à |
| 129 | HOP (high octet preset) | 161 | ¡ | 193 | Á | 225 | á |
| 130 | BPH (break permitted here) | 162 | ¢ | 194 | Â | 226 | â |
| 131 | NBH (no break here) | 163 | £ | 195 | Ã | 227 | ã |
| 132 | IND (index) | 164 | ¤ | 196 | Ä | 228 | ä |
| 133 | NEL (next line) | 165 | ¥ | 197 | Å | 229 | å |
| 134 | SSA (start of selected area) | 166 | ¦ | 198 | Æ | 230 | æ |
| 135 | ESA (end of selected area) | 167 | § | 199 | Ç | 231 | ç |
| 136 | HTS (character tabulation set) | 168 | ¨ | 200 | È | 232 | è |
| 137 | HTJ (character tabulation with justification) | 169 | © | 201 | É | 233 | é |
| 138 | VTS (line tabulation set) | 170 | ª | 202 | Ê | 234 | ê |
| 139 | PLD (partial line forward) | 171 | « | 203 | Ë | 235 | ë |
| 140 | PLU (partial line backward) | 172 | ¬ | 204 | Ì | 236 | ì |
| 141 | RI (reverse line feed) | 173 | soft (optional) hyphen | 205 | Í | 237 | í |
| 142 | SS2 (single-shift two) | 174 | ® | 206 | Î | 238 | î |
| 143 | SS3 (single-shift three) | 175 | ¯ | 207 | Ï | 239 | ï |
| 144 | DCS (device control string) | 176 | ° (degree) | 208 | Ð | 240 | ð |
| 145 | PU1 (private use one) | 177 | ± | 209 | Ñ | 241 | ñ |
| 146 | PU2 (private use two) | 178 | ² | 210 | Ò | 242 | ò |
| 147 | STS (set transmit state) | 179 | ³ | 211 | Ó | 243 | ó |
| 148 | CCH (cancel character) | 180 | ´ | 212 | Ô | 244 | ô |
| 149 | MW (message waiting ) | 181 | µ | 213 | Õ | 245 | õ |
| 150 | SPA (start of guarded area) | 182 | ¶ | 214 | Ö | 246 | ö |
| 151 | EPA (end of guarded area) | 183 | · | 215 | × | 247 | ÷ |
| 152 | SOS (start of string) | 184 | , (cedilla) | 216 | Ø | 248 | ø |
| 153 | SGI (single graphic character introducer) | 185 | ¹ | 217 | Ù | 249 | ù |
| 154 | SCI (single character introducer) | 186 | º | 218 | Ú | 250 | ú |
| 155 | CSI (control sequence introducer) | 187 | » | 219 | Û | 251 | û |
| 156 | ST (string terminator) | 188 | ¼ | 220 | Ü | 252 | ü |
| 157 | OSC (operating system command) | 189 | ½ | 221 | Ý | 253 | ý |
| 158 | PM (privacy message) | 190 | ¾ | 222 | Þ | 254 | þ |
| 159 | APC (application program command) | 191 | ¿ | 223 | ß | 255 | ÿ |

Characters 128 through 159 are nonprinting control characters, much like characters 0 through 31 of the ASCII set. Unicode does not specify any meanings for these 32 characters, but their common interpretations are listed in the table. On Windows, most of these positions are used for noncontrol characters not included in Latin-1. These alternate interpretations are given in Table A-3.

Table A-3. Windows characters between 128 and 159

| Code | Character | Code | Character | Code | Character | Code | Character |
|------|-----------|------|-----------|------|-----------|------|-----------|
| 128 | € | 136 | ˆ | 144 | undefined | 152 | ~ |
| 129 | undefined | 137 | ‰ | 145 | ' | 153 | ™ |
| 130 | ‚ | 138 | Š | 146 | ' | 154 | š |
| 131 | ƒ | 139 | ‹ | 147 | " | 155 | › |
| 132 | „ | 140 | Œ | 148 | " | 156 | œ |
| 133 | … | 141 | undefined | 149 | • | 157 | undefined |
| 134 | † | 142 | Žª | 150 | – | 158 | ž |
| 135 | ‡ | 143 | undefined | 151 | — | 159 | Ÿ |

Values beyond 255 encode characters from various other character sets. Where possible, character blocks describing a particular group of characters map onto established encodings for that set of characters by simple transposition. For instance, Unicode characters 884 through 1011 encode the Greek alphabet and associated characters like the Greek question mark (;). This is a direct transposition by 720 of characters 128 through 255 of the ISO 8859-7 character set, which is in turn based on the Greek national standard ELOT 928. For example, the small letter delta, δ, Unicode character 948, is ISO 8859-7 character 228. A small epsilon, ε, Unicode character 949, is ISO 8859-7 character 229. In general, the Unicode value for a Greek character equals the ISO 8859-7 value for the character plus 720. Other character sets are included in Unicode in a similar fashion whenever possible.

As much as I'd like to include complete tables for all Unicode characters, if I did so, this book would be little more than that table. For complete lists of all the Unicode characters and associated glyphs, the canonical reference is *The Unicode Standard Version 4.0* by the Unicode Consortium, ISBN 0-321-18578-1. Updates to that book can be found at *http://www.unicode.org/*. Online charts can be found at *http://unicode.org/charts*.

# Index

We'd like to hear your suggestions for improving our indexes. Send email to *index@oreilly.com*.

## About the Author

**Elliotte Rusty Harold** is originally from New Orleans, to which he returns periodically in search of a decent bowl of gumbo. However, he currently resides in the Prospect Heights neighborhood of Brooklyn with his wife, Beth, and cats Charm (named after the quark) and Marjorie (named after his mother-in-law). He's an adjunct professor of computer science at Polytechnic University, where he teaches Java, XML, and object oriented programming. His Cafe au Lait web site (*http://www.cafeaulait.org*) is one of the most popular independent Java sites on the Internet, and his spin-off site, Cafe con Leche (*http://www.cafeconleche.org*), has become one of the most popular XML sites. He's currently working on the XOM library for XML, the Jaxen XPath engine, and the Amateur media player. His previous books include *Java Network Programming* (O'Reilly) and *Processing XML with Java* (Addison-Wesley).

## Colophon

The animal appearing on the cover of *Java I/O*, Second Edition, is the cottontail rabbit, American cousin to the European or "true" rabbit. Cottontails are stocky compared to hares and have short, fluffy tails. Their long, coarse coats vary in color from reddish-brown to black or grayish-brown. In the summer, they feed almost entirely on tender grasses, herbs, and farm crops, including peas, beans, and lettuce; in the winter, they eat bark, twigs, and buds of shrubs. Rabbits live in thickets, forests, meadows, woods, and rabbit cages. Some other interesting things about rabbits are that they can't see directly in front of them, and they can't vomit even if they want to.

Breeding occurs from March through early fall, with a gestation period of about 28 days. Cottontails normally produce between two and four litters per year, with three to eight bunnies per litter. Due to predation, weather, habitat destruction, disease, and parasites, only about 15 percent of the young survive their first year.

Wild rabbits live in many parts of the world, but typically prefer moderate climates, which is one reason why about half of the world's rabbits live in North America. In general, rabbits stay busy fulfilling various human expectations (as pets, food, and pests), as well as maintaining their reputation as both innocent and sexy. The notion of the rabbit's innocence may be due to its place in the food chain as an animal of prey, while its prolific breeding has made it a symbol of playful sexuality. The rabbit is also a common folklore archetype of the trickster, and in Japanese tradition, rabbits live on the Moon where they make mochi (mashed sticky rice).

The cover font is Adobe ITC Garamond. The text font is Linotype Birka; the heading font is Adobe Myriad Condensed; and the code font is LucasFont's TheSans Mono Condensed. This colophon was written by Lydia Onofrei.

# Better than e-books

Buy *Java I/O*, 2nd Edition, and access the
digital edition FREE on Safari for 45 days.

Go to www.oreilly.com/go/safarienabled
and type in coupon code XZEM-8USF-NNCJ-K8FF-ULZY

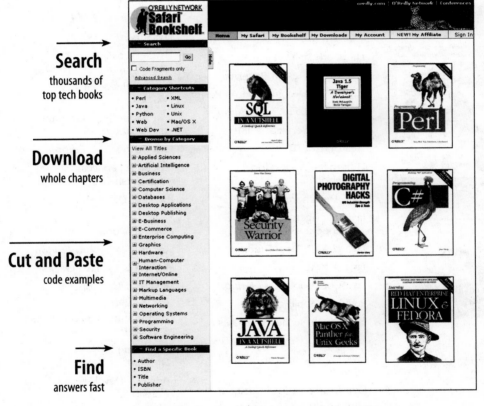

**Search**
thousands of
top tech books

**Download**
whole chapters

**Cut and Paste**
code examples

**Find**
answers fast

Search Safari! The premier electronic reference
library for programmers and IT professionals.

# Related Titles from O'Reilly

## Java

Ant: The Definitive Guide,
  *2nd Edition*

Better, Faster, Lighter Java

Beyond Java

Eclipse

Eclipse Cookbook

Eclipse IDE Pocket Guide

Enterprise JavaBeans 3.0,
  *5th Edition*

Hardcore Java

Head First Design Patterns

Head First Design Patterns Poster

Head First Java, *2nd Edition*

Head First Servlets & JSP

Head First EJB

Hibernate: A Developer's
  Notebook

J2EE Design Patterns

Java 5.0 Tiger: A Developer's
  Notebook

Java & XML Data Binding

Java & XML

Java Cookbook, *2nd Edition*

Java Data Objects

Java Database Best Practices

Java Enterprise Best Practices

Java Enterprise in a Nutshell,
  *3rd Edition*

Java Examples in a Nutshell,
  *3rd Edition*

Java Extreme Programming
  Cookbook

Java Generics and Collections

Java in a Nutshell, *5th Edition*

Java Management Extensions

Java Message Service

Java Network Programming,
  *2nd Edition*

Java NIO

Java Performance Tuning,
  *2nd Edition*

Java RMI

Java Security, *2nd Edition*

JavaServer Faces

JavaServer Pages,
  *2nd Edition*

Java Servlet & JSP
  Cookbook

Java Servlet Programming,
  *2nd Edition*

Java Swing, *2nd Edition*

Java Web Services
  in a Nutshell

JBoss: A Developer's
  Notebook

JBoss at Work: A Practical Guide

Learning Java, *2nd Edition*

Mac OS X for Java Geeks

Maven: A Developer's
  Notebook

Programming Jakarta Struts,
  *2nd Edition*

QuickTime for Java: A
  Developer's Notebook

Spring: A Developer's
  Notebook

Swing Hacks

Tomcat:
  The Definitive Guide

WebLogic: The Definitive Guide

Our books are available at most retail and online bookstores.
To order direct: 1-800-998-9938 • *order@oreilly.com* • *www.oreilly.com*
Online editions of most O'Reilly titles are available by subscription at *safari.oreilly.com*